The Chicago Manual of Style

The Chicago Manual of Style

15th edition

The University of Chicago Press

CHICAGO AND LONDON

The University of Chicago Press, Chicago 60637
The University of Chicago Press, Ltd., London
© 1982, 1993, 2003 by The University of Chicago
All rights reserved. Published 2003
First edition published 1906. Thirteenth edition 1982. Fourteenth edition 1993. Fifteenth edition 2003.
Printed in the United States of America

12 11 10 09 08 07 06 05   2 3 4 5

ISBN: 0-226-10403-6 (CLOTH)
ISBN: 0-226-10405-2 (CLOTH AND CD-ROM)
ISBN: 0-226-10404-4 (CD-ROM)

Library of Congress Cataloging-in-Publication Data

The Chicago manual of style. — 15th ed.
        p. cm.
Includes bibliographical references and index.
      ISBN 0-226-10403-6 (alk. paper)
    1. Printing—Style manuals.   2. Authorship—Style manuals.
Z253 .U69 2003
808'.027'0973—dc21

                                                          2003001860

⊚ The paper used in this publication meets the minimum requirements of the American National Standard for Information Sciences—Permanence of Paper for Printed Library Materials, ANSI Z39.48-1992.

www.chicagomanualofstyle.org

Contents

Preface

In preparing this fifteenth edition of *The Chicago Manual of Style,* we have sought to address the increasing proportion of our users who work with magazines, newsletters, corporate reports, proposals, electronic publications, Web sites, and other nonbook or nonprint documents. We have continued, nonetheless, to focus on the specific needs of our core constituency—writers and editors of scholarly books and journals. Because new needs, both technological and literary, prompted a major revision, Chicago consulted a wider range of advisers than ever before. We enlisted scholars, publishing professionals, and writers familiar with book and journal publishing, journalism, and—particularly valuable—electronic publication. Their counsel informs this edition.

Computer technology and the increasing use of the Internet mark almost every chapter. New sections have been added on preparing electronic publications (in chapters 1, 2, and 3), including the kind of editing and proofreading these require. Guidance on citing electronic works, accompanied by many examples, is offered in chapter 17. The differing demands of print and nonprint works are noted wherever relevant. We assume throughout that most writers and editors, whether preparing print or nonprint works, use computer software. The figure in chapter 2 that both explains and illustrates how to edit a manuscript on paper is now accompanied by an example of a redlined manuscript edited on screen.

New to this edition is a chapter on grammar and usage by Bryan A. Garner, author of *A Dictionary of Modern American Usage* (1998). While most of the *Chicago Manual* deals with "house style" (consistent forms of capitalization, punctuation, spelling, hyphenation, documentation, and so forth), Garner outlines the grammatical structures of English, shows how to put words and phrases together to achieve clarity, warns against pomposity, and identifies common errors. Included in this chapter are a glossary of troublesome expressions; guidance on bias-free language; and a list of words with their associated prepositions. As elsewhere in this manual, a conservative approach is tempered by pragmatism. Some elements in this chapter reappear elsewhere in different contexts; for example, restrictive versus nonrestrictive clauses are discussed in chapter 5 from a syntactical point of view and in chapter 6 as part of the treatment of commas.

Other important revisions include a section (in chapter 1) on the various elements that make up a scholarly journal; updated and expanded coverage of copyright and permissions matters (chapter 4); a reorganized section on compounds and hyphenation that contains new material but occupies less space (in chapter 7); more attention to Canadian terms and usage (in chapters 8 and 17 and elsewhere); a new section prepared by editors of Gallaudet University Press on the typographic presentation of American Sign Language (in chapter 10); and a largely rewritten chapter on mathematics (chapter 14), which recognizes the almost universal use of computer software by both authors and editors. We have reorganized the chapters on documentation: chapter 16 now outlines the two main systems preferred by Chicago (notes and bibliography on the one hand and the author-date style on the other), and chapter 17 discusses specific elements and subject matter, with examples of both systems in almost every paragraph. In the area of design and manufacture, we have streamlined coverage to reflect what writers and editors need to know about current procedures. This material is presented in appendix A, which includes a list of key terms used in typesetting, printing, and binding. Appendix B diagrams the editing and production processes for both books and journals. The "For Further Reference" sections have been eliminated in favor of a more comprehensive bibliography; the entries, thoroughly updated, are classified by type.

To aid navigation, every numbered paragraph now opens with a run-in subhead identifying the subject matter of the paragraph. For a more detailed overview of the manual than chapter titles alone can provide, we have added first-level subheads to the table of contents. As in earlier editions, each chapter opens with a full list of its contents.

As for the rules that many of us either know or know how to look up, we have changed only a few, and mainly those that have never caught on. For example, in line with almost universal usage in the United States, we now recommend the month-day-year form of dates (January 1, 2003) and present our formerly preferred day-month-year style as a useful option. And we no longer urge deletion of the *n* in *2nd* or the *r* in *3rd*. As always, most Chicago rules are guidelines, not imperatives; where options are offered, the first is normally our preference. Users should break or bend rules that don't fit their needs, as we often do ourselves. Some advice from the first edition (1906), quoted in the twelfth and thirteenth editions and invoked in the fourteenth, bears repeating: "Rules and regulations such as these, in the nature of the case, cannot be endowed with the fixity of rock-ribbed law. They are meant for the average case, and must be applied with a certain degree of elasticity."

This manual had its origins in the 1890s as a single sheet of typographic fundamentals drawn up by a University of Chicago Press proofreader. From its first publication as a book in 1906 to this fifteenth edition, it has retained its occasionally arbitrary character, for it reflects Chicago's house style. Ideas generated from within the press and, increasingly, from outside have modified its tone and the thrust of its guidelines over the years. The twelfth edition, the most radically revised, was virtually a new book. The thirteenth and fourteenth continued to draw ideas from authors and editors, from responses to questionnaires, and from letters and telephone calls from (sometimes perplexed) readers. The present edition benefited not only from similar sources but also from a circle of advisers connected by e-mail, from a listserv for university press managing editors, and from the Q&A page in the University of Chicago Press's own Web site. Many who contributed ideas, words, sections, and examples are listed in the acknowledgments that follow.

On behalf of the University of Chicago Press
Margaret D. F. Mahan
Spring 2003

Acknowledgments

We are indebted first to Catharine Seybold and Bruce Young, who compiled the pathbreaking twelfth edition of this manual as well as the thirteenth edition, and to John Grossman, who compiled the fourteenth. Their efforts set a high standard that we have sought to emulate in the present edition, which was principally revised by Margaret Mahan.

Over the course of the revision, we have benefited from the advice of scholars, authors, and publishing professionals who reviewed material in their areas of expertise or offered fruitful suggestions. These include Ria Ahlström, Susan Allan, Michael Allen, Bruce Barton, Rudolph M. Bell, Laurence L. Bongie, Michael Boudreau, Therese Boyd, T. David Brent, Joseph Brown, Thomas Cable, Gordon Calhoun, Erik Carlson, Perry Cartwright, Rachel Chance, Alicja Chwals, Charlie Clark, Everett Conner, Bruce D. Craig, Anthony Crouch, Bruce O. Dancik, Philippe Desan, Erin DeWitt, Janet Dodd, Wendy Doniger, Fred Donner, Andrei Draganescu, Kate Duff, Jean Eckenfels, Richard Eckersley, Janet Emmons, June P. Farris, Thomas Fischer, Mark Fowler, Beth Garrison, Constance Hale, Holly Halliday, Terence Halliday, Kathleen Hansell, Eugene Harnack, Anthony Hoskins, Joann Hoy, Bob Hudnut, Cheryl Iverson, Tiger Jackson, Elizabeth Jewell, Leslie Keros, Michael Koplow, Kathryn Kraynik, Kathryn Krug, Josh Kurutz, Barbara Lamb, Karen Larsen, John Lipski, Gordon Meade, Julia Melvin, Ineke Middeldorp-Crispijn, Tess Mullen, Nancy Mulvany, David Nadziejka, Jeff Newman, Christina von Nolcken, Eizaburo Okuizumi, Donald O'Shea, David Pharies, Cameron Poulter, Brian Prestes, Mary Beth Protomastro, Frank Reynolds, Claudia Rex,

Robert J. Richards, Norma Roche, Carol Saller, Jessie Scanlon, Christine Schwab, Lys Ann Shore, Brian Simpson, Barbara Sivertsen, Beverly Sperring, Lynn Stafford-Yilmaz, Marta Steele, Sem Sutter, Martin Tanner, Sandy Thatcher, John W. Velz, Lila Weinberg, Paul Wheatley, Martin White, Bob Williams, Bruce Young, and Yuan Zhou. We are also grateful to others, too many to name individually, who responded to queries and informal polls about specific sections of the manual.

The entire penultimate draft of the manuscript was read by the members of our Advisory Board, a panel of experts representing various communities of readers:

Howard S. Becker, San Francisco
David Bevington, Department of English, University of Chicago
David Stanford Burr, St. Martin's Press
Patricia L. Denault, Harvard University
Bryan A. Garner, LawProse Inc.
Ann Goldstein, *New Yorker*
John Hevelin, Sun Microsystems
Deanna LaValle High, Association of Governing Boards of Universities and Colleges
Mary Knoblauch, *Chicago Tribune*
Ruth Melville, Editor
June Smith, Houghton Mifflin
Justine Burkat Trubey, R. R. Donnelley and Sons
B. Tommie Usdin, Mulberry Technologies Inc.
Robert Wald, Department of Physics, University of Chicago

We acknowledge with thanks the work of those who contributed chapters or parts of chapters to this edition: Geraldine Brady, Jenni Fry, Bryan A. Garner, DeLloyd J. Guth, Greg Hajek, Russell Harper, Sylvia Mendoza Hecimovich, Sharon Jennings, Jane Jiambalvo, Mary E. Laur, Mary E. Leas, John Muenning, Colleen Mullarkey, Margaret Perkins, Anita Samen, Jill Shimabukuro, Lys Ann Shore, Steven N. Shore, Philip Smith, Julie Steffen, William S. Strong, Ivey Pittle Wallace, and Martin L. White.

Within the University of Chicago Press, special thanks go to Linda J. Halvorson and Mary E. Laur, who coordinated the entire process after the departure of Penelope Kaiserlian in July 2001. Many others have contributed their knowledge and skills to the project on a continuing basis: from manuscript editing, Margaret Perkins and Anita Samen; from production and design, Sylvia Mendoza Hecimovich and Jill Shimabukuro; from information technology, John Muenning and Evan Owens; from marketing, Ellen Gibson and Carol Kasper; and from the press administration, A. M. (Lain) Adkins and Mary Summerfield. Amy Collins and Christopher Rhodes provided editorial assistance. M. Sue Ormuz, Siobhan Drummond, and Michael Brehm contributed to various aspects of the production process. Alice Bennett copyedited the final manuscript. On behalf of the press, Jenni Rom proofread the book, and Margie Towery prepared the index.

Paula Barker Duffy
Director, The University of Chicago Press
Spring 2003

I

The Parts of a Published Work

~~~~~~

Introduction

1.1   *A historical note.* The history of publishing since the end of the fifteenth century has been shaped by the application of technology to the conception and manufacture of printed texts. The evolution of this technology has been largely incremental, with occasional revolutionary developments followed by periods of relative stability. The most recent revolution started with the introduction of computer technology into mainstream society—and into the publishing field—in the last quarter of the twentieth century. This technology has transformed the means of editing and producing traditional print texts and has allowed the development of new and still evolving modes of electronic delivery. Everything that follows in this manual is shaped by a recognition of the lasting impact of the electronic revolution on the publishing industry.

1.2   *Published works.* A published work may be produced and delivered in the traditional way—printed on paper and bound—or conveyed in a digital format and displayed on a screen. Because many publishers have been guided by the history and traditions of print publishing even as they have moved toward electronic publishing, and because many of these traditions, including the logical order of elements in a printed work, can be a useful starting point in the design and production of electronic works, each of the major sections that follow begins with the components of printed paper-and-ink publications and then discusses those of electronic publications. Much of what is covered also applies to works other than journals and books. For printed books, see 1.4–116; for electronic books, see 1.117–37; for printed journals, see 1.138–68; for electronic journals, see 1.169–91; for manuscript preparation, see chapter 2.

1.3   *Leaves and pages, rectos and versos.* The trimmed sheets of paper that make up a printed book or journal are often referred to as leaves. A page is one side of a leaf. The front of the leaf, the side that lies to the right in an open book, is called the recto. The back of the leaf, the side that lies to the left when the leaf is turned, is the verso. Rectos are always odd-numbered, versos always even-numbered. For definitions of these and other terms mentioned throughout this chapter, see the list of key terms in appendix A.

Books

DIVISIONS

1.4   *Outline of divisions and parts.* The interior of a printed book usually comprises three major divisions: the front matter (also called preliminary matter or "prelims"), the text, and the back matter (or end matter). An appropriate sequence for all the component parts of these divisions is presented below; some parts have alternative placements. Few books contain all these parts, and some books have parts not listed. All the listed parts will be discussed in this chapter. Lowercase roman numerals are assigned to pages in the front matter and arabic numerals to all the rest, including the back matter. Starting pages that cannot be determined in manuscript because of the variable lengths of certain parts are simply indicated as recto, the right-hand page being the traditional choice. Note that every page is counted in the page sequence, even those on which no number actually appears, such as the title and half-title pages, copyright page, and blank pages.

FRONT MATTER

Book half title	i
Series title, frontispiece, or blank	ii
Title page	iii

FRONT MATTER

Half Title and Its Verso

1.5   *Half title.* The half title (on p. i, the first recto) normally consists only of the main title. The subtitle is omitted, and the author's name does not appear. The verso of the half title (p. ii) is usually blank but may contain text or an illustration. For example, some title pages are presented as a two-page spread across pages ii and iii.

1.6 *Additional uses of page ii.* If the book is part of a series, the title of the series, the volume number in the series, the name of the general editor of the series, and sometimes the titles of books already published may appear on page ii. (A series title may appear on the title page instead.)

Women in Culture and Society
A Series Edited by Catharine R. Stimpson

If the book is the published proceedings of a symposium, the title of the symposium, the name of the city where it was held, the date when it was held, the committee that planned the symposium, and sometimes the sponsor of the symposium may appear on page ii.

1.7 *List of previous publications.* Some publishers list an author's previous publications on page ii; Chicago generally lists these on the copyright page (see 1.14) or on the cover (if a paperback) or jacket.

1.8 *Frontispiece.* Page ii sometimes carries an illustration, called a frontispiece. If the frontispiece is printed on a different stock from the text, and thus is inserted separately, it will not constitute page ii, though it will still appear opposite the title page, which is normally page iii (1.9).

Title Page

1.9 *Information displayed.* The title page (p. iii or, if a two-page spread, pp. ii–iii) presents the full title of the book; the subtitle, if any (note that there should never be more than one subtitle); the name of the author, editor, or translator; and the name and location of the publisher. If the type size or style of the subtitle differs from that of the main title, no colon or other mark of punctuation is needed to separate them.

1.10 *New edition.* In a new edition of a work previously published, the number of the edition (e.g., Third Edition) should also appear on the title page, usually following the title. See also 1.21–24.

1.11 *Author(s).* The author's name, or authors' names, may appear below or above the title. Given names should not be shortened to initials unless the author's name is widely known in such a form (e.g., O. Henry, P. D. James). Using a full first name helps to ensure that a name will not be conflated with another in bibliographic listings and library catalogs. Chicago does not print academic degrees or affiliations after an author's name on the title page, with the exception of MD, which may be retained in the field of medicine. For multiauthor works, see 1.89.

1.12 *Volume editor(s) or translator(s).* The usual form for giving the name of a volume editor or translator on the title page is "Edited by John Doe" (not "John Doe, Editor") or "Translated by Eric Wachthausen."

1.13 *Publisher.* The publisher's full name (imprint) should be given on the title page and is usually followed by the name of the city (or cities) where the principal offices are located. The publisher's logo may also appear there. The year of publication is best avoided on the title page, particularly if it conflicts with copyright information on page iv (see 1.18).

Copyright Page

1.14 *Biographical note.* A brief note on the author or authors ("author" here includes editors, compilers, and translators), listing previous publications and, if relevant, academic affiliation, may appear at the top of the copyright page (see fig. 1.1). It must correspond to related information given on the jacket or cover, though the wording need not be identical. (The biographical note may appear on a separate page, either in the front matter or the back matter, according to the publisher's preference.) See also 1.120.

1.15 *Publisher's address.* The address of the publisher—and sometimes the addresses of overseas agents—may also be given on the copyright page. Chicago usually puts these above the copyright notice. An address may be abbreviated, consisting, for example, only of city and perhaps postal code.

1.16 *Copyright notice.* The Copyright Act of 1989 does not require that published works carry a copyright notice in order to secure copyright protection. Nevertheless, most publishers continue to carry the notice to discourage infringement. The usual notice consists of three parts: the symbol ©, the year the book is published, and the name of the copyright owner (see fig. 1.1). For electronic books, see 1.119; for journals, see 1.141, 1.177–79; for a full discussion, see 4.38–44.

1.17 *Copyright owner versus publisher.* The name of the copyright owner is not necessarily the name of the publisher. Books published by the University of Chicago Press, for example, are usually copyrighted in the name of the university ("© 2006 by The University of Chicago"). Some authors prefer to copyright their works in their own names ("© 2006 by Alison A. Author"), a preference also discussed in 4.41.

Frank F. Furstenberg Jr. is the Zellerbach Family Professor of Sociology at the University of Pennsylvania. Thomas D. Cook is professor of sociology, psychology, education, and policy research at Northwestern University. Jacquelynne Eccles is professor of education and psychology at the University of Michigan. Glen H. Elder Jr. is the Odum Professor of Sociology at the University of North Carolina, Chapel Hill. Arnold Sameroff is professor of psychology at the University of Michigan.

The University of Chicago Press, Chicago 60637
The University of Chicago Press, Ltd., London
© 1999 by The University of Chicago
All rights reserved. Published 1999
07 06 05 04 03 02 01 00 99   1 2 3 4 5

ISBN (cloth): 0-226-27391-1

The University of Chicago Press gratefully acknowledges a subvention from the John D. and Catherine T. MacArthur Foundation in partial support of the costs of production of this volume.

Library of Congress Cataloging-in-Publication Data

Managing to make it : urban families and adolescent success / [edited by] Frank F. Furstenberg Jr. . . . [et al.].
    p. cm.—(John D. and Catherine T. MacArthur Foundation series on mental health and development. Studies in successful adolescent development)
      Includes bibliographical references and index.
      ISBN 0-226-27391-1 (alk. paper)
      1. Urban youth—Pennsylvania—Philadelphia—Family relationships.   2. Urban youth—Pennsylvania—Philadelphia—Longitudinal studies.   3. Parenting—Pennsylvania—Philadelphia—Longitudinal studies.   4. Socially handicapped teenagers—Pennsylvania—Philadelphia—Longitudinal studies.   5. Success—Pennsylvania—Philadelphia—Longitudinal studies.   I. Furstenberg, Frank F., 1940–   .
    II. Series.
    HQ796.M268   1999
    649′.125′0974811—dc21

                                                 98-27071
                                                   CIP

⊗ The paper used in this publication meets the minimum requirements of the American National Standard for Information Sciences—Permanence of Paper for Printed Library Materials, ANSI Z39.48-1992.

Fig. 1.1. A typical copyright page, including identification of author, copyright notice, impression date and number (denoting 1999 for the first impression), International Standard Book Number (ISBN), publisher's acknowledgment of a subvention, Library of Congress Cataloging-in-Publication data (CIP), and paper durability statement.

1.18   *Year of publication.* The year of publication should correspond to the copyright date. From a marketing point of view, if a book is physically available near the end of a year but not formally published until the beginning of the next, the later date is preferred as both copyright and publication date.

© 2010 by Millennial Publishing House
All rights reserved. Published 2010

The University of Chicago Press, Chicago 60637
The University of Chicago Press, Ltd., London

© 1961, 1983 by The University of Chicago
All rights reserved. First edition 1961
Second edition 1983

Printed in the United States of America
04 03 02 01 00 99 98   6 7 8 9

Fig. 1.2. Copyright notice of a second edition (1983), with impression line indicating that this edition was reprinted for the sixth time in 1998.

1.19 *Subsequent editions.* Each new edition (as distinct from a new impression, or reprinting) of a book is copyrighted, and the copyright dates of all previous editions should appear in the copyright notice (see fig. 1.2). If the new edition is so extensive a revision that it virtually constitutes a new publication, previous copyright dates may be omitted. See also 1.21, 4.40.

1.20 *Additional copyright information.* The date of copyright renewal or a change in the name of the copyright owner is sometimes reflected in the copyright notice if the work is reprinted. (Copyright may be assigned to the author or someone else after the initial copyright has been registered and printed in the first impression.) Copyright renewal is shown in the following manner:

© 1943 by Miriam Obermerker. © renewed 1971 by Miriam Obermerker

To indicate a change in copyright ownership, the name of the new copyright owner is substituted for that of the previous owner. The copyright date remains the same unless the copyright has been renewed. Copyrights remain legally valid even if renewal or reassignment information cannot, for some reason, appear in a new edition or printing.

1.21 *Publishing history.* The publishing history of a book, which usually follows the copyright notice, begins with the date (year) of original publication. If a book is reprinted, the number and date of the current impression are usually indicated. Corrections are sometimes made in new impressions, but if significant revisions are made, the result may be a new edition. The number and date of the new edition become part of the publishing history. The copyright dates of all editions may be accumulated in the copyright notice (see 1.19), but usually only the original edition and latest editions are reflected in the publishing history (see fig. 1.2 and the copyright notice to this manual).

1.22 *Edition versus impression.* "Edition," as opposed to "impression," is used in at least two senses. (1) A new edition may be defined as one in which a substantial change has been made in one or more of the essential elements of the work (e.g., text, notes, appendixes, or illustrations). As a rule of thumb, at least 20 percent of a new edition should consist of new or revised material. A work that is republished with a new preface or afterword but is otherwise unchanged except for corrections of typographical errors is better described as a new impression or a reissue; the title page may include such words as "With a New Preface." (2) "Edition" may be used to designate a reissue in a new format—for example, a paperback, deluxe, or illustrated version—or under the imprint of a different publisher.

1.23 *Edition number.* A new edition is best designated on the title page by its number: Second Edition, Third Edition, and so forth. Such phrases as "revised and expanded" are redundant on the title page, since the nature and extent of the revision are normally described in the prefatory material or on the cover. For electronic books, see 1.121.

1.24 *Format of publishing history.* The sequence of items in the publishing history is as follows: date (year) of first publication or first edition; number and date of current edition; number and date of impression if other than the first (see 1.26). These items may each be on a separate line, or they may be run together. There should be no period at the end of a line, but if the items are run together, they are separated within a line by a period (see figs. 1.1, 1.2). A previous publisher's name need not be given unless the licensing agreement requires that it appear in the new edition.

First edition published 1995. Second edition 2005

Revised edition originally published 1985
University of Chicago Press edition 2002

1.25 *Country of printing.* The country in which a book is printed is traditionally identified inside the work. If a book is printed in a country other than the country of publication, the jacket or cover must so state: for example, "Printed in China."

1.26 *Impression.* The impression is usually identified by a line of numerals running below the publishing history (see fig. 1.1). The first group of numerals, reading from right to left, represents the last two digits of suc-

FRANÇOIS FURET (1927–97), educator and author, was a Chevalier of the Legion of Honor and was elected, in 1997, to become one of the "Forty Immortals" of the Académie Française, the highest intellectual honor in France. His many books include *Interpreting the French Revolution, Marx and the French Revolution,* and *Revolutionary France.* DEBORAH FURET, his widow, collaborated with him on several projects.

The University of Chicago Press, Chicago 60637
The University of Chicago Press, Ltd., London
© 1999 by The University of Chicago
All rights reserved. Published 1999
07 06 05 04 03 02 01 00 99   1 2 3 4 5

ISBN: 0-226-27340-7 (cloth)

Originally published as *Le passé d'une illusion: Essai sur l'idée communiste au XXe siècle,* © Éditions Robert Laffont, S.A., Paris, 1995

The University of Chicago Press gratefully acknowledges the generous contribution of the French Ministry of Culture to the translation of this book.

Fig. 1.3. Part of the copyright page of a translation, including title and copyright of the original edition (as required by contract with the original publisher), and biographical notes on both author (François Furet) and translator (Deborah Furet).

ceeding years starting with the date of original publication. The second set, following a space of an em (see appendix A) or more and reading from left to right, represents the numbers of possible new impressions. The lowest number in each group indicates the present impression and date. In figure 1.1, therefore, the impression is identified as the first, and the year of printing as 1999; in figure 1.2, the numbers indicate a sixth printing in 1998. This method involves minimal resetting in each new impression, since the typesetter merely deletes the lowest number. Indicating a new impression not only reflects the sales record of a book but also signals that corrections may have been made.

1.27 *Translation.* If the book is a translation, the original title, publisher, and copyright information should be recorded on the copyright page (see fig. 1.3).

1.28 *International Standard Book Number (ISBN).* An ISBN is assigned to each book by its publisher under a system set up by the R. R. Bowker Company and the International Organization for Standardization (ISO). The ISBN uniquely identifies the book, thus facilitating order fulfillment and computer tracking of inventory. For example, in ISBN 0-226-07522-2, the first digit, 0, tells us that the book was published in an English-speaking country; the second group of digits, 226, identifies the publisher (in this in-

The University of Chicago Press, Chicago 60637
The University of Chicago Press, Ltd., London
© 1942, 1953, 1956, 1991 by The University of Chicago

Agamemnon
© 1947 by Richmond Lattimore

All rights reserved
Volume 1 published 1992
Printed in the United States of America

00 99 98 97 96 95 94 93 92   1 2 3 4 5

ISBN (4-vol. set) 0-226-30763-8
ISBN (vol. 1) 0-226-30764-6

Fig. 1.4. Part of a copyright page for volume 1 in an edition having an ISBN for the complete set and separate ISBNs for each volume. This practice is followed with works that are as likely to be sold as individual volumes as in a set.

stance the University of Chicago Press); the third group identifies the book; and the last digit is the check digit, which mathematically discloses any error in the preceding group. (The ISBN Agency proposes to change the current ten-digit format to a thirteen-digit format in January 2005.) The ISBN is included in the Cataloging-in-Publication (CIP) data received from the Library of Congress (see 1.32–34 and figs. 1.1 and 1.3). If the CIP data are printed elsewhere in the book, or not included at all, the ISBN should nevertheless be included on the copyright page. The ISBN should also be printed on the book jacket and on the back cover of a paperback book. If a book is issued in both cloth and paper bindings, a separate ISBN is assigned to each. When a work comprises two or more volumes, separate ISBNs are assigned to individual volumes that are likely to be sold separately (see fig. 1.4). If the complete work is to be sold as a set only, the same ISBN applies to all volumes. Additional information about the assignment and use of ISBNs may be obtained from the ISBN United States Agency, R. R. Bowker. For electronic books, see 1.125. Note that each version of a book should list the ISBNs for all other versions that were available when the current version was produced.

1.29   *International Standard Serial Number (ISSN).* An ISSN is assigned to serial publications, which include journals, magazines, yearbooks, and certain monograph series. The ISSN remains the same for each issue of the publication and is printed either on the page containing the copyright notice for the issue or with the instructions for ordering the publication. An electronic edition must carry an ISSN different from that assigned to the

The University of Chicago Press, Chicago 60637
The University of Chicago Press, Ltd., London
© 1990 by The University of Chicago
All rights reserved. Published 1990
Printed in the United States of America
99 98 97 96 95 94 93 92 91 90   1 2 3 4 5

Chapter 3 contains a slightly revised version of "On Reading
'Incompatibility' in Plato's *Sophist.*" *Dialogue* 14, no. 1 (March
1975): 143–46, reprinted with the permission of the editor of *Dia-*
logue. An earlier version of chapter 4 appeared as "Plato on
Not-Being: Some Interpretations of the συμπλοχὴ εἰδῶν (259E)
and Their Relation to Parmenides' Problem," *Midwest Studies in*
Philosophy 8 (1983): 35–65. Reprinted with the permission of
the University of Minnesota Press.

Fig. 1.5. Part of a copyright page acknowledging earlier publication of certain chapters.

print edition (see 1.125). If the publications are books, each is also assigned an International Standard Book Number, and both the ISSN (for
the series) and the ISBN (for the book) are printed in the book. Journals
and other nonbook serial publications are not assigned an ISBN; each issue of such a series carries only an ISSN. The Library of Congress does not
issue CIP data for books with an ISSN.

1.30 *Acknowledgments, permissions, and other credits.* The copyright page, if space
permits, may include acknowledgments of previously published parts of
a book, illustration credits, and permission to quote from copyrighted
material (figs. 1.5, 1.6) unless such acknowledgments appear elsewhere in
the book (see 2.45). For source notes, see 16.68.

The photographs in this book are by Kevin Wideangle and are reproduced by permission.

The illustration on the title page is a detail from a photograph of Nietzsche in Basel, ca.
1876. Photo Stiftung Weimarer Klassik. GSA 101/17.

For a full discussion of permissions, see chapter 4.

1.31 *Grants.* Grants of financial assistance toward publication that are made
to the publisher (rather than the author) should be acknowledged on the
copyright page unless they require more space or greater prominence, in

Albert Boime is professor of art history at the University of California, Los Angeles.

The University of Chicago Press, Chicago 60637
The University of Chicago Press, Ltd., London
© 1993 by The University of Chicago
All rights reserved. Published 1993
Printed in the United States of America
02 01 00 99 98 97 96 95 94 93   1 2 3 4 5

ISBN (cloth): 0-226-06330-5

Library of Congress Cataloging-in-Publication Data

Boime, Albert.
    The art of the Macchia and the Risorgimento : representing culture and
    nationalism in nineteenth-century Italy / Albert Boime.
        p.   cm.
    Includes index.
    ISBN 0-226-06330-5
    1. Macchiaioli.   2. Painting, Modern—19th century—Italy.   3. Art and
    society—Italy.   I. Title
    ND617.5.M3B65   1993
    759.5'51'09034—dc20   92-17169
                                                                    CIP

Photo credits—4.6: © Arch. Phot. Paris/S.P.A.D.E.M.; 3.1–3.3, 3.16:
Soprintendenza per i B.A.S. di Napoli; 3.21: Bequest of Collis P. Huntington
(25.110.66); 4.2: Gift of Mrs. J. W. Simpsom, 42.22; 4.1, 4.5, 4.10, 4.12, 4.13,
4.33, 6.14: © Photo R.M.N.; 5.8: Purchase in memory of Ralph Cross Johnson;
7.26, 7.23: Galleria d'arte moderna di Palazzo Pitti; 7.34: Alinari/Art Resource
N.Y.; 7.44: Instituto Centrale per il Catalogo e la Documentazione

This book is printed on acid-free paper.

Fig. 1.6. Copyright page including photo credits. Note the short paper durability statement, used where coated paper stock precludes the claim made in the fuller statement.

which case they may appear on a separate page, usually following the copyright page. Wording should be as requested (or at least approved) by the grantors (see fig. 1.3).

1.32   *Cataloging-in-Publication (CIP) data.* Since 1971 most publishers have printed the Library of Congress CIP data on the copyright pages of their books. The CIP data may appear elsewhere in the book as long as a note is added to the copyright page (e.g., "Library of Congress Cataloging-in-

Publication data will be found at the end of this book"). The Library of Congress does not provide CIP data for serial publications (see 1.29) or for musical scores.

1.33   *CIP data.* The cataloging data printed in a book correspond substantially to the catalog file in the Library of Congress. The *CIP Publishers Manual,* issued by the Cataloging in Publication Division of the Library, provides information and instruction for participants in the program. Examples of CIP data may be found in figures 1.1, 1.3, 1.6.

1.34   *Application for CIP data.* As soon as the final title has been decided on, the contents page completed, and the ISBN (see 1.28) assigned, the publisher may fill out a form provided by the Library of Congress and send it to the Cataloging in Publication Division, Library of Congress, together with either a complete set of proofs or copies of enough material from the manuscript to enable the library to classify the book properly (all available front matter, introduction or first chapter, etc.). Application may also be made in electronic form; consult the CIP manual. The library requires at least ten working days after receiving the material to complete the cataloging and send the data to the publisher. To discharge their purpose the printed CIP data should appear substantially as provided by the library. After the data have been received, any necessary corrections can be made using forms provided by the CIP Division or by personal correspondence.

1.35   *Paper durability statement.* Included on the copyright page is a statement relating to the durability of the paper the book is printed on. Acid-free paper has a longer life expectancy, and paper that is somewhat alkaline is more durable still. Durability standards for paper have been established by the American National Standards Institute (ANSI), which has issued statements to be included in books meeting these standards (see figs. 1.1, 1.3). For uncoated paper that is alkaline and that meets the standards for folding and tearing, ANSI authorizes the following notice, which must include the circled infinity symbol:

⊗ The paper used in this publication meets the minimum requirements of the American National Standard for Information Sciences—Permanence of Paper for Printed Library Materials, ANSI Z39.48-1992.

If a book is printed on coated stock—for example, a book containing color illustrations—the following notice may be carried (see also fig. 1.6):

This book is printed on acid-free paper.

Dedication

1.36 *Format and placement.* If a dedication is to be included, it should appear by itself, preferably on page v. The phrasing, to be determined by the author, is best kept simple. There is no need to say "Dedicated to." Such forms as "To George," "For my children," or "In memory of my mother, Mary Stephens" are appropriate.

1.37 *Appropriate use.* It is not customary for editors of contributed volumes to include a dedication unless it is jointly offered by all contributors. Nor do translators generally offer their own dedication unless it is made clear that the dedication is not that of the original author.

Epigraph

1.38 *Placement.* An author may wish to include an epigraph—a quotation that is pertinent but not integral to the text—at the beginning of the book. If there is no dedication, the epigraph may be placed on page v. When there is also a dedication, the epigraph may follow on page vi (opposite the table of contents); more rarely, it may appear on a blank verso facing the first page of the text. Epigraphs are also occasionally used at chapter openings and even at the beginnings of sections within chapters.

1.39 *Source.* The source of an epigraph is usually given on a line following the quotation, sometimes preceded by a dash (see 11.40). Only the author's name (only the last name of a well-known author) and, usually, the title of the work need appear. A book epigraph should never be annotated. If a footnote or an endnote to a chapter epigraph is required, the reference number should follow the source, or, to avoid the intrusion of a number, the supplementary documentation may be given in an unnumbered note (see 16.66).

Table of Contents

1.40 *Placement.* The table of contents (usually titled simply Contents) begins on page v or, if page v carries a dedication or an epigraph, on page vii.

1.41 *Format.* The table of contents for a printed work should include all preliminary material that follows it but exclude anything that precedes it. It should list the title and *beginning* page number of each section of the book: front matter, text divisions, and back matter, including the index (see fig. 1.7). If the book is divided into parts as well as chapters, the part titles appear in the contents, but their page numbers are omitted (see fig. 1.7).

Contents

Photographs follow page 158

Fig. 1.7. Table of contents showing front matter, introduction, parts, chapters, back matter, and location of photo gallery.

If the parts have separate introductions, however, these should also be shown in the table of contents. Page numbers in the manuscript of the table of contents are typically indicated by 000, XXX, or ●●●; the actual numbers can be inserted only after pages have been made up. Subheads within chapters are usually omitted from the table of contents, but if they provide valuable signposts for readers, they may be included (see table of contents to this manual, pp. v–x, which lists the first-level subheads and omits the second and third levels).

1.42 *Chapters with different authors.* In a volume consisting of chapters by different authors, the name of each author should be given in the table of contents with the title of the chapter:

The Supreme Court as Republican Schoolmaster
Ralph Lerner 127
or
Self-Incrimination and the New Privacy, *Robert B. McKay* 193

1.43 *Grouped illustrations.* In a book containing illustrations that are printed together in a gallery or galleries (see 12.7), it is seldom necessary to list them separately in a list of illustrations. Their location may be noted at the end of the table of contents; for example, "Illustrations follow pages 130 and 288." See also figure 1.7.

List of Illustrations and List of Tables

1.44 *Is a list needed?* In a book with either very few or very many illustrations or tables, all tied closely to the text, it is not essential to list them in the front matter. Multiauthor books, proceedings of symposia, and the like commonly do not carry lists of illustrations or tables. See also 12.52.

1.45 *List of illustrations.* Where a list is appropriate, the list of illustrations (usually titled Illustrations but entered in the table of contents as List of Illustrations to avoid ambiguity) should match the table of contents in type size and general style. In books containing various kinds of illustrations, the list may be divided into sections headed, for example, Figures, Tables (see 1.47 and fig. 1.8) or Plates, Drawings, Maps. Page numbers are given for all illustrations printed with the text and counted in the pagination, even when the numbers do not actually appear on the text page. When pages of illustrations are printed on different stock and not counted in the pagination, their location is indicated by "Facing page 000" or "Following page 000" in the list of illustrations (see fig. 1.9) or in the table of contents (fig. 1.7). A frontispiece, because of its prominent position at the front of the book, is not assigned a page number; its location is simply given as "frontispiece."

ILLUSTRATIONS

Fig. 1.8. Partial list of illustrations, with subheads. If the book contained no tables, the subhead "Figures" would be omitted. If it contained many tables, these would probably be listed on a new page under the heading "Tables." How best to list illustrations of various sorts depends as much on space as on logic.

1.46 *Illustration titles.* Titles given in the list of illustrations may be shortened or otherwise adjusted. For capitalization of titles, headline style versus sentence style, see 8.166–67. See also 12.52–55.

1.47 *List of tables.* Listing tables in the front matter is helpful mainly in books with frequent references to them. If a list of tables (titled Tables but entered in the table of contents as List of Tables) is needed, it follows the table of contents or, if there is one, the list of illustrations. Titles may be short-

Illustrations

Following Page 46

1. Josaphat's first outing
2. Portrait of Marco Polo
3. Gold–digging ant from Sebastian Münster's *Cosmographei*, 1531
4. An Indian "Odota" from Sebastian Münster's *Cosmographei*, 1531

. . . .

Following Page 520

84. *Doctrina christam* printed at Quilon
85. First book printed at Macao by Europeans, 1585
86. First book printed in China on a European press, 1588
87. Title page of *Doctrina Christiana* printed at Manila, 1593, in Tagalog and Spanish
88. Final page of above
89. Title page of *Doctrina Christiana* printed at Manila, 1593, in Spanish and Chinese

Fig. 1.9. Partial list of illustrations showing numbers, titles, and placement of unpaginated plates. (Compare fig. 1.7.)

ened (see 1.46). Tables are occasionally listed under a subhead in the list of illustrations (see 1.45 and fig. 1.8).

Foreword, Preface, Acknowledgments, and Introduction

1.48 *Foreword.* A foreword is usually a statement by someone other than the author, sometimes an eminent person whose name may be carried on the title page: "With a Foreword by John Quincy." The author's own statement about the work is usually called a preface. Both are set in the same size and style of type as the text. A foreword normally runs only a few pages, and its author's name appears at the end, flush right, with a line space (or less) between it and the text. The title or affiliation of the author of a foreword may appear under the name, often in smaller type. If a foreword runs to a substantial length, with or without a title of its own, its author's name may be given at the beginning instead of at the end. For place and date with a foreword, see 1.50. See also 1.53, 1.60.

1.49 *Preface.* Material normally contained in an author's preface includes reasons for undertaking the work, method of research (if this has some bearing on readers' understanding of the text), acknowledgments (but see

1.52), and sometimes permissions granted for the use of previously published material.

1.50   *Author's signature.* A preface need not be signed, since readers logically assume that an unsigned preface was written by the author whose name appears on the title page. If there might be some doubt about who wrote it, however, or if an author wishes to sign the preface (sometimes just with initials), the signature normally appears at the end, flush right, with a line space (or less) between it and the text. When a place and date are included at the end of a preface or foreword, these may appear flush left, with space between them and the text.

1.51   *New preface.* When a new preface is written for a new edition or for a reprinting of a book long out of print, it should precede the original preface. The original preface is then usually retitled Preface to the First Edition, and the new preface may be titled Preface to the Second Edition, Preface to the Paperback Edition, Preface 1993, or whatever fits. In a book containing both an editor's preface and an author's preface, the editor's preface, which may be titled as such or retitled Editor's Foreword, comes first and should bear the editor's name at its conclusion.

1.52   *Acknowledgments.* If the acknowledgments are long, they may be put in a separate section following the preface; if a preface consists only of acknowledgments, its title should be changed to Acknowledgments. Acknowledgments are occasionally put at the back of a book, preceding the other back matter. In multivolume works, acknowledgments that apply to all volumes need appear only in the first. Should they vary from volume to volume, separate acknowledgments may be required in each. See also 4.95–96.

1.53   *Introduction.* Most introductions belong not in the front matter but at the beginning of the text, paginated with arabic numerals (see 1.60). Material about the book—its origins, for example—rather than about the subject matter should be included in the preface or in the acknowledgments (see 1.49–52). A substantial introduction by someone other than the author is usually included in the front matter, following the acknowledgments, but if it is not more than three to five pages, it may more appropriately be called a foreword (see 1.48) and placed before the preface.

Other Front Matter

1.54   *Additional elements.* Other items that may be placed either in the front matter or, sometimes more suitably, in the back matter include a list of abbreviations, a publisher's note, a translator's note, and a note on editorial method. See 1.85 and 1.89 for placement of chronologies and lists of contributors.

1.55 *List of abbreviations.* Not every work that includes abbreviations needs a separate list of abbreviations with the terms or names they stand for. If many are used, or if a few are used frequently, a list is useful; its location should always be given in the table of contents. If abbreviations are used in the text or footnotes, the list may appear in the front matter. If they are used only in the back matter, the list should appear before the first element in which abbreviations are used, whether the appendixes, the endnotes, or the bibliography.

1.56 *Publisher's or translator's notes.* Elements such as a publisher's note or a translator's note are usually treated typographically in the same way as a preface or foreword. A publisher's note, used rarely and only to state something that cannot be included elsewhere, should either precede or immediately follow the table of contents. A translator's note, like a foreword, should precede any element, such as a preface, that is by the original author.

1.57 *Editorial method.* An explanation of an editor's method or a discussion of variant texts, often necessary in scholarly editions, may appear either in the front matter (usually as the last item there) or in the back matter (as an appendix or in place of one). Brief remarks about editorial method, however—such as noting that spelling and capitalization have been modernized—should be incorporated in the editor's preface.

TEXT

1.58 *Organization of text.* In general, the front matter serves as a guide to the contents and nature of the book, and the back matter provides reference material. The text proper should contain everything necessary for a reader to understand the author's argument. The organization of the text material can help or hinder comprehension. The following paragraphs deal with principal divisions found in most nonfiction books. Details of handling special elements in the text—quotations, illustrations, tables, mathematics, notes—are discussed in chapters 11–17.

1.59 *Second half title.* Where the front matter is extensive, a second half title, identical to the one on page i, may be added before the text. The second half title may be counted as page 1, the beginning of the pages bearing arabic page numbers, or (less desirable but sometimes demanded by page makeup problems) as the last recto of the front matter, with an odd-numbered roman page number. In either case, the page number does not appear (an unexpressed folio or blind folio). The page following the second half title (its verso) is usually blank, though it may contain an illustration or an epigraph. A second half title, counted as arabic page 1, is also useful when the book design specifies a double-page spread for chapter openings; in such a case, chapter 1 starts on page 2. See also 1.100.

Introduction in Text

1.60 *Format.* Unlike the kind of introduction that may be included in the front matter (see 1.53), a text introduction is integral to the subject matter of the book and should not include acknowledgments, an outline of the contents ("In the first two chapters I discuss . . ."), or other material that belongs in the front or back matter. (This rule may not apply in the case of a reprint or facsimile edition, where the front matter is furnished by a volume editor.) A text introduction carries arabic page numbers. A new introduction to a classic work may be considered a text introduction even if it includes biographical or other material about the original author. If titled simply Introduction, an introduction does not normally carry a chapter number and is usually considerably shorter than a chapter. An author who has titled chapter 1 Introduction should be encouraged to give the chapter a more graphic title. An introduction is occasionally titled Prologue, Prelude, or some other term. See also 1.64.

Parts

1.61 *Division into parts.* Some books are divided into parts (see fig. 1.7). Each part usually carries a number and a title and should contain at least two chapters. A part title, bearing the number (if it has one) and title of the part, appears on a page by itself, usually recto, preceding the first chapter in the part, which also usually starts recto. Chapters are numbered consecutively throughout the book; they do *not* begin over with 1 in each part. Parts are sometimes called sections, though "section" is more commonly used for a subdivision within a chapter (see 1.71–73).

1.62 *Part titles and pagination.* Part titles and their versos are counted in the pagination, even though their page numbers do not appear (unless a part introduction begins on either of these pages; see 1.63).

1.63 *Part introduction.* Each part may have an introduction, usually short, titled or untitled. The part introduction may begin on a new recto following the part title, or on the verso of the part title, or on the part title itself.

1.64   *Omission of part title or other uses of it.* A text introduction to a book that is divided into parts precedes the part title to part 1 and needs no part title of its own. Also, no part title need precede the back matter of a book divided into parts, though one may be useful before a series of appendixes or a notes section.

Chapters

1.65   *Division into chapters.* Most nonfiction prose works are divided into numbered chapters, which should be of approximately the same length. At least in scholarly works, chapter titles too should be similar in length and tone. Short titles are generally preferable to long ones, and descriptive titles to whimsical ones, which can cloy or mislead. (These guidelines are not intended to stifle humor, satire, and so forth.)

1.66   *Format, placement, and pagination.* Each chapter normally starts on a new page, verso or recto, and its opening page should carry a drop folio (see 1.100)—or sometimes no folio—and no running head (see 1.93–99). The first chapter ordinarily begins on a recto (but see 1.59). The chapter display usually consists of the chapter number ("chapter" is often omitted); the chapter title; the chapter subtitle, if any; and sometimes an epigraph (see 1.38, 11.40). Footnote reference numbers or symbols should not appear anywhere in the chapter display except, if unavoidable, after an epigraph (see 1.39). A note that refers to the chapter as a whole should be unnumbered and should precede the numbered notes, whether it appears on the first page of the chapter or in the endnotes (see 16.66).

1.67   *Multiple authors and affiliations.* In multiauthor books, the chapter author's name is always given in the chapter display. An affiliation or other identification is put in an unnumbered footnote on the first page of the chapter (see 16.69) or in a list of contributors (1.89). An unnumbered footnote is also used to disclose the source of a chapter or other contribution that is being reprinted from an earlier publication. When both the author's affiliation and the source of the contribution are given in the note, it is customary, but not essential, that the affiliation come first.

1.68   *Chapter offprints.* When offprints of individual chapters are planned, each chapter should begin on a recto.

Other Divisions

1.69   *Poetry.* In a book of previously unpublished poetry, each poem usually begins on a new page. Any part titles provided by the poet should appear on separate pages (rectos) preceding the poems grouped under them. In a collection of previously published poems, more than one poem, or the end of one and the beginning of another, may appear on the same page.

1.70   *Letters and diaries.* Letters and diaries are usually presented in chronological order, so they are seldom amenable to division into chapters or parts. For diary entries dates may be used as headings, and in published correspondence the names of senders or recipients of letters (or both) may serve as headings. The date of a letter may be included in the heading if it does not appear in the letter itself. Such headings in diaries and correspondence do not usually begin a new page.

Subheads

1.71   *Use of subheads.* Long chapters may include several subheads in the text as guides. Subheads should be short and meaningful and, like chapter titles, parallel in structure and tone. They rarely begin a new page.

1.72   *Levels of subheads.* Many works require only one level of subhead throughout the text. Some, particularly scientific or technical works, require further subdivision. Where more than one level is used, the subheads are referred to as the A-level subhead (the first-level heading after the chapter title), the B-level, the C-level, and so on (or A-head, B-head, C-head, etc.). Only the most complicated works need more than three levels. The number of subhead levels required may vary from chapter to chapter.

1.73   *Number of subheads.* When a section of text is subdivided, there should ordinarily be at least two subsections. A single subhead in a chapter or a single B-level subhead under an A-level subhead may be viewed as illogical and asymmetrical. (There are cases, however, when a single subdivision is needed.)

1.74   *Placement and typographic style.* Subheads, except the lowest level, are each set on a line separate from the following text, the levels differentiated by type style and placement. The lowest level is often run in at the beginning of a paragraph, usually set in italics and followed by a period (as in the paragraphs in this manual). It is then referred to as a run-in subhead (or run-in sidehead). Run-in sideheads are usually capitalized sentence style (see 8.166).

1.75   *Titles versus numbers.* Unless sections in a chapter are cited in cross-references elsewhere in the text, numbers are usually unnecessary with subheads. In general, subheads are more useful to a reader than section numbers alone. If numbers are used, they begin with 1 (or, if roman numerals are used, I) in each chapter.

1.76 *Numbering sections and subsections.* In scientific and technical works, however, the numbering of sections, subsections, and sometimes sub-subsections provides easy reference. There are various ways to number sections. The most common is double numeration or multiple numeration. In this system sections are numbered within chapters, subsections within sections, and sub-subsections within subsections. The number of each division is preceded by the numbers of all higher divisions, and all division numbers are separated by periods,[1] colons, or hyphens. Thus, for example, the numbers 4.8 and 4.12 signify the eighth section and the twelfth section of chapter 4. The series 4.12.3 signifies the third subsection in the twelfth section of chapter 4, and so on. The system employed by this manual is chapter number followed by *paragraph* number for easy cross-referencing. The multiple-numeration system may also be used for illustrations, tables, and mathematical equations (see, respectively, 12.13, 13.13, and 14.20–21).

1.77 *Omission of note numbers in subheads.* No note reference number should appear within or at the end of a subhead. Such a reference number should be placed at an appropriate location in the text.

1.78 *First sentence after subhead.* The first sentence of text following a subhead should not refer syntactically to the subhead; words should be repeated where necessary. For example:

SECONDARY SPONGIOSA
The secondary spongiosa, a vaulted structure . . .
not
SECONDARY SPONGIOSA
This vaulted structure . . .

1.79 *Other ways to break text.* Where a break stronger than a paragraph but not as strong as a subhead is required, a set of asterisks or a type ornament, or simply a blank line, may be inserted between paragraphs. Using a blank line has the disadvantage that it may be missed if the break falls at the bottom of a page.

---

1. Multiple numeration using periods should not be confused with decimal fractions. Paragraph or section 4.9 may be followed by 4.10—quite unlike the decimal fraction system.

Epilogues, Afterwords, and Conclusions

1.80　*Concluding elements.* Epilogues and afterwords are relatively brief sections that sometimes end a text. They bear no chapter numbers. Conclusions tend to be more extensive and may assume the significance and proportions of final chapters, with or without chapter numbers. In such concluding sections the author may make some final statement about the subject presented, the implications of the study, or questions inviting further investigation. Epilogues, afterwords, and conclusions may begin either recto or verso unless the book is divided into parts, in which case they must begin recto so that they do not appear to belong to the final part only. Typographically they are usually treated like forewords or prefaces.

BACK MATTER

Appendixes

1.81　*Content of an appendix.* An appendix may include explanations and elaborations that are not essential parts of the text but are helpful to a reader seeking further clarification, texts of documents, long lists, survey questionnaires, or sometimes even charts or tables. The appendix should not be a repository for odds and ends that the author could not work into the text.

1.82　*Multiple appendixes.* When two or more appendixes are required, they should be designated by either numbers (Appendix 1, Appendix 2, etc.) or letters (Appendix A, Appendix B, etc.), and each should be given a title as well. The first appendix should begin recto; subsequent appendixes may begin verso or recto.

1.83　*Placement.* In the back matter, appendixes precede the notes. An appendix may be placed at the end of a chapter if what it contains is essential to understanding the chapter. Here it should be introduced by an A-level subhead. In multiauthor books and in books from which offprints of individual chapters will be required, any appendix must follow the chapter it pertains to.

1.84　*Type size.* Appendixes may be set either in the same type size as the text proper or in smaller type.

MADISON CHRONOLOGY
1787

27 May–17 September	JM attends Federal Convention at Philadelphia; takes notes on the debates
29 May	Virginia Plan presented
6 June	JM makes first major speech, containing analysis of factions and theory of extended republic
8 June	Defends "negative" (veto) on state laws
19 June	Delivers critique of New Jersey Plan
27 June–16 July	In debate on representation, JM advocates proportional representation for both branches of legislature
16 July	Compromise on representation adopted
26 July	Convention submits resolutions to Committee of Detail as basis for preparing draft constitution
6 August	Report of Committee on Detail delivered
7 August	JM advocates freehold suffrage
7 August–10 September	Convention debates, then amends, report of 6 August
31 August	JM appointed to Committee on Postponed Matters
8 September	Appointed to Committee of Style
17 September	Signs engrossed Constitution; Convention adjourns
ca. 21 September	Leaves Philadelphia for New York
24 September	Arrives in New York to attend Congress
26 September	Awarded Doctor of Laws degree in absentia by College of New Jersey

Fig. 1.10. Opening page of a chronology. For date style, see 6.46.

Chronology

1.85   *Placement.* A chronological list of events may be useful in certain works. It usually appears in the back matter, sometimes as an appendix, but if essential to readers it is better placed in the front matter, immediately before the text. For an example, see figure 1.10.

Endnotes

1.86   *Format and placement.* Endnotes, simply headed Notes, follow any appendix material and precede the bibliography or reference list (if there is one). The notes to each chapter are introduced by a subhead indicating the chapter number and sometimes the chapter title. The running heads to

1.59). *Not* paginated are leaves or signatures—such as color illustrations or photo galleries—that are inserted after pages have been made up (see 1.45).

Front Matter

1.101 *Roman numerals.* The front matter of a book, especially in the United States, is paginated with lowercase roman numerals (see 1.4). This traditional practice is also expedient, for some of these pages (for example, the preface, acknowledgments, and dedication) may be expanded or even added at the last moment. If arabic numbering were to begin with the half title, no page could be added to the front matter once the book was in page proofs.

1.102 *Display pages and succeeding front matter.* No page number appears on display pages (half title, title, copyright, dedication, epigraph). A drop folio (or no folio) is used on the opening page of each succeeding section of the front matter. Blank pages show no page number.

Text and Back Matter

1.103 *Beginning of the text.* The text begins with arabic page 1. If the text begins with a second half title (see 1.59) or with a part title, the half title or part title counts as page 1, its verso counts as page 2, and the first arabic number to appear is the drop folio (3) on the first page of text (see 1.66). If there is no part title or half title, the first page of the text proper becomes page 1. Page numbers generally do not appear on part titles, but if text appears on a part title, a drop folio may be used.

1.104 *Chapter openings and back matter.* The opening page of each chapter and of each section in the back matter carries either a drop folio or no page number. Page numbers and running heads are usually omitted on pages containing only illustrations or tables, except in books with long sequences of figures or tables.

More Than One Volume

1.105 *Separate versus consecutive pagination.* When a work runs to more than one volume, the publisher must decide how to paginate volume 2: Begin with page 1 on the first page of text, or carry on from where the numbering left off in volume 1? When an index to two volumes is to appear at the end of volume 2, it is often useful to paginate consecutively through both volumes so that the index entries need not include volume as well as page numbers. More than two volumes, regardless of index placement, are best paginated separately because page numbers in four digits are unwieldy (though necessary in large single-volume reference works). For readers' convenience, any reference to a specific page in a work with volumes paginated separately must include the volume number as well as the page number.

1.106 *Front and back matter.* Even if the pagination is consecutive through more than one volume, the front matter in each volume begins with page i. In rare cases where back matter, such as an index, must be added to volume 1 later in the production process, lowercase roman folios may be used; these should continue the sequence from the front matter in that volume—if, for example, the last page of the front matter, even if blank, is xii, the back matter would start with page xiii.

ERRATA

1.107 *Format and placement.* Lists of errors and their corrections may take the form of loose, inserted sheets or bound-in pages. An errata sheet should never be supplied to correct simple typographical errors (which may be corrected in a later printing) or to insert additions to, or revisions of, the printed text (which should wait for the next edition of the book). It should be used only in extreme cases where errors severe enough to cause misunderstanding are detected too late to correct in the normal way but before the finished book is distributed. Then the errors, with their locations and their corrections, may be listed on a sheet that is laid in loose, usually inside the front cover. (The sheet must be inserted by hand, adding considerably to the cost of the book.) If the corrected material can be pasted over the incorrect material, it should be printed on adhesive paper. The following form may be adapted to suit the particulars:

Errata

PAGE	FOR	READ
37, line 5	Peter W. Smith	John Q. Jones
182, line 15	is subject to	is not subject to
195, line 8	figure 3	figure 15
23, 214	Transpose captions of plates 2 and 51.	

1.108 *Bound-in errata page.* A bound-in errata page may be justified when all or part of a book is photographically reproduced from an earlier publication (see fig. 1.12). Such a page must be prepared in time to be set in type and printed and bound with the book. It may be placed either at the end of the

---

Errata

Chapters 1 through 6 and chapters 8 and 9 have been photographically reproduced from the original journal articles. The following are corrections for typographical errors in those articles.

Chap. 1
P. 43, n. 16: "*wirtschaftsmenschen*" should be capitalized.
P. 72, line 12: "1226" should read "1225."

Chap. 2
P. 91, n. 2: "Appendix IV" should read "Appendix III."
P. 91, n. 4: "Appendix IV" should read "Appendix III."
P. 96, line 19: "*stamai uoli*" should read "*stamaiuoli.*"
P. 107, n. 3: "Appendix IV" should read "Appendix III."
P. 114, Appendix II: "Vencenzo" should read "Vincenzo."

Chap. 3
P. 130, line 19: "*sopracorpo*" should read "*sopraccorpo.*"
P. 134, line 31: "*sovracorpo*" should read "*sovraccorpo.*"
P. 155, n. 1: "Accerito" should read "Accerrito"; the date of Folco's death should be 1431.
P. 158, line 24: "*sopracorpo*" should read "*sopraccorpo.*"

Chap. 4
P. 198, col. 1, line 21: "enforcible" should read "enforceable."

Chap. 5
P. 201, line 1: "*bancum*" should read "*bancus.*"
P. 202, line 1: "sought" should read "found."
P. 203, line 20: "became" should read "become."
P. 208, n. 31: "*Verlagsystem*" should read "*Verlagssystem.*"
P. 213, n. 51: "*Tujdschrift*" should read "*Tijdschrift.*"
P. 216, n. 64: "Maine" should read "Maino."
P. 221, n. 107: "*Sicilio*" should read "*Sicilie*"; "*1908*" should read "*1808.*"
P. 227, n. 125: "Publication" should read "Publicatiën."
P. 237, line 15: "wors" should read "worse."

Chap. 6
P. 240, line 22: "Masarozzo" should read "Masaiozzo"; insert "Martellini" after "d'Agnolo."
P. 240, n. 3: "wich" should read "wish."

Fig. 1.12. Page of errata printed and bound with photographically reproduced material.

front matter or at the end of the book and should be listed in the table of contents. For electronic books, see 1.123.

EXTERIOR STRUCTURE

Cover

1.109 *Hard versus soft.* A book is protected, identified, and often promoted by its cover. A clothbound book has a hard cover, a paperback a soft cover.

Hard covers are usually constructed of laminated cardboard over which is stretched an integument of cloth, treated paper, or vinyl or some other plastic. Soft covers are usually made of rather thick but flexible paper whose printed and decorated outside surface is coated with varnish or with a synthetic resin or plastic laminate. For jackets, see 1.112.

1.110   *Front, back, and spine.* A book cover has three parts: front, back, and spine. In hardbound books the spine is most often printed with the author's (or editor's) full name, or the last name only if space is tight; the title of the book; and the publisher's name. Note that the spine copy reads from the top down (cf. 12.58). The subtitle is usually omitted. The publisher's name is often shortened or replaced by an emblem or device known as a colophon or logo. (For another meaning of colophon see 1.92.) The front cover may be blank, especially when there is a jacket, but it sometimes bears stamped or printed material, such as author and title or the publisher's colophon or some other decoration. The back cover of an unjacketed book must bear a bar code (see 1.115–16).

1.111   *Paperback covers.* Paperback covers usually carry printing on all three parts. The author's or editor's name, the publisher's name or colophon or both, and the title are ordinarily printed on the spine. The front cover carries the author's or editor's name, the title and (usually) the subtitle, and sometimes the name of a translator, a contributor of a foreword, or the like. The back cover usually carries promotional copy, such as a description of the book or quotations from reviews; a brief biographical statement about the author; the series title if the book is part of a series; and sometimes the publisher's name, Web site, and other relevant material. Artwork may appear on any or all of the cover parts. For placement of bar codes, see 1.116.

Jacket

1.112   *Content of the jacket.* Hardcover books are often protected by a coated paper jacket (or dust jacket). In addition to the three parts to be found on the book cover itself, the jacket also has flaps that tuck inside the front and back covers. The front and spine carry the same kind of material as the front and spine of paperback covers (see 1.111). The material included on the back of a paperback cover is begun on the front flap of the hardcover jacket and completed either on the back flap or the back panel of the jacket. The back panel is sometimes used to promote other books by the publisher. For placement of bar codes, see 1.116.

Fig. 1.13. Left: A Bookland EAN bar code and a five-digit side bar, or add-on, code. Above the bar codes, in numerals that are optically readable as well as machine readable, is the ISBN. The bar codes are also presented in optically readable numerals. In this example the price is identified as $20.00 in U.S. currency. Right: A Bookland EAN bar code with a five-digit side bar code of 90000, indicating that this auxiliary bar code is not being used by the publisher.

Copy and Artwork for the Cover and Jacket

1.113　*Credit for artwork.* If a credit line is required for artwork included on a jacket or cover, it should appear on the back flap of the jacket or the back cover of a paperback book. Credit for artwork on a paperback cover or on the actual cover (as opposed to the jacket) of a hardcover book may also appear inside the book, usually on the copyright page, since the cover is a permanent part of the bound book. See 12.48 for styling of credit lines.

1.114　*ISBN, Bookland EAN bar code.* Two additional elements should appear on the back cover of a paperback or the back panel of a jacket. The first is the International Standard Book Number (ISBN), which serves as a convenient identifier of both publisher and title (see 1.28). On the cover or jacket, the ISBN is usually given in numerals that are both machine readable and optically readable. The second is the Bookland EAN (European Article Number) bar code, which is equivalent to the Universal Product Code printed on merchandise packages and used by retailers to identify item and price and record each item sold. The Bookland EAN bar code presents a thirteen-digit number in laser-readable form (see fig. 1.13). The first three digits identify the item either as a book (978) or as a periodical (977). Following this prefix are the first nine digits of the ISBN, with hyphens omitted. The last digit of the ISBN, the check digit, is replaced by a new check digit mathematically related to the composite number represented by the bar code.

1.115　*Price code.* The basic Bookland EAN code is now augmented by a five-digit bar code used primarily, but optionally, as a currency and price indicator (fig. 1.13). The first digit identifies the currency in which the price is specified (e.g., the digit 5 stands for U.S. dollars); the following four digits represent the price. The digits 2000, following the digit 5, indicate a price of $20.00 in U.S. currency. A price exceeding $98.98 is indicated by the four-digit series 9999, in which case the actual price must be entered manually. Some publishers use the five-digit side bar code for other purposes. If the publisher does not wish to use this auxiliary bar code, the digits 90000 are entered.

1.116 *Printed bar codes.* In printing the bar codes, the precision with which the thickness of the bars is reproduced is critical, as are the dimensions of the code itself. For this reason, publishers that do not generate their own bar codes may wish to obtain negative film or positive prints from specialized suppliers. Standard locations for the codes are the back cover for a paperback book and, for a hardcover book, either the back cover or, if the book is jacketed, the back panel of the jacket. Wherever it appears, the code must be printed against a white or very light background, and the surface must be smooth enough to accept the printing effectively. Bar codes must be printed in a color that can be read by a scanner. (Additional information about the Bookland EAN bar code system may be obtained from the Book Industry Study Group.)

ELECTRONICALLY PUBLISHED BOOKS

1.117 *Printed versus electronic books.* Many of Chicago's guidelines for printed books also apply to electronically published books; most electronic books are to some degree analogous to traditional print publications. A book can be presented online or in a storage medium (such as a CD-ROM) in almost the same format as a printed book, including all the traditional elements—title page, copyright page, table of contents, notes, and bibliography—along with the text itself. But electronic books need not be presented in the traditional linear fashion. Both the content and the organization can be transformed by the electronic environment. While this section does not discuss the constantly evolving software that drives these transformations, it does address the essential parts of any electronic book.

Front Matter

1.118 *Elements included.* The front matter for an electronic book contains all the elements recommended for a printed book, with the exception of anything related purely to the print tradition or the limitations of the linear bound book. An electronic book, for example, need not have anything resembling a half title or a frontispiece. The front matter may be one "page," or it may include several subdocuments that can be reached from that page by means of hypertext (text that contains electronic links; see also 1.182). Although there is no "right way" to organize an electronic book, its organization must be logical: when in doubt, make an analogy to print. For example, a preface is still a preface, and the way it is presented should make it clear that it is to be read before the body of the book. Front matter may not be literally up front in an electronic book, but the order in which the book as a whole is intended to be read should be clearly indicated through a combination of traditional terms and logical navigational aids.

1.119 *Copyright information.* Copyright information for an electronic book need be presented only once. Some books, however—for example, those posted on the Internet—are designed so that one part may be read separately from the work as a whole, without any clear statement of what it is or who owns it. In such cases it may be advisable, in addition to the main copyright notice, to include a short copyright notice with each separate page or subdocument, to discourage infringement; for example:

© 2001 by The University of Chicago
All rights reserved. Electronic edition published 2005

This example refers to a book published and therefore copyrighted as a printed work in 2001, then published in electronic form in 2005.

1.120 *Author biographies.* Author biographies, which typically appear on the copyright page, cover, or jacket of a printed book, often become a separate item in electronic books, reached by means of a link to a statement "about the author(s)."

1.121 *Publication details.* The publisher's address and the copyright notice should follow the guidelines for printed books (see 1.15–16). The publishing history (see 1.21) should include any previously published print or electronic editions of the work. An electronic edition of a printed work is considered a new edition and should carry the designation "electronic edition" (see 1.119).

1.122 *Production details.* Electronic books available on CD-ROM carry information about where the CD-ROM was manufactured (analogous to "Printed in the United States"); electronic books posted on the Internet need not carry information about where they were produced.

1.123 *Impression numbers.* Impression numbers do not apply to electronic books. Publishers should, however, maintain a record of minor revisions similar to those incorporated into new impressions of print works. If an electronic book undergoes major revisions, publishers should assign revision numbers (e.g., first revised edition, second revised edition, etc.). If a book posted on the Internet is subject to continuous revision, the publisher should so indicate, perhaps by providing revision dates.

1.124 *Cataloging-in-Publication (CIP) data.* Books published only in electronic form were not, when this edition of *The Chicago Manual of Style* was published, eligible for the Library of Congress's CIP program. Editors should check with the Library of Congress for its current policies regarding electronic books.

1.125 *International Standard Book Number (ISBN).* Every electronic book must carry a unique ISBN, separate from any print version. Moreover, if a particular book is published in more than one electronic format, each should carry a unique ISBN. Finally, each version of a book should provide the ISBNs for all other available versions. For more information on ISBNs, see 1.28.

1.126 *Table of contents.* The table of contents (together with an index, if any; see 1.133–34) provides the key to navigating a printed work. This navigation function is just as important in an electronic book, in which the items listed are linked to specific sections of the work, serving as a useful home base. The table of contents also shows the size and scope of the work: a reader may not be able to flip through the pages of an electronic book or gauge its size, especially if it is not presented on screen as a linear set of traditional-sized pages with running heads and folios or as one scrollable file. The table of contents therefore may be a more elaborate menu than the typical list of chapter titles recommended for printed works.

1.127 *Lists of illustrations and tables.* Lists of illustrations and tables, linked to each item listed, should be provided according to the guidelines for printed works (1.44–47). Thumbnail versions of illustrations, also linked to the illustrations themselves, may be included in the list.

1.128 *Forewords and prefaces, dedications and epigraphs, and other front matter.* The linear presentation of printed books is especially suited to such items as dedications, forewords, and other items that set the stage for a book or provide crucial information about, for example, abbreviations used. Publishers of electronic books have greater freedom in presenting these elements but should bear in mind the logical order in which the material was meant to be read; when in doubt, make an analogy to print.

Text

1.129   *Organization.* Most of the recommendations regarding the main text of a printed book (1.58–80) also apply to electronic books. Parts, chapters, and subheads all provide a useful organizational model.

1.130   *Nonprint elements.* An electronic book can incorporate much more content than its ink-on-paper counterpart, almost always including some form of hypertext (see 1.182) and metadata (literally, information about information—e.g., such document-related data as keywords or permissions—which can be embedded in the electronic file). It might also include sound, such as background music that varies according to the dramatic course of the narrative; animation; the author's working notes; or whatever can be delivered digitally. Although there is no standard course that an electronic book should take, the integrity of such books should be considered, at least initially, in terms of their traditional printed counterparts.

Notes

1.131   *Hypertext links.* Notes are transformed in the electronic environment by means of hypertext links to and from the main text. It is unnecessary, therefore, to consider them in terms of the position-related analogy to footnotes or endnotes. Publishers should ensure that links provide a seamless and transparent method for shuttling back and forth between a note and its reference in the text; readers should not be required to search or scroll through the document to get to notes and back to text.

Back Matter

1.132   *Elements.* Such traditional elements of the printed book as appendixes, chronologies, glossaries, bibliographies and reference lists, lists of contributors, and even colophons have counterparts in electronic books, and they provide a logical basis for organizing comparable materials in an electronic book.

1.133   *Index.* A good search engine—not to mention the basic search capabilities of any electronic environment—allows readers to query a text about its contents. No search engine, however, can tell a reader what questions to ask. Moreover, a mechanical calculation of relevance will not always replace the judgment professional indexers bring to bear when deciding which terms—and which occurrences or discussions of them—an index should include. Chicago therefore strongly recommends indexes for electronic books whose printed counterparts would merit them.

1.134 *Page references.* Although page references cannot be used for indexes of electronic works that do not carry fixed page numbers, there are several software-determined strategies for providing links to discrete occurrences of an entry in the text. Page numbers need not be purged from an index derived from a print document but published electronically; they may be useful, and they may themselves be linked to the material cited.

Running Heads

1.135 *Need for running heads.* An electronic book can be designed to look like its printed counterpart (though recto and verso pages are almost never a part of the design), but even if it is not, some variation on the traditional running head should be used to keep readers oriented.

Page Numbers

1.136 *Method of numbering.* An electronic book may employ screen-sized pages with fixed page numbers, or it may instead be a series of subdocuments or consist of one large, scrollable document. Publishers merely need to ensure that, for books consisting of unpaginated subdocuments, each subdocument is readily identifiable—by chapter number, subhead, or other organizational division—both to keep readers oriented and to allow proper citation of the work.

Documentation and Technical Help

1.137 *Types of help.* Some electronic books require documentation that provides instructions related to special features of the book—documentation that goes beyond that accompanying the hardware and software used to create and display the book. Some books place unique demands on the software, such as those involving complex queries to databases, and the publisher may need to provide a fuller explanation of the functionality of the publication. Such information might be in the form of answers to questions that a publisher anticipates readers might have in mind and, in the case of Internet books, answers to actual questions raised by readers and posted after the book is published (these are sometimes known as "frequently asked questions," or FAQs). Or more comprehensive, annotated help systems and tutorials may be necessary. Finally, publishers should consider providing an avenue for technical support for especially complex works.

Journals

COVERS AND SPINE

1.138   *Accuracy and current information.* A printed journal is usually bound in soft covers, like a paperback. The spine and covers of a journal contain important information that must be checked as carefully as the text within. Journals follow their own editorial and typographic styles, which differ widely. See also 1.167, 2.38, 3.17, 3.39.

1.139   *Spine.* The spine contains the name of the journal, the volume and issue numbers, and the date, month, or season and year of publication. It may also note the beginning and ending page numbers of that issue. Consistent placement of these elements from issue to issue ensures a pleasing visual alignment when the issues are shelved together.

1.140   *Cover 1.* The front cover, called cover 1, has the same general design for every issue. As part of the design, a color scheme is chosen for the covers and spine. Often one color is used for every issue, and that color becomes identified with the journal. Sometimes several are chosen, the color(s) changing with each issue or each volume. Cover 1 displays the name of the journal; the volume and issue numbers; the date, month, or season, and the year of the issue; the publisher's name; and sometimes the table of contents or an illustration (whose caption or credit line appears either on cover 2 or on the contents page; see 1.141, 1.147). The title of a special issue, along with the name(s) of the editor(s) of the special issue, appears on cover 1.

1.141   *Cover 2.* The inside front cover usually contains the masthead with the names of the editor(s) and staff, the editorial board, the journal's International Standard Serial Number (ISSN; see 1.29), its dates or frequency of publication, subscription information, addresses for business and editorial correspondence, and the copyright line for the entire issue (see also 1.161). Cover 2 may also include information about postage; a statement about paper durability; a statement about copying beyond fair use; information about obtaining microfilm copies of back issues; mention of a submission fee, if that is part of the journal's practice; information about indexing of the journal's articles; a statement about advertising policy; and a caption for any illustration that appears on cover 1. If the journal is sponsored by a scholarly society or other organization, cover 2 may supply the name and address of the society and the names of officers (which must, of course, be kept up to date). Occasionally on cover 2 but more often in the

43

front or back matter of each issue (see 1.144–46), there may be a statement of editorial policy for the journal indicating what kind of articles the journal publishes as well as information for contributors about how and in what form to submit a manuscript.

1.142 *Cover 3.* The inside back cover is often given over to advertising, or it may be used for information for contributors. If the table of contents begins on cover 4 (see 1.143), it may be completed on cover 3.

1.143 *Cover 4.* The back cover carries the bar code for the journal issue in the lower right-hand corner. (If there is advertising on cover 4, the bar code may be put on cover 2 or cover 3.) It may also carry the table of contents or titles of articles scheduled to appear in a forthcoming issue, or advertising. If the table of contents begins on cover 1, it may be completed on cover 4.

FRONT MATTER

1.144 *Placement of elements.* The elements discussed in 1.140–43 can equally occur in the front matter, or preliminary ("prelim") pages. Some journals, because they have a large staff and a large number of editors on their advisory board, have space on cover 2 only for the masthead and advisory board editors; the other items then appear in the front matter.

1.145 *Information for contributors.* If not included on cover 2 (see 1.141) or cover 3 (see 1.142), information for potential contributors may appear in the front or back matter; it can vary in length from a sentence to several pages. A statement of editorial policy may appear in either the front or the back matter.

1.146 *Acknowledgments.* Acknowledgments of reviewers, announcements of awards or conferences, calls for papers, and errata are published periodically in the preliminary pages or at the end of a journal issue. If the issue is a supplement or special issue on a single topic, perhaps representing the proceedings of a conference or symposium, the issue may begin with a title page that contains the title of the supplement, the name(s) of any guest editor(s), information about the source of the articles (perhaps a conference or symposium), and sponsorship information, if any.

1.147 *Table of contents.* The table of contents, usually headed Contents, may appear in the front matter or on the cover(s) of the issue (see 1.141–43). It bears the title of the journal; the date, month, or season and the year; the

Ethics

An International Journal of Social, Political, and Legal Philosophy

VOLUME 109   JANUARY 1999   NUMBER 2

Fig. 1.14. Partial table of contents for a scholarly journal. Note that the page numbers, as in most scholarly journals, are sequential throughout a volume.

volume and issue numbers; and the titles of the articles in the issue along with the authors' names and the page number on which each article begins. It also lists review articles, book reviews, book notes, commentaries, editorials, or other substantive items, and it may either list articles published in electronic form only (e-articles) or direct readers to the journal's Web site for a list of those articles. See figure 1.14.

1.148   *Section titles.* The table of contents may contain section titles, such as Reviews or, where there are enough items to warrant a special section, Announcements (see 1.158).

1.149   *Special issues.* In a special issue, the table of contents carries the title of the special issue and the names of its editors. See also 1.150.

1.150   *Editorials.* An editorial is not a regular feature in most academic journals but appears on a particular occasion. When there is a change of some sort—a new editor, modifications in editorial policy or style, features added or dropped, or graphic redesign of the journal (see 1.162)—an editorial announces and explains the change. A journal may provide an annual editorial summing up the year's activity. Some journals publish invited editorials, written by someone who is neither the journal's editor-in-chief nor a member of its editorial board, that comment on a particular article or group of articles. A special issue usually includes an introduction by the special issue's editor(s). The heading Editorial or Introduction is used, and the editor's name appears at the end of the piece.

MAJORS AND MINORS

1.151   *Categories.* Items published in a journal are often described as being majors or minors. The majors, principally the articles, are the items set in the major (or regular) type size and style of the journal. Special kinds of articles, such as review essays, survey articles, or articles grouped as a symposium, are typically treated as majors. Minors, often set in smaller type, are items such as brief reports, letters to the editor, book reviews, book notes, announcements, calls for papers, errata, and notes on contributors.

1.152   *First page.* The first page of an article includes the title of the article, the author's or authors' name(s), the affiliation of each author (sometimes), an address for correspondence and reprints (sometimes), dates of submission and acceptance of the article (most commonly in scientific journals), an abstract (sometimes), the beginning of the text, an acknowledgment note (sometimes), an editor's note (occasionally), any footnotes that are referenced on that page, and the copyright line for the particular article (see 1.161). A general section heading such as Articles, Review Essay, or Symposium or a specific heading such as Medical Microbiology may appear above the article title.

1.153   *Subheads.* An article, like a chapter in a book, may be divided into sections and subsections headed by subheads, sub-subheads, and so on (see 1.71–

78). The number of subhead levels required may vary from article to article.

1.154   *Illustrations, appendixes, and other elements.* In addition to text, an article may contain illustrations, extracts, equations, and tables. It may also be followed by one or more appendixes, which in turn may contain text, tables, and the like.

1.155   *Documentation.* One of the fundamental identifying marks of a journal is its documentation style—either notes or references. Notes still prevail in many humanities journals. References—used mostly by journals in science and the social sciences—appear at the end of the article to which they pertain. Notes may be footnotes or endnotes; if the latter, they appear at the end of the article, with the heading Notes. For a discussion of different styles of documentation, see chapter 16.

1.156   *Book reviews.* Many journals include a book review section. Such sections, usually headed Reviews or Book Reviews, vary greatly in length from journal to journal. Within a section, each review carries a heading that lists information about the book being reviewed. The heading includes the author's name, the title of the book, place and date of publication, publisher's name, number of pages (including front matter), and price. If the book is part of a series, the series name may be given. Some journals include reviews of other journals and of new media. The name of the reviewer usually appears at the end of the review but occasionally follows the heading.

1.157   *Book notes.* Book notes use the same form of headings as book reviews, but the text is much shorter and reviewers may be listed by their initials. Some journals also publish a list of books or other materials received for review from publishers.

1.158   *Announcements.* Announcements include such items as notices of future conferences and symposia; calls for papers, award nominations, or research subjects; and employment opportunities.

1.159   *Contributors.* Some journals have a special section with information about the contributors to the issue, such as their affiliations and publications or fields of study. The names must be checked against the authors' names on the first page of every article to be sure they are spelled correctly (see also 2.38).

1.160   *Letters.* Letters to the editor(s), rare in a humanities journal, are usually treated as a minor. In some scientific journals, however, letters appear as a regular, lively feature, often with replies, and may contain equations, tables, and figures. (In Chicago's *Astrophysical Journal*, letters appear so frequently that they have become a separate publication with a schedule of its own.)

1.161 *Copyright lines.* In addition to the copyright line that appears on cover 2, each substantive article or element in the journal normally carries its own copyright line. This usually appears at the bottom of the first page of the article, below any footnotes on that page. It contains three basic parts: (1) information on the current issue, including the name of the journal, the volume number, the month and year of publication, and the inclusive page numbers of the article; (2) the actual copyright notice, containing the copyright symbol, the year, the name of the copyright owner (usually either the publisher or the sponsoring society), and the words "all rights reserved"; and (3) a series of numbers (the Copyright Clearance Center code) containing the journal's unique identification number (its ISSN), the year, the volume and issue numbers, the article number (each article has its own assigned number, with articles numbered in sequence through an issue), and the per copy fee for photocopying, payable through the Copyright Clearance Center (CCC; see below).

The Journal of Modern History 74 (March 2002): 1–27
© 2002 by The University of Chicago. All rights reserved.
0022-2801/2002/7401-0001$10.00

Most but not all journals use the CCC, which provides systems through which copyright owners can license the reproduction and distribution of those materials in both print and electronic form. Its relations with equivalent agencies in other countries enable the CCC to collect fees for uses in those countries. Note that fees apply only to copyrighted material and not to articles in the public domain. Since book reviews and book notes are not usually copyrighted by the publisher, the first page of the relevant section typically carries a disclaimer stating that permission to reprint a book review (book note, etc.) printed in the section may be obtained only from the author.

DESIGN AND STYLE

1.162 *Design.* A printed journal's design—its physical, visual, and editorial features—is determined when the journal is founded. At that time, a designer creates a design for the cover and the overall look of a journal and specifications for all its regular features. Because the designer designs not for a specific text but for categories of text—article title, author's name, text, heads, subheads, and such—the design of a journal should be simple and flexible as well as being visually pleasing and easy to read. It is then the job of the manuscript editor to fit the items for a particular issue into the overall design. For electronically published journals, see 1.169–91.

1.163   *Editorial style.* A journal's editorial style (see 2.52) governs such things as when to use numerals or percent signs, how to treat abbreviations or special terms, and how tables are typically organized. Consistency of design and style contributes to a journal's identity; readers know what to expect, and the substantive contribution of each article stands out more sharply when typographical distractions are at a minimum.

1.164   *Redesign.* A long-running journal may occasionally be redesigned typographically. More rarely, the editors may introduce minor alterations in style to accommodate changing needs. Once established, however, a new design or style must be adhered to as carefully as the one it replaces.

VOLUME AND INDEX

1.165   *Volume.* A volume of a journal usually comprises the issues published in a calendar year. For a journal published quarterly, a volume has four issues; for one published monthly, twelve issues. Some journals, however, publish two or more volumes in one year, depending on the frequency and length of issues. Chicago's *Astrophysical Journal*, for example, has published as many as eighteen volumes in one year. A library could not bind a whole year's issues of a massive journal into a single volume.

1.166   *Index.* At the end of a volume, most journals publish an index to the articles and other pieces published in that volume. The index appears in the volume's last issue. Names of authors, titles of articles, and titles and authors of books reviewed are indexed. In the sciences, subject indexes are sometimes included (but see 1.186).

1.167   *Page numbers.* Page numbers in a journal usually start with 1 in the volume's first issue and run continuously to the end of the volume. An issue always begins on a right-hand page (recto) and ends on a left-hand page (verso); thus the last page of an issue is an even number and the first page an odd one. If issue 1 ends with page 264, then issue 2 starts on page 265. It is important to keep track of the ending page number of an issue so as to determine the first page number of the next issue. For articles that are published only in electronic form but can be printed as pages formatted to look like those in the print journals, a separate page-numbering system is used (E1, E2, etc.), again running continuously to the end of the volume.

1.168 *Running heads or running feet.* Running heads or feet bear the name of the journal (either spelled out or in abbreviated form); the author's surname or, for more than one author, a shortened version of the author list (such as "Aldrich et al."); the title of the article, usually shortened, or the name of the journal section (such as Brief Reports). Arrangement of these pieces of information on rectos and versos varies among journals. For more on running heads and for their occasional omission, see 1.93–94, 1.99.

ELECTRONICALLY PUBLISHED JOURNALS

1.169 *Definition.* Electronically published journals include journals that are published in both print and electronic versions and those that are published in electronic form only (e-journals).

1.170 *Compared with print.* Electronically published journals typically contain all the material included in print journals except, in some cases, advertising. Electronic journals may present the material in much the same way as print journals—as page images (e.g., portable document format [PDF] or files) that can be printed and that correspond to the pages of the journal's print issues—or they may present searchable, full-text versions replete with internal and external hypertext links, high-resolution images, data that can be downloaded to the user's computer for analysis, and other features not available in the print edition. Some journals make articles available in multiple formats, including full-text, PDF, and other versions; some even release, upon acceptance of an article, an initial "in press" version consisting of the author's accepted but unedited file, perhaps including the comments of anonymous peer reviewers (see 1.173).

1.171 *Articles and issues.* Electronic journals are typically not used in the way a reader might flip through an issue of a printed journal; the electronic format encourages random access to single articles, without the context of an issue as a whole. Users can navigate by various means within a journal's Web site and can move freely from the journal's site to other online resources and back again, perhaps never looking at an issue's table of contents.

1.172 *Articles as individual publications.* Aside from the richness of full-text electronic files and multifaceted Web sites, the primary difference between print and electronic journals has been the increasing tendency to publish articles electronically as discrete items that are not associated—at least initially—with a particular issue of a journal. In many journals, electronic articles become items in what is essentially a growing database of published works. Although print journals serve an important archival function for libraries, are traditionally used for promotion and tenure decisions, and are considered by many people to be easier to read, in some fields the association between individual articles and particular print issues of a journal has become almost incidental. This is especially true of journals that publish articles electronically before publishing them in print; for such articles, the real date of publication is the date of electronic publication (which should be included as part of the article's history), not the date, month, or season named on the cover of the print journal. Especially in the sciences, where initial publication online is increasingly common, many readers may read and in fact cite articles before issues have been printed or page numbers have even been assigned.

1.173   *Preprints.* Manuscripts are sometimes released before publication: authors themselves may circulate drafts within a research community, or they may circulate versions submitted to a journal. They may post drafts on a preprint server—as is standard practice in the physics community—or on their own Web pages. Some journals post accepted but not yet edited articles on their Web sites.

Front Matter and Home Pages

1.174   *Front matter.* Most journal home pages include hypertext links to all material typically found in the front matter of a printed journal.

1.175   *Additional resources.* Journal home pages may also provide some or all of the following resources: a fuller description of the journal and its policies; information about the history of the journal and, if applicable, the sponsoring society; more extensive information about preparation and submission of electronic text, tables, math, art, and other files (e.g., animations or large data sets); links to other home pages (e.g., the publisher's home page, the sponsoring society's home page, other relevant societies' home pages, and databases or other online resources associated with the journal or the field); individual and institutional subscription forms; lists of institutional subscribers; site license agreement and registration forms; links to tables of contents for all issues of the journal or for those currently available online; lists of articles scheduled for upcoming issues; a link to a journal-specific or broader search engine; society meeting abstracts and information about upcoming meetings; society membership information and application forms; information about special services for subscribers (e.g., tables of contents distributed by e-mail before publication in print); and e-mail links for questions about manuscript submission and review, subscriptions, back issues, advertising, copyright and permissions, books and new media for review, passwords and other technical issues, and other topics. These resources typically are not associated with a particular issue of the journal but are simply updated as needed.

1.176 *Issues as context.* There is a potential loss of information that comes with the uncoupling of articles from issues of a journal. Editors of electronic journals should seek to preserve the historical context by maintaining, in connection with each article, information that might affect interpretation of its contents or its selection for publication. Information such as the names of the editors and editorial board, any sponsors or advertisers in the journal, and the information for contributors—as they existed at the time of the article's publication—are as relevant as the date of publication in assessing the import of a work.

Copyright Information and Date of Publication

1.177 *Copyright of individual articles.* Journals typically contain copyright information for each article. This is especially important for journals that release articles individually in electronic form well before the print edition, which contains copyright information for an issue, has been assembled, printed, and distributed. See also 1.16.

1.178 *Publication history.* For all articles that are published electronically before they are published in print, the date of electronic publication should appear as part of the article's history, in both the print and the electronic versions. This date is also part of the context for interpretation of the article; in the sciences, especially, what is known—or at least what has been reported—can change rapidly.

1.179 *International Standard Serial Number (ISSN).* An electronically published journal should have an ISSN (see 1.29) that is distinct from the ISSN assigned to its print version (if there is a print version). Each version of a journal should provide the ISSN(s) for any other available version(s).

Running Heads

1.180 *Location and function.* In electronic articles, the shortened versions of an article's title and author name(s) typically included in a print journal's running heads may be displayed on each screen; their location on the screen depends on the browser and on the electronic journal's design. As is the case in print journals, this information orients readers.

Text

1.181   *Printed versus electronic text.* The text of an electronically published article is typically identical to the article's print version (if there is a print version). The content and organization are the same. However, the electronic format allows the document to contain not just standard text but hypertext.

1.182   *Hypertext.* Hypertext is text that contains links—to other elements within the document (perhaps illustrations, tables, and the reference list, notes, or bibliography) and often to outside resources such as field-specific indexes or databases. Display of a full-text journal article typically includes a list of linked items, consisting of an article-specific list (or menu) that allows readers to move directly to other sections or elements of the article and a standard menu that allows them to move to the issue's table of contents, to the previous or next article in the issue, to the journal's home page, to a search page, or elsewhere. The display may also include thumbnail versions of the article's tables and illustrations (see 1.184–85).

Reference Lists, Notes, and Bibliographies

1.183   *Links.* In full-text electronic articles, text citations of references, notes, or items in a bibliography are typically linked to the items themselves, allowing readers to move from the text citation to the cited item and back to the text. Reference lists and bibliographies may also contain links to resources outside the article—for example, to cited articles or to an outside index or database (see 1.186).

Tables

1.184   *Electronic versus print.* In electronic articles, tables display the same information as in the print journal. Tables in electronic articles can be presented in multiple formats, however, such as an image of the typeset table, a searchable hypertext version with links, or a machine-readable version that allows readers to download the data and either repeat the analyses used in the article or use the data, perhaps in combination with data from other sources, for their own analyses. Table footnote citations can be linked to the table footnotes themselves; this is especially useful for navigation in very large tables. Links also allow readers to move freely from text to tables and back again, as well as from one table to another. Very large tables may be published in electronic form only; if there is also a print version of the article, both versions should make this difference explicit (see 1.188–90). In some cases it may be more appropriate to present data as machine-readable data sets rather than rendering them in traditional two-dimensional tables.

Illustrations

1.185 *Electronic versus print.* An electronic article may simply display the same illustrations available in the print version of the article. Illustrations may be displayed in the text as thumbnails, with links that allow readers to move about as described for tables (1.184). However, the range of types of illustrations that can be offered in electronic journals is richer than the range possible in print. Static images may be offered in various resolutions that can allow readers to look more closely. Videos and animations, represented in the print version as still frames, can allow them to view movement and understand processes. Illustrations may include an audio component. An electronic article can include more illustrations than would be practical in print. Color can be used freely, without the costs associated with color printing, although "accuracy" of color can vary considerably between display devices.

Indexes

1.186 *Types of indexes.* Some electronic journals, especially in the sciences, have dispensed with subject indexes; in some fields, journal subject indexes have been almost completely superseded by large online databases (such as the National Library of Medicine's bibliographic database of journal articles, PubMed) that allow readers to search an entire field of indexed journals, perhaps using terms from a standard list of keywords, rather than searching individually at each journal's or each journal publisher's Web site. In some fields, more readers may reach an article by this means than by subscribing to the journal. If they lack such capabilities, however, journals should continue to publish a subject index regularly. For journals that publish a traditional subject index electronically, the index can be offered simply as a rendition of the printed index or as hypertext.

Publication Policy

1.187 *Corrections.* Chicago considers the electronic version of its journal articles to be the version of record; the print version, which should contain all elements that are essential to the article, may nevertheless include only a subset of the material available electronically. Because the electronic version as it existed on the date of electronic publication is the version of record, it is extremely important not to make tacit changes to the electronic file. Despite the ease with which electronic documents can be corrected and updated, errors should be corrected by means of errata, as the journal normally would correct errors; online, errata and articles in need of correction can be linked electronically. Note that release of electronic articles before they are published in print means that errors may turn up well before the print issue has been assembled; consequently, an issue may include an erratum that concerns an article in the same issue. In this case, the erratum should state that the article is in the current issue and should specify the date of electronic publication.

Differences between Print and Electronic Versions

1.188   *Making differences explicit.* Chicago recommends that all differences between the print and electronic versions of an article be noted in both. The print version should specify any electronic-only features, and the electronic version should state how the print version differs.

1.189   *Electronic-only articles.* Some journals designate certain articles for publication in electronic form only. These may be articles that merit publication in the journal but have been assigned a lower priority than articles to be published in both print and electronic form, or they may be articles with substantial electronic-only features whose absence would render print versions much less useful. Any articles published as part of an issue but only in electronic form should be listed in the print edition of the journal.

1.190   *Electronic-only features.* Although a printed article should include all elements that are essential to understanding, interpreting, and documenting the text, many journals publish special materials electronically that are not available in the print version. These features may include very large tables, supplemental reading lists, animations, audio components, or color versions of figures published in black and white in the printed journal. Differences between versions must be noted in all other versions (see 1.188).

Identification of Digital Material

1.191   *Unique identifiers.* All electronic publications must be citable. Chicago's electronic journals publish articles that are associated with page ranges, either print pages or e-pages (which are assigned numbers that begin with the prefix *E* or, less desirably, *e*). Articles themselves also have numbers that can be found in the Copyright Clearance Center code (for journals that are registered with the Copyright Clearance Center, see 1.161), and new schemes of identifiers, such as the Digital Object Identifier (DOI), are being developed. Although industry practice in this area is evolving, the fundamental need is clear: persistent, citable, permanent identifiers for electronic content.

2

Manuscript Preparation and Manuscript Editing

~~~~~~

Introduction

2.1 *Overview.* The first part of this chapter (2.3–46) is addressed primarily to authors, conceived broadly to include compilers, translators, volume editors, editors of journals, and contributors to journals or books. It deals with what most publishers expect in the physical preparation of manuscripts. Although many of the guidelines apply to all forms of publication, most pertain primarily to printed books. Authors preparing works for electronic publication should consult their publishers for additional instructions. Those writing for scholarly journals or other periodicals should consult the specific publication's instructions for authors. The second part of the chapter (2.47–103) relates primarily to manuscript editors—often called copyeditors—and explains what they do to manuscripts. All the guidelines given may be modified according to the publisher's needs and the nature of the publication. For an illustration of how the stages described in this chapter fit into the overall publishing process for books and journals, see appendix B.

2.2 *Terminology.* "Manuscript" is used here to include electronic files, hard copy (also called printout), cut-and-pasted copy, photocopied material, and typescript. "Typing" is used interchangeably with "keyboarding" or "keying." And although most on-screen editing does not technically take place online, the term "editing online" is used, since it has become standard within the publishing industry.

The Author's Responsibilities

2.3 *Elements to be furnished.* Before editing begins, the author should provide any of the following elements that are to be included in the work:

- Title page
- Dedication
- Epigraph
- Table of contents

- List of illustrations
- List of tables
- Preface
- Acknowledgments
- Any other front matter
- All text matter, including introduction and part titles
- Notes
- Appendixes
- Glossary
- URLs for all Web sites cited
- Bibliography or reference list
- Any other back matter
- All illustrations and all tables
- Illustration captions
- All permissions, in writing, that may be required to reproduce illustrations or previously published material or to cite unpublished data or personal communications (see chapter 4)

The publisher usually furnishes the half-title page, the copyright page, and copy for the running heads. The list above, except for most of the front and back matter, also applies to authors contributing an article to a journal or a chapter to a book.

PHYSICAL FORM AND NUMBER OF COPIES REQUIRED

2.4 *Electronic files.* After a book manuscript has been accepted for publication, publishers usually require the electronic files for the work (except for the index) in its latest version, often in disk form, along with two sets of hard copy (one may be a photocopy), which must correspond exactly to the electronic files submitted. Discrepancies can cause major problems, since a manuscript editor working with the electronic files will frequently refer to the hard copy. The disk must be labeled with the author's name, the title of the work, parts of the work included on the disk if more than one is required for the whole work, software used, and date when the disk was made. If files are submitted as e-mail attachments, the relevant information should be furnished in the author's cover letter. The author should retain backup files but must make no further changes to them, since the files sent to the publisher will be the ones used by the manuscript editor (see 2.5). Any material (such as certain types of illustrations) that cannot be included in electronic form must accompany the hard copy, and any additional material that cannot be printed out (such as videos, animations, or large data files) must be noted and described in the cover letter. For all such material, the software used, the number of items, their type(s), and the individual file names must be specified. Check with your publisher or journal editorial office for additional instructions. The index, which cannot be completed until page proofs are available, should be furnished in electronic form as well as hard copy. For preparation of the electronic files, see 2.10–35. For paper-only manuscripts, see 2.6. For manuscripts consisting largely of previously published material, see 2.7 and 2.41–46. For journals, the physical form of the manuscript and the number of copies required are usually specified in the journal's instructions for authors.

2.5 *Changes to manuscript.* An author who needs to make further changes after submitting the files must alert the publisher immediately, before editing has begun. For major changes, the author must submit revised files and hard copy. Minor changes can be entered later on the edited manuscript (see 2.74) or redlined printout (see 2.83) that the author will receive from the editor. For journals, major changes are rarely permitted after an article has been accepted; schedules do not allow for them. Peer-reviewed articles that require major changes may also require additional review.

2.6 *Paper manuscripts, or typescripts.* In the absence of electronic files, the author should provide the publisher with two identical paper copies of the manuscript; one may be a photocopy. All copy must be vertically double-spaced. Anything added by hand must be clearly written, in upper- and lowercase letters, directly above the line or in the margin, *never* on the back of the page. Corrections longer than a short phrase must be typed and inserted where they belong by cutting the page and taping the pieces to fresh sheets of paper, using transparent tape that can be written on. See also 2.94.

2.7 *Previously published material.* If previously published material is submitted in the form of printed pages, a photocopy is also required. See 2.42–43.

2.8 *Paper.* Paper copies should be submitted on good-quality paper that can be written on and is of standard size—in the United States, $8^{1}/_{2} \times 11$ inches. A4 paper (210×297 mm) is also acceptable for authors from countries in which A4 is standard. Print on only one side of the sheet.

2.9 *Preparing the files: an overview.* The following discussion (2.10–35) assumes that, after being edited, the electronic files furnished by an author will be converted into printed form by the publisher's typesetter, an in-house typesetter, or an in-house automated typesetting system. Some of the discussion also applies to paper-only or electronic-only manuscripts. *All authors should consult their publishers or, if publishing in a journal, study* *the journal's instructions for authors before preparing final copy*; some of the steps recommended in the following paragraphs may be unnecessary or unsuitable for certain publications, and some, if difficult for the author to perform, may better be done by the publisher.

KEYBOARDING: GENERAL INSTRUCTIONS

2.10   *Some admonitions.* Consistency is essential. Keep formatting to a minimum. The publisher wants your keystrokes, not a fancy printout. Never type lowercase el (l) where the numeral one (1) is intended. Never type capital oh (O) where zero (0) is intended. In general, use the correct character if your software allows rather than a makeshift keyboard substitute—for example, if you want the prime symbol, insert the prime symbol from your word processor's list of symbols rather than using an apostrophe. If in doubt, consult your publisher.

2.11   *Software.* All files (except for those containing illustrations) should be submitted in the same software and in the same font. If you have used more than one font, or if you have problems converting from one software to another, consult your publisher. Avoid sans serif fonts, since these do not clearly distinguish between 1, l, and I.

2.12   *Line spacing and word spacing.* For the hard copy, the entire text and, if possible, all extracts, notes, bibliography, index, and other material should be vertically double-spaced. A single character space, not two spaces, should be left after periods at the ends of sentences (both in manuscript and in final, published form) and after colons. (For colons in bibliographic forms, see 16.15, 17.169.) No extra character space should be left after the final punctuation at the end of a paragraph; the hard return should follow the punctuation immediately. (If you cannot remove all such extra spaces, the publisher or typesetter will delete them.) No extra vertical space (blank lines) should be left between paragraphs unless a break must appear in the printed version (see 1.79).

2.13   *Justification and margins.* Only the left-hand margin should be justified. Right-hand justification should be turned off, leaving the margin unjustified (ragged right), so that correct word spacing is preserved. Margins of at least one inch should appear on all four sides of the hard copy.

2.14   *Paragraph indention, tabs, and hard returns.* Use the tab key (*not* the space bar) to indent the first line of a paragraph and the first line of each item in a vertical list. Never use the tab key to indent runover lines in flush-and-hang (or hanging-indention) setting (see 2.29). Use hard returns *only* when the following line must appear as a new line in the printed version, as in a new paragraph, a subhead, or a set-off extract. For extracts, both prose and verse, see 2.25–26.

2.15   *Hyphenation.* The hyphenation function on your word processor should be turned off. The only hyphens that should appear in the manuscript are hard hyphens, that is, hyphens in compound forms; don't worry if, in the hard copy, such hyphens happen to fall at the end of a line or the right-hand margin is extremely ragged. See also 2.99.

2.16   *Dashes.* For an em dash—one that indicates a break in a sentence like this—either use the em dash character on your word processor or type two hyphens (leave no space on either side). For the long dash (three-em dash) in bibliographies, use six unspaced hyphens. (For more on the em dash, see 6.87–93.)

2.17   *Italics, underlining, and boldface.* Unless your publisher decrees otherwise, use italics, not underlining, for words that are to be italicized in the printed version. (In a redlined version [see 2.88 and fig. 2.2] underlining may denote editorial changes.) If you have underlined words that are to appear in italics in the published version, make your intent clear to the publisher, and be consistent. (Some software uses underlining for italics.) Likewise, if you intend underlining rather than italics to appear in the published work, say so in a letter to the publisher or a note to the copy-editor. (Some file-conversion processes automatically change all under-lined terms to italics.) Use boldface only for words that must appear thus in the published version.

2.18   *Special characters.* If your word processor cannot print a particular charac-ter that you need, devise a code (e.g., *er<mac>os* for *erōs*) and list it in a let-ter to the publisher or a note to the editor. Your publisher may be able to provide a preferred code for the character you want. Consult your pub-lisher before using a special font (see 2.11).

NAMING THE ELECTRONIC FILES AND NUMBERING PAGES

2.19   *How many files?* For books, separate electronic files should be created for the various elements—front matter through table of contents, preface, chapters, appendixes, and so on—but not, unless the publisher requests it, for the notes (see 2.27). Chapters or similar divisions are best named "ch-01," "ch-02," and so forth (or something similar) so that they appear in correct order if there are more than nine. Ask your publisher about file-naming preferences. A list of all file names, including any electronic-only elements, should accompany the manuscript. (In the hard copy the various divisions should be arranged in the order specified in the table of contents, which is not necessarily the order of the electronic directory.) Files for color illustrations may include the word *color* in their names, especially if black-and-white prints have also been submitted. For journals, procedures may differ; many journals specify that all elements of an article manuscript, including tables but excluding other illustrations, should be stored in a single file.

2.20 *Front matter.* The front-matter pages need not be numbered except for elements such as a preface that run more than a page, in which case, "pref-1, pref-2," or some such designation may be used. The editor will indicate the appropriate roman numerals for the typesetter (see 2.78).

2.21 *Numbering by chapter or whole book.* Book manuscript pages may be numbered by chapter as long as the chapter number or other element also appears (for example, "intro. 1," "intro. 2"; "chap. two, 1"; "chap. two, 2"). Some publishers prefer that they be numbered consecutively from page 1 through the end of the book, including endnotes and other back matter. In a paper-only manuscript, pages added after the initial numbering may be numbered with *a* or *b* (for example, 55, 55a, 55b).

2.22 *Pages of tables or illustrations.* For book manuscripts, tables or illustrations should be on separate pages, not interspersed with lines of text. These pages should not be numbered consecutively with the manuscript pages but should be keyed to the chapter or section they belong to. Their approximate placement should be marked in the text (see 2.30–33). For data files or illustrations that cannot be printed but will be published in electronic form, see 2.4. For manuscripts of journal articles, consult the specific journal's instructions for authors.

CHAPTER TITLES AND SUBHEADS

2.23 *Chapter titles.* "Chapter 1," "Chapter 2," and so on should appear flush left above the title. The chapter title, as well as its subtitle if it has one, should be typed in roman type, starting flush left, and with initial capitals only (headline style; see 8.167), never in full capitals. A colon should separate subtitle from title. Only words that are italicized in the text should be italicized in a title or subtitle. A title should never be followed by a period.

2.24   *Subheads.* A subhead should begin on a line by itself with one or two lines of space above, usually flush left, and typed with initial capitals only (see 8.167). The levels of subhead, if more than one, must be distinguished by type style, such as italics versus roman or whatever works best (don't use full capitals). Each level of subhead must always be in the same style. If the publisher prefers, they may be identified by codes—for example, <a> for the first level, <b> for the second, and so on (see 2.88)—inserted immediately before the first word of the subhead. The codes will not appear in the published version. Except for run-in heads (1.74), which are simply italicized and given initial capitals for the first word and proper names only (sentence style; see 8.166), subheads are never followed by a period.

EXTRACTS

2.25   *Prose extracts.* Prose extracts (also known as block quotations) should be double-spaced vertically and indented. Use the indent feature on your word processor. Use the tab key only for indenting paragraphs within a prose extract, after using the indent feature (the first line of a prose extract should not have a paragraph indent). Use a hard return only at the end of the extract or, if there is more than one paragraph within the extract, at the end of each paragraph. For ellipses, see 11.51–65. See also 11.23–27, 11.43.

2.26   *Poetry extracts.* Poetry extracts should also be double-spaced and indented, *not* centered (even if they are to appear centered in the printed version). Let runover lines wrap normally; do *not* use the tab key to indent them. Use a hard return only at the end of each full line of poetry. Only if certain new lines of a poem are to receive deeper indention than others should you use the tab key. You must clearly distinguish between runover lines and indented lines of poetry. If there are either runover or double-indented lines, or if there is any unusual spacing or indention in your hard copy, append a photocopy of the original printed poem. For ellipses, see 11.61. The source, if given after the extract, should appear in parentheses on a separate line, aligned vertically with the beginning of the first line of the poem. (In the printed version, the source may appear flush right.) See also 11.28–32.

DOCUMENTATION AND OTHER SCHOLARLY APPARATUS

2.27   *Notes.* Unless your publisher instructs otherwise, you can create notes by using the footnote or endnote function of your word processor. In the manuscript they may appear either as footnotes or as chapter endnotes, regardless of how they are to appear in the published version. Keeping the notes embedded rather than placing them in a separate file may facilitate additions or deletions in the editing stage; check with your publisher. For note form, see chapter 16. For footnotes to tables, see 2.32.

2.28 *Glossaries and lists of abbreviations.* In typing a glossary or a list of abbreviations, however these are to appear in the published version, you may, but need not, use the hanging-indention function of your word processor. Avoid two-column format. Start each entry on a new line, flush left, capitalized only if the term is capitalized in the text. (For an example of a glossary, see the key terms list in appendix A.) Place a period or a colon (or less desirably an em dash) after the term and begin the definition with a capital letter, as if it were a new sentence. If the definition runs to a second line, let it wrap normally; do not indent it. Entries need closing punctuation only if they have interior punctuation; for examples, see key terms in appendix A. Any term or abbreviation that is repeatedly italicized in the text (not just on first use) should also be italicized in the glossary or list of abbreviations. The file should be double-spaced vertically. See also 1.87.

2.29 *Bibliographies and reference lists.* Although a bibliography or reference list will appear in flush-and-hang (or hanging-indention) style in the published version (like the bibliography in this manual), you may either use the hanging-indention function on your word processor or allow each entry to run over (or wrap) normally. Never use the tab key to indent runovers. The material should be double-spaced vertically. For capitalization, use of italics, and other matters of bibliographic style, see chapters 16 and 17.

TABLES AND ILLUSTRATIONS

2.30 *Text references and callouts.* A *text reference* is addressed to the reader ("table 5," or "see fig. 3.2"), is run into the text, and will appear in the published version. A *callout* is an instruction, which will not appear in the published work, telling where a table or an illustration is to appear. In the manuscript, a callout should be enclosed in angle brackets or some other delimiter and placed on a separate line following the paragraph in which the table or illustration is first referred to ("<table 5 here>"; "<fig. 3.2 here>") or, if a later location is preferable, where the table or illustration is to appear. For a full discussion of table preparation, see chapter 13.

2.31 *Table numbering and callouts.* In book manuscripts, tables, whether ultimately to appear in text or in a separate section, should be grouped in a separate electronic file. Journals may require authors to group text and tables together in a single file; consult the specific journal's instructions for authors. If tables are to appear in text, their location must be shown by a callout (see 2.30). If tables are numbered consecutively throughout a book, the numbering must be carefully checked, since an error will entail renumbering throughout. Alternatively, use double numeration (see 1.76). The word "Table" and the table number, an arabic numeral, are typed on a line by themselves. The next line contains the table title, typed in upper- and lowercase (never in full capitals), sentence style (see 8.166), and with no final period. A parenthetical explanation such as "(in millions)" may follow the title, but longer explanations should go in a note. If tabular material is very brief and simple, little more than a list, it may be typed at its location in the text without a table number. For details on table preparation, see chapter 13.

2.32   *Table notes.* Notes to a table must appear immediately below the table body and must carry their own numbering (preferably letters; see 13.47), keyed to that table. They must never be numbered along with the notes to the text. See 13.43–50.

2.33   *Illustration callouts and captions.* Unless grouped in a section separate from the regular text, illustrations such as graphs and diagrams require both a text reference and a callout (see 2.30). Photographs and maps—at least in printed books—do not always need a text reference but do need a callout if they are to appear in text (see 12.10–16). As with tables, illustrations may either be numbered consecutively throughout the book or carry double numbers (see 1.76, 12.12–13). The numbers must be carefully checked in either case. Illustrations that will be published in electronic form typically need a text reference that will be linked to the illustration itself; consult your publisher for instructions. Captions for all illustrations (as distinct from a list of illustrations following the table of contents; see 1.44–47) should be furnished in a separate file. For journals, follow the instructions provided by the journal in question. See also 12.31–51. For a full discussion of illustrations and how to prepare them for publication, see chapter 12.

2.34   *Electronically prepared illustrations.* Text figures that have been prepared electronically, such as graphs and diagrams, should be submitted in separate files, clearly identified. Figures may be numbered consecutively throughout a book or double-numbered (see 12.12–13). If they are very simple and can easily be typeset as part of the text, they may need neither a number nor a caption (but check with your publisher). Working (or temporary) numbers should be assigned for placement. Videos, animations, and data files submitted in electronic but not print form—along with color figures for which only black-and-white prints have been prepared—

must be noted and described in the author's cover letter (see 2.4). For further discussion, see chapter 12.

2.35 *Photographs, paintings, and the like.* Text figures that are to be reproduced photographically, such as paintings and maps, should be furnished in whatever form the publisher requests. Glossy prints must be clearly labeled, usually on the back of the print or on a self-sticking label, in a manner that does not impair their quality (see 12.17). They may be either numbered consecutively throughout a book or double-numbered (see 12.12–13). Plates grouped in a gallery (see 12.7) are numbered separately from figures appearing in the text. If numbers are not to appear in the published version, working numbers should be assigned for identification and should accompany the captions (see 12.15). For further discussion, see chapter 12.

CROSS-CHECKING

2.36 *Checking quotations.* All quoted matter should be checked against the original source, for both content and citation, before a manuscript is submitted for publication.

2.37 *Cross-references.* Before a manuscript is submitted for publication, all cross-references, whether to a chapter, a section, an appendix, or even a sentence of text, should be verified. A chapter number or title may have been changed, or a passage deleted, after the original reference to it. Cross-references are best made to chapter or section numbers, which can be entered at the manuscript stage. For printed works, references to page numbers are strongly discouraged on grounds of cost and time, since the correct number can be supplied only when a work is in page proof. Where absolutely necessary, a page number should be indicated by three bullets ("see p. ●●●"). In printed books, a good index should eliminate the need for most cross-references. In books, journals, or individual articles published electronically, online search capabilities may further reduce the need for cross-references. Requiring readers to perform a search and to weed out irrelevant results, however, may be less helpful than simply providing a link. Where links are used, they must be checked online as carefully as cross-references in printed works (see 3.43) to ensure that they lead to the intended material.

2.38 *Cross-checking the manuscript.* All parts of the manuscript must be cross-checked to avoid discrepancies. The following list includes major items to check:

- All titles and subtitles (introduction, parts, chapters, etc.) against table of contents
- Subheads against table of contents
- Illustrations against their captions, text references, and callouts
- Illustration captions against list of illustrations
- Tables against their text references and callouts
- Table titles against list of tables
- All cross-references
- In an electronic work, all links
- Notes against their text references
- Notes against bibliography
- Parenthetical text citations against reference list
- Abbreviations against list of abbreviations
- In a multivolume work or a journal issue, authors' names in table of contents against chapter or article headings and list of contributors
- In an issue of a journal that is paginated consecutively throughout a volume, the first page against the last page of the previous issue

MULTIAUTHOR BOOKS AND JOURNALS

2.39 *Volume editor's responsibilities.* The specific responsibilities of the volume editor, contributors, and publisher must be determined before a multiauthor manuscript is submitted. If there is more than one volume editor, the responsibilities of each must be spelled out. After ensuring that the contributors furnish their papers in a uniform style agreed to by all parties, the volume editor is usually responsible for the following:

1. Getting manuscripts, including illustrations, from all contributors in a form acceptable to the publisher well before the date for submitting the volume
2. Sending a publishing agreement (provided by the publisher) to each contributor (see 4.52)
3. Getting written permission from copyright owners to reproduce material in copyrighted works published elsewhere, illustrations taken from another work, and the like (see chapter 4)
4. Editing each contribution for sense and checking references and other documentation for uniformity of style, then sending edited manuscripts to the contributors for their approval *before* the volume is submitted to the publisher (an activity distinct from the manuscript editing that will be done later by the publisher)
5. Editing any discussions to be included in the volume and getting any necessary approval for such editing

6. Providing a list of contributors with their affiliations and brief biographical notes to be included in the volume
7. Providing a title page, table of contents, and any necessary prefatory material
8. Sending the complete manuscript to the publisher in a form acceptable for publication (see 2.3–38)
9. Preparing the index
10. Adhering to the publisher's schedule, ensuring that contributors do likewise, keeping track of the contributors' whereabouts at all stages of publication, and assuming the responsibilities of any contributor who cannot fulfill them

Most if not all of these responsibilities also apply to journal editors.

2.40 *Further responsibilities.* Depending on the arrangement with the publisher, the volume editor may also be responsible for the following:

1. Checking the edited manuscript and responding to all queries, or distributing the edited manuscript to the contributors and checking it after their review to ensure that all queries have been answered
2. Reading the master proofs or distributing master proofs to the contributors and then checking their corrections

PREPARING A MANUSCRIPT FROM PRINTED MATERIAL

2.41 *Retyped copy.* If a manuscript, or parts of a manuscript, for an anthology or other work consisting largely of published material is retyped by the compiler, the guidelines for preparing the files (2.9–35) should be followed.

2.42 *Printed copy.* If a manuscript is presented in the form of printed pages, the compiler needs *two* clean sets of the original pages to make *one* copy of the manuscript, since sheets with printing on both sides are unacceptable for editing and typesetting. Each original page should be pasted or taped to an $8\frac{1}{2} \times 11$ inch sheet of paper. If two clean copies of the original pages are unavailable, clear photocopies are acceptable, provided all words at both ends of the lines are clear and the paper can be written on with pencil.

2.43 *Notes.* If footnotes on the original pages are to remain substantially unchanged and to appear as footnotes in the new version, they may be left at the foot of the pasted-up pages. If a compiler's or volume editor's notes are intermingled with the original notes (see 16.28, 16.65) or if the notes appeared at the end of the book in the original, all the notes should be pasted or typed on new sheets in the order in which they are to appear. If footnotes in the original are to appear as endnotes, they should be cut from the foot of the page and pasted on new sheets.

2.44 *Illustrations.* Photocopies of illustrations are not acceptable for reproduction. The compiler should procure glossy prints (see 2.35). If these are unavailable, the publisher may be able to reproduce an illustration from the original publication. For journals, consult the journal's instructions.

2.45 *Source notes.* Each selection of previously published material should be accompanied by either a headnote (a brief introduction preceding the selection) or, more commonly, an unnumbered footnote on the first page of text, giving the source (see 16.68), the name of the copyright owner if the selection is in copyright (see chapter 4, esp. 4.2–6), and the original title if it has been changed. If a selection has previously appeared in various places and different versions, the source note need not give the entire publishing history but must state which version is being reprinted. Obtaining permissions is time consuming; compilers should seek expert help with permissions long before submitting a manuscript. See 4.67–73, 4.98.

2.46 *Permissible changes to published material.* The following changes to published material may be made without editorial comment: notes may be renumbered; cross-references to parts of the original work that are no longer relevant may be deleted; obvious typographical errors and inadvertent grammatical slips may be corrected. See 11.8. If changes are made in spelling, capitalization, or footnote style, the compiler should note such changes in the preface or elsewhere. For deletions indicated by ellipsis points, see 11.51–65. Unless there is ample space to insert corrections above the printed lines, any corrections should be written in the margins, as if in proofs (see 3.20–21).

The Manuscript Editor's Responsibilities

PRINCIPLES OF MANUSCRIPT EDITING

2.47 *Overview and terminology.* The following paragraphs deal generally with what manuscript editing is and with the things manuscript editors do. For details on how they do it physically, see 2.81–91 (for editing electronic files) and 2.92–103 (for editing on paper). "Editor" is used here to refer to the manuscript editor (or copyeditor); "publisher" refers to the publishing house and its policies.

2.48 *Manuscript editing as opposed to developmental editing.* Manuscript editing, also called copyediting or line editing, requires attention to every word in a manuscript, a thorough knowledge of the style to be followed (see 2.52), and the ability to make quick, logical, and defensible decisions. It is undertaken only when a manuscript has been accepted for publication. It may include both mechanical editing (see 2.51) and substantive editing (see 2.55). It is distinct from developmental editing (not discussed in this manual), which addresses more radically the content of a work, the way material should be presented, the need for more or less documentation and how it should be handled, and so on. Since editing of this kind may involve total rewriting or reorganization of a work, it should be done—if needed—*before* manuscript editing begins.

2.49 *Estimating time.* The amount of editing a manuscript needs depends not only on how it has been prepared but also on the audience for which the work is intended and the publication schedule. Estimating how long the editing will take, which requires looking at all parts of a manuscript and, often, editing a small sample, can be based on page count or on total number of words; in either case the editor should take into account any complexities in the text, documentation, or illustrations as well as the medium in which the editing will be done—on paper or in an electronic file. The nature of the material, along with the capabilities of the software and the editor's own skills, will influence the choice of medium. Editing online, which often involves certain typesetting functions such as coding or tagging, may take longer than editing by hand, but production time may be shortened. Also pertinent is information about the author's availability, amenability to being edited, propensity to revise, and so forth. As a very rough estimate, a 100,000-word book manuscript, edited online by an experienced editor, may take seventy-five to one hundred hours of work before being sent to the author, plus ten to twenty additional hours after the author's review. (If an author has made substantial changes to the edited manuscript, as much as a week's additional work may be needed.)

2.50 *Stages of editing.* Editors usually go through a manuscript three times—once to do the initial editing, easily the longest stage; a second time to review, refine, and sometimes correct the editing; and a third time after the author's review (see 2.75). Careful editors begin the initial editing stage by looking through the entire document to assess the nature and scope of the work that will be required, to identify any matters that should be clarified with the author before editing begins, and to reduce the number of surprises that could cause delays if discovered later in the process. Most edit each element in a work (text, notes, tables, bibliography, etc.) separately to help attain consistency; others edit the apparatus, or a part of it, along with the text. Whatever the procedure, all elements must be compared to ensure that the notes match their text references, the tables correspond to any discussion of them in the text, and so on.

2.51 *Mechanical editing.* Copyediting involves two processes. The first, being concerned with the mechanics of written communication, is known as mechanical editing. It refers to consistency in capitalization, spelling, hyphenation, table format, use of abbreviations, and so forth; correctness of punctuation, including ellipsis points, parentheses, and quotation marks; the way numbers are treated; consistency between text, tables, and illustrations; citation format; and other matters of style in the sense described in 2.52. Mechanical editing also includes attention to grammar, syntax, and usage at the most basic level. Such editing may include either preparing an electronic file according to the requirements of the production process and the medium in which the work will be published or, if the editing is done by hand, marking up the hard copy for a typesetter. For the second process, substantive editing, see 2.55–56.

2.52 *Style.* As generally used in this manual, style refers to the mechanics discussed in 2.51 and expanded upon in chapters 6–18. Journal editors follow the established style of the periodical they are editing for, and they may often consult additional style resources specific to the subject area, including specialized style manuals as well as other periodicals, either in print or online. Book editors may follow the house style of the publisher or of a particular discipline—sometimes with agreed-on variations. If a book is part of a series or a multivolume work, it should conform to the style set by earlier volumes. For a multiauthor work, whose chapters may have been prepared in different styles (despite the publisher's pleas to the contrary), the editor will have to impose an agreed-on style on maverick chapters. The style of any work, as well as occasional deviations from it, must be determined by author, editor, and publisher before editing begins. For style in the sense of verbal expression, see 2.55–56 and chapter 5; for styles in lieu of typographic coding, see 2.90.

2.53 *Reference works.* A good dictionary is essential. Chicago recommends *Webster's Third New International Dictionary* and the latest edition of its desk version, *Merriam-Webster's Collegiate Dictionary* (see bibliog. 3.1). Editors also need printed reference works or access to online sources that furnish reliable spellings and identifications of persons, places, historical events, technical terminology, and the like. Unfamiliar terms or little-known persons should be defined or identified on their first appearance unless a work is addressed to a specialized readership. The first name is normally given the first time a person is mentioned, though it may be inappropriate if the person is well known by last name alone. For some basic reference works, see section 4 of the bibliography.

2.54   *Style sheet.* To ensure consistency, for each manuscript the editor must keep an alphabetical list of words or terms to be capitalized, italicized, hyphenated, spelled, or otherwise treated in any way unique to the manuscript. Changes that are made simply for consistency with the house style being followed need not be noted on the style sheet. It is enough to say, for example, "In all other respects, Chicago style is followed." It is useful—indeed, essential for a manuscript edited on paper—to add the page or paragraph number (or other appropriate locator) of the first occurrence of each item, since an item added from the middle or end of a manuscript may have escaped attention earlier and will need to be corrected on the editor's second pass (see 2.50). Editing online greatly simplifies this aspect of an editor's work. When the editor makes a new decision and notes it on the style sheet, every instance of the item affected by the decision can be found by an electronic search and changed as needed. (Beware of making global changes that might affect material that should not be altered, such as quoted material or entries in a bibliography.) Special punctuation, unusual diacritics, and other items should also be noted on the style sheet. Not only the editor but also the author and the typesetter may need to refer to the style sheet at various stages of editing and production. See figure 2.1.

2.55   *Substantive editing.* Substantive editing deals with the organization and presentation of existing content. It involves rephrasing for smoothness or to eliminate ambiguity, reorganizing or tightening, reducing or simplifying documentation, recasting tables, and other remedial activities. (It should not be confused with developmental editing, a more drastic process; see 2.48.) In general, no substantive work should be undertaken without agreement between publisher and editor, especially for book-length works; if major substantive work is needed, the author should be consulted and perhaps invited to approve a sample before the editing proceeds, to avoid delays later. Journal editors, however, working on rigid schedules, may need to do substantive editing without prior consultation with authors if problems of organization, presentation, and verbal expression have not been addressed at earlier stages.

2.56   *Discretion in substantive editing.* A light editorial hand is nearly always more effective than a heavy one. An experienced copyeditor will recognize and not tamper with unusual figures of speech or idiomatic usage and will know when to make an editorial change and when simply to suggest it, whether to delete a repetition or an unnecessary recapitulation or simply to point it out to the author, and how to suggest tactfully that an expression

action plans	Parliament
antiracist	pro-immigrant
	pro-multicultural
child welfare workers	Progress Party
co-citizen	
Conservative Party (Norwegian)	situation analysis
Convention on Human Rights	Somali, Somalis
	Students' Antiracist Movement
first person singular	
ghetto-like	Third World
government	
	Ungdom mot vold (rom)
jinns (plur. of jinn)	
King and Queen (per author's request)	Western Europe
Labor Party (Norwegian)	Youth Against Violence (Ungdom mot vold)
Labor government	
minister of child and family affairs	*Mechanical matters*
Ministry of Child and Family Affairs	(1995:47–48) colon betw. year and pp.
	Ellipses: three-dot method, not three-plus-four
north (of Norway)	Quoted newspaper headlines: sentence style
northerners	"emphasis mine"
Norwegian Pakistanis	
non-word	

Fig. 2.1. Manuscript editor's style sheet. When prepared for a hand-marked manuscript, the style sheet usually indicates the page number for the first appearance of each item. With online editing and the consequent ease of searching, this may be unnecessary, though another appropriate locator (section, paragraph, sentence number) may be helpful, depending on the program's search capabilities.

may be inappropriate. An author's own style should be respected, whether flamboyant or pedestrian. Although fact checking is not usually expected of a manuscript editor (at least in most university presses), obvious errors, including errors in mathematical calculations, should always be pointed out, and questionable proper names, bibliographic references, and the like should be verified or queried. All manuscript editors should know whether the publishers or journals they work for have strict policies on terms relating to race or ethnicity, sex, age, and other areas of potential bias or whether individual discretion is allowed (see 5.203–6). For communicating with the author and querying, see 2.69–75, 2.84, 2.94.

2.57 *Editing part titles and chapter or article titles.* The editor of a book manuscript should ensure that part and chapter titles, and their subtitles if any, are consistent with the text in spelling, hyphenation, and italics. Part and chapter titles must be checked against the table of contents, and any discrepancy must be queried. Unless the typographic style is already known (as in a journal or series), all titles should be in headline style (see 8.167). All should be coded for the typesetter (if the manuscript is to be typeset traditionally). Chicago, for example, often uses the following codes, enclosed in angle brackets (see 2.89): <pn> (part number), <pt> (part title), <pst> (part subtitle), <cn> (chapter number), <ct> (chapter title), <cst> (chapter subtitle). Other publishers may prescribe different codes for such purposes. See also 2.91, 2.102.

2.58   *Editing subheads.* Subheads should be checked for uniformity of style and for pertinence (see 1.71–79) as well as for consistency with the text in spelling, hyphenation, and italics. If there is more than one level of subhead, is the hierarchy logical? If there are more than three levels, can the lowest be eliminated? The typographic form of a subhead in the manuscript does not always reflect its intended level. If subheads are to appear in the table of contents, they must be cross-checked for consistency. Unless the typographic style is already known (as in a journal or series), subheads should normally be in headline style (see 8.167); subtitles should be separated by a colon. But if an author has consistently used sentence style (see 8.166) for subheads, that style should not be altered without consultation with the author and publisher, since it may be more appropriate in the particular work. Where subheads consist of full sentences, sentence capitalization is preferable. Subheads are typically coded for the typesetter: for example, <a> (first-level subhead), <b> (second-level subhead). For details on coding, see 2.88–89. If the editing is done on paper, the first level should be marked by a circled A, the second by a circled B, and so on.

2.59   *Cross-references.* All references to tables, figures, appendixes, bibliographies, or other parts of a work should be checked by the editor. If the author, for example, mentions a statistic for 2001 and refers readers to table 4, which gives statistics only through 2000, the editor must point out the discrepancy. Place-names on a map that illustrate the text must be spelled as in the text. Cross-references to specific pages should be minimized or eliminated (see 2.37). Some authors need to be discouraged from commenting too frequently on the structure of their work ("This is what I did earlier, this is what I am doing now, and this is what I will do later"); chapter titles, subheads, the table of contents, and the index should provide sufficient signposts.

2.60   *Quotations and previously published material.* Aside from adjusting quotation marks and ellipsis points to conform to house style (see 11.8–10), the editor must do nothing to quoted material unless the author is translating it from another language, in which case it may be lightly edited. Misspelled words and apparent transcription errors should be queried. An author who appears to have been careless in transcribing should be asked to check all quotations for accuracy, including punctuation. The editor should ensure that sources are given for all quoted material, whether following the quotation or in a note. In editing previously published material, especially if it has been abridged, the editor should read for sense to ensure that nothing is out of order or has inadvertently been omitted. Discrepancies should be queried. If the previously published material has been provided on paper only, any ambiguous end-of-line hyphens should be marked for the typesetter (see 2.99).

2.61 *Editing notes.* Each note must be checked against the text to ensure that its text reference is correct and in the right place and that any terms used in the note are treated the same way as in the text. When notes are to be printed as footnotes, the author may be asked to shorten excessively long ones or absorb them into the text or an appendix. Lists, tables, and figures should be placed not in footnotes but in the text or in an appendix. Editors may sometimes request an additional note to accommodate a needed source or citation. More frequently, in consultation with the author, they will combine notes or delete unneeded ones. See 16.36–39. When notes are added, combined, or dropped, it is essential that note numbers be adjusted both in text and in the notes themselves. When editing online, keeping the notes embedded during editing prevents disasters. An editor working on paper must take special care in renumbering notes.

2.62 *Editing note citations.* If notes contain citations, these must be carefully checked for style (but see 2.63). Further, every subsequent reference to a work previously cited must be given in the same form as the first reference or in the same shortened form (see 16.41–48). In a work containing a bibliography as well as notes, each citation in the notes should be checked against the bibliography and any discrepancy resolved or, if necessary, queried in both contexts so that the author can easily compare them (see 2.71). A bibliography (as opposed to a reference list; see 2.64) need not include every work cited in the notes (see 16.74–76) and may properly include some entries that are not cited.

2.63 *Flexibility in citation style.* Imposing house style on notes prepared in another style can be immensely time consuming and, if the existing form is consistent and clear to the reader, is often unnecessary. In journal editing, however, such flexibility may not be feasible, especially for electronic articles in which citations may be linked to an outside database, requiring absolute consistency of format. Before making sweeping changes, the editor should consult the author or the publisher or both.

2.64 *Editing bibliographies and reference lists.* The editor must ensure that each entry in a bibliography or reference list conforms to the same style: order of items in each entry, punctuation, and so on (see chapters 16 and 17). Alphabetizing should be checked, or dates if the bibliography is in chronological order. If a reference list is used, the editor will have checked all text citations against the list while editing the text and will have queried or resolved discrepancies (see 2.62, 2.71). Many editors find it helpful to edit the bibliography or reference list before the text and notes.

2.65 *Editing tables.* The editor should verify that the author has taken the steps described in 2.3, 2.22, and 2.31–32 and should either complete them or have the author do so. A manuscript edited on paper with no electronic files provided may require some cutting and pasting, with callouts written on the relevant text pages (2.22). For guidelines on editing tables, see 13.68–71. For cross-checking between text and tables, see 2.59.

2.66 *Checking illustrations and their placement and editing captions.* The editor should verify that the author has taken the steps described in 2.33–35. Illustrations are frequently added, dropped, or renumbered during editing, so it is essential to check all illustrations against their text references and callouts and against the captions and list of illustrations to be sure that they match and that the illustrations show what they say they do. Captions must conform to the style of the text. Source information should be edited in consultation with the publisher. If permissions are outstanding, the publisher, not the editor, should take up the matter with the author. Any wording on a diagram or chart should conform to the spelling and capitalization used in the caption or the text. (If the wording on the illustration cannot be changed, it is sometimes acceptable to adjust the spelling in the caption or text.) For details on preparing illustrations and captions, see chapter 12. For checking credits, see 12.48.

2.67 *Preparing front matter for a printed book.* The publisher normally provides copy for the series title (if any) and copyright page. An editor may need to produce clean copy for the half title, title page, table of contents, and list of illustrations, carefully checking all against the text and captions. If subheads are to be dropped from the table of contents, the author should be consulted. For the sequence and form of front matter, see 1.5–57; for items always or sometimes required on the copyright page, see 1.14–35. Some or all of these elements may also be required for electronic books; consult your publisher. For printed books, the editor should indicate the pages where particular elements are to begin (e.g., "dedication, p. v") and which pages are to remain blank (e.g., "page ii blank").

2.68 *Editing indexes.* When the index arrives, it should be edited and typeset immediately, since the rest of the book or journal is now in page proof. For preparing an index, see chapter 18; for editing an index, see 18.135–37. An index should begin on a right-hand page (see 1.91).

COMMUNICATING WITH THE AUTHOR

2.69 *Early contact.* A book editor should, if possible, get in touch with an author at the time editing begins, to establish good relations, ask any necessary questions, and thereby avoid nasty surprises. If imposing house style involves a global change such as lowercasing a term the author has capitalized throughout, the author should be alerted early. Journal editors too, to expedite production, sometimes notify authors of global changes early in the game. Most authors are content to submit to a house style; those who are not may be willing to compromise. Unless usage is determined by journal or series style, the author's wishes should be respected. For a manuscript that requires extensive changes, it may be wise, if the schedule allows, to send a sample of the editing for the author's approval before proceeding (see 2.55).

2.70 *When to query.* If the editor has merely tried to bring mechanical consistency to a manuscript, there is no need to query the author. Nor is there any need to explain the correction of solecisms unless the author challenges the correction when reviewing the editing. Queries should be brief and, wherever possible, answerable by yes or no. Or they may be more specific: "Do you mean X or Y?" A query must never sound pedantic, condescending, or indignant. Specialized terms, whether editorial, typographic, or grammatical, should be avoided unless familiar to the author. Queries to the author need be prefaced by "au:" only if the editor is including notes to others, for example, the typesetter. Some journals, working on tight deadlines, use a standard memorandum to inform the author that the manuscript has been edited for clarity, consistency, grammar, journal style, and so forth and that routine changes have not been queried; in addition, the author will receive a list of specific queries. Book editors sometimes do likewise; see also 2.73.

2.71 *What to query.* Any discrepancies should be queried (or corrected if obvious): for example, "George Jessell OK? See John Jessell, chap. 2, par. beginning 'War seemed certain'"; "Repetition intentional? See chap. 3, par.

beginning 'Later that year'"; "Where do closing quote marks belong?" If the editor feels confident in deleting a repetition or correcting a discrepancy or minor error, a simple "OK?" is enough. For bibliographic discrepancies, see 2.61–64. Name spellings that look wrong ("Pricilla," "Napolean") are not necessarily typos and should be queried. Foreign-language words, including proper names, should be queried unless easily verified.

2.72 *How to mark queries.* For the mechanics of typing or marking queries on a manuscript, see 2.84 (for editors working online) and 2.94 (for those working on paper).

2.73 *The cover letter.* The letter sent to the author with the edited manuscript, or sometimes separately, should include some or all of the following items (unless already communicated):

1. What the editing has involved: adjustment of spelling to conform to house style; occasional rephrasing for clarity or to eliminate inadvertent repetition, and so forth
2. Whether and how the editing has been shown—as a redlined printout (see 2.83) or a hand-marked manuscript—and what the markings and codes mean
3. How the author should respond to queries, veto any unwanted editing, and make any further adjustments on the printout or manuscript (see 2.5, 2.85, 2.103)
4. A warning that the author should now make any last-minute changes, additions, or deletions; check quoted matter and citations if necessary; and carefully review the editing, since even editors are fallible and any errors missed in editing and not caught until proofs may be deemed "author's alterations" and charged to the author (see 3.15)
5. The deadline for return of the edited copy
6. An approximate date when the author may expect to receive proofs and the kind of proofs to expect (galleys or, more likely, page proofs; see 3.1, 3.16)
7. A brief discussion about the index, if any—whether the author is to prepare it, whether instructions are needed (see chapter 18), or whether a freelance indexer is to be engaged at the author's expense
8. A request for confirmation of the author's mailing and e-mail addresses and telephone and fax numbers throughout the publishing process

2.74 *Sending the edited manuscript to the author.* If edited online, a book manuscript is usually sent to the author in the form of a redlined printout (see 2.83), which the author reads, marks as necessary, and returns to the editor. Journal articles may be either made available to authors as PDF files or sent to them as typeset proofs, redlined printouts, or hand-marked manuscripts. A hand-marked manuscript is a one-of-a-kind document; if it is lost, the manuscript must be reedited. To avert such a disaster, it should be photocopied before it is mailed or sent by some traceable means—preferably both.

2.75   *Checking the author's final changes.* When the manuscript comes back from the author, the editor goes through once again to see what the author has done, check that all queries have been answered, and edit any new material. Except for style adjustments, the author's version should prevail; if that version is unacceptable for any reason, a compromise should be sought. The editor then updates the electronic files, marks the typeset proofs (if journal articles have been sent in that form; see 2.74), or, if a manuscript is to be typeset from paper, clarifies or retypes the new material and crosses out the queries.

PUTTING A MANUSCRIPT INTO PRODUCTION

2.76   *Type specifications and coding.* When a book manuscript goes to the typesetter, it should be accompanied by a designer's layout (formally referred to as "composition and page layout specifications"; see fig. A.14 for an example), which specifies the typeface and type size for the various elements in the manuscript—text, extracts, subheads, and so forth—and the amount of vertical space required at chapter openings, between text and footnotes, and elsewhere. These specifications ("specs") are keyed to the generic codes (see 2.89), styles (see 2.90), or tags (see 2.91) used in the manuscript. The typesetter will then convert the codes, styles, or tags into type codes. Occasionally a manuscript editor will need to do a little more than coding. For example, if the layout calls for the first few words of each chapter to be set in caps and small caps (e.g., WHAT IN SHAKESPEARE MAY APPALL US), the editor should mark precisely which words should be so treated. Journal manuscripts are usually typeset according to the journal's typesetting specifications.

2.77   *Type specifications and hand markup.* In the rare event that no designer's layout or list of specifications is available—for example, in an informally published brochure—the editor should mark up the hard copy with appropriate type specifications at the first occurrence of the element they apply to. For example, in the margin next to the first block of regular text, "text: 10/12 Times Roman × 26" (meaning 10-point type with 12-point leading, each line 26 picas long); and next to the first extract, "extract: 9/11

Times Roman; indent 2 pi from left." As long as all extracts have been coded "ext," all first-level subheads "A," and so forth, markup can be kept to a minimum. For more on hand markup, see 2.92–103.

2.78 *Ensuring correct pagination.* However the manuscript is paginated, the editor should make clear to the typesetter where roman page numbers end and arabic numbers begin. It is important to mark on the manuscript what page will constitute arabic 1 of the printed version, whether or not the number will actually appear (whether the folio is to be "expressed" or "blind"; see 1.59). If there is a part title and the first chapter begins on page 3, "arabic p. 3" should be specified at the chapter opening. The editor should specify whether subsequent elements are to begin on a recto or, if the design calls for a double-page spread, on a verso. To avoid expensive repagination in proof, the editor should check that all elements—in the front matter, the text, and the back matter—are in their correct order and that the order is reflected in the table of contents. For journals, see 1.147.

2.79 *Running heads.* The editor provides copy from which running heads (or feet) will be set (see 1.93–99). The copy must clearly indicate which heads are to appear on versos and which on rectos. For a book, running heads must be included for any material that will occupy more than one printed page; journals may require running heads for all copy, regardless of length. To fit on a single line, usually containing the page number as well, a chapter or article title may have to be shortened for a running head but must include the key terms in the title. The author's approval may be needed; if possible, the editor should send the running head copy along with the edited manuscript. In shortened foreign-language titles, no word may be omitted that governs the case ending of another word in the running head. Running-head copy normally accompanies the manuscript to the typesetter and should be included with the other electronic files. If the running heads are to reflect the content of particular pages (rather than chapters or sections), the copy cannot be prepared until page proofs are available. For running heads to notes, the page numbers they apply to (Notes to Pages •••–••• or XXX–XXX) must be supplied in proof (see 1.86, 1.98).

2.80 *Information for the typesetter.* Information accompanying a book manuscript to the typesetter, usually prepared by the editor in the form of a checklist, a memorandum, a transmittal form, or a combination of such documents, should include at least some of the following:

· Name of author and title of work
· What is included in the package: disk, clean printout (see 2.83), illustrations, etc.

- How the work is to be typeset: electronically from the publisher's files or rekeyed
- The software used in editing the manuscript, the number of files, file names, and codes or styles used
- The total number of pages in a manuscript to be typeset from paper
- The number of chapters, illustrations, tables, and other matter, and what, if anything, is still to come
- Which elements are to be included in the front matter, the text, and the end matter
- Whether the notes are to be footnotes or endnotes
- Whether the illustrations will be interspersed in the text or will appear in a gallery
- Which elements must start recto
- How many sets of proofs will be needed, and whether galleys as well as page proof are needed
- Any special characters needed

It may also be useful to include the style sheet (see 2.54) and a list of non-dictionary words and proper names with preferred word breaks (see 3.7). Editors are sometimes required to furnish spine copy (see 1.110) and cover or jacket copy (see 1.112–13).

EDITING ONLINE: SOME MECHANICS

2.81 *Backup and conversion.* Before editing begins, a backup copy must be made of the author's files, which must be stored, not altered in any way, and used *only* for reference. The files are then converted, if necessary, to the software the editor uses. If special characters (e.g., letters in a non-Latin alphabet) fail to convert, expert help must be sought (from a typesetter, a librarian, or the author). The publisher may decide to have the manuscript edited on paper and rekeyed by a typesetter.

2.82 *Cleanup.* Before editing the manuscript, the editor should ensure that the files represent the author's latest version (see 2.4–5), check that the author has followed the steps outlined in 2.4–8, and make any necessary repairs. Many tasks can be automated and combined in a single electronic tool set; some publishers make such tools available to authors and freelance editors.

2.83 *Redlining, or tracking changes.* To enable the author to approve the editing, the edited files are often printed out in a redlined version (created by means of "track changes" or a similar feature of text-editing software; see fig. 2.2). Depending on the software and printer the editor uses, added or changed material may appear literally in red (as it does on screen), or double underlined, or shaded, or in boldface—in any case in a distinct form. Deleted material usually is struck through. Queries to the author appear either as footnotes or run into the text (see 2.84). Whether *all* the editing, mechanical as well as substantive, is redlined depends on the software and on the editor. Editors whose software has a built-in redlining function will usually keep it turned on as they work; the author thus sees every change. Those who use keystrokes to produce redlining may prefer to alert the author to global changes (such as capitalization of a certain term) the first time each such change is made and to redline only changes the author must approve individually. Still others may enter changes as if they were editing their own work and see only the results of their editing on the screen, not what was there before; the edited files then are compared with the original, unedited files by means of a software program that prints out a redlined version. Some authors may receive both a redlined version and a clean printout (a hard copy of the edited manuscript that does not show the editing), or only a clean printout with queries. If an element such as a bibliography has been heavily redlined, the editor may send a clean printout of that element for the author to approve, as well as the redlined printout for reference. If redlining is not used, the editor must let the author know what has been done to the manuscript (see 2.69, 2.70, 2.73).

2.84 *Queries to the author.* Editors working online can query the author in three ways; the first is usually the simplest. The editor may use a "comment mechanism" that creates footnotes distinct from the author's footnotes (letters or asterisks rather than numbers if the program permits). Or the editor may run the query into the text in an easily searchable form (enclosed in brackets or other delimiters and appearing in boldface or some font not used elsewhere in the text). A third method, best reserved for manuscripts that require extensive queries and comments, is to create a separate file of queries, keyed to the manuscript by some symbol easily seen by the author. After queries have been responded to, they (and any text symbols referring to them) must be deleted from the files to be used for typesetting, lest they appear in proof or (disastrously) in the published version. See figure 2.2.

2.85 *Retaining the edited files.* In general, the edited electronic files should not be sent to the author. An author who does review files online must redline any final adjustments in such way that they are distinct from the editor's changes, so that they in turn can be edited before the manuscript is typeset. Some text-editing software can protect editorial changes from alteration ("read only").

2.86 *The author's review.* Some editors do their second reading on a printout of the redlined version or, if none is produced, a clean printout of the manuscript with the editing incorporated. They can then mark additional changes or, if necessary, stets, in the way they want the author to make final adjustments—in a bright color, fully legible, in upper- and lower-case. If the author adds more than a sentence or two, the new material may be furnished either as a printout or in electronic form with a hard copy, but the printout or file must contain *only* the new material; it must never be a revised form of the chapter or article, which would require a total reediting. The editor should make this procedure clear to the author when sending the edited manuscript.

2.87 *What is sent to the typesetter.* When the editor has reviewed the files to ensure that all queries have been answered and has updated the files accordingly (see 2.75, 2.84), a clean copy of the final version is usually printed out. This printout accompanies the final files that are sent to the typesetter and must exactly correspond to them. (Typesetters often read proof against the clean printout; unless a redlined printout contains all last-minute adjustments by the publisher, it cannot be relied on as "final" copy.) The redlined printout with the author's handwritten emendations, whether or not it is sent to the typesetter, typically goes to the author with the proofs (see 3.5).

2.88 *Generically marking the typographic elements.* Depending on how the manuscript is to be typeset and what software the editor is using, the various elements in the manuscript—chapter display, subheads, text, prose extracts, poetry, notes, captions, and so forth—are marked generically by coding (see 2.89), by assigning styles (see 2.90), or by inserting tags (see 2.91). See also 2.76. The editor usually does the type marking as part of the editing. The typesetter or typesetting program then converts the generic marking to the type specifications given by the journal or book design. It is essential that editor, publisher, and typesetter confer before this marking is done.

2.89 *Coding.* Generic codes are often mnemonic in form (see fig. 2.2). They are usually enclosed in angle brackets or, if angle brackets are used in the text, in curly brackets or some other delimiters. Publishers differ not only in what codes they recommend but also in what elements to code. Some require that every element be coded, including regular text; others regard regular text as a default but require exit codes at the end of coded elements. Consistency is essential. The copyeditor may need to invent codes for unusual elements. Whether a manuscript is typeset in house or by an outside supplier, the editor must furnish a list of codes used, with their definitions; for example:

<cn>	chapter number
<ct>	chapter title
<a>	first-level subhead (A-head)
<b>	second-level subhead (B-head)
<ext>	block quotation (prose extract)
<po>	poetry extract
<sc>	small caps
<mac>	macron on following letter
<n>	en dash
<na>	subhead in endnotes section
<![comment]!>	instruction to the typesetter
<!help!>	signal to typesetter to consult hard copy at this point

Exit codes may be necessary for elements not followed by a hard return, depending on the publisher's or typesetter's requirements. Exit codes may be made by adding a slash: </cn> for the end of a chapter number, </sc> for the end of small caps, </list> for the end of a list, and so on.

2.90 *Assigning styles.* In some circumstances, software-generated style tags may be applied to a manuscript instead of generic codes. Depending on the typesetting program used, such style tags may even be preferable. Authors and copyeditors should ask the publisher what kind of style tags to use for a given manuscript. Each tag has a name and is applied to either the paragraph level or the character level. A paragraph is defined as any string of text that follows a hard return and ends with a hard return. Paragraph styles should be given descriptive names (e.g., "chapter number," "chapter title," "first-level subhead," "body text," "extract"). Character-level styles are used primarily to differentiate characters from their neighbors in the surrounding text (e.g., when an individual word or letter is set in Courier within an otherwise Times Roman paragraph). Common character attributes such as boldface and italics need not be styled separately. If there are special characters or text elements that do not lend themselves easily to style tags, it may be necessary to combine style tags and generic codes with instructions or messages to the typesetter. A list of styles and any generic codes should always accompany the manuscript.

2.91 *Using formal markup languages.* Some manuscripts, especially those that will be published in electronic as well as printed form, may be edited in or converted to a formal markup language (e.g., XML or SGML) in which tags mark the structure of the document. In this type of markup, each element, including the document as a whole, is enclosed between an opening tag and a closing tag that identify the type of element and may contain unique identifiers that create links used in navigating the electronic version. Tags are "nested"; for example, the body of the document, enclosed between an opening and a closing "body" tag, will include all sections and subsections of the document, with each of those parts also enclosed between an opening and a closing tag that identify the element and its place in the hierarchy. Tags for larger elements are typically used to mark what the elements are rather than how they are to be presented; this practice streamlines subsequent presentation of the document in various forms. Smaller portions of text may be marked either according to how they are to be presented (e.g., in italic type) or according to the intent of the presentation (e.g., emphasis). If editing takes place after conversion to a formal markup language, the editor's responsibility is to make sure that the tags correspond logically to the document's structure and that the markup is true to the intent of the tagging scheme. The editor may check each tag or use a script designed to identify and perhaps correct errors. If markup errors are not corrected there may be problems in the published versions of the document (see 3.42–43).

EDITING ON PAPER: SOME MECHANICS

2.92   *Keeping a clean copy.* Before beginning to edit, the editor should make sure there is a clean copy of the original, unedited version for reference or in case any reediting is necessary.

2.93   *Marking the manuscript.* Editing a manuscript that is going to be rekeyed requires a technique distinct from that of proofreading (see chapter 3). Editing appears not in the margin but above the word or words it pertains to. An exception may be made only if there is too little space between the lines (as in a manuscript that contains previously printed material). For marking queries, see 2.94. For a sample of a correctly marked manuscript, see figure 2.3.

2.94   *Queries to the author.* In manuscripts edited on paper, queries are best written in the margin, especially if the manuscript is to be photocopied. When the author has responded, they can simply be crossed out. Chicago discourages the use of gummed slips: they cannot be easily photocopied, and they have to be detached before typesetting (and thus are no longer in place when the manuscript is sent to the author with the proofs). The third method described in 2.84 is also an option in otherwise hand-marked manuscripts. See figure 2.3.

2.95 *Circling.* Circling has several meanings to the typesetter. (1) Circling a number or an abbreviation in the text and writing "sp" in the margin means that the element is to be spelled out; but if a number can be spelled out in different ways, or if an abbreviation may be unfamiliar to the typesetter, the editor should write out the form required. (2) Circling a comma or a colon means that a period is to be set; when a period is inserted by hand, it should be circled so it will not be missed by the typesetter. (3) Circling a marginal comment shows that the comment is not to be set in type but is either an instruction to the typesetter or a query to the author.

2.96 *Inserting, deleting, and substituting.* A regular caret (peak upward $\wedge$) should be carefully distinguished from an inverted caret (V-shaped $\vee$) used to mark superscripts, apostrophes, and the like. The conventions for deleting and substituting material should also be kept distinct.

2.97 *Transposing, closing up, and separating.* Special attention should be paid to punctuation when words are transposed or deleted; the new position of commas, periods, and the like must be clearly shown.

2.98 *Changing punctuation.* Any added or changed punctuation should be clearly marked for the typesetter—for example, by circling an added period, placing a caret over an added comma, or placing an inverted caret under added quotation marks. If necessary, write (and circle) "colon," "exclamation point," or whatever applies, either in the margin or close to the punctuation change.

2.99 *Dashes and hyphens.* Em dashes, if typed as two hyphens with no space between or on either side, need not be marked. Two- or three-em dashes, even if consistently typed, should be marked, as should en dashes, unless the typesetter is given a global instruction:—for example, "all hyphens between inclusive numbers are to be set as en dashes." End-of-line hyphens should be marked to distinguish between soft and hard hyphens. Soft hyphens are used merely to break a word at the end of a line; hard hyphens are "permanent" hyphens (such as that in twenty-first) and must remain no matter where the hyphenated word or term appears. See also 2.15.

2.100 *Capitalizing, lowercasing, and marking for italics or boldface.* To capitalize a lowercase letter, triple underline it; to make it a small capital, double underline it. To lowercase a capital letter, run a slanted line through it. To mark for italics, run a horizontal line under the word(s) to be italicized; for

<ct>How ~~and~~ an Editor ~~marks~~ Marks an Electronic Manuscript</ct>

~~EDITING~~ Editing an electronic manuscript is ~~a~~ more straightforward ~~process~~ than editing on paper. One could say it's a binary process; most markup is a matter of indicating one of two things: delete, or add. The trick is showing an author what you've done ~~to an author~~ and communicating stylistic instructions to the compositor.

<a>~~Specific Marks~~ Showing Your Work</a>

An electronic manuscript should first be cleaned up to get rid of extra spaces, errant hard returns, and superfluous formatting. This may be done "silently." Subsequent modifications can be communicated using the features built into most word-processing programs. Deleted text is most often struck through~~, like this~~; added text, underlined or double underlined. Often, a vertical line will appear in the margin next to a line that has been altered. Some programs have been designed to slash through ~~unwanted~~ deleted text or to highlight additions or other changes. Make sure your presentation is legible (a hyphen, for example, cannot be struck through with a midlevel horizontal line; ~~strike-out~~ strike out the whole compound instead and replace it with the corrected text). Choose a method that is easy to clean up. An editor should be able to remove redlining in just a few steps, certain that words will not be "gluedtogether" or inadvertently deleted. Though the dream of a universal standard~~ization~~ for electronic text has yet to be achieved, what you see is what you get. SMALL CAPITALS, ~~boldface,~~ **boldface,** *italics*—even em dashes and en dashes (e.g., 2003–2010)—not to mention special characters of an ever-increasing variety, may be communicated by software rather than description or coding. If you do need to comment, there are a variety of options for inserting "marginal" comments to authors. Built-in ~~comment~~ annotation functions or embedded footnotes,[A] being easiest to remove from a manuscript before publication, are often preferred to bracketed comments inserted in the text.

<a>Markup</a>

The other aspect of online editing involves markup, described by a longtime copyeditor as follows:

<ext>Mark the various elements of a manuscript with your word processor's "style palette," defining and assigning discrete names to chapter titles, subheads, prose extracts, and the like, or delimit such things manually with angle-bracketed codes (e.g., "<ext>" and "</ext>" for an extract, "<a>" and "</a>" for a first-level subhead). Consistent manual markup can always be converted across software platforms by some form of pattern recognition, and it can also form the basis for more sophisticated tagging in dedicated markup languages such as XML (for "Extensible Markup Language").</ext>

Whatever method you choose, include a list of styles or codes with the edited manuscript.

[A]This is a sample of a footnoted comment or query to an author.

Fig. 2.2. A redlined manuscript page, illustrating some alternative ways to show editing. For example, changed or added words are underlined, double-underlined, or highlighted; deletions are shown by horizontal strike-through lines or by slashes. In an actual manuscript, changes would be expressed in a uniform manner, usually determined by the software used. A manuscript may be almost literally redlined if a color printer is used; substituted words will appear in red or some other color.

How and Editor marks a Manuscript

[——EDITING A MANUSCRIPT, whether in the form of a typescript or a computer printout, requires a different method from that used in correcting proof. A correction or an operational sign is inserted in a line of type, not in the margin as in proof reading. The operator looks at every line of the manuscript word for word, and so any editor's change must be in it's proper place and clearly written.

Specific Marks

A caret between two words shows where additional material is to be inserted. three lines under a lowercase letter tell the typesetter to make it a capital; 2 lines mean a small capital (A.D.); one line means italic; a wavy line means boldface; and a stroke through a capital letter means lowercase. Unwanted underlining is removed thus. A small circle around a comma indicates a period. A straight line between parts of a closed compound, or between two words acidentally run together, will request space between the two words—to be doubly sure, add a space mark as well. two short parallel lines mean a hyphen is to be added between two words, as in two-thirds of a well done fish.

(run in) A circle around an abbrev. or numeral instructs the typesetter to spell it out. abbreviations that are ambiguous or not likely to be recognized by a typesetter should be spelled out by the editor (Biol. Biology or Biological; gen. gender, genitive, or genus) as should figures that might be spelled out more than one way (2500 twenty-five hundred or two thousand five hundred). Dots under a crossed-out word or passage mean stet (let it stand). Hyphens apearing when dashes should be used—except double hyphens representing an em dash—should always be marked; otherwise a hyphen may be used between continuing numbers like 15-18 or may confusingly be used to set off parenthetical matter. Whenever it is ambiguous or likely to confuse the typesetter, an end-of-line hyphen should be underlined or crossed out so that the typesetter will know whether to retain the hyphen in the line or close up the word.

(Au: OK?)
(equals signs)
(equals sign)

Fig. 2.3. An example of a hand-marked manuscript page.

boldface, make the horizontal line wavy. There is no need to underline words that appear in italics in the manuscript as long as the typesetter is instructed to italicize them. If an author has used both underlining and italics, special instructions are needed (see 2.17). For mathematical copy, see 14.61–67.

2.101 *Paragraph indention, flush left or right setting, and vertical spacing.* For indicating a paragraph indention, moving material to the left or right, and marking vertical space, see figure 2.3. In typographic usage the sign # means space, not number. To indicate a blank line, write "one-line #" and circle it (see 2.95).

2.102 *Coding.* For the kinds of elements that need coding, and for examples of codes, see 2.89. Handwritten codes are circled (see 2.95) rather than enclosed in angle brackets or other delimiters.

2.103 *Color of pencil or ink.* All editorial changes should be made in a color that will reproduce clearly if the edited manuscript is photocopied or faxed. The author should be asked to respond to the editing in a color distinct from that used by the editor. For querying the author, see 2.94.

3

Proofs

Introduction

3.1   *Definitions.* Unless otherwise specified, "proofs" here are first proofs, usually in page form; the proofreader is whoever has primary responsibility for proofreading (often an author); and the typesetter is whoever sets type based on the publisher's composition and page layout specifications (see 2.76–77), generates proof, and enters corrections (sometimes an editor or even an author). Further, although this chapter is addressed largely to those who proofread on paper, works to be published in a form other than print on paper must be checked with equal care in that form (see 3.42–43). For more on page layout and the various stages and kinds of proofs, see appendix A. For an illustration of how the stages described in this chapter fit into the overall publishing process for books and journals, see appendix B.

3.2　*Who checks proofs.* No matter who checks proofs, painstaking reading and consistent marking remain essential. A record must be kept of when each stage of proof has been corrected and by whom; the best record is a set of carefully marked proofs, preferably dated and signed (see figs. 3.1, 3.2). Proofreading functions may be shared: for example, an author may read and mark the proof, a manuscript editor may ensure that the author's corrections are indeed made, and a designer or production assistant may check type quality and general appearance, both on paper and on screen.

3.3　*Master proofs.* The master proofs are the single set of proofs marked and returned to the typesetter. If proofs other than the master set are corrected, all marks should be transferred to the master set. Some publishers send the master set to the author; others send a duplicate and then transfer the author's corrections to the master set. After the typesetter has made the corrections, the publisher should retain the master set as a record until the work has been published.

3.4　*Schedule.* Since many people are involved in the production of a journal or a book, a few days' delay in returning proof to the publisher or typesetter can cause a major delay in publication. Some journals allow the author as little time as forty-eight hours to make corrections. When the time scheduled for proofreading appears to conflict with the demands of accuracy, or if any other problem arises that might affect the schedule, the proofreader should immediately confer with the publisher.

What to Look For

3.5　*Reading against copy.* In proofreading parlance, "copy" refers to edited manuscript. If type has been set from electronic files, proof should be checked against the version of the manuscript that contains the author's final changes and responses to queries (see 2.75). If type has been set from a paper-only manuscript, hence totally rekeyed, the proofreader must read word for word against the edited manuscript, noting all punctuation, paragraphing, capitalization, italics, and so forth and ensuring that any handwritten editing has been correctly interpreted. This task may be easier if a second person reads from the manuscript while the proofreader follows and marks the proof. Whether type has been set from electronic files or from paper, the proofreader must mark *only* the proofs, *never* the manuscript, which is now known as "dead" (or "foul") copy. To correctly assign responsibility for error (see 3.14), the manuscript as earlier approved by the author must be kept intact. For systemic errors resulting from conversion of electronic files, see 3.8. For checking revised proofs, see 3.18.

3.6 *Spelling.* The proofreader should watch for the kind of errors missed by computer spell checkers—"it's" where "its" is meant, "out" where "our" is meant, and so forth—as well as any other misspellings. The manuscript editor's style sheet (see 2.54) may be a useful reference.

3.7 *Word breaks.* End-of-line hyphenation should be checked, especially in proper names and foreign terms. Chicago recommends the word breaks given in *Merriam-Webster's Collegiate Dictionary* (see bibliog. 3.1). (There are electronic dictionaries, including Webster, that can be used in conjunction with automated typesetting systems.) For words or names not listed in a dictionary, a liberal rather than a rigid approach is advisable, since formal usage varies widely and any change requested may entail further breaks or create tight or loose lines (lines with too little or too much space between words). Such problems may be avoided if a list of nondictionary words and their preferred hyphenation (or an editor's style sheet if it includes this information) is submitted to the typesetter along with the manuscript. See also 2.15, 7.33–45.

3.8 *Typeface and font.* All material in italics, boldface, small capitals, or any font different from that of the regular text should be looked at to be sure the new font starts and stops as intended. All heads and subheads should be checked for the typographic style assigned to their level (see 2.24, 2.58). All set-off material (excerpts, poetry, equations, etc.) should be checked for font, size, and indention. Note that conversion of electronic files for typesetting can result in unexpected systemic errors, such as the dropping or transmutation of a special character throughout the work or even the disappearance of all heads of a particular level. Such errors may be marked with a single, or "global," instruction to the typesetter, since the typesetter's solution is likely to be a global one; using this shortcut avoids cluttering the proofs with corrections of each instance. When a major systemic problem of this sort is identified, the typesetter should be consulted immediately.

3.9 *Page numbers and running heads.* Page numbers and running heads must be checked to ensure that they are present where they are supposed to be and absent where they are not (see 1.93–99, 2.79), that the correct page number appears following a blank page, and that the typesetter has followed instructions as to what should appear on a recto, a verso, or a double-page spread. Running heads must be both proofread and checked for placement. For running heads to endnotes, the page numbers must be supplied or verified by checking the text pages the notes pertain to (Notes to Pages ●●●–●●●; see 1.86, 1.98, 2.79).

3.10 *Illustrations and tables.* The proofreader must verify that all illustrations appear in the right location in the text, in the right size, right side up, not "flopped" (turned over left to right, resulting in a mirror image), and with their own captions. Captions should be read as carefully as the text. Tables must be proofread both for content and for alignment. Where an illustration or a table occupies a full page, no running head or page number should appear; but if several full pages of illustrations or tables appear in sequence, the proofreader may request that page numbers, and sometimes running heads as well, be added to better orient readers (see 1.99, 1.104). If an illustration or a table is still to come, the proofreader must mark the proof (e.g., "fig. 2 here") and ensure that enough space is left in the text to accommodate it. If there are lists of illustrations and tables, all captions and titles should be checked against the lists, and page numbers must be added. At this stage, someone must check that all needed permissions and credits for illustrations are in hand. If any are missing, material may have to be dropped or replaced.

3.11 *Overall appearance.* Each page or, better, each pair of facing pages should be checked for length (see 3.12), vertical spacing, position of running heads and page numbers, and so forth. Conformity to design must be verified. Such apparent impairments as fuzzy type, incomplete letters, and blocks of type that appear lighter or darker than the surrounding text may be due to poor photocopying. If in doubt, the proofreader may query "Type OK?" or "Too dark?" When four or more lines end with a hyphen or the same word, word spacing should be adjusted to prevent such "stacks." A page should not begin with the last line of a paragraph unless it is full measure and should not end with the first line of a new paragraph. Nor should the last word in any paragraph be broken—that is, hyphenated, with the last part of the word beginning a new line. To correct any of these occurrences, page length may be adjusted. (A very short line at the top of a page is known as a "widow"; a single word or part of a word at the end of a paragraph is an "orphan.")

3.12 *Adjusting page length.* Although facing pages of text must align, it is usually acceptable for each page in a two-page spread to run a line or two long or short to avoid "widows" and "orphans" (see 3.11) or to accommodate corrections. For example, if a correction on page 68 requires an added line, the typesetter may be asked to add space above a subhead on page 69 so that the two pages wind up the same length. Type can sometimes be rerun more loosely or more tightly to add ("save") or eliminate ("lose") a line.

3.13 *Sense.* The proofreader must query—or correct, if possible—illogical, garbled, repeated, or missing text. Any rewriting, however, must be limited to the correction of fact or of gross syntactical error, since all source checking and substantive and stylistic changes should have been done at the editing stage. No change should be made that would alter page makeup, since repagination not only is expensive but, for books, can affect the index (see 3.19).

3.14 *Assigning responsibility for error.* The proofreader may be asked to distinguish between errors introduced by the typesetter and errors that were left uncorrected in the manuscript or even introduced during editing. In such cases, corrections should be accompanied by codes determined by the publisher or typesetter, such as PE (printer's error),[1] AA (author's alteration), and EA (editor's alteration). All such codes should be circled. See 3.15.

3.15 *Author's alterations (AAs).* A publisher's contract may allow an author to make, without penalty, alterations in proof in terms of a percentage of the initial cost of the typesetting. Since the cost of corrections is far higher relatively than that of the original typesetting, an AA allowance of (for example) 5 percent does *not* mean that 5 percent of the proof may be altered. An author may be asked to pay the cost of AAs beyond the AA allowance stipulated in the contract. Page numbers added to cross-references in proof are usually considered AAs. Corrections of errors uncaught in editing are considered AAs if the author reviewed and approved the edited manuscript. Correction of an error introduced into the manuscript by the publisher *after* the author's review—made by the manuscript editor, for example, in entering the author's final adjustments—is an editor's alteration (EA) and not chargeable to the author. Supplying page numbers in lists of tables and illustrations and in running heads to notes constitutes an EA.

3.16 *Galley proofs.* If proofs are likely to require many corrections, or if illustrations or other material are to be interspersed after the text has been typeset, first proofs are sometimes issued in the form of galleys. Galleys are numbered for reference but do not include page numbers or, usually, running heads (which will be inserted when corrected galleys are made up

---

1. The term printer's error (PE), still in common use, reflects the time when typesetting was done by the same person or firm that did the printing.

into page proofs). Nor do they include illustrations. They do include text, chapter or article headings, subheads, tables, notes, and all other typeset matter. They should be read and marked with the same care as any other first proofs.

3.17   *Double-checking.* In addition to the tasks outlined in 3.5–14, the proofreader must also perform the following checks, according to the needs of the particular work:

1. For a book, ensure that the table of contents is complete; query—or delete, if necessary—any item listed that does not appear in the work
2. Check article or chapter titles and, if necessary, subheads or other heads against the table of contents to ensure consistent wording, and add beginning page numbers to the table of contents
3. If footnotes are used, ensure that each footnote appears, or at least begins, on the page that includes its callout number or symbol
4. Complete any cross-references (see 2.37)
5. For a book, check the half title and the title page to be sure the title is correct and the author's or volume editor's name is spelled right; verify that the information on the copyright page is accurate and complete
6. For a journal, check the covers, spine, and any front or back matter copy that is unique to the particular journal; check the elements that change with each issue, such as volume and issue numbers and date, month, or season of publication; ensure that the inclusive page numbers that appear on the spine are accurate; check front and back matter for any elements that may have changed, such as subscription prices or names of editors and members of the editorial board; ensure that copyright lines are included and accurate on all individual articles or other elements of the journal that carry them

For additional checking of electronic works, see 3.43.

3.18   *Revised proofs.* After corrections have been entered on first proofs, a set of revised proofs is usually issued. This second set must be compared with the first set (now known as "foul" proofs) to be sure all corrections have been properly typeset. (A proofreader checking revised proofs against galleys [see 3.16] must now perform the tasks listed in 3.9–12, 3.17.) Only the passages that contain corrected or new material need be proofread, but the proofreader should scan whatever has been rerun (lines whose opening and closing words do not correspond to the first proofs), since hyphenation or even page makeup may have been changed. If all rerun copy has been circled or bracketed, the proofreader can check revised proof more efficiently. Any corrections that have resulted in repagination may require adjustment to the index. To maintain a proper record, nothing must be marked on the foul proofs at this stage; any final corrections must be marked only on the revised set. The proofreader should bear in mind that any errors not caught at this stage may have to go uncorrected (see 3.40).

3.19   *Index.* An index set from well-prepared files (see 18.134) can be proofread quickly. If any repagination has taken place, however, all entries referring to the renumbered pages must be checked against revised proof and, if necessary, corrected. Index proof should be read and returned to the type-setter promptly, usually within twenty-four hours, so it is usually proof-read by a member of the publisher's staff.

How to Mark Proofs

3.20   *Where to mark.* Corrections to proof must always be written in the margin, left or right, next to the line concerned. A mark must also be placed in the text—a caret for an addition, a line through a letter or word to be deleted or replaced—to indicate where a correction is to be made. *Never* should a correction be written between the lines, where it could be missed. If a line requires two or more corrections, these should be marked in the margin in the order in which they occur, separated by vertical lines (see fig. 3.2). A guideline should be used only when a correction cannot be written next to the line in which it occurs.

3.21   *Major changes.* Where many errors occur in a line or two, the whole pas-sage should be crossed out and rewritten correctly in the margin. Longer changes should be typed on separate sheets, clearly labeled to show where they are to be inserted, and attached to the proof. A note in the margin should refer to the attachment. Every effort must be made to match the number of words in the new material to the number deleted from the old, so as not to affect page length. Material to be transposed from one page to another should be so marked in the margin; proofs must never be literally cut and pasted.

3.22   *Color and legibility.* Red proof markings are often preferred for visibility, but any color will do as long as the corrections are distinct from any type-setter's query. All corrections must be written clearly in upper- and lower-case letters. Either a pen or an erasable pencil may be used; in either case, the proofreader must be prepared to eradicate unwanted marks. Messy corrections may lead to further errors. If a small number of late-stage proof corrections must be transmitted to the typesetter by fax, the marks must be dark enough to transmit clearly, and they must not extend to the edges of the paper lest they be incomplete on the recipient's copy.

3.23   *Proofreader's marks.* The marks explained in the following paragraphs and illustrated in figures 3.1 and 3.2 are commonly understood by typesetters working in English. Other instructions provided by printers and publishers are unlikely to differ much from what is given here. Note that all verbal instructions to the typesetter—such as "see attached typescript" as well as "ital" or "rom"—are best circled. Otherwise such words, even if abbreviated, may be erroneously keyed in.

3.24   *Deleting copy.* To remove a letter, a word, or more, draw a diagonal line through a letter or a straight line through a word and write the delete mark (see fig. 3.1) in the margin. No part of the text should be obliterated. A punctuation mark that is to be removed should be circled rather than crossed through, so that it is still visible to the typesetter. The form of the delete mark in the margin need not be exactly as shown in figure 3.1, but it should be made in such a way as not to be confused with a *d*, an *e*, or an *l*. The mark for "delete and close up" should be used when a letter or a hyphen is deleted from within a word. The delete mark is used only when something is to be removed. When something is to be substituted for the deleted matter, it is simply written in the margin next to the line or lines that have been struck through (see fig. 3.2).

3.25   *Deleting space.* To delete space between letters or words, use the close-up mark (see fig. 3.1) in the text as well as in the margin.

3.26   *Adding or adjusting space.* To call for more space between words or letters, insert a vertical line in the text where the space is to be inserted and make a *space* mark (#) in the margin. The space mark is also used to show where more vertical space (or "leading," a term derived from the lead that was used in hot-metal typesetting) is needed between lines. All words in the same line should be separated by the same amount of space, though the spacing will vary from line to line in justified setting. When word spaces within a line are unequal, insert carets in the problem areas of the text and write the equal-space mark (eq #) in the margin.

3.27   *Paragraphs.* To indicate a new paragraph, insert an L-shaped mark in the text to the left and partly under the word that is to begin a new paragraph and write the paragraph mark (¶) in the margin. To run two paragraphs together, draw a line in the text from the end of one paragraph to the beginning of the next and write "run in" in the margin.

3.28 *Indention.* To indent a line one em space from the left or right margin, draw a small square (□) to the left of the material to be indented and repeat the square in the margin. To indent two or more ems, draw a rectangle divided into two or more squares. To indent more than one line, draw a line down from the square.

3.29 *Moving type.* Use the marks for moving type right ( ]) or left ([ ) or for centering ( ][ ) when a line of type, a title, an item in a table, or a letter appears too far to the left or right. Use the marks for moving type up (⌐) or down (⌐) when something appears vertically out of place. All these marks must be inserted in the text as well as in the margin.

3.30 *Marking for flush left or right.* To indicate that an indented line of type should start flush left (at the left-hand margin), insert a move-left ([ ) mark at the left of the first word in that line and write "fl" (flush left) in the margin, circled. To indicate that an element should appear flush right, do the same thing but with the move-right ( ]) mark and marginal "fr."

3.31 *Alignment.* The mark for vertical alignment (‖) is used mainly to indicate inaccurate alignment in tabular matter.

3.32 *Transposing.* To move letters, words, phrases, lines, paragraphs, or any other material from one place to another, use the transpose mark in the text (as in hand editing; see fig. 2.3) and write "tr" (circled) in the margin.

3.33 *Spelling out.* When abbreviations or numerals are to be spelled out, circle them in the line and write the spell-out mark (circled "sp") in the margin. If there is any ambiguity about the spelling (see 2.95), write the full word in the margin.

3.34 *"Stet."* To undelete or restore something that has earlier been marked for deletion or correction, place a row of dots in the text under the material that is to remain, cross out the marginal mark or correction, and write "stet" ("let it stand")—or to avoid any ambiguity, "stet as set"—in the margin, circled.

3.35 *Capitalization and font.* To lowercase a capital letter, draw a slash through the letter and write "lc" in the margin. To capitalize a lowercase letter, draw three lines under it and write "cap" in the margin. For small caps, draw two lines under the letters or words and write "sc" in the margin. For italics, draw a single line under the word or words and write "ital" in the margin. To remove italics, circle the italicized word or words and write "rom" in the margin. For boldface, draw a wavy line under the word or words and

Proofreaders' Marks

ᔫ Delete

⟲ Close up; delete space

ᶐ Delete and close up (use only when deleting letters *within* a word)

(stet) Let it stand

Insert space

(eq #) Make space between words equal; make space between lines equal

(hr #) Insert hair space

(ls) Letterspace

⁋ Begin new paragraph

☐ Indent type one em from left or right

] Move right

[Move left

][Center

⌐ Move up

⌊⌋ Move down

(fl) Flush left

(fr) Flush right

═ Straighten type; align horizontally

‖ Align vertically

(tr) Transpose

(sp) Spell out

TYPOGRAPHICAL SIGNS

(ital) Set in italic type

(rom) Set in roman type

(bf) Set in boldface type

(lc) Set in lowercase

(caps) Set in capital letters

(sc) Set in small capitals

(wf) Wrong font; set in correct type

X Check type image; remove blemish

∨ Insert here *or* make superscript

∧ Insert here *or* make subscript

PUNCTUATION MARKS

⩗ Insert comma

⩖ ⩗ Insert apostrophe *or* single quotation mark

⩔ ⩕ Insert quotation marks

⊙ Insert period

(set)? Insert question mark

;| Insert semicolon

⩔ or :| Insert colon

═ Insert hyphen

M̲ Insert em dash

N̲ Insert en dash

{|} or (|) Insert parentheses

Fig. 3.1. Proofreaders' marks.

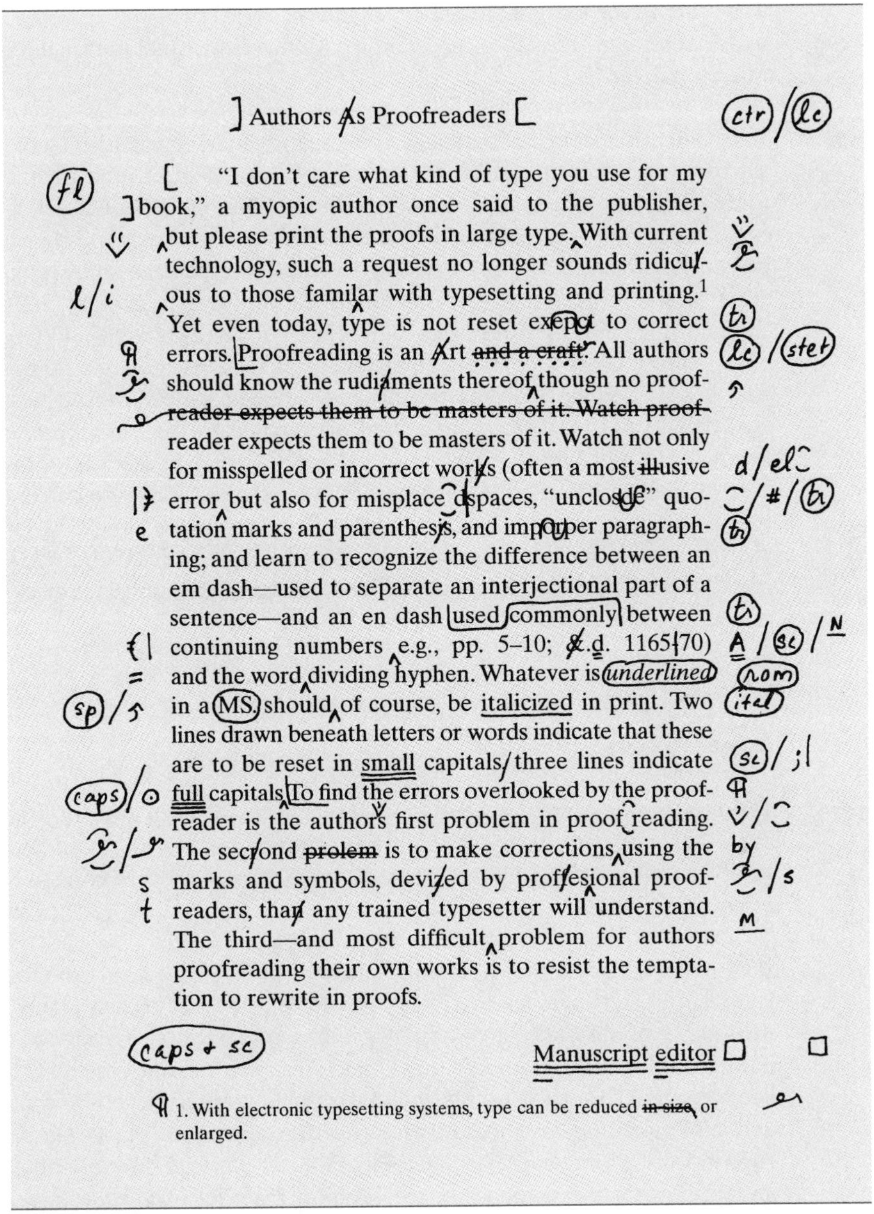

] Authors As Proofreaders [

["I don't care what kind of type you use for my book," a myopic author once said to the publisher, but please print the proofs in large type. With current technology, such a request no longer sounds ridiculous to those familiar with typesetting and printing.[1] Yet even today, type is not reset except to correct errors. Proofreading is an Art and a craft. All authors should know the rudiments thereof though no proofreader expects them to be masters of it. Watch proofreader expects them to be masters of it. Watch not only for misspelled or incorrect works (often a most illusive error but also for misplace dspaces, "unclosd" quotation marks and parenthesis, and improper paragraphing; and learn to recognize the difference between an em dash—used to separate an interjectional part of a sentence—and an en dash used commonly between continuing numbers e.g., pp. 5–10; q.d. 1165–70) and the word dividing hyphen. Whatever is underlined in a MS should, of course, be italicized in print. Two lines drawn beneath letters or words indicate that these are to be reset in small capitals/three lines indicate full capitals To find the errors overlooked by the proofreader is the authors first problem in proof reading. The second prolem is to make corrections using the marks and symbols, devised by proffesional proofreaders, that any trained typesetter will understand. The third—and most difficult problem for authors proofreading their own works is to resist the temptation to rewrite in proofs.

Manuscript editor

1. With electronic typesetting systems, type can be reduced in size or enlarged.

Fig. 3.2. Marked proof.

write "bf" in the margin. To remove boldface, circle the boldface word or words and write "not bf" in the margin. All these marginal instructions must be circled.

3.36   *Punctuation and accents.* To change a punctuation mark, circle it and write the correct mark in the margin. To add a mark, insert a caret and write the mark in the margin. Lest they be missed or misinterpreted, all punctuation marks in the margin may be clarified thus: a comma should have a caret over it; an apostrophe or a quotation mark should have an inverted caret under it; a parenthesis should have two short horizontal lines through it; a period should be circled; semicolons and colons should be followed by a short vertical line; question marks and exclamation points should be accompanied by the circled word "set"; and hyphens, en dashes, em dashes, and minuses should be differentiated by their appropriate symbols (see fig. 3.1). If an accent or a diacritical mark is missing or incorrect, the entire letter should be crossed out in the text and written in the margin with its correct accent; *never* must the accent alone appear in the margin. For clarity, the name of any unusual accent or diacritical mark (e.g., "breve") should also be written and circled in the margin. For examples of all these matters, see figures 3.1 and 3.2.

Cover Proofs

3.37   *Die copy.* Proof of die copy—author's name, title, publisher's imprint, and any other matter to be stamped on the spine or cover of a hardbound book—should be checked with extreme care. Any error must be corrected *before* the die is made.

3.38   *Book jacket and paperback cover proof and other promotional copy.* Proof of jacket copy and paperback cover copy should be read and checked against the interior of the work for consistency in content and style. The author's name and the title of the work must match those on the title page of the book (though the subtitle may be omitted from the cover or jacket). Author and title must also be checked wherever they appear on the jacket or cover—front, spine, back, or flaps. Biographical material on the author should be checked against any biographical material inside the book, though the wording need not be identical. If the work is part of a series or a multivolume set, the series title or volume number must match its counterpart inside the book. The price (if it is to appear), the ISBN, and any necessary credit line for a photograph of the author or for artwork used on the cover or jacket must be verified. Catalog copy, advertising copy, and any other promotional material should be similarly proofread and checked.

3.39 *Journal cover proof.* Although the elements that appear on the covers of academic journals vary considerably, the following suggestions should apply to most journals. The front cover (called cover 1) must be checked carefully to ensure that elements that change with each issue, such as the volume and issue numbers and the month, date, or season of publication, are accurate and up to date. The spine must be similarly checked. If the contents of the issue are listed on cover 1, they must be checked against the interior to be sure that authors' names and article titles match exactly and, for journals that publish various types of articles, that articles have been listed in the correct section of the journal. If inclusive page numbers appear on the spine, these must be verified. The inside of the front cover (cover 2) often includes subscription prices and information on how to subscribe, names of editors and members of the editorial board, or copyright information; all such information must be checked. Covers 3 (inside of back cover) and 4 (back cover) may contain advertisements, instructions to authors on submitting articles, or a list of articles to appear in future issues. They all must be verified by the proofreader.

Bluelines and Folded and Gathered Sheets

3.40 *Bluelines.* Bluelines, or "blues," are photographic proofs in the form of unbound signatures furnished not by the typesetter but by the printer. They are normally checked only for completeness of contents; page sequence; margins; location, sizing, position, and cropping (if any) of illustrations; and any spots or smudges. Any correction that would involve typesetting should be avoided at this stage for reasons of schedule and expense. Bluelines should therefore *not* be treated as revised proofs (see 3.18). Only to avoid such a grave error as an incorrect title or a misspelled author's name should a typesetting correction be made in blues. Digital proofs, generated by a technology different from that used for bluelines, should be checked in the same way as blues except that it is not necessary to check for spots and smudges (film imperfections that result from handling), which do not occur in digital proofs.

3.41 *Folded and gathered sheets.* Folded and gathered sheets (F&Gs), also called press sheets, are not proofs but the first printed sheets of a book or journal. (For full-color illustrations, press sheets are occasionally sent to the publisher to approve before the entire work is printed.) By the time the publisher sees a complete set of F&Gs, copies of the work are off the press and may be in the bindery. Since any correction at this stage would involve reprinting an entire signature, the publisher may prefer to turn a blind eye or, if absolutely necessary, resort to an errata sheet (see 1.107–8).

Checking Works for Electronic Publication

3.42 *Evidence of incorrect markup.* If codes or markup that are used to produce an electronic work are incorrect in kind, in scope, in relation to each other, or in the context of the document type, the electronic work may manifest problems either in its appearance or in the functioning of its parts (see 2.91). Such problems may occur even when typeset proofs for a work to be published both in print and in electronic form appear to be correct.

3.43 *Presence and functioning of all elements of the work.* Works to be published in electronic form should be checked in electronic form with the same care that is applied to printed proofs. Checking electronic copy may include some or all of the following steps: (1) looking carefully at layout to make sure that no elements are missing, that all elements are presented as intended, and that no markup added for another purpose (e.g., for a print version) adversely affects the electronic version; (2) confirming that all special characters have been converted correctly (see 3.8); (3) verifying that hypertext links work—both links within the work and links to other sites or resources; (4) making sure that any illustrations or other nontext features of the work are present and function as desired; and (5) for a work that will be published in more than one medium, making sure that the forms either match exactly—if that is the intent—or vary as intended (e.g., if a work to be published in both print and electronic forms includes features designated for inclusion in the electronic form only, both versions must be checked to ensure that these features are present in the electronic version and only in that version; see 1.188–90). Although some initial checking may have been done during the editing stage, the person responsible for checking electronic copy must identify any incorrect or missing elements; problems identified later, during the final stages of production, may delay publication.

Rights and Permissions   WILLIAM S. STRONG

Introduction

4.1 *Overview.* The foundation on which the entire publishing industry rests is the law of copyright, and a basic knowledge of it is essential for both authors and editors. This chapter gives readers that basic knowledge: how copyright is acquired, how it is owned, what it protects, what rights it comprises, how long it lasts, how it is transferred from one person to another. Once that foundation is laid, the key elements of publishing contracts are discussed, as well as the licensing of rights (what publishers call the "rights and permissions" function). The treatment of rights and permissions includes some guidelines for "fair use." While every effort is made here to be accurate, copyright law is both wide and intricate, and this chapter makes no claim to be exhaustive. Also, this chapter should not be considered legal advice or substitute for a consultation with a knowledgeable attorney in any particular circumstance. (For more detailed treatment of specific issues, see the works listed in section 2.2 of the bibliography.)

Copyright Law and the Licensing of Rights

4.2 *Relevant law.* For most publishing purposes the relevant law is the Copyright Act of 1976 (Public Law 94-553), which took effect on January 1, 1978, and the various amendments enacted since then. The 1976 act was a sweeping revision, superseding previous federal law and eliminating (though not retroactively) the body of state law known as common-law copyright. It did not, however, make old learning obsolete. Because prior law continues to govern most pre-1978 works in one way or another, anyone involved with publishing should understand both the old and the new regimes. Both will affect publishing for decades to come. Note that the law discussed in this chapter is that of the United States. The United States and most other countries are members of the Berne Convention, the oldest international copyright treaty. While the Berne Convention and certain other treaties have fostered significant uniformity around the world, anyone dealing with foreign copyrights should bear in mind that, conventions aside, the laws of other countries may contain significant differences from United States law.

4.3   *How copyright comes into being.* Whenever a book or article, poem or lecture, database or drama comes into the world, it is automatically covered by copyright so long as it is "fixed" in some "tangible" form. The term *tangible* is broader than paper and traditional media; it includes things such as electronic memory. A copyrightable work is "fixed" as long as it is stored in some manner that is not purely transitory. Thus an e-mail message that is stored in the sender's computer is fixed and copyrightable, but an extemporaneous lecture that is broadcast without being recorded is not.

4.4   *Registration not required.* Although it is advisable to register works with the United States Copyright Office, registration is not a prerequisite to legal protection. The practical reasons for registering are discussed in 4.48.

4.5   *Original expression.* Copyright protects the original expression contained in a work. *Originality* for copyright purposes has a very low threshold. Only a modicum of creativity is required; the law protects such minimal intellectual effort as the selection and arrangement of entries in a guide to prices of used automobiles. What counts is not quality or novelty, but only that the work be original with the author and not copied, consciously or unconsciously, from some other source. The term *expression* means the words, sounds, or images that an author uses to express an idea or convey information. Copyright protects the expression but not the underlying conceptual or factual material.

4.6   *Author the original owner.* Whoever is the author (a term not synonymous with *creator*, as will be seen) controls copyright at the outset and automatically possesses certain rights in the work. How these rights are owned, transferred, and administered is the focus of this chapter.

VARIETIES OF AUTHORSHIP

4.7   *Individual and joint authors.* In popular (or "trade") publishing and in the humanities, the typical author is likely to be an individual. In scientific, technical, and medical publishing, especially in the realm of journals, a work will more likely than not involve the efforts of more than one author. Such works are typically joint works. As defined by the statute, a joint work is "a work prepared by two or more authors with the intention that their contributions be merged into inseparable or interdependent parts of a unitary whole."

4.8   *Collective works.* Works in which the independent contributions of two or more authors are combined are considered collective rather than joint works. Copyright in them, which covers the selection and arrangement of materials, belongs to the compiler or editor and is separate from the copyright in the each of the various components. Typical examples of collective works are newspapers and anthologies.

Works Made for Hire

4.9   *Employer as author.* Another type of authorship is work made for hire. The law regards the employer or other controlling party as the "author" of any such work and hence as the initial owner of the copyright.

4.10   *The three categories of work made for hire.* Present law defines much more stringently than previous law the conditions that must be met for a work to be considered made for hire. First, the work may be prepared within the scope of a person's employment, such as the editorial column in a scholarly journal, a news story in a weekly magazine, or the entry for "aardvark" written by a person on an encyclopedia's paid staff. Second, someone *not* on the payroll will in certain instances be treated as an "employee" in determining authorship if that person is acting as the agent of another party. Determining agency is a difficult and somewhat ad hoc task, and this area of works made for hire is likely to be murky for some time to come. The third type is the specially ordered or commissioned work that both hiring party and creator agree *in writing* is to be considered a work made for hire. This sort of arrangement is available for only a few narrowly defined types of work:

- contributions to collective works, such as a book review commissioned for a journal
- contributions to motion pictures and sound recordings
- translations

· instructional texts
· tests
· answer materials for tests
· atlases
· compilations of existing materials such as anthologies
· "supplementary works" such as forewords, bibliographies, indexes, textual notes, and illustrations

A work that qualifies for such treatment will not be considered made for hire unless the written agreement between the commissioning party and the creative party expressly says so. The written agreement can be signed retroactively, although the safer practice is to obtain the parties' signatures before the work is created.

4.11 *Ineligible works.* It bears emphasizing that many kinds of works that could conceivably be commissioned do *not* qualify as works made for hire, no matter what agreement may be made between writer and publisher. Monographs and novels, for example, would not be eligible because they are not in any of the specific categories listed above.

4.12 *Joint authorship.* Although the law is not entirely clear on this point, it appears that any work that is partially made for hire will be treated as made for hire for copyright duration (see 4.22–23) and certain other purposes, even though a joint coauthor might be independent and not writing "for hire."

RIGHTS OF THE COPYRIGHT OWNER

4.13 *Rights of reproduction and distribution.* The author of a work possesses, at the beginning, a bundle of rights that collectively make up copyright. When a work is to be published, the author normally transfers some or all of these rights to the publisher, by formal agreement. Two of these rights are basic from the publisher's point of view: the right to make copies of the work (traditionally by printing, and now often by digital reproduction) and the right to distribute such copies to the public—in sum, to publish the work. In the case of online publishing, reproduction and distribution blend into the act of transmitting the work on demand to the reader's computer.

4.14 *Other copyright rights.* A third important right is the right to make what the law terms derivative works—that is, works based on the original work, such as translations, abridgments, dramatizations, or other adaptations.

A fourth right, the right of public display, is becoming increasingly important to publishers insofar as online publishing constitutes "display" of the work. Taken together, these rights (along with the right of public performance, which is not usually germane to publishing) constitute what are known as the copyright rights in a work. They exist from the time the work is created—that is, put in tangible form—and they belong to the author, who can sell, rent, give away, will, or transfer them in some other way, individually or as a package, to whomever the author wishes.

4.15 *Moral rights: integrity of copyright management information.* In addition to the foregoing rights, the law also gives the creators of certain works of fine art a so-called moral right against mutilation and misattribution. A dozen or more states have enacted legislation to the same effect as the federal law but generally broader. This moral right, however, whether federal or state, has little effect on publishers (except perhaps while in possession of original artwork) and will not be dealt with further here. The only quasi-moral right given to authors of literary works is the right to prohibit false attribution. This right, found to varying degrees in both state and federal unfair competition law, prevents a publisher from crediting an author with material he or she has not written and, conversely, from failing to credit an author as the source of the work, except where the publisher is acting with the author's acquiescence. Similar to the moral right of attribution is the right to protect the integrity of "copyright management information." This information, for publications, consists of the following:

- the title and other information identifying the work, including the content of the copyright notice
- the name of, and other identifying information about, the author
- the name of, and other identifying information about, the copyright owner, including the content of the copyright notice
- terms and conditions for use of the work
- identifying numbers or symbols referring to such information or links to such information

Copyright management information, to the extent it is included in a work, cannot be removed or altered without the permission of the copyright owner, and no work on which the information has been altered or removed may be distributed, or imported for distribution, without the permission of the copyright owner. Furthermore, it is unlawful to affix false copyright management information to a work or to distribute or import for distribution a work bearing false copyright management information. Significantly, *anyone* who is injured by a violation of these restrictions—

including the author, even if the author has assigned the copyright—may bring suit against the wrongdoer. Thus, this provision of the law functions much like the moral right of attribution, but is applicable to all published works and therefore free of the narrow confines that apply to the moral right per se.

4.16 *Trademark protection of titles.* In addition to copyright, a publishable work may have trademark protection, covering its title and arguably, in the case of fiction, the names of its characters and imaginary locales. (Copying only the title or character names of a work would not be considered a copyright infringement.) Trademark rights can arise under either federal or state law or both. Book titles are harder to protect as trademarks than journal or lecture titles, because of a judicial and administrative reluctance to give trademark protection to names that are used only once. Nevertheless, it is fair to say that some book titles are clearly protectible; *Gone with the Wind* and *Winnie-the-Pooh* are titles that cannot be used without permission.

4.17 *Basic versus subsidiary rights.* Whoever controls the copyright in a work, whether author or publisher, may not only exercise those rights directly but also empower others to exercise them. If, for example, the author of a book has transferred the whole bundle of rights to a publishing house, the publishing house will itself exercise the basic rights of printing and publishing the book, compensating the author by paying a percentage of the sales receipts (a royalty) from each copy sold. It will also be responsible for administering subsidiary rights. These rights (discussed in 4.60) usually involve exploiting markets in which the publishing house is not active. For example, foreign-language, book-club, and motion-picture rights involve specialized markets and require special expertise. For this reason, subsidiary rights are likely to be exercised by third parties under license from the publisher, although, if the publisher is part of a large media conglomerate, licensing is often intramural. Part of the publisher's responsibility to the author should be to see that subsidiary rights are exploited as effectively as possible. Licensing subsidiary rights also includes granting what the publishing industry calls permissions, a term that refers to such things as the licensing of photocopying for classroom use and quoting or reproducing in a new work small parts of another work.

4.18 *Author retention of subsidiary rights.* Authors of "trade" books—fiction, biography, and other books for the general reader—are more likely than scholarly authors to be represented by agents and more likely to retain some or all subsidiary rights. In such cases, subsidiary rights are licensed directly by the author (through his or her agent) to foreign publishers, motion picture producers, and the like. Typically, however, "permissions" are still handled by the publisher rather than the agent or author.

COPYRIGHT AND THE PUBLIC DOMAIN

4.19   *Copyright duration before 1978.* Until January 1, 1978, a dual system of copyright existed in the United States. Common-law copyright, created by the individual states of the Union, protected works from the time of their creation until publication, however long that might be. A personal letter written in the eighteenth century but never published was protected as effectively as a 1977 doctoral thesis in the making. In neither case could the document be copied and distributed (that is, published) without the express permission of either the creator of the work or the creator's legal heirs. Statutory, or federal, copyright protected works at the moment of publication and for twenty-eight years thereafter, provided that a proper copyright notice appeared in the published work. Thereafter, copyright in the work could be renewed for another twenty-eight years if the original copyright claim had been registered with the United States Copyright Office (a department of the Library of Congress) and if a renewal claim was filed by the appropriate person(s) during the final year of the first term of copyright. Thus in the normal course of things federal copyright in a work was intended to last for a total of fifty-six years from the date of publication, after which time the work went into the public domain—that is, it became public property and could be reproduced freely. See 4.20–21, 4.44.

4.20   *Lengthening of copyright duration in 1978.* To enter the public domain is of course the ultimate fate of all copyrighted works. However, the elaborate system described in 4.19 was replaced as of 1978 by a unitary federal copyright of substantially greater length. Subsequent amendments have lengthened the term yet further and eliminated a number of formalities that used to be required. All these changes have made entering the public domain almost theoretical for works currently being created. As will be discussed below, other changes to the law have given many older works, particularly those of foreign origin, an unexpected reprieve (see 4.28).

4.21   *Uses of public-domain works.* Once in the public domain, a work may never again be protected and is free for all to use. The use may be direct and simple; for example, Mark Twain's novels have now lost their copyrights and may be republished free of royalty. Or the public-domain works may be the compost from which new works, adaptations or other derivative works, spring in due course. Such new works are entitled to copyright, but their copyright is limited to the new material they contain. The new copyright entitles the new publisher to put a copyright notice on the resulting derivative work, and nothing requires that such notice delineate what is and is not covered by the copyright. This sometimes has the unfortunate by-product (not always unintended, let it be said) of making users think that the scope of copyright extends to the public-domain material. For government-produced works in the public domain, see 4.43.

Duration of Copyright for Works Created after 1977

4.22   *"Life plus seventy."* Enacted in 1976 and effective on January 1, 1978, the present copyright law did away with this dual system of federal/common-law copyright. Present law is both simpler and more complex regarding copyright duration. It is simpler in that we now have only one unified, federal system protecting all works fixed in tangible form from the moment so fixed. It is more complex in that terms of protection are different depending on authorship, and in that works existing before 1978 are subject to a variety of special rules. The paradigmatic copyright term, under the new law, is "life plus seventy," that is, life of the author plus seventy years. (In the case of joint authors, the seventy years are added to the life of the last author to die.) As will be seen below, however, there are many exceptions to this rule.

4.23   *Works made for hire.* Since the owner of the copyright in a work made for hire is not the actual creator of the work (often, indeed, the copyright owner is a corporate entity), the law specifies a fixed term of years for the duration of copyright. This term is 95 years from the date of publication or 120 years from the date of creation, whichever is the shorter.

4.24   *Anonymous and pseudonymous works.* As in the case of works made for hire, the regular rule for duration of copyright cannot be applied if an author publishes anonymously or under a pseudonym. Again, the law prescribes the same fixed term of copyright for these works—95 years from the date of publication or 120 years from creation, whichever is the shorter. If after publication, however, such an author's name is revealed and recorded in the documents of the Copyright Office, the regular "life plus seventy" rule takes over, unless, of course, the work is made for hire.

Duration of Copyright for Works Created before 1978

4.25   *Pre-1978 unpublished works.* For unpublished works that were still under common-law copyright when the new law went into effect, there is a transitional rule. Such works are given the same copyright terms as post-1977 works, but with the proviso that copyright in them lasted at least until December 31, 2002; if the works were published before that date, expiration is postponed at least until December 31, 2047. Thus, these published works have a copyright term of not less than seventy years from the date the new law went into effect and a longer term if their authors' lives extended beyond 1977.

4.26 *Pre-1978 published U.S. works.* Works published before December 31, 1922, are now in the public domain. Works published during the years 1923 through 1963 are still under copyright if their copyrights were properly renewed in the twenty-eighth year after first publication. (The safest way to determine this is to commission a search of the Copyright Office records through a copyright attorney or a reputable search firm.) The renewal term for such works is now sixty-seven years rather than twenty-eight. Works published from 1964 through 1977 will be protected without fail for ninety-five years from first publication, because renewal for such works is automatic. All the above assumes that these works were at all times published with proper copyright notice. For a discussion of copyright notice, see 4.38–44.

4.27 *New copyright for new editions.* In deciding whether a work may be republished without permission, bear in mind that each time a work is materially revised a new copyright comes into being, covering the new or revised material. Thus a seminal treatise published in 1920 is now in the public domain, but the author's revision published in 1934 may not be. One is free to republish the 1920 version, but that may be an empty privilege.

4.28 *Pre-1978 published foreign works.* The rules just described do not apply to foreign works. Such works are protected in their own countries for the life of the author plus fifty or seventy years, depending on the country concerned. In the United States, a pre-1978 foreign work automatically receives the same term of copyright as a pre-1978 U.S. work, but without regard to whether proper copyright notice ever appeared on it, and without regard to whether copyright was renewed in the twenty-eighth year after publication. This is so because, effective January 1, 1996, Congress restored to copyright all foreign works that had forfeited copyright as a result of noncompliance with U.S. notice and renewal requirements. Copyrights restored in this manner are subject to certain protections given to those who produced copies or derivative works before December 8, 1994, relying on the apparent forfeiture of copyright. It should be noted that the U.S. copyright term for foreign works, even after restoration, does not synchronize with the protection of those works outside the United States. If a French author of a work published in 1922 lived until 1970, the work would now be in the public domain in the United States but would remain under copyright in France until 2040. If the same author had published another work in 1923, that work would retain copyright in the United States until 2018, still twenty-two years less than in France. Publishers who wish to reissue or otherwise make use of foreign public-domain works need to be aware that foreign markets may be foreclosed to them.

4.29   *Definition of "foreign."* For purposes of the special restoration rules discussed in 4.28, a work is a foreign work if it was first published outside the United States. The only substantial exception is for works published in the United States within a thirty-day period after foreign publication, as used to be done by some U.S. publishers to get Berne Convention treatment by "the back door" before the United States became a member of Berne. Such works are not eligible for copyright restoration.

Renewing Copyright in Pre-1978 Works

4.30   *Benefits of renewal.* Although renewal is now automatic, the law retains certain benefits for those who take the trouble to file actively for renewal. Filing for renewal fixes the ownership of the second-term copyright on the date of filing; automatic renewal fixes ownership in whoever could have renewed on the *last day* of the first term. A renewal that has been actively obtained constitutes prima facie evidence of copyright and its ownership; the evidentiary value of an automatically renewed copyright is discretionary with the courts. Finally, and most important, if the renewal is allowed to happen automatically, existing derivative works can continue to be exploited for the second term of copyright, whereas active renewal gives the renewal-term owner—unless he or she signed a derivative work license explicitly covering the renewal term—the right to relicense derivative work rights.

4.31   *Renewal by the author.* The author, if living, is the person entitled to file for renewal. Publishers who have obtained renewal-term rights from authors should continue to file for renewal on the author's behalf as they have traditionally done.

4.32   *Renewal if the author is deceased.* Whether renewal occurs by filing or automatically, if the author is not alive the law allocates the copyright to his or her surviving spouse, children, or other heirs according to complex rules that will not be parsed here.

ASSIGNING OR LICENSING COPYRIGHT

4.33 *Subdividing a copyright.* Copyright is often referred to as a "bundle" of rights. The basic components, as noted above, are the right to reproduce, the right to distribute copies of a work to the public, the right to make derivative works, and the right to perform or display a work publicly. Each of these rights may be separately licensed or assigned. Furthermore, each of them may be carved up into smaller rights along lines of geography, time, or medium. Thus, for example, the right to publish a treatise may be carved up so that Publisher A gets North American rights while Publisher B gets United Kingdom rights. A French translation license may be given to Librairie C for a ten-year fixed term. Or Publisher A may receive print rights while D-DISC gets CD-ROM rights and E-NET gets online publication rights. There is theoretically no end to the ways of subdividing a copyright, other than the limits of human ingenuity and the marketplace.

4.34 *Exclusive versus nonexclusive licenses.* Finally, licenses may be exclusive or nonexclusive. Typically, anyone making a substantial investment will insist on exclusive rights, whereas persons making ephemeral use at low marginal cost—a typical case being classroom photocopying—need no more than nonexclusive rights. An exclusive licensee is treated in general like an owner of copyright, and has standing to sue any infringer of that right. A nonexclusive licensee is more like the holder of a personal privilege than the holder of a property interest, and cannot sue infringers or even, without the permission of the licensor, transfer the license to someone else. While most authorities believe that, by contrast, an exclusive licensee has the power to assign and sublicense the right concerned, a federal court opinion in mid-2002 cast doubt on that presumption. As a precaution, anyone drafting an exclusive license should expressly state that the license may be assigned and sublicensed at the discretion of the licensee.

4.35 *Goals of the parties to a license.* The goal of a licensor of rights is to define them as narrowly as possible so that the maximum revenue may be wrung from the property. The goal of a licensee is to define the license as broadly as possible so as to cover all foreseeable contingencies. Both sides, though, have a common interest in seeing that the license is clear and understandable. Disputes between licensors and licensees usually result from the use of jargon that is not understood by both, or failure to specify when payment is due and for what, or misunderstanding of the facts and the technology concerned. The failure of some older licenses to anticipate, or least accommodate, new media has led to many lawsuits. Drafting a license demands and deserves care and skill, as well as good communication between lawyers and their clients.

4.36 *Payment.* A license and the obligation to pay for that license are usually treated as reciprocal obligations, not mutually dependent ones. Thus the failure of a licensee to pay royalties does not automatically terminate the license and turn the licensee into an infringer. It gives the licensor a claim for contract damages, not a copyright infringement claim. Shrewd licensors will whenever possible reverse this presumption in their contracts, and shrewd licensees will usually resist.

4.37 *Termination of transfers.* Apart from contractual rights, the statute itself gives individual authors the right to terminate licenses and assignments of copyright under certain conditions. The law specifically grants authors the right to terminate any post-1977 copyright arrangement after thirty-five years, and a roughly comparable termination right applies to licenses signed before 1978. The mechanics of termination, including the determination of who has the right to terminate, are extraordinarily complicated and are of importance to only the most lucrative of copyrights, so no more will be said here.

COPYRIGHT NOTICE

4.38 *The old rules.* No aspect of copyright has caused more grief than the rules of copyright notice. These rules have been responsible for most forfeitures of copyright. Largely a trap for the unwary, they were softened somewhat in 1978 and removed almost entirely in 1989. They were not without purpose or utility, but the rules prevented the United States from joining the Berne Convention, and in the end their utility was outweighed by this and other disadvantages.

4.39 *Three different regimes.* Congress could not easily dispense with the rules retroactively, however, and the resulting 1989 legislation means that we now operate simultaneously under three doctrines: (1) for works first published on or after March 1, 1989, no copyright notice is required; (2) for works first published in the United States between January 1, 1978, and February 28, 1989, copyright notice must have been used on all copies published before March 1, 1989, with the proviso that certain steps could be taken to redeem deficient notice (see 4.44); and (3) for United States works first published before January 1, 1978, the copyright was almost certainly forfeited if the notice was not affixed to all copies; few excuses were or are available. (As noted above, foreign works have been retroactively exempted from these rules.) Notwithstanding the liberality of the new law, continued use of notice is strongly advised to deprive infringers of any possible defense of ignorance. The rules in 4.40–43 should therefore still be followed.

Content of Notice

4.40 *Three elements of the notice.* Under present law, as under the old, the notice consists of three parts: (1) either the symbol © (preferred because it also suits the requirements of the Universal Copyright Convention), or the word *copyright*, or the abbreviation *copr.*; (2) the year of first publication; and (3) the name of the copyright owner. Many publishers also add the phrase "all rights reserved," and there is no harm in doing so, but the putative advantages of it (which were limited to Latin America) have all but vanished. The year of first publication is not needed for greeting cards, postcards, stationery, and certain other works not germane to the publishing industry. Where a work is in its renewal term of copyright, it is customary, but not required, to include the year of renewal as well as the year of first publication. Many publishers also include the publication years of various editions of a work if the work has been revised. Technically this is not necessary: if a revision is substantial enough to constitute a derivative work, only the publication year of the derivative work need be used. See also 1.16–27.

4.41 *Name used in the notice.* The name used in the notice should be the name of the author unless the author has assigned all rights to the publisher. However, it is not uncommon to see the publisher's name in the notice when it does not own all rights. Conversely, authors sometimes insist on notice in their names even when they have assigned all rights—and publishers sometimes acquiesce, thereby giving up something that has no value except to the ego of the author. Such vagaries are regrettable but, unless they mislead those seeking permission to use the copyrighted material, quite harmless.

4.42 *Placement of notice.* The copyright notice should be placed so as to give reasonable notice to the consumer. The old law was very specific about its location: for books, on either the title page or the page immediately following, and for journals and magazines, on the title page, the first page of text, or the front cover. Present law simply states that the notice should be so placed as "to give reasonable notice of the claim of copyright," but most publishers continue to place it in the traditional locations required by the old law. See also 1.119, 1.141, 1.152, 1.161, 1.177.

4.43 *United States government materials.* Works created by employees of the United States government in the course of their official duties are in the public domain. When a work consists "preponderantly" of materials created by the federal government, this must be stated in the notice. This may be done either positively (e.g., "Copyright is claimed only in the introduction, notes, appendixes, and index of the present work") or negatively (e.g., "Copyright is not claimed in 'Forest Management,' a publication of the United States government reprinted in the present volume"). Works produced by state or local governments or by foreign governments are not per se in the public domain and are not subject to this notice provision.

4.44 *Correcting mistakes.* Under pre-1978 law, no mechanism was available to cure the effects of a defective notice: copyright was forfeited and that was that, unless the omission of notice was accidental and occurred in a very small number of copies. For publication between January 1, 1978, and March 1, 1989 (when the notice requirement was finally dropped altogether), a more lenient regime prevailed. A mistake in the owner's name, or a mistake by no more than a year in the date element of the notice, was largely excused. Any more serious mistake was treated as an omission of notice. Any omission of one or more of the necessary three elements would be excused if the omission was from a "relatively small" number of copies. If more extensive omission occurred, the copyright owner could still save the copyright from forfeiture by registering it (see 4.45–48) within five years after the defective publication and making a "reasonable effort" to add the notice to all copies distributed to the public after the omission was discovered. Very few cases have discussed what a "reasonable effort" is, and their explanations, being somewhat ad hoc, give limited guidance to anyone trying to determine if a work in this category is still protected by copyright.

DEPOSIT AND REGISTRATION

4.45 *Deposit requirements.* The law requires copyright owners to send copies of their published works to the Copyright Office for deposit and use in the Library of Congress. The copies must be sent within three months of publication. Although failure to make the required deposit does not forfeit the copyright, the copyright owner is subject to a fine for noncompliance if a specific request from the Library of Congress is ignored. For printed works, the deposit of two copies of the "best edition" is required. If, for example, clothbound and paperback editions of a book are published simultaneously, the cloth edition must be sent. If the work is a very expensive or limited edition, relief from the requirement of depositing two copies of each book may be obtained by applying to the Library of Congress, in which case only one copy need be sent. Databases published only online are exempt. When sending deposit copies to the Copyright Office, publishers usually have the copyright registered as well. In the case of printed materials, the two deposit copies also serve the requirements for registration. In the case of electronic publications, the submission of certain "identifying material" will suffice.

4.46   *Registration forms and fees.* To register a work the author or other claimant must fill out the appropriate application form. There are several forms, tailored to different types of works. Form TX (see fig. 4.1) is used for books and other works in the broad category called literary works, other than periodicals. For all periodicals, including but not limited to newspapers, magazines, newsletters, journals, and even annuals, use form SE. The Copyright Office offers forms and intelligible explanations of its registration rules, including its complex deposit requirements, on its Web site. The fee for registration is a modest amount per work. For a group of works, one fee covers the entire group. Group registration is available for multiple photographs or multiple contributions to periodicals by a single author, and for certain serial publications. Publishers with large lists tend to keep funds on deposit at the Copyright Office and to charge their registration fees against their deposit accounts.

4.47   *Need for accuracy and candor.* It is important to answer all questions on the application accurately. Copyright owners have been sanctioned by courts for misleading the Copyright Office by (for example) failing to disclose that a work is based on preexisting materials. Statements on the application do not need to be exhaustive, but they must be correct and not evasive. However, in contrast to patent applications, there is no requirement for disclosure of adverse claims or any other information not specifically called for on the form.

4.48   *Benefits of registration.* Registration is not necessary to "obtain" a copyright (which exists in the work from the moment it is fixed in tangible form; see 4.3) or to ensure its validity, but responsible publishers seldom publish without registering copyright because of the added protection registration affords. Unlike the copyright notice, registration puts on public record the exact details of a copyright claim. In cases of infringement, registration is a prerequisite to bringing suit unless the work was written by a non-U.S. author and first published abroad. Moreover, if registration has been

Copyright Office Registration Forms

FORM NAME	DESCRIPTION
TX	Application for copyright registration for a nondramatic literary work
SE	Application for copyright registration for serials (includes periodicals, newspapers, annuals, journals, and proceedings of societies)
SE/Group	Application for copyright registration for a group of serials
G/DN	Application for copyright registration for a group of daily newspapers or newsletters
VA	Application for copyright registration for a work of the visual arts
PA	Application for copyright registration for a work of the performing arts
SR	Application for copyright registration for a sound recording
GR/CP	Adjunct application for copyright registration for a group of contributions to periodicals (for a collection of works by the same author previously published with notice of copyright—used only in conjunction with one of the foregoing, such as TX)
CA	Application for supplementary copyright registration to correct or amplify information given in the Copyright Office record of an earlier registration (useful for correcting errors made in the initial, basic registration)
RE	Application for renewal registration (to register claim for renewal of copyright in works published between January 1, 1950, and December 31, 1977)
GATT	Application for foreign works restored to U.S. copyright (see 4.28–29)

Fig. 4.1. List of the various application forms for copyright registration. The form used for literary and scholarly books is TX. Publishers of periodicals can effect group registration by using SE/Group (for serials) or G/DN (for daily newspapers and newsletters). Authors who publish frequently in periodicals can register their works in groups, using GR/CP.

made within three months of publication, or before an infringement begins, the copyright owner, instead of going through the difficulties of proving actual damages, can sue for "statutory damages" (in effect, an award of damages based on equity rather than on proof of loss) and, most significantly, is eligible to be reimbursed for attorney's fees.

The Publishing Agreement

4.49 *Basic rights.* No publishing house may legally publish a copyrighted work unless it first acquires the basic rights to copy the work and distribute it to the public. Although in theory a publisher could proceed with no more than a nonexclusive license of these rights, and although this is done in rare circumstances, for obvious reasons publishers generally insist on exclusive rights. In most instances these rights are acquired from the author by means of a contract called the publishing agreement.

NEW BOOKS

4.50 *Basic book-contract provisions.* In book publishing the publisher typically draws up the contract for a new book, to be signed by both the publisher and the author or, in the case of a joint work, by all authors. In this contract the publisher and author agree to certain things. The publisher undertakes to publish the book after acceptance of the manuscript and to pay the author a stipulated royalty out of the proceeds. The author, in addition to granting rights to the publisher, typically guarantees that the work is original and has never before published and that it does not violate copyright or libel anyone or otherwise expose the publisher to legal liability. The author usually agrees to correct and return proofs and to cooperate in future revisions of the work. Book-publishing agreements are generally fairly lengthy and detailed documents and include many other points of agreement. Among the common areas of negotiation are royalty schedules; royalty advances and expense allowances; the standards for acceptance of the manuscript; the period following acceptance within which the publisher must issue the work; what rights, beyond North American print rights, are granted to the publisher; what share of royalties the author receives for revised editions to which he or she does not contribute; how rights revert to the author if the book goes out of print; and on what terms the author may audit the publisher's financial records to ensure full payment of royalties due. Typically, publishing agreements prohibit the author from publishing works that compete with the work under contract.

4.51 *Option clauses.* In former years publishing agreements often contained binding options on the author's next book. These are almost a thing of the past. Some publishers insist on a right of first refusal or a right to match outstanding offers on the author's next book, but such provisions are becoming rare.

4.52   *Edited works.* The agreement just described is intended for books with one or a few authors. Another type of book, common in scholarly but not in trade publishing, is one in which the chapters are contributed by various authors, chosen and guided by an editor who is an authority in the relevant field. The editor, by selecting and arranging the contributions included in the work, adds another layer of authorship. As author of the collective work, the book as a whole, he or she should sign an agreement similar to the standard author agreement described above. In dealing with the chapter contributors, a publisher may in some circumstances use an agreement of the same type, especially if the contributors are to receive royalty shares. All such agreements, though, need to be modified to reflect the particular allocation of responsibilities between editor and contributors. Alternatively, in appropriate circumstances, publishers can use simpler forms (such as that in fig. 4.3), closer in style to journal author forms (see fig. 4.2). Finally, it is possible to use work-made-for-hire agreements for all these persons, although that is the least common solution. For symposia, see 4.57.

4.53   *Other contracts.* In scholarly publishing, in addition to contracts with the authors of new books, several other types of agreement are in use for special kinds of works. Two of the common ones cover contributions to scholarly journals (see 4.54–56 and fig. 4.2) and to symposia (see 4.57 and fig. 4.3).

JOURNAL ARTICLES

4.54   *Transfers of rights.* Contributors to a journal possess at the beginning exactly the same rights in their work as authors of books. Consequently, when an article has been accepted for publication in a scholarly journal, the author is usually asked to sign a formal transfer of rights in the contribution to the publisher. In the absence of a written copyright transfer agreement, all that the publisher acquires from the agreement to publish is the privilege of printing the contribution in the context of that journal. Contributors frequently do not know this and do not understand that without broad rights the publisher cannot license anthology, database, classroom photocopying, or other uses that spread the author's message. They will sometimes balk at the breadth of the copyright transfer they are asked to make until these legalities are explained. In the agreement currently in use at the University of Chicago Press, the publisher returns to the contributor the right to reprint the article in other scholarly works (see fig. 4.2). Such a provision is fair to both sides and is to be encouraged.

PUBLICATION AGREEMENT

FROM:

TO: DATE:

The University of Chicago Press is pleased to undertake the publication of your contribution, entitled

("the Contribution"), to its journal,

. We ask you to assign the copyright, thus granting us all rights for the Contribution, so that you as author and we as sponsor of the Journal may be protected from the consequences of unauthorized use. You will have the right, however, after publication in the Journal, to reprint the Contribution without charge in any book of which you are the author or editor.

Accordingly, the following terms of publication are submitted for your consideration.

Copyright Assignment: Whereas The University of Chicago, acting through its Press, is undertaking to publish the Contribution in its journal, named above, and whereas you desire to have the Contribution so published, now therefore you grant and assign the entire copyright for the Contribution to the University for its exclusive use. The copyright consists of any and all rights of whatever kind or nature now or hereafter protected by the copyright laws of the United States and of all foreign countries, in all languages and forms of communication, and the University shall be the sole proprietor thereof. The University, in turn, grants to you the right to reprint the Contribution in any book of which you are the author or editor, subject to your giving proper credit in the book to the original publication of the Contribution in the Journal. To protect the copyright in the Contribution, the original copyright notice as it appears in the Journal should be included in the credit.

Warranty: You warrant that the Contribution is original with you; that it contains no matter which is defamatory or is otherwise unlawful or which invades individual privacy or infringes any proprietary right or any statutory copyright; and you agree to indemnify and hold the University harmless against any claim to the contrary. Further, you warrant that you have the right to assign the copyright to the University and that no portion of the copyright to the Contribution has been assigned previously. It is understood that the copyright to the Contribution has not been registered with the Library of Congress, but that in the event such registration has taken place you will promptly transfer the copyright to the University.

Previous Publication and Permission: You warrant that the Contribution has not been published elsewhere in whole or in part (except as may be set out in a rider annexed hereto and signed by the University) and that no agreement to publish is outstanding. Should the Contribution contain material which requires written permission for inclusion in the Contribution, such permission shall be obtained at your own expense from the copyright proprietor and submitted for review to the editor of the Journal with the manuscript.

Proofhandling: You will be given an opportunity to read and correct the edited manuscript and/or proofs, but if you fail to return them to the editor of the Journal by the date set by the editor, production and publication may proceed without your corrections.

Subsidiary Rights and Compensation: It is understood that you will receive no monetary compensation from the University for the assignment of copyright and publication of the Contribution in the Journal. However, fees received from licenses to reprint the Contribution in readers, anthologies, and/or textbooks will be divided equally between you and the Press. You will receive no monetary compensation for other licenses which may be granted for the use of your Contribution, nor will you receive any share of fees amounting to $50.00 or less. Your share of fees collected by the Press will be paid to you (in the case of joint authors, to the first named) within three months of receipt.

If the foregoing terms are satisfactory, please sign and date this agreement. (*All* joint authors should sign, and every author's Social Security number and year of birth should be included. Use the other side of this white page if necessary.) *Please return the white copy to the editor immediately and retain the yellow copy for your own files.*

For The University of Chicago

PAULA BARKER DUFFY, *Director*
The University of Chicago Press

Author signature:________________ Date:________

U.S. Social Security Number (if applicable):____________ Year of Birth:________

Address:________________________

08/00

Fig. 4.2. Agreement for publication of a journal article, currently in use by the University of Chicago Press. Here the author transfers all copyright rights to the publisher of the journal, and the publisher transfers back to the author the right to reprint the article in other scholarly contexts.

4.55   *Less than full rights.* Some journal publishers, when an author refuses to transfer copyright in toto, ask instead for a license more closely tailored to their specific needs. Care must be taken in such cases to ensure that the contract covers all the subsidiary rights that the publisher may want to exercise or sublicense and that the publisher's rights are exclusive where they need to be. This is especially true for electronic database rights. A recent Supreme Court decision has made clear that the right to publish an article in a journal does not carry with it ipso facto the right to include that article in an electronic database. Journal publishers who wish to put their publications up on their Web sites, or license them to database publishers, need to ensure that their contracts give them that right. In general, the trends toward narrowing or customization of licenses from journal authors to their publishers imposes on publishers a need to keep careful records of what rights they have obtained in each article, so as not to grant subsidiary rights that they do not in fact control.

4.56   *Journal editors.* The role of the journal editor must not be forgotten. Unless he or she is an employee or agent of the company or society that owns the journal, the editor has a separate copyright in each issue as a collective work. Journal publishers should be sure ownership of that separate copyright is clearly agreed on.

CONTRIBUTIONS TO SYMPOSIA

4.57   *Symposium proceedings.* Symposium proceedings, made up of papers by different authors, are sometimes published as special issues of journals and sometimes as stand-alone books. The editor of the proceedings, in either case, has a separate status as author because the proceedings, as a whole, are a collective work. If the proceedings are being published as a journal issue, the publisher needs to make clear who owns copyright in the editor's work and to secure from every contributor a contract more or less identical to that used for authors of articles published in regular issues of the journal concerned. If the proceedings are being published as a book, the editor should sign a standard book author agreement, modified as appropriate, and the contributors should sign separate forms covering their own papers (see fig. 4.3). Either the volume editor or the publisher will send these forms to all contributors. When these have been signed, they are returned to the publisher and filed with the contract for the volume. See also 4.52.

The University of Chicago Press

1427 East 60th Street, Chicago, Illinois 60637-2954
Since 1891 Publishers of Scholarly Books and Journals

Telephone: (773) 702-7700
Fax: (773) 702-9756
http://www.press.uchicago.edu

CONTRACTS AND SUBSIDIARY RIGHTS

PUBLICATION AGREEMENT
Date

Name
Address

Dear

The University of Chicago, acting through its Press, is pleased to undertake the publication of your contribution:

(the "Contribution") to be included in the volume now entitled

written/edited by: (the "Work").

As a condition of publication, it is essential that you grant us all rights, including the copyright, for the Contribution. Accordingly, the following terms of publication are submitted for your consideration:

APPROVAL AND ACCEPTANCE: We mutually agree that publication of the Contribution is contingent upon its acceptance for publication by the Press volume/manuscript editor and upon its meeting Press editorial standards. Publication is additionally contingent upon the formal and final approval for publication of the Contribution and the Work by the Board of University Publications, without whose approval no publication by us takes place.

COPYRIGHT ASSIGNMENT: Whereas the University of Chicago, acting through its Press, undertakes to publish the Contribution as above, and whereas you desire to have the Contribution so published, now, therefore, you grant and assign to the University for its exclusive use the entire copyright for the Contribution. The copyright consists of any and all rights of whatever kind or nature now or hereafter protected by the copyright laws of the United States and of all foreign countries in all forms of communication, and the University shall be the sole proprietor thereof.

WARRANTY: You warrant that the Contribution is original with you; that it contains no matter which is libelous or is otherwise unlawful or which invades individual privacy or infringes any proprietary right or any statutory copyright; and you agree to indemnify and hold the University harmless against any claim or judgment to the contrary. Further, you warrant that you have the right to assign the copyright to the University, and that no right protected by copyright to the

Fig. 4.3. Agreement, or consent, for publication of an article or a chapter commissioned as a contribution to a collective work, such as a symposium. Different forms of agreement are required for "works made for hire," such as translations, forewords, or indexes.

126

Contribution has been previously assigned. It is understood that the copyright to the Contribution has not been registered with the United States Copyright Office, but in the event that such registration has taken place, you will promptly transfer the copyright to the University.

PREVIOUS PUBLICATION AND PERMISSION: You warrant that the Contribution has not been published elsewhere in whole or in part (except as may be set out in a rider annexed hereto and signed by the University) and that no agreement to publish the Contribution or any part or version thereof is outstanding. Should the Contribution contain any material which requires written permission for inclusion in the Contribution, such permission shall be obtained at your own expense from the copyright proprietor and submitted for review by the University with the manuscript.

PROOFHANDLING: You will be given an opportunity to read and correct the edited manuscript and/or proofs, but if you fail to return them by the date separately agreed, production and publication may proceed without your corrections.

COMPENSATION: As total compensation for your preparation of the Contribution and the above grant and assignment of rights, the University will publish the Contribution and you will receive, upon publication, _____ free copies of the hardcover edition of the Work and _____ free copies of the paperbound edition when published by the University. You may purchase additional copies of the Work for your own use by direct order to the University of Chicago Press at 40% discount from the then prevailing list price.

If the foregoing terms are satisfactory, please sign and date this Agreement; return the University's copy to _____ immediately, retaining the Contributor's Copy for your files.

ACCEPTED AND APPROVED: FOR THE UNIVERSITY OF CHICAGO

_____ _____

Name: Paula Barker Duffy, Director
               The University of Chicago Press
Date: _____

_____
Federal Tax Identification (Social Security) Number

_____
Citizenship

_____
Permanent address

_____

The Publisher's Responsibilities

COPYRIGHT TASKS

4.58 *Notice and registration.* When a publisher accepts an author's assignment of rights in a publishing contract, it normally assumes the responsibility of performing all the tasks associated with copyright. These include seeing that appropriate copyright notice is included in the published work, supplying and forwarding the deposit copies of the work to the Copyright Office, registering the copyright, and (for works published before 1978) helping the author renew the copyright at the appropriate time.

4.59   *Licensing of subsidiary rights.* Since the assignment of rights in most instances includes some or all subsidiary rights as well as the basic right to publish the work, publishers also become engaged in licensing subsidiary rights. Increasingly, as publishers expand their reach and competencies through merger and acquisition, they are exercising subsidiary rights as well as basic rights.

HANDLING SUBSIDIARY RIGHTS

4.60   *Categories.* Subsidiary rights are usually thought of as including the following categories; some apply to all types of published works and others to books only:

Foreign rights, whereby a foreign publisher may be licensed to sell the book in its original version in that publisher's own territory. The licensor should be careful to limit the license to the print medium, because electronic distribution cannot easily, if at all, be limited geographically. (And a work that the original publisher makes available online will be of less appeal to foreign print distributors.)

Translation rights, whereby a foreign publisher may be licensed to translate the work into another language and to have standard publisher's rights in the translation (other than live stage rights, motion picture rights, and perhaps electronic rights).

Serial rights, whereby a magazine or newspaper publisher may be licensed to publish the book or excerpts from it in a series of daily, weekly, or monthly installments. First serial rights refers to publication before the work has come out in book form; second serial rights to publication afterward.

Paperback rights, whereby a publisher is licensed to produce and sell a paperback version of the book. So-called quality, or trade, paperbacks are normally sold in bookstores, like clothbound books. Mass-market paperbacks are typically marketed through newsstands and supermarkets, although many now find their way into bookstores. Where the publisher of the paperback is the original publisher, paperback rights are not subsidiary but primary, usually with their own royalty scale. Some books are published only in paper, with no previously published clothbound version; these are called original paperbacks.

Book-club rights, whereby a book club is given the right to distribute the book to its members for less than the regular trade price. Copies generally are sold to the book club in bulk at a steep discount.

Reprint rights, whereby another publisher is licensed to reprint the work, in whole or in part, in an anthology or some other collection or (usually if the work has gone out of print in English) in a cheap reprint edition. This category also includes licensing document delivery companies to reproduce chapters of works on demand.

Live-stage rights, whereby a theatrical producer is given the right to produce a play or musical based on the work.

Motion-picture rights, whereby a movie producer or studio is given the right to make a motion picture based on the work.

Audio rights, whereby the work is licensed for recording on cassette tape or compact disc.

Electronic rights, whereby the work, or portions of it, is licensed for distribution online, for publication in CD-ROM format, or for dissemination via other electronic means. However, if the publisher itself intends to issue the work in electronic form, electronic rights should be considered not subsidiary rights but part of the publisher's basic publication right and subject to a primary royalty. Publishers should normally assign new ISBNs for the electronic versions of their works, just as they have always done when (for example) issuing a hardcover work in paperback form (see 1.28). Publishers should bear in mind that electronic versions may sometimes be considered derivative works rather than mere copies of the print version. The addition of substantial hyperlinks and the like may create a derivative work. If the publisher is for any reason not acquiring general derivative work rights in the contract, it should make sure to obtain at least the right, when making an electronic version of the work, to embed links and other codes in the electronic version.

Rights for scholarly use, whereby the publisher grants others permission to quote text or copy charts and other illustrations from the original.

Rights for educational use, whereby teachers are permitted to make copies of the work for their classes or to include excerpts from the work in course-specific anthologies ("course packs"). Until recently, photocopying was the standard medium for classroom use, but electronic reproduction is becoming more common and blurring some of the boundaries of subsidiary rights. Educational use may also include such things as inclusion in electronic reserves in libraries or distribution over campus intranets.

Subsidiary rights in the context of journals also include microform (including microfilm and microfiche) and the right to make summaries of articles in so-called abstract form. Reproduction by document delivery houses and licensing of electronic database rights are particularly relevant to journals.

4.61   *Electronic-rights licensing.* The term *electronic rights* covers a wide range of possibilities, and the number is constantly growing. Among the users of electronic rights are aggregators, who make available online a large number of publications in a given field or fields; research services, both current and archival, that permit access to databases of publications, often by subscription; and services that allow users to purchase or "borrow" electronic copies of works. The decision whether to license some or all of such uses is both an economic and a strategic one. For the most part, electronic delivery services are too new for publishers to predict with any certainty what income may flow from them. Rather, the economic issue is whether the availability of a work through these services may "cannibalize" the publisher's projected print sales. The strategic issue is even harder to quantify, involving the need to be on the cutting edge of publishing or not to be seen as a laggard in such matters. In entering into electronic rights licenses, the publisher should satisfy itself that the delivery mechanism of the particular licensee has safeguards against excessive downloading—or that such downloading is something the publisher can tolerate. The publisher should also ensure that no electronic license lasts more than a few years, for the pace of change is such that all of these issues need to be revisited frequently.

4.62   *Authors' electronic use of their own works.* In scholarly journals, the right of authors to make electronic use of their own works has become contentious. For example, publishers that have traditionally allowed their authors to make unlimited photocopies for their own students now face an analogous demand: that authors be permitted to post their works on campus Web sites. If the Web site is accessible only by password and only to members of the university, the publisher may well decide that the risk of lost revenue is modest and less important than the goodwill of the author. But there is no standard answer to this question, and no one knows what impact such uses will have on publishers' revenues.

4.63   *Economic considerations.* This list by no means exhausts the various forms of subsidiary rights the publisher may handle, but it includes the major ones. Depending on the administrative structure of the publishing house and the importance and marketability of the work involved, various persons or departments may handle different aspects of subsidiary-rights work—a special rights and permissions department, the sales or marketing department, the acquiring editor, or even the chief executive officer. When the publisher sells or licenses rights to others, money is paid, either in a lump sum or as a royalty, and these proceeds are normally split between the publisher and the author according to whatever terms are specified in the publishing contract. In a typical book-publishing agreement the author receives at least 50 percent of such income. Some publishers have tried to avoid paying the author so much by licensing at an artificially low royalty to a sister company or other affiliate, but such "sweetheart" arrangements are suspect and of doubtful legality. In general, licenses between related companies should be handled in the same way as those between unrelated companies unless the author agrees otherwise in advance.

GRANTING PERMISSION

4.64   *Handling permission requests.* A publisher with a relatively large backlist of books and journals, such as the University of Chicago Press, may receive dozens of communications every day from people seeking to license material from its list. Some requests are for standard subsidiary rights licenses, as described above. Others are for permission to reproduce snippets of prose or verse, or an illustration or two, from a book or journal. Most publishers have a "rights and permissions" staff to handle these requests. Rights and permissions can be a major source of income but also a major item of expense. As will be discussed later in this chapter, the Internet offers a way to boost income and lower expense.

4.65   *Author's role in licensing.* Depending on the terms of the author's contract or on editorial custom, a publisher will either grant rights and permissions subject to the author's approval (which the requester is often asked to obtain) or handle the request itself. Before any request, large or small, can be granted, the material requested must be checked to make sure that the publisher does indeed hold the necessary copyright. And to be unequivocally sure of this the publisher needs to have had the author's full cooperation when the book or article was first published.

The Author's Responsibilities

4.66 *Author's warranties.* In signing a contract with a publisher an author warrants (guarantees) that the work is original, that the author owns it, that no part of it has been previously published, and that no other agreement to publish it or part of it is outstanding. The author should also warrant that the work does not libel anyone or infringe any person's right of privacy. If the work contains scientific formulas or practical advice, the author should also be asked to warrant that all instructions in the work will, if accurately followed, not cause injury to anyone. Some publishers ask for a further warranty that any statement of fact in the work is indeed accurate.

OBTAINING PERMISSIONS

4.67 *General principles.* Budget permitting, an author may wish to commission illustrations on a work-made-for-hire basis, using forms supplied by the publisher. With this exception, to use anyone else's copyrighted work, whether published or unpublished, an author must have the copyright owner's permission unless the intended use is a "fair use" (see 4.75–84). Technically, permission need not be gotten in writing, but it would be most unwise to rely on oral permission. No permission is required to quote from works of the United States government or works in which copyright has expired. See 4.26–29 for guidelines to determine whether copyright in old material has expired. Bear in mind that although the original text of a classic reprinted in a modern edition may be in the public domain, recent translations and abridgments, as well as editorial introductions, notes, and other apparatus, are protected by copyright. But whether permission is needed or not, the author should always, as a matter of good practice, credit any sources used.

4.68 *Author's role in obtaining permissions.* Publishing agreements place on the author the responsibility to request any permission needed for the use of material owned by others. In the course of writing a book or article, the author should keep a record of all copyright owners whose permission may be necessary before the work is published. For a book containing many illustrations, long prose passages, or poetry, obtaining permissions may take weeks, even months. For example, the author may find that an American publisher holds rights only for distribution in the United States and that European and British Commonwealth rights are held by a British publisher. The author, wishing worldwide distribution for the book (world rights), must then write to the British publisher requesting permission to reprint, mentioning (if true) that permission has already been obtained from the American publisher. If the author of copyrighted material has died, or if the copyright owner has gone out of business, a voluminous correspondence may ensue before anyone authorized to grant permission can be found (see 4.73). The author therefore should begin requesting permissions as soon as a manuscript is accepted for publication. Most publishers wisely decline to start setting type for a book until all the author's permissions are in hand.[1]

4.69 *Author's own work.* The author should remember that permission is sometimes needed to reuse or even to revise his or her own work. If the author has already allowed a chapter or other significant part to appear in print elsewhere—as a journal article, for example—then written permission to reprint it, or to update or revise it, will need to be secured from the copyright owner of the other publication, unless the author secured the right of reuse in the contract with that earlier publisher. The law does not require that the prior publication be credited in the new publication, but it is a common courtesy to give credit on the copyright page of the book, in a footnote on the first page of the reprinted material, or in a special list of acknowledgments. And if the first publisher owns copyright in the material, it may make credit a condition of permission to reprint. Also, if the first publisher owns copyright, the new publisher will need to flag its files so that subsequent permissions requests for that material are referred to the original copyright owner.

4.70 *Fees and record keeping.* Most publishing agreements stipulate that any fees to be paid will be the author's responsibility. When all permissions have been received, the author should send them, or copies of them, to the publisher, who will note and comply with any special provisions they contain. The publisher will file all permissions with the publishing contract, where they may be consulted in the event of future editions or of requests for permission to reprint from the work. The copyeditor will check the permissions against the manuscript to be sure all necessary credits have been given. See 1.30, 2.45, 4.95, 16.68.

---

1. It is possible to engage professional help in obtaining permissions for a large project. Specialists in this work are listed under "Consultants" in the annual publication *LMP (Literary Market Place;* see bibliog. 2.7).

4.71 *Permissions beyond the immediate use.* Many publishers, when giving permission to reprint material they control, will withhold the right to sublicense that material, even if the sublicensing is of the new author's work as a whole. Some publishers will also limit their licenses to a single edition (though not a single printing). Where this is so, the publisher receiving the permission will have to go back to the source for new permission, usually for an additional fee, for any new edition, paperback reprint, serialization, or whatever. Alternatively, the publisher granting permission can stipulate up front what fees are to be paid for further uses and permit the new publisher to secure such permission automatically on payment of the agreed fee.

4.72 *Unpublished works.* Getting permission for unpublished works presents an entirely different problem. Instead of a publishing corporation, one must deal with the author or author's heirs, who may not be easily identified or found. If the writer is dead, it may be especially difficult to determine who controls the copyrights.

4.73 *The missing copyright owner.* The problem presented by unpublished works whose authors are dead is, in a larger sense, just an example of the problem of the missing copyright owner. Another typical example is the publisher that has gone out of business or at least is no longer doing business under a given imprint. A reasonable (and well-documented) effort must be made to locate such a copyright owner. The elements of a bona fide search will vary with the circumstances but could well include a search of the Copyright Office records, an attempt to communicate with the copyright owner at whatever address is last stated in the file for the work concerned, and perhaps an Internet search for the author or publishers. If such efforts yield no results, there is still some risk in going forward. Technically, use of the work might still be ruled an infringement of copyright should a copyright owner surface, but it is unlikely that any court would do more than require the payment of a reasonable permissions fee. Anyone proceeding with publication under these conditions should certainly be prepared to offer and pay a reasonable fee on receiving any objection from the rediscovered owner.

4.74 *Noncopyright restrictions on archives.* Authors who wish to include unpublished material in their works should be aware that private restrictions, unrelated to copyright, may limit its use. The keeper of a collection, usually a librarian or an archivist, is the best source of such information, including what permissions must be sought and from whom. Bear in mind that copyright in a manuscript is different from ownership of the actual paper. Most often a library or collector will own the physical object itself but not the right to reproduce it. Thus there may be two permissions required: one for access to the material and one for the right to copy. It is important not to mistake one for the other.

Fair Use: Quoting without Permission

4.75 *Overview of the legal doctrine.* The doctrine of fair use was originally developed by judges as an equitable limit on the absolutism of copyright. Although incorporated into the new copyright law, the doctrine still does not attempt to define the exact limits of the fair use of copyrighted work. It does state, however, that in determining whether the use made of a work in any particular case is fair, the factors to be considered must include the following:

1. The purpose and character of the use, including whether such use is of a commercial nature or is for nonprofit educational purposes
2. The nature of the copyrighted work
3. The amount and substantiality of the portion used in relation to the copyrighted work as a whole
4. The effect of the use on the potential market for, or value of, the copyrighted work

Essentially, the doctrine excuses copying that would otherwise be infringement. For example, it allows authors to quote from other authors' work or to reproduce small amounts of graphic or pictorial material for purposes of review or criticism or to illustrate or buttress their own points. Authors invoking fair use should transcribe accurately and give credit to their sources. They should not quote out of context, making the author of the quoted passage seem to be saying something opposite to, or different from, what was intended.

4.76 *Validity of "rules of thumb."* Although the law lays out no boundaries or ironclad formulas for fair use, some publishers have their own rules of thumb. Such rules, of course, have no validity outside the publishing house: courts, not publishers, adjudicate fair use. The rules exist in part to give an overworked permissions department, which often cannot tell whether a proposed use of a quotation is actually fair, something to use as a yardstick.

4.77 *A few general rules.* Fair use is use that is fair—simply that. Uses that are tangential in purpose to the original, and uses that transform the copied material by changing its context or the way it is perceived, will always be judged more leniently than those that merely parallel or parrot the original. For example, extensive quotation of the original is acceptable in the context of a critique but may well not be acceptable if one is simply using the first author's words to reiterate the same argument or embellish one's own prose. Use of any literary work in its entirety—a poem, an essay, a chapter of a book—is hardly ever acceptable. Use of less than the whole will be judged by whether the second author appears to be taking a free ride on the first author's labor. As a general rule, one should never quote more than a few contiguous paragraphs of prose or lines of poetry at a time or let the quotations, even if scattered, begin to overshadow the quoter's own material. Quotations or graphic reproductions should not be so long that they substitute for, or diminish the value of, the copyright owner's own publication. Proportion is more important than the absolute length of a quotation: quoting five hundred words from an essay of five thousand is likely to be riskier than quoting that amount from a work of fifty thousand. But an even smaller percentage can be an infringement if it constitutes the heart of the work being quoted.

4.78 *Epigraphs and interior monologues.* Quotation in the form of an epigraph does not fit neatly into any of the usual fair-use categories but is probably fair use by virtue of scholarly and artistic tradition. The same can be said of limited quotation of song lyrics, poetry, and the like in the context of an interior monologue or fictional narrative. Of course, this would not excuse the publication of a collection of epigraphs or lyrics without permission of the various authors being quoted.

4.79 *Unpublished works.* Where the work to be quoted has never been published, the same considerations apply. But if the author or the author's spouse or children are still living, some consideration should be given to their interest in controlling when the work is disclosed to the public.

4.80 *Paraphrasing.* Bear in mind that although fair use will protect verbatim copying, unfair use will not be excused by paraphrasing. Traditional copyright doctrine treats extensive paraphrase as merely disguised copying. Thus, fair-use analysis will be the same for both. Paraphrase of small quantities of material, on the other hand, may not constitute copying at all, so that fair-use analysis would never come into play.

4.81 *Pictorial and graphic materials.* With respect to pictorial and graphic materials, there is little legal precedent to navigate by. At the level of intuition, it seems that a monograph on Picasso should be free to reproduce details from his paintings in order, for example, to illustrate the critic's discussion of Picasso's brushwork. Reproducing the entire image in black and white may also be reasonably necessary to illustrate the author's analysis of

Picasso's techniques of composition. However, justification wears thin where a painting is reproduced in vivid color occupying a full page; the result begins to compete with large-scale reproductions of artwork that have no scholarly purpose. Likewise, reproduction on the cover would probably be seen as commercial rather than scholarly use and therefore unjustified. As for photographs, using them merely as illustrations would require permission, but use as described above in a scholarly treatment of photography might not.

4.82   *Charts, tables, and graphs.* Reproduction of charts, tables, and graphs presents a difficult judgment call. An aggressive approach would justify copying a single item on the ground that one chart is the pictorial equivalent of a few sentences. A more conservative approach would argue that a graph is a picture worth a thousand words and that reproducing it without permission is taking a free ride on the first author's work. This latter approach has the flaw of being too absolute in practice, for it is difficult under this rationale to imagine *any* fair use of such an image. Where the item in question represents a small portion of the original work and a small portion of the second work, the harm seems minimal, outweighed by the benefits of open communication. Certainly, reproduction of a single graph, table, or chart that simply presents data in a straightforward relationship, in contrast to reproduction of a graph or chart embellished with pictorial elements, should ordinarily be considered fair use. Indeed, some graphs that merely present facts with little or no expressive input—the equivalent, in two dimensions, of a mere list—may even be beyond the protection of copyright.

4.83   *Importance of attribution.* With all reuse of others' materials, it is important to identify the original as the source. This not only bolsters the claim of fair use, it also helps avoid any accusation of plagiarism. Nothing elaborate is required; a standard footnote will suffice, or (in the case of a graph or table, for example) a simple legend that says "Source: [author, title, and date of earlier work]." Note that such a legend is not always clear: Does it mean that the data are taken from the original but reformatted by the second author or that the graph or table has itself been copied? If the latter, it is preferable to say "Reprinted from [author, title, and date of earlier work]" rather than merely "Source." See also 12.40–43, 13.45, 16.68.

4.84   *Unnecessary permissions.* Given the ad hoc nature of fair use and the absence of rules and guidelines, many publishers tend to seek permission if they have the slightest doubt whether a particular use is fair. This is unfortunate. The right of fair use is valuable to scholarship, and it should not be allowed to decay because scholars fail to employ it boldly. Furthermore, excessive permissions processing tends to slow down the gestation of worthwhile writings. Even if permission is sought and denied, that should not necessarily be treated as the end of the matter. The U.S. Supreme Court has held that requesting permission should not be regarded as an admission that permission is needed. In other words, where permission is denied, or granted but for an unreasonable price, there is an opportunity for a second look.

Library and Educational Copying as Fair Use

4.85 *The Copyright Act.* Fair use has been much in dispute as applied to photocopying for classroom and library use. The Copyright Act contains specific guidelines for library photocopying, and the legislative history of the act contains specific, though not official, guidelines for classroom photocopying.

4.86 *Library photocopying.* The new law does attempt to define minimum fair-use limitations on machine copying by libraries, in a long section with many exemptions and caveats too complex to discuss here. In general, it allows libraries to make single copies of copyrighted works, provided each copy bears the original copyright notice and provided the copies are made for one of the purposes specifically defined in the statute, including the following:

1. If the copy is made for a library's own use because the library's own copy of the work is damaged or missing and a replacement cannot be obtained at a fair price
2. If the copy is made for a patron's use and is limited to an article or a small part of a larger work—or the whole of a larger work if a printed copy cannot be obtained at a fair price—and only if the copy is intended for use by the patron in "private study, scholarship, or research"

The law specifically forbids "systematic" copying by libraries. Presumably this includes but is not limited to (1) making copies of books or periodicals as a substitute for buying them and (2) making copies for patrons indiscriminately without regard to the patrons' identity or intended use of the material.

4.87 *Educational photocopying.* The Copyright Act does not include similar guidelines for educational photocopying. But a congressional report published at the time the law was being written includes privately negotiated guidelines, implicitly approved by Congress, for fair use of copyrighted material. These guidelines are available at the Web site of the United States Copyright Office. "Brevity" and "spontaneity" are the guiding principles; the latter reflects the premise that photocopying for classroom use should be done only when there is too little time to obtain permission. Multiple copies should not exceed the number of students in the class. They should not substitute for anthologies or regular school purchases. The same items should not be copied from year to year or semester to semester, but once only and at the instance of a particular teacher for immediate use in the classroom. Workbooks and other consumable materials should not be copied, and the students should not be charged more than the actual copying cost. Any copy must include the copyright notice used in the original. As for the widespread practice of making customized anthologies ("course packs") for individual teachers' classes, cases subsequent to the guidelines make clear that this is an infringement if express permission is not received from the copyright owners of all materials included in them.

4.88   *Digitizing and automating the permissions process.* The technologies of photocopying and electronic reproduction present a major institutional challenge to publishers. The volume of license requests under these headings exceeds the ability of traditional techniques to process them. Publishers have customarily processed such requests by hand, case by case, evaluating each request on its own merits and often tailoring a fee to the specific circumstances. Whether this approach can or should survive is an open question. The Internet—the very electronic technology that publishers have often regarded as a threat—provides a powerful tool for handling requests rapidly and with little or no staff involvement. A properly designed Web site, coupled with the adoption of standard, publicly quoted fees, can create a highly efficient marketplace for copying, to the benefit of both the publisher and its customers. Authors seeking permission for use of other authors' work can obtain that permission immediately and can realistically budget for permission fees in advance. The marketplace can be even more efficient when an outside vendor such as the Copyright Clearance Center (to name one of several; see 1.161) enables users to obtain online permissions from multiple publishers through a single Web site. Whether these services become the standard, or inspire publishers to move their own rights and permissions work to the Web, remains to be seen.

REQUESTING PERMISSION

4.89   *Information required.* Would-be users can help reduce delay and miscommunication by submitting their requests for permission in the best possible form. All requests for permission to reprint should be sent to the copyright holder in writing and in duplicate. The request should contain the following explicit information:

1. The title of the original work and exact identification, with page numbers, of what is to be reprinted. Identification should include, in the case of a table or figure, its number and the page it appears on (e.g., figure 6 on page 43); in the case of a poem, the title and the page on which the poem appears; in the case of a prose passage, the opening and closing phrases in addition to the page numbers (e.g., "from 'The military genius of Frederick the Great' on page 110 through 'until the onset of World War I' on page 112"). The requester should be sure to cite the original source of the material, not any subsequent reprinting of it.

2. Information about the publication in which the author wishes to reproduce the material: title, approximate number of printed pages, form of publication (clothbound book, paperback book, journal, electronic journal), publisher, probable date of publication, approximate print run, and list price (if available).

3. The kind of rights requested. The most limited rights a user ought to accept are "nonexclusive world rights in the English language, for one edition." The best opening gambit would be "nonexclusive world rights in all languages and for all editions in print and other media, including the right to grant customary permissions requests but only where the licensed material is incorporated in [the requester's work]." The request for "the rights to grant customary permissions" would, if granted, greatly simplify the downstream licensing of the new work. Unfortunately, such a right is not implicit in any nonexclusive license (see 4.34) and is seldom granted, and licensees of works in which earlier material is used end up needing to get multiple layers of permission.

In granting permission, the copyright holder either will sign and return to the author one copy of the request or will counter by sending the author the copyright owner's standard form. In either case the person responding to the request should state clearly what fee is demanded for the proposed use and what special conditions apply to the grant. The second copy of the permission form will be retained in the copyright owner's files. The requesting author should give the original to the publisher and keep a third copy for reference.

4.90   *Sample permissions letters.* The University of Chicago Press supplies authors or editors of books requiring many permissions with a model re-

The University of Chicago Press

1427 East 60th Street, Chicago, Illinois 60637-2954
Since 1891 Publishers of Scholarly Books and Journals

Telephone: (773) 702-7700
Fax: (773) 702-9756
http://www.press.uchicago.edu

CONTRACTS AND SUBSIDIARY RIGHTS

To: Reference:
                                                     Date:

I am writing to request permission to reprint the following material:

    Author/Title/Date of publication:

    Pages as they appear in your publication:

    Other identifying information and remarks:

This material is to appear as originally published (any changes or deletions are noted on the reverse side of this letter) in the following work that the University of Chicago Press is presently preparing for publication:

    Author (Editor)/Title:

    Proposed date of publication:

    Remarks:

We request nonexclusive world rights, as part of our volume only, in all languages and for all editions.

If you are the copyright holder, may I have your permission to reprint the above material in our book? If you do not indicate otherwise, we will use the usual scholarly form of acknowledgment, including publisher, author, title, etc.

If you are not the copyright holder, or if additional permission is needed for world rights from another source, please indicate so.

Thank you for your consideration of this request.

Sincerely yours,

_____

The above request is hereby approved on the conditions specified below, and on the understanding that full credit will be given to the source.

Date:_____. Approved by:_____

Fig. 4.4. Suggestions for a letter seeking permission to reprint material in a scholarly book. Some of the information about the proposed book may be lacking when the author begins to request permissions, but as much information as possible should be supplied. Note that spaces are left so that the person addressed can use the letter itself for granting or denying the request or for referring the author elsewhere.

quest letter (fig. 4.4) but suggests that they write on their own personal or (when appropriate) institutional letterhead. Every publisher would be well advised to adopt some variation of this practice, for authors typically are rudderless at sea without it.

Illustrations

4.91   *Rights holders.* Permission to reproduce pictorial works—as opposed to charts, graphs, or the like that are usually created by the same author(s) as the text—will sometimes, but not reliably, be available from the publisher. A publisher who has used the pictorial work to illustrate text that someone is seeking to reprint may very well not have the right to sublicense use of the illustration. Even a publisher of, say, a collection of the artist's work may not have rights to the individual images. In such a case the permission seeker must deal with the owner of the object or the artist or both. Copyright ownership of artworks sold before 1978 is not always easy to determine, because before 1978 the law generally, but not always, assumed that so long as an original artwork remained unpublished, its copyright passed from hand to hand with ownership of the object itself. For post-1977 works, copyright belongs to the artist unless the artist has explicitly assigned it to someone else. But even for such works, the person seeking permission to reproduce the artwork in a book or journal may, as a practical matter, need to deal with a museum that expects a fee for the privilege of allowing reproduction. Where the museum can deny permission to photograph the object, such a fee is the tariff one pays for physical access if nothing else. Where the museum is licensing its own reproduction or photograph of the work, it has less justification, for the law denies copyright to photographs that merely reproduce another two-dimensional image. Be that as it may, authors and publishers are generally loath to antagonize museums by challenging their positions.

4.92   *Stock agencies and image archives.* The only kind of pictorial work for which permissions are easily granted is photographs, at least where one is dealing with a stock agency or other commercial image archive. Such agencies have vast inventories of images and published, easy-to-understand fee structures. There are also Web sites that act as clearinghouses for photographic permissions.

4.93   *Information required.* A permission request for an illustration should be sent to the picture agency, museum, artist, or private individual controlling reproduction rights. Again, the request should be as specific as possible regarding the identity of what is to be reproduced, the form of publication in which it will appear, and the kind of rights requested. If the author making the request knows that the illustration will also be used elsewhere than in the text proper (such as on the jacket or in advertising), this fact should be noted. Whether the publisher or the author should pay whatever additional fee is charged for cover use is a matter for negotiation.

4.94 *Fees.* Fees paid for reproducing material, especially illustrations procured from a stock photo agency, normally cover one-time use only—in, say, the first edition of a book. If an illustration is also to be used on the jacket or in advertising, a higher fee is customary. And if a book is reprinted as a paperback or goes into a second edition, another fee is usually charged. Ideally such a fee should be agreed to in advance, at the time of the initial permission.

Acknowledging Sources

4.95 *Credit lines.* Whether or not the use of others' material requires permission, an author should give the exact source of such material: in a note or internal reference in the text, in a source note to a table, or in a credit line under an illustration. Where formal permission has been granted, the author should, within reason, follow any special wording stipulated by the grantor. For a text passage complete in itself, such as a poem, or for a table, the full citation to the source may be followed by:

Reprinted by permission of the publisher.

A credit line below an illustration may read, for example:

Courtesy of The Newberry Library, Chicago, Illinois.

For examples of various kinds of credit lines, see 12.42, 12.45–47, 12.50, 12.51, 13.45, 16.68.

4.96 *Acknowledgments sections.* In a work that needs many permissions, acknowledgments are often grouped in a special Acknowledgments section at the front or back of the work (see 1.52). Some citation of the source should still, however, be made on the page containing the relevant material.

Fees

4.97 *Responsibility for payment.* As noted above, publishing agreements generally make the author responsible for any fees charged for use of others' material. A publisher may agree to pay the fees and to deduct them from the author's royalties or—in rare instances—to split the fees with the author. If it appears that a book would be enhanced by illustrations not provided by the author, many publishing agreements enable the publisher to find the illustrations and (with the author's consent) charge any fees involved to the author's royalty account. One exception to these generalizations is school and college textbooks, where it is common for the publisher to provide a certain amount of its own funds to pay for illustrations.

4.98 *Anthologies.* A book made up entirely of other authors' copyrighted materials—stories, essays, poems, documents, selections from larger works—depends for its existence on permissions from the various copyright owners. The compiler of such a volume therefore should begin seeking permissions as soon as a contract for publication of the volume has been executed or a "letter of intent" has been received from the prospective publisher. Informal inquiries to copyright owners may be initiated before that time, but no sensible publisher of material to be anthologized is likely to grant permission for its use or to set fees without knowing the details of eventual publication. Once those details are known, the compiler must act quickly. Permission for a selection may be refused, or the fee charged may be so high that the compiler is forced to drop that selection and substitute another. And until all permissions have been received and all fees agreed on, the table of contents cannot be final.

5

Grammar and Usage

BRYAN A. GARNER

Grammar

INTRODUCTION

5.1 *Definition.* Grammar consists of the rules governing how words are put together into sentences. These rules, which native speakers of a language learn largely by osmosis, govern most constructions in a given language. The small minority of constructions that lie outside these rules fall mostly into the category of idiom and usage.

5.2 *Schools of thought.* There are many schools of grammatical thought—and differing vocabularies for describing grammar. Grammatical theories are in flux, and the more we learn, the less we seem to know: "An entirely adequate description of English grammar is still a distant target and at present seemingly an unreachable one, the complications being what they are."[1] In fact, the more detailed the grammar (it can run to many large volumes), the less likely it is to be of use to most writers and speakers.

5.3 *Parts of speech.* As traditionally understood, grammar is both a science and an art. Often it has focused—as it does here—on parts of speech and their syntax. Traditional grammar has held that there are eight parts of speech: nouns, pronouns, adjectives, verbs, adverbs, prepositions, conjunctions, and interjections.[2] Each of those word classes is treated below. Somewhat surprisingly, modern grammarians cannot agree on precisely how many parts of speech there are in English. At least one grammarian says there are as few as three.[3] Another insists that there are "about fifteen," noting that "the precise number is still being debated."[4] This section deals with the traditional eight, sketching some of the main lines of English grammar using traditional grammatical terms.

1. Robert W. Burchfield, *Unlocking the English Language* (New York: Hill and Wang, 1991), 22.
2. See Robert L. Allen, *English Grammar and English Grammars* (New York: Charles Scribner's Sons, 1972), 7.
3. Ernest W. Gray, *A Brief Grammar of Modern Written English* (New York: World, 1967), 70.
4. R. L. Trask, *Language: The Basics* (London: Routledge, 1996), 35.

NOUNS

Definitions

5.4 *Nouns.* A noun is a word that names something, whether abstract (intangible) or concrete (tangible). It may be a common noun (the name of a generic class or type of person, place, or thing) or a proper noun (the formal name of a specific person, place, or thing). A concrete noun may be a count noun (if what it names can be counted) or a mass noun (if what it names is uncountable or collective).

5.5 *Common nouns.* A common noun is the informal name of one item in a class or group {a chemical} {a river} {a pineapple}.[5] It is not capitalized unless it begins a sentence or appears in a title.

5.6 *Proper nouns.* A proper noun is a person's name or the official name of a place or thing {John Doe} {Moscow} {the Hope Diamond}. It is always capitalized, regardless of how it is used. A common noun may become a proper noun {Nelson's flagship was the *Victory*}, and sometimes a proper noun may be used figuratively and informally, as if it were a common noun {like Moriarty, he is a Napoleon of crime} (*Napoleon* here connoting an ingenious mastermind who is ambitious beyond limits). Proper nouns may be compounded when used as a unit to name something {the Waldorf-Astoria Hotel} {*Saturday Evening Post*}. Over time, some proper nouns (called eponyms) have developed common-noun counterparts, such as *sandwich* (from the Earl of Sandwich) and *china* (from the country of China). See also 8.65.

5.7 *Count nouns.* A count noun has singular and plural forms and expresses enumerable things {dictionary–dictionaries} {hoof–hooves} {newspaper–newspapers}. As the subject of a sentence, a singular count noun takes a singular verb {the jar is full}; a plural count noun takes a plural verb {the jars are full}.

5.8 *Mass nouns.* A mass noun (sometimes called a noncount noun or a collective noun) is one that denotes something uncountable, either because it is abstract {cowardice} {evidence} or because it refers to an indeterminate aggregation of people or things {the faculty} {the bourgeoisie}. As the subject of a sentence, a mass noun usually takes a singular verb {the litigation is varied}. But in a collective sense, it may take either a singular or

---

5. Note that the examples in this chapter only are presented in curly brackets to save space.

a plural verb form {the ruling majority is unlikely to share power} {the majority of voters are satisfied}. A singular verb emphasizes the group; a plural verb emphasizes the individual members. If a collective noun appears throughout a piece of writing, use one verb form consistently.

Properties of Nouns

5.9 *Four properties.* Nouns have four properties: case, gender, number, and person.

5.10 *Case.* In English, only nouns and pronouns have case. Case denotes the relationship between a noun (or pronoun) and other words in a sentence. The three cases are nominative, objective, and possessive. Except in the possessive, nouns do not change form to indicate case {the doctor is in} (nominative), {see the doctor} (objective), {the doctor's office} (possessive). See 5.22–27.

5.11 *Gender.* Gender classifies nouns into masculine, feminine, and neuter. In English, the masculine and feminine genders occur almost exclusively with (1) nouns that refer specifically to male or female humans or animals {king} {queen} {ram} {ewe}; (2) compound nouns that contain specifically masculine or feminine nouns or pronouns {boyfriend} {horsewoman}; (3) nouns that have a feminine suffix such as *ess* or *ix* (many of which are archaic) {actress} {executrix}; and (4) nouns used in personification (see 5.49). Almost all other words are neuter {monarch} {sheep}. If gender is to be indicated, descriptive adjectives such as *male* and *female* may be needed if there is no gender-specific term: for example, a female fox is a *vixen*, but there is no equivalent term for a female goldfish.

5.12 *Number.* Number shows whether one object or more than one object is referred to, as with *clock* (singular) and *clocks* (plural). See 5.14–21.

5.13 *Person.* Person shows whether an object is speaking (first person) {we the voters will decide} (*voters* is first person), spoken to (second person) {children, stop misbehaving} (*children* is second person), or spoken about (third person) {a limo carried the band} (*limo* and *band* are third person).

Plurals

5.14 *Dictionaries.* Because exceptions abound, a good dictionary is essential for checking the correct plural form of a noun. But there are some basic rules for forming plurals. See also 7.6–16.

5.15 *Adding "s" or "es."* Most plurals are formed by adding *s* or *es*. If a noun ends with a letter whose sound readily combines with the *s* sound, then use *s* to form the plural {siren–sirens} {club–clubs} {toy–toys}. If the noun ends in a letter that is not euphonious with *s* alone (e.g., it ends in a sibilant such as *s*, *sh*, *x*, *z*, or a soft *ch*), then use *es* to form the plural {box–boxes} {moss–mosses} {birch–birches}.

5.16 *Nouns ending in "f" or "fe."* Some nouns ending in *f* or *fe* take an *s* {reef–reefs} {dwarf–dwarfs} {safe–safes}. Other nouns change the *f* to *v* and add *es* {hoof–hooves} {knife–knives} {wolf–wolves}. A few words have one preferred form in American English {wharf–wharves} and another in British English {wharf–wharfs}. Even if one knows a word's etymology, the correct forms are unpredictable. Consult a reliable dictionary.

5.17 *Nouns ending in "o."* Some nouns ending in *o* take an *s* {avocado–avocados} {memento–mementos} {tuxedo–tuxedos}. But others take an *es* {mango–mangoes} {cargo–cargoes} {volcano–volcanoes}. There is no firm rule for determining whether the plural is formed with *s* or *es*, but two guidelines may prove helpful: (1) Nouns used as often in the plural as in the singular usually form the plural with *es* {vetoes} {heroes}. *Zeros* is an exception (and therefore hard to remember). (2) Nouns usually form the plural with *s* if they appear to have been borrowed from some other language {intaglio–intaglios}; if they are proper names {Fazio–Fazios}; if they are rarely used as plurals {bravado–bravados}; if they end in *o* preceded by a vowel {portfolio–portfolios}; or if they are shortened words {photo–photos}.

5.18 *Nouns ending in "y."* Nouns ending in *y* follow one of two rules: (1) If the noun is common and the *y* is preceded by *qu* or by a consonant, change the *y* to *i* and add *es* to form the plural {soliloquy–soliloquies} {berry–berries} {folly–follies}. (2) If the noun is proper or if the *y* is preceded by a vowel, add *s* to form the plural {Teddy–Teddys} {ploy–ploys} {buoy–buoys}.

5.19 *Compound nouns.* Compound nouns that consist of separate words (with or without hyphens) form the plural by adding the appropriate ending to the noun or, if there is more than one, to the main noun {brother in arms–brothers in arms} {court-martial–courts-martial} {motion picture–motion pictures}.

5.20 *Irregular plurals.* Some nouns have irregular plurals {child–children} {basis–bases}. With some of these irregular words, the plural form depends on the meaning. Take the noun *louse*, for example: people may be infested with *lice* (insects), but contemptible people are *louses* (by metaphorical extension). Some nouns are ordinarily the same in both the singular and the plural, especially those denoting fish, game, and livestock {one fish, two fish} {I hoped to see many deer, but I saw only one deer}.

5.21 *Plural form with singular sense.* Some nouns are plural in form but singular in use and meaning {the good news is} {politics is a complicated subject}.

Case

5.22 *Function.* Case denotes the relationship between a noun or pronoun and other words in a sentence. Because English nouns do not change form between the nominative case and the objective case, some grammarians hold that English nouns do not have the property of case. But most personal pronouns (and *who*) do have distinct nominative and objective forms (see 5.47). And since pronouns stand in for nouns, some grammarians recognize these cases in nouns as well. Determining the "case" of a noun is a matter of distinguishing a subject from an object.

5.23 *Subjects.* A noun functioning as a subject (nominative case) is the actor or the person or thing about which an assertion is made in a clause, as in *the governor delivered a speech* (*governor* being the subject) or *the shops are crowded because the holiday season has begun* (*shops* and *season* being the subjects of their respective clauses). The subject of a clause controls the number of the verb and typically precedes it {the troops retreated in winter} (*troops* is the subject), although it can appear anywhere in the sentence {high in the tree sat a leopard} (*leopard* is the subject). A noun or pronoun that follows a form of *to be* and refers to the same thing as the subject is called a predicate nominative {my show dogs are Australian shepherds} (*Australian shepherds* is a predicate nominative). Generally, a sentence's predicate is the part that contains a verb and makes an assertion about the subject; in the example just given, the complete predicate is *are Australian shepherds.*

5.24 *Objects.* A noun functioning as an object (objective case) is either (1) the person or thing acted on by a transitive verb in the active voice {the balloon carried a pilot and a passenger} (*pilot* and *passenger* are objective) or (2) the person or thing related to another element by a connective such as a preposition {place the slide under the microscope} (*under* is a preposition, *microscope* is objective). An object typically follows the verb {the queen consulted the prime minister} (*queen* is nominative and *prime minister* is objective). But with an inverted construction, an object can appear elsewhere in the sentence {everything else was returned; the medicine the villain withheld} (*medicine* is objective and *villain* is nominative). A noun functioning as an object is never the subject of the following verb and does not control the number of the verb. In the sentence *an assembly of strangers was outside,* the plural noun *strangers* is the object of the preposition *of.* The singular noun *assembly* is the subject and agrees with the singular verb *was.*

5.25 *Possessive case.* The possessive case (sometimes called the genitive case) denotes (1) ownership, possession, or occupancy {the architect's drawing board} {Arnie's room}; (2) a relationship {the philanthropist's secretary}; (3) agency {the company's representative}; or (4) an idiomatic shorthand form of an *of*-phrase (e.g., *one hour's delay* is equal to *a delay of one hour*). The possessive case is formed in different ways depending on the noun or nouns and their usage in a sentence. The possessive of a singular noun is formed by adding *'s* {driver's seat} {engineer's opinion}. The possessive of a plural noun that ends in *s* or *es* is formed by adding an apostrophe {parents' house} {foxes' den}. The possessive of an irregular plural noun is formed by adding *'s* {women's rights} {mice's cage}. The possessive of a multiword compound noun is formed by adding the appropriate ending to the last word {parents-in-law's message}. See also 7.17–29.

5.26 *Possessives of titles and names.* The possessive of a title or name is formed by adding *'s* {Lloyd's of London's records} {National Geographic Society's headquarters} {Dun & Bradstreet's rating}. This is so even when the word ends in a sibilant {Dickens's novels} {Dow Jones's money report}, unless the word itself is formed from a plural {General Motors' current production rate} {Applied Materials' financial statements}. But if a word ends in a sibilant, it is acceptable (especially in journalism) to use a final apostrophe without the additional *s* {Bill Gates' testimony}. See also 7.19–23.

5.27 *Joint and separate possessives.* If two or more nouns share possession, the last noun takes the possessive ending. For example, *Peter and Harriet's correspondence* refers to the correspondence between Peter and Harriet. If two or more nouns possess something separately, each noun takes its own possessive ending. For example, *Peter's and Harriet's correspondence* refers to Peter's correspondence and also to Harriet's correspondence.

Agent and Recipient Nouns

5.28 *Definitions and use.* An agent noun denotes a person who performs some action. It is usually indicated by the suffix *er* {adviser} or *or* {donor}. The most common agent nouns end in *er;* generally, *or* appears in words that were brought into English directly from Latin. Consult a good dictionary. A recipient noun denotes a person who receives some thing or action, or one for whom something is done. It is usually indicated by the suffix *ee,* derived from the passive-voice verb. For example, an *honoree* is one who is honored. In legal usage, a recipient noun often means "one to whom"; for example, a *lessee* is one to whom property is leased. In recent years there has been a fad in coining new *ee* words, and sometimes the meaning is not at all passive; for example, an *attendee* is one who attends. Because these words unnecessarily displace their active-voice equivalents and can be ambiguous (What is the difference between an attender and an attendee?), they should be avoided.

Appositives

5.29   *Definition and use.* An appositive noun is one that immediately follows another noun or noun phrase in order to define or further identify it {George Washington, our first president, was born in Virginia} (*our first president* is an appositive of the proper noun *George Washington*). Commas frame an appositive noun unless it is restrictive—for example, compare *Robert Burns, the poet, wrote many songs about women named Mary* (*poet* is a nonrestrictive appositive noun) with *the poet Robert Burns wrote many songs about women named Mary* (*Robert Burns* restricts *poet* by precisely identifying which poet). See also 6.31.

Functional Variation

5.30   *Nouns as adjectives.* Words that are ordinarily nouns sometimes function as other parts of speech, such as adjectives or verbs. A noun-to-adjective transition takes place when a noun modifies another noun {the morning newspaper} {a state legislature} {a varsity sport} (*morning, state,* and *varsity* are adjectives). Occasionally, using a noun as an adjective can produce an ambiguity. For example, the phrase *fast results* can be read as meaning either "rapid results" or (less probably but possibly) "the outcome of a fast." Sometimes the noun and its adjectival form can be used interchangeably—for example, *prostate cancer* and *prostatic cancer* both refer to cancer of the prostate gland. But sometimes using the noun instead of the adjective may alter the meaning—for example, *a study group* is not necessarily *a studious group.* A preposition may be needed to indicate a noun's relation to other sentence elements. But if the noun functions as an adjective, the preposition must be omitted; at times this can result in a vague phrase—for example, *voter awareness* (awareness *of* voters or *by* them?). Context might suggest what preposition is missing, but a reader may have to deduce the writer's meaning.

5.31   *Nouns as verbs.* It is fairly common in English for nouns to pass into use as verbs; it always has been. For example, in 1220 the noun *husband* meant one who tilled and cultivated the earth {the husband has worked hard to produce this crop}. About 1420 it became a verb meaning to till, cultivate, and tend crops {you must husband your land thoughtfully}. New noun-to-verb transitions often occur in dialect or jargon. For example, the noun *mainstream* is used as a verb in passages such as *more school districts are mainstreaming pupils with special needs*. In formal prose, such recently transformed words should be used cautiously if at all.

5.32   *Other functional shifts.* Words that ordinarily function as other parts of speech, as well as various types of phrases, may function as nouns. Aside from the obvious instance of pronouns (see 5.34), these include adjectives such as *poor* {the poor are always with us} (see 5.94), adverbs such as *here* and *now* {we cannot avoid the here and now}, participles (gerunds) such as *swimming* {swimming in that lake can be dangerous} (see 5.110), infinitives such as *to discover* {to discover the truth is our goal} (see 5.107), and clauses such as *what the people want* {what the people want is justice}.

Formation of New Nouns

5.33   *How new nouns are coined.* Nouns are often coined in one of two ways. (1) A compound noun is often created by stringing together two or more existing words to form one unit, with or without hyphens {toothpick} {railroad} {meltdown} {sister-in-law} {motion picture}. (2) A derivative noun is formed by adding a suffix or prefix to a noun, adjective, or verb. Some suffixes commonly used for this purpose are *ness* {kindness}, *ship* {relationship}, *dom* {kingdom}, *th* {warmth}, and *er* {finder}. Examples of prefixes include *cross* {crosswind}, *half* {half-length}, *mid* {midair}, and *self* {self-reliance}. See also 7.90.

PRONOUNS

Definition and Uses

5.34   *Definition.* A pronoun is a word used as a substitute for a noun or, sometimes, another pronoun. It is used in one of two ways. (1) A pronoun may substitute for an expressed noun or pronoun, especially to avoid needless repetition. For example, most of the nouns in the sentence *The father told the father's daughter that the father wanted the father's daughter to do some chores* can be replaced with pronouns: *The father told his daughter that he wanted her to do some chores*. (2) A pronoun may also stand in the place of an understood noun. For example, if the person addressed has been identified elsewhere, the question *Susan, are you bringing your boots?* can be more simply stated as *Are you bringing your boots?* And in the sentence *It is too hot*, the indefinite *it* is understood to mean *the temperature (of something)*.

5.35 *Antecedents of pronouns.* A pronoun typically refers to an antecedent—that is, an earlier noun, pronoun, phrase, or clause in the same sentence or, if the reference is unambiguous, in a previous sentence. An antecedent may be explicit or implicit, but it must be clear. Miscues and ambiguity commonly arise from (1) a missing antecedent (as in *the clown with his dog made it a pleasure to watch*, where *it* is intended to refer to the circus, not explicitly mentioned in context); (2) multiple possible antecedents (as in *Scott visited Eric after his discharge from the army*, where it is unclear who was discharged—Eric or Scott); and (3) multiple pronouns and antecedents in the same sentence (e.g., *When the bottle is empty or the baby stops drinking, it must be sterilized with hot water because if it drinks from a dirty bottle, it could become ill*—where one hopes that the hot-water sterilization is for the bottle).

5.36 *Pronouns without antecedents.* Some pronouns do not require antecedents. The first-person pronoun *I* stands for the speaker, so it almost never has an antecedent. Similarly, the second-person pronoun *you* usually needs no antecedent {Are you leaving?}, although one is sometimes supplied in direct address {Katrina, do you need something?}. As an expletive pronoun, *it* often has no antecedent {it's time to go}. And the relative pronoun *what* and the interrogative pronouns (*who, which, what*) never take an antecedent {Who cares what I think?}. In colloquial usage, *they* often appears without an antecedent {they say she's a good golfer}, but vigilant listeners and readers often demand to know who "they" are.

5.37 *Position in sentence.* A pronoun should generally follow the word it refers to. Some writers foreshadow a point before the predicate by placing the pronoun before the antecedent, but this device can cause confusion {whether they agreed with her or not, most participants in the survey said the senator made some good points} (the pronoun *they* precedes *most participants*, and *her* comes before the antecedent *senator*; the writer leaves the reader hanging awhile). Such an anticipatory reference often permissibly occurs in constructions involving *like, as do*, or *as have* {like his colleagues, Mr. Turino hopes to win reelection}.

5.38 *Sentence meaning.* The presence or absence of a pronoun may affect the meaning of a sentence. For example, if a noun is used in the first person, a first-person pronoun must also be used or else the sense will shift to the third person. Compare *I, Claudius, once ruled the Roman Empire* with *Claudius once ruled the Roman Empire*. Or *talk to me, your physician*, with *talk to your physician*. As an imperative, the second-person pronoun *you* may usually be either used or omitted without changing the meaning: *You come here!* is the same as *Come here!* although the pronoun adds an aggressive tone that may not be appropriate. When *you* is not used imperatively, however, the word cannot be omitted without shifting the sentence to the third person—compare, for example, *you children rake the yard* (speaking to the children) with *children rake the yard* (speaking about the children—but in direct address: *Children, rake the yard*).

Properties of Pronouns

5.39 *Four properties.* A pronoun has the same properties as a noun: number, person, gender, and case (see 5.9–13). A pronoun must agree with its antecedent in number, person, and gender. A few special uses of pronouns should be noted.

5.40 *Number and antecedent.* A pronoun's number is guided by that of its antecedent noun or nouns {a book and its cover} {the dogs and their owner}. A collective noun takes a singular pronoun if the members are treated as a unit {the audience showed its appreciation} but a plural if they act individually {the audience rushed back to their seats}. A singular noun that is modified by two or more adjectives to denote different varieties, uses, or aspects of the object may take a plural pronoun {British and American writing differ in more ways than just their spelling}. Two or more singular nouns or pronouns that are joined by *and* are taken jointly and referred to by a plural pronoun {the boy and girl have left their bicycles outside}.

5.41 *Exceptions regarding number.* There are several refinements to the rules stated just above: (1) When two or more singular antecedents connected by *and* together denote a single thing or each refer to the same thing, the pronoun referring to the antecedents is singular {red, white, and blue is the color scheme} {a lawyer and role model received her richly deserved recognition today}. (2) When two or more singular antecedents are connected by *and* and modified by *each, every,* or *no,* the pronoun referring to the antecedents is singular {every college and university encourages its students to succeed}. (3) When two or more singular antecedents are connected by *or, nor, either–or,* or *neither–nor,* they are treated separately and referred to by a singular pronoun {neither the orange nor the peach tastes as sweet as it should}. (4) When two or more antecedents of different numbers are connected by *or* or *nor,* the pronoun's number agrees with that of the nearest (usually the last) antecedent; if possible, cast the sentence so that the plural antecedent comes last {neither the singer nor the dancers have asked for their paychecks}. (5) When two or more antecedents of different numbers are connected by *and*, they are usually referred to by a plural pronoun regardless of the nouns' order {the horses and the mule kicked over their water trough}.

5.42 *Pronoun with multiple antecedents.* When a pronoun's antecedents differ in person from the pronoun and the antecedents are connected by *and*, *or*, or *nor*, the pronoun must take the person of only one antecedent. The first person is preferred to the second, and the second person to the third. For example, in *you or I should get to work on our experiment*, the antecedents are in the first and second person. The following pronoun *our* is in the first person, as is the antecedent *I*. In *you and she can settle your dispute*, the antecedents are in the second and third person, so the following pronoun *your* takes the second person. If the pronoun refers to only one of the connected nouns or pronouns, it takes the person of that noun {you and Marian have discussed her trip report}. At times the pronoun may refer to an antecedent that is not expressed in the same sentence; it takes the number of that antecedent, not of any connected noun or pronoun that precedes it {neither they nor I could do his work} (*his* referring to someone named in a preceding sentence).

5.43 *Antecedents of different genders.* If the antecedents are of different genders and are joined by *and*, a plural pronoun is normally used to refer to them {the sister and brother are visiting their aunt}. But if a pronoun refers to only one of the antecedent nouns connected by *and*, the pronoun's gender is that of the noun referred to {the uncle and niece rode in his car}. A special problem arises when the antecedent nouns are singular, are of different genders or an indeterminate gender, and are joined by *or* or *nor*. Using *he*, *his*, and *him* as common-sex pronouns is now widely considered sexist, if not misleading, and picking the gender of the nearest antecedent may be equally misleading (e.g., *some boy or girl left her lunch box on the bus*). A good writer can usually recast the sentence to eliminate the need for any personal pronoun at all {some child left a lunch box on the bus}. See 5.49, 5.51, 5.204.

Classes of Pronouns

5.44 *Six classes.* There are six classes of pronouns:

- · Personal—*I, you, he, she, it, we,* and *they*
- · Demonstrative—*that* and *this*
- · Interrogative—*what, which,* and *who*
- · Relative—*that, what, which,* and *who*

- Indefinite—for example, *another, any, each, either,* and *none*
- Adjective—for example, *any, each, that, this, what,* and *which*

Many pronouns, except personal pronouns, may function as more than one type—for example, *that* may be a demonstrative, relative, or adjective pronoun—depending on their purpose in a particular sentence.

Personal Pronouns

5.45 *Form.* A personal pronoun shows by its form whether it is referring to the speaker (first person), the person or thing spoken to (second person), or the person or thing spoken of (third person). It also displays the other properties of nouns: number, gender, and case.

5.46 *Identification.* As with nouns, the first person is the speaker or speakers {I need some tea} {we heard the news}. The first-person singular pronoun *I* is always capitalized no matter where it appears in the sentence {if possible, I will send you an answer today}. All other pronouns are capitalized only at the beginning of a sentence, unless they are part of an honorific title {a toast to Her Majesty}. (See also 8.35.) The second person shows who is spoken to {you should write that essay tonight}. And the third person shows who or what is spoken of {she is at work} {it is in the glove compartment}.

5.47 *Changes in form.* Personal pronouns change form (or "decline") according to person, number, and case. Apart from the second person, all personal pronouns show number by taking a singular and plural form. Although the second-person pronoun *you* is both singular and plural, it always takes a plural verb, even if only a single person or thing is addressed.

The Forms of Pronouns

SINGULAR PRONOUNS

	Nominative	Objective	Possessive
First Person	I	me	my, mine
Second Person	you	you	your, yours
Third Person	he, she, it	him, her, it	his, her, hers, its

PLURAL PRONOUNS

	Nominative	Objective	Possessive
First Person	we	us	our, ours
Second Person	you	you	your, yours
Third Person	they	them	their, theirs

Only the first- and most third-person pronouns show a change of case (the second-person *you* and third-person *it* keeping the same form as both subject and object, just as nouns do). In fact, the English language has only seven words that have different nominative and objective forms: *I/me, we/us, he/him, she/her, they/them, who/whom,* and *whoever/whomever*. A pronoun in the nominative case is either the subject of a verb {I like this china} {he has good posture} or, especially in formal English, a predicate nominative (after a linking verb) {this is he} {it was she who recommended the books}. (See 5.101.) A pronoun in the objective case is either the object of a verb {the crowd liked her} or the object of a preposition {the teachers were beside her}. In less formal English, pronouns in the objective case often encroach on the strictly correct nominative form in the predicate {it was her}. The opposite trend can be seen with an interrogative pronoun at the beginning of the sentence {Who are you going with?}. Grammarians believe that this gradual shift in the language, now ensconced in informal usage, has resulted from a widespread sense among speakers of English that the beginning of a sentence is "subject territory," whereas the end of a sentence is "object territory." And, of course, the irregularity of pronoun cases—there being so few in English—is not conducive to maintaining all the distinctions in the long term. But formal writers and speakers do maintain most of them strictly and will continue to do so in the foreseeable future. Meanwhile, ill-schooled and insecure writers and speakers engage in what linguists call "hypercorrection," misapplying the rules governing pronouns by using the nominative where the objective is called for (as in the mistaken form *between you and I* for *between you and me*) and vice versa (as in the mistaken form *May I ask whom is calling?* for *May I ask who is calling?*). For more on case, see 5.22–24. For more on *who/whom*, see 5.202.

5.48 *Gender, number, and case.* If a personal pronoun follows a relative pronoun and both refer to the same antecedent in the main clause, the personal pronoun takes the gender and number of that antecedent {I saw a farmer who was plowing his fields with his mule}. If the personal pronoun refers to a different antecedent from that of the relative pronoun, it takes the gender and number of that antecedent {I saw the boy and also the girl who pushed him down}. (See 5.59–60.) A personal pronoun does not govern the case of a relative pronoun. Hence an objective pronoun such as *me* may be the antecedent of the nominative pronoun *who*, although a construction formed in this way sounds increasingly archaic or (to the nonliterary) incorrect {she was referring to me, who never graduated from college}.

5.49 *Expressing gender.* Only the third-person singular pronouns directly express gender. In the nominative and objective cases, the pronoun takes the antecedent noun's gender {the president is not in her office today; she's at a seminar}. In the possessive case, the pronoun always takes the gender of the possessor, not of the person or thing possessed {the woman loves her husband} {Thomas is visiting his sister} {the puppy disobeyed its owner}. Some nouns may acquire gender through personification, a figure of speech that refers to a nonliving thing as if it were a person. Pronouns enhance personification when a feminine or masculine pronoun is used as if the antecedent represented a female or male person (as was traditionally done, for example, when a ship or other vessel was referred to as *she* or *her*).

5.50 *Special rules.* Some special rules apply to personal pronouns. (1) If a pronoun is the subject of a clause, or follows a conjunction but precedes the verb, it must be in the nominative case {she owns a tan briefcase} {Delia would like to travel, but she can't afford to}. (2) If a pronoun is the object of a verb, or of a preposition, it must be in the objective case {the rustic setting helped him relax} {that's a matter between him and her}. (3) If a prepositional phrase contains more than one object, then all the objects must be in the objective case {Will you send an invitation to him and me?}. (4) If a pronoun is the subject of an infinitive, it must be in the objective case {Does Tina want me to leave?}.

5.51 *Special uses.* Some personal pronouns have special uses. (1) *He, him,* and *his* have traditionally been used as pronouns of indeterminate gender equally applicable to a male or female person {if the finder returns my watch, he will receive a reward}. Because these pronouns are also masculine-specific, they have long been regarded as sexist when used generically, and their indeterminate-gender use is declining. (See 5.43, 5.204.) (2) *It* eliminates gender even if the noun's sex could be identified. Using *it* does not mean that the noun has no sex—only that the sex is unknown or unimportant {the baby is smiling at its mother} {the mockingbird is building its nest}. (3) *We, you,* and *they* can be used indefinitely, that is, without antecedents, in the sense of "persons," "one," or "people in general." *We* is sometimes used by an individual who is speaking for a group {the council's representative declared, "We appreciate your concern"} {the magazine's editor wrote, "In our last issue, we covered the archaeological survey of Peru"}. This latter use is called the editorial *we*. Some writers also use *we* to make their prose appear less personal and to draw in the reader or listener {from these results we can draw only one conclusion}. *You* can apply indefinitely to any person or all persons {if you read this book, you will learn how to influence people} (*you* is indefinite—anyone who reads the book will learn). The same is true of *they* {they say that Stonehenge may have been a primitive calendar} (*they* are unidentified and, perhaps, unimportant). (4) *It* also has several uses as an indefinite pronoun: (a) *it* may refer to a phrase, clause, sentence, or implied thought {he said that the Web site is down, but I don't believe it} (the clause might be rewritten *I don't believe what he said*); (b) *it* can be the subject of a verb (usually a form of *to be*) without an antecedent noun {it was too far}, or an introductory word or expletive for a phrase or clause that follows the verb {it is possible that Dody is on vacation}; (c) *it* can be the grammatical subject in an expression about time or weather {it is almost midnight} {it is beginning to snow}; and (d) *it* may be an expletive that anticipates the true grammatical subject or object {I find it hard to wake up}. Using the indefinite *it* carelessly may result in obscurity—for example, *Paul asked about my cough again; it is starting to annoy me* (What is annoying, Paul's asking or the cough?); *My cousin is a doctor. It is an interesting profession* (there is no noun naming the profession [medicine], so *it* lacks a necessary antecedent).

Possessive Pronouns

5.52 *Uses and forms.* The possessive pronouns, *my, our, your, his, her, its,* and *their,* are used as limiting adjectives to qualify nouns {my dictionary} {your cabin} {his diploma}. Each has a corresponding absolute (also called independent) form that can stand alone without a noun: *mine, ours, yours, his, hers, its,* and *theirs.* The independent form does not require an explicit object: the thing possessed may be either an antecedent or something understood {this dictionary is mine} {this cabin of yours} {Where is hers?}. An independent possessive pronoun can also stand alone and be treated as a noun: it can be the subject or object of a verb {hers is on the table} {pass me yours}, or the object of a preposition {put your coat with theirs}. When used with the preposition *of,* a double possessive is produced: *that letter of Sheila's* becomes *that letter of hers.* Such a construction is unobjectionable with names, and mandatory with pronouns. Note that none of the possessive personal pronouns are spelled with an apostrophe.

5.53 *Compound personal pronouns.* Several personal pronouns form compounds by taking the suffix *self* or *selves.* These are *my–myself; our–ourselves; your–yourself; your–yourselves; him–himself; her–herself; it–itself;* and *them–themselves.* These compound personal pronouns are the same in both the nominative case and the objective case. They have no possessive forms. They are used for three purposes: (1) for emphasis (they are then termed intensive pronouns) {I saw Queen Beatrice herself} {I'll do it myself}; (2) to refer to the subject of the verb (they are then termed reflexive pronouns) {he saved himself the trouble of asking} {we support ourselves}; and (3) to substitute for a simple personal pronoun {this getaway weekend is just for myself}. This third use is not well established in modern usage, so if a simple personal pronoun will suffice, use that word {this getaway weekend is just for me}.

5.54 *Reflexive and intensive pronouns.* The distinction between reflexive and intensive personal pronouns is useful and important. A reflexive pronoun reflects the action that the verb describes by renaming the subject. It is similar in appearance to an intensive pronoun but differs in function. An intensive pronoun is used in apposition to its referent to add emphasis {I myself have won several writing awards}. Intensive pronouns lend force to a sentence. Unlike reflexive pronouns, they are in the nominative case. Compare the intensive pronoun in *I burned the papers myself* (in which the object of *burned* is *papers*) with the reflexive pronoun in *I burned myself* (in which the object of *burned* is *myself*).

Demonstrative and Interrogative Pronouns

5.55 *Demonstrative pronouns.* A demonstrative pronoun (or, as it is sometimes called, a deictic pronoun) is one that points directly to its antecedent: *this* and *that* for singular antecedents {this is your desk} {that is my office}, and *these* and *those* for plural antecedents {these have just arrived} {those need to be answered}. *This* and *these* point to objects that are close by in time, space, or thought, while *that* and *those* point to objects that are comparatively remote in time, space, or thought. The antecedent of a demonstrative pronoun can be a noun, phrase, clause, sentence, or implied thought, as long as the antecedent is clear. *Kind* and *sort*, each referring to "one class," are often used with an adjectival *this* or *that* {this kind of magazine} {that sort of school}. The plural forms *kinds* and *sorts* should be used with the plural demonstratives {these kinds of magazines} {those sorts of schools}.

5.56 *Interrogative pronouns.* An interrogative pronoun asks a question. The three interrogatives are *who, what,* and *which.* Only one, *who,* declines: *who* (nominative), *whom* (objective), *whose* (possessive) {Who starred in *Casablanca*?} {To whom am I speaking?} {Whose cologne smells so nice?}. In the nominative case, *who* is used in two ways: (1) as the subject of a verb {Who washed the dishes today?}; and (2) as a predicate nominative after a linking verb {It was who?}. In the objective case, *whom* is used in two ways: (1) as the object of a verb {Whom did you see?}; and (2) as the object of a preposition {For whom is this building named?}.

5.57 *Referent of interrogative pronouns.* To refer to a person, either *who* or *which* can be used, but they are not interchangeable. *Who* is universal or general and asks for any one or more persons of all persons; the answer may include any person, living or dead, present or absent {Who wants to see that movie?}. *Who* also asks for a particular person's identity {Who is that person standing near the samovar?}. *Which* is usually selective or limited; it asks for a particular member of a group, and the answer is limited only to the group addressed or referred to {Which explorers visited China in the sixteenth century?}. *Which* should not indiscriminately displace *who* or *whom* {Of the five finalists, who would be the best dean?} (*who* is better than *which*). To refer to a person, animal, or thing, either *which* or *what* may be used {Which one of you did this?} {What kind of bird is that?}. When applied to a person, *what* asks for the person's character, occupation, qualities, and the like {What do you think of our governor?}. When applied to a thing, *what* is broad and asks for any one thing, especially of a set {What is your quest?} {What is your favorite color?}.

Relative Pronouns

5.58   *Definition.* A relative pronoun is one that introduces a subordinate (or relative) clause and relates it to the main clause. Relative pronouns in common use are *who*, *which*, *what*, and *that*. *Who* is the only relative pronoun that declines: *who* (nominative), *whom* (objective), *whose* (possessive) {the woman who presented the award} {an informant whom he declined to name} {the writer whose book was a best-seller}. Although *who* refers only to a person (but see 5.62), it can be used in the first, second, or third person. *Which* refers only to an animal or a thing. *What* refers only to a nonliving thing. *Which* and *what* are used only in the second and third person. *That* refers to a person, animal, or thing, and can be used in the first, second, or third person. See also 5.48.

5.59   *Antecedent.* Usually, a relative pronoun's antecedent is a noun or pronoun in the main clause on which the relative clause depends. For clarity, it should immediately precede the pronoun {the diadem that I told you about is in this gallery}. The antecedent may also be a noun phrase or a clause, but the result can sometimes be ambiguous: in *the bedroom of the villa, which was painted pink*, does the *which* refer to the bedroom or to the villa?

5.60   *Omitted antecedent.* If no antecedent noun is expressed, *what* can be used to mean *that which* {Is this what you were looking for?}. But if there is an antecedent, use a different relative pronoun: *who* {Where is the man who spoke?}, *that* (if the relative clause is restrictive, i.e., essential to the sentence's basic meaning) {Where are the hunters that Jones told us about?}, or *which* (if the relative clause is nonrestrictive, i.e., could be deleted without affecting the sentence's basic meaning) {the sun, which is shining brightly, feels warm on my face}. See also 5.38.

5.61 *Possessive forms.* The forms *of whom* and *of which* are possessives {the child, the mother of whom we talked about, is in kindergarten} {this foal, the sire of which Belle owns, will be trained as a hunter/jumper}. (These forms have an old-fashioned sound and can often be rephrased more naturally {the child whose mother we talked about is in kindergarten}.) The relative *what* forms the possessive *of what* {The purpose of what?}. The relative *that* forms the possessive *of that* (the preposition being placed at the end of the phrase) {no legend that we know of} or *of which* {no legend of which we know}. On ending a sentence with a preposition, see 5.169.

5.62 *"Whose" and "of which."* The relatives *who* and *which* can both take *whose* as a possessive form (*whose* substitutes for *of which*) {a movie the conclusion of which is unforgettable} {a movie whose conclusion is unforgettable}. Some writers object to using *whose* as a replacement for *of which*, especially when the subject is not human, but the usage is centuries old and widely accepted as preventing unnecessary awkwardness. Compare *the company whose stock rose faster* with *the company the stock of which rose faster*. Either form is acceptable, but the possessive *whose* is smoother.

5.63 *Compound relative pronouns. Who, whom, what,* and *which* form compound relative pronouns by adding the suffix *ever.* The compound relatives *whoever, whomever, whichever,* and *whatever* apply universally to any or all persons or things {whatever you do, let me know} {whoever needs to write a report about this book may borrow it}. See also 5.202 under *whoever; whomever.*

Other Types of Pronouns

5.64 *Indefinite pronouns.* An indefinite pronoun is one that generally or indefinitely represents an object, usually one that has already been identified or doesn't need specific identification. The most common are *another, any, both, each, either, neither, none, one, other, some,* and *such.* There are also compound indefinite pronouns, such as *anybody, anyone, anything, everybody, everyone, everything, nobody, no one, oneself, somebody,* and *someone. Each, either,* and *neither* are also called distributive pronouns because they separate the objects referred to from others referred to nearby. Indefinite pronouns have number. When an indefinite pronoun is the subject of a verb, it is usually singular {everyone is enjoying the dinner} {everybody takes notes during the first week}. But sometimes an indefinite pronoun carries a plural sense {nobody could describe the music; they hadn't been listening to it} {everyone understood the risk, but they were lured by promises of big returns}. The forms of indefinite pronouns are not affected by gender or person, and the nominative and objective forms are the same. To form the possessive, the indefinite pronoun may take *'s* {that is no one's fault} {Is this anyone's jacket?} or the adverb *else* plus *'s* {don't interfere with anybody else's business} {no one else's cups were broken}.

5.65   *Adjective pronouns.* An adjective pronoun (also called a pronominal adjective) functions as a noun modifier. All pronouns other than personal pronouns, *who*, and *none* may serve as adjectives {those windows} {some coyotes}.

ADJECTIVES

5.66   *Definition.* An adjective is a word that adds a new idea to a noun or pronoun either by describing it more definitely or fully (a descriptive adjective) or by narrowing a noun's or pronoun's meaning (a limiting adjective). Some suffixes that distinguish adjectives are *able* {manageable}, *al* {mystical}, *ary* {elementary}, *en* {wooden}, *ful* {harmful}, *ible* {inaccessible}, *ic* {artistic}, *ish* {foolish}, *ive* {demonstrative}, *less* {helpless}, *like* {childlike}, *ous* {perilous}, *some* {lonesome}, and *y* {sunny}.

5.67   *Proper adjectives.* A proper adjective is one that, being or deriving from a proper name, begins with a capital letter {a New York minute} {a Cuban cigar} {a Canadian dollar}. The proper name used attributively is still capitalized, but it does not cause the noun it modifies to be capitalized. Where the connection between the proper noun and its attributive use is weak or obscure, the noun is often lowercase {french fry} {diesel engine}. See also 8.65, 8.85. A place-name containing a comma—such as *Toronto, Ontario,* or *New Delhi, India*—should generally not be used as an adjective because a second comma may be deemed obligatory {we met in a Toronto, Ontario, restaurant} (the comma after *Ontario* is awkward). Compare the readability of *a New Delhi, India, marketplace* with *a New Delhi marketplace* or *a marketplace in New Delhi, India* (substituting a prepositional phrase for the proper adjective). See also 6.43.

5.68   *Participial adjectives.* A participial adjective is simply a participle (see 5.108) that modifies a noun. It can be a present participle (verb ending in *ing*) {the dining room} {a walking stick} {a rising star} or a past participle (usually a verb ending in *ed*) {an endangered species} {a completed assignment} {a proven need}. Some irregular past participles have only this adjectival function {a shaven face} {a graven image}, the past-participial verb having taken a different form {shaved} {engraved}. See also 5.84.

Articles as Limiting Adjectives

5.69 *Definition of an article.* An article is a limiting adjective that precedes a noun or noun phrase and determines the noun's or phrase's use to indicate something definite (*the*) or indefinite (*a* or *an*). An article might stand alone or be used with other adjectives {a road} {a brick road} {the yellow brick road}. When present, it is always the first word in a noun phrase.

5.70 *Definite article.* The definite article points to a definite object that (1) is so well understood that it does not need description (e.g., *the package is here* is a shortened form of *the package that was expected is here*); (2) is a thing that is about to be described {the sights in Chicago}; or (3) is important {won the grand prize}. The definite article may precede a singular or a plural noun. Mass nouns may also take the definite article {the evidence} {the herd}.

5.71 *Indefinite article.* An indefinite article points to nonspecific objects, things, or persons that are not distinguished from the other members of a class. The thing may be singular {a student at Princeton}, or uncountable {a multitude}, or generalized {an idea inspired by Milton's *Paradise Lost*}.

5.72 *Exceptions.* In a few usages, the indefinite article provides a specific reference {I saw a great movie last night} and the definite article a generic reference {the Scots are talking about independence} (generalizing by nationality).

5.73 *Choosing "a" or "an."* With the indefinite article, the choice of *a* or *an* depends on the sound of the word it precedes. *A* comes before words with a consonant sound, including /y/, /h/, and /w/, no matter how the word is spelled {a eulogy} {a hotel suite} {a Ouachita tribe member}. *An* comes before words with a vowel sound {an LSAT exam room} {an *X-Files* episode} {an hour ago}. See also 5.202, 7.46, 15.9.

5.74 *Articles with coordinate nouns.* With a series of coordinate nouns, an article should appear before each noun {the rosebush and the hedge need trimming} {a letter and a magazine came in the mail today}. If the things named make up a single idea, the article need not be repeated {in the highest degree of dressage, the horse and rider appear to be one entity}. And if the named things are covered by one plural noun, the definite article should not be repeated with each modifier {in the first and second years of college}.

5.75   *Effect on meaning.* Because articles have a demonstrative value, the meaning of a phrase may shift depending on the article used. For example, *an officer and gentleman escorted Princess Plum to her car* suggests (though ambiguously) that the escort was one man with two descriptive characteristics. But *an officer and a friend escorted Princess Plum to her car* suggests that two people acted as escorts. Similarly, *Do you like the red and blue cloth?* suggests that the cloth contains both red and blue threads. But *Do you like the red and the blue cloth?* suggests that two different fabrics are being discussed. If ambiguity is likely in a given context, the clearest way to express the idea that the cloth contains both red and blue is to hyphenate the phrase as a compound modifier: *red-and-blue cloth*; and with two kinds of cloth, the clear expression is either to repeat the word *cloth* (*the red cloth and the blue cloth*) or to use *cloth* with the first adjective rather than the second (*the red cloth and the blue*).

5.76   *Zero article.* Some usages call for a zero article, an article implicitly present, usually before a mass or plural noun {although both new and washed bottles are stacked nearby, cider is poured into new bottles only} (*the* is implicit before *new bottles*).

5.77   *Omitted article.* The absence of an article may alter a sentence's meaning— for example, the meaning of *the news brought us little comfort* (we weren't comforted) changes if *a* is inserted before *little*: *the news brought us a little comfort* (we felt somewhat comforted).

5.78   *Article as pronoun substitute.* An article may sometimes substitute for a pronoun. For example, the blanks in *a patient who develops the described rash on _____ hands should inform _____ doctor* may be filled in with the pronoun phrase *his or her* or the article *the*. See also 5.204.

Dates as Adjectives

5.79   *Use and punctuation.* Dates are often used as descriptive adjectives, more so today than in years past. If a month-and-year or month-and-day date is used as an adjective, no hyphen or comma is needed {October 31 festivities} {December 2003 financial statement}. If a full month-day-year date is used, then a comma is considered necessary both before and after the year {the May 18, 2002, commencement ceremonies}. But this construction seems awkward because the adjective (which is forward-looking) contains two commas (which are backward-looking); the construction is therefore best avoided {commencement ceremonies on May 18, 2002}. See also 6.46.

Position of Adjectives

5.80 *Basic rules.* An adjective that modifies a noun or noun phrase usually precedes it {perfect storm} {spectacular view} {good bowl of soup}. An adjective may follow the noun if (1) special emphasis is needed {reasons innumerable} {captains courageous}; (2) it occurs in this position in standard usage {court-martial} {notary public}; (3) it is normally a predicate adjective (see 5.83) {the city is asleep}; or (4) the noun is of a type usually followed by the adjective {anything good} {everything yellow} {nothing important} {something wicked}.

5.81 *After possessive noun or pronoun.* When a noun phrase includes a possessive and an adjective, both modifying the same noun, the adjective typically follows the possessive {children's athletic shoes} {the company's former president}.

5.82 *Adjective modifying pronoun.* When modifying a pronoun, an adjective usually follows the pronoun {the searchers found him unconscious} {some like it hot}, sometimes as a predicate adjective {it was insensitive} {Who was so jealous?}.

5.83 *Predicate adjective.* A predicate adjective is an adjective that follows a linking verb (see 5.101) but modifies the subject {the child is afraid} {the night became colder} {this tastes delicious} {I feel bad}. If an adjective in the predicate modifies a noun or pronoun in the predicate, it is not a predicate adjective. For example, in *the train will be late,* the adjective *late* modifies the subject *train.* But in *the train will be here at a late hour,* the adjective *late* modifies the predicate noun *hour.*

5.84 *Dangling participle.* A participial adjective often correctly appears before a main clause {watching constantly, the lioness protected her cubs from danger}. But such a participial phrase is said to "dangle" when the participle lacks grammatical connection to a noun that performs the action denoted by the participle. This occurs when a participial form is not immediately followed by the noun it modifies—for example, *before receiving the medal, the general congratulated the soldier (receiving* is meant to apply to *soldier,* not *general).* The same problem arises when a possessive follows the participial phrase—for example, *dodging the traffic, his cell phone got dropped in the street* (the cell phone wasn't dodging traffic). Recasting the sentence to eliminate the dangler will improve the style {the general congratulated the soldier before awarding the medal} {dodging the traffic, he dropped his cell phone in the street}. For certain participles functioning as prepositions (or subordinating conjunctions) and therefore exempt from the rule against dangling, see 5.164.

Degrees of Adjectives

5.85 *Three degrees.* An adjective has three degrees of comparison: the positive {hard}, the comparative {harder}, and the superlative {hardest}. A positive adjective simply expresses an object's quality without reference to any other thing {a big balloon} {bad news}.

5.86 *Comparative forms.* A comparative adjective expresses the relationship between two things in terms of a specified quality they share, often to determine which has more or less of that quality {a cheaper ticket} {a happier ending}. The suffix *er* usually signals the comparative form of a common adjective having one or sometimes two syllables {light–lighter} {merry–merrier}. An adjective with three or more syllables takes *more* instead of a suffix to form the comparative {intelligent–more intelligent} {purposeful–more purposeful}. Some adjectives with two syllables take the *er* suffix {lazy–lazier} {narrow–narrower}, but most take *more* {more hostile} {more careless}.

5.87 *Superlative forms.* A superlative adjective expresses the relationship between at least three things and denotes an extreme of intensity or amount in a particular shared quality {the biggest house on the block} {the bitterest pill of all}. The suffix *est* usually signals the superlative form of a common adjective having one or sometimes two syllables {lighter–lightest} {narrower–narrowest}. An adjective with three or more syllables takes *most* instead of a suffix to form the superlative {quarrelsome–most quarrelsome} {humorous–most humorous}. Some adjectives with two syllables take the *est* suffix {holy–holiest} {noble–noblest}, but most take *most* {most fruitful} {most reckless}.

5.88 *Forming comparatives and superlatives.* There are a few rules for forming a short regular adjective's comparative and superlative forms. (1) If the adjective is a monosyllable ending in a single vowel followed by a single consonant, the final consonant is doubled before the suffix is attached {red–redder–reddest}. (2) If the adjective ends in a silent *e*, the *e* is dropped before adding the suffix {polite–politer–politest}. (3) A participle used as an adjective requires *more* or *most* before the participle; no suffix is added to form the comparative or the superlative {this teleplay is more boring than the first one} {I am most tired on Fridays}. Many adjectives are irregular—there is no rule that guides their comparative and superlative forms {good–better–best} {less–lesser–least}. A good dictionary will show the forms of an irregular adjective.

Special Types of Adjectives

5.89 *Past-participial adjectives.* When a past participle functioning as an adjective has a modifier, that modifier is usually modified with an adverb such as *quite* {quite surprised}, *barely* {barely concealed}, or *little* {little known}, or an adverbial phrase such as *very much* {very much distrusted}. If the past participle has gained a strong adjectival quality, *very* will do the job alone without the quantitative *much* {very tired} {very drunk}. But if the participial form seems more like a verb, *very* needs *much* to help do the job {very much appreciated} {very much delayed}. A few past participles (such as *bored, interested, pleased, satisfied*) are in the middle of the spectrum between those having mostly adjectival qualities and those having mostly verbal qualities. With these few, the quantitative *much* is normally omitted. See 5.159.

5.90 *Uncomparable adjectives.* An adjective that, by definition, describes an absolute state or condition—for example, *entire, impossible, pregnant, unique*—is called uncomparable. It cannot take a comparative suffix and cannot be coupled with one of the comparative terms *more, most, less,* and *least*. Nor can it be intensified by a word such as *very, largely,* or *quite*. But on the rare occasion when a particular emphasis is needed, a good writer may depart from this rule and use a phrase such as *more perfect,* as the framers of the United States Constitution did in composing its preamble {We the People of the United States, in order to form a more perfect Union . . .}.

5.91 *Coordinate adjectives.* A coordinate adjective is one that appears in a sequence with one or more related adjectives to modify the same noun. Coordinate adjectives should be separated by commas or by *and* {skilled, experienced chess player} {nurturing and loving parent}. But if one adjective modifies the noun and another adjective modifies the idea expressed by the combination of the first adjective and the noun, the adjectives are not considered coordinate and should not be separated by a comma. For example, *a lethargic soccer player* describes a soccer player who is lethargic. Likewise, phrases such as *red brick house* and *wrinkled canvas jacket* are unpunctuated because the adjectives are not coordinate: they have no logical connection in sense (a red house could be made of many different materials; so could a wrinkled jacket). The most useful test is this: if *and* would fit between the two adjectives, a comma is necessary. See also 6.39–40.

5.92 *Phrasal adjectives.* A phrasal adjective (also called a compound modifier) is a phrase that functions as a unit to modify a noun. A phrasal adjective follows these basic rules: (1) Generally, if it is placed before a noun, you should hyphenate the phrase to avoid misdirecting the reader {dog-eat-dog competition}. There may be a considerable difference between the hyphenated and the unhyphenated forms. For example, compare *small animal hospital* with *small-animal hospital.* (2) If a compound noun is an element of a phrasal adjective, the entire compound noun must be hyphenated to clarify the relationship among the words {video-game-magazine dispute} {college-football-halftime controversy}. (3) If more than one phrasal adjective modifies a single noun, hyphenation becomes especially important {nineteenth-century song-and-dance numbers} {state-inspected assisted-living facility}. (4) If two phrasal adjectives end in a common element, the ending element should appear only with the second phrase, and a suspension hyphen should follow the unattached words to show that they are related to the ending element {the choral- and instrumental-music programs}. But if two phrasal adjectives *begin* with a common element, a hyphen is usually inappropriate, and the element should be repeated {left-handed and left-brained executives}. (5) If the phrasal adjective denotes an amount or a duration, plurals should be dropped. For instance, *pregnancy lasts nine months* but is *a nine-month pregnancy,* and a shop *open twenty-four hours a day* requires *a twenty-four-hour-a-day schedule.* The plural is retained only for fractions {a two-thirds majority}. (6) If a phrasal adjective becomes awkward, the sentence should probably be recast. For example, *The news about the lower-than-expected third-quarter earnings disappointed investors* could become *The news about the third-quarter earnings, which were lower than expected, disappointed investors.* Or perhaps this: *Investors were disappointed by the third-quarter earnings, which were lower than expected.* See also 7.82–90.

5.93 *Exceptions for hyphenating phrasal adjectives.* There are exceptions for hyphenating phrasal adjectives: (1) If the phrasal adjective follows a verb, it is usually unhyphenated—for example, compare *a well-trained athlete* with *an athlete who is well trained.* (2) When a proper name begins a phrasal adjective, the name is not hyphenated {the Monty Python school of comedy}. (3) A two-word phrasal adjective that begins with an adverb ending in *ly* is not hyphenated {a sharply worded reprimand} (but *a not-so-sharply-worded reprimand*).

Functional Variation

5.94 *Adjectives as nouns.* Adjective-to-noun transitions are relatively common in English. Some adjectives are well established as nouns and are perfectly suitable for most contexts. For example, *a postmortem examination* is often called *a postmortem*; *collectible objects* are *collectibles*; and *French citizens* are *the French*. Any but the most established among such nouns should be used only after careful consideration. If there is an alternative, it will almost certainly be better. For example, there is probably no good reason to use the adjective *collaborative* as a noun (i.e., as a shortened form of *collaborative enterprise*) when the perfectly good *collaboration* is available.

5.95 *Adjectives as verbs.* Adjective-to-verb transitions are uncommon in English but occur once in a while, usually as jargon or slang {the cargo tanks were *inerted* by introducing carbon dioxide into them} {it would be silly to *low-key* the credit for this achievement}. They are not acceptable in formal prose.

5.96 *Other parts of speech functioning as adjectives.* Words that ordinarily function as other parts of speech, but sometimes as adjectives, include nouns (see 5.30), pronouns (see 5.52), and verbs (see 5.107).

VERBS

Definitions

5.97 *Verbs.* A verb shows the performance or occurrence of an action or the existence of a condition or a state of being, such as an emotion. Action verbs include *walk, shout, taste,* and *fly.* Nonaction verbs include *imagine, exist,* and *dread.* A verb is the most essential part of speech—the only one that can express a thought by itself, in a complete grammatical sentence (with the subject understood) {Run!} {Enjoy!} {Think!}.

5.98 *Transitive and intransitive verbs.* Depending on its relationship with objects, a verb is classified as transitive or intransitive. A transitive verb requires an object to express a complete thought; the verb indicates what action the subject exerts on the object (but see 5.99). For example, in *the cyclist hit a curb,* the verb *hit* expresses what the subject (*cyclist*) did to the object (*curb*). An intransitive verb does not require an object to express a complete thought {the rescuer jumped}, although it may be followed by a prepositional phrase {the rescuer jumped to the ground}. Many verbs are both transitive and intransitive. The different usages are distinguishable by their meanings. For example, when used transitively, as in *the king's heir will succeed him, succeed* means "to follow and take the place of"; when used intransitively, as in *the chemist will succeed in identifying the toxin*, it means "to accomplish a task." A verb that is normally used transitively may sometimes be used intransitively to emphasize the verb and leave the object undefined or unknown {the patient is eating poorly} (*how well* the patient eats is more important than *what* the patient eats).

5.99 *Ergative verbs.* Some verbs, called ergative verbs, can be used transitively or intransitively with a noun that becomes the object when the verb's use is transitive, and the subject when the verb's use is intransitive. For example, with the noun *door* and the verb *open*, one can say *I opened the door* (transitive) or *the door opened* (intransitive). Many words undergo ergative shifts. For example, the verb *ship* was once exclusively transitive {the company shipped the books on January 16}, but in commercial usage it is now often intransitive {the books shipped on January 16}. Likewise, *grow* (generally an intransitive verb) was transitive only in horticultural contexts {the family grew several types of crops}, but commercial usage now makes it transitive in many other contexts {how to grow your business}. Careful writers and editors employ such usages cautiously if at all, preferring well-established idioms.

5.100 *Regular and irregular verbs.* Depending on its inflections (changes of form), a verb is classified as regular or irregular. The irregular verbs are among the most challenging. Although an irregular verb usually forms the present participle in the same way as a regular verb {ride–riding} {spring–springing}, there are no modern rules on how an irregular verb forms the past tense and past participle {ride–rode–ridden} {spring–sprang–sprung}. A good dictionary of usage or general dictionary is an essential aid. Fortunately, the great majority of English verbs are regular and are inflected according to rules. A regular verb that ends in a double consonant {block}, two vowels and a consonant {cook}, or a vowel other than *e* {veto} forms the present participle by adding *ing* to its simple form {blocking} {cooking} {vetoing}. It forms the past tense and past participle by adding *ed* to its simple form {block–blocked–blocked} {cook–cooked–cooked} {veto–vetoed–vetoed}. If a regular verb ends in a single vowel before a consonant, the consonant is doubled before taking the present or past form's ending {drip–dripping–dripped}. If a regular verb ends in a silent *e*, the *e* is dropped to form the present participle {bounce–bouncing}; only a *d* is added to form the past tense and past participle {bounce–bounced}. If a regular verb ends in *y* preceded by a consonant, the *y* changes to an *i* before forming the past tense and past participle with *ed* {hurry–hurried}. A few regular verbs have an alternative past tense and past participle formed by adding *t* to the simple verb form {dream–dreamed} {dream–dreamt}. When these alternatives are available, American English tends to prefer the forms in *ed* (e.g., *dreamed, learned, spelled*), while British English tends to prefer the forms in *t* (*dreamt, learnt, spelt*).

5.101 *Linking verbs.* A linking verb (also called a copula or connecting verb) is one that links the subject to an equivalent word in the sentence—a predicate pronoun, predicate noun, or predicate adjective. The linking verb itself does not take an object. There are two kinds of linking verbs: forms of *to be* and intransitive verbs that are used in a weakened sense, such as *seem, smell, appear, feel,* and *look.* When used as a link, the weakened intransitive verb often has a figurative sense akin to that of *became,* as in *he fell heir to a large fortune* (he didn't physically fall on or into anything) or *the river ran dry* (a waterless river doesn't run—it has dried up). See 5.158.

5.102 *Phrasal verbs.* A phrasal verb is usually a verb plus a preposition (or particle) {settle down} {get up}. A phrasal verb is not hyphenated, even though its equivalent noun or phrasal adjective might be—compare *to flare up* with *a flare-up,* and compare *to step up the pace* with *a stepped-up pace.* Three rules apply: (1) if the phrasal verb has a sense distinct from the component words, use the entire phrase—e.g., *hold up* means "to rob" or "to delay," and *get rid of* and *do away with* mean "to eliminate"; (2) avoid the phrasal verb if the verb alone conveys essentially the same meaning—e.g., *rest up* is equivalent to *rest*; and (3) don't compress the phrase into a one-word verb, especially if it has a corresponding one-word noun form—e.g., one *burns out* and suffers *burnout.*

5.103 *Principal and auxiliary verbs.* Depending on its uses, a verb is classified as principal or auxiliary (also termed modal). A principal verb is one that can stand alone to express an act or state {he jogs} {I dreamed about Xanadu}. If combined with another verb, it expresses the combination's leading thought {a tiger may roar}. An auxiliary verb is used with a principal verb to form a verb phrase that indicates mood, tense, or voice {You must study for the exam!} {I will go to the store} {the show was interrupted}. The most commonly used auxiliaries are *be, can, do, have, may, must, ought, shall,* and *will.* For more on auxiliary verbs, see 5.132–40.

5.104 *Verb phrases.* The combination of an auxiliary verb with a principal verb is a verb phrase, such as *could happen, must go,* or *will be leaving.* When a verb phrase is modified by an adverb, the modifier typically goes directly after the first auxiliary verb, as in *could certainly happen, must always go,* and *will soon be leaving.* The idea that verb phrases should not be "split" in this way is quite mistaken (see 5.160). A verb phrase is negated by placing *not,* the negative adverb, after the first auxiliary {we have not called him}. In an interrogative sentence, the first auxiliary begins the sentence and is followed by the subject {Must I repeat that?} {Do you want more?}. An interrogative can be negated by placing *not* after the subject {Do you not want more?}, but contractions are often more natural {Don't you want more?}. Most negative forms can be contracted {we do not–we don't} {I will not–I won't} {he has not–he hasn't} {she does not–she doesn't}, but *I am not* is contracted to *I'm not* (or, jocularly or in dialect, *I ain't*—but never *I amn't*). The corresponding interrogative form is *aren't I.* Sometimes the negative is emphasized if the auxiliary is contracted with the pronoun and the negative is left standing alone {he is not–he isn't–he's not} {we are not–we aren't–we're not} {they have not–they haven't–they've not}.

Infinitives

5.105 *Definition.* An infinitive, also called a verb's root or stem, is the part of a verb that in its principal uninflected form may be preceded by *to* {to dance} {to dive}. In the active voice, *to* is generally dropped when the infinitive follows an auxiliary verb {you must flee} and can be dropped after several verbs, such as *bid, dare, feel, hear, help, let, make, need,* and *see* {You dare say that to me!}. But when the infinitive follows one of these verbs in the passive voice, *to* should be retained {she saw him leave, but he was seen to return later} {they cannot be made to listen}. The *to* should also be retained after *ought* (see 5.138).

5.106 *Split infinitive.* Although from about 1850 to 1925 many grammarians stated otherwise, it is now widely acknowledged that adverbs sometimes justifiably separate the *to* from the principal verb {they expect to more than double their income next year}. See 5.160.

5.107 *Uses of the infinitive.* The infinitive has great versatility. It is sometimes called a verbal noun because it can function as a verb or a noun. The infinitive also has limited uses as an adjective or an adverb. As a verb, it can take (1) a subject {we wanted the lesson to end}; (2) an object {to throw the javelin}; (3) a predicate complement {to race home}; or (4) an adverbial modifier {to think quickly}. As a noun, the infinitive can perform as (1) the subject of a finite verb {to fly is a lofty goal}; or (2) the object of a transitive verb or participle {I want to hire a new assistant}. The infinitive can be used as an adjective to modify a noun {a compulsion to steal}. It can also be used adverbially to indicate a motive or purpose or to denote a result {he's too nice to do such awful things}.

Participles and Gerunds

5.108   *Forming participles.* Two participles are formed from the verb stem: the present participle invariably ends in *ing,* and the past participle usually ends in *ed.* The present participle denotes the verb's action as in progress or incomplete at the time expressed by the sentence's principal verb {watching intently for a mouse, the cat settled in to wait} {hearing his name, Jon turned to answer}. The past participle denotes the verb's action as completed {planted in the spring} {written last year}.

5.109   *Participial phrases.* A participial phrase is made up of a participle plus any closely associated word or words, such as modifiers or complements. It can be used (1) as an adjective to modify a noun or pronoun {nailed to the roof, the slate will stop the leaks}, or (2) as an adverb to modify the predicate, or any adverb or adjective in the predicate {she will succeed, persevering despite discouragement} {she pointed to the chef drooping behind the counter}. For more on participial adjectives, see 5.68, 5.84.

5.110   *Gerunds.* A gerund is a present participle used as a noun. Being a noun, the gerund can be used as (1) the subject of a verb {complaining about it won't help}; (2) the object of a verb {I don't like your cooking}; (3) a predicate nominative or complement {his favorite hobby is sleeping}; or (4) the object of a preposition {reduce erosion by terracing the fields}.

Properties of Verbs

5.111   *Five properties.* A verb has five properties: voice, mood, tense, person, and number.

5.112   *Active and passive voice.* Voice shows whether the subject acts (active voice) or is acted on (passive voice)—that is, whether the subject performs or receives the action of the verb. Only transitive verbs are said to have voice. The clause *the judge levied a $50 fine* is in the active voice because the subject (*judge*) is acting. But *the tree's branch was broken by the storm* is in the passive voice because the subject (*branch*) does not break itself—it is acted on by the object (*storm*). The passive voice is always formed by joining an inflected form of *to be* (or, in colloquial usage, *to get*) with the verb's past participle. Compare *the ox pulls the cart* (active voice) with *the cart is pulled by the ox* (passive voice). A passive-voice verb in a subordinate clause often has an implied *be*: in *the advice given by the novelist,* the implied (or understood) words *that was* come before *given*; so the passive construction is *was given*. Although the inflected form of *to be* is sometimes implicit, the past participle must always appear. Sometimes the agent remains unnamed {his tires were slashed}. As a matter of style, passive voice {the matter will be given careful consideration} is typically, though not always, inferior to active voice {we will consider the matter carefully}.

5.113 *Progressive conjugation and voice.* If an inflected form of *to be* is joined with the verb's present participle, a progressive conjugation is produced {the ox is pulling the cart}. The progressive conjugation is in active voice because the subject is performing the action, not being acted on.

5.114 *Mood.* Mood (or mode) indicates the way in which the verb expresses an action or state of being. The three moods are indicative, imperative, and subjunctive. The indicative mood makes statements or asks questions {amethysts cost very little} {the botanist lives in a garden cottage} {Does that bush produce yellow roses?}. The imperative mood expresses commands or requests and usually has an understood *you* as the sentence's subject {give me the magazine} {take good care of yourself}. The subjunctive mood expresses an action or state not as a reality but as a mental conception. Typically, this means that the subjunctive expresses an action or state as doubtful, imagined, desired, conditional, or otherwise contrary to fact {if I were wealthy, I could travel} {I wish I had some alternatives}. It also often expresses a suggestion {I suggest that you be early} or a requirement {the requirement that all exams be completed by 2:00 p.m.}. The subjunctive appears in the base form of the verb (*be* in the example just given, instead of an inflected form. Note that not every *if* takes a subjunctive verb: when the action or state might be true but the writer does not know, the indicative is called for {if I am right about this, please call} {if Napoleon was in fact poisoned with arsenic, historians will need to reconsider his associates}. See also 5.127, 5.130.

5.115 *Tenses.* Tense shows the time in which an act, state, or condition occurs or occurred. The three major divisions of time are present, past, and future. (Some modern grammarians hold that English has no future tense; see 5.118.) Each division of time breaks down further into a perfect tense that indicates a comparatively more remote time: present perfect, past perfect, and future perfect.

5.116 *Present tense.* The present-tense form is the infinitive verb's stem (with an added *s* in the third-person singular), also called the present indicative {walk} {drink}. It primarily denotes acts, conditions, or states that occur in the present {I see} {you understand} {the water runs}. It is also used (1) to express a habitual action or general truth {cats prowl nightly} {polluted water is a health threat}; (2) to refer to memorable persons and to works of the past that are still extant or enduring {Julius Caesar describes his strategies in *The Gallic War*} {the Pompeiian mosaics are exquisite}; and (3) to narrate a fictional work's plot {the scene takes place aboard the *Titanic*}. This third point is important for those who write about literature. Characters in books, plays, and films *do* things—not *did* them. If you want to distinguish between present action and past action in literature, the present perfect tense is helpful {Hamlet, who has spoken with his father's ghost, reveals what he has learned to no one but Horatio}. See 5.119. The present continuous tense denotes continuing or progressive action and consists of the present tense of the verb *to be* plus a present participle {the children are swimming} {the water is evaporating}. See also 5.141.

5.117   *Past tense.* The past tense is formed by inflection (see 5.100); the basic inflected form is called the past indicative {walked} {drank}. It denotes an act, state, or condition that occurred or existed at some point in the past {the auction ended yesterday} {we returned the shawl}.

5.118   *Future tense.* The future tense is formed by using *will* with the verb's stem form {will walk} {will drink}. It refers to an expected act, state, or condition {the artist will design a wall mural} {the restaurant will open soon}. *Shall* may be used instead of *will* in the first person {I shall arrive tomorrow} {we shall see}, but in American English *shall* typically appears only in first-person questions {Shall we go?} and in third-person legal commands {the debtor shall pay within thirty days}. In most contexts, *will* is preferred. Incidentally, some linguists are now convinced that English has no future tense at all—that *will* is simply a modal verb that should be treated with all the others (see 5.132).[6] Yet the future tense remains a part of traditional grammar and is discussed here in the familiar way. See also 5.140.

5.119   *Present perfect tense.* The present perfect tense is formed by using *have* or *has* with the principal verb's past participle {have walked} {has drunk}. It denotes an act, state, or condition that is now completed or continues up to the present {I have put away the clothes} {it has been a long day}. The present perfect is distinguished from the past tense because it refers to (1) a time in the indefinite past {I have played golf there before}, or (2) a past action that comes up to and touches the present {I have worked here for eighteen years}. The past tense, by contrast, indicates a more specific or a more remote time in the past.

5.120   *Past perfect tense.* The past perfect (or pluperfect) tense is formed by using *had* with the principal verb's past participle {had walked} {had drunk}. It

---

6. R. L. Trask, *Language: The Basics* (London: Routledge, 1996), 58.

refs to an act, state, or condition that was completed before another specified past time or past action {the engineer had driven the train to the roundhouse before we arrived} {by the time we stopped to check the map, the rain had begun falling}.

5.121 *Future perfect tense.* The future perfect tense is formed by using *will have* with the verb's past participle {will have walked} {will have drunk}. It refers to an act, state, or condition that is expected to be completed before some other future act or time {the entomologist will have collected sixty more specimens before the semester ends} {the court will have adjourned by five o'clock}. *Shall have* can also be used in the first person, but is usually avoided for the reasons discussed in 5.118.

5.122 *Person.* A verb's person reflects whether the act, state, or condition is that of (1) the person speaking (first person, *I* or *we*), (2) the person spoken to (second person, *you*), or (3) the person or thing spoken of (third person, *he, she, it,* or *they*).

5.123 *Number.* The number of a verb must agree with the number of the noun or pronoun used with it. In other words, the verb must be singular or plural. Only the third-person present-indicative singular changes form to indicate number and person {you sketch} {she sketches} {they sketch}. The second-person verb is always plural in form, whether one person or more than one person is spoken to {you are a wonderful person} {you are wonderful people}.

Conjugation of Verbs

5.124 *Seven parts.* Conjugation is the changing (inflecting) of a verb's form to reflect voice, mood, tense, person, and number. A verb has seven conjugated parts: the present indicative, the present participle, the present subjunctive, the past indicative, the past participle, the past subjunctive, and the imperative. Except for the auxiliary verbs, the rules for conjugation are explained in the following sections.

5.125 *Verb stem (present indicative).* The present indicative is the verb stem for all persons, singular and plural, in the present tense—except for the third-person singular, which adds an *s* to the stem {takes} {strolls}. If the verb ends in *o*, an *es* is added {goes} {does}. If the verb ends in *y*, the *y* is changed to *i* and then an *es* is added {identify–identifies} {carry–carries}.

5.126 *Forming present participles.* The present participle is formed by adding *ing* to the stem of the verb {reaping} {wandering}. If the stem ends in *ie*, the *ie* usually changes to *y* before the *ing* is added {die–dying} {tie–tying}. If the stem ends in a silent *e*, that *e* is usually dropped before the *ing* is added {giving} {leaving}. There are two exceptions: the silent *e* is retained when (1) the word ends with *oe* {toe–toeing} {hoe–hoeing} {shoe–shoeing}, and (2) the verb has a participle that would resemble another word but for the distinguishing *e* (e.g., *dyeing* means something different from *dying*, and *singeing* means something different from *singing*). The present participle is the same for all persons and numbers {I am studying} {they are leaving}.

5.127   *Present subjunctive.* Apart from a few set phrases (e.g., *so be it, be they, she need not*), in present-day English the present subjunctive typically appears in the form *if I (he, she, it) were* {if I were king} {if she were any different}. That is, the present subjunctive ordinarily uses a past-tense verb (e.g., *were*) to connote uncertainty or impossibility. Compare *if I am threatened, I will quit* (indicative) with *if I were threatened, I would quit* (subjunctive), or *if the canary sings, I smile* (indicative) with *if the canary sang* (or *should sing*, or *were to sing*), *I would smile* (subjunctive). See also 5.114.

5.128   *Past indicative.* The past indicative is formed by adding *ed* to a regular verb's stem {like–liked} {spill–spilled}. Irregular verbs form the past tense in various ways {give–gave} {stride–strode} {read–read}. A good dictionary will show an irregular verb's past indicative form.

5.129   *Forming past participles.* With regular verbs, the past participle is formed in the same way as the past indicative—that is, the past-indicative and past-participial forms are always identical {stated–stated} {pulled–pulled}. For irregular verbs, the forms are sometimes the same {paid–paid} {sat–sat} and sometimes different {forsook–forsaken} {shrank–shrunk}. A good dictionary will show the past participles.

5.130   *Past subjunctive.* The past subjunctive typically appears in the form *if I (he, she, it) had* {if I had gone} {if he had been there}. That is, the past subjunctive ordinarily uses a past-perfect verb (e.g., *had been*) to connote uncertainty or impossibility. Compare *if it arrived, it was not properly filed* (indicative) with *if it had arrived, it could have changed the course of history* (subjunctive). See also 5.114.

5.131   *Imperative.* The imperative is the verb's stem used to make a command, a request, an exclamation, or the like {Please come here.} {Give me a clue.} {Help!}.

Auxiliary Verbs

5.132   *Definition.* An auxiliary verb (sometimes termed a modal or helping verb) is a highly irregular verb that is used with other verbs to form voice, tense, and mood. The main ones are explained in the following sections. See also 5.103.

5.133   *"Can."* This verb uses only its stem form in the present indicative {I can} {it can} {they can}. In the past indicative, *can* becomes *could* for all persons {he could see better with glasses}. *Can* does not have an infinitive form (*to be able to* is substituted) or a present or past participle. Because it denotes ability or permission, *can* is always followed by an explicit or implicit principal verb {Can you carry the trunk? Yes, I certainly can.}.

5.134   *"Do."* This verb has two forms in the present indicative: *does* for the third-person singular, and *do* for all other persons. In the past indicative, the only form for all persons is *did*. The past participle is *done*. As an auxiliary verb, *do* is used only in the present and past indicative {Did you speak?} {we do plan some charity work}. When denoting performance, *do* can also act as a principal verb {he does well in school} {they do good work}. *Do* can sometimes substitute for a verb, thereby avoiding repetition {Marion dances well, and so do you} {he caught fewer mistakes than you did}.

5.135   *"Have."* This verb has two forms in the present indicative: *has* for the third-person singular, and *have* for all other persons. In the past indicative, the only form for all persons is *had*; the past participle is also *had*. As an auxiliary verb, when the present or past indicative of *have* precedes the past participle of any verb, that verb's present-perfect or past-perfect indicative mood is formed {I have looked everywhere} {he had looked for a better rate}. When denoting possession, *have* can also be a sentence's principal verb {she has a car and a boat} {you have a mosquito on your neck}.

5.136   *"May."* This verb has only its stem form in the present indicative {I may} {it may} {they may}. The past indicative, *might* {he asked if he might bring a friend}, is also used with a present or present-perfect meaning to express greater uncertainty than *may* {we may be delayed} {we might win the lottery} {the jeweler may have forgotten to call} {the jeweler might have given you the wrong diamond}. *May* does not have an infinitive form or a present or past participle. As an auxiliary, *may*, denoting wishfulness or purpose, forms a subjunctive equivalent {may you always be happy} {give so that others may live}.

5.137   *"Must."* This verb does not vary its form in either the present or past indicative. It does not have an infinitive form (*to have to* is substituted) or a present or past participle. Denoting obligation, necessity, or inference, *must* is always used with an express or implied infinitive {we must finish this design} {everyone must eat} {the movie must be over by now}.

5.138 *"Ought."* This verb does not vary its form in either the present or past indicative. It has no infinitive form or present or past participle. Denoting a duty or obligation, *ought* is nearly always used with an infinitive, even in the negative {we ought to invite some friends} {the driver ought not to have ignored the signal}. Although *to* is occasionally omitted after *not* {you ought not worry}, the better usage is to include it {you ought not to worry}. See also 5.105.

5.139 *"Shall."* This verb uses only its stem form in the present indicative. It is a relatively rare word in present-day American English, except in first-person questions (see 5.118) {Shall we dance?} {Shall I fetch you some coffee?}. The past indicative form, *should*, is used for all persons, and always with a principal verb {they should be at home} {Should you read that newspaper?}. *Should* does not have an infinitive form or a present or past participle. *Should* often carries a sense of duty or compulsion {I should review those financial-planning tips} {you should clean the garage today}; sometimes it carries a sense of inference {the package should have been delivered today}.

5.140 *"Will."* This verb uses only its stem form in the present indicative {she will} {they will}. In the past indicative, the only form for all persons is *would* {we would go fishing on Saturdays} {She would say that!}. *Would* sometimes expresses a condition {I would slide down the hill if you lent me your sled}. *Will* often carries a sense of the future (see 5.118) {she will be at her desk tomorrow} or, in the past form *would*, expresses a conditional statement {I would recognize the house if I saw it again}.

The Verb *to Be*

5.141 *Forms.* The verb *to be* has eight forms (*is, are, was, were, been, being, be,* and *am*) and has several special uses. First, it is sometimes a sentence's principal verb meaning "exist" {I think, therefore I am}. Second, it is more often used as an auxiliary verb {I was born in Lubbock}. When joined with a verb's present participle, it denotes continuing or progressive action {the train is coming} {the passenger was waiting}. When joined with a past participle, the verb becomes passive {a signal was given} {an earring was dropped} (see 5.112). Often this type of construction can be advantageously changed to active voice {he gave a signal} {she dropped her earring}. Third, *to be* is the most common linking verb that connects the subject with something affirmed about the subject {truth is beauty} {we are the champions}. Occasionally, a form of *to be* is used as part of an adjective {a would-be hero} or noun {a has-been} {a rock-star wannabe [want to be]}.

5.142 *Conjugation. To be* is conjugated differently from other verbs. (1) The stem is not used in the present-indicative form. Instead, *to be* has three present-tense forms: for the first-person singular, *am*; for the third-person singular, *is*; and for all other persons, *are*. (2) The present participle is formed by adding *ing* to the root *be* {being}. It is the same for all persons, but the present continuous requires also using *am*, *is*, or *are* {I am being} {it is being} {you are being}. (3) The past indicative has two forms: the first- and third-person singular use *was*; all other persons use *were* {she was} {we were}. (4) The past participle for all persons is *been* {I have been} {they have been}. (5) The imperative is the verb's stem {Be yourself!}.

ADVERBS

Definition and Formation

5.143 *Definition.* An adverb is a word that qualifies, limits, describes, or modifies a verb, an adjective, or another adverb {she studied constantly} (*constantly* qualifies the verb *studied*); {the juggler's act was really unusual} (*really* qualifies the adjective *unusual*); {the cyclist pedaled very swiftly} (*very* qualifies the adverb *swiftly*). An adverb may also qualify a preposition, a conjunction, or a clause {the birds flew right over the lake} (*right* qualifies the preposition *over*); {this is exactly where I found it} (*exactly* qualifies the conjunction *where*); {apparently you forgot to check your references} (*apparently* qualifies the rest of the clause). Finally, grammarians have traditionally used the term "adverb" as a catchall to sweep in words that aren't readily put into categories (such as the *to* in an infinitive [see 5.105] and the particle in a phrasal verb [see 5.102]).

5.144 *With suffixes.* Many adjectives have corresponding adverbs distinguished by the suffix *ly* or, after most words ending in *ic*, *ally* {slow–slowly} {careful–carefully} {pedantic–pedantically} but {public–publicly}. But adjectives ending in *le* or *ly* do not make appealing adverbs {juvenile–juvenilely} {silly–sillily}. If an *ly* adverb looks clumsy (e.g., *juvenilely* or *uglily*), either rephrase the sentence or use a phrase (e.g., *in a juvenile manner* or *in an ugly way*).

5.145 *Without suffixes.* Many adverbs do not have an identifying suffix (e.g., *almost, never, here, now, just, seldom, late, near, too*). And not every word ending in *ly* is an adverb—some are adjectives (e.g., *lovely, curly*). A few nouns form adverbs by taking the ending *ways* {side–sideways}, *ward* {sky–skyward}, or *wise* {clock–clockwise}.

5.146 *Distinguished from adjectives.* An adverb is distinguishable from an adjective because an adverb doesn't modify a noun or pronoun {we made an early start and arrived at the airport early} (the first *early* is an adjective modifying the noun *start*; the second is an adverb modifying *arrived*). Some adverbs are identical to prepositions (e.g., *up* or *off*) but are distinguishable because they are not attached to a following noun {he ran up a large bill} {let's cast off}. These prepositional adverbs (sometimes called particles or particle adverbs) are typically parts of phrasal verbs. See 5.102.

Simple versus Compound Adverbs

5.147 *Simple and flat adverbs.* A simple adverb is a single word that qualifies a single part of speech {hardly} {now} {deep}. A flat or bare adverb is one that has an *ly* form but whose adjective form may work equally well or even better, especially when used with an imperative in an informal context {drive slow} {hold on tight} {tell me quick}. Some flat adverbs are always used in their adjective form {work fast} because the *ly* has become obsolete (although it may linger in derived words—e.g., *steadfast* and *steadfastly*). And the flat adverb may have a different meaning from that of the *ly* adverb. Compare *I am working hard* with *I am hardly working.*

5.148 *Phrasal and compound adverbs.* A phrasal adverb consists of two or more words that function together as an adverb {in the meantime} {for a while} {here and there}. A compound adverb appears to be a single word but is a combination of several words {notwithstanding} {heretofore} {thereupon}. Compound adverbs should be used cautiously and sparingly because they make the tone stuffy.

Adverbial Degrees

5.149 *Three degrees.* Like adjectives (see 5.85), adverbs have three degrees: the positive, the comparative, and the superlative. A positive adverb simply expresses a quality without reference to any other thing {the nurse spoke softly} {the choir sang merrily}.

5.150 *Comparative forms.* Most one-syllable adverbs that do not end in *ly* form the comparative by taking the suffix *er* {sooner} {harder}. Multisyllable adverbs usually form the comparative with *more* or *less* {the Shakespearean villain fenced more ineptly than the hero} {the patient is walking less painfully today}. A comparative adverb compares the quality of a specified action or condition shared by two things {Bitey worked longer than Arachne} {Rachel studied more industriously than Edith}.

5.151 *Superlative forms.* Most one-syllable adverbs that do not end in *ly* form the superlative by taking the suffix *est* {soonest} {hardest}. Multisyllable adverbs usually form the superlative with *most* or *least* {everyone's eyesight was acute, but I could see most acutely} {of all the people making choices, he chose least wisely}. A superlative adverb compares the quality of a specified action or condition shared by at least three things {Sullie bowled fastest of all the cricketers} {of the three doctoral candidates, Rebecca defended her dissertation the most adamantly}. In a loose sense, the superlative is sometimes used for emphasis rather than comparison {the pianist played most skillfully}.

5.152 *Irregular adverbs.* A few adverbs have irregular comparative and superlative forms {badly–worse–worst} {little–less–least}. A good dictionary is the best resource for finding an irregular adverb's forms of comparison.

5.153 *Uncomparable adverbs.* Many adverbs are uncomparable. Some, by their definitions, are absolute and cannot be compared {eternally} {never} {singly} {uniquely} {universally}. Most adverbs indicating time {now} {then}, position {on}, number {first} {finally}, or place {here} are also uncomparable.

5.154 *Intensifiers.* An adverb can be intensified with words such as *very* and *quite* {the very fashionably dressed actor} {everyone ate quite heartily}.

Position of Adverbs

5.155 *Placement as affecting meaning.* To avoid miscues, the adverb should generally be placed as near as possible to the word it is intended to modify. For example, in *the marathoners submitted their applications to compete immediately,* what does *immediately* modify—*compete* or *submitted*? Placing the adverb with the word it modifies makes the meaning clear {*the marathoners immediately submitted their applications to compete*}. A misplaced adverb can completely change a sentence's meaning. For example, *we nearly lost all our camping equipment* states that the equipment was saved; *we lost nearly all our camping equipment* states that almost everything was lost.

5.156 *Modifying words other than verbs.* If the adverb qualifies an adjective, an adverb, a preposition, or a conjunction, it should immediately precede the word or phrase qualified {our vacation was very short} {the flight took too long} {your fence is partly over the property line} {leave only when the bell rings}.

5.157 *Modifying intransitive verbs.* If the adverb qualifies an intransitive verb, it should immediately follow the verb {the students sighed gloomily when homework was assigned} {the owl perched precariously on a thin branch}. Some exceptions are *always, never, often, generally, rarely,* and *seldom,* which may precede the verb {mountaineers seldom succeed in climbing K2}.

5.158 *Adverbs and linking verbs.* Adverbs do not generally follow linking verbs (see 5.101) such as *be, appear, seem, become, look, smell, taste, hear,* and *feel.* A verb of this kind connects a descriptive word with the clause's subject; the descriptive word applies to the subject, not the verb {he seems modest}. To determine whether a verb is a linking verb, consider whether the descriptive word describes the action or condition rather than the subject. For example, *the sculptor feels badly* literally describes the act of feeling or touching as not done well. But *the sculptor feels bad* describes the sculptor as unwell or perhaps experiencing guilt.

5.159 *Adverbs with past-participial adjectives.* If a past participle is used to describe something, use a single adverb as a modifier {a very distinguished speaker} {too tired to continue} {badly beaten challenger}. If the past participle is part of the predicate and expresses deep feeling or emotion or strong force, then use a phrase as a modifier {too densely packed to remove} {very much distressed by the failure}. See 5.89.

5.160 *Adverb within verb phrase.* When an adverb qualifies a verb phrase, the natural place for the adverb is between the auxiliary verb and the principal verb {the administration has consistently repudiated this view} {the reports will soon generate controversy} {public opinion is sharply divided}. See 5.104. Some adverbs may follow the principal verb {you must go quietly} {Are you asking rhetorically?}. There is no rule against adverbial modifiers between the parts of a verb phrase. In fact, it's typically preferable to put them there {the heckler was abruptly expelled} {the bus had been seriously damaged in the crash}. And sometimes it is perfectly appropriate to split an infinitive verb with an adverb to add emphasis or to produce a natural sound. See 5.106. A verb's infinitive or *to* form is split when an intervening word immediately follows *to* {to bravely assert}. If the adverb bears the emphasis in a phrase {to boldly go} {to strongly favor}, then leave the split infinitive alone. But if moving the adverb to the end of the phrase doesn't suggest a different meaning or impair the sound, then it is an acceptable way to avoid splitting the verb. Recasting a sentence just to eliminate a split infinitive or avoid splitting the infinitive can alter the nuance or meaning: for example, *it's best to always get up early* (*always* modifies *get up*) is not quite the same as *it's always best to get up early* (*always* modifies *best*). Or an unnatural phrasing can result: *it's best to get up early always.*

5.161   *Importance of placement.* An adverb's placement is also important because adverbs show time {we'll meet again}, place or source {put the flowers here} {Where did you get that idea?}, manner {speak softly}, degree or extent {sales are very good} {How far is it to the pub?}, reason {I don't know how Patricia found the right answer}, consequence {I want to be on time so we can get good seats}, and number {fool me twice, shame on me}.

PREPOSITIONS

Definition and Types

5.162   *Definition.* A preposition is a word or phrase that links an object (a noun or noun equivalent) to another word in the sentence to show the relationship between them. A preposition's object is usually a noun or pronoun in the objective case {between me and them}, but an adjective, adverb, verb, or phrase may follow instead. Usually a preposition comes before its object, but there are exceptions. For example, the preposition can end a clause, especially a relative clause, or sentence {this isn't the pen that Steve writes with}. And a preposition used with the relative pronoun *that* (or with *that* understood) always follows the object {this is the moment [that] I've been waiting for}. It also frequently, but not always, follows the pronouns *which* {Which alternative is your decision based on?} {this is the alternative on which my decision is based} and *whom* {there is a banker [whom] I must speak with} {I can't tell you to whom you should apply}.

5.163   *Simple and compound.* Many prepositions are relatively straightforward. A simple preposition consists of a single monosyllabic word such as *as, at, by, down, for, from, in, like, of, off, on,* plus *since, through, to, toward, up,* or *with.* A compound preposition has two or more syllables; it may be made up of two or more words {into} {outside} {upon}. Some examples are *about, above, across, after, against, alongside, around, before, below, beneath, between, despite, except, inside, onto, opposite, throughout, underneath, until,* and *without.*

5.164   *Participial prepositions.* A participial preposition is a participial form that functions as a preposition (or sometimes as a subordinating conjunction). Examples include *assuming, barring, concerning, considering, during, notwithstanding, owing to, provided, regarding, respecting,* and *speaking.* Unlike other participles, these words do not create dangling modifiers when they have no subject {Considering the road conditions, the trip went quickly} {Regarding Watergate, he had nothing to say}. See 5.84.

5.165   *Phrasal prepositions.* A phrasal preposition consists of two or more separate words used as a prepositional unit. These include *according to, because of, by means of, by reason of, by way of, contrary to, for the sake of, in accordance with, in addition to, in case of, in consideration of, in front of, in regard to, in respect to, in spite of, instead of, on account of, out of, with reference to, with regard to,* and *with respect to.* Many of these phrasal prepositions are symptoms of officialese, bureaucratese, or other verbose styles. If a simple preposition will do in context, use it. For example, if *about* will replace *with regard to* or *in connection with,* prefer the simpler expression.

Prepositional Phrases

5.166   *Definition.* A prepositional phrase consists of a preposition, its object, and any words that modify the object. A prepositional phrase can be used as a noun {for James to change his mind would be a miracle}, an adverb (in which case it is also called an adverbial phrase) {we strolled through the glade}, or an adjective (also called an adjectival phrase) {the cathedrals of Paris}.

5.167   *Placement.* A prepositional phrase with an adverbial or adjectival function should be as close as possible to the word it modifies to avoid awkwardness, ambiguity, or unintended meanings {Is a person with blond hair named Sandy here?}.

5.168   *Refinements on placement.* If a prepositional phrase equally modifies all the elements of a compound construction, the phrase follows the last element in the compound {the date, the place, and the budget for the wedding have been decided}. If the subject is singular and followed by a plural prepositional phrase, the predicate is singular: compare the predicate in *the man and two daughters have arrived* with that in *the man with two daughters has arrived* and in *the man has arrived with his two daughters.*

5.169   *Ending a sentence with a preposition.* The traditional caveat of yesteryear against ending sentences with prepositions is, for most writers, an unnecessary and pedantic restriction. As Winston Churchill famously said, "That is the type of arrant pedantry up with which I shall not put." A sentence that ends in a preposition may sound more natural than a sentence carefully constructed to avoid a final preposition. Compare *Those are the guidelines an author should adhere to* with *Those are the guidelines to which an author should adhere*. The "rule" prohibiting terminal prepositions was an ill-founded superstition.

5.170 *Clashing prepositions.* If a phrasal verb {give in} precedes a prepositional phrase {in every argument}, the back-to-back prepositions will clash {he gives in in every argument}. Recast the sentence when possible to avoid juxtaposed prepositions: *rather than continue arguing, he always gives in;* or *in every argument, he gives in.* For more on phrasal verbs, see 5.102.

5.171 *Elliptical phrases.* Sometimes a prepositional phrase is elliptical, being an independent expression without an antecedent. It often starts a clause and can usually be detached from the statement without affecting the meaning. Elliptical prepositional phrases include *for example, for instance, in any event, in a word, in the last analysis,* and *in the long run* {in any event, call me when you arrive}.

Other Prepositional Issues

5.172 *Functional variation.* Some words that function as prepositions may also function as other parts of speech. The distinguishing feature of a preposition is that it always has an object. A word such as *above, behind, below, by, down, in, off, on,* or *up* can be used as either an adverb or a preposition. When used as a preposition, it takes an object {let's slide down the hill}. When used as an adverb, it does not {we sat down}. Some conjunctions may serve as prepositions (e.g., *than* and *but*). The conjunction joins a clause containing an explicit or implied separate action. Compare the prepositional *but* in *everyone but Fuzzy traveled abroad last summer* (*but* is used to mean "except") with the conjunctive *but* in *I like the cut but not the color* (*but* joins a clause containing an implied separate action: *I don't like the color*).

5.173 *Use and misuse of "like."* *Like* is probably the least-understood preposition. Its traditional function is adjectival, not adverbial, so that *like* governs nouns and noun phrases {teens often see themselves as star-crossed lovers like Romeo and Juliet}. As a preposition, *like* is followed by a noun or pronoun in the objective case {the person in that old portrait looks like me}. Increasingly (but loosely) today in ordinary speech, *like* displaces *as* or *as if* as a conjunction to connect clauses. For example, in *it happened just like I said it would happen, like* should read *as;* and in *you're looking around like you've misplaced something, like* should read *as if.* Because they are conjunctions, *as* and *as if* are followed by nouns or pronouns in the nominative case {Do you work too hard, as I do?}.

Limiting Prepositional Phrases

5.174 *Avoiding overuse.* Prepositions can easily be overused. Stylistically, a good ratio to strive for is one preposition for every ten to fifteen words. Five editorial methods can reduce the number of prepositions in a sentence.

5.175 *Cutting prepositional phrases.* If the surrounding prose permits, a prepositional phrase can be eliminated. For example, *the most important ingredient in this recipe* could be reduced to *the most important ingredient* when it appears within a passage focused on a particular recipe.

5.176 *Cutting unnecessary prepositions.* A noun ending in *ance, ence, ity, ment, sion,* or *tion* is often formed from a verb {qualification–qualify} {performance–perform}. These nouns are sometimes called "nominalizations" or "buried verbs," and they often require additional words, especially prepositions. *During her performance of the concerto* is essentially equivalent to *while she performed the concerto.* Using the verb form often eliminates more than one preposition. For example, *toward maximization of* becomes simply *to maximize,* so that *our efforts toward maximization of profits failed* might be edited down to *our efforts to maximize profits failed.*

5.177 *Replacing with adverbs.* A strong adverb can often replace a weak prepositional phrase. For example, *the cyclist pedaled with fury* is weak compared with *the cyclist pedaled furiously.*

5.178 *Replacing with possessives.* A possessive may replace a prepositional phrase, especially an *of*-phrase. For example, *I was dismayed by the complexity of the street map* essentially equals *The street map's complexity dismayed me.* See 5.25.

5.179 *Using active voice.* Changing from passive voice to active almost always eliminates a preposition—that is, whenever the actor appears in a *by*-phrase. For example, *the ship was sailed by an experienced crew* equals *an experienced crew sailed the ship.*

CONJUNCTIONS

5.180 *Definition and types.* A conjunction connects sentences, clauses, or words within a clause {my daughter graduated from college in December, and my son will graduate from high school in May} (*and* connects two independent clauses); {I said hello, but no one answered} (*but* connects two independent clauses); {we're making progress slowly but surely} (*but* joins two adverbs within an adverbial clause). The two main classes of conjunctions are coordinate and subordinate. Some words that are typically considered adverbs also serve as conjunctions; among these are *nevertheless* (see 5.184), *otherwise* (see 5.185), and *consequently* (see 5.186). See also 6.19–20, 6.32–34, 6.36–37, 6.58–59.

5.181 *Coordinating conjunctions.* Coordinating conjunctions join words or groups of words of equal grammatical rank, that is, independent elements such as two nouns, two verbs, two phrases, or two clauses {Are you speaking to him or to me?} {the results are disappointing but not discouraging}. A coordinating conjunction may be either a single word or a correlative conjunction.

5.182 *Correlative conjunctions.* Correlative conjunctions are used in pairs, often to join successive clauses that depend on each other to form a complete thought. Correlative conjunctions must frame structurally identical or matching sentence parts {an attempt both to win the gold medal and to set a new record}; in other words, each member of the pair should immediately precede the same part of speech {they not only read the book but also saw the movie} {if the first claim is true, then the second claim must be false}. Some examples of correlative conjunctions are *as–as, if–then, either–or, neither–nor, both–and, where–there, so–as,* and *not only–but also.*

5.183 *Copulative conjunctions.* Copulative (or additive) coordinating conjunctions denote addition. The second clause states an additional fact that is related to the first clause. The conjunctions include *and, also, moreover,* and *no less than* {one associate received a raise, and the other was promoted} {the jockeys' postrace party was no less exciting than the race itself}.

5.184 *Adversative conjunctions.* Adversative or contrasting coordinating conjunctions denote contrasts or comparisons. The second clause usually qualifies the first clause in some way. The conjunctions include *but, still, yet,* and *nevertheless* {the message is sad but inspiring} {she's earned her doctorate, yet she's still not satisfied with herself}.

5.185 *Disjunctive conjunctions.* Disjunctive or separative coordinating conjunctions denote separation or alternatives. Only one of the statements joined by the conjunction may be true; with some conjunctions, both may be false. The conjunctions include *either, or, else, but, nor, neither, otherwise,* and *other* {that bird is neither a heron nor a crane} {you can wear the blue coat or the green one}.

5.186 *Final conjunctions.* Final (or illative) coordinating conjunctions denote inferences or consequences. The second clause gives a reason for the first clause's statement, or it shows what has been or ought to be done in view of the first clause's expression. The conjunctions include *consequently, for, hence, so, thus, therefore, as a consequence, as a result, so that,* and *so then* {he had betrayed the king; therefore he was banished} {it's time to leave, so let's go}.

5.187 *Subordinating conjunctions.* A subordinating conjunction connects clauses of unequal grammatical rank. The conjunction introduces a clause that is dependent on the main clause {follow this road until you reach the highway} {that squirrel is friendly because people feed it} {Marcus promised that he would help}. A pure subordinating conjunction has no antecedent and is not a pronoun or an adverb {take a message if someone calls}.

5.188 *Special uses of subordinating conjunctions.* Subordinating conjunctions or conjunctive phrases often denote the following relationships: (1) Comparison or degree: *than* (if it follows comparative adverbs or adjectives, or if it follows *else, rather, other,* or *otherwise*), *as, else, otherwise, rather, as much as, as far as,* and *as well as* {Is a raven less clever than a magpie?} {these amateur musicians play as well as professionals} {it's not true as far as I can discover}. (2) Time: *since, until, as long as, before, after, when, as,* and *while* {while we waited, it began to snow} {the tire went flat as we were turning the corner} {we'll start the game as soon as everyone understands the rules} {the audience returned to the auditorium after the concert's resumption was announced}. (3) Condition or assumption: *if, though, unless, except, without,* and *once* {once we agree on a design, we can begin remodeling the house} {your thesis must be presented next week unless you have a good reason to postpone it} {I'll go on this business trip if I can fly first class}. (4) Reason or concession: *as, inasmuch as, why, because, for, since, though, although,* and *albeit* {since you won't share the information, I can't help you} {Sir John decided to purchase the painting although it was very expensive} {she deserves credit because it was her idea}. (5) Purpose or result: *that, so that, in order that,* and *such that* {we dug up the yard so that a new water garden could be laid out} {he sang so loudly that he became hoarse}. (6) Place: *where* {I found a great restaurant where I didn't expect one to be}. (7) Manner: *as if* and *as though* {he swaggers around the office as if he were an executive}. (8) Appositions: *and, or, what,* and *that* {the buffalo, or American bison, was once nearly extinct} {we received a message that everything went well} {the supervisor explained what had gone wrong}. (9) Indirect questions: *whether, why,* and *when* {he could not say whether we were going the right way}. See also 6.36.

5.189 *Relative pronouns and interrogative adverbs as conjunctions.* In addition to its pronoun function, a relative pronoun serves a conjunctive function. So do interrogative adverbs. In fact, relative pronouns and interrogative adverbs may be treated as a special class of subordinating conjunctions when they join sentences. A relative conjunction has an antecedent in the main clause {bring me the suitcase that is upstairs} (*that* refers to *suitcase*). A relative adverbial conjunction does the same job as an adverbial conjunction, but the conjunction has an antecedent {Do you recall the place where we first met?} (*where* has the antecedent *place* and also modifies *met*). Some common examples of conjunctive relative adverbs are *after, as, before, until, as, now, since, so, when,* and *where.* Interrogative adverbs are used to ask direct and indirect questions; the most common are *why, how, when, where,* and *what* {Barbara asked when we were supposed to leave} {I don't see how you reached that conclusion}.

5.190 *"With" used loosely as a conjunction.* The word *with* is sometimes used as a quasi-conjunction meaning *and.* This construction is slovenly because the *with*-clause appears to be tacked on as an afterthought. For example, the sentence *everyone else grabbed the easy jobs with me being left to scrub the oven* could be revised as *since everyone else grabbed the easy jobs, I had to scrub the oven.* Or it could be split into two sentences joined by a semicolon: *Everyone else grabbed the easy jobs; I had to scrub the oven.* Instead of *with,* find the connecting word, phrase, or punctuation that best shows the relationship between the final thought and the first, and then recast the sentence.

5.191 *Beginning a sentence with a conjunction.* There is a widespread belief—one with no historical or grammatical foundation—that it is an error to begin a sentence with a conjunction such as *and, but,* or *so.* In fact, a substantial percentage (often as many as 10 percent) of the sentences in first-rate writing begin with conjunctions. It has been so for centuries, and even the most conservative grammarians have followed this practice. Charles Allen Lloyd's 1938 words fairly sum up the situation as it stands even today: "Next to the groundless notion that it is incorrect to end an English sentence with a preposition, perhaps the most wide-spread of the many false beliefs about the use of our language is the equally groundless notion that it is incorrect to begin one with 'but' or 'and.' As in the case of the superstition about the prepositional ending, no textbook supports it, but apparently about half of our teachers of English go out of their way to handicap their pupils by inculcating it. One cannot help wondering whether those who teach such a monstrous doctrine ever read any English themselves."[7] Still, *but* as an adversative conjunction can occasionally be unclear at the beginning of a sentence. Evaluate the contrasting force of the *but* in question and see whether the needed word is really *and*; if *and* can be substituted, then *but* is almost certainly the wrong word. Consider this example: *He went to school this morning. But he left his lunchbox on the kitchen table.* Between those sentences is an elliptical idea, since the two actions are in no way contradictory. What is implied is something like this: *He went to school, intending to have lunch there, but he left his lunch behind.* Because *and* would have made sense in the passage as originally stated, *but* is not the right word. To sum up, then, *but* is a perfectly proper way to open a sentence, but only if the idea it introduces truly contrasts with what precedes. For that matter, *but* is often an effective way of introducing a paragraph that develops an idea contrary to the one preceding it.

INTERJECTIONS

5.192 *Definition.* An interjection or exclamation is a word, phrase, or clause that denotes strong feeling {Never again!} {You don't say!}. An interjection has little or no grammatical function in a sentence; it is used absolutely {really, I can't understand why you put up with the situation} {Oh no, how am I going to fix the damage?} {Hey, it's my turn next!}. It is frequently allowed to stand as a sentence by itself {Oh! I've lost my wallet!} {Ouch! I think my ankle is sprained!} {Get out!} {Whoa!}. Introductory words such as *well* and *why* may also act as interjections when they are meaningless utterances {well, I tried my best} {why, I would never do that}. The punctuation offsetting the interjections (see 6.29) distinguishes them. Compare the different meanings of *Well, I didn't know him* with *I didn't know him well* and *Why, here you are!* with *I have no idea why you are here* and *Why? I have no idea.*

5.193 *Usage.* Interjections are natural in speech {your order should be shipped, oh, in eight to ten days} and are frequently used in poetry and dialogue. They may also imply irony or a range of emotions, from humor to disappointment {because our business case was, ahem, poorly presented, our budget will not be increased this year}.

---

7. Charles Allen Lloyd, *We Who Speak English: And Our Ignorance of Our Mother Tongue* (New York: Thomas Y. Crowell, 1938), 19.

5.194   *Functional variation.* Because interjections are usually grammatically independent of the rest of the sentence, most parts of speech may be used as interjections. A word that is classified as some other part of speech but used with the force of an interjection is called an exclamatory noun, exclamatory adjective, and so forth. Some examples are *Good!* (adjective); *Idiot!* (noun); *Help!* (verb); *Indeed!* (adverb); *Dear me!* (pronoun); *If only!* (conjunction).

5.195   *Words that are exclusively interjections.* Some interjections are used only as such. Words such as *ouch, whew, ugh, psst,* and *oops* are not used as any other parts of speech (except when referred to as words, as here, and therefore functioning as nouns).

5.196   *Punctuating interjections.* An exclamation mark usually follows an interjection {Oh no!} or the point where the strong feeling ends {Oh no, I've forgotten the assignment!}. A comma follows *oh* only when a natural pause occurs {Oh yes!} {Oh, my new books!}

5.197   *"Oh" and "O."* The interjection *oh* takes the place of other interjections to express an emotion such as pain {Ow!}, surprise {What!}, wonder {Strange!}, or aversion {Ugh!}. It is lowercase if it doesn't start the sentence, and it is typically followed by a comma {Oh, why did I have to ask?} {The scenery is so beautiful, but, oh, I can't describe it!}. The vocative *O,* a form of classically stylized direct address, is always capitalized and is typically unpunctuated {O Jerusalem!}. It most often appears in poetry. See 7.47.

Word Usage

INTRODUCTION

5.198   *Grammar versus usage.* The great mass of linguistic issues that writers and editors wrestle with don't really concern grammar at all—they concern usage: the collective habits of a language's native speakers. It is an arbitrary fact, but ultimately an important one, that *corollary* means one thing and *correlation* something else. And it seems to be an irresistible law of language that two words so similar in sound will inevitably be confounded by otherwise literate users of language. Some confusions, such as the one just cited, are relatively new. Others, such as *lay* versus *lie* and *infer* versus *imply,* are much older.

5.199   *Standard Written English.* In any age, careful users of language will make distinctions; careless users will blur them. We can tell, by the words someone uses and the way they go together, something about the education and background of that person. We know whether people speak educated English and write what is commonly referred to as Standard Written English.

5.200   *Dialect.* Of course, some writers and speakers prefer to use dialect, and they use it to good effect. Will Rogers is a good example. He had power as a speaker of dialect, as when he said: "Liberty don't work near as good in practice as it does in speeches." And fiction writers often use dialect in dialogue. They may even decide to put the speaker's voice in dialect.

5.201   *Focus on tradition.* In the short space of this chapter, only the basics of Standard Written English can be covered. Because no language stands still—because the standards of good usage change, however slowly—no guide could ever satisfy all professional editors. What is intended here is a guide that steers writers and editors toward the unimpeachable uses of language—hence it takes a fairly traditional view of usage. For the writer or editor of most prose intended for a general audience, the goal is to stay within the mainstream of literate language as it stands today.

GLOSSARY OF TROUBLESOME EXPRESSIONS

5.202   *Good usage versus common usage.* Although this book recommends *Merriam-Webster's Collegiate Dictionary* (see bibliog. 3.1), one must use care and judgment in consulting *any* dictionary. The mere presence of a word in the dictionary's pages does not mean that the word is in all respects fit for print. The dictionary merely describes how speakers of English use the language; despite occasional usage notes, lexicographers generally disclaim any intent to guide writers and editors on the thorny points of English usage—apart from collecting evidence of what others do. So *infer* is recorded as meaning, in one of its senses, *imply*; *irregardless* may mean *regardless*; *restauranteur* may mean *restaurateur*, and on and on. That is why, in the publishing world, it is generally necessary to consult a usage guide in addition to a dictionary. The standards of good usage make demands on writers and editors, whereas common usage can excuse any number of slipshod expressions. Even so, good usage should make reasonable demands—not set outlandishly high standards. The following glossary sets out the reasonable demands of good usage as it stands today. It focuses on how the terms are commonly misused and is not intended as an exhaustive list of the terms' definitions and uses.

a; an. Use the indefinite article *a* before any word beginning with a consonant sound {a utopian dream}. Use *an* before any word beginning with a vowel sound {an officer} {an honorary degree}. The word *historical* and its variations cause missteps, but since the *h* in these words is pronounced, it takes an *a* {an hourlong talk at a historical society}. Likewise, an initialism (whose letters are sounded out individually) may be paired with one article, while an acronym (which is pronounced as a word) beginning with the same letter is paired with the other {an HTML document describing a HUD program}. See 5.73.

ability; capability; capacity. *Ability* refers to a person's physical or mental skill or power to achieve something {the ability to ride a bicycle}. *Capability* refers more generally to power or ability {she has the capability to play soccer professionally} or to the quality of being able to use or be used in a certain way {a jet with long-distance-flight capability}. *Capacity* refers especially to a vessel's ability to hold or contain something {a high-capacity fuel tank}. Used figuratively, *capacity* refers to a person's physical or mental power to learn {an astounding capacity for mathematics}.

abjure; adjure. To *abjure* is to deny or renounce under oath {the defendant abjured the charge of murder} or to declare one's permanent abandonment of a place {abjure the realm}. To *adjure* is to require someone to do something as if under oath {I adjure you to keep this secret} or to urge earnestly {the executive committee adjured all the members to approve the plan}.

about; approximately. When idiomatically possible, use the adverb *about* instead of *approximately*. In the sciences, however, *approximately* is preferred {approximately thirty coding-sequence differences were identified}. Avoid coupling either word with another word of approximation, such as *guess* or *estimate*.

abstruse. See **obtuse.**

accord; accordance. The first word means "agreement" {we are in accord on the treaty's meaning}; the second word means "conformity" {the book was printed in accordance with modern industry standards}.

accuse; charge. A person is *accused of* or *charged with* a misdeed. *Accused* is less formal than *charged* (which suggests official action). Compare *Jill accused Jack of eating her chocolate bar* with *Maynard was charged with theft.*

actual fact, in. Redundant. Try *actually* instead, or simply omit.

addicted; dependent. One is physically *addicted* to something, but psychologically *dependent* on something. Still, to avoid the harsh connotations of *addiction,* we say that victims of diseases are physically *dependent* on medications, some of them habit-forming, that they must routinely take.

adduce; deduce; induce. To *adduce* is to give as a reason, offer as a proof, or cite as an example {as evidence of reliability, she adduced her four years of steady volunteer work as a nurse's aide}. *Deduce* and *induce* are opposite processes. To *deduce* is to reason from general principles to specific conclusions, or to draw a specific conclusion from general bases {from these clues, one deduces that the butler did it}. To *induce* is to form a general principle based on specific observations {after years of studying ravens, the researchers induced a few of their social habits}.

adequate; sufficient; enough. *Adequate* refers to the suitability of something in a particular circumstance {an adequate explanation}. *Sufficient* refers to an amount of material (always with a mass noun) {sufficient water} {sufficient information}. *Enough* modifies both count nouns {enough people} and mass nouns {enough oil}.

adherence; adhesion. With a few exceptions, the first term is figurative, the second literal. Your *adherence* to the transportation code requires the *adhesion* of an inspection sticker to your windshield.

adjure. See **abjure.**

admission; admittance. *Admission* is figurative, suggesting particularly the rights and privileges granted upon entry {the student won admission to a first-rate university}. *Admittance* is purely physical {no admittance beyond this point}.

adverse; averse. *Adverse* means either "strongly opposed" or "unfortunate" and typically refers to things (not people) {adverse relations between nations} {an adverse wind blew the ship off course}. *Averse* means "feeling negatively about" and refers to people {averse to asking for directions}.

affect; effect. *Affect,* almost always a verb, means "to influence, have an effect on" {the adverse publicity affected the election}. (The noun *affect* has a specialized meaning in psychology: an emotion or mood. Consult your dictionary.) *Effect,* usually a noun, means "an outcome, result" {the candidate's attempted explanations had no effect}. But it may also be a verb meaning "to make happen, produce" {the goal had been to effect a major change in campus politics}.

affirmative, in the; in the negative. These are slightly pompous ways of saying *yes* and *no.* They result in part because people are unsure how to punctuate *yes* and *no.* The ordinary way is this: *he said yes* (without quotation marks about *yes,* and without a capital); *she said no* (ditto).

afflict. See **inflict.**

affront. See **effrontery.**

after having (plus past participle). Though common, this phrasing is redundant. Try instead *after* (plus present participle): change *after having passed the audition, she . . .* to *after passing the audition, she . . . ;* or, *having passed the audition, she. . . .* See 5.108.

afterward, adv.; **afterword,** n. The first means "later"; the second means "an epilogue." On *afterward(s),* see **toward.**

aged (four) years old. Redundant. Write *aged four years, four years old,* or *four years of age.*

aggravate. Traditionally, *aggravate* means "to intensify (something bad)" {aggravate an injury} {an aggravated crime}. If the sense is "to bother," use *annoy* or *irritate*.

alibi. Avoid this as a synonym for *excuse*. The traditional sense is "the defense of having been elsewhere when a crime was committed."

all (of). Delete the *of* whenever possible {all the houses} {all my children}. The only common exceptions occur when *all of* precedes a nonpossessive pronoun {all of us} and when it precedes a possessive noun {all of North Carolina's players}.

all ready. See **already.**

all right. Two words. Avoid *alright.*

all together. See **altogether.**

allude; elude; illude. To *allude* is to refer to something indirectly {allude to a problem}. It is often loosely used where *refer* or *quote* would be better— that is, where there is a direct mention or quotation. To *elude* is to avoid capture {elude the hunters}. To *illude* (quite rare) is to deceive {your imagination might illude you}.

allusion; reference. An *allusion* is an indirect or casual mention or suggestion of something {the cockroach in this story is an allusion to Kafka}. A *reference* is a direct or formal mention {the references in this scholarly article have been meticulously documented}.

alongside. This term, meaning "at the side of," should not be followed by *of.*

a lot. Two words, not one.

already; all ready. The first refers to time {the movie has already started}; the second refers to people's preparation {Are the actors all ready?}.

alright. See **all right.**

altar, n.; **alter,** vb. An *altar* is a table or similar object used for sacramental purposes. To *alter* is to change.

alternate, adj. & n.; **alternative,** adj. & n. *Alternate* implies (1) substituting for another {we took the alternate route} or (2) taking turns with another {her alternate chaired the meeting}. *Alternative* implies a choice between two or more things {I prefer the second alternative}.

altogether; all together. *Altogether* means "wholly" or "entirely" {that story is altogether false}. *All together* refers to a unity of time or place {we were all together at Thanksgiving}.

ambiguous; ambivalent. Language that has more than one reasonable meaning is *ambiguous* {the question is ambiguous}. Views that express contradictory ideas or mixed feelings are *ambivalent* {Bjay expressed an ambivalent opinion about the value of vitamin G} {Nancy's reaction to the news was ambivalent}.

amend; emend. The first is the general term, meaning "to change or add to" {the city amended its charter to abolish at-large council districts}. The second means "to correct (text, etc.)" {for the second printing, the author emended several typos that had reached print in the first}. The noun corresponding to *amend* is *amendment*; the one corresponding to *emend* is *emendation*.

amiable; amicable. Both mean "friendly," but *amiable* refers to people {an amiable waiter} and *amicable* to relationships {an amicable divorce}.

amid. See **between.**

among. See **between.**

amount; number. *Amount* is used with mass nouns {a decrease in the amount of pollution}, *number* with count nouns {a growing number of dissidents}.

an. See **a.**

and. Popular belief to the contrary, this conjunction usefully begins sentences, typically outperforming *moreover, additionally, in addition, further*, and *furthermore*. See 5.191.

and/or. This Janus-faced term can often be replaced by *and* or *or* with no loss in meaning. Where it seems needed {take a sleeping pill and/or a warm drink}, try *or . . . or both* {take a sleeping pill or a warm drink or both}, or think of other possibilities {take a sleeping pill with a warm drink}.[8] Only in nonliterary contexts where it unambiguously means *or . . . or both* and where elegance must give way to economy should a writer resort to *and/or.*

anticipate. Avoid this word as a loose synonym for *expect*. Strictly, it means "to foresee, take care of in advance, or forestall."

anxious. Avoid it as a synonym for *eager*. The standard sense is "worried, distressed."

anyone; any one. The one-word *anyone* is a singular indefinite pronoun {anyone would know that}. The two-word phrase *any one* is a more emphatic form of *any*, referring to a single person or thing in a group {Do you recognize any one of those boys?} {I don't know any one of those stories}.

any place. See **anywhere.**

anywhere; any place. The first is preferred for an indefinite location {my keys could be anywhere}. But *any place* (two words) is narrower when you mean "any location" {they couldn't find any place to sit down and rest}. Avoid the one-word *anyplace.*

appertain. See **pertain.**

appraise; apprise. To *appraise* is to put a value on something {the jeweler appraised the necklace}. To *apprise* is to inform or notify someone {keep me apprised of any developments}.

appreciate. Three senses: (1) to understand fully; (2) to increase in value;

---

8. See Bryan A. Garner, *Legal Writing in Plain English* (Chicago: University of Chicago Press, 2001), 112–13.

(3) to be grateful for (something). Sense 3 often results in verbose constructions; instead of *I would appreciate it if you would let me know*, use *I would appreciate your letting me know* or, more simply, *please let me know*.

apprise. See **appraise.**

approve; endorse. *Approve* implies positive thought or a positive attitude rather than action apart from consent. *Endorse* implies both a positive attitude and active support.

approve (of). *Approve* alone connotes official sanction {the finance committee approved the proposed budget}. *Approve of* suggests favor {she approved of her sister's new hairstyle}.

approximately. See **about.**

apt; likely. Both mean "fit, suitable," but *apt* is used for general tendencies or habits {the quarterback is apt to drop the football}. *Likely* expresses probability {because he didn't study, it's likely that he'll do poorly on the exam}. Although *likely* is traditional as a synonym of *probable*, many writers and editors object to its use as a synonym of *probably*.

area. Often a nearly meaningless filler word, as in *the area of partnering skills*. Try deleting *the area of*. In the sciences, however, its more literal meaning is often important.

as far as. Almost always wordy. Avoid the nonstandard phrasing that uses *as far as* in place of *as for*—that is, using *as far as* without the completing verb *is concerned* or *goes*. Compare *as far as change is concerned, it's welcome* with *as for change, it's welcome*.

as is. In reference to an acquisition, *as is* is framed in quotation marks and refers to the acceptance of something without guarantees or representations of quality {purchased "as is"}. The phrase *on an "as is" basis* is verbose.

as of yet. See **as yet.**

as per. This phrase, though common in the commercial world, has long been considered nonstandard. Instead of *as per your request*, write *as you requested* or (less good) *per your request*.

assault; battery. These are popularly given the same meaning. But in traditional common law, *assault* refers to a threat that causes someone to reasonably fear physical violence, and *battery* refers to a violent or repugnant intentional physical contact with another person. Assault doesn't involve touching; battery does.

assemblage; assembly. An *assemblage* is an informal collection of people or things. An *assembly* is a group of people organized for a purpose.

assent; consent. The meanings are similar, but *assent* connotes enthusiasm; *consent* connotes mere allowance.

as such. This pronominal phrase always requires an antecedent for *such* {satellite TV is a luxury and, as such, has a limited market}. The phrase is now often loosely used as a synonym for *therefore*.

assumption; presumption. An *assumption* is not drawn from evidence; typically, it is a hypothesis {your assumption can be tested by looking at the public records}. A *presumption* implies a basis in evidence; if uncontradicted, a *presumption* may support a decision {the legal presumption of innocence}.

assure. See **ensure.**

as to. This two-word preposition is best used only to begin a sentence that could begin with *on the question of* or *with regard to* {as to those checks, she didn't know where they came from}. Otherwise, use *about* or some other preposition.

as yet; as of yet. Stilted and redundant. Use *yet, still, so far,* or some other equivalent.

at the present time; at this time; at present. These are turgid substitutes for *now, today, currently,* or even *nowadays* (a word of perfectly good literary standing). Of the two-word versions, *at present* is least suggestive of bureaucratese.

at the time that; at the time when. Use the plain and simple *when* instead.

avenge, vb.; **revenge,** vb. & n. *Avenge* connotes a just exaction for a wrong {historically, family grudges were privately avenged}. The corresponding noun is *vengeance. Revenge* connotes the infliction of harm on another out of anger or resentment {the team is determined to revenge its humiliating loss in last year's championship game}. *Revenge* is much more commonly a noun {they didn't want justice—they wanted revenge}.

averse. See **adverse.**

avocation; vocation. An *avocation* is a hobby {stamp collecting is my weekend avocation}. A *vocation* is one's profession or, especially in a religious sense, one's calling {she had a true vocation and became a nun}.

awhile; a while. The one-word version is adverbial {let's stop here awhile}. The two-word version is a noun phrase that follows the preposition *for* or *in* {she worked for a while before beginning graduate studies}.

backward(s). See **toward.**

based on. This phrase has two legitimate and two illegitimate uses. It may unimpeachably have verbal force (*base* being a transitive verb, as in *they based their position on military precedent*) or, in a passive sense, adjectival force (*based* being read as a past-participial adjective, as in *a sophisticated thriller based on a John Le Carré novel*). Two uses, however, are traditionally considered slipshod. *Based on* should not have adverbial force {rates are adjusted annually, based on the ninety-one-day Treasury bill} or prepositional force (as a dangling participle) {Based on this information, we decided to stay}. Try other constructions {rates are adjusted annually on the basis of the ninety-one-day Treasury bill} {with this information, we decided to stay}.

basis. Much overworked, this word most properly means "foundation." It often appears in the phrase *on a ___ basis* or some similar construction. When possible, substitute adverbs (*personally*, not *on a personal basis*) or simply state the time (*daily*, not *on a daily basis*). The plural is *bases* {the legislative bases are complicated}.

battery. See **assault.**

behalf. *In behalf of* means "in the interest or for the benefit of" {the decision is in behalf of the patient}. *On behalf of* means "acting as agent or representative of" {on behalf of Mr. Scott, I would like to express heartfelt thanks}.

between; among; amid. *Between* indicates one-to-one relationships {between you and me}. *Among* indicates undefined or collective relationships {honor among thieves}. *Between* has long been recognized as being perfectly appropriate for more than two objects if multiple one-to-one relationships are understood from the context {trade between members of the European Union}. *Amid* is used with mass nouns {amid talk of war}, *among* with plurals of count nouns {among the children}. Avoid *amidst* and *amongst*.

bi; semi. Generally, *bi* means "two" (*biweekly* means "every two weeks"), while *semi* means "half" (*semiweekly* means "twice a week"). Because these prefixes are often confounded, writers should be explicit about the meaning.

biannual; semiannual; biennial. *Biannual* and *semiannual* both mean "twice a year" {these roses bloom biannually}. But *biennial* means "once every two years" or "every other year" {the state legislature meets biennially}. To avoid confusion, write *semiannual* (instead of *biannual*), and consider writing *once every two years* (instead of *biennial*).

billion; trillion. The meanings vary in different countries. In the United States, a *billion* is 1,000,000,000. In Great Britain, Canada, and Germany, a *billion* is a thousand times more than that (a million millions, or what Americans call a *trillion*). Further, in Great Britain a *trillion* is a million million millions, what Americans would call a *quintillion* (1,000,000,000,000,000,000). The American definitions are gaining acceptance, but writers need to remember the historical geographic distinctions. See 9.10.

born; borne. *Born* is used only as an adjective {a born ruler} or in the fixed passive-voice verb *to be born* {the child was born into poverty}. *Borne* is the past participle of *bear* {this donkey has borne many heavy loads} {she has borne three children}. It is also used as a suffix in the sciences {foodborne} {vectorborne}.

breach, n. & vb.; **breech,** n. A *breach* is a gap in or violation of something {a breach of contract}. To *breach* is to break, break open, or break through {breach the castle walls}. A *breech* refers to the lower or back part of something, especially the buttocks {a breech birth}.

bring; take. The distinction may seem obvious, but the error is common. The simple question is Where is the action directed? If it's toward you, use *bring* {bring home the bacon}. If it's away from you, use *take* {take out the trash}. You *take* (not *bring*) your car to the mechanic.

but. Popular belief to the contrary, this conjunction usefully begins contrasting sentences, typically better than *however*. See 5.191.

by means of. Often verbose. Use *by* or *with* if either one suffices.

by reason of. Use *because* or *because of* unless *by reason of* is part of an established phrase {by reason of insanity}.

can; could. *Can* means "to be able to" and expresses certainty {I can be there in five minutes}. *Could* is better for a sense of uncertainty or a conditional statement {Could you stop at the cleaners today?} {if you send a deposit, we could hold your reservation}. See 5.133.

can; may. *Can* most traditionally applies to physical or mental ability {she can do calculations in her head} {the dog can leap over a six-foot fence}. In colloquial English, *can* also expresses a request for permission {Can I go to the movies?}, but this usage is not recommended in formal writing. *May* suggests possibility {the class may have a pop quiz tomorrow} or permission {you may borrow my car}. A denial of permission is properly phrased formally with *may not* {you may not borrow my credit card} or with *cannot* or *can't* {you can't use the computer tonight}. See 5.133, 5.136.

capability. See **ability.**

capacity. See **ability.**

capital; capitol. A *capital* is a seat of government (usually a city) {Austin is the capital of Texas}. A *capitol* is a building in which a legislature meets {the legislature opened its new session in the capitol today}.

carat; karat; caret. *Carat* measures the weight of a gemstone; *karat* measures the purity of gold. To remember the difference, think of 24K. *Caret* is a mark on a manuscript indicating where matter is to be inserted.

career; careen. The word *career*'s career as a verb meaning "to go full speed" may be about over. Its duties have been assumed by *careen* ("to tip to one side while moving"), even though nothing in that verb's definition denotes high speed. Still, careful writers recognize the distinction.

caret. See **carat.**

case. This word is often a sign of verbal inflation. For example, *in case* means *if*; *in most cases* means *usually*; *in every case* means *always*. The word is justifiably used in law (in which a *case* is a lawsuit or judicial opinion) and in medicine (in which the word refers to an instance of a disease or disorder).

censer; censor, n.; **sensor.** The correct spellings can be elusive. A *censer* is either a person who carries a container of burning incense or the container itself. A *censor* is a person who suppresses objectionable subject matter. A *sensor* is a mechanical or electronic detector.

censor, vb.; **censure,** vb. To *censor* is to review and cut out objectionable material—that is, to suppress {soldiers' letters are often censored in wartime}. To *censure* is to criticize strongly or disapprove, or to officially reprimand {the House of Representatives censured the president for the invasion} {In some countries the government *censors* the press. In the United States the press often *censures* the government.}.

center around. Although this illogical phrasing does have apologists, stylists tend to use either *center on* or *revolve around.*

certainty; certitude. If you are absolutely sure about something, you display both *certainty* (firm conviction) and *certitude* (cocksureness). That fact you are sure about, however, is a *certainty* but not a *certitude*—the latter is a trait reserved for people.

chair; chairman; chairwoman; chairperson. *Chair* is widely regarded as the best gender-neutral choice. Since the mid-seventeenth century, *chair* has referred to an office of authority. See 5.204.

charge. See **accuse.**

childish; childlike. *Childlike* is used positively to connote innocence, mildness, and freshness {a childlike smile}. *Childish* is pejorative; it connotes immaturity and unreasonableness {childish ranting}.

circumstances. Both *in the circumstances* and *under the circumstances* are acceptable, but *under* is now much more common.

cite, n.; **site.** As a noun, *cite* is colloquial for *citation*, which refers to a source of information {a cite to *Encyclopaedia Britannica*}. A *site* is a place or location {building site} {Web site}.

citizen; subject. In a governmental sense, these are near synonyms that should be distinguished. A *citizen* owes allegiance to a nation whose sovereignty is a collective function of the people {a citizen of Germany}. A *subject* owes allegiance to an individual sovereign {a subject of the queen}.

class. This word denotes a category or group of things {the class of woodwind instruments}, never one type {an oboe is a type of woodwind} or one kind of thing {a drum is one kind of percussion instrument}.

classic; classical. *Classic* means "important, authoritative" {*The Naked Night* is one of Bergman's classic films}. *Classical* applies to the traditional "classics" of literature, music, and such {classical Greek} {a classical composer}. *Classical* is also used in the sciences to refer to the best- or earliest-characterized form {classical physics} {classical EEC syndrome} {classical sporadic Creutzfeldt-Jakob disease}.

cleave. This verb was originally two different words, and that difference is reflected in its opposite meanings: (1) to cut apart {to cleave meat}, and

(2) to cling together {standing in the rain, his clothes cleaving to his body}. The conjugations are (1) *cleave, cleft* (or *clove*), *cloven*, and (2) *cleave, cleaved, cleaved*.

clench; clinch. *Clench* connotes a physical action {he clenched his hand into a fist}. *Clinch* generally has figurative uses {she clinched the victory with her final putt}.

climactic; climatic. *Climactic* is the adjective corresponding to *climax* {during the movie's climactic scene, the projector broke}. *Climatic* corresponds to *climate* {the climatic conditions of northern New Mexico}.

clinch. See **clench.**

close proximity. Redundant. Write either *close* or *in proximity.*

cohabit; cohabitate. *Cohabit* is the traditional verb. *Cohabitate*, a backformation from *cohabitation*, is best avoided.

collegial; collegiate. *Collegial* answers to *colleague; collegiate* answers to *college.*

commendable; commendatory. What is done for a worthy cause is *commendable* {commendable dedication to helping the poor}. What expresses praise is *commendatory* {commendatory plaque}.

common; mutual. What is *common* is shared by two or more people {born into different families but having a common ancestor}. What is *mutual* is reciprocal or directly exchanged by and toward each other {mutual obligations}. Strictly, *friend in common* is better than *mutual friend* in reference to a third person who is a friend of two others.

commonweal; commonwealth. The *commonweal* is the public welfare. A *commonwealth* is a nation or state.

compare. To *compare with* is to discern both similarities and differences between things. To *compare to* is to note primarily similarities between things.

compelled; impelled. If you are *compelled* to do something, you have no choice in the matter {Nixon was compelled by the unanimous Supreme Court decision to turn over the tapes}. If you are *impelled* to do something, you still may not like it, but you are convinced that it must be done {the voter disliked some candidates but was impelled by the income-tax issue to vote a straight party ticket}.

compendious; voluminous. These are not synonyms, as many apparently believe. *Compendious* means "concise, abridged." *Voluminous*, literally "occupying many volumes," most commonly means "vast" or "extremely lengthy."

complacent; complaisant; compliant. To be *complacent* is to be content with oneself and one's life—with the suggestion that one may be smug and unprepared for future trouble. To be *complaisant* is to be easygoing and eager to please. To be *compliant* is to be amenable to orders or to a regimen.

compliment; complement. A *compliment* is a flattering or praising remark {a compliment on your skill}. A *complement* is something that completes or brings to perfection {the lace tablecloth was a complement to the antique silver}. The words are also verbs: to *compliment* is to praise, while to *complement* is to supplement adequately or to complete.

comprise; compose. Use these with care. To *comprise* is "to be made up of, to include" {the whole comprises the parts}. To *compose* is "to make up, to form the substance of something" {the parts compose the whole}. The phrase *comprised of*, though increasingly common, is poor usage. Instead, use *composed of* or *consisting of.*

concept; conception. Both words may refer to an abstract thought, but *conception* also means "the act of forming an abstract thought." Avoid using either word as a high-sounding equivalent of *idea, design, thought,* or *program.*

condole, vb.; **console,** vb. These are closely related, but not identical. To *condole with* is to express sympathy to {community leaders condoled with the victims' families}. The corresponding noun is *condolence* {they expressed their condolences at the funeral}. To *console* is to comfort {the players consoled their humiliated coach}. The corresponding noun is *consolation* {their kind words were little consolation}.

confidant; confidante; confident. *Confidant* is a close companion, someone (male or female) you confide in. *Confidante,* a feminine form, is a fading alternative spelling of *confidant* (used only in reference to a female confidant). It reflects French gender spellings. *Confident* is the adjective meaning "having faith, being certain."

congruous; congruent. Both terms mean "in harmony, in agreement." The first is seen most often in its negative form, *incongruous.* The second is used in geometry to describe figures that are identical in size and shape and in arithmetic to describe two numbers whose difference is evenly divisible by a given modulus.

connive; conspire. A person who secretly allows or deliberately avoids noticing something objectionable *connives* {the parents connived at the child's misbehavior}. But a person who makes secret plans with another to do something harmful or illegal *conspires* {he conspired with his friend to spoil the reunion}.

connote; denote. To *connote* (in reference to language) is to convey an additional meaning, especially an emotive nuance {the new gerund "parenting" and all that it connotes}. To *denote* (again in reference to language) is to specify the literal meaning of something {the phrase "freezing point" denotes thirty-two degrees Fahrenheit or zero degrees Celsius}. Both words have figurative uses {all the joy that young love connotes} {a smile may not denote happiness}.

consent. See **assent.**

consequent; subsequent. The first denotes causation; the second does not. A *consequent* event always happens after the event that caused it, as does a *subsequent* event. But a *subsequent* event is not necessarily a consequence of the first event.

consider. Add *as* only when you mean "to examine or discuss for a particular purpose" {handshaking considered as a means of spreading disease}. Otherwise, omit *as* {we consider him qualified}.

consist. There are two distinct phrases: *consist of* and *consist in*. The first applies to the physical components that make up a tangible thing {the computer-system package consists of software, the CPU, the monitor, and a printer}. The second refers to the essence of a thing, especially in abstract terms {moral government consists in rewarding the righteous and punishing the wicked}.

console. See **condole.**

conspire. See **connive.**

contact, vb. If you mean *write* or *call* or *e-mail,* say so. But *contact* is undeniably a useful way of referring to communication without specifying the means.

contagious; infectious. *Contagious* refers to mode of transmission; a *contagious* disease spreads by contact, direct or nearly direct, with an infected person or animal {rabies is a contagious disease}. *Infectious* refers to cause; an infection involves invasion by and multiplication of a pathogen, regardless of how transmission occurs. An *infectious* disease may or may not be contagious {influenza is infectious and contagious} {tetanus is infectious but not contagious}.

contemporary; contemporaneous. Both express coinciding time, but *contemporary* usually applies to people, and *contemporaneous* only to things or actions. Because *contemporary* has the additional sense "modern," it is unsuitable for contexts involving multiple times. That is, a reference to *Roman, Byzantine, and contemporary belief systems* is ambiguous; change *contemporary* to *modern.*

contemptuous; contemptible. If you are *contemptuous,* you are feeling contempt for someone or something. If you are *contemptible,* others will have that attitude toward you.

content; contents. *Content* applies to the topic of a written or oral presentation {the lecture's content was offensive to some who were present}. *Contents* usually denotes physical ingredients {the package's contents were easy to guess}. If the usage suggests many items, material or nonmaterial, *contents* is correct {table of contents} {the investigative report's contents}.

continual; continuous. What is *continual* is intermittent or frequently repeated. What is *continuous* never stops—it remains constant or uninterrupted.

contravene; controvert. To *contravene* is to conflict with or violate {the higher speed limit contravenes our policy of encouraging fuel conservation}. To *controvert* is to challenge or contradict {the testimony controverts the witness's prior statement}.

convince. See **persuade.**

copyright, vb. The verb is conjugated *copyright–copyrighted–copyrighted.* Note the spelling, which has nothing to do with *write.*

corollary; correlation. A *corollary* is either (1) a subsidiary proposition that follows from a proven mathematical proposition, often without requiring additional evidence to support it, or (2) a natural or incidental result of some action or occurrence. A *correlation* is a positive connection between things or phenomena. If used in the context of physics or statistics, it denotes the degree to which the observed interactions and variances are not attributable to chance alone.

corporal; corporeal. What is *corporal* relates in some way to the body {corporal punishment}; what is *corporeal* has a body {not our spiritual, but our corporeal existence}.

correlation. See **corollary.**

could. See **can.**

couldn't care less. This is the standard phrasing. Avoid the illogical form *could care less.*

councillor; counselor. A *councillor* is one who sits on a council {city councillor}. A *counselor* is a person who gives advice {personal counselor}.

couple of. Using *couple* as an adjective is poor phrasing. Add *of* {we watched a couple of movies).

court-martial. The two words are joined by a hyphen, whether the phrase functions as a noun or as a verb. Because *martial* acts as an adjective meaning "military," the plural of the noun is *courts-martial.*

credible; credulous; creditable. A trustworthy person or a believable story is *credible* ("believable"). A person who will believe anything is *credulous* (cf. **incredible; incredulous**). Something that brings one honor or deserves respect is *creditable* ("meritorious").

crevice; crevasse. Size matters. A crack in the sidewalk is a *crevice* (accent on the first syllable); a fissure in a glacier or a dam is a *crevasse* (accent on the second syllable).

criminal. See **unlawful.**

criteria. This is the plural form of *criterion* ("a standard for judging"). One *criterion,* two *criteria.*

damp, vb.; **dampen.** Both words convey the sense "to moisten." *Damp* also means "to reduce with moisture" {damp the fire} or "to diminish vibration or oscillation of (a wire or voltage)" {damp the voltage}. In a figurative sense, *dampen* means "to depress, curtail" {dampen one's hopes}.

data. Though originally this word was a plural of *datum,* it is now commonly treated as a mass noun and coupled with a singular verb. In formal writing (and always in the sciences), use *data* as a plural.

deadly; deathly. *Deadly* means "capable of causing death" {deadly snake venom}. *Deathly* means "deathlike" {deathly silence}.

decide whether; decide if. See **determine whether.**

decimate. This word literally means "to kill every tenth person," a means of repression that goes back to Roman times. But the word has come to mean "to inflict heavy casualties," and that use is accepted. Less accepted is the further extension to mean "to inflict heavy damage." Avoid *decimate* (1) when you are referring to complete destruction or (2) when a percentage is specified. That is, don't say that a city was "completely decimated," and don't say that some natural disaster "decimated 23 percent of the city's population."

deduce. See **adduce.**

defamation; libel; slander. *Defamation* is the communication of a falsehood that damages someone's reputation. If it is recorded, especially in writing, it is *libel*; otherwise it is *slander*.

definite; definitive. *Definite* means "clear, exact" {a definite yes}. *Definitive* means "conclusive, final, most authoritative" {a definitive treatise}.

delegate. See **relegate.**

denote. See **connote.**

denounce; renounce. To *denounce* is either to criticize harshly or to accuse. To *renounce* is either to relinquish or to reject.

dependent. See **addicted.**

deprecate. In general, to *deprecate* is to disapprove. But in the phrase *self-deprecating*—which began as a mistaken form of *self-depreciating* but is now standard—the sense of *deprecate* is "to belittle." In the computer-software world, *deprecate* serves as a warning: a *deprecated* feature or function is one that will be phased out of future release of software, so that users should quickly begin looking for alternatives.

derisive; derisory. What is *derisive* ridicules {derisive laughter}. What is *derisory* invites or deserves ridicule {that derisory "banana" hat}.

deserts; desserts. The first are deserved {your just deserts}, the second eaten {the many desserts on the menu}.

despite; in spite of. For brevity, prefer *despite*.

determine whether; determine if. The first phrasing is irreproachable style; the second is acceptable, though less formal. The same is true of *decide whether* versus *decide if*. See also **whether.**

different. The phrasing *different from* is generally preferable to *different than* {this company is different from that one}, but sometimes the adverbial phrase *differently than* is all but required {she described the scene differently than he did}.

disburse; disperse. To *disburse* is to distribute money. To *disperse* can be to distribute other things or to break up, as an unruly crowd.

disc. See **disk.**

discomfort; discomfit. *Discomfort* is a noun meaning "uncomfortableness." It can also be used as a verb meaning "to make ill at ease." But doing so often invites confusion with *discomfit*, which originally meant "to defeat utterly." Today it means "to thwart or confuse" {the ploy discomfited the opponent}. The distinction has become a fine one, since a *discomfited* person is inevitably uncomfortable. *Discomfiture* is the corresponding noun.

discreet; discrete. *Discreet* means "circumspect, judicious" {a discreet silence}. *Discrete* means "separate, distinct, unconnected" {six discrete parts}.

discriminating, adj.; **discriminatory.** The word *discrimination* can be used in either a negative or a positive sense, and these adjectives reflect that ambivalence. *Discriminating* means "analytical, discerning, tasteful" {a discriminating palate}. *Discriminatory* means "reflecting a biased treatment" {discriminatory employment policy}.

disinterested. This word should be reserved for the sense "not having a financial or personal interest at stake, impartial." Avoid it as a replacement for *uninterested* (which means "unconcerned, bored").

disk; disc. *Disk* is the usual spelling {floppy disk}. But *disc* is preferred in a few specialized applications {compact disc} {disc brakes} {disc harrow}.

disorganized; unorganized. Both mean "not organized," but *disorganized* suggests a group in disarray, either thrown into confusion or inherently unable to work together {the disorganized 1968 Democratic National Convention in Chicago}.

disperse. See **disburse.**

distinctive; distinguished; distinguishable. A *distinctive* feature is something that makes a person (or place or thing) easy to distinguish (pick out) from others. But it does not necessarily make that person *distinguished* (exalted) {the distinguished professor wears a distinctive red bow tie}. It does, however, make the person *distinguishable*, a term that does not carry the positive connotation of *distinguished*.

dive, vb. The preferred conjugation is *dive–dived–dived*. The form *dove*, though common in certain regions and possibly on the rise, has not traditionally been considered good form.

doctrinal; doctrinaire. *Doctrinal* means "of, relating to, or constituting a doctrine"; it is neutral in connotation {doctrinal differences}. *Doctrinaire* means "dogmatic," suggesting that the person described is stubborn and narrow-minded {a doctrinaire ideologue}.

doubtless, adv. Use this form—not *doubtlessly*.

doubt that; doubt whether; doubt if. *Doubt that* conveys a negative sense of skepticism or questioning {I doubt that you'll ever get your money back}. *Doubt whether* also conveys a sense of skepticism {the official says that he doubts whether the company could survive}. *Doubt if* is a casual phrasing for *doubt that*.

drag. Conjugated *drag–dragged–dragged*. The past form *drug* is dialectal.

dream. Either *dreamed* (more typical in American English) or *dreamt* (more typical in British English) is acceptable for the past-tense and past-participial forms.

drink, vb. Correctly conjugated *drink–drank–drunk* {they had not drunk any fruit juice that day}.

drown, vb. Conjugated *drown–drowned–drowned*.

drunk, adj.; **drunken.** *Drunk* describes a current state of intoxication {drunk driver}. (By contrast, a *drunk*—like a *drunkard*—is someone who is habitually intoxicated.) *Drunken* describes either a trait of habitual intoxication {drunken sot} or intoxicated people's behavior {a drunken brawl}.

due to. In strict traditional usage, *due to* should be interchangeable with *attributable to* {the erratic driving was due to some prescription drugs that the driver had taken} {coughs due to colds}. When used adverbially, *due to* is often considered inferior to *because of* or *owing to*. So in the sentence *due to the parents' negligence, the entire family suffered*, the better phrasing would be *because of* [or *owing to*] *the parents' negligence, the entire family suffered*.

due to the fact that. Use *because* instead.

dumb. This word means either "stupid" or "unable to speak." In the second sense, *mute* is clearer for most modern readers.

dying; dyeing. *Dying* is the present participle of *die* ("to cease living"); *dyeing* is the present participle of *dye* ("to color with a liquid").

each other; one another. Traditionalists use *each other* when two things or people are involved, *one another* when more than two are involved.

eatable. See **edible.**

economic; economical. *Economic* means "of or relating to large-scale finances" {federal economic policy}. *Economical* means "thrifty; financially efficient" {an economical purchase}.

edible; eatable. What is *edible* is fit for human consumption {edible flowers}. What is *eatable* is at least minimally palatable {the cake is slightly burned but still eatable}.

effect. See **affect.**

effete. Traditionally, it has meant "decadent, worn out, sterile." Today it is often used to mean either "snobbish" or "effeminate." Because of its ambiguity, the word is best avoided altogether.

effrontery; affront. *Effrontery* is an act of shameless impudence or audacity. An *affront* is a deliberate insult.

e.g. See **i.e.**

elemental; elementary. Something that is *elemental* is an essential constituent {elemental ingredients} or a power of nature {elemental force}. Something that is *elementary* is basic, introductory, or easy {an elementary math problem}.

elicit; illicit. *Elicit* ("to draw out [an answer, information, etc.]") is a verb {to elicit responses}; *illicit* ("illegal") is an adjective {an illicit scheme}. Writers often use *illicit* when they mean *elicit*.

elude. See **allude.**

emend. See **amend.**

emigrate. See **immigrate.**

empathy; sympathy. *Empathy* is putting yourself in someone else's shoes to understand that person's situation. *Sympathy* is compassion and sorrow one feels for another.

endemic. See **epidemic.**

endorse. See **approve.**

enervate; innervate. These words are antonyms. To *enervate* is to weaken or drain of energy. To *innervate* is to stimulate or provide with energy.

enormity; enormousness. *Enormity* means "monstrousness, moral outrageousness, atrociousness" {the enormity of the Khmer Rouge's killings}. *Enormousness* means "abnormally great size" {the enormousness of Alaska}.

enough. See **adequate.**

ensure; insure; assure. *Ensure* is the general term meaning to make sure that something will (or won't) happen. In best usage, *insure* is reserved for underwriting financial risk. So we *ensure* that we can get time off for a vacation, and *insure* our car against an accident on the trip. We *ensure* events and *insure* things. But we *assure* people that their concerns are being addressed.

enthused, adj. Use *enthusiastic* instead. And avoid *enthuse* as a verb.

enumerable; innumerable. These are nearly opposite near-homonyms. *Enumerable* means "able to be counted"; *innumerable* means "too many to count."

envy. See **jealousy.**

epidemic; endemic; pandemic. An *epidemic* disease breaks out, spreads through a limited area (such as a state), and then subsides {an epidemic outbreak of measles}. (The word is frequently used as a noun {a measles epidemic}.) An *endemic* disease is perennially present within a region or population {malaria is endemic in parts of Africa}. (Note that *endemic* describes a disease and not a region: it is incorrect to say *this region is endemic for* [a disease].) A *pandemic* disease is prevalent over a large area, such as a nation or continent, or the entire world {the 1919 flu pandemic}.

equally as. This is typically faulty phrasing. Delete *as*.

et al. This is the abbreviated form of *et alii* ("and others")—the *others* being people, not things. Since *al.* is an abbreviation, the period is required. Cf. **etc.**

etc. This is the abbreviated form of *et cetera* ("and other things"); it should never be used in reference to people. *Etc.* implies that a list of things is too extensive to recite. But often writers seem to run out of thoughts and tack on *etc.* for no real purpose. Also, two redundancies often appear with this abbreviation: (1) *and etc.*, which is poor style because *et* means "and," and (2) *etc.* at the end of a list that begins with *e.g.*, which properly introduces a short list of examples. Cf. **et al.**

event. The phrase *in the event that* is a long and formal way of saying *if.*

eventuality. This term often needlessly displaces more specific everyday words such as *event, result,* and *possibility.*

every day, adv.; **everyday,** adj. The first is adverbial, the second adjectival. One may wear one's *everyday* clothes *every day.*

every one; everyone. The two-word version is an emphatic way of saying "each" {every one of them was there}; the second is a pronoun equivalent to *everybody* {everyone was there}.

exceptional; exceptionable. What is *exceptional* is uncommon, superior, rare, or extraordinary {an exceptional talent}. What is *exceptionable* is objectionable or offensive {an exceptionable slur}.

explicit; implicit. If something is *explicit,* it is deliberately spelled out, as in the writing of a contract or the text of a statute. If it is *implicit,* it is not specifically stated but either is suggested in the wording or is necessary to effectuate the purpose. Avoid *implicit* to mean "complete, unmitigated."

fact that, the. This much-maligned phrase is not always avoidable. But hunt for a substitute before deciding to use it. Sometimes *that* alone suffices.

farther; further. The traditional distinction is to use *farther* for a physical distance {we drove farther north to see the autumn foliage} and *further* for a figurative distance {let's examine this further} {look no further}.

fax, n. & vb. Derived from *facsimile transmission,* the foreshortened *fax* is almost universally preferred for convenience. The plural is *faxes.* Note that the word is governed by the same rules of capitalization as other common nouns. *FAX* is incorrect: the word is not an acronym.

faze; phase, vb. To *faze* is to disturb or disconcert {Jones isn't fazed by insults}. To *phase* (usually *phase in* or *phase out*) is to schedule or perform a plan, task, or the like in stages {phase in new procedures} {phase out the product lines that don't sell}.

feel. This verb is weak when used as a substitute for *think* or *believe.*

feel bad. Invariably, the needed phrase is *feel bad* (not *badly*). See 5.158.

fewer. See **less.**

fictional; fictitious; fictive. *Fictional* (from *fiction* as a literary genre) means "of, relating to, or characteristic of imagination" {a fictional story}. *Fictitious* means "imaginary; counterfeit; false" {a fictitious name}. *Fictive* means "possessing the talent for imaginative creation" {fictive gift}.

finalize. Meaning "to make final or bring to an end," this word has often been associated with inflated jargon. Although its compactness may recommend it in some contexts, use *finish* or *make final* when possible.

first. In enumerations, use *first, second, third*, and so forth. Avoid the *ly* forms.

fit. This verb is undergoing a shift. It has traditionally been conjugated *fit–fitted–fitted*, but today *fit–fit–fit* is prevalent in American English {when she tried on the dress, it fit quite well}. In the passive voice, however, *fitted* is still normal {the horse was fitted with a new harness}.

flair. See **flare.**

flammable; inflammable. *Flammable* was invented as an alternative to the synonymous word *inflammable*, which some people misunderstood—dangerously—as meaning "not combustible." Today *flammable* is the standard term.

flare; flair. A *flare* is an unsteady and glaring light {an emergency flare} or a sudden outburst {a flare-up of fighting}. A *flair* is an outstanding talent {a flair for mathematics} or originality and stylishness {performed with flair}.

flaunt; flout. The first word, meaning "to show off ostentatiously" {they flaunted their wealth}, should not be confused with the second, *flout*, meaning "to treat with disdain or contempt" {flouting the rules}.

flounder; founder. Keep the figurative meanings of these terms straight by remembering their literal meanings. To *flounder* is to struggle awkwardly, as though walking through deep mud {the professor glared while the unprepared student floundered around for an answer}. To *founder* is to sink or to fall to the ground {with no editorial expertise, the publisher soon foundered}.

flout. See **flaunt.**

following. Avoid this word as an equivalent of *after*. Consider: *Following the presentation, there was a question-and-answer session. After* is both simpler and clearer. Where causation is implied, however, *following* may be preferable {organ rejection following transplantation}.

forbear, vb.; **forebear,** n. The terms are unrelated, but the spellings are frequently confused. To *forbear* is to refrain {he wanted to speak but decided to forbear}. (The conjugation is *forbear–forbore–forborne*.) A *forebear* is an ancestor {the house was built by Murray's distant forebears}.

forego; forgo. To *forego* is to go before {the foregoing paragraph}. (The word appears most commonly in the phrase *foregone conclusion*.) To *forgo*, by contrast, is to do without or renounce {they decided to forgo that opportunity}.

foreword; preface. A *foreword* (not *forward*) is a book's introduction that is written by someone other than the book's author. An introduction written by the book's author is called a *preface*. See 1.48–49.

forgo. See **forego.**

former; latter. In the best usage, these words apply only to pairs. The *former* is the first of two, the *latter* the second of two.

fortuitous; fortunate. *Fortuitous* means "by chance," whether the fortune is good or bad {the rotten tree could have fallen at any time; it was just fortuitous that the victims drove by when they did}. *Fortunate* means "blessed by good fortune" {we were fortunate to win the raffle}.

forward(s). See **toward.**

founder. See **flounder.**

fulsome, adj. Although some dictionaries give "characterized by abundance" or a variation as one definition for this word, many readers (and writers) adhere to the sense "too much, excessive to the point of being repulsive." Avoid using *fulsome* to mean "very full."

further. See **farther.**

future, in the near. Use *soon* or *shortly* instead.

gentleman. This word is a vulgarism when used as a synonym for *man*. When used in reference to a cultured, refined man, it is susceptible to some of the same objections as those leveled against *lady*. Use it cautiously. Cf. **lady.**

get. Though shunned by many writers as too casual, *get* often sounds more natural than *obtain* or *procure* {get a divorce}. It can also substitute for a stuffy *become* {get hurt}. The verb is conjugated *get–got–gotten* in American English, and *get–got–got* in British English.

gibe; jibe. A *gibe* is a biting insult or taunt; *gibes* are figuratively thrown at their target {the angry crowd hurled gibes as the suspect was led into the courthouse}. *Jibe* means "to fit or coincide" {the verdict didn't jibe with the judge's own view of the facts}.

gild. See **guild.**

go. This verb is conjugated *go–went–gone*. *Went* appears as a past participle only in dialect.

gourmet; gourmand. Both are aficionados of good food and drink. But a *gourmet* knows and appreciates the fine points of food and drink, whereas a *gourmand* is a glutton.

graduate, vb. Whereas *graduate* means "to grant a diploma to or confer a degree on," *graduate from* means "to receive a diploma or degree from (a school, university, or other institution)." A school can *graduate* a student or a student can *graduate from* a school, but a student can never *graduate* a school.

grateful; gratified. To be *grateful* is to be thankful or appreciative. To be *gratified* is to be pleased, satisfied, or indulged.

grisly; grizzly; grizzled. What is *grisly* is gruesome or horrible {grisly details}. What is *grizzly* is grayish; one subspecies of brown bear gets its name from its silver-tipped fur {grizzly bear}. On people, gray hair is more often described as *grizzled* {the hermit's grizzled beard}.

guild, n.; gild, vb. A *guild* is an organization of persons with a common interest or profession {a guild of goldsmiths}. To *gild* is to put a thin layer of gold on something {gild a picture frame}.

half (of). Delete the *of* whenever possible {half the furniture}.

handful. If *handful* applies to a mass noun, use a singular verb {a handful of trouble is ahead}. But if *handful* applies to a plural count noun, use a plural verb {there are only a handful of walnut trees lining Main Street}.

hangar; hanger. One finds *hangars* at an airport {airplane hangars}. Everywhere else, one finds *hangers* {clothes hangers} {picture hangers}.

hanged; hung. *Hanged* is used as the past participle of *hang* only in its transitive form when referring to the killing (just or unjust) of a human being by suspending him or her by the neck {criminals were hanged at Tyburn Hill}. But if death is not intended or likely, or if the person is suspended by a body part other than the neck, *hung* is correct {he was hung upside down as a cruel prank}. In most senses, of course, *hung* is the past form of *hang* {Mark hung up his clothes}.

hanger. See **hangar.**

harebrained. So spelled (after the timid, easily startled animal)—not *hairbrained.*

healthy; healthful. Traditionally, a living thing that is *healthy* enjoys good health; something that is *healthful* promotes health {a healthful diet will keep you healthy}. But *healthy* is gradually taking over both senses.

help (to). Omit the *to* when possible {talking will help resolve the problem}.

he or she. To avoid sexist language, many writers use this alternative phrasing (in place of the generic *he*). Use it sparingly—preferably after exhausting all less obtrusive methods of achieving gender neutrality. But *he or she* is preferable to *he/she, s/he, (s)he,* and the like. See also 5.43, 5.203–6.

historic; historical. *Historic* refers to what is momentous in history {January 16, 1991, was a historic day in Kuwait}; *historical* refers simply to anything that occurred in the past.

holocaust. When capitalized, this word refers to the Nazi genocide of European Jews in World War II. When not capitalized, it refers (literally or figuratively) to extensive devastation caused by fire, or to the systematic and malicious killing of human beings on a vast scale.

home in. This phrase is frequently misrendered *hone in.* (*Hone* means "to sharpen.") *Home in* refers to what homing pigeons do; the meaning is "to come closer and closer to a target."

hopefully. The old meaning of the word ("in a hopeful manner") seems unsustainable; the newer meaning ("I hope" or "it is to be hoped") seems here to stay. But many careful writers deplore the new meaning.

hung. See **hanged.**

I; me. When you need the first person, use it. It's not immodest to use it; it's superstitious not to.

idyllic. An *idyll* is a short pastoral poem, and by extension *idyllic* means "charming" or "picturesque." It is not synonymous with *ideal* (perfect).

i.e.; e.g. The first is the abbreviation for *id est* ("that is"); the second is the abbreviation for *exempli gratia* ("for example"). The English equivalents are preferable in formal prose, though sometimes the quickness of these two-letter abbreviations makes them desirable. Always put a comma after either of them.

if; whether. See **determine whether.**

illegal. See **unlawful.**

illegible; unreadable. Handwriting or printing that is *illegible* is not clear enough to be read {illegible scrawlings}. Writing that is *unreadable* is so poorly composed as to be either incomprehensible or intolerably dull.

illicit. See **elicit; unlawful.**

illude. See **allude.**

immigrate; emigrate. To *immigrate* is to enter a country to live, leaving a past home. To *emigrate* is to leave one country to live in another one. The cognate forms also demand attention. Someone who moves from Ireland to the United States is an *immigrant* here, and an *emigrant* there. An *émigré* is also an *emigrant*, but especially one in political exile.

impact. Resist using this word as a verb unless in a physical context. Try *affect* or *influence* instead. Besides being hyperbolic, *impact* is widely considered a solecism (though it is gaining ground).

impelled. See **compelled.**

implicit. See **explicit.**

imply; infer. The writer or speaker *implies* (hints, suggests); the reader or listener *infers* (deduces). Writers and speakers often use *infer* as if it were synonymous with *imply*, but careful writers always distinguish between the two words.

in actual fact. See **actual fact, in.**

inasmuch as. *Because* or *since* is almost always a better choice.

in behalf of. See **behalf.**

in connection with. This is a vague, fuzzy phrase {she explained the financial consequences in connection with the transaction} {a liking for everything in connection with golf} {Phipson was compensated in connection with its report}. Try replacing the phrase with *of, related to,* or *associated* *with* {she explained the financial consequences of the transaction}, *about* {a liking for everything about golf}, or *for* {Phipson was compensated for its report}.

incredible; incredulous. *Incredible* properly means "unbelievable." Colloquially, it is used to mean "astonishing (in a good way)" {it was an incredible trip}. *Incredulous* means "disbelieving, skeptical" {people are incredulous about the rising gas costs}.

inculcate; indoctrinate. One *inculcates* values *into* a child but *indoctrinates* the child *with* values. That is, *inculcate* always has a value or values as its object, followed by the preposition *into* {inculcate courage into soldiers}. *Indoctrinate* takes a person as its object {indoctrinate children with the habit of telling the truth}.

indicate. Often vague. When possible, use a more direct verb such as *state*, *comment, show, suggest,* or *say.*

individual. Use this word to distinguish a single person from a group. When possible, use a more specific term, such as *person, adult, child, man,* or *woman.*

indoctrinate. See **inculcate.**

induce. See **adduce.**

in excess of. Try replacing this verbose phrase with *more than* or *over.*

infectious. See **contagious.**

infer. See **imply.**

inference. Use the verb *draw,* not *make,* with *inference* {they drew the wrong inferences}. Otherwise, readers may confuse *inference* with *implication.*

inflammable. See **flammable.**

inflict; afflict. Events, illnesses, punishments, and such are *inflicted on* living things or entities {an abuser inflicts cruelty}. The sufferers are *afflicted with* or *by* disease or troubles {agricultural communities afflicted with drought}.

ingenious; ingenuous. These words are similar in form but not in meaning. *Ingenious* describes what is intelligent, clever, and original {an ingenious invention}. *Ingenuous* describes what is candid, naive, and without dissimulation {a hurtful but ingenuous observation}.

innervate. See **enervate.**

innumerable. See **enumerable.**

in order to; in order for. Often these expressions can be reduced to *to* and *for.* When that is so, and rhythm and euphony are preserved or even heightened, use *to* or *for.*

in proximity. See **close proximity.**

in regard to. This is the phrase, not *in regards to.* Try a single-word substitute instead: *about, regarding, concerning.*

in spite of. See **despite.**

insure. See **ensure.**

intense; intensive. *Intense* is always preferred outside philosophical and scientific usages. But *intensive* should be retained in customary phrases
such as *labor-intensive* and *intensive care.*

in the affirmative. See **affirmative, in the.**

in the event that. See **event.**

in the near future. See **future.**

in the negative. See **affirmative, in the.**

irregardless. An error. Use *regardless* (or possibly *irrespective*).

it is I; it is me. Both are correct and acceptable. The first phrase is strictly
grammatical (and stuffy); the second is idiomatic (and relaxed), often
contracted to *it's me.* In the third-person constructions, however, a
greater stringency holds sway in good English {this is he} {it isn't she
who has caused such misery}.

its; it's. *Its* is the possessive form of *it; it's* is the contraction for *it is* {it's a
sad dog that scratches its fleas}.

jealousy; envy. *Jealousy* connotes feelings of resentment toward another,
particularly in matters relating to an intimate relationship. *Envy* refers to
covetousness of another's advantages, possessions, or abilities.

jibe. See **gibe.**

karat. See **carat.**

lady. When used as a synonym for *woman*—indeed, when used anywhere
but in the phrase *ladies and gentlemen*—this word will be considered objectionable by some readers who think of it as a patronizing stereotype.
This is especially true when it is used for unprestigious jobs {cleaning
lady} or as a condescending adjective {lady lawyer}. Some will insist on
using it to describe a refined woman. If they've consulted this entry,
they've been forewarned. Cf. **gentleman.**

latter. See **former.**

laudable; laudatory. *Laudable* means "praiseworthy" {a laudable effort}.
Laudatory means "expressing praise" {laudatory phone calls}.

lay; lie. *Lay* is a transitive verb—it demands a direct object {lay your pen-
cils down}. It is inflected *lay–laid–laid* {I laid the book there yesterday}
{these rumors have been laid to rest}. *Lie* is an intransitive verb—it never
takes a direct object {lie down and rest}. It is inflected *lie–lay–lain* {she
lay down and rested} {he hasn't yet lain down}.

leach; leech. To *leach* is to percolate or to separate out solids in solution by
percolation. A *leech* is a bloodsucker (both literal and figurative).

lend, vb.; **loan,** vb. & n. *Lend* is the correct term for letting someone use
something with the understanding that it (or its equivalent) will be returned. The verb *loan* is standard only when money is the subject of the
transaction. *Loan* is the noun corresponding to both *lend* and *loan,* vb.
The past-tense and past-participial form of *lend* is *lent.*

less; fewer. Reserve *less* for mass nouns, or amounts—for example, less salt, dirt, water. Reserve *fewer* for countable things—fewer people, calories, grocery items, suggestions. One easy guideline is to use *less* with singular nouns and *fewer* with plural nouns.

libel. See **defamation.**

lie. See **lay.**

life-and-death; life-or-death. Logic aside (life and death being mutually exclusive), the first phrase is the standard idiom {a life-and-death decision}.

likely. See **apt.**

literally. This word means "actually; without exaggeration." It should not be used oxymoronically in figurative senses, as in *they were literally glued to their seats* (unless glue had in fact been applied).

loan. See **lend.**

loathe, vb.; **loath,** adj. To *loathe* something is to detest it or to regard it with disgust {I loathe tabloid television}. Someone who is *loath* is reluctant {Tracy seems loath to admit mistakes}.

lose; loose, vb.; **loosen.** To *lose* something is to be deprived of it. To *loose* something is to release it from fastenings or restraints. To *loosen* is to make less tight or to ease a restraint. *Loose* conveys the idea of complete release, whereas *loosen* refers to only a partial release.

luxuriant; luxurious. The two terms are fairly often confused. What is *luxuriant* is lush and grows abundantly {a luxuriant head of hair}. What is *luxurious* is lavish and extravagant {a luxurious resort}.

malevolent; maleficent. *Malevolent* means "evil in mind" {with malevolent intent}. *Maleficent* means "evil in deed" {a maleficent bully}.

malodorous. See **odious.**

maltreatment. See **mistreatment.**

mantle; mantel. A *mantle* is a long, loose garment like a cloak. A *mantel* is a wood or stone structure around a fireplace.

masterful; masterly. *Masterful* describes a person who is dominating and imperious. *Masterly* describes a person who has mastered a craft, trade, or profession; the word often means "authoritative" {a masterly analysis}.

may; can. See **can.**

may; might. *May* expresses what is possible, is factual, or could be factual {I may have turned off the stove, but I can't recall doing it}. *Might* suggests something that is uncertain, hypothetical, or contrary to fact {I might have won the marathon if I had entered}. See 5.136.

me. See **I.**

media; mediums. In scientific contexts and in reference to mass communications, the plural of *medium* is *media* {some bacteria flourish in several types of media} {the media are now issuing reports}. But if *medium* refers to a spiritualist, the plural is *mediums* {several mediums have held séances here}.

memoranda; memorandums. Both plural forms are correct, although *memoranda* is more common. *Memoranda* is sometimes misused as if it were singular.

might. See **may.**

militate. See **mitigate.**

mistreatment; maltreatment. *Mistreatment* is the more general term. *Maltreatment* denotes a harsh form of *mistreatment,* involving abuse by rough or cruel handling.

mitigate; militate. *Mitigate,* like its synonym *extenuate,* means "to lessen or soften"; so *mitigating circumstances* lessen the seriousness of a crime. *Militate,* by contrast, means "to have a marked effect on" and is usually followed by *against* {his nearsightedness militated against his ambition to become a commercial pilot}.

much; very. *Much* generally intensifies past-participial adjectives {much obliged} {much encouraged} and some comparatives {much more} {much worse} {much too soon}. *Very* intensifies adverbs and most adjectives {very carefully} {very bad}, including past-participial adjectives that have more adjectival than verbal force {very bored}. See 5.89.

mutual. See **common.**

myself. Avoid using *myself* as a pronoun in place of *I* or *me.* Use it reflexively {I did myself a favor} or emphatically {I myself have tried to get through that tome!}.

nauseous; nauseated. Whatever is *nauseous* induces a feeling of nausea—it makes us feel sick to our stomachs. To feel sick is to be *nauseated.* The use of *nauseous* to mean *nauseated* may be too common to be called error anymore, but strictly speaking it is poor usage. Because of the ambiguity in *nauseous,* the wisest course may be to stick to the participial adjectives *nauseated* and *nauseating.*

necessary; necessitous. *Necessary* means "required under the circumstances" {the necessary arrangements}. *Necessitous* means "impoverished" {living in necessitous circumstances}.

no. See **affirmative, in the.**

noisome. This word has nothing to do with *noise.* It means "noxious, offensive, foul-smelling" {a noisome factory}.

none. This word may take either a singular or a plural verb. A guideline: if it is followed by a singular noun, treat it as a singular {none of the building was painted}; if by a plural noun, treat it as a plural {none of the guests were here when I arrived}. But for special emphasis, it is quite proper (though possibly stilted) to use a singular verb when a plural noun follows {none of the edits was accepted}.

notable; noticeable; noteworthy. *Notable* ("readily noticed") applies both to physical things and to qualities {notable sense of humor}. *Noticeable* means "detectable with the physical senses" {a noticeable limp}. *Noteworthy* means "remarkable" {a noteworthy act of kindness}.

notwithstanding. One word. Less formal alternatives include *despite, although*, and *in spite of*. The word *notwithstanding* may precede or follow a noun {notwithstanding her bad health, she decided to run for office} {her bad health notwithstanding, she decided to run for office}.

number. See **amount.**

numerous. This is typically a bloated word for *many*.

observance; observation. *Observance* means "obedience to a rule or custom" {the family's observance of Passover}. *Observation* means either "a study of something" or "a remark based on such a study" {a keen observation about the defense strategy}. Each term is sometimes used when the other would be better.

obtuse; abstruse. *Obtuse* describes a person who can't understand; *abstruse* describes an idea that is hard to understand. A person who is *obtuse* is dull and, by extension, dull-witted. What is *abstruse* is incomprehensible or nearly so.

odious; odorous; odoriferous; malodorous. *Odious* means "hateful" {odious Jim Crow laws}. It is not related to the other terms, but it is sometimes misused as if it were. *Odorous* means "detectable by smell, for better or worse." *Odoriferous* means essentially the same thing, although it has meant "fragrant" as often as it has meant "foul." *Malodorous* means "smelling quite bad." The mistaken form *odiferous* is often used as a jocular equivalent of *smelly*, but most dictionaries don't record it.

odoriferous. See **odious.**

off. Never put *of* after this word {we got off the bus}.

officious. A person who is *officious* is aggressively nosy and meddlesome. The word has nothing to do with an *officer* and should not be confused with *official*.

on; upon. Prefer *on* to *upon* unless introducing an event or condition {put that on the shelf, please} {you'll get paid upon the job's completion}. For more about *on*, see **onto.**

on behalf of. See **behalf.**

one another. See **each other.**

oneself. One word—not *one's self.*

onto; on to; on. When is *on* a preposition and when is it an adverb? The sense of the sentence should tell, but the distinction can be subtle. *Onto* implies a movement, so it has an adverbial flavor even though it is a preposition {the gymnast jumped *onto* the bars}. When *on* is part of the verbal phrase, it is an adverb and *to* is the preposition {the gymnast held *on to* the bars}. One trick is to mentally say "up" before *on*: if the sentence still makes sense, then *onto* is probably the right choice. Alone, *on* does not imply motion {the gymnast is good *on* the parallel bars}.

oppress; repress. *Oppress*, meaning "to persecute or tyrannize," is more negative than *repress*, meaning "to restrain or subordinate."

oral. See **verbal.**

oration. See **peroration.**

orient; orientate. To *orient* is to get one's bearings (literally to find east) {it took the new employee a few days to get oriented to the firm's suite}. Unless used in the sense "to face or turn to the east," *orientate* is a poor variation to be avoided.

ought; should. Both express a sense of duty, but *ought* is stronger. Unlike *should*, *ought* requires a fully expressed infinitive, even in the negative {you ought not to see the movie}. See 5.138–39.

outside. In spatial references, no *of* is necessary—or desirable—after this word. But *outside of* is acceptable as a colloquialism meaning "except for" or "aside from."

over. As an equivalent of *more than*, this word is perfectly good idiomatic English.

overly. Avoid this word, which is widely considered poor usage. Try *over* as a prefix or *unduly*.

pair. This is a singular form, despite the inherent sense of twoness. The plural is *pairs* {three pairs of shoes}.

pandemic. See **epidemic.**

parameters. Though it may sound elegant or scientific, this word is usually just pretentious when it is used in nontechnical contexts. Stick to *boundaries, limits, guidelines, grounds, elements*, or some other word.

partake in; partake of. To *partake in* is to participate in {the new student refused to partake in class discussions}. To *partake of* is either to get a part of {partake of the banquet} or to have a quality, at least to some extent {this assault partakes of revenge}.

partly; partially. Both words convey the sense "to some extent; in part" {partly disposed of}. *Partly* is preferred in that sense. But *partially* has the additional senses of "incomplete" {partially cooked} and "unfairly; in a way that shows bias toward one side" {he treats his friends partially}.

peaceable; peaceful. A *peaceable* person or nation is inclined to avoid strife {peaceable kingdom}. A *peaceful* person, place, or event is serene, tranquil, and calm {a peaceful day free from demands}.

peak; peek; pique. These three sometimes get switched through writerly blunders. A *peak* is an apex, a *peek* is a quick or illicit glance, and a fit of *pique* is an episode of peevishness and wounded vanity. To *pique* is to annoy or arouse: an article *piques* (not *peaks*) one's interest.

pendant, n.; **pendent,** adj. A *pendant* is an item of dangling jewelry, especially one worn around the neck. What is *pendent* is hanging or suspended.

penultimate. This word means "the next to last." Many people have started misusing it as a fancy equivalent of *ultimate*.

people; persons. The traditional view is that *persons* is used for smaller numbers {three persons}, and *people* with larger ones {millions of people}. But today most people use *people* even for small groups {only three people were there}.

period of time; time period. Avoid these phrases. Try *period* or *time* instead.

peroration; oration. A *peroration*, strictly speaking, is the conclusion of an *oration* (speech). Careful writers avoid using *peroration* to refer to a rousing speech or writing.

perpetuate; perpetrate. To *perpetuate* something is to sustain it or prolong it indefinitely {perpetuate the species}. To *perpetrate* is to commit or perform (an act) {perpetrate a crime}.

personally. Three points. First, use this word only when an actor does something that would normally be done through an agent {the president personally signed this invitation} or to limit other considerations {Jean was affected by the decision but was not personally involved in it}. Second, *personally* is redundant when combined with an activity that necessarily requires the actor's presence {the senator personally shook hands with the constituents}. Third, *personally* shouldn't appear with *I* when stating an opinion; it weakens the statement and doesn't reduce the speaker's liability for the opinion. The only exception arises if a person is required to advance someone else's view but holds a different personal opinion {in the chamber I voted to lower taxes because of the constituencies I represented; but I personally believed that taxes should have been increased}.

persons. See **people**.

persuade; convince. *Persuade* is associated with actions {persuade him to buy a suit}. *Convince* is associated with beliefs or understandings {she convinced the auditor of her honesty}. The phrase *persuade to (do)* has traditionally been considered better than *convince to (do)*. But either verb will take a *that*-clause {the committee was persuaded that an all-night session was necessary} {my three-year-old is convinced that Santa Claus exists}.

pertain; appertain. *Pertain to*, the more common term, means "to relate to" {the clause pertains to assignment of risk}. *Appertain to* means "to belong to by right" {the defendant's rights appertaining to the Fifth Amendment}.

phase. See **faze**.

phenomenon. This is a singular form. The plural is *phenomena*.

pique. See **peak.**

pitiable; pitiful. To be *pitiable* is to be worthy of pity. To be *pitiful* is to be contemptible.

pleaded; pled. The first is the standard past-tense and past-participial form {he pleaded guilty} {they have pleaded with their families}. Avoid *pled.*

pore. To *pore over* something written is to read it intently. Some writers confuse this word with *pour.*

practicable; possible; practical. These terms differ in shading. What is *practicable* is capable of being done; it's feasible. What is *possible* might be capable of happening or being done, but there is some doubt. What is *practical* is fit for actual use.

precipitate, adj.; **precipitous.** What is *precipitate* occurs suddenly or rashly; it describes demands, actions, or movements. What is *precipitous* is dangerously steep; it describes cliffs and inclines.

precondition. Try *condition* or *prerequisite* instead.

predominant; predominate. Like *dominant, predominant* is an adjective {a predominant point of view}. Like *dominate, predominate* is a verb {a point of view that predominates throughout the state}. Using *predominate* as an adjective is common but loose usage.

preface. See **foreword.**

prejudice, vb. Although *prejudice* is a perfectly normal English noun to denote an all-too-common trait, and *prejudiced* is an unobjectionable adjective, the verb *to prejudice* is a legalism. For a plain-English equivalent, use *harm* or *hurt.*

preliminary to. Make it *before, in preparing for,* or some other natural phrasing.

prescribe. See **proscribe.**

presently. This word is ambiguous. Write *at present, now,* or *soon,* whichever you really mean.

presumption. See **assumption.**

preventive. Although the corrupt form *preventative* is fairly common, the strictly correct form is *preventive.*

previous to. Make it *before.*

prior to. Make it *before* or *until.*

process of, in the. You can almost always delete this phrase without affecting the meaning.

propaganda. This is a singular noun {propaganda was everywhere}. The plural is *propagandas.*

prophesy; prophecy. *Prophesy* is the verb {the doomsayers prophesied widespread blackouts for Y2K}. *Prophecy* is the noun {their prophecies did not materialize}. *Prophesize* is an erroneous form sometimes encountered.

proscribe; prescribe. To *proscribe* something is to prohibit it {legislation that proscribes drinking while driving}. To *prescribe* is to appoint or dictate a rule or course of action {Henry VIII prescribed the order of succession to include three of his children} or to specify a medical remedy {the doctor prescribed anti-inflammatory pills and certain exercises}.

protuberance. So spelled. Perhaps because *protrude* means "to stick out," writers want to spell *protuberance* (something that bulges out) with an extra *r* (after the *t*). But the words are from different roots.

proved; proven. *Proved* is the preferred past-participial form of *prove* {it was proved to be true}. Use *proven* as an adjective {a proven success}.

proximity. See **close proximity.**

purposely; purposefully. What is done *purposely* is done intentionally, or "on purpose." What is done *purposefully* is done with a certain goal in mind. An action may be done *purposely* without any particular interest in a specific result—that is, not *purposefully*.

question whether; question of whether; question as to whether. The first phrasing is the best, the second is next best, and the third is to be avoided. See **as to.**

quick(ly). *Quickly* is the general adverb. But *quick* is properly used as an adverb in the idiomatic phrases *get rich quick* and *come quick*. See 5.147.

quote; quotation. Traditionally a verb, *quote* is often used as an equivalent of *quotation* in speech and informal writing. Also, writers (especially journalists) tend to think of *quotes* as contemporary remarks usable in their writing and of *quotations* as being wisdom of the ages expressed pithily.

rack. See **wrack.**

reason why. Although some object to the supposed redundancy of this phrase, it is centuries old and perfectly acceptable English. And *reason that* is not always an adequate substitute.

reference. See **allusion.**

refrain; restrain. To *refrain* is to restrain yourself (or *refrain from* doing something); it is typically an act of self-discipline. Other people *restrain* you {if you don't refrain from the disorderly conduct, the police will restrain you}.

regrettable; regretful. What is *regrettable* is unfortunate or deplorable. A person who is *regretful* feels regret or sorrow for something done or lost. The adverb *regrettably*, not *regretfully*, is the synonym of *unfortunately*.

relegate; delegate. To *relegate* is to assign a lesser position {the officer was relegated to desk duty pending an investigation} or to hand over for decision or execution {the application was relegated to the human services committee}. To *delegate* is to authorize another to act on one's behalf {Congress delegated environmental regulation to the EPA}.

renounce. See **denounce.**

repellent; repulsive. *Repellent* and *repulsive* both denote the character of driving others away. But *repulsive* has strong negative connotations of being truly disgusting.

repetitive; repetitious. Both mean "occurring over and over." But whereas *repetitive* is fairly neutral in connotation, *repetitious* has taken on an air of tediousness.

repress. See **oppress.**

repulsive. See **repellent.**

restive; restful. *Restive* has two senses: "impatient, stubborn" and "restless, agitated." *Restful* means "conducive to rest."

restrain. See **refrain.**

reticent. This word should not be used as a synonym for *reluctant*. It means "inclined to be silent; reserved; taciturn" {when asked about the incident, the congressional representative became uncharacteristically reticent}.

revenge. See **avenge.**

seasonal; seasonable. *Seasonal* means either "dependent on a season" {snow skiing is a seasonal hobby} or "relating to the seasons or a season" {the seasonal aisle stays stocked most of the year, starting with Valentine's Day gifts in January}. *Seasonable* means "timely" {seasonable motions for continuance} or "fitting the season" {it was unseasonably cold for July}.

self-deprecating. See **deprecate.**

semi. See **bi.**

semiannual. See **biannual.**

sensor. See **censor.**

sensual; sensuous. What is *sensual* involves indulgence of the senses—especially sexual gratification. What is *sensuous* usually applies to aesthetic enjoyment; only hack writers imbue the word with salacious connotations.

shine. When this verb is intransitive, it means "to give or make light"; the past tense is *shone* {the stars shone dimly}. When it is transitive, it means "to cause to shine"; the past tense is *shined* {the caterer shined the silver}.

should. See **ought.**

sight; site. A *sight* may be something worth seeing {the sights of London} or a device to aid the eye {the sight of a gun}, among other things. A *site* is a place, whether physical {a mall will be built on this site} or electronic {Web site}. The figurative expression meaning "to focus on a goal" is *to set one's sights.* See also **cite.**

since. This word may relate either to time {since last winter} or to causation {since I'm a golfer, I know what "double bogey" means}. Some writers erroneously believe that the word relates exclusively to time. But the causal *since* was a part of the English language before Chaucer wrote in the fourteenth century, and it is useful as a slightly milder way of expressing causation than *because*. But if there is any possibility of confusion with the temporal sense, use *because*.

site. See **cite; sight.**

slander. See **defamation.**

slew; slough; slue. *Slew* is an informal word equivalent to *many* or *lots* {you have a slew of cattle}. It is sometimes misspelled *slough* (a legitimate noun meaning "a grimy swamp") or *slue* (a legitimate verb meaning "to swing around").

slow. This word, like *slowly*, may be an adverb. Generally, prefer *slowly* {go slowly}. But when used after the verb in a pithy statement, especially an injunction, *slow* often appears in colloquial usage {Go slow!} {take it slow}. See 5.147.

slue. See **slew.**

sneak. This verb is conjugated *sneak–sneaked–sneaked*. Reserve *snuck* for dialect and tongue-in-cheek usages.

spit. If used to mean "to expectorate," the verb is inflected *spit–spat–spat* {he spat a curse}. But if used to mean "to skewer," it's *spit–spitted–spitted* {the hens have been spitted for broiling}.

stanch. See **staunch.**

stationary; stationery. *Stationary* describes a state of immobility or of staying in one place {if it's stationary, paint it}. *Stationery* denotes writing materials {love letters written on perfumed stationery}. To remember the two, try associating the *er* in *stationery* with the *er* in *paper*; or remember that a *stationer* is someone who sells the stuff.

staunch; stanch. *Staunch* is an adjective meaning "ardent and faithful" {a staunch Red Sox supporter}. *Stanch* is a verb meaning "to stop the flow"; it is almost always used in regard to bleeding, literally and metaphorically {after New Hampshire the campaign was hemorrhaging; only a big win in South Carolina could stanch the bleeding}.

subject. See **citizen.**

subsequent. See **consequent.**

subsequently. Try *later*.

subsequent to. Make it *after*.

such. This word, when used to replace *this* or *that*—as in "such building was later condemned"—is symptomatic of legalese. *Such* is actually no more precise than *the, this, that, these,* or *those*. It is perfectly acceptable, however, to use *such* with a mass noun or plural noun when the meaning is "of that type" or "of this kind" {such impudence galled the rest of the family} {such vitriolic exchanges became commonplace in later years}.

sufficient. See **adequate.**

sympathy. See **empathy.**

systematic; systemic. *Systematic* means "according to a plan or system, methodical, or arranged in a system." *Systemic* is limited in use to physiological systems {a systemic disease affecting several organs} or, by extension, other systems that may be likened to the body {systemic problems within the corporate hierarchy}.

take. See **bring.**

tantalizing; titillating. A *tantalizing* thing torments us because we want it badly and it is always just out of reach. A *titillating* thing tickles us pleasantly, either literally or figuratively.

thankfully. This word traditionally means "appreciatively; gratefully." It is not in good use as a substitute for *thank goodness* or *fortunately*.

that; which. These are both relative pronouns (see 5.58–62). In polished American prose, *that* is used restrictively to narrow a category or identify a particular item being talked about {any building that is taller must be outside the state}; *which* is used nonrestrictively—not to narrow a class or identify a particular item but to add something about an item already identified {alongside the officer trotted a toy poodle, which is hardly a typical police dog}. *Which* should be used restrictively only when it is preceded by a preposition {the situation in which we find ourselves}. Otherwise it is almost always preceded by a comma, a parenthesis, or a dash. In British English, writers and editors seldom observe the distinction between the two words.

therefore; therefor. The words have different senses. *Therefore*, the common word, means "as a consequence; for that reason" {the evidence of guilt was slight; the jury therefore acquitted the defendant}. *Therefor*, a legalism, means "in return for" or "for it" {he brought the unworn shirt back to the store and received a refund therefor}.

thus. *Thus* is the adverb—not *thusly*.

till. This is a perfectly good preposition and conjunction {open till 10:00 p.m.}. It is not a contraction of *until* and should not be written *'til*.

timbre; timber. *Timbre* is a musical term meaning tonal quality. *Timber* is the correct spelling in all other uses.

time period. See **period of time.**

titillating. See **tantalizing.**

tolerance; toleration. *Tolerance* is the habitual quality of being tolerant; *toleration* is a particular instance of being tolerant.

torpid. See **turbid.**

tortious; tortuous; torturous. What is *tortious* relates to torts (civil wrongs) or to acts that give rise to legal claims for torts {tortious interference with a contract}. What is *tortuous* is full of twists and turns {a tortuous path through the woods}. What is *torturous* involves torture {a torturous exam}.

toward; towards. The preferred form is without the *s* in American English, with it in British English. The same is true for other directional words, such as *upward, downward, forward,* and *backward,* as well as *afterward.* The use of *afterwards* and *backwards* as adverbs is neither rare nor incorrect. But for consistency it is better to stay with the shorter forms.

transcript; transcription. A *transcript* is a written record, as of a trial or a radio program. *Transcription* is the act or process of creating a transcript.

trillion. See **billion.**

triumphal; triumphant. Things are *triumphal* {a triumphal arch}, but only people feel *triumphant* {a triumphant Caesar returned to Rome}.

turbid; turgid; torpid. *Turbid* water is thick and opaque from churned-up mud {a turbid pond}; by extension, *turbid* means "unclear, confused, or disturbed" {a turbid argument}. *Turgid* means "swollen" and, by extension, "pompous and bombastic" {turgid prose}. *Torpid* means "idle and lazy" {a torpid economy}.

unique. Reserve this word for the sense "one of a kind." Avoid it in the sense "special, unusual." Phrases such as *very unique, more unique, somewhat unique,* and so on—in which a degree is attributed to *unique*—are poor usage. See 5.90.

unlawful; illegal; illicit; criminal. This list is in ascending order of negative connotation. An *unlawful* act may even be morally innocent (for example, letting a parking meter expire). But an *illegal* act is something that society formally condemns, and an *illicit* act calls to mind moral degeneracy {illicit drug use}. Unlike *criminal,* the first three terms can apply to civil wrongs.

unorganized. See **disorganized.**

unreadable. See **illegible.**

upon. See **on.**

utilize. Try the verb *use* instead. And instead of *utilization,* try the noun *use.*

venal; venial. A person who is *venal* is mercenary or open to bribery {a venal government official}; a thing that is *venal* is purchasable {venal livestock}. (The latter usage is archaic.) What is *venial* is pardonable or excusable {a venial offense} {a venial error}.

verbal; oral. If something is put into words, it is *verbal.* Technically, *verbal* covers both written and spoken utterance. But if you wish to specify that something was conveyed by word of mouth, use *oral.*

very. See **much.**

vocation. See **avocation.**

voluminous. See **compendious.**

whether. Generally, use *whether* alone—not with the words *or not* tacked on {they didn't know whether to go}. The *or not* is necessary only when you mean to convey the idea of "regardless of whether" {we'll finish on time whether or not it rains}. *Whether* is sometimes replaced by *if* in informal usage {we didn't know if we would finish}; in more formal usage, *whether* is preferred. See also **determine whether**.

which. See **that**.

while. *While* may substitute for *although* or *whereas*, especially if a conversational tone is desired {while many readers may disagree, the scientific community has overwhelmingly adopted the conclusions here presented}. Yet because *while* can denote either time or contrast, the word is occasionally ambiguous; when a real ambiguity exists, *although* or *whereas* is the better choice.

who; whom. Here are the traditional rules: *Who* is a nominative pronoun used as (1) the subject of a finite verb {it was Jim who bought the coffee today}, or (2) a predicate nominative when it follows a linking verb {that's who}. *Whom* is an objective pronoun that may appear as (1) the object of a verb {I learned nothing about the man whom I saw}, or (2) the object of a preposition {the woman to whom I owe my life}. Today there are two countervailing trends: first, there's a decided tendency to use *who* colloquially in most contexts; second, among those insecure about their grammar, there's a tendency to overcorrect and use *whom* when *who* would be correct. Writers and editors of formal prose often resist the first of these; everyone should resist the second. See also 5.58.

whoever; whomever. Avoid the second unless you are certain of your grammar {give this book to whoever wants it} {give it to whomever you choose}. If you are uncertain why both these examples are correct, use *anyone who* in the first example and just *anyone* in the second.

whom. See **who**.

who's; whose. The first is a contraction {Who's on first?}, the second a possessive {Whose life is it, anyway?}. Unlike *who* and *whom*, *whose* may refer to things as well as people {the Commerce Department, whose bailiwick includes intellectual property}. See 5.62.

whosever; whoever's. The first is correct in formal writing {we need to talk to whosever bag that is}; the second is acceptable in casual usage {whoever's dog got into our garbage can should clean up the mess}.

wrack; rack. To *wrack* is to severely or completely destroy {a storm-wracked ship}. (*Wrack* is also a noun denoting wreckage {the storm's wrack}.) To *rack* is to torture by stretching with an instrument {rack the prisoner until he confesses} or to stretch beyond capacity {to rack one's brains}.

wrong; wrongful. These terms are not interchangeable. *Wrong* has two senses: (1) "immoral, unlawful" {it's wrong to bully smaller children}; and (2) "improper, incorrect, unsatisfactory" {the math answers are wrong}. *Wrongful* likewise has two senses: (1) "unjust, unfair" {wrongful conduct}; and (2) "unsanctioned by law; having no legal right" {it was a wrongful demand on the estate}.

yes. See **affirmative, in the.**

your; you're. *Your* is the possessive form of *you*. *You're* is the contraction for *you are*.

BIAS-FREE LANGUAGE

5.203   *Maintaining credibility.* Biased language—language that is either sexist or suggestive of other conscious or subconscious prejudices that are not central to the meaning of the work—distracts and may even offend readers, and in their eyes it makes the work less credible. Few texts warrant the deliberate display of linguistic biases. Nor is it ideal, however, to call attention to the supposed absence of linguistic biases, since this will also distract readers and weaken credibility.

5.204   *Gender bias.* Consider the issue of gender-neutral language. On the one hand, it is unacceptable to a great many reasonable readers to use the generic masculine pronoun (*he* in reference to no one in particular). On the other hand, it is unacceptable to a great many readers either to resort to nontraditional gimmicks to avoid the generic masculine (by using *he/she* or *s/he*, for example) or to use *they* as a kind of singular pronoun. Either way, credibility is lost with some readers. What is wanted, in short, is a kind of invisible gender neutrality. There are many ways to achieve such language, but it takes thought and often some hard work. See 5.43, 5.51, 5.78.

5.205   *Other biases.* The same is true of other types of biases, such as slighting allusions, assumptions, or stereotypes based on characteristics such as race, ethnicity, disability, religion, age, sexual orientation, or birth or family status. Careful writers avoid language that reasonable readers might find offensive or distracting—unless the biased language is central to the meaning of the writing.

5.206   *Editor's responsibility.* A careful editor points out to authors any biased terms or approaches in the work (knowing, of course, that the bias may have been unintentional), suggests alternatives, and ensures that any biased language that is retained is retained by choice. Although some publishers prefer to avoid certain terms or specific usages in all cases, Chicago does not maintain a list of words or usages considered unacceptable. Rather, its editors adhere to the reasoning presented here and apply it to individual cases. They consult guides to avoiding bias in writing (see bibliog. 1.2) and work with authors to use the most appropriate language for the work.

PREPOSITIONAL IDIOMS

5.207 *Idiomatic uses.* Among the most persistent word-choice issues are those concerning prepositions. Which prepositions go with which words? You *imbue* A *with* B but *instill* B *into* A; you *replace* A *with* B but *substitute* B *for* A; you *prefix* A *to* B but *preface* B *with* A; you *force* A *into* B but *enforce* B *on* A; finally, A *implies* B, so you *infer* B *from* A. And that's only the beginning of it.

5.208 *Shifts in idiom.* While prepositional idioms often give nonnative speakers of English nightmares, even native speakers sometimes need to double-check them. Often the language undergoes some shifting. There may be a difference between traditional literary usage (*oblivious of*) and prevailing contemporary usage (*oblivious to*). Sometimes the writer may choose one or the other preposition for reasons of euphony. (Is it better, in a given context, to *ruminate on, about,* or *over* a specified problem?) Sometimes, too, the denotative and connotative differences can be striking: it's one thing to be *smitten with* another and quite a different thing to be *smitten by* another.

5.209 *List of words and prepositions.* Listed here are the words that most often give writers trouble. Where more than one preposition is given, the bracketed terms show the context where each is appropriate. Where two prepositions are followed by a single bracketed term, either can be used in a similar context. The notation *"none (transitive)"* indicates that no preposition is used when a verb is transitive. Examples of the first item in the list might be *abide with me; to abide by an agreement; I can't abide him.*

abide (vb.): with [stay]; by [obey]; *none* (transitive)
abound (vb.): in, with [resources]
absolve (vb.): from [guilt]; of [obligation]
abut (vb.): on, against [land]; *none* (transitive)
accompanied (adj.): by (not *with*) [something else]
accord (vb.): in *or* with [an opinion]; to [a person]
account (vb.): to [a person]; for [a thing or a person]
acquiesce (vb.): in [a decision]; to [pressure]
acquit (vb.): of (not *from*) [a charge]; *none* (transitive)
adept (vb.): at [an activity]; in [an art]
admit (vb.) ("acknowledge"): *none* (not *to*) (transitive)
admit (vb.) ("let in"): to, into
admit (vb.) ("allow"): of
agree (vb.): to, on, upon [terms]; about [concur]; with [a person]; in [a specified manner (e.g., *in general* or *in principle*)]
answer (vb.): to [a person]; for [an act]

anxious (adj.): about [a concern] (preferably not *to* [do something])

argue (vb.): with [a person]; over, about [a situation or thing]; for, against [a position]

badger (vb.): into [doing something]; about [a situation]

ban (n.): on [a thing; an activity]; from [a place]

ban (vb.): from [a place]

bank (vb.): on [rely]; off [carom]; at, with [a financial institution]

based (adj.): on (preferably not *upon*) [a premise]; in [a place; a field of study]

beguile (vb.): into [doing something]; with [gifts, flattery, etc.]

bestow (vb.): on (preferably not *upon*) [an honoree]

binding (adj.): on (preferably not *upon*) [a person]

blasphemy (n.): against [a religious tenet]

cajole (vb.): into [doing something]; out of [a possession]

caution (vb.): about [a situation]; against [doing something]

center (vb.): on, upon (not *around*) [a primary issue]

chafe (vb.): at [doing something]; under [an irritating authority]

coalesce (vb.): into [a unit]

coerce (vb.): into [doing something]

cohesion (n.): between, among [things; groups]

coincide (vb.): with [an event]

collude (vb.): with [a person to defraud another]

comment (n.): on [a thing]; about [another person]; to [a person]

commiserate (vb.): with [a person]

compare (vb.): with (literal comparison); to (poetic or metaphorical comparison)

comply (vb.): with (not *to*) [a rule; an order]

confide (vb.): to, in [a person]

congruence (n.): with [a standard]

connive (vb.): at [a bad act]; with [another person]

consider (vb.): *none* (transitive); as [one of several possible aspects (*not* as a substitute for "to be")]; for [a position]

consist (vb.): of [components (said of concrete things)]; in [qualities (said of abstract things)]

contemporary (adj.): with [another event]

contemporary (n.): of [another person]

contiguous (adj.): with, to [another place]

contingent (adj.): on (preferably not *upon*)

conversant (adj.): with, in [a field of study]

convict (vb.): of, for [not *in*]

depend (vb.): on (preferably not *upon*)

differ (vb.): from [a thing or quality]; with [a person]; about, over, on [an issue]

different (adj.): from (but when an independent clause follows *different*, the conjunction *than* is a defensible substitute for *from what*: "movies today are different than they were in the fifties")

dissent (n. & vb.): from, against (preferably not *to* or *with*)

dissimilar (adj.): to (not *from*)

dissociate (vb.): from

enamored (adj.): of (not *with*)

equivalent (adj.): to, in (preferably not *with*)

excerpt (n. & vb.): from (not *of*)

forbid (vb.): to (formal); from (informal)

foreclose (vb.): on [mortgaged property]

fraternize (vb.): with [certain people]

hail (vb.): as [an esteemed person]; from [a place]

hale (vb.): to, into [a place]; before [a magistrate]

hegemony (n.): over [rivals]; in [a region, a field]

identical (adj.): with (preferred by purists); to [something else]

impatience (n.): with [a person]; with, at, about [a situation]

impose (vb.): on (preferably not *upon*) [a person]

inaugurate (vb.): as [an officer]; into [an office]

inculcate (vb.): into, in [a person]

independent (adj.): of (not *from*) [something else]

infringe (vb.): *none* (transitive); on (preferably not *upon*) [a right]

inhere (vb.): in (not *within*) [a person; a thing]

inquire (vb.): into [situations]; of [people]; after [people]; about [a thing]

instill (vb.): in, into (not *with*) [a person]

lull (vb.): into [deception]; to [sleep]

mastery (n.): of [a skill]; over [people]

meant (vb.): as [an intention]; for [a destination, literal or figurative]

militate (vb.): against [an outcome]

mitigate (vb.): *none* (transitive)

oblivious (adj.): of (preferred); to [a danger; an opportunity]

off (prep. & adv.): *none* (not *of*)

predilection (n.): for [a preferred thing]

predominate (vb.) (not transitive): in [a field]; over [a rival]

preferable (adj.): to [not *than*]

pregnant (adj.): with [the child]; by [the father]

pretext (n.): for [a true intention]

purge (vb.): of [bad elements]; from [an organization; a society]

reconcile (vb.): with [a person]; to [a situation]

reticent (adj.): about [speaking; a topic]; in [manner]

sanction (n.): for [misbehavior]; of [a sponsoring body]; to [a person; an event]

shiver (vb.): from [cold]; at [something frightening]

skillful (adj.): at, in [an activity]; with [tools]

stigmatize (vb.): *none* (transitive); as [dishonorable]

subscribe (vb.): to [a periodical or an opinion]; for [stock]

succeed (vb.): in [an endeavor]; to [an estate]; as [a person in some position]

trade (vb.): for [swap]; in [sell]; with [do business with]; at [patronize]; on [buy and sell at]

trust (n.): in [faith]; for [beneficial trust]

undaunted (adj.): in [a task]; by [obstacles]

unequal (adj.): to [a challenge]; in [attributes]

used (adj.): to [accustomed]; for [applied]

vexed (adj.): with [someone]; about, at [something]

6

Punctuation

Introduction

6.1   *Function.* Punctuation should be governed by its function, which is to promote ease of reading. Although punctuation, like word usage, allows for subjectivity, authors and editors should be aware of certain principles lest the subjective element obscure meaning. The guidelines offered in this chapter draw for the most part from traditional American practice.

6.2   *Coverage.* The rules and examples given below apply largely to regular text. For the special punctuation recommended in mathematics, foreign languages, notes, bibliographies, indexes, Internet publications, and so on, see the appropriate chapters in this manual and consult the index.

Typographic and Aesthetic Considerations

6.3   *Punctuation and font: primary system.* All punctuation marks should appear in the same font—roman or italic—as the main or surrounding text, except for punctuation that belongs to a title or an exclamation in a different font. This departure from Chicago's former usage serves both simplicity and logic. For parentheses and brackets, see 6.6. For an alternative system, see 6.5.

> Smith played the title role in *Hamlet, Macbeth,* and *King Lear;* after his final performance,
>   during which many in the audience wept, he announced his retirement.
> Many editors admire *Wired Style*: it is both elegant and easy to use.
> *An Apache Life-way: The Economic, Social, and Religious Institutions of the Chiricahua
>   Indians*
> Are you saying the wound was *self-inflicted?*
> She is the author of *What Next?*
> For light entertainment he reads *King Lear*!
> The manual *Online!* is always at my elbow.
> We heard his cries of "*Help!*"

6.4   *Boldface.* Punctuation marks following *boldface* should be dealt with case by case, depending on how the boldface word is used.

> **head margin**. Top margin of a page.
> **Note:** In what follows . . .
> **Danger!** Take only as directed.
> What is the point of clicking on **Help**? It seldom helps me.

6.5   *Punctuation and font: alternative system.* According to a more traditional system, periods, commas, colons, and semicolons should appear in the same font as the word, letter, character, or symbol immediately preceding them if different from that of the main or surrounding text. In the first example in 6.3, the first two commas and the semicolon would be italic. Question marks and exclamation points, however, should appear in the same font as the immediately preceding word only if they belong to a title or an exclamation (see examples in 6.3).

6.6   *Parentheses and brackets.* Even if the alternative system (see 6.5) is used, parentheses and brackets should appear in the same font—roman or italic—as the surrounding text, not in that of the material they enclose. This system, though it may occasionally cause typefitting problems when a slanting italic letter touches a nonslanting roman parenthesis or bracket, has two main virtues: it is easy to use, and it has long been practiced. A typesetter can be instructed to add a thin space between touching characters.

The Asian long-horned beetle (*Anoplophora glabripennis*) attacks maples.
The letter stated that my check had been "recieved [*sic*] with thanks."

When a phrase in parentheses or brackets appears on a line by itself, the parentheses or brackets are usually in the same font as the phrase.

[To be concluded]

6.7 *Another practice.* Another option is to have parentheses and brackets appear in the same font as the words they enclose, or at least the first and last words. If the first and last words are in different fonts, however, both the opening and the closing parentheses or brackets should appear in the font of the surrounding text, not each in a different font.

CLOSING QUOTATION MARKS IN RELATION TO OTHER PUNCTUATION

6.8 *Periods and commas.* Periods and commas precede closing quotation marks, whether double or single. This is a traditional style, in use well before the first edition of this manual (1906). As nicely expressed in William Strunk Jr. and E. B. White's *Elements of Style,* "Typographical usage dictates that the comma be inside the [quotation] marks, though logically it often seems not to belong there" (p. 36; see bibliog. 1.1). The same goes for the period. (An apostrophe at the end of a word should never be confused with a closing single quotation mark; punctuation always follows the apostrophe.) In the kind of textual studies where retaining the original placement of a comma in relation to closing quotation marks is essential to the author's argument and scholarly integrity, the alternative system described in 6.10 could be used, or rephrasing might avoid the problem. In computer-related writing, in which a file name or other character string enclosed in quotation marks might be rendered inaccurate or ambiguous by the addition of punctuation within the quotation marks, the alternative system may be used, or the character string may be set in another font, without quotation marks (see 7.79). For single versus double quotes, see 7.52, 7.58, 11.8, 11.33–35. For related matters in computer writing, see Eric S. Raymond, "Hacker Writing Style," in *The New Hacker's Dictionary* (bibliog. 5).

6.9 *Colons, semicolons, question marks,* and *exclamation points.* Unlike periods and commas, these all follow closing quotation marks unless a question mark or an exclamation point belongs within the quoted matter. (This rule applies the logic absent in 6.8.)

Take, for example, the first line of "To a Skylark": "Hail to thee, blithe spirit!"
I was asked to state my "name and serial number"; I have no serial number.
Which of Shakespeare's characters said, "All the world's a stage"?
"Where are you from?"
"Watch out!"

6.10   *Alternative system.* According to what is sometimes called the British style (set forth in *The Oxford Guide to Style* [the successor to *Hart's Rules*; see bibliog. 1.1]), a style also followed in other English-speaking countries, only those punctuation points that appeared in the original material should be included within the quotation marks; all others follow the closing quotation marks. This system, which requires extreme authorial precision and occasional decisions by the editor or typesetter, works best with single quotation marks. (The British tend to use double quotation marks only for quotations within quotations.)

OTHER TYPOGRAPHIC MATTERS

6.11   *Space between sentences.* In typeset matter, one space, not two (in other words, a regular word space), follows any mark of punctuation that ends a sentence, whether a period, a colon, a question mark, an exclamation point, or closing quotation marks.

6.12   *Display type.* As long as no confusion results, commas may sometimes be omitted for aesthetic reasons at the ends of lines set in large display type (the kind of type used for title pages, chapter or article openings, subheads, and other elements different from the body text).

Period

6.13   *Use of the period.* A period marks the end of a declarative or an imperative sentence. It is followed by a single space (see 2.12, 6.11). In colloquial style it is sometimes used with an incomplete sentence. For the many other uses of the period, consult the index.

The two faced each other in silence.
Wait here.
A hurricane was rapidly approaching. Which prompted us to leave.

6.14 *Location of period.* When an entire independent sentence is enclosed in parentheses or square brackets, the period belongs inside the closing parenthesis or bracket. When matter in parentheses or brackets, even a grammatically complete sentence, is included within another sentence, the period belongs outside (but see also 6.103). For the location of a period with quotation marks, see 6.8.

> Fiorelli insisted on rewriting the paragraph. (He loved to alter others' drafts.)
> Farnsworth had left an angry message for Isadora on the mantel (she noticed it while glancing in the mirror).
> "She was determined never again to speak to him [her former employer]."

6.15 *Omission of period.* No period should follow display lines (chapter titles, subheads, and similar headings), running heads, column heads in tables, brief captions, datelines in correspondence, signatures, or addresses. Run-in subheads, however, such as the one at the beginning of this paragraph, are followed by periods. When an expression that takes a period ends a sentence, no additional period follows (see 6.122). For use or omission of the period in outline style, see 6.127. For periods in URLs and e-mail addresses, see 6.17.

> Avoid using *op. cit.* Readers prefer a more precise reference.

6.16 *Ellipses.* For the use of ellipsis points (a series of periods), see 11.51–65.

6.17 *URLs and e-mail addresses.* In Internet addresses, no space follows a period (also known as a dot). If it is necessary to break a URL or an e-mail address at the end of a printed line, the period should appear on the new line, never at the end of the line above. See also 7.44, 17.11.

> Chicago's Q&A Web site, which can be found at http://www.chicagomanualofstyle.org, has attracted much constructive comment.

Comma

6.18 *Use of the comma.* The comma, aside from its technical uses in mathematical, bibliographical, and other contexts, indicates the smallest break in sentence structure. It denotes a slight pause. Effective use of the comma involves good judgment, with ease of reading the end in view.

SERIES AND THE SERIAL COMMA

6.19   *Comma needed.* Items in a series are normally separated by commas (but see 6.60). When a conjunction joins the last two elements in a series, a comma—known as the serial or series comma or the Oxford comma—should appear before the conjunction. Chicago strongly recommends this widely practiced usage, blessed by Fowler and other authorities (see bibliog. 1.2), since it prevents ambiguity. If the last element consists of a pair joined by *and*, the pair should still be preceded by a serial comma and the first *and* (see the last two examples below).

> She took a photograph of her parents, the president, and the vice president.
> The owner, the agent, and the tenant were having an argument.
> I want no ifs, ands, or buts.
> Paul put the kettle on, Don fetched the teapot, and I made tea.
> The meal consisted of soup, salad, and macaroni and cheese.
> John was working, Jean was resting, and Alan was running errands and furnishing food.

6.20   *Comma not needed.* In a series whose elements are all joined by conjunctions, no commas are needed unless the elements are long and pauses helpful.

> Is it by Snodgrass or Shapiro or Brooks?
> You can turn left at the second fountain and right when you reach the temple, or turn left at the third fountain and left again at the statue of Venus, or just ask a local person how to get there.

6.21   *Semicolons within series.* When elements in a series involve internal punctuation, or when they are very long and complex, they should be separated by semicolons (see 6.60).

6.22   *"Etc." and "and so forth."* The abbreviation *etc.* (*et cetera*, literally "and others of the same kind") is traditionally both preceded and followed by a comma when it is the final item in a series. Such English equivalents as *and so forth, and the like,* are usually treated the same way. (The use of *etc.* in formal prose is frowned on, though it is acceptable in lists and tables and within parentheses. When used, it should not be italicized.) See also 5.202 under *etc.*

> Cats, dogs, parrots, etc., in transit must be confined to cages.
> The carpenter's saw, hammer, level, and so forth, were found in the attic.

An alternative and quite acceptable usage is to omit the second comma (after *etc.*), punctuating such expressions in the same way as the final element in any series.

6.23   *"Et al."* The abbreviation *et al.* (*et alia* [neut.], *et alii* [masc.], or *et aliae* [fem.], literally "and others"), whether used in regular text or (more often) in bibliographical references (see 16.44, 16.118, 17.29–30), should be treated as one would treat "and her colleagues" or "and their group." When it follows a single item, it requires no preceding or following comma; when it follows two or more names, it is treated the same way as any final element in a series. Note that it is not italicized and that no period follows *et* (which is not an abbreviation).

Zonana et al. (2000) stated that HED-ID affects only males.
In swept the chair, the treasurer, et al., to announce their resignation.

6.24   *Ampersand.* When an ampersand is used instead of the word *and* (as in company names), the serial comma is omitted (except in legal style, with reference to three or more authors; see 17.280).

Winken, Blinken & Nod are experts in nightwear.

INTRODUCTORY WORDS AND PHRASES

6.25   *Introductory phrase with comma.* An adverbial or participial phrase at the beginning of a sentence is usually followed by a comma, especially if a slight pause is intended. A single word or a very short introductory phrase does not require a comma except to avoid misreading.

After reading the note, Henrietta turned pale.
On the other hand, his vices could be considered virtues.
Exhausted by the morning's work, she lay down for a nap.
Having eaten the cat's dinner, Fido ate his own.
On Tuesday he tried to see the mayor.
but
Before eating, the members of the committee met in the assembly room.
To Anthony, Blake remained an enigma.

6.26   *Introductory phrase without comma.* A comma is not used after an introductory adverbial or participial phrase that immediately precedes the verb it modifies.

Out of the Mercedes stepped the woman we were looking for.
Running along behind the wagon was the archduke himself!

6.27 *"Oh" and "ah."* A comma follows an exclamatory *oh* or *ah* only if a slight pause is intended. No comma follows vocative *oh* or (mainly poetic and largely archaic) *O*. See also 5.197.

"Oh, what a beautiful mornin' . . ."   Oh mighty king!
Ah, here we are at last!   "O wild West Wind . . ."
Oh no! Ah yes! Oh yeah?

6.28 *Direct address.* A comma follows names or words used in direct address and informal correspondence.

Ms. Jones, will you please take a seat.
Friends, I am not here to discuss personalities.
Ma'am, your order is ready.
Dear Judy,

6.29 *"Yes," "no," and the like.* A comma usually follows *yes, no, well,* and the like, at the beginning of a sentence if a slight pause is intended.

Yes, I admit that Benson's plan has gained a following.
No, that item is not on the agenda.
Well then, we shall have to take a vote.
but
No no no!

INTERJECTIONS AND DESCRIPTIVE PHRASES

6.30 *Parenthetical elements.* Commas set off parenthetical elements if a slight break is intended. If a stronger break is needed or if there are commas within the parenthetical element, em dashes (6.88) or parentheses (6.97) should be used. An adverb essential to the meaning of the clause (as in the last two examples below) should not be enclosed in commas. See also 5.202 under *that; which.*

This, indeed, was exactly what Scali had feared would happen.
All the test animals, therefore, were reexamined.
We shall, however, take up the matter at a later date.
The Hooligan Report was, to say the least, a bombshell.
Wolinski, after receiving his instructions, left immediately for Algiers.

The most provocative, if not the most important, part of the statement came last.
Her words were true, if not compelling.
This road leads away from, rather than toward, your destination.
She knew that, in the end, truth would prevail.
but
The storehouse was indeed empty.
Two students cheated and were therefore disqualified.

6.31   *Restrictive and nonrestrictive phrases.* A phrase that is restrictive, that is, essential to the meaning of the noun it belongs to, should not be set off by commas. A nonrestrictive phrase, however, *should* be enclosed in commas or, if at the end of a sentence, preceded by a comma. See also 5.29.

The woman wearing a red coat is my sister.
but
My sister, wearing a red coat, set off for the city.
She set off for the city, wearing a red coat.

INDEPENDENT CLAUSES

6.32   *Conjunctions between clauses.* When independent clauses are joined by *and, but, or, so, yet,* or any other conjunction, a comma usually precedes the conjunction. If the clauses are very short and closely connected, the comma may be omitted. (For the use of a semicolon between independent clauses, see 6.57.)

We bolted the door, but the intruder was already inside.
Everyone present was startled by the news, and one man fainted.
Do we want to preserve law and order, or are we interested only in our property?
The bus never came, so we took a taxi.
but
Timothy played the guitar and Betty sang.

6.33   *Conjunctions in a series.* When a sentence is composed of a series of short independent clauses with a conjunction joining the last two, commas should appear both between the clauses and before the conjunction (see 6.19).

Donald cooked, Sally trimmed the tree, and Maddie and Cammie offered hors d'oeuvres.

If independent clauses in a series themselves contain commas, they should be separated by semicolons (see 6.60).

6.34 *Compound predicate.* A comma is not normally used between the parts of a compound predicate—that is, two or more verbs having the same subject, as distinct from two independent clauses—though it may occasionally be needed to avoid misreading or to indicate a pause.

> He had accompanied Sanford and had volunteered to write the report.
> Kelleher tried to see the mayor but was told he was out of town.
> *but*
> She recognized the man who entered the room, and gasped.

DEPENDENT CLAUSES

6.35 *Comma preceding main clause.* A dependent clause that precedes a main clause should be followed by a comma.

> If you accept our conditions, we shall agree to the proposal.

6.36 *Comma following main clause.* A dependent clause that follows a main clause should *not* be preceded by a comma if it is restrictive, that is, essential to the meaning of the main clause. If it is merely supplementary or parenthetical, it should be preceded by a comma. (Note that the distinction is occasionally tenuous; if in doubt, use a comma to indicate a pause.)

> We will agree to the proposal if you accept our conditions.
> Paul was astonished when he heard the terms.
> He didn't run because he was afraid; he ran because it had started to rain.
> *but*
> She ought to be promoted, if you want my opinion.
> At last she arrived, when the food was cold.
> He didn't run, because he was afraid to move.

6.37 *"And if," "that if," and the like.* When two conjunctions appear next to each other (e.g., *and if, but if*), they should not be separated by a comma if there would be no pause between them if they were spoken aloud—or, in grammatical terms, if the dependent clause is restrictive in meaning (see 6.38).

> Burton examined the documents for over an hour, and if Smedley had not intervened, the forgery would have been revealed.
> They decided that if it rained, they would reschedule the game.

RELATIVE CLAUSES

6.38 *Restrictive and nonrestrictive.* A relative clause that is restrictive—that is, essential to the meaning of the sentence—is neither preceded nor followed by a comma. But a relative clause that could be omitted without essential loss of meaning (a nonrestrictive clause) should be both preceded and (if the sentence continues) followed by a comma. Although *which* can be used restrictively, many careful writers preserve the distinction between restrictive *that* (no commas) and nonrestrictive *which* (commas). (The word *that* may be omitted in contexts that are clear without it.) See also 5.202 under *that; which.*

The report that the committee submitted was well documented.
The book I have just finished is due back tomorrow; the others can wait.
That is the woman who mistook my coat for hers.
but
The report, which was well documented, was submitted to the committee.
This book, which I finished last night, is due back tomorrow.
The woman, who was extremely embarrassed, returned my coat.

TWO OR MORE ADJECTIVES PRECEDING A NOUN

6.39 *Comma or no comma between adjectives.* When a noun is preceded by two or more adjectives that could, without affecting the meaning, be joined by *and,* the adjectives are normally separated by commas. But if the noun and the adjective immediately preceding it are conceived as a unit, such as "little girl," "political science," or "glass ceiling," no comma should be used. See also 5.91.

Shelly had proved a faithful, sincere friend.
It is going to be a long, hot, exhausting summer.
She has a young, good-looking friend.
but
She has many young friends.
He has rejected traditional religious affiliations.

6.40 *Repeated adjective.* When an adjective is repeated before a noun, a comma normally appears between the pair.

"You're a bad, bad dog!"
Many, many people have enjoyed the book.

CONSTRUCTIONS WITH *NOT, NOT ONLY,* *THE MORE, THE LESS*

6.41 *"Not," "not only," and the like.* Whether to place commas around an interjected phrase beginning with *not* depends largely on whether pauses are intended. Normally, either two commas or none should be used.

> We hoped the mayor herself, not her assistant, would attend the meeting.
> They marched to Washington, not only armed with petitions and determined to get their senators' attention, but also hoping to demonstrate their solidarity with one another.
> *but*
> They were armed not only with petitions but also with evidence.
> The judge dismissed not only the parking ticket cases but several others as well.
> She decided not to march but merely to collect signatures.

6.42 *"The more," "the less," and so on.* A comma should be used between clauses of the *more . . . the more* type but not between short phrases of that type.

> The more I read about Winterbottom, the more I like her.
> The higher Fisher climbed, the dizzier he felt.
> The less you eat, the better you'll feel.
> *but*
> The more the merrier.
> The sooner the better.

APPOSITIVES

6.43 *Appositives with or without commas.* A word, abbreviation, phrase, or clause that is in apposition to a noun is set off by commas if it is nonrestrictive—that is, omittable, containing supplementary rather than essential information. If it is restrictive—essential to the noun it belongs to—no commas should appear. See also 5.29.

> The committee chair, Gloria Ruffolo, called for a resolution.
> Stanley Groat, president of the corporation, spoke first.
> Sheila Fitzpatrick, PhD, introduced the speaker.
> Ursula's husband, Clifford, had been a student of Norman Maclean's. (In informal prose, "Ursula's husband Clifford had . . ." is acceptable)
> My older sister, Betty, taught me the alphabet.
> *but*
> My sister Enid lets me hold her doll. (I have two sisters.)
> O'Neill's play *The Hairy Ape* was being revived. (O'Neill wrote several plays.)

A problem arises when a proper name includes a comma before the final element, as in "the [Canadian] Constitution Act, 1982" or "California State University, Northridge." Because such a comma is part of the name and not part of the surrounding sentence, a second comma is not, strictly speaking, required when the name appears in the middle of a clause. But its absence may be sufficiently disturbing to most readers to suggest recasting the sentence (as in the first example below), slipping in a mildly illegal comma (as in the second), or adding a nonrestrictive clause or phrase after the proper name (as in the third). See also 8.176.

the 1982 Constitution Act was hailed . . .
California State University, Northridge, has an enrollment of . . .
California State University, Northridge, often called CSUN, has an enrollment of . . .

THAT IS, NAMELY, FOR EXAMPLE, OR, AND SIMILAR EXPRESSIONS

6.44 *Commas customary.* Expressions of the *that is* type are usually followed by a comma. They may be preceded by a comma, an em dash, or a semicolon; or the entire phrase they introduce may be enclosed in parentheses or em dashes. When *or* is used in the sense of "in other words," it is preceded by a comma.

He had coopted several of his friends, namely, Jones, Burdick, and Fauntleroy.
The committee—that is, its more influential members—wanted to drop the matter.
Keesler managed to change the subject; that is, he introduced a tangential issue.
Bones from various small animals (e.g., a squirrel, a cat, a pigeon, a muskrat) were found
in the doctor's cabinet.
The compass stand, or binnacle, must be situated within the helmsman's field of vision.

Note that "e.g." and "i.e." are not italicized.

SEPARATING HOMONYMS

6.45 *Commas between homonyms.* For ease of reading, two words that are spelled alike but have different functions may be separated by a comma if a slight pause is intended.

Let us march in, in twos.
Whatever is, is good.
but
He gave his life that that cause might prevail.

DATES

6.46 *Commas needed or omitted.* In the month-day-year style of dates, the style most commonly used in the United States and hence now recommended by Chicago, commas are used both before and after the year. In the day-month-year system—sometimes awkward in regular text, though useful in material that requires many full dates—no commas are needed. Where month and year only are given, or a specific day (such as a holiday) with a year, neither system uses a comma. See also 5.79, 9.33–35.

The ship sailed on October 6, 1999, for Southampton.
The April 1, 2000, press conference elicited little new information.
Bradford gradually came to accept the verdict. (See his journal entries of 6 October 1999 and 4 January 2000.)
In March 2003 she turned seventy.
On Thanksgiving Day 1998 they celebrated their seventy-fifth anniversary.

ADDRESSES AND NAMES

6.47 *Addresses and place-names in text.* Commas are used to set off the individual elements in addresses or place-names that are run into the text. No comma appears between a street name and an abbreviation such as SW or before a postal code.

Proofs were sent to the author at 743 Olga Drive NE, Ashtabula, OH 44044, on May 2.
Waukegan, Illinois, is not far from the Wisconsin border.
The plane landed in Kampala, Uganda, that evening.

In a mailing address, commas should be used as sparsely as possible. For place-names used adjectivally, see 5.67.

6.48 *Personal names plus place-names.* Commas are used to set off a place of residence immediately following a person's name unless the place is essential to the meaning of the sentence or is considered part of the person's name.

Patricia Birkholz, of Saugatuck, was easily elected.
Gerald Ford, from Grand Rapids, ascended to the White House.
but
The Kennedys of Orange County are unrelated to John F. Kennedy.
Clement of Alexandria

6.49 *"Jr.," "Sr.," and the like.* Commas are no longer required around *Jr.* and *Sr.* If commas are used, however, they must appear both before and after the element. Commas never set off *II, III,* and such when used as part of a name.

George W. Wilson Jr. has eclipsed his father's fame.
or
George W. Wilson, Jr., has eclipsed his father's fame.
John A. Doe III is the son of John A. Doe Jr.

6.50 *"Inc.," "Ltd.," and the like.* Commas are not required around *Inc., Ltd.,* and such as part of a company's name. As with *Jr.,* however, if commas are used, they must appear both before and after the element.

The president of Millennial Products Inc. was the first speaker.
or, less desirably,
The president of Millennial Products, Inc., was the first speaker.

ELLIPTICAL CONSTRUCTIONS

6.51 *Comma indicating ellipsis.* A comma is often used to indicate the omission of a word or words readily understood from the context.

In Illinois there are seventeen such schools; in Ohio, twenty; in Indiana, thirteen.
Thousands rushed to serve him in victory; in defeat, none.

The comma may be omitted if the elliptical construction is clear without it.

One child is good at composition, another at mathematics, and the third at sports.
Ronald adored her and she him.

QUOTATIONS, MAXIMS, AND QUESTIONS

6.52 *Placement of comma.* The comma in relation to quoted material is discussed only briefly below. For the location of a comma in relation to closing quotation marks, see 6.8. For detailed discussion and illustration of the use or omission of commas before and after quoted material, including dialogue, see 11.21, 11.55, 11.58. See also 7.52.

6.53 *Comma with quoted material.* Quoted material, if brief, is usually introduced by a comma; if longer or more formal, by a colon (see 6.66, 11.20).

If a quotation is introduced by *that, whether,* or a similar conjunction, no comma is needed.

> It was Emerson who wrote, "Blessed are those who have no talent!"
> She replied, "I hope you are not referring to me."
> Was it Stevenson who said that "the cruelest lies are often told in silence"?
> He is now wondering whether "to hold, as 'twere, the mirror up to nature."

6.54 *Comma with maxims and such.* With maxims, proverbs, mottoes, and other familiar expressions, commas are used or omitted in the same way as with appositives (6.43) and quotations (6.53). Whether such expressions are enclosed in quotation marks depends largely on the syntax of the sentence in which they appear. See also 8.210.

> The motto "All for one and one for all" appears over the door.
> Tom's favorite proverb, "A rolling stone gathers no moss," proved wrong.
> It is untrue that a rolling stone gathers no moss.

6.55 *Comma with questions.* A direct question included within another sentence is usually preceded by a comma; it need not begin with a capital letter (see first two examples), but if the question is relatively long or has internal punctuation, an initial capital helps (see third example). An indirect question takes no comma (see fourth and fifth examples). See also 6.70–75.

> Suddenly he asked himself, where am I headed?
> The question, how are we going to tell her? was on everyone's mind.
> Legislators had to confront the issue, Can the fund be used for the current emergency, or must it remain dedicated to its original purpose?
> Anselm wondered why he was feeling faint.
> What to do next is the question.

COMMA WITH PARENTHESES AND BRACKETS

6.56 *Location of comma.* When the context calls for a comma at the end of material in parentheses or brackets, the comma should follow the closing parenthesis or bracket. A comma never precedes a closing parenthesis. (For its rare appearance before an opening parenthesis, see fifth example in 6.126.)

> Although he rejected the first proposal (he could not have done otherwise), he made it clear that he was open to further negotiations.
> He gives a careful, though stilted (and somewhat obscure), exposition.
> "Conrad told his assistant [Martin], who was clearly exhausted, to rest."

Semicolon

6.57 *Use of the semicolon.* The semicolon, stronger than a comma but weaker than a period, can assume either role, though its function is usually closer to that of a period. Its most common use is between two independent clauses not joined by a conjunction.

> The controversial portrait had been removed from the entrance hall; in its place had been hung a realistic landscape.
>
> Mildred intends to go to Europe; her plans, however, are still quite vague.

6.58 *Before an adverb.* The following adverbs, among others, should be preceded by a semicolon when used transitionally between independent clauses: *then, however, thus, hence, indeed, accordingly, besides,* and *therefore.*

> The controversial portrait had been removed from the entrance hall; indeed, it had disappeared entirely from the building.
>
> Mildred intends to go to Europe; however, she has made no plans.
>
> Joe had forgotten his reeds; therefore he could not play the oboe solo.

"I think, therefore I am" (Descartes) remains an exception to this usage.

6.59 *Before a conjunction.* An independent clause introduced by a conjunction may be preceded by a semicolon, especially when the independent clause has internal punctuation. For the more common use of a comma with conjunctions, see 6.32.

> Frobisher had always assured his grandson that the house would be his; yet there was no provision for this bequest in his will.
>
> Maria had determined to question the ambassador; but bodyguards surrounding him, as well as the presence of dancing girls, prevented him from noticing her.

6.60 *In a series.* When items in a series involve internal punctuation, they should be separated by semicolons. See also 6.126.

> The membership of the international commission was as follows: France, 4; Germany, 5; Great Britain, 1; Italy, 3; United States, 7.
>
> The defendant, in an attempt to mitigate his sentence, pleaded that he had recently, and quite unexpectedly, lost his job; that his landlady—whom, incidentally, he had once saved from attack—had threatened him with eviction; and that he had not eaten for several days.

6.61 *With "that is" and the like.* A semicolon may be used before expressions such as *that is* or *namely.* See also 6.44.

We need to set priorities; that is, we must respond to immediate needs as well as to long-term goals.

6.62   *With parentheses or brackets.* When the context calls for a semicolon at the end of material enclosed in parentheses or brackets, the semicolon should follow the closing parenthesis or bracket. For the location of a semicolon with quotation marks, see 6.9.

She enclosed a check for $145 (her final payment); then, with relief, she sealed the envelope.
"He dismissed his assistant [Martin]; he then turned to his visitor."

Colon

6.63   *Use of the colon.* A colon introduces an element or a series of elements illustrating or amplifying what has preceded the colon. Between independent clauses it functions much like a semicolon, though more strongly emphasizing sequence. The colon may be used instead of a period to introduce a series of related sentences (as in the fourth example below). Colons are also used in URLs; no space precedes or follows a colon in a URL. For use of the em dash instead of a colon, see 6.88. (A colon should never be immediately followed by a dash: either a colon or a dash alone suffices.)

The study involves three food types: cereals, fruits and vegetables, and fats.
They even relied on a chronological analogy: just as the Year II had overshadowed 1789, so the October Revolution had eclipsed that of February.
Many of the police officers held additional jobs: thirteen of them, for example, moonlighted as security guards.
Henrietta was faced with a hideous choice: Should she reveal what was in the letter and ruin her reputation? Or should she remain silent and compromise the safety of her family?
You should be able to find an archived version of the article at http://www.nytimes.com.

6.64   *Lowercase or capital letter after a colon?* When a colon is used within a sentence, as in the first three examples in 6.63, the first word following the colon is lowercased unless it is a proper name. When a colon introduces two or more sentences (as in the fourth example in 6.63 or the second example in 6.65), or when it introduces a speech in dialogue or an extract (as in the examples in 6.66), the first word following it is capitalized.

6.65   *With "as follows" and the like.* A colon is normally used after *as follows, the following,* and similar expressions. (For lists, see 6.124–30.)

> The steps are as follows: first, make grooves for the seeds; second, sprinkle the seeds; third, push the earth back over the grooves; fourth, water generously.
> I argue the following propositions: First, . . . Second, . . . Third, . . .

6.66   *Introducing speech.* A colon is often used to introduce speech in dialogue or an extract. See also 11.20. For use of the comma in dialogue, see 6.53, 11.21.

> Michael: The incident has already been reported.
> Timothy: Then, sir, all is lost!

> Julian Duguid, author of *Green Hell* (1931), starts his book boldly: "When a man yields to the urge of Ishmael . . ."

6.67   *With introductory phrase.* At the beginning of a speech or a formal communication, a colon usually follows the identification of those addressed. For use of a comma, see 6.28.

> Ladies and Gentlemen: Dear Credit and Collections Manager:
> To Whom It May Concern:

6.68   *Inappropriate uses of colon.* A colon is *not* normally used after *namely, for example,* and similar expressions. Nor is it used before a series introduced by a verb or a preposition.

> The study involved the three most critical issues, namely, voter registration, voter turnout, and referendums.
> A résumé should include educational background, work experience, other relevant experience, and knowledge of any foreign languages.
> This manual is concerned with (1) the components of a publication, (2) copyright law, (3) formal style, (4) documentation, and (5) indexes.

For various list forms and their punctuation, see 6.124–30.

6.69   *With parentheses or brackets.* When the context calls for a colon at the end of material enclosed in parentheses or brackets, the colon should follow the closing parenthesis or bracket. For the location of a colon with quotation marks, see 6.9.

> A change occurred in the behavior of two of the animals (rhesus monkeys): they had become hypersensitive to sound.

Question Mark

6.70   *Use of the question mark.* The question mark is used to mark a direct question, to indicate an editorial doubt, or (occasionally) to express surprise or disbelief. A double question mark, sometimes used humorously to express total surprise or confusion, is generally to be avoided. See also 6.77, 6.121, 6.123.

> Who will represent the poor?
> Thomas Kraftig (1610?–66) was the subject of the final essay.
> This is your reply?

6.71   *Within a sentence.* A question mark is used within a sentence at the end of a direct question (see also 6.55). If the question does not begin the sentence, it need not start with a capital letter (but see 6.55).

> Is it worth the risk? he wondered.
> The question, how can the two be reconciled? was on everyone's mind.

For the omission of a comma following a question mark, see 6.123.

6.72   *Indirect question.* An indirect question never takes a question mark. See also 6.55.

> He wondered whether it was worth the risk.
> How the two could be reconciled was the question on everyone's mind.

6.73   *Indirect one-word question.* When a question within a sentence consists of a single word, such as *who, when, how,* or *why,* a question mark may be omitted, and the word is sometimes italicized. See also 6.55.

> She asked herself why.
> The question was no longer *how* but *when.*

6.74   *Courtesy question.* A request courteously disguised as a question does not require a question mark.

> Would you kindly respond by March 1.   Will the audience please rise.

6.75   *With quotation marks, parentheses, or brackets.* A question mark should be placed inside quotation marks, parentheses, or brackets only when it is part of the quoted or parenthetical matter. See also 6.9.

The ambassador asked, "Has the Marine Corps been alerted?"
Why was Farragut trembling when he said, "I'm here to open an inquiry"?
Emily (had we met before?) winked at me.
Why did she tell him only on the morning of his departure (March 18)?
"What do you suppose he had in mind," inquired Newman, "when he said, 'You are all greater fools than I thought'?"

Exclamation Point

6.76   *Use of the exclamation point.* An exclamation point (which should be used sparingly to be effective) marks an outcry or an emphatic or ironic comment. For its use as a code in instructions for typesetting, see 2.89. See also 6.121, 6.123.

> Look out!
> The emperor, it seems, had forgotten to notify his generals!

6.77   *Exclamation rather than question.* A question that is essentially an exclamation usually ends with an exclamation point.

> How could you possibly believe that!   When will I ever learn!

6.78   *Inappropriate use.* An exclamation point added in brackets to quoted matter to indicate editorial protest or amusement is strongly discouraged, since it appears contemptuous. The Latin expression *sic* (thus) is preferred (see 7.56, 11.69).

6.79   *With quotation marks, parentheses, or brackets.* An exclamation point should be placed inside quotation marks, parentheses, or brackets only when it is part of the quoted or parenthetical matter.

> The woman cried, "Those men are beating that child!"
> Her husband actually responded, "It's no concern of mine"!
> Janet Laslow (I could have died!) repeated the whole story.
> Tichnick's angry reply, "I do not know the man!" took us all by surprise.

Hyphens and Dashes

6.80   *Hyphens and dashes compared.* Hyphens and the various dashes all have their specific appearance (shown below) and uses (discussed in the following paragraphs). The hyphen, the en dash, and the em dash are the most commonly used and must be typeset correctly; an en dash appearing where a hyphen is called for bespeaks editorial or typographic confusion. In typing, as opposed to typesetting, writers are advised (unless otherwise instructed by their editors or publishers) to use a single hyphen both for a hyphen and for an en dash, two hyphens for an em dash, four hyphens for a 2-em dash, and six hyphens for a 3-em dash. The publisher will convert these to the appropriate forms. See 2.15–16, 2.89, 2.99.

hyphen -   en dash –   em dash —   2-em dash ——   3-em dash ———

HYPHEN

6.81   *Compounds.* The use of the hyphen in compound words and names and in word division is discussed in 5.92–93 and in chapter 7, especially 7.33–45 and 7.82–90. See also 6.85.

6.82   *To separate characters.* A hyphen is used to separate numbers that are not inclusive, such as telephone numbers, social security numbers, and ISBNs. It is also used—in dialogue, in reference to American Sign Language (see 10.147, 10.149, 10.154), and elsewhere—to separate letters when a word is spelled out.

1-800-621-2376 *or* (1-800) 621-2376
0-226-10389-7
"My name is Phyllis; that's p-h-y-l-l-i-s."
A proficient signer can fingerspell C-O-L-O-R-A-D-O in less than two seconds.

In URLs, careful distinction must be made between a hyphen (-), a tilde (~), and an underline (_).

http://www.rz.uni-karlsruhe.de/~szm/woerterbuch1.html
www.niu.edu/univ_press

E-mail addresses and URLs that include hyphens must be typeset with care; to avoid ambiguity, not only should no hyphen be added at line breaks, but no line breaks should be allowed to occur at existing hyphens. See 7.44.

EN DASH

6.83   *En dash as "to."* The principal use of the en dash is to connect numbers and, less often, words. In this use it signifies *up to and including* (or *through*).

For the sake of parallel construction the word *to*, never the en dash, should be used if the word *from* precedes the first element; similarly, *and*, never the en dash, should be used if *between* precedes the first element. For more on dates and times, see 9.38, 9.43. For the slash, see 6.114.

Her college years, 1998–2002, were the happiest in her life
For documentation and indexing, see chapters 16–18.
In Genesis 6:13–22 we find God's instructions to Noah.
Join us on Thursday, 11:30 a.m.–4:00 p.m., to celebrate the New Year.
The London–Paris train leaves at two o'clock.
I have blocked out December 2002–March 2003 to complete my manuscript.
Her articles appeared in *Postwar Journal* (3 November 1945–4 February 1946).
Green Bay beat Denver 31–24.
The legislature voted 101–13 to adopt the resolution.
but
She was in college from 1998 to 2002.
She published her articles between November 3, 1945, and February 4, 1946.

6.84 *With nothing following.* An en dash may be used by itself after a date to indicate that something (a publication or a person's life) is still going on. No space follows the en dash.

Professor Plato's survey (1999–) will cover the subject in the final volume.
Jane Doe (1950–); *or* Jane Doe (b. 1950)

6.85 *In place of a hyphen.* The en dash is used in place of a hyphen in a compound adjective when one of its elements is an open compound or when two or more of its elements are open compounds or hyphenated compounds (see 7.83). As illustrated by the first four examples below, en dashes separate the main elements of the new compounds more clearly than hyphens would ("hospital" versus "nursing home," "post" versus "World War II," etc.), thus preventing ambiguity. In the last two examples, however, to have used en dashes between "non" and "English" and between "user" and "designed" would merely have created an awkward asymmetry; the meaning is clear with hyphens.

the post–World War II years
a hospital–nursing home connection
a nursing home–home care policy
a quasi-public–quasi-judicial body (*or, better*, a judicial body that is quasi-public and quasi-judicial)
but
non-English-speaking peoples

a wheelchair-user-designed environment (*or, better,* an environment designed for wheelchair users)

(Abbreviations for compounds are treated as single words, so a hyphen, not an en dash, is used in such phrases as "U.S.-Canadian relations.")

6.86 *Other uses.* The en dash is sometimes used as a minus sign, but minus signs and en dashes are distinct characters. Since both the characters themselves and the spacing around them may differ when typeset, it is best to use the correct character, especially in mathematical copy. In electronic documents, substituting any character for another may hinder searches. In certain scientific disciplines, the en dash may sometimes be used where one would normally expect a hyphen (see *Scientific Style and Format*; bibliog. 1.1). In some instances an en dash is used to link a city name to the name of a university that has more than one campus.

the University of Wisconsin–Madison   the University of Wisconsin–Milwaukee

EM DASH

6.87 *Versatility and frequency of use.* The em dash, often simply called the dash, is the most commonly used and most versatile of the dashes. To avoid confusion, no sentence should contain more than two em dashes; if more than two elements need to be set off, use parentheses (see 6.98).

6.88 *Amplifying or explaining.* An em dash or a pair of em dashes sets off an amplifying or explanatory element. (Commas, parentheses, or a colon may perform a similar function.)

It was a revival of the most potent image in modern democracy—the revolutionary idea.
The influence of three impressionists—Monet, Sisley, and Degas—is obvious in her
   work.
The chancellor—he had been awake half the night—came down in an angry mood.
She outlined the strategy—a strategy that would, she hoped, secure the peace.
My friends—that is, my former friends—ganged up on me.

6.89 *Separating subject from pronoun.* An em dash may be used to separate a subject, or a series of subjects, from a pronoun that introduces the main clause. Note its use after a series separated by semicolons in the last example.

Consensus—that was the will-o'-the-wisp he doggedly pursued.
Broken promises, petty rivalries, and false rumors—such were the obstacles he encountered.

Darkness, thunder, a sudden scream—nothing alarmed the child.

Kingston, who first conceived the idea; Barber, who organized the fundraising campaign; and West, who conducted the investigation—those were the women most responsible for the movement's early success.

6.90 *Indicating sudden breaks.* An em dash or a pair of em dashes may indicate a sudden break in thought or sentence structure or an interruption in dialogue. (Ellipsis points may also serve this purpose; see 11.45.)

"Will he—can he—obtain the necessary signatures?" asked Mill.

"Well, I don't know," I began tentatively. "I thought I might—"
"Might what?" she demanded.

If the break belongs to the surrounding sentence rather than to the quoted material, the em dashes must appear outside the quotation marks.

"Someday he's going to hit one of those long shots, and"—his voice turned huffy— "I won't be there to see it."

6.91 *Used in place of, or with, a comma.* If the context calls for an em dash where a comma would ordinarily separate a dependent clause from an independent clause, the comma should be omitted. But if an em dash is used at the end of quoted material to indicate an interruption, a comma should be used before the words that identify the speaker.

Because the data had not been fully analyzed—the reason for this will be discussed later—the publication of the report was delayed.
but
"I assure you, we shall never—," Sylvia began, but Mark cut her short.

6.92 *With other punctuation.* A question mark or an exclamation point—but never a comma, a colon, or a semicolon, and rarely a period (see 16.65)— may precede an em dash.

All at once Richardson—can he have been out of his mind?—shook his fist in the ambassador's face.
Only if—heaven forbid!—you lose your passport should you call home.

6.93 *Used instead of quotation marks.* Em dashes are occasionally used instead of quotation marks (mainly by French writers) to set off dialogue. Each speech starts a new paragraph.

— Will he obtain the necessary signatures?
— Of course he will!

6.94　*In an index.* For the use of em dashes in an index, see 18.27.

2-EM AND 3-EM DASHES

6.95　*2-em dash.* A 2-em dash represents a missing word or part of a word, either omitted to disguise a name (or occasionally an expletive) or else missing or illegible in quoted or reprinted material. When a whole word is missing, space appears on both sides of the dash. When only part of a word is missing, no space appears between the dash and the existing part (or parts) of the word; when the dash represents the end of a word, a normal word space follows it. See also 7.66, 11.66–67.

> "The region gives its —— to the language spoken there."
> Admiral N—— and Lady R—— were among the guests.
> David H——h [Hirsch?] voted aye.

(Although a 2-em dash sometimes represents material to be supplied, it should not be confused with a blank line to be filled in; a blank in a form should appear thus ____.)

6.96　*3-em dash.* In a bibliography, a 3-em dash followed by a period represents the same author or editor named in the preceding entry (see 16.84–89, 16.103–5).

> ———. *The Last Dinosaur Book.* Chicago: University of Chicago Press, 1998.

Parentheses

6.97　*Characteristics of parentheses.* Parentheses usually set off material that is less closely related to the rest of the sentence than that enclosed in em dashes or commas. For parenthetical references to a list of works cited, see 16.107–20. For parenthetical references following quoted material, see 11.72–84. For parentheses in notes and bibliographies, see chapters 16 and 17. For parentheses in mathematics, see chapter 14, especially 14.25–31. For roman versus italic type, see 6.6.

> He suspected that the inert gases (helium, etc.) could produce a similar effect.
> Intelligence tests (e.g., the Stanford-Binet) are no longer widely used.
> The final sample that we collected (under difficult conditions) contained an impurity.
> Wexford's analysis (see chapter 3) is more to the point.

> *Dichtung und Wahrheit* (also known as *Wahrheit und Dichtung*) has been translated as *Poetry and Truth.*
>
> The disagreement between Johns and Evans (its origins have been discussed elsewhere) ultimately destroyed the organization.

6.98   *With em dashes.* A combination of parentheses and em dashes may be used if called for.

> The Whipplesworth conference—it had already been interrupted by three demonstrations (the last bordering on violence)—was adjourned promptly.

6.99   *Glosses or translations.* Parentheses are used to enclose glosses of unfamiliar terms or translations of foreign terms—or, if the term is given in English, to enclose the original word. In quoted matter, brackets should be used (see 6.104). See also 7.52, 10.6.

> A drop folio (a page number printed at the foot of a page) is useful on the opening page of a chapter.
>
> The word used was not *une poêle* (frying pan) but *un poêle* (stove).
>
> German has two terms for eating—one for the way humans eat (*essen*) and another for the way animals eat (*fressen*).

6.100   *Run-in lists.* Parentheses are used to enclose numerals or letters marking divisions in lists that are run into the text. See 6.126.

6.101   *Telephone numbers.* Parentheses are sometimes used to set off the area code from the rest of a telephone or fax number. (A hyphen is more common, however.)

> (1-800) 555-8476 *or* 1-800-555-8476

6.102   *Parentheses within parentheses.* Although the use of parentheses within parentheses (usually for bibliographic purposes) is permitted in some publications—especially in law—Chicago prefers brackets within parentheses (see 6.106). For parentheses within em dashes, see 6.98. For parentheses in mathematics, see 14.25.

6.103   *With other punctuation.* An opening parenthesis should be preceded by a comma or a semicolon only in an enumeration (see 6.126); a closing parenthesis should never be preceded by a comma or a semicolon. A question mark, an exclamation point, and closing quotation marks precede a closing parenthesis if they belong to the parenthetical matter; they follow it if they belong to the surrounding sentence. A period precedes the closing parenthesis if the entire sentence is in parentheses; otherwise it follows. (A parenthetical enclosure of more than one sentence should not be included within another sentence. If a final period is needed at the end of such an enclosure, rewording may be necessary to keep the enclosure independent of the surrounding text, as is this one.) Parentheses should rarely appear back to back. Different kinds of material may, if necessary, be enclosed in a single set of parentheses, usually separated by a semicolon. For parentheses in documentation, see chapters 16 and 17.

Having entered (on tiptoe), we sat down on the nearest seats we could find.
Come on in (quietly, please!) and take a seat.
(see Smith and Hawkins 1990; *t*-tests are used here)

Brackets

SQUARE BRACKETS

6.104 *Use of square brackets.* Square brackets (in the United States usually just called brackets) are used mainly to enclose material—usually added by someone other than the original writer—that does not belong to the surrounding text. In quoted matter, reprints, anthologies, and other nonoriginal material, square brackets enclose editorial interpolations, explanations, translations of foreign terms, or corrections. Sometimes the bracketed material replaces rather than amplifies the original word or words. For brackets in mathematical copy, see 14.25. See also 11.66–68.

"They [the free-silver Democrats] asserted that the ratio could be maintained."
"Many CF [cystic fibrosis] patients have been helped by the new therapy."
Satire, Jebb tells us, "is the only [form] that has a continuous development."
[This was written before the discovery of the Driscoll manuscript.—Ed.]

If quoted matter already includes brackets of its own, the editor should so state in the source citation (e.g., "Brackets in the original"); see 11.70 for an analogous situation with italics.

6.105 *In translations.* In a translated work, square brackets are sometimes used to enclose a word or phrase in the original language to avoid ambiguity. (Translators should use this device sparingly.)

The differences between society [*Gesellschaft*] and community [*Gemeinde*] will now be analyzed.

6.106   *Within parentheses.* Square brackets are used as parentheses within parentheses, usually for bibliographic purposes. (For parentheses within em dashes, see 6.98.)

> (For further discussion see Richardson's excellent analysis [1999] and Danneberger's survey [2000].)

6.107   *In phonetics.* Square brackets may be used to enclose a phonetic transcription.

> The verb *entretenir* [ātrətnir], like *keep*, is used in many idioms.

6.108   *With other punctuation.* For brackets with other punctuation, the same principles apply as for parentheses (see 6.103).

ANGLE BRACKETS AND BRACES

6.109   *Use of angle brackets.* Angle brackets (< >) are used in electronic manuscript preparation to enclose codes for the typesetter (see 2.89). The mathematical signs for *less than* (<) and *greater than* (>), also used in etymology to mean *derived from* (<) and *gives* or *has given* (>), look the same as angle brackets but are not to be confused with them (see 14.2). *Braces* ({ }), often called *curly brackets,* are heavily used in programming languages as well as in mathematical and other specialized writing (see, e.g., 14.27). They are not interchangeable with parentheses or brackets. See the examples in chapter 5 for one possible use of braces.

6.110   *When to avoid angle brackets.* Although angle brackets are sometimes used to set off URLs and e-mail addresses, this use should be avoided, since some identifiers include angle brackets as part of their internal punctuation (see 17.10). To avoid ambiguity, reserve angle brackets for delimiting typesetting codes (see, e.g., 2.89).

> Visit Williams and Wilkins on the Internet, http://www.wwilkins.com, or contact our customer service department at custserv@wwilkins.com.

Slash

6.111   *Terminology.* The slash (/)—also known as virgule, solidus, slant, or forward slash, to distinguish it from a backward slash, or backslash (\)—has various distinct uses. For a discussion of the niceties associated with the various terms, see Richard Eckersley et al., *Glossary of Typesetting Terms* (bibliog. 2.6).

6.112 *Signifying alternatives.* A slash most commonly signifies alternatives. In certain contexts it proves convenient shorthand for *or* (but see 6.113). It is also used for alternative spellings or names. Where one or more of the terms separated by slashes is an open compound, a thin space before and after the slash is helpful.

he/she	Hercules/Heracles
his/her	Margaret/Meg/Maggie
and/or	World War I / First World War

6.113 *Technical use.* A slash is used in certain contexts to mean *and*.

an insertion/deletion mutation	a Jekyll/Hyde personality
an MD/PhD student	

6.114 *With years.* A slash is sometimes used in dates instead of an en dash (see 6.83), or even in combination with an en dash, to indicate the last part of one year and the first part of the next.

The winter of 1966/67 was especially severe.
Enrollment has increased between 1998/99 and 2001/2.
The fiscal years 1991/92–1998/99 were encouraging in several respects.

6.115 *With dates.* Slashes are used informally in all-numeral dates (e.g., 3/10/02), but this device should be avoided in formal style since ambiguity can arise: Americans usually put the month first, whereas Canadians and Europeans put the day first. The same problem occurs when hyphens or en dashes are used in all-numeral dates. (In a context where the events of September 11, 2001, are being discussed, 9/11 is quite acceptable. See also 8.81.) See 9.35.

6.116 *With abbreviations.* A slash may stand as shorthand for *per*, as in "110 km/sec," "$450/week" (see 15.46, 15,62), or in certain abbreviations, in lieu of a period, as in "c/o" (in care of).

6.117 *With fractions.* A slash can be used to mean "divided by" when a fraction bar is inappropriate. See 14.44.

6.118 *In poetry.* When two or more lines of poetry are quoted in regular text, slashes with space on each side are used to show line breaks.

"Thou hast not missed one thought that could be fit, / And all that was improper dost omit."

6.119   *Computer and Internet use.* Single and double slashes are used in URLs. No space should precede or follow them. In typeset URLs, line breaks may occur after a slash but not between two slashes. Slashes as well as backward slashes, or backslashes (\), are used in computer directory paths; the type of slash used depends on the operating system. See also 17.10–11.

http://sports.espn.go.com/nfl/index
c:\office\wpwin\wpdocs

Quotation Marks

6.120   *Other discussions.* For the location of closing quotation marks in relation to other punctuation, see 6.8–9. For the use of quotation marks with a comma, see 6.53; with a colon, 6.66; with a question mark, 6.75; with an exclamation point, 6.79. For a full discussion of quotation marks with dialogue and quoted matter, see 11.11–16, 11.20–21, 11.33–39. For the use of quotation marks with single words or phrases to signal some special usage, see 7.58, 7.60–62. For quotation marks in French, see 10.32–33; in German, 10.45; in Italian, 10.53.

Multiple Punctuation and When to Avoid It

6.121   *Likely combinations.* The use of more than one mark of punctuation at the same location usually involves quotation marks, em dashes, parentheses, or brackets in combination with periods, commas, colons, semicolons, question marks, or exclamation points. For quotation marks see 6.8–10, 6.52–54, 6.66, 6.75, 6.79. For em dashes see 6.91, 6.92, 6.96. For parentheses and brackets see 6.98, 6.102, 6.103, 6.106, 6.108, 6.126.

6.122   *No double period.* When an expression that takes a period ends a sentence, no additional period follows (see 6.15). When such an expression is followed by a comma, however, both period and comma appear.

The study was funded by Mulvehill & Co.
Her wallet contained U.S., Canadian, and Bahamian currency.
Johnson et al., in *How to Survive*, describe such an ordeal.

6.123   *When to omit comma or period.* Neither a period (aside from an abbreviating period) nor a comma ever accompanies a question mark or an exclamation point. The latter two marks, being stronger, take precedence over the first two. If a question mark and an exclamation point are both called for, only the mark more appropriate to the context should be retained.

"Have you read the platform?" asked Mark.
What did she mean when she said, "The foot now wears a different shoe"?
Who shouted, "Up the establishment!"
Her favorite songs are "Hello Dolly!" "Chicago," and "Come with Me."
That is your answer?

Lists and Outline Style

6.124   *Format.* Lists may be either run into the text or set vertically (outline style). Short, simple lists are usually better run in, especially if the introduction and the items form a complete grammatical sentence (see 6.126). Lists that require typographic prominence, that are extremely long (as in 2.73 and 4.60 of this manual), or that contain items of several levels (see 6.130) should be set vertically.

6.125   *General principles.* Where similar lists are fairly close together, consistency is essential. All items in a list should be syntactically alike—that is, all should be noun forms, phrases, full sentences, or whatever the context requires. Unless numerals or letters serve a purpose—to indicate the order in which tasks should be done, to suggest chronology or relative importance among the items, or, in a run-in list, to clearly separate the items—they may be omitted.

6.126   *Run-in lists.* Numerals or letters that mark divisions in a run-in list are enclosed in parentheses. If letters are used, they are sometimes italicized. No punctuation precedes the first parenthesis if the last word of the introductory material is a verb or a preposition. If the introductory material is an independent clause, a colon should precede the first parenthesis. The items are separated by commas unless any of the items require internal commas, in which case all the items should be separated by semicolons. When each item in a list consists of a complete sentence or several sentences, the list is best set vertically (see 6.127).

The qualifications are as follows: a doctorate in physics, five years' experience in a national laboratory, and an ability to communicate technical matter to a lay audience.

Compose three sentences illustrating the uses of (1) commas, (2) em dashes, and (3) parentheses.

The lecturer will expound on (a) glyceraldehyde, (b) erythrose, (c) arabinose, and (d) allose.

You are advised to pack (1) warm, sturdy outer clothing and enough underwear to last ten days; (2) two pairs of boots, two pairs of sneakers, and plenty of socks; and (3) binoculars and a camera.

Data are available on three groups of counsel: (1) the public defender of Cook County, (2) the member attorneys of the Chicago Bar Association's Defense of Prisoners Committee, and (3) all other attorneys.

Specifically, the committee set down fundamental principles, which in its opinion were so well established that they were no longer open to controversy: (1) the commerce power was complete, except as constitutionally limited; (2) the power included the authority absolutely to prohibit specified persons and things from interstate transit; (3) the only limitation upon this authority, as far as the Keating-Owen bill was concerned, was the Fifth Amendment, which protected against arbitrary interference with private rights; and (4) this authority might be exercised in the interest of the public welfare as well as in the direct interest of commerce.

6.127 *Vertical lists: punctuation and format.* A vertical list is best introduced by a complete grammatical sentence, followed by a colon (but see 6.128). Items carry no closing punctuation unless they consist of complete sentences. If the items are numbered, a period follows the numeral and each item begins with a capital letter. To avoid long, skinny lists, short items may be arranged in two or more columns. If items run over a line, the second and subsequent lines are usually indented (flush-and-hang style, also called hanging indention, as used in bibliographies and indexes). In a numbered list, runover lines are aligned with the first word following the numeral. Instead of indenting runover lines, extra space may be inserted between the items. Bullets (heavy dots, as in the fifth example below and elsewhere in this manual, e.g., 2.38) make good visual signposts in unnumbered lists but can lose their force if used too frequently.

Your application must include the following documents:

a full résumé
three letters of recommendation
all your diplomas, from high school to graduate school

a brief essay indicating why you want the position and why you consider yourself qualified
for it
two forms of identification

.   .   .   .   .

An administrative facility can be judged by eight measures:

image	quality
security	functional organization
access	design efficiency
flexibility	environmental systems

Each of these measures is discussed below.

.   .   .   .   .

Compose three sentences:
1. To illustrate the use of commas in dates
2. To distinguish the use of semicolons from the use of periods
3. To illustrate the use of parentheses within dashes

.   .   .   .   .

To purge files protected by Delete Sentry, start with the following steps:
1. From the Microsoft Tools group, choose the Undelete icon.
2. To select the directory from which you want to purge files, choose the
   Drive/Dir button.
3. In the Undelete screen, select the files you want to purge.

.   .   .   .   .

Use the Remote Control Panel if your software cannot send printer commands for any of
the following:
- Control toner usage by turning **EconoMode** on or off
- Adjust print quality by changing the **Resolution Enhancement** technology and
  Print Density settings
- Manage printer memory by changing the **Image Adapt** and **Page Protect** settings

6.128   *Vertical lists in paragraph style.* When items in a numbered list consist of
very long sentences, or of several sentences, and the list does not require
typographic prominence, the items may be set in regular text style as

numbered paragraphs, with only the first line indented, punctuated as normal prose.

6.129 *Vertical lists punctuated as a sentence.* In a numbered vertical list that completes a sentence begun in an introductory element and consists of phrases or sentences with internal punctuation, semicolons may be used between the items, and a period should follow the final item. Each item begins with a lowercase letter. Such lists, often better run into the text, should be set vertically only if the context demands that they be highlighted.

Reporting for the Development Committee, Jobson reported that
1. a fundraising campaign director was being sought;
2. the salary for this director, about $50,000 a year, would be paid out of campaign funds;
3. the fundraising campaign would be launched in the spring of 2005.

If bullets were used instead of numbers in the example above, the punctuation and capitalization would remain the same.

6.130 *Vertical lists with subdivided items.* Where items in a numbered list are subdivided, both numerals and letters may be used. Any runover lines should be aligned with the first word following the numeral.

Applicants will be tested for their skills in the following areas:

1. Punctuation
    a. Using commas appropriately
    b. Deleting unnecessary quotation marks
    c. Distinguishing colons from semicolons
2. Spelling
    a. Using a dictionary appropriately
    b. Recognizing homonyms
    c. Hyphenating correctly
3. Syntax
    a. Matching verb to subject
    b. Recognizing and eliminating misplaced
       modifiers
    c. Distinguishing phrases from clauses

In the following example, note that the numerals or letters denoting the top three levels are set off by periods and those for the lower four by single or double parentheses, thus distinguishing all seven levels by punctuation as well as indention. Note also that numerals are aligned vertically on the last digit. The parenthetical letters, here shown in italics, could also be set in roman.

I. Historical introduction
II. Dentition in various groups of vertebrates
    A. Reptilia
        1. Histology and development of reptilian teeth
        2. Survey of forms
    B. Mammalia
        1. Histology and development of mammalian teeth
        2. Survey of forms
            a) Primates
                (1) Lemuroidea
                (2) Anthropoidea
                    (*a*) Platyrrhini
                    (*b*) Catarrhini
                        i) Cercopithecidae
                        ii) Pongidae
            b) Carnivora
                (1) Creodonta
                (2) Fissipedia
                    (*a*) Ailuroidea
                    (*b*) Arctoidea
                (3) Pinnipedia
             c) Etc. . . .

In a list with fewer levels, the capital roman numerals, capital letters (except for proper names), or parenthetical arabic numerals could be dispensed with. What is important is that readers see at a glance the level to which each item belongs.

7

Spelling, Distinctive Treatment of Words, and Compounds

~~~~~~

Introduction

7.1   *Recommended dictionaries.* For general matters of spelling, Chicago recommends using *Webster's Third New International Dictionary* and its chief abridgment, *Merriam-Webster's Collegiate Dictionary* (referred to below as Webster) in its latest edition.[1] If more than one spelling is given, or more than one form of the plural (see 7.7), Chicago normally opts for the first form listed, thus aiding consistency. If, as occasionally happens, the *Collegiate* disagrees with the *Third International*, the *Collegiate* should be followed, since it represents the latest lexical research.

7.2   *Other dictionaries.* For further definitions or alternative spellings, refer to a standard dictionary such as the *American Heritage Dictionary of the English Language* or the *Random House Dictionary of the English Language*. At least for spelling, one source should be used consistently throughout a single work.

7.3   *Topics covered.* The following paragraphs discuss matters not easily found in the dictionary: how to form the plural and possessive forms of certain nouns and compounds; how to break words (at the end of a printed line) that are not listed in the dictionary; when to use capitals, italics, or quotation marks for distinctive treatment of words and phrases; and, perhaps most important but placed at the end of the chapter for easy reference (7.90), how to deal with compound words, prefixes, and suffixes.

Variant Spellings

7.4   *Spellings peculiar to particular disciplines.* Where a variant spelling carries a special connotation within a discipline, the author's preference should be

---

1. For full bibliographic information on these and other English dictionaries, see bibliog. 3.1.

respected. For example, "archeology," though it is listed second in Webster, is the spelling insisted on by certain specialists. In the absence of such a preference, spell it "archaeology."

7.5 *Non-U.S. spelling.* In English-language works by non-U.S. authors that are edited and typeset in the United States, editors at the University of Chicago Press generally change spelling used in other English-speaking countries to American spelling (e.g., *colour* to *color*, *analyse* to *analyze*). Since consistency is more easily maintained by this practice, few authors object. In quoted material, however, spelling is left unchanged (see 11.8).

Plurals

7.6 *Standard forms.* Most nouns form their plural by adding *s* or—if they end in *ch, j, s, sh, x,* or *z*—by adding *es*. Since no English speakers should need help with such plural forms as *thumbs, churches, fixes,* or *boys,* these are not listed in Webster. Webster does, however, give plural forms for words ending in *y* that change to *ies* (*baby*, etc.); for words ending in *o* (*ratio, potato,* etc.); for words such as *crocus, datum,* or *alumna;* and for all words with irregular plurals (*child, leaf,* etc.). See also 5.14–21.

7.7 *Alternative plurals.* Where Webster gives two forms of the plural (*zeros* or *zeroes, millennia* or *millenniums*) Chicago normally opts for the first. Different forms of the plural, however, are occasionally used for different purposes. A book may have two *indexes* and a mathematical expression two *indices,* as indicated in Webster's entry for "index."

7.8 *Compound nouns.* Webster gives the plural form of most compounds that are tricky (*fathers-in-law, coups d'état, courts-martial, chefs d'oeuvre,* etc.). For those not listed, common sense can usually provide the answer.

masters of arts	history majors	child wives

7.9 *Proper nouns.* Names of persons and other capitalized nouns normally form the plural by adding *s* or *es* (but see 7.10).

five Toms, four Dicks, and three Harrys	the two Germanys reunited
keeping up with the Joneses	Romanys were persecuted
rainy Sundays	Afghans and Pakistanis

An apostrophe is never used to form the plural of a family name: "The Jeffersons live here" (*not* "Jefferson's"). With names such as Waters or

Rogers, consider rewording to avoid the awkwardness of "Waterses" or "Rogerses." For the apostrophe in the possessive form of proper nouns, see 7.18–22.

7.10 *Tribal names.* According to current preference, names of Native American tribes form their plural by adding *s*. In earlier writings the *s* was often omitted (indeed, Webster gives the *s* form as the second spelling).

> the Hopis of northeastern Arizona (*not* Hopi)
> Many Cherokees work in this town.

7.11 *Singular form used for the plural.* Names ending in an unpronounced *s* or *x* are best left in the singular form.

> the seventeen Louis of France
> the two Dumas, father and son
> two Charlevoix (*or, better*, two towns called Charlevoix)
> three Velázquez (*or, better*, three works by Velázquez)

7.12 *Italicized words.* If italicized terms—names of newspapers, titles of books, and the like—are used in the plural, the *s* is normally set in roman. A title already in plural form, however, may be left unchanged. In case of doubt, avoid the plural by rephrasing.

> two *Chicago Tribune*s and three *Milwaukee Journal-Sentinel*s
> several *Madame Bovary*s
> too many *sic*s
> four *New York Times*

Foreign words in their plural form should be set entirely in italics.

> *Blume, Blumen*   *cheval, chevaux*   *señor, señores*

7.13 *Words in quotation marks.* The plural of a word or phrase in quotation marks may be formed by the addition of an apostrophe before the *s*, with the closing quotation marks following the *s* (though rewording is usually a better option). A plural ending should never follow closing quotation marks.

> How many more "To be continued's" can we expect? (*not* "To be continued"s)

7.14 *Noun coinages.* Words and hyphenated phrases that are not nouns but are used as nouns form the plural by adding *s* or *es*. To avoid an awkward appearance, an adjustment in spelling (or sometimes an apostrophe) may be needed.

Ifs and buts	dos and don'ts	threes and fours	thank-yous
but			
maybe's	yesses and noes (*or* yes's and no's, *especially if* maybe's *is also used*)		

7.15   *Letters, abbreviations, and numerals.* Capital letters used as words, abbreviations that contain no interior periods, and numerals used as nouns form the plural by adding *s*. But see 15.45 (for some exceptions) and 15.58 (for the International System).

the three Rs	*but*
the 1990s	p. (page), pp. (pages)
IRAs	n. (note), nn. (notes)
vol., vols.	MS (manuscript),
URLs	MSS (manuscripts)
ed., eds.	

7.16   *Use of apostrophe.* To avoid confusion, lowercase letters and abbreviations with two or more interior periods or with both capital and lowercase letters form the plural with an apostrophe and an *s*. See also 7.63–65.

x's and *y*'s
M.A.'s and Ph.D.'s (*or* MAs and PhD's)

For the omission of periods, see 15.4.

Possessives

THE GENERAL RULE

7.17   *Most nouns.* The possessive of most *singular* nouns is formed by adding an apostrophe and an *s*, and the possessive of *plural* nouns (except for a few irregular plurals that do not end in *s*) by adding an apostrophe only. This practice, used in conjunction with the exceptions and options outlined in 7.19–22, reflects the way possessive forms are generally pronounced and is largely faithful to Strunk and White's famous rule 1 ("Form the possessive singular of nouns by adding *'s*"). Since feelings on these matters sometimes run high, users of this manual may wish to modify or add to the exceptions. For an alternative practice, see 7.23. See also 5.25–27.

the horse's mouth
a bass's stripes
puppies' paws
children's literature
a herd of sheep's mysterious disappearance

7.18   *Proper nouns, letters, and numbers.* The general rule covers most proper nouns, including names ending in *s*, *x*, or *z*, in both their singular and plural forms, as well as letters and numbers.

Kansas's legislature	the Williamses' new house
Chicago's lakefront	Malraux's masterpiece
Burns's poems	Inez's diary
Marx's theories	the Martinezes' daughter
Berlioz's works	Josquin des Prez's motets
Strauss's Vienna	dinner at the Browns' (*that is, at the Browns' home*)
Dickens's novels	FDR's legacy
the Lincolns' marriage	1999's heaviest snowstorm
Williams's reputation	

The rule applies equally to company names that include a punctuation point.

Yahoo!'s chief executive

Rewording may be advisable to avoid such awkward possessives as "the Rogerses' address" (see 7.9).

EXCEPTIONS TO THE GENERAL RULE AND SOME OPTIONS

7.19   *Nouns plural in form, singular in meaning.* When the singular form of a noun ending in *s* looks like a plural and the plural form is the same as the singular, the possessive of both singular and plural is formed by the addition of an apostrophe only. If ambiguity threatens, use *of* to avoid the possessive.

politics' true meaning
economics' forerunners
this species' first record (*or, better*, the first record of this species)

The same rule applies when the name of a place or an organization (or the last element in the name) is a plural form ending in s, such as *the United States*, even though the entity is singular.

the United States' role in international law
Highland Hills' late mayor
Calloway Gardens' former curator
the National Academy of Sciences' new policy

7.20 *Names like "Euripides."* The possessive is formed without an additional *s* for a name of two or more syllables that ends in an *eez* sound.

Euripides' tragedies   the Ganges' source   Xerxes' armies

7.21 *Words and names ending in unpronounced "s."* To avoid an awkward appearance, an apostrophe without an *s* may be used for the possessive of singular words and names ending in an unpronounced *s*. Opt for this practice *only* if you are comfortable with it and are certain that the *s* is indeed unpronounced.

Descartes' three dreams
the marquis' mother
François' efforts to learn English
Vaucouleurs' assistance to Joan of Arc
Albert Camus' novels (the s is unpronounced)
but
Raoul Camus's anthology (the s is pronounced)

7.22 *Other exceptions.* For . . . *sake* expressions traditionally omit the *s* when the noun ends in an *s* or an *s* sound.

for righteousness' sake
for goodness' sake
for Jesus' sake
but
Jesus's contemporaries

Where neither an *s* nor an apostrophe alone looks right (as with such names as Isis), avoid the possessive and use *of* instead.

7.23 *An alternative practice.* Those uncomfortable with the rules, exceptions, and options outlined above may prefer the system, formerly more common, of simply omitting the possessive *s* on all words ending in *s*—hence "Dylan Thomas' poetry," "Maria Callas' singing," and "that business' main concern." Though easy to apply, that usage disregards pronunciation and thus seems unnatural to many.

PARTICULARITIES OF THE POSSESSIVE

7.24 *Two nouns as a unit.* Closely linked nouns are considered a single unit in forming the possessive when the entity "possessed" is the same for both; only the second element takes the possessive form. When the entities are different, both nouns take the possessive form. See also 5.27.

> my aunt and uncle's house
> Gilbert and Sullivan's *Iolanthe*
> Minneapolis and Saint Paul's transportation system
> *but*
> my aunt's and uncle's specific talents
> New York's and Chicago's transportation systems
> our friends' and neighbors' children

7.25 *Compounds.* In compound nouns and noun phrases the final element usually takes the possessive form. If plural compounds pose problems, opt for *of*.

> a cookbook's index
> student assistants' time cards
> my daughter-in-law's profession
> *but*
> the professions of both my daughters-in-law

7.26 *Genitive.* Analogous to possessives, and formed like them, are certain expressions based on the old genitive case. The genitive here implies *of*.

> an hour's delay
> in three days' time
> six months' leave of absence (*or* a six-month leave of absence)

7.27 *Possessive versus attributive forms.* The line between a possessive or genitive form (see 7.26) and a noun used attributively—as an adjective—is sometimes fuzzy, especially in the plural. Although terms such as *employees' cafeteria* sometimes appear without an apostrophe, Chicago dispenses with the apostrophe only in proper names (often corporate names) or where there is clearly no possessive meaning.

a consumers' group	*but*
taxpayers' associations	*Publishers Weekly*
children's rights	Diners Club
the women's team	Department of Veterans Affairs
a boys' club	a housewares sale

7.28   *Gerunds.* A noun (or more commonly a pronoun) followed by a gerund may take the possessive form in contexts where, if a pronoun was used, it would be in the possessive case. This practice, elegant if followed appropriately, requires caution. For an excellent discussion, see "Possessive with Gerund," in *The New Fowler's Modern English Usage* (bibliog. 1.2). See also 5.110. In the first two examples below, the possessive form is clearly needed.

Eleanor's revealing her secret resulted in a lawsuit.
Fathers' assuming the care of children has changed many lives.

In the following three examples, the possessive form (given in parentheses) might sound pedantic to some. In the fourth, however, use of the pronoun *their* is unlikely to seem so.

She was worried about her daughter (*or* daughter's) going there alone.
I won't put up with Jefferson and Franklin (*or* Jefferson's and Franklin's) being denigrated.
The problem of authors (*or* authors') finding the right publisher can be solved.
but
The problem of their finding the right publisher can be solved.

In the following two examples, where "Randy" and "Guests" could not be replaced by "his" and "their," the possessive would clearly be incorrect.

We listened to Randy singing a solo.
Guests wishing to park their own cars should check with the management.

7.29   *Possessive with "of."* The possessive form may be preceded by *of* where *one of several* is implied. "A friend of Dick's" and "a friend of his" are equally acceptable. See also 5.52.

a cousin of Jim's
a favorite phrase of Professor Deam's

7.30   *Italicized or quoted terms.* As with plurals, when an italicized term appears in roman text, the possessive *s* should be set in roman. A term enclosed in quotation marks, however, should never be made into a possessive.

the *Atlantic Monthly*'s editor
Gone with the Wind's admirers
but
admirers of "Ode on a Grecian Urn"

Contractions and Interjections

7.31   *Contractions.* In contractions, an apostrophe normally replaces omitted letters. Some contractions, such as *won't* or *ain't*, are formed irregularly. Colloquialisms such as *gonna* or *wanna* take no apostrophe (there being no obvious place for one). Webster lists many common contractions, along with alternative spellings and, where appropriate, plurals. Since some word processors automatically change an apostrophe at the beginning of a word to an opening single quotation mark, caution is needed; a code in angle brackets can be added, or it may be possible to fool the system either by typing a letter before the apostrophe and then deleting the letter or by some other means.

singin'   meet'n   'tis (*not* 'tis)
dos and don'ts   rock 'n' roll

7.32   *Interjections.* As with contractions, Webster lists such interjections as *ugh* and *pshaw*. For those not found in the dictionary, plausible spellings should be sought in literature or invented.

tsk, tsk!   atchoo!   um . . . er . . .   shh!

Word Division

7.33   *Dictionary system.* For end-of-line word breaks, as for spelling and plural forms, Webster should be the primary guide. The dots between syllables in Webster indicate where breaks may be made; in words of three or more syllables, there is usually a choice of breaks. The following paragraphs are intended merely to supplement, not to replace, the dictionary's system of word division. For word division in foreign words (other than those given in an English dictionary), see chapter 10.

7.34   *Words that should not be divided.* Single-syllable words, including verb forms such as *aimed* and *helped,* are never divided. Since one-letter divisions are not permissible, such words as *again, enough,* and *unite* cannot be divided. Words that may be misread if divided, such as *water, women,* and *prayer,* should be divided only with reluctance.

7.35   *Dividing according to pronunciation.* In the usage preferred by Chicago and reflected in Webster, most words are divided according to pronunciation rather than derivation.

knowl-edge (*not* know-ledge)
democ-racy *or* de-mocracy (not *demo-cracy*)

7.36   *Dividing after a vowel.* Unless a resulting break affects pronunciation, words are best divided after a vowel. When a vowel forms a syllable in the middle of a word, it should run into the first line if possible. Diphthongs are treated as single vowels.

criti-cism (*rather than* crit-icism)
liga-ture (*rather than* lig-ature)
aneu-rysm (*or* an-eurysm)

7.37   *Compounds, prefixes, and suffixes.* Hyphenated or closed compounds and words with prefixes or suffixes are best divided at the natural breaks.

poverty-/stricken (*rather than* pov-/erty-stricken)
thanks-giving (*rather than* thanksgiv-ing)
dis-pleasure (*rather than* displea-sure)
re-inforce (*rather than* rein-force)

7.38   *Gerunds.* Most gerunds and present participles may be divided before the *ing.* When the final consonant before the *ing* is doubled, however, the break occurs between the consonants. For words ending in *ling,* check the dictionary.

certify-ing	dab-bing	fiz-zling
giv-ing	run-ning	bris-tling

7.39   *Two-letter word endings.* Two-letter word endings are best *not* carried over to a second line.

losses (*rather than* loss-es)
sur-prises (*rather than* surpris-es)

7.40   *Proper nouns and personal names.* Proper nouns of more than one element, especially personal names, should be broken, if possible, between the elements rather than within any of the elements. If a break within a name is needed, consult the dictionary. Many proper nouns appear, with suggested divisions, in the listings of biographical and geographical names at the back of *Merriam-Webster's Collegiate Dictionary.* Those that cannot be found in a dictionary should be broken (or left unbroken) according to the guidelines in 7.34–39. If pronunciation is not known or easily guessed, the break should usually follow a vowel.

Alek-sis
Jean- / Paul Sartre (*or, better,* Jean-Paul / Sartre)
Ana-stasia

A personal name with one or more middle initials should be broken after the initial or initials. If initials are given instead of first names, the break should follow the initials. A break before a number, *Jr.,* or *Sr.* should be avoided (unless *Jr.* or *Sr.* is enclosed in commas).

Frederick L. / Anderson
M. F. K. / Fisher
Elizabeth II (*or, if necessary,* Eliz- / abeth II)

7.41   *Numerals.* Large numbers expressed as numerals are best left intact. To avoid a break, reword the sentence. If a break must be made, however, it should come only after a comma and never after a single digit.

1,365,- / 000,000 *or* 1,365,000,- / 000

7.42   *Abbreviations.* Abbreviations used with numerals are best left intact; either the numeral should be carried over to the next line or the abbreviation should be moved up.

345 m   24 kg   55 BCE   6:35 p.m.

7.43   *Run-in lists.* A number or letter, such as (3) or (c), used in a run-in list should not be separated from the beginning of what follows it. If it occurs at the end of a line, it should be carried over to the next line.

7.44 *URLs and e-mail addresses.* Where it is necessary to break a URL or an e-mail address, no hyphen should be used. The break should be made between elements, after a colon, a slash, a double slash, or the symbol @ but before a period or any other punctuation or symbols. To avoid confusion, a URL that contains a hyphen should never be broken at the hyphen. If a particularly long element must be broken to avoid a seriously loose line, it should be broken between syllables according to the guidelines offered above. See also 6.17, 17.11.

http://
www.salonmagazine.com
or
http://www
.salonmagazine.com
or
http://www.salon
magazine.com

7.45 *Typographic considerations.* An abundance of hyphenated lines on one printed page is usually frowned on. Moreover, no more than three succeeding lines should be allowed to end in hyphens. Even in material with an unjustified right-hand margin, word breaks are needed to avoid exceedingly uneven lines. (In manuscript preparation, however, word breaks should always be avoided; see 2.15.)

A and *An*, O and *Oh*

7.46 *"A" and "an."* The indefinite article *a*, not *an*, is used in American English before words beginning with a pronounced *h*. See also 5.73.

a hotel   a historical study
but
an honor   an heir

Before an abbreviation, a numeral, or a symbol, the use of *a* or *an* depends on how the term is pronounced. In the first example below, MS would be pronounced *em ess*; in the second, it would be pronounced *manuscript*.

an MS treatment (a treatment for multiple sclerosis)
a MS in the National Library
an NBC anchor   a CBS anchor   a URL
an @ sign   an 800 number

7.47 *"O" and "oh."* The vocative *O* (largely obsolete) is always capitalized, whereas the interjection *oh* is capitalized only when beginning a sentence or standing alone. See also 5.197.

"Thine arm, O Lord, in days of old . . ."
She has been director for . . . oh . . . ten or twelve years.
Oh! It's you!

Ligatures

7.48 *Use of ligatures.* The ligatures æ (*a* + *e*) and œ (*o* + *e*) should not be used in Latin or transliterated Greek words. Nor should they be used in words adopted into English from Latin, Greek, or French (and thus to be found in English dictionaries).

aesthetics   a trompe l'oeil mural
Encyclopaedia Britannica   a tray of hors d'oeuvres
oedipal   Emily Dickinson's oeuvre

The ligature æ (along with other special characters) is, however, needed for spelling Old English words in an Old English context. And the ligature œ is needed for spelling French words in a French context (see 10.41).

es hæl   Ælfric   le nœud gordien   *Œuvres complètes*

Italics, Capitals, and Quotation Marks

EMPHASIS

7.49 *Italics for emphasis.* Good writers use italics for emphasis only as an occasional adjunct to efficient sentence structure. Overused, italics quickly lose their force. Seldom should as much as a sentence be italicized for emphasis, and never a whole passage. In the first example below, the last three words, though clearly emphatic, do not require italics because of their commanding position in the sentence.

The damaging evidence was offered not by the arresting officer, not by the injured plaintiff, but by the boy's own mother.

In the following examples the emphasis would be lost without the italics.

Let us dwell for a moment on the idea of *conscious* participation.
How do we learn to think in terms of *wholes*?

7.50   *Capitals for emphasis.* Initial capitals, once used to lend importance to certain words, are now used only ironically.

"OK, so I'm a Bad Mother," admitted Mary cheerfully.

Capitalizing an entire word or phrase for emphasis is rarely appropriate. If capitals are wanted—in dialogue or in representing newspaper headlines, for example—small caps rather than full capitals look more graceful.[2] (For the use of small capitals in representing terms in American Sign Language, see 10.147–54.)

"Be careful—WATCH OUT!" she yelled.
We could not believe the headline: PRESIDENT DEAD.

FOREIGN WORDS

7.51   *Italics.* Italics are used for isolated words and phrases in a foreign language if they are likely to be unfamiliar to readers.

The *grève du zèle* is not a true strike but a nitpicking obeying of work rules.
Honi soit qui mal y pense is the motto of the Order of the Garter.

An entire sentence or a passage of two or more sentences in a foreign language is usually set in roman and enclosed in quotation marks (see 11.85).

7.52   *Parentheses and quotation marks.* A translation following a foreign word, phrase, or title is enclosed in parentheses or quotation marks. See also 6.99, 10.6, 17.66.

The word she wanted was *pécher* (to sin), not *pêcher* (to fish).
The Prakrit word *majjao,* "the tomcat," may be a dialect version of either of two Sanskrit words: *madjaro,* "my lover," or *marjaro,* "the cat" (from the verb *mrij,* "to wash," because the cat constantly washes itself).
Leonardo Fioravanti's *Compendio de i secreti rationali* (Compendium of rational secrets) became a best-seller.

---

2. Note that "capitalizing" a word means setting only the initial letter as a capital. Capitalizing a whole word, LIKE THIS, is known as "setting in full caps." Setting a word in small capitals (or "small caps") results in THIS STYLE.

In linguistic and phonetic studies a definition is often enclosed in single quotation marks with no intervening punctuation; any following punctuation is placed *after* the closing quotation mark. (For a similar usage in horticultural writing, see 8.138.)

The gap is narrow between *mead* 'a beverage' and *mead* 'a meadow'.

7.53 *Proper nouns.* Foreign proper nouns are not italicized in an English context.

A history of the Comédie-Française has just appeared.
Leghorn—in Italian, Livorno—is a port in Tuscany.

7.54 *Familiar foreign words.* Foreign words and phrases familiar to most readers and listed in Webster are not italicized if used in an English context; they should be spelled as in Webster. German nouns, if in Webster, are lowercased. If confusion might arise, however, foreign terms are best italicized and spelled as in the original language.

pasha	in vitro	recherché	de novo
weltanschauung	a priori	the kaiser	eros and agape
but			

He never missed a chance to *épater les bourgeois*.

If a familiar foreign term, such as *mise en scène*, should occur in the same context as a less unfamiliar one, such as *mise en abyme* (not listed in Webster), either both or neither should be italicized, so as to maintain internal consistency. The decision to italicize should not be based solely on whether a term appears in Webster.

7.55 *Italics at first occurrence.* If a foreign word not listed in an English dictionary is used repeatedly throughout a work, it need be italicized only on its first occurrence. If it appears only rarely, however, italics may be retained.

7.56 *Scholarly words and abbreviations.* Commonly used Latin words and abbreviations should not be italicized.

ibid.	et al.	ca.	passim

Because of its peculiar use in quoted matter, *sic* is best italicized.

"mindful of what has been done here by we [*sic*] as agents of principle"

HIGHLIGHTING TERMS IN SPECIFIC CONTEXTS

7.57   *Italics.* Key terms in a particular context are often italicized on their first occurrence. Thereafter they are best set in roman.

> The two chief tactics of this group, *obstructionism* and *misinformation*, require careful analysis.

7.58   *"Scare quotes."* Quotation marks are often used to alert readers that a term is used in a nonstandard, ironic, or other special sense. Nicknamed "scare quotes," they imply, "This is not my term" or "This is not how the term is usually applied." Like any such device, scare quotes lose their force and irritate readers if overused. See also 7.59, 7.62.

> In disk-to-film technology, "repros" are merely revised proofs.
> "Child protection" sometimes fails to protect.

In works of philosophy, single quotation marks are sometimes used for similar purposes, but Chicago discourages that practice unless it is essential to the author's argument and not confusing to readers. (For punctuation with quotation marks, double or single, see 6.8–10.)

7.59   *"So-called."* A word or phrase preceded by *so-called* should not be enclosed in quotation marks. The expression itself indicates irony or doubt.

> So-called child protection sometimes fails to protect.
> Her so-called mentor induced her to embezzle from the company.

QUOTED PHRASES, COMMON EXPRESSIONS, AND SLANG

7.60   *Quoted phrases.* Phrases quoted from another context, recognizable to readers, are often enclosed in quotation marks, with no source given. Discretion is required, however; in the last two examples below, quotation marks are not needed (though they would not be incorrect), since the phrases have become common expressions.

> Marilyn did not willingly "suffer the little ones" to enter her studio.
> *but*
> The pursuit of happiness is a practice more often defended than defined.
> Myths of paradise lost are common in folklore.

7.61 *Slang.* Terms considered slang or argot should be enclosed in quotation marks only if they are foreign to the normal vocabulary of the writer or likely to be unfamiliar to readers. Quotation marks should not be used for mere colloquialisms.

Had it not been for Bryce, the "copper's nark," Collins would have made his escape.
but
I grew up in a one-horse town.
Only techies will appreciate this joke.
What is he beefing about this time?

WORDS AND LETTERS USED AS WORDS

7.62 *Words and phrases used as words.* When a word or term is not used functionally but is referred to as the word or term itself, it is either italicized or enclosed in quotation marks.

The term *critical mass* is more often used metaphorically than literally.
What is meant by *neurobotics*?

Although italics are the traditional choice, quotation marks may be more appropriate in certain contexts. In the first example below, italics set off the foreign term and quotation marks are used for the English. In the second, italicizing the terms and abbreviations might seem to contradict what is being said. And in the third, the terms in quotation marks are in fact quoted material.

The Spanish verbs *ser* and *estar* are both rendered by "to be."
Common foreign terms such as "amour-propre" or "coup d'état" are not italicized; nor are the abbreviations "e.g." and "i.e."
Young children use "her and me" more freely than "she and I" as subject pronouns.

7.63 *Letters as letters.* Individual letters and combinations of letters of the Latin alphabet are usually italicized.

the letter *q*   a lowercase *n*   a capital *W*
The plural is usually formed in English by adding *s* or *es*.
He signed the document with an *X*.
I need a word with two *e*'s and three *s*'s.

Roman type, however, is traditionally used in two common expressions.

Mind your p's and q's!
dotting the i's and crossing the t's

Roman type is always used for phonetic symbols.

7.64 *Scholastic grades.* Letters used to denote grades are usually capitalized and set in roman type.

She finished with one A, three Bs, and two Cs.

7.65 *Plurals of letters.* To avoid confusion, the plural of single lowercase letters is formed by adding an apostrophe before the *s*. The *s* is roman even when the letter is italic. Capital letters do not normally require an apostrophe in the plural.

There really are two *x*'s in Foxx.
the three Rs

7.66 *Letters standing for names.* A letter used in place of a name is usually capitalized and set in roman type. If it is used in a hypothetical statement, it is not followed by a period.

Let us assume that A sues B for breach of contract . . .

If a single initial is used as an abbreviation for a name, it is followed by a period; if used to conceal a name, it may be followed by a 2-em dash and no period (see 6.95). If no punctuation follows the dash, a word space must appear before the next word.

Professor D. will be making his entrance shortly.
Senator K—— and Representative L—— were in attendance.

If two or more initials are used as an abbreviation for an entire name, no periods are needed. See also 8.6.

Kennedy and Johnson soon became known as JFK and LBJ.

7.67 *Letters as shapes.* Letters that are used to represent shape are capitalized and set in roman type (an S curve, an L-shaped room). (To use a sans serif font, as is sometimes done, does not aid comprehension and may present difficulties in typesetting.)

7.68 *Names of letters.* The name of a letter, as distinct from the letter itself, is usually set in roman type, without quotation marks (a dee, an aitch). The following spellings, drawn from *Merriam-Webster's Collegiate Dictionary*, should be used only where a single italicized letter is inappropriate. Editors and proofreaders occasionally need to name letters ("a cue, not a gee"). Since vowels are not named in Webster, invention is called for (an ee, not an oh; lc A; "eye," not "one"; "oh," not zero; "you").

b	bee	*j*	jay	*q*	cue	*x*	ex
c	cee	*k*	kay	*r*	ar	*y*	wye
d	dee	*l*	el	*s*	ess	*z*	zee
f	ef	*m*	em	*t*	tee		
g	gee	*n*	en	*v*	vee		
h	aitch	*p*	pee	*w*	double-u		

7.69 *Rhyme schemes.* Lowercase italic letters, with no space between, are used to indicate rhyme schemes or similar patterns.

The Shakespearean sonnet's rhyme scheme is *abab, cdcd, efef, gg.*

MUSIC: SOME TYPOGRAPHIC CONVENTIONS

7.70 *Reference works.* Music publishing is too specialized to be more than touched on here. Authors and editors requiring detailed guidelines may refer to D. Kern Holoman, *Writing about Music* (bibliog. 1.1). For an illustration of typeset music, see figure 12.7. For names of musical works, see 8.202–5.

7.71 *Musical pitches.* Letters standing for musical pitches (which in turn are used to identify keys, chords, and so on) are usually set as roman capitals. The terms *sharp, flat,* and *natural,* if spelled out, are set in roman type and preceded by a hyphen. Editors unfamiliar with musicological conventions should proceed with caution. In the context of harmony, for example, some authors may regard a "C-major triad" as being based on the note rather than the key of C. See also 7.74.

middle C
the key of G major
the D-major triad *or* D major triad
an F augmented triad (an augmented triad on the note F)
G-sharp *or* G♯
the key of B-flat minor *or* B♭ minor

Beethoven's E-flat-major symphony (the *Eroica*)
an E string

A series of pitches are joined by en dashes.

The initial F–G–F–B♭

7.72 *Octaves.* In technical works, various systems are used to designate octave register. Those systems that group pitches by octaves begin each ascending octave on C. In one widely used system, pitches in the octave below middle C are designated by lowercase letters: c, c♯, d, . . . , a♯, b. Octaves from middle C up are designated with lowercase letters bearing superscript numbers or primes: c^1, c^2, and so on, or c′, c″, and so on. Lower octaves are designated, in descending order, by capital letters and capital letters with subscript numbers: C, C_1, C_2. Because of the many systems and their variants in current use, readers should be alerted to the system employed (for example, by an indication early in the text of the symbol used for middle C). Technical works on the modern piano usually designate all pitches with capital letters and subscripts, from A_1 at the bottom of the keyboard to C_{88} at the top. Scientific works on music usually designate octaves by capital letters and subscripts beginning with C_0 (middle C = C_4). When pitches are otherwise specified, another designation system is unnecessary.

middle C   A 440   the soprano's high C

To indicate simultaneously sounding pitches (as in chords), the pitches are listed from lowest to highest and are sometimes joined by plus signs.

C + E + G

7.73 *Chords.* In the analysis of harmony, chords are designated by roman numerals indicating what degree of the scale the chord is based on.

V (a chord based on the fifth, or dominant, degree of the scale)
V^7 (dominant seventh chord)
iii (a chord based on the third, or mediant, degree of the scale)

Harmonic progressions are indicated by capital roman numerals separated by en dashes: IV–I–V–I. While roman numerals for all chords suffice for basic descriptions of chordal movement, in more technical writing, minor chords are distinguished by lowercase roman numerals and other distinctions in chord quality and content are shown by additional symbols and arabic numerals.

7.74   *Major and minor.* In some works on musical subjects where many keys are mentioned, capital letters are used for major keys and lowercase for minor. If this practice is followed, the words *major* and *minor* are usually omitted.

7.75   *Dynamics.* Terms indicating dynamics are usually given in lowercase, often italicized: *piano, mezzoforte,* and so on. Where space allows, the spelled-out form is preferred in both text and musical examples. Symbols for these terms are rendered in lowercase boldface italics with no periods: ***p, mf,*** and so on. "Editorial" dynamics—those added to a composer's original by an editor—are sometimes distinguished by another font or by parentheses or brackets.

COMPUTER TERMS

7.76   *Variation.* Typographic conventions for expressing the names of particular keys, commands, and other computer terms vary widely. The following paragraphs merely offer a few common patterns. What is important is the consistent use of a particular style or font to refer to a particular element.

7.77   *Capitalization.* The basic alphabet keys as well as all named keys (Ctrl, Home, Shift, Command, etc.), menu items (Save, Print, Exit, etc.), and icon names (the Cut button, the Italic button, etc.) are capitalized and spelled as on the keys or in the software.

> The function key F2 has no connection with the keys F and 2.
> Choosing Cut from the Edit menu is an alternative to pressing Ctrl+X.

7.78   *The plus sign.* The plus sign, without a space either side, is used when different keys are to be pressed simultaneously.

> If the screen freezes, press Ctrl+Alt+Delete.

7.79   *Font.* Italics, boldface, or some other font may be used to distinguish elements needing greater prominence than capitalization. Quotation marks are best avoided, given their specialized use in computer languages. Sans serif type should never be used (see 2.11). File names may be italicized if italics are not used for other elements. Ideally, they should appear in a form that most closely represents the way they look to someone using the language or system under discussion.

> Choose **Tutorial** from the **Help** menu, and open the file *introduction.*

If keys need to be distinguished from options, a mixture of fonts may be used.

Click on *Insert* (or press **Alt+I**) and select *Bookmark*.

7.80 *Words to be typed.* Words that are to be typed should appear in a font distinct from that used for keys, functions, and so forth. Avoid quotation marks unless they are actually to be typed. Sans serif type must not be used (see 2.11).

Type **win** after the prompt. Then press Enter to return to Windows.

7.81 *Names and terms.* Proper names of computer hardware, software, networks, systems, and languages are capitalized. Generic terms are lowercased. For spelling, consult a dictionary; if you prefer an alternative form (*hardcopy* rather than *hard copy*, etc.), use it consistently. For names of keys, functions, and such, see 7.77; for file names, see 7.79. For terms such as *e-mail*, see 7.90, section 2. For further guidance, consult Constance Hale and Jessie Scanlon, eds., *Wired Style* (bibliog. 1.2).

APL
BASIC
Dell Low-Profile 486; personal computer
Hewlett Packard LaserJet 4L; laser printer
the Internet; the Net
Netscape; a browser
Pascal
UNIX
Windows 2000; operating system
WordPerfect 8.1; word-processing software
the World Wide Web; the Web; a Web site; a Web page

Compounds and Hyphenation

INTRODUCTION

7.82 *Overview.* Probably the most common spelling questions for writers and editors concern compound terms—whether to spell as two words, hyphenate, or close up as a single word. Prefixes and suffixes can be troublesome also. The first place to look for answers is the dictionary. The following paragraphs and the hyphenation guide in 7.90 offer guidelines for spelling compounds not necessarily found in the dictionary (though some of the examples are drawn from Webster), and for treatment of compounds according to their grammatical function (as nouns, adjectives, or adverbs) and their position in a sentence. See also 5.92–93.

7.83   *Some definitions.* An open compound is spelled as two or more words (*high school, lowest common denominator*). A hyphenated compound is spelled with one or more hyphens (*mass-produced, kilowatt-hour, non-English-speaking*). A closed (or solid) compound is spelled as a single word (*birthrate, notebook*). A permanent compound is one that has been accepted into the general vocabulary and can be found in the dictionary. A temporary compound is a new combination created for some specific, often one-time purpose (*dictionary-wielding, impeachment hound*); such compounds, though some eventually become permanent, are not normally found in the dictionary. Not strictly compounds but often discussed with them are words formed with prefixes (*antigrammarian, postmodern*); these also are dealt with in 7.90, section 3.

7.84   *The trend toward closed compounds.* With frequent use, open or hyphenated compounds tend to become closed (*on line* to *on-line* to *online*). Chicago's general adherence to Webster does not preclude occasional exceptions when the closed spellings have become widely accepted, pronunciation and readability are not at stake, and keystrokes can be saved. See 7.90, section 2.

7.85   *Hyphens and readability.* A hyphen can make for easier reading by showing structure and, often, pronunciation. Words that might otherwise be misread, such as *re-creation*, should be hyphenated. Hyphens can also eliminate ambiguity. Although *decision making* as a noun is not normally hyphenated, to add one in *fast decision-making* shows that decisions (not snap judgments) must be made soon. Similarly, the hyphen in *much-needed clothing* shows that the clothing is badly needed rather than abundant and needed. Where no ambiguity could result, as in *public welfare administration* or *graduate student housing*, hyphenation is not mandatory, though it is quite acceptable and preferred by many writers and editors.

7.86   *Compound modifiers before or after a noun.* When compound modifiers (also called phrasal adjectives) such as *open-mouthed* or *nicotine-free* come later in a phrase than the noun they describe, ambiguity is unlikely and the hyphen dispensable (though not incorrect). When such compounds precede a noun, hyphenation usually makes for easier reading. With the exception of proper nouns (such as *United States*) and compounds formed by an adverb ending in *ly* plus an adjective (see 7.87), it is never incorrect to hyphenate adjectival compounds before a noun. Hyphenated adjectival compounds that appear in Webster (such as *well-read* or *ill-humored*) may be spelled without a hyphen when they follow a noun. (To avoid repeated "either–or" suggestions, the comments in 7.90 generally recommend hyphenation only before a noun.)

7.87   *Adverbs ending in "ly."* Compounds formed by an adverb ending in *ly* plus an adjective or participle (such as *largely irrelevant* or *smartly dressed*) are not hyphenated either before or after a noun, since ambiguity is virtually impossible.

7.88   *Multiple hyphens.* Although two or more hyphens are standard in such phrases as *a matter-of-fact approach* or *an over-the-counter drug*, there is no consensus—nor need there be—on the need for more than one hyphen in longer and less common adjectival compounds. Readability and semantic logic are sometimes judged differently by equally literate writers or editors. Thus, *early nineteenth-century literature* and *early-nineteenth-century literature* are both in good standing. Using one hyphen or two does not affect the meaning of the phrase as a whole. Likewise, *late twentieth-century politicians* will surely not be understood as "recently deceased twentieth-century politicians," but those who prefer to hyphenate *early-nineteenth* will logically hyphenate *late-twentieth* also. Some are more comfortable with the additional hyphen (which logic indicates), others without it (to avoid a lengthy string). Consistency must be maintained within any one work. See also 7.90, section 2, under *century*.

7.89   *Hyphen with word space.* When the second part of a hyphenated expression is omitted, the hyphen is retained, followed by a word space.

fifteen- and twenty-year mortgages
Chicago- or Milwaukee-bound passengers
five- to ten-minute intervals
but
a five-by-eight-foot rug (a single entity)

Omission of the second part of a solid compound follows the same pattern.

both over- and underfed cats
but
overfed and overworked mules (*not* overfed and -worked mules)

HYPHENATION GUIDE FOR COMPOUNDS, COMBINING FORMS, AND PREFIXES

7.90   *Overview.* Before using this guide, please refer to 7.82–89 above. The guide illustrates not hard-and-fast rules but general patterns. Writers and editors are bound to make their own exceptions according to context or personal taste. For reasons of space, the comments following each item do not attempt to provide rationales. Although much of the suggested hyphenation is logical and aids readability, some is traditional rather than logical. Each of the three sections is arranged alphabetically. The first deals with compounds according to type, the second with words commonly used as elements in compounds, and the third with prefixes. Compounds formed with suffixes (e.g., nationhood, penniless) are almost always closed.

1. Compounds according to Type

adjective + noun: *small-state* senators, a *high-quality* alkylate, a *middle-class* neighborhood, the neighborhood is *middle class*. (Hyphenated before but not after a noun.)

adjective + participle: *tight-lipped* person, *high-jumping* grasshoppers, *open-ended* question, the question was *open ended*. (Hyphenated before but not after a noun.)

adverb ending in *ly* + participle or adjective: *highly paid, utterly useless*. (Open whether before or after a noun.)

adverb not ending in *ly* + participle or adjective: a *much-loved* woman, she was *much loved*, a very *well-read* child, *little-understood* rules, a *too-easy* answer, the *best-known* author, the *highest-ranking* officer, the *worst-paid* job, a *lesser-paid* colleague, the *least skilled* workers, the *most efficient* method. (Hyphenated before but not after a noun; compounds with *most* and *least* usually open.)

age terms: a *three-year-old*, a *five-year-old* child, a *fifty-five-year-old* woman, *eight-* to *ten-year-olds*. (Hyphenated in both noun and adjective forms; for space after first hyphen, see 7.89.)

chemical terms: *sodium chloride* solution. (Open in both noun and adjective forms.)

colors: *emerald green, bluish green, coal black*, a *green and red* dress, a *black-and-white* print, the truth isn't *black and white*. (Open whether before or after a noun except for such established expressions as *black-and-white*, which are usually hyphenated before a noun.)

combining forms: *electrocardiogram, socioeconomic, politico-scientific* studies, the *practico-inert*. (Usually closed if permanent, hyphenated if temporary.)

compass points and directions: *northeast, southwest, east-northeast*, a *north–*

south street, the street runs *north–south*. (Closed in noun, adjective, and adverb forms unless three directions are combined, in which case a hyphen is used after the first. When *from . . . to* is implied, an en dash is used.)

ethnic terms. See **proper nouns and adjectives.**

fractions, simple: *one-half, three-quarters,* I'm *three-quarters* done, a *two-thirds* majority, *one and three-quarters, three fifty-thirds*. (Traditionally hyphenated in noun, adjective, and adverb forms, except when second element is already hyphenated. See also 9.15)

fractions, compounds formed with: a *half hour*, a *half-hour* session, a *quarter mile*, a *quarter-mile* run, an *eighth note*. (Noun form open, adjective form hyphenated. See also **numbers** in this section and **half** in section 2.)

gerund + noun: *running shoes, cooking class, running-shoe* department. (Noun form open, adjective form hyphenated. See also **noun + gerund**.)

noun + adjective: *computer-literate*, a *debt-free* year, the stadium is *fan friendly*, she is *HIV-positive*. (Hyphenated before a noun, usually open after a noun.)

noun + gerund: *decision making*, a *decision-making* body, *mountain climbing, time-clock-punching* employees, a *Nobel Prize–winning* chemist (for use of the en dash, see 6.85), *bookkeeping, caregiving, policymaking*. (Noun form usually open; adjective form hyphenated before a noun. Some permanent compounds closed.)

noun + noun, single function: *student nurse, master builder, directory path, tenure track, tenure-track* position, *home-rule* governance. (Noun form open, adjective form hyphenated before a noun.)

noun + noun, two functions: *nurse-practitioner, city-state, city-state* governance. (Both noun and adjective forms always hyphenated.)

noun + numeral or enumerator: the *round II* meetings, a *type A* executive. (Both noun and adjective forms always open.)

noun + participle: a *Wagner-burdened* repertoire, *flower-filled* garden, a *clothes-buying* grandmother, I am *software challenged*. (Hyphenated before a noun, otherwise open.)

number + abbreviation: the *33 m* distance, a *2 kg* weight, a *3 ft. high* wall. (Always open.)

number + percentage: *50 percent*, a *10 percent* raise. (Both noun and adjective forms always open.)

number, ordinal, + noun: *third-floor* apartment, *103rd-floor* view, *fifth-place* contestant, *twenty-first-row* seats. (Adjective form hyphenated before a noun. See also **century** in section 2.)

number, ordinal, + superlative: a *second-best* decision; *third-largest* town; *fourth-to-last* contestant; he arrived *fourth to last*. (Hyphenated before a noun, otherwise open.)

number, spelled out, + noun: a *hundred-meter* race, a *250-page* book, a *fifty-year* project, a *three-inch-high* statuette, it's *three inches high, five- to ten-*

minute intervals. (Hyphenated before a noun, otherwise open. Note the space after the first number in the last example.)

numbers, spelled out: *twenty-eight, three hundred, nineteen forty-five, five hundred and fifty.* (Twenty-one through ninety-nine hyphenated; others open. See also **fractions, simple.**)

participle + noun: *chopped-liver* pâté, *cutting-edge* methods, their approach was *on the cutting edge.* (Adjective form hyphenated before a noun, seldom used after a noun.)

participle + preposition: a frequently *referred-to* paragraph, this book is often *referred to.* (Hyphenated before but not after a noun.)

participle + *up, out,* and the like: *dressed-up* children, *spelled-out* numbers, fractions that are *spelled out.* (Adjective form hyphenated before but not after a noun.)

phrases, adjectival: an *over-the-counter* drug, her approach was *matter-of-fact,* a *quicker-than-usual* reply, her reply was *quicker than usual.* (Familiar phrases hyphenated whether before or after a noun; other phrases hyphenated only before a noun. See also **phrases, familiar; phrases, foreign.**)

phrases, familiar: *stick-in-the-mud, jack-of-all-trades,* a *flash in the pan.* (Hyphenated, with rare exceptions.)

phrases, foreign, used adjectivally: an *a priori* argument, a *Sturm und Drang* drama, *in vitro* fertilization, a *tête-à-tête* approach. (Open unless hyphens appear in the original language.)

proper nouns and adjectives, hyphenated: the *Franco-Prussian War, Anglo-American* cooperation, the *Scotch-Irish.* (Hyphenated in both noun and adjective forms.)

proper nouns and adjectives, open: *African Americans,* an *African American,* a *Chinese American* child, *French Canadians,* the *North Central* region, *Middle Eastern* countries, *State Department* employees, *World War II* history. (Open in both noun and adjective forms. See also 8.42.)

relationships: See **foster, grand, in-law,** and **step** in section 2.

time: at *three thirty,* the *three-thirty* train, a *four o'clock* train, the *5:00 p.m.* news. (Usually open; hyphenated only for easier reading.)

2. Compounds Formed with Specific Terms

ache: *toothache, stomachache.* (Always closed.)

all: *all out, all along, all in, all over,* an *all-out* effort, an *all-American* player, the book is *all-encompassing.* (Adverbial phrases open; adjectival phrases hyphenated both before and after a noun.)

book: *reference book, coupon book, checkbook, cookbook* (Open if not in the dictionary.)

borne: *waterborne, foodborne, cab-borne, mosquito-borne.* (Normally closed, but hyphenated after words ending in *b* and after words of three or more syllables. See also **like** and **wide**.)

century: *twentieth-century* literature, *twenty-first-century* history, *fourteenth-century* monastery, a *mid-eighteenth-century* poet, *late nineteenth-century* politicians; her style was *nineteenth century*. (Adjectival compounds hyphenated before but not after a noun. See **old** below, and **mid** in section 3; see also 7.88.)

cross: a *cross-reference, cross-referenced, cross-grained, cross-country, crossbow, crossover*. (Noun, adjective, and adverb forms hyphenated, except for some permanent compounds.)

e: *e-mail, e-article, e-commerce, e-marketing, e-zine, e–graduate school*. (Hyphenated; use en dash if *e-* precedes an open compound. See also 7.85, 8.163.)

elect: *president-elect, mayor-elect, county assessor elect*. (Hyphenated unless the name of the office consists of two or more words.)

ever: *ever-ready* help, *ever-recurring* problem, *everlasting*. (Usually hyphenated before a noun; some permanent compounds closed.)

ex: *ex-boyfriend, ex-marine, ex–corporate executive*. (Hyphenated, but use en dash if *ex-* precedes an open compound; see 7.83.)

fold: *fourfold, hundredfold, twenty-five-fold, 150-fold*. (Closed unless formed with a hyphenated number or a numeral.)

foster: *foster mother, foster parents*, a *foster-family* background. (Noun forms open, adjective forms hyphenated.)

free: *toll-free* number, *accident-free* driver; the number is *toll free*; the driver is *accident free*. (Compounds formed with *free* as second element are hyphenated before a noun, open after a noun.)

full: *full-length* mirror, three *bags full*, a *suitcase full*. (Hyphenated when *full* precedes a noun, open after a noun. Use *ful* only in such permanent compounds as *a cupful, a handful*.)

general: *attorney general, postmaster general, lieutenants general*. (Always open; in plural forms, *general* remains singular.)

grand, great-grand: *grandfather, granddaughter, great-grandmother, great-great-grandson*. (*Grand* compounds closed, *great* compounds hyphenated.)

half: *half-asleep, half-finished*, a *half sister*, a *half hour*, a *half-hour* session, *halfway, halfhearted*. (Adjective forms hyphenated, noun forms open. Some permanent compounds closed, whether nouns, adjectives, or adverbs. Check the dictionary. See also **fractions** in section 1.)

house: *schoolhouse, courthouse* (*court house* in some jurisdictions), *rest house*. (Permanent compounds often closed. If not in the dictionary, open.)

in-law: *sister-in-law, parents-in-law*. (All compounds hyphenated; only the first element takes a plural form.)

like: *catlike, childlike, mattresslike, bell-like, Whitman-like* poetry, a *penitentiary-like* institution. (Normally closed, but hyphenated after words ending in *l*, after most proper nouns (but *Christlike*), after most words of three or more syllables, or simply to avoid a cumbersome appearance. Hyphenated compounds retain the hyphen both before and after a noun. See also **borne** and **wide**.)

mid. See section 3.

near: a *near accident*, a *near-dead* language. (Open before a noun, hyphenated before an adjective.)

odd: a *hundred-odd* manuscripts; *350-odd* books. (Always hyphenated.)

old: *decade-old*, a *three-year-old*, a *105-year-old* woman, a *centuries-old* debate, the debate is *centuries old*. (Hyphenated, especially before a noun. See also **age terms** in section 1.)

on: *online, onstage, ongoing, on-screen, on-site*. (Sometimes closed, sometimes hyphenated. Check dictionary, and hyphenate if term is not listed. See also 7.84.)

percent: *5 percent*, a *10 percent* increase. (Both noun and adjective forms always open.)

pseudo. See section 3.

quasi: a *quasi corporation*, a *quasi-public* corporation. (Open before a noun, hyphenated before an adjective.)

self: *self-restraint, self-realization, self-sustaining, self-conscious*, the behavior is *self-destructive, selfless, unselfconscious*. (Both noun and adjective forms hyphenated, except where *self-* is followed by a suffix or preceded by *un*. Note that *unselfconscious*, Chicago's preference, is contrary to Webster.)

step: *stepmother, stepgranddaughter*. (Always closed.)

style: *kindergarten-style, Chicago-style* hyphenation, dancing *1920s-style*. (Always hyphenated.)

vice: *vice-consul, vice-chancellor, vice president, vice-presidential* duties, *vice admiral, viceroy*. (Sometimes hyphenated, sometimes open, occasionally closed. Check dictionary and hyphenate if term is not listed.)

Web: *Web site, Web-related* matters, he is *Web-happy*. (Noun form open, adjective form hyphenated.)

wide: *worldwide, citywide, Chicago-wide*, the canvass was *university-wide*. (Normally closed, but hyphenated after proper nouns, after most words of three or more syllables, or simply to avoid a cumbersome appearance. Hyphenated compounds retain the hyphen both before and after a noun. See also **borne** and **like.**)

3. Words Formed with Prefixes

Compounds formed with prefixes are normally closed, whether they are nouns, verbs, adjectives, or adverbs.

A hyphen should appear, however, (1) before a capitalized word or a numeral, such as sub-Saharan, pre-1950; (2) before a compound term, such as non-self-sustaining, pre–Vietnam War (before an open compound, an en dash is used; see 7.83); (3) to separate two *i*'s, two *a*'s, and other combinations of letters or syllables that might cause misreading, such as anti-intellectual, extra-alkaline, pro-life; (4) to separate the repeated terms in a double prefix, such as sub-subentry; (5) when a prefix or combining form stands alone, such as over- and underused, macro- and microeconomics.

The spellings shown below conform largely to *Merriam-Webster's Collegiate Dictionary*. Compounds formed with combining forms not listed here, such as *auto*, *tri*, and *para*, follow the same pattern.

ante: antebellum, antenatal, antediluvian
anti: antihypertensive, antihero, *but* anti-inflammatory, anti-Hitlerian
bi: binomial, bivalent, bisexual
bio: bioecology, biophysical, biosociology
co: coequal, coauthor, coeditor, coordinate, cooperation, *but* co-opt, co-worker
counter: counterclockwise, counterrevolution
cyber: cyberspace, cyberstore
extra: extramural, extrafine, *but* extra-administrative
hyper: hypertension, hyperactive, hypertext
infra: infrasonic, infrastructure
inter: interorganizational, interfaith
intra: intrazonal, intramural, *but* intra-arterial
macro: macroeconomics, macromolecular
mega: megavitamin, megamall, mega-annoyance (hyphenate before words beginning with *a*)
meta: metalanguage, metaethical, *but* meta-analysis (not the same as metanalysis)
micro: microeconomics, micromethodical
mid: midthirties, a midcareer event, midcentury, *but* mid-July, the mid-1990s, the mid-twentieth century, mid-twentieth-century history
mini: minivan, minimarket
multi: multiauthor, multiconductor, *but* multi-institutional
neo: neonate, neoorthodox, Neoplatonism
non: nonviolent, nonevent, nonnegotiable, *but* non-beer-drinking
over: overmagnified, overshoes, overconscientious
post: postdoctoral, postmodernism, posttraumatic, *but* post-Vietnam
pre: premodern, preregistration, prewar, preempt, *but* Pre-Raphaelite
pro: proindustrial, promarket, but pro-life, pro-Canadian
proto: protolanguage, protogalaxy, protomartyr

pseudo: pseudotechnocrat, pseudomodern, *but* pseudo-Tudor
re: reedit, reunify, reproposition, *but* re-cover, re-creation (as distinct from *recover, recreation*)
semi: semiopaque, semiconductor, *but* semi-invalid
socio: socioeconomic, sociocultural, sociolinguistics
sub: subbasement, subzero, subcutaneous
super: superannuated, supervirtuoso, superpowerful
supra: supranational, suprarenal, supraorbital, *but* supra-American
trans: transsocietal, transmembrane, transcontinental, transatlantic, *but* trans-American
ultra: ultrasophisticated, ultraorganized, ultraevangelical
un: unfunded, unneutered, *but* un-English, un-unionized
under: underemployed, underrate, undercount

8

Names and Terms

Historical and Cultural Terms

Introduction

8.1   *Patterns.* This chapter helps to establish patterns in the use of names and of terms associated with names: names of persons and places; of events and movements; of governmental or corporate bodies and their actions; of vessels, species, and other entities; and, finally, of literary and other creative works. Which of these should always be capitalized? Which should generally be lowercased? Which are commonly italicized? Consistency in such matters aids readability in any publication, long or short.

8.2   *The "down" style.* Chicago generally prefers a "down" style—the parsimonious use of capitals. Although proper names are capitalized, many words derived from or associated with proper names (brussels sprouts, board of trustees), as well as the names of significant offices (presidency, papacy), may be lowercased with no loss of clarity or respect.

8.3   *Names versus generic terms.* Many proper names combine a given name with a generic (or descriptive) term (Albion College, the Circuit Court of Lake County, President Bush). After the first mention, an official name is often replaced by the generic term alone, which (no longer strictly a proper name) may safely be lowercased.

Albion College was founded in 1835. The college has some illustrious alumni.

Her suit was filed with the Circuit Court of Lake County. Appearing in court made her nervous, since she had little experience of circuit court procedures.

They asked to speak with President Bush, but the president was unavailable that day.

8.4   *Context.* Although the pattern of capitalization chosen for the various categories illustrated in this chapter may prove adaptable to most publications, no such pattern can be universally applied. In certain official (as opposed to literary) contexts, *the College* or *the President* may appropriately be capitalized. Writers and editors must use discretion and judgment in deciding when to follow the guidelines.

Personal Names

8.5   *Spelling.* For names of well-known deceased persons, Chicago generally follows the spelling in *Merriam-Webster's Biographical Dictionary* or the biographical section of *Merriam-Webster's Collegiate Dictionary.* For living persons, consult *Who's Who* or *Who's Who in America,* among other sources. (See bibliog. 4.1 for these and other useful reference works.) Where different spellings appear in different sources (e.g., W. E. B. DuBois *versus* W. E. B. Du Bois), the writer or editor must make a choice and stick with it.

8.6   *Capitalization.* Names and initials of persons, real or fictitious, are capitalized. The space between initials should be the same as the space between the last initial and the name, except when initials are used alone, with or without periods.

Jane Doe   George S. McGovern   P. D. James   M. F. K. Fisher   LBJ

The names of certain writers occasionally appear without capitals—for example, bell hooks. If such unconventional spelling is the strong preference of the bearer of the name, it should be respected in appropriate contexts. E. E. Cummings can be capitalized, however, since one of his publishers, not he himself, lowercased his name. (Library catalogs usually capitalize all such names.) For obvious reasons, a lowercased name should not begin a sentence. Also, names used in such expressions as "by george!" are usually lowercased.

ENGLISH NAMES

8.7   *English names with particles.* Many names borne by people in English-speaking countries include particles such as *de, d', de la, von, van,* and *ten.* Practice with regard to capitalizing and spacing the particles varies widely, and confirmation should be sought in a biographical dictionary or other authoritative source. When the surname is used alone, the particle is generally retained, capitalized or lowercased (though always capitalized when beginning a sentence) and spaced as in the full name. *Le* is always capitalized, as are *La* and *L'*, when not preceded by *de*. See also 8.10–20.

Thomas De Quincey; De Quincey	Robert M. La Follette; La Follette
Diana DeGette; DeGette	John Le Carré; Le Carré
Alfonse D'Amato; D'Amato	Pierre-Charles L'Enfant; L'Enfant
Walter de la Mare; De la Mare	Abraham Ten Broeck; Ten Broeck
Daphne du Maurier; Du Maurier	Wernher von Braun; von Braun
Page duBois; duBois	Stephen Van Rensselaer; Van Rensselaer
W. E. B. Du Bois; Du Bois (but see 8.5)	Robert van Gulik; van Gulik

8.8 *Hyphenated and extended names.* A hyphenated last name or a last name that consists of two or more elements should never be shorn of one of its elements. For names of prominent or historical figures, Webster and other reliable alphabetical listings usually indicate where the last name begins.

Victoria Sackville-West; Sackville-West
Ralph Vaughan Williams; Vaughan Williams (*not* Williams)
Ludwig Mies van der Rohe; Mies van der Rohe (*not* van der Rohe); Mies
but
John Hope Franklin; Franklin
Charlotte Perkins Gilman; Gilman

8.9 *Native American names.* When the English form of a Native American name is formed with the definite article, *the* remains lowercase.

the Little Turtle	the Prophet

NON-ENGLISH NAMES

8.10 *Context.* The following paragraphs focus on non-English personal names as these would be used in an English-language context.

8.11 *French names.* The particles *de* and *d'* are lowercased (except at the beginning of a sentence). When the last name is used alone, *de* (but not *d'*) is often dropped. Its occasional retention, in *de Gaulle*, for example, is suggested by tradition rather than logic. (When a name begins with closed-up *de*, such as *Debussy*, the *d* is always capitalized.)

Alexis de Tocqueville; Tocqueville
Alfred de Musset; Musset

but
Charles de Gaulle; de Gaulle
Jean d'Alembert; d'Alembert

When *de la* precedes a name, *la* is usually capitalized and is always retained when the last name is used alone. The contraction *du* is usually lowercased in a full name but is retained and capitalized when the last name is used alone. (When a name begins with closed-up *Du,* such as *Dupont,* the *d* is always capitalized.)

Jean de La Fontaine; La Fontaine
René-Robert Cavelier de La Salle; La Salle
Philippe du Puy de Clinchamps; Du Puy de Clinchamps

When the article *le* accompanies a name, it is capitalized with or without the first name.

Gustave Le Bon; Le Bon

Initials standing for a hyphenated given name should also be hyphenated.

Jean-Paul Sartre; J.-P. Sartre; Sartre

Since there is considerable variation in French usage, the guidelines and examples above merely represent the most common forms.

8.12 *German, Italian, and Portuguese names.* In the original languages, particles in German, Italian, and Portuguese names are lowercased and are usually dropped when the last name is used alone. But if the form with the particle is the one familiar to English speakers, it should be used.

Alexander von Humboldt; Humboldt
Maximilian von Spee; Spee
Heinrich Friedrich Karl von und zum Stein; Stein
Ludwig van Beethoven; Beethoven
Giovanni da Verrazano; Verrazano
Friedrich von Steuben; von Steuben
Vasco da Gama; da Gama
Luca della Robbia; della Robbia
but
Leonardo da Vinci; Leonardo

8.13   *Dutch names.* In English usage, the particles *van, van den, ter,* and the like are lowercased when full names are given but usually capitalized when only the last name is used.

Joannes van Keulen; Van Keulen
Pieter van den Keere; Van den Keere
Vincent van Gogh; Van Gogh
Gerard ter Borch; Ter Borch

8.14   *Spanish names.* Many Spanish names are composed of both the father's and the mother's family names, in that order, sometimes joined by *y* (and). When the given name is omitted, persons with such names are usually referred to by both family names but sometimes by only one, according to their own preference. It is never incorrect to use both.

José Ortega y Gasset; Ortega y Gasset *or* Ortega
Pascual Ortiz Rubio; Ortiz Rubio *or* Ortiz
Federico García Lorca; García Lorca (known among Anglophones, however, as Lorca)

Spanish family names that include an article, a preposition, or both are treated in the same way as analogous French names.

Tomás de Torquemada; Torquemada
Manuel de Falla; Falla
Bartolomé de Las Casas; Las Casas
Gonzalo Fernández de Oviedo; Fernández de Oviedo

Traditionally, married women replaced their mother's family name with their husband's (first) family name, sometimes preceded by *de*. If, for example, María Carmen Mendoza Salinas married Juan Alberto Peña Montalvo, she could change her legal name to María Carmen Mendoza (de) Peña or, if the husband was well known by both family names, to María Carmen Mendoza (de) Peña Montalvo. Many modern women in Spanish-speaking countries, however, no longer take their husband's family name. For alphabetizing, see 18.82.

8.15   *Russian names.* Russian family names, as well as middle names (patronymics), sometimes take different endings for male and female members of the family. For example, Lenin's real name was Vladimir Ilyich Ulyanov; his sister was Maria Ilyinichna Ulyanova. In text, often only the given name and patronymic are used; in the index the name should be listed under the family name, whether or not this appears in the text.

8.16   *Hungarian names.* In Hungarian practice the family name precedes the given name—for example, Molnár Ferenc, Kodály Zoltán. In English contexts, however, such names are usually inverted—Ferenc Molnár, Zoltán Kodály.

8.17   *Arabic names.* Surnames of Arabic origin (which are strictly surnames rather than family names) are often prefixed by such elements as *Abu, Abd, ibn, al-,* or *el-*. Since these are integral parts of a name, just as *Mc* or *Fitz* are parts of certain English names, they should not be dropped when the surname is used alone. See also 10.98, 18.74.

> Syed Abu Zafar Nadvi; Abu Zafar Nadvi
> Aziz ibn Saud; Ibn Saud
> Tawfiq al-Hakim; al-Hakim

Names of rulers of older times, however, are often shortened to the first part of the name rather than the second.

> Harun al-Rashid; Harun (al-Rashid, "Rightly Guided," was Harun's *kunyah,* a name taken on his accession to the caliphate)

8.18   *Chinese names.* In Chinese practice, the family name comes before the given name. (This practice should be followed in English contexts with names of Chinese persons but not with those of persons of Chinese origin whose names have been anglicized.) For use of the pinyin and Wade-Giles systems of transliteration, see 10.100–103.

> Chiang Kai-shek; Chiang (Wade-Giles)
> Mao Tse-tung; Mao (Wade-Giles)
> Li Bo; Li (pinyin)
> Du Fu; Du (pinyin)
> *but*
> Anthony Yu; Yu
> Tang Tsou; Tsou

8.19   *Japanese names.* In Japanese usage the family name precedes the given name. Japanese names are sometimes westernized, however, by authors writing in English or persons of Japanese origin living in the West.

> Tajima Yumiko; Tajima
> Yoshida Shigeru; Yoshida
> *but*
> Noriaki Kurosawa; Kurosawa

8.20   *Other Asian names.* In some Asian countries, people are usually known by their given name rather than by a surname or family name. The Indonesian writer Pramoedya Ananta Toer, for example, would be referred to in short form as Pramoedya (not as Toer). For further examples, see 18.75, 18.79, 18.83, 18.84. If in doubt, use the full form of a name in all references or consult an expert.

Titles and Offices

8.21   *Capitalization: the general rule.* Civil, military, religious, and professional titles are capitalized when they immediately precede a personal name and are thus used as part of the name (usually replacing the title holder's first name). Titles are normally lowercased when following a name or used in place of a name (but see 8.22). See 8.25–29 for many examples. For abbreviated forms, see 15.11–18.

President Lincoln; the president   Dean Mueller; the dean
General Bradley; the general   Governors Edgar and Ryan; the governors
Cardinal Newman; the cardinal

Although both first and second names may be used after a title (e.g., Vice President Dick Cheney), such usage is generally avoided in formal prose. Note also that once a title has been given, it need not be repeated each time a person's name is mentioned.

Dick Durbin, senator from Illinois; Senator Durbin; Durbin

8.22   *Exceptions to the general rule.* In formal contexts as opposed to running text, such as a displayed list of donors in the front matter of a book or a list of corporate officers in an annual report, titles are usually capitalized even when following a personal name. Exceptions may also be called for in promotional or other contexts for reasons of courtesy or politics.

Maria Martinez, Director of International Sales

A title used alone, in place of a personal name, is capitalized only in such contexts as a toast or a formal introduction, or when used in direct address.

Ladies and Gentlemen, the Prime Minister.
I would have done it, Captain, but the ship was sinking.
Thank you, Mr. President.

8.23 *Titles used in apposition.* When a title is used in apposition before a personal name, not as part of the name but as a descriptive tag, and often with *the,* it is lowercased.

the empress Elizabeth of Austria
German chancellor Gerhard Schröder
the globe-trotting pope John Paul II
former presidents Reagan and Clinton
chief operating officer Susan Raymond
the then secretary of state Madeleine Albright
but
Secretary of State Albright (see 8.25)

8.24 *Text use.* The lists in the sections that follow, obviously not exhaustive, show various titles and words related to them as they might appear in text rather than in a formal listing or heading. See also 8.3–4.

8.25 *Civil titles*

the president; George Washington, first president of the United States; President Washington; the presidency; presidential; the Washington administration (see also 8.23); Chandrika Kumaratunga, president of Sri Lanka; President Kumaratunga *or* Mrs. Kumaratunga

the vice president; Richard Cheney, vice president of the United States; Vice President Cheney; vice-presidential duties; Jorge Quiroga, vice president of Bolivia; Vice President Quiroga

the secretary of state; Colin Powell, secretary of state; Secretary of State Powell *or* Secretary Powell

the senator; the senator from West Virginia; Senator Robert C. Byrd; Senators Byrd and Trent; Sen. John Glenn, Democrat from Ohio (*or* D-OH; see 15.31)

the representative; the congressman; the congresswoman; Henry Hyde, representative from Illinois *or* congressman from Illinois; Congressman Hyde *or* Rep. Henry Hyde (R-IL) *or* Rep. Henry Hyde (R-Ill.); Maxine Waters, representative from California; Congresswoman Waters; the congresswoman *or* the representative; Representatives Hyde and Waters

the Speaker; Dennis Hastert, Speaker of the House of Representatives; Speaker Hastert (*Speaker* is traditionally capitalized)

the chief justice; William H. Rehnquist, chief justice of the United States; Chief Justice Rehnquist (see also 8.69)

the associate justice; Ruth Bader Ginsburg, associate justice; Justice Ginsburg; Justices Ginsburg and Souter

the chief judge; Henry Tonigan, chief judge; Judge Tonigan

the ambassador; Philip Lader, ambassador to the Court of St. James's *or* ambassador to the United Kingdom; Ambassador Lader

the governor; Ruth Ann Minner, governor of the state of Delaware; Governor Minner

the mayor; Richard M. Daley, mayor of Chicago; Mayor Daley

the state senator; Olga Parker, Ohio state senator; the Honorable Olga Parker

the state representative (same pattern as state senator)

the governor-general of Canada; the Right Honourable Edward Richard Schreyer

the minister; Heize Takenaka, Japanese economics minister; Mr. Takenaka

the prime minister; the Right Honourable Pierre Elliott Trudeau, former prime minister of Canada; Tony Blair, the British prime minister (not normally used as a title preceding the name)

the premier (of a Canadian province); the Right Honourable Roy Romanow

the member of Parliament (UK and Canada); Jane Doe, member of Parliament *or, more commonly,* Jane Doe, MP (not used as a title preceding the name); Jane Doe, the member for West Hamage

the chief whip; Tony Yengeni, chief whip of the African National Congress; Yengeni

the foreign secretary (UK); the foreign minister (other nations); the British foreign secretary; the German foreign minister (not used as a title preceding the name)

the chancellor; Gerhard Schröder, chancellor of Germany; Chancellor Schröder

the chancellor of the exchequer (UK); Gordon Brown; Chancellor Brown

the Lord Privy Seal (UK; always capitalized)

For use of *the Honorable* and similar terms of respect, see 8.35, 15.18.

8.26   *Titles of sovereigns and other rulers.* See also 8.34.

King Abdullah; the king of Jordan

Queen Elizabeth; Elizabeth II; the queen (in a British or Canadian context, the Queen)

the Holy Roman Emperor

Hamad bin Isa al-Khalifa, emir of Bahrain; Sheik Hamad

the shah of Iran

the sharif of Mecca

the paramount chief of Basutoland

Wilhelm II, emperor of Germany; Kaiser Wilhelm II; the kaiser

the führer (Adolf Hitler)

Il Duce (used only of Benito Mussolini; both *i* and *d* capitalized)

8.27   *Military titles*

the general; General Ulysses S. Grant, commander in chief of the Union army; General Grant; the commander in chief

the General of the Army; Omar N. Bradley, General of the Army; General Bradley (*General of the Army* always capitalized to avoid ambiguity)

the admiral; Chester W. Nimitz, Fleet Admiral; Admiral Nimitz, commander of the Pacific
  Fleet (*Fleet Admiral* always capitalized to avoid ambiguity)
the chairman; Richard B. Myers, chairman of the Joint Chiefs of Staff
the captain; Captain Frank LeClaire, company commander
the sergeant; Sergeant Carleton C. Singer; a noncommissioned officer (NCO)
the warrant officer; Warrant Officer John Carmichael; Mr. Carmichael
the chief petty officer; Chief Petty Officer Tannenbaum
the private; Private T. C. Alhambra
the British general; General Sir Guy Carleton, British commander in New York City; General Carleton

For abbreviations, often used when a title precedes a name and appropriate in material in which many military titles appear, see 15.15.

8.28 *Quasi-military titles.* Titles and ranks used in organizations such as the police, the merchant marine, or the Salvation Army are treated the same way
as military titles.

the chief of police; Frederick Day, Lake Bluff chief of police; Chief Day
the warden; Jane Doe, warden of the state penitentiary; Warden Doe

8.29 *Religious titles*

the rabbi; Rabbi Avraham Yitzhak ha-Kohen Kuk; the rabbinate
the cantor *or* hazzan; Deborah Bard, cantor; Cantor Bard
the sheikh; Sheikh Ibrahim el-Zak Zaky
the imam; Imam Shamil
the ayatollah; Ayatollah Khomeini
the Dalai Lama (traditionally capitalized); *but* previous dalai lamas
the sadhu; the guru; the shaman
the pope; Pope John Paul II; the papacy; papal
the cardinal; Francis Cardinal George *or, less formally,* Cardinal George; the sacred college
  of cardinals
the patriarch; Cyrillus Lucaris, patriarch of Constantinople; the patriarchate
the archbishop; the archbishop of Canterbury; Archbishop Temple
the bishop; the bishop of Toledo; Bishop Donovan; bishopric; diocese
the minister; the Reverend Shirley Stoops (see also 15.18)
the rector; the Reverend James Williams (see also 15.18)

See also 8.35.

8.30 *Corporate and organizational titles.* Titles of persons holding offices such as
those listed below are rarely used as part of a name. If a short form is re-

quired, either the generic term or simply a personal name suffices. For appositional use, see 8.23.

> the chief executive officer; Susan Franklin, chief operating officer of Caterham Corporation; the CEO of the corporation
> the director; Beverly Jarrett, director of the University of Missouri Press
> the school superintendent; Allan Alson, superintendent of Evanston Township High School District
> the secretary-treasurer; Georgina Fido, secretary-treasurer of the Kenilworth Kennel Society

8.31 *Academic titles*

> the professor; Françoise Meltzer, professor of comparative literature; Professor Meltzer
> the chair; James R. Norris, chair of the Department of Chemistry; Professor Norris
> the provost; Richard P. Saller, provost of the University of Chicago; Mr. Saller
> the president; Don Michael Randel, president of the University of Chicago; Mr. Randel *or* President Randel
> the dean; Joyce Feucht-Haviar, dean of the College of Extended Learning; Dean Feucht-Haviar
> named professorships; Wendy Doniger, Mircea Eliade Distinguished Service Professor in the Divinity School; Professor Doniger; Anthony Grafton, Dodge Professor of History, Princeton University; Professor Grafton
> the professor emeritus (masc.); the professor emerita (fem.); professors emeriti (masc. or masc. and fem.); professors emeritae (fem.); Professor Emerita Neugarten (Note that *emeritus* and *emerita* are honorary designations and do not simply mean *retired*.)

8.32 *Other academic designations.* Terms denoting student status are lower-cased.

> freshman *or* first-year student   sophomore   junior   senior

Names of degrees, fellowships, and the like are lowercased when referred to generically. See also 15.21.

> a master's degree; a doctorate; a fellowship; master of business administration (MBA)

8.33 *Civic and academic honors.* Titles denoting civic or academic honors are capitalized when following a personal name. For awards, see 8.89; for abbreviations, see 15.22.

> Laurence L. Bongie, Fellow of the Royal Society of Canada; the fellowship

8.34   *Titles of nobility.* Unlike most of the titles mentioned in the previous paragraphs, titles of nobility do not denote offices (such as that of a president
or an admiral). Whether inherited or conferred, they form an integral and,
with rare exceptions, permanent part of a person's name and are therefore
usually capitalized. The generic element in a title, however (the duke, the
earl, etc.), is lowercased when used alone as a short form of the name. (In
British usage, the generic term used alone remains capitalized in the case
of royal dukes but not in the case of nonroyal dukes; in North American
usage such niceties may be disregarded.) For further advice consult *The
Times Guide to English Style and Usage* (bibliog. 1.1), and for a comprehensive listing consult the latest edition of *Burke's Genealogical and Heraldic
History of the Peerage* (bibliog. 4.1). See also 8.26.

the prince; Prince Charles; the Prince of Wales

the duke; the duchess; the Duke and Duchess of Windsor

the marquess; the Marquess of Bath; Lord Bath

the marchioness; the Marchioness of Bath; Lady Bath

the earl; the Earl of Shaftesbury; Lord Shaftesbury; Anthony Ashley Cooper, 7th (*or* seventh) Earl of Shaftesbury; previous earls of Shaftesbury;

the countess (wife of an earl); the Countess of Shaftesbury; Lady Shaftesbury

the viscount; Viscount Eccles; Lord Eccles

Baroness Thatcher; Lady Thatcher (a conferred title)

Dame Judi Dench; Dame Judi (a conferred title)

the baron; Lord Rutland

the baronet; the knight; Sir John Euston; Sir John

Lady So-and-So (wife of a marquess, earl, baron, or baronet)

Lady Olivia So-and-So (daughter of a duke, marquess, or earl)

the Honourable Jessica So-and-So (daughter of a baron)

the duc de Guise (lowercased in accordance with French usage); François de Lorraine,
duc de Guise

the count; Count Helmuth von Moltke *or* Graf Helmuth von Moltke; the comte de
Toulouse

Note that marquesses, earls, viscounts, barons, and baronesses are addressed, and referred to after first mention, as Lord or Lady So-and-So, at
least in British usage. The following entry, drawn from *Burke's Genealogical and Heraldic History of the Peerage*, illustrates the complexities of
British noble nomenclature.

The 5th Marquess of Salisbury (Sir Robert Arthur James Gascoyne-Cecil, K.G., P.C.), Earl
of Salisbury, Wilts; Viscount Cranborne, Dorset, and Baron Cecil of Essendon, Rutland;
co-heir to the Barony of Ogle

8.35   *Terms of respect.* Honorific titles and respectful forms of address are capitalized. For the use of many such terms in formal correspondence, see "Forms of Address," a comprehensive listing at the back of *Merriam-Webster's Collegiate Dictionary.* For abbreviations, see 15.18. The following examples are intended merely to illustrate capitalization. See also 8.29.

the Honorable Olympia J. Snowe (U.S. senator, member of congress, etc.)
the Right Honourable Joseph-Jacques Jean Chrétien (Canadian governor-general, prime
     minister, premier, etc.)
the First Lady
the Queen Mother
Pandit Nehru
Mahatma Gandhi
Her (His, Your) Majesty; His (Her, Your) Royal Highness
the Most Reverend John A. Donovan (Roman Catholic bishop)
Your (Her, His) Excellency
Mr. President
Madam Speaker
Your Honor
but
sir, ma'am
my lord, my lady

Epithets, Kinship Names, and Personifications

8.36   *Epithets, or nicknames.* A characterizing word or phrase used as part of, or instead of, a person's name is capitalized.

the Great Emancipator	the Young Pretender	Babe Ruth
the Sun King	the Great Commoner	the Swedish Nightingale
the Wizard of Menlo Park	Catherine the Great	Ivan the Terrible
Stonewall Jackson		

When used in addition to a name, an epithet is enclosed in quotation marks and placed either within or after the name. Parentheses are unnecessary.

George Herman "Babe" Ruth
Jenny Lind, "the Swedish Nightingale"
Ivan IV, "the Terrible"

8.37 *Temporary epithets.* When preceding a name, role-denoting epithets such as *citizen* or *historian* should be lowercased and treated as if in apposition (see 8.23).

the historian William McNeill (*not* Historian McNeill)

8.38 *Epithets as names of characters.* In references to works of drama or fiction, epithets or generic titles used in place of names are normally capitalized.

John Barrymore performed brilliantly as Chief Executioner.
Alice's encounters with the Red Queen and the Mad Hatter

8.39 *Kinship names.* Kinship names are lowercased unless they immediately precede a personal name or are used alone, in place of a personal name. Pet names, however, are always lowercased.

my father and mother
the Brontë sisters
Let's write to Aunt Maud.
I believe Grandmother's middle name was Marie.
Please, Dad, let's go.
but
No, my son, I'm afraid not. (Lowercased after a pronoun)
She adores her aunt Maud. (Appositional use; see 8.23)
Sorry, sweetheart!

Kinship terms used in connection with religious offices or callings are treated similarly.

We asked Mother Superior to speak first.
A certain Brother Thomas, one of the brothers from the Franciscan monastery, . . .
They welcomed their new rector, Father Smith.
We learned that the Holy Father was on his way.

8.40 *Personification.* The poetic device of giving abstractions the attributes of persons, and hence capitalizing them, is rare in today's writing. The use of capitals for such a purpose is best confined to quoted material.

"The Night is Mother of the Day, / The Winter of the Spring" (John Greenleaf Whittier)
but
In springtime, nature is at its best.
It was a battle between head and heart; reason finally won.

Ethnic, Socioeconomic, and Other Groups

8.41   *Capitalization.* Names of ethnic and national groups are capitalized. Adjectives associated with these names are also capitalized. For hyphenation or its absence, see 8.42.

> Aborigines; an Aborigine; Aboriginal art
> African Americans; African American culture (see also 8.42–43)
> American Indians; an American Indian (see text below)
> Arabs; Arabian
> Asians; Asian influence in the West; an Asian American
> the British; a British person *or, colloquially,* a Britisher, a Brit
> Caucasians; a Caucasian (see also 8.43)
> Chicanos; a Chicano; a Chicana
> European Americans
> the French; a Frenchman; a Frenchwoman
> French Canadians
> Hispanics; a Hispanic
> Inuits; Inuit sculpture
> Italian Americans; an Italian American neighborhood (see also 8.42)
> Jews; a Jew; Jewish ethnicity (see also 8.104)
> Latinos; a Latino; a Latina; Latino immigration
> Native Americans; Native American poetry (see text below)
> New Zealanders; New Zealand immigration
> Hopis; a Hopi; Hopi customs
> Pygmies; a Pygmy; Pygmy peoples
> Romanys; a Romany; the Romany people

Many American Indians prefer *American Indians* to the more current term *Native Americans,* and in certain historical works *Indians* may be more appropriate. Canadians often speak of *First Nations* or *First Peoples.*

8.42   *Use of hyphen.* Whether terms such as *African American, Italian American, Chinese American,* and the like should be spelled open or hyphenated has been the subject of considerable controversy, the hyphen being regarded by some as suggestive of bias. Chicago doubts that hyphenation represents bias, but since the hyphen does not aid comprehension in such terms as those mentioned above, it may be omitted unless the writer prefers it. See also 7.90, section 1, under *proper nouns and adjectives.*

8.43   *Color.* Designations based loosely on color are usually lowercased, though capitalization may be appropriate if the writer strongly prefers it. See also 8.41.

black people, blacks, people of color
white people, whites
but
Negro, Negroes
Caucasian, Caucasians

8.44   *Class.* Terms denoting socioeconomic classes or groups are lowercased.

the middle class; a middle-class neighborhood
the upper-middle class; an upper-middle-class family
blue-collar workers
the aristocracy
the proletariat
homeless people

8.45   *Physical characteristics.* Terms describing groups or individuals according to a physical characteristic or a disability are usually lowercased.

wheelchair users   blind persons   deaf children

Some writers capitalize *deaf* when referring to people who identify themselves as members of the distinct linguistic and cultural group whose primary language is ASL—the Deaf community—and lowercase it when referring to people who have a hearing loss or to those deaf people who prefer oral methods of communication. See also 10.145.

Names of Places

8.46   *Spelling.* For the spelling of names of places, consult *Merriam-Webster's Geographical Dictionary* (bibliog. 4.2). Since names of countries and cities often change, however, even the most recent edition of such a reference work cannot be current in every detail. Writers and editors should attempt to use the form of names appropriate to the period under discussion. Note that when *the* precedes a name, it is capitalized with a city name (e.g., "The Hague") but not with other names ("the Philippines"; "the Vatican"; "the Himalayas").

PARTS OF THE WORLD

8.47   *Continents, countries, cities, oceans, and such.* Entities that appear on maps are always capitalized, as are adjectives and nouns derived from them.

Asia; Asian	California; Californian	Atlantic Ocean; Atlantic
Ireland; Irish	Chicago; Chicagoan	South China Sea
the Netherlands; Dutch		

8.48   *Points of the compass. Compass points* and terms derived from them are lowercased if they simply indicate direction or location. But see 8.50.

> pointing toward the north; a north wind; a northern climate
> to fly east; an eastward move; in the southwest of France; southwesterly

8.49   *Regional terms. Regional terms* (often based on points of the compass) that are accepted as proper names but do not normally appear on maps are usually capitalized. Adjectives and nouns derived from such terms, however, are usually lowercased. See also 8.48, 8.50.

> the Northwest; northwestern
> the East; eastern; an easterner (but see also 8.50)

8.50   *Patterns and variations.* The following examples illustrate not only the principles sketched in 8.2–4 but also variations (not always logical) based on context and usage.

> the Swiss Alps; the French Alps; an Alpine Village (if in the Alps), *but* alpine pastures in the Rockies (see also 8.57)
> Antarctica; the Antarctic Circle; the Antarctic Continent
> the Arctic; the Arctic Circle; Arctic waters; a mass of Arctic air (but lowercased when used metaphorically, as in "We are having arctic weather in Chicago"; see 8.65)
> Central America, Central American countries; central Asia; central Illinois; central France; central Europe (*but* Central Europe when referring to the political division of World War I)
> the continental United States; the continent of Europe, *but* on the Continent (meaning in continental Europe as opposed to Great Britain); Continental cuisine, *but* continental breakfast
> the East, eastern, an easterner, the eastern seaboard, East Coast (referring to the eastern United States); the East, the Far East, Eastern (referring to the Orient and Asian culture); the Middle East (*or,* formerly more common, the Near East), Middle Eastern (referring to Iran, Iraq, etc.); the Eastern Hemisphere; eastern Europe (*but* Eastern Europe when referring to the post–World War II division of Europe); eastward, to turn east (direction)
> the equator, equatorial climate; the Equatorial Current; Equatorial Guinea (formerly Spanish Guinea)
> the Great Plains; the northern plains; the plains (*but* Plains Indians)
> the Midwest, midwestern, a midwesterner
> the North, northern; Northern, Northerner (in American Civil War contexts); the North-

west, the Pacific Northwest, the Northwest Passage, northwestern; North Africa, North African countries, in northern Africa; North America, North American, the North American continent; the North Atlantic, a northern Atlantic route; the Northern Hemisphere; northern California (see below for Southern California); Northeast Brazil (a political division); the Far North

the poles; the North Pole, the North Polar ice cap; the South Pole; polar regions (see also Antarctica; the Arctic)

the South, southern; Southern, a Southerner (in American Civil War contexts); the Deep South; the south of France; the Southeast, the Southwest, southeastern, southwestern (U.S.); Southeast Asia; South Africa, South African (referring to the Republic of South Africa); southern Africa (referring to the southern part of the continent); *but* Southern California (considered a cultural entity as much as a geographical term)

the tropics, tropical; the Tropic of Cancer; the Neotropics, Neotropical; subtropical

Upper Egypt; the Upper Peninsula (of Michigan); the upper reaches of the Thames

the West; the Occident; the Western world (considered a cultural entity); the West, West Coast (of the U.S.); west, western, westward (direction), a westerner

8.51 *Popular names.* Popular names of places, or epithets, are usually capitalized. Quotation marks are not needed. Some of the following examples may be used of more than one place. None should be used in contexts where they will not be readily understood. See also 8.36.

Back Bay	the Gaza Strip	Skid Row
the Badger State	the Gulf	the South Side
the Badlands	the Holy City	the South Seas
the Bay Area	the Jewish Quarter	the Sun Belt
the Beltway	the Lake District	the Twin Cities
the Bible Belt	the Left Bank	the Upper West Side
the Cape	the Loop (Chicago)	the Village
the Delta	the Old World	the West End
the Eastern Shore	the Panhandle	the Wild West
the East End	the Promised Land	the Windy City
the Eternal City	the Rust Belt	
the Fertile Crescent	Silicon Valley	

Certain terms considered political rather than geographical entities are lowercased.

the iron curtain   the third world

8.52 *Generic terms.* Generic terms used for parts of urban areas are not capitalized.

the business district   the inner city

8.53   *"Greater."* When *greater* is used with the name of a city to denote a whole metropolitan area, it is capitalized.

Greater Chicago   Greater London

8.54   *Real and metaphorical names. Mecca* is capitalized when referring to the Islamic holy city, as is *Utopia* when referring to Thomas More's imaginary country. Both are lowercased when used metaphorically. See also 8.65.

Stratford-upon-Avon is a mecca for Shakespeare enthusiasts.
She is trying to create a utopia for her children.

POLITICAL DIVISIONS

8.55   *Capitalization.* Words denoting political divisions—from *empire, republic,* and *state* down to *ward* and *precinct*—are capitalized when they follow a name and are used as an accepted part of the name. When preceding the name, such terms are usually capitalized in names of countries but lowercased in entities below the national level. Used alone, they are almost always lowercased. But see 8.56.

the Ottoman Empire; the empire
the British Commonwealth; Commonwealth nations; the commonwealth
the United States; the Republic; the Union
the United Kingdom; Great Britain; Britain (*not* the kingdom)
the Russian Federation (formerly the Union of Soviet Socialist Republics; the Soviet Union); Russia; the federation
the Republic of South Africa (formerly the Union of South Africa); South Africa; the republic
the Fifth Republic (France)
the Republic of Indonesia; the republic
the Republic of Lithuania; the republic
the Federal Democratic Republic of Ethiopia; the republic
the State of the Harari Peoples; the state
the Commonwealth of Australia; the commonwealth
the state of New South Wales
the Australian Capital Territory
the Commonwealth of Puerto Rico
Washington State; the state of Washington
the New England states
the province of Ontario (in Canadian usage, the Province of Ontario)

Jiangxi Province
Massachusetts Bay Colony; the colony at Massachusetts Bay
the British colonies; the thirteen colonies
the Indiana Territory; the territory of Indiana
the Northwest Territory; the Old Northwest
the Western Reserve
Lake County; the county of Lake; the county; county Kildare (Irish usage)
New York City; the city of New York
the City (the old city of London, now the financial district, always capitalized)
Shields Township; the township
the Eleventh Congressional District; the congressional district
the Fifth Ward; the ward
the Sixth Precinct; the precinct

8.56 *Governmental entities.* Where the government rather than the place is meant, the words *state, city,* and the like are usually capitalized.

She works for the Village of Forest Park
That is a City of Chicago ordinance.
but
Residents of the village of Forest Park enjoy easy access to the city of Chicago.

TOPOGRAPHICAL DIVISIONS

8.57 *Mountains, rivers, and the like.* Names of mountains, rivers, oceans, islands, and so forth are capitalized. The generic term (*mountain,* etc.) is also capitalized when used as part of the name. In the plural, it is capitalized when it is part of a single name (Hawaiian Islands) and when it is used of two or more names, both beginning with the generic term (Mounts Washington and Rainier). When the generic term comes second and applies to two or more names, it is usually lowercased (the Illinois and the Chicago rivers).

Cape Kennedy
the Nile Delta
the Continental Divide
the Black Forest
the Hawaiian Islands; Hawaii; *but* the island of Hawaii
the Windward Islands; the Windwards
Silver Lake
Lake Michigan; Lakes Michigan and Erie; the Great Lakes

the Rocky Mountains; the Rockies (see also 8.50)
Stone Mountain
Mount Washington; Mount Rainier; Mounts Washington and Rainier
the Pacific Ocean; the Pacific and the Atlantic oceans
the Iberian Peninsula
Walden Pond
the Great Barrier Reef
the Illinois River; the Illinois and the Chicago rivers
the Mediterranean Sea; the Mediterranean
the Bering Strait
the Indian Subcontinent
the Nile Valley; the valley; the Mississippi River valley
Death Valley; the Valley of Kings
the Horn of Africa

8.58   *Generic terms.* When a generic term is used descriptively (or in apposition; see 8.23) rather than as part of name, or when used alone, it is lowercased.

the Amazon basin
along the Pacific coast (*but* the Pacific Coast *if the region is meant*)
the California desert
the river Thames
the Hudson River valley

8.59   *Foreign terms.* When a foreign generic term forms part of a geographic name, the English term should not be included.

the Rio Grande (*not* the Rio Grande River)
Fujiyama (*not* Mount Fujiyama)
Mauna Loa (*not* Mount Mauna Loa)
the Sierra Nevada (*not* the Sierra Nevada Mountains)

PUBLIC PLACES AND MAJOR STRUCTURES

8.60   *Thoroughfares and the like.* The names of streets, avenues, squares, parks, and so forth are capitalized. The generic form is lowercased when used alone. In the plural, *street, avenue,* and such are usually lowercased. See also 9.55–56.

Broadway
Fifty-fifth Street; Fifty-seventh and Fifty-fifth streets

Hyde Park Boulevard; the boulevard
Interstate 80; I-80; an interstate highway
Jackson Park; the park
the Lion's Gate
London Bridge; the bridge
the Mall (in London)
Pennsylvania Avenue; Carnegie and Euclid avenues
Park Lane
Piccadilly Circus
Tiananmen Square; the square
the Spanish Steps; the steps
U.S. Route 66; Routes 1 and 2; a state route

8.61   *Buildings and monuments.* The names of buildings and monuments are capitalized. The generic form is lowercased when used alone.

the Babri Mosque; the mosque
Buckingham Fountain; the fountain
the Capitol (*as distinct from* the capital city)
the Chrysler Building; the building; the Empire State and Chrysler buildings
Hadrian's Wall (*but* the Berlin wall)
the Houses of Parliament
the Jefferson Memorial; the memorial
the Leaning Tower of Pisa
the Pyramids (*but* the Egyptian pyramids)
Shedd Aquarium; the aquarium
the Stone of Scone
Symphony Center; the center
Tribune Tower; the tower
the Washington Monument; the monument
Westminster Abbey; the Abbey (a short form rather than a generic term)
the White House

Some massive works of sculpture are regarded primarily as monuments and therefore not italicized (see 8.206).

the Statue of Liberty; the statue
Mount Rushmore National Memorial; Mount Rushmore
the Colossus of Rhodes; the colossus

8.62   *Rooms, offices, and such.* Official names of rooms, offices, and the like are capitalized.

<table>
<tr><td>the Empire Room (*but* room 421)</td><td>the Oval Office</td></tr>
<tr><td>the Amelia Earhart Suite (*but* suite 219)</td><td>the West Wing of the White House</td></tr>
<tr><td>the Lincoln Bedroom</td><td></td></tr>
</table>

8.63 *Foreign names.* Foreign names of thoroughfares and buildings are not italicized and may be preceded by English *the* if the definite article is used in the original language.

<table>
<tr><td>the Champs-Elysées</td><td>Unter den Linden (never preceded by *the*)</td></tr>
<tr><td>the Bibliothèque nationale</td><td>the Marktstrasse</td></tr>
<tr><td>the Bois de Boulogne</td><td>the Piazza delle Terme</td></tr>
</table>

Words Derived from Proper Names

8.64 *When to capitalize.* Adjectives derived from personal names are normally capitalized. Those in common use may be found in Webster, sometimes in the biographical names section (e.g., *Aristotelian, Jamesian, Machiavellian, Shakespearean*). If not in the dictionary, adjectives can sometimes be coined by adding *ian* (to a name ending in a consonant) or *an* (to a name ending in *e* or *i*). Many names, however, do not lend themselves to such coinages, which should then be avoided. See also 8.65, 8.85.

<table>
<tr><td>Baudelaire, Baudelairean</td><td>Rabelais, Rabelaisian</td></tr>
<tr><td>Bayes, Bayesian</td><td>Sartre, Sartrean</td></tr>
<tr><td>Dickens, Dickensian</td><td>Shaw, Shavian</td></tr>
<tr><td>Mendel, Mendelian</td><td></td></tr>
</table>

8.65 *When not to capitalize.* Personal, national, or geographical names, and words derived from such names, are often lowercased when used with a *nonliteral* meaning. For example, "an excellent Swiss gruyère" refers to a cheese made in Switzerland, whereas "swiss cheese" is an American cheese with holes in it. (Although some of the following terms are capitalized in Webster, Chicago prefers to lowercase them in their nonliteral use.) See also 8.85.

<table>
<tr><td>anglicize</td><td>cheddar</td></tr>
<tr><td>arabic numerals</td><td>diesel engine</td></tr>
<tr><td>arctics (boots)</td><td>delphic</td></tr>
<tr><td>bohemian</td><td>dutch oven</td></tr>
<tr><td>brie</td><td>epicure</td></tr>
<tr><td>brussels sprouts</td><td>frankfurter</td></tr>
</table>

french fries	pasteurize
french dressing	pharisaic
french windows	philistine, philistinism
gruyère	platonic (but see 8.85)
herculean	quixotic
homeric	roman numerals
india ink	roman type
italic type	scotch whisky; scotch
italicize	stilton
jeremiad	swiss cheese (not made in Switzerland)
lombardy poplar	venetian blinds
manila envelope	vulcanize
morocco leather	wiener

Names of Organizations

GOVERNMENTAL AND JUDICIAL BODIES

8.66 *Overview.* The full names of legislative, deliberative, administrative, and judicial bodies, departments, bureaus, and offices, and often their short forms, are capitalized. Adjectives derived from them are usually lower-cased, as are the generic names for such bodies when used alone. See also 10.8.

8.67 *Legislative and deliberative*

the United Nations General Assembly; the UN General Assembly; the assembly
the League of Nations; the League
the United Nations Security Council; the Security Council; the council
the United States Congress; the U.S. Congress; the Ninety-seventh Congress; Congress; 97th Cong.; congressional
the United States Senate; the Senate; senatorial; the upper house of Congress
the House of Representatives; the House; the lower house of Congress
the Electoral College
the Committee on Foreign Affairs; the Foreign Affairs Committee; the committee
the General Assembly of Illinois; the assembly; the Illinois legislature; the state senate
the Chicago City Council; the city council
Parliament; parliamentary; an early parliament; the British parliament; the House of Commons; the Commons; the House of Lords; the Lords
the Crown (the British monarchy); Crown lands

the Privy Council (*but* a Privy Counsellor)

the Parliament of Canada; the Senate (upper house); the House of Commons (lower house)

the Legislative Assembly of British Columbia; the Quebec National Assembly

the Dail Eireann (lower house of the Irish parliament)

the Assemblée nationale *or* the National Assembly (present-day France); the (French) Senate; the parliamentary system; the Parlement de Paris (historical)

the States General *or* Estates General (France and Netherlands, historical)

the Cortes (Spain; a plural form in Spanish but used as a singular in English)

the Cámera de Diputados (Mexico)

the Bundestag (German parliament); the Bundesrat (German upper house); the Reichstag (imperial Germany)

the House of People's Representatives; the House of Federation; the Council of Ministers (Ethiopia)

the Dewan Perwakilon Rakyat *or* House of Representatives; the Majelis Permusyawaratan Rakyat *or* People's Consultative Assembly (Indonesia)

the European Parliament; the parliament

8.68 *Administrative*

the Department of State; the State Department; the department; departmental

the Department of the Interior; Interior (a short form, not a generic term)

the Federal Bureau of Investigation; the bureau; the FBI

the Bureau of the Census; census forms; the census of 2000

the Occupational Safety and Health Administration; OSHA

the National Institutes of Health; the NIH; the National Institute of Mental Health; the NIMH

the Office of Human Resources; Human Resources (a short form, not a generic term)

the Federal Reserve System; the Federal Reserve Board; the Federal Reserve

the United States Postal Service; the postal service; the post office

the County Board of Lake County; the Lake County Board; the county board

the Peace Corps

the Centers for Disease Control and Prevention; the CDC (abbreviation did not change when "and Prevention" was added to name)

8.69 *Judicial*

the United States (*or* U.S.) Supreme Court; the Supreme Court; the Court (traditionally capitalized in reference to the U.S. Supreme Court)

the Arizona Supreme Court; the supreme court; the supreme courts of Arizona and New Mexico

the United States Court of Appeals for the Seventh Circuit; the court of appeals

the District Court for the Southern District of New York; the district court
the Court of Common Pleas (Ohio); the court
the Circuit Court of Lake County, Family Division (Illinois); family court
the Supreme Court of Canada
the Birmingham Crown Court; Dawlish Magistrates' Court (England)
the Federal Supreme Court (Ethiopia)

States, counties, and cities vary in the way they name their courts. For example, *court of appeals* in New York State and Maryland is equivalent to *supreme court* in other states; and such terms as *district court, circuit court, superior court,* and *court of common pleas* are used for similar court systems in different states. Generic names should therefore be used only when the full name or jurisdiction has been stated.

8.70   *Lowercased entities.* Certain terms associated with governmental bodies are lowercased.

administration; the Carter administration
brain trust
cabinet (*but* the Kitchen Cabinet in the Jackson administration)
city hall (the municipal government)
civil service
court (a royal court)
executive, legislative, or judicial branch
federal; the federal government; federal agencies
government
monarchy
parlement (French; *but* the Parlement of Paris)
state; church and state; state powers

POLITICAL AND ECONOMIC ORGANIZATIONS AND MOVEMENTS

8.71   *Organizations and parties.* Names of national and international organizations, alliances, and political movements and parties are capitalized (e.g., "the Socialist Party in France"). The words *party* and *movement* are capitalized when part of the name of an organization. Names of systems of thought and of the adherents to such systems are often lowercased (e.g., "an eighteenth-century precursor of socialism"; "the communism of the early Christians"). Nonliteral, or metaphorical, references are also lowercased (e.g., "fascist tendencies; nazi tactics"). For consistency, however— as in a work about communism in which the philosophy, its adherents, the political party, and party members are discussed—capitalizing the organization, philosophy, and adherents, in both noun and adjective forms, will prevent editorial headaches.

the African National Congress party (*party* is not part of official name); the ANC

The Arab League; the league

Bolshevik(s); the Bolshevik (*or* Bolshevist) movement; bolshevism *or* Bolshevism (see text above)

the Communist Party (*but* Communist parties); the party; Communist(s); Communist countries; communism *or* Communism (see text above)

the Democratic Party; the party; Democrat(s) (party members or adherents); democracy; democratic nations

the Entente Cordiale; the Entente

the Ethiopian Somali Democratic League; the league; the party

the European Union; the EU; the Common Market

the Fascist Party; Fascist(s); fascism or Fascism (see text above)

the Federalist Party; Federalist(s) (U.S. history); federalism or Federalism (see text above)

the Free-Soil Party; Free-Soiler(s)

the General Agreement on Tariffs and Trade; GATT

the Green Party; the party; Green(s)

the Hanseatic League; Hansa; a Hanseatic city

the Holy Alliance

the Know-Nothing Party; Know-Nothing(s)

the Labour Party; Labourite(s) (members of the British party)

the Libertarian Party; Libertarian(s); libertarianism *or* Libertarianism (see text above)

Loyalist(s) (American Revolution; Spanish civil war)

Marxism-Leninism; Marxist-Leninist(s)

the National Socialist Party; National Socialism; the Nazi Party; Nazi(s); Nazism

the North American Free Trade Association; Nafta (see 15.7)

the North Atlantic Treaty Organization; NATO

the Organization of Economic Cooperation and Development; the OECD; the organization

the Popular Front; the Front

the Populist Party; Populist(s); populism *or* Populism (see text above)

the Progressive Party; Progressive movement; Progressive(s); progressivism *or* Progressivism (see text above)

the Quadruple Alliance; the alliance

the Republican Party; the party; the GOP (Grand Old Party); Republican(s) (party members or adherents); republicanism; a republican form of government

the Socialist Party (*but* Socialist parties); the party; Socialist(s) (party members or adherents); socialism *or* Socialism (see text above)

the Social Democratic Party; the party; Social Democrat(s)

the United Democratic Movement; the movement
the World Health Organization; WHO

8.72 *Political groups and movements.* Names of political groups or movements
other than recognized parties are usually lowercased.

anarchist(s)
independent(s)
centrist(s)
moderate(s)
mugwump(s)
opposition (*but* the Opposition, in British and Canadian contexts, referring to the party
    out of power)
but
the Left; members of the left wing; left-winger(s); on the left
the Right; members of the right wing; right-winger(s); on the right
the Far Left
the Far Right
the radical Right

INSTITUTIONS AND COMPANIES

8.73 *What to capitalize.* The full names of institutions and companies and of
their departments, and sometimes their short forms, are capitalized. A *the*
preceding a name, even when part of the official title, is lowercased in running text. Such generic terms as *school* and *company* are usually lowercased when used alone but are sometimes capitalized to avoid ambiguity
or for promotional purposes.

the University of Chicago; the university; the University of Chicago and Harvard Univer-
    sity; Northwestern and Princeton universities; the University of Wisconsin–Madison
the Department of History; the department; the Law School
the University of Chicago Press; the press *or* the Press
the Board of Trustees of the University of Chicago; the board of trustees; the board
the Art Institute of Chicago; the Art Institute
the Cleveland Orchestra; the orchestra
Captain Beefheart and the Magic Band; the band
the Beach Boys; the Beatles; the Grateful Dead (*but* Tha Eastsidaz)
the General Foods Corporation; General Foods; the corporation
the Hudson's Bay Company; the company
the Illinois Central Railroad; the Illinois Central; the railroad
the Library of Congress; the library

the Manuscripts Division of the library

the Museum of Modern Art; MOMA; the museum

the New York Stock Exchange; the stock exchange

Skidmore, Owings & Merrill; SOM; the architectural firm

the Smithsonian Institution; the Smithsonian

Waukegan West Middle School; the middle school

8.74 *Names with unusual capitalization.* Parts of names given in full capitals on the letterhead or in the promotional materials of particular organizations may be given in upper- and lowercase when referred to in other contexts (e.g., "the Rand Corporation" rather than "the RAND Corporation"). Company names that are spelled without an initial capital (e.g., drkoop.com, which is not a URL) or with a capital following a lowercase letter (e.g., eBay) should remain thus in text. For obvious reasons, however, a name beginning with a lowercase letter should not begin a sentence; if it must, it should be capitalized. See also 8.163.

ASSOCIATIONS AND CONFERENCES

8.75 *Associations and the like.* The full names of associations, societies, unions, meetings, and conferences, and sometimes their short forms, are capitalized. A *the* preceding a name, even when part of the official title, is lowercased in running text. Such generic terms as *society* and *union* are usually lowercased when used alone.

Girl Scouts of the United States of America; a Girl Scout; a Scout

the Congress of Industrial Organization; CIO; the union

the Fifty-seventh Annual Meeting of the American Historical Association; the annual
    meeting of the association

the Green Bay Packers; the Packers

the Independent Order of Odd Fellows; IOOF; an Odd Fellow

Industrial Workers of the World; IWW; the Wobblies

the International Olympic Committee; the IOC; the committee

the League of Women Voters; the league

the National Conference of Christians and Jews; the conference

the National Organization for Women; NOW; the organization

the New-York Historical Society (note the hyphen); the society

the Textile Workers Union of America; the union

the Quadrangle Club; the club

8.76 *Conferences.* A substantive title given to a single conference is enclosed in quotation marks. For lecture series, see 8.93.

"Planning for Computer Chaos at the Turn of the Millennium," a symposium held at Future City, Atlantis, February–March 1999.
but
the 1999 International Conference on Y2K

Historical and Cultural Terms

PERIODS

8.77 *Numerical designations.* A numerical designation of a period is lowercased unless it is considered part of a proper name. For the use of numerals, see 9.37.

the twenty-first century
the nineteen hundreds
the nineties
the quattrocento
the second millennium BCE
but
the Eighteenth Dynasty
the Fifth Republic

8.78 *Descriptive designations.* A descriptive designation of a period is usually lowercased, except for proper names. For traditionally capitalized forms, see 8.79.

ancient Greece	the Hellenistic period
the antebellum period	imperial Rome
antiquity	modern history
the baroque period	the romantic period (see also 8.85)
the colonial period	the Shang dynasty
a golden age	the Victorian era

8.79 *Traditional names.* Some names of periods are capitalized, either by tradition or to avoid ambiguity. See also 8.81.

the Age of Reason	the Gay Nineties
the Augustan Age	the Gilded Age
the Common Era	the Grand Siècle
the Counter-Reformation	the High Middle Ages (*but* the late
the Dark Ages	Middle Ages)
the Enlightenment	the High Renaissance

the Jazz Age	the Progressive Era
the Mauve Decade	the Reformation
the Middle Ages (*but* the medieval era)	the Renaissance
the Old Kingdom (ancient Egypt)	the Restoration
the Old Regime (*but* the ancien régime)	the Roaring Twenties

8.80 *Cultural periods.* Names of prehistoric cultural periods are capitalized. For geological periods, see 8.142–45.

the Bronze Age	the Ice Age	the Iron Age	the Stone Age

Analogous terms for modern periods are best lowercased.

the age of steam	the nuclear age	the information age

EVENTS

8.81 *Historical events.* Names of many major historical events and projects are capitalized. Others, more recent or known by their generic descriptions, are usually lowercased. If in doubt, do not capitalize. For wars and battles, see 8.121–22; for religious events, 8.116; for acts and treaties, 8.86.

the Boston Tea Party	the South Sea Bubble
the Cultural Revolution	the War on Poverty
the Great Depression; the Depression	*but*
(President Johnson's) Great Society	the baby boom
the Industrial Revolution	the civil rights movement
the New Deal	the cold war
Prohibition	the crash of 1929
Reconstruction	the Dreyfus affair
the Reign of Terror; the Terror	the gold rush
September 11; 9/11 (see also 6.115)	

8.82 *Major speeches.* A very few speeches have attained the status of titles and are thus traditionally capitalized. Others are usually lowercased.

Washington's Farewell Address
the Gettysburg Address
the annual State of the Union address
Franklin Roosevelt's second inaugural address
the Checkers speech
Martin Luther King Jr.'s "I have a dream" speech

8.83   *Natural phenomena.* Names of natural phenomena or disasters of historic dimensions are often capitalized. If identified by a place-name or a year, they are usually lowercased.

the Great Plague; the plague
the Great Fire of London; the Great Fire
the Chicago Fire; the fire

El Niño
Hurricane Mitch; the 1998 hurricane
the Northridge earthquake of 1994

Use the pronoun *it*, not *he* or *she*, when referring to named storms, hurricanes, and the like.

8.84   *Sporting events.* The full names of major sporting events are capitalized.

the Kentucky Derby; the derby
the NBA World Championship Series; the championship series
the Olympic Games; the Olympics; the Winter Olympics
the World Cup

CULTURAL MOVEMENTS AND STYLES

8.85   *What to capitalize.* Nouns and adjectives designating cultural styles, movements, and schools—artistic, architectural, musical, and so forth—and their adherents are capitalized if derived from proper nouns. (The word *school* remains lowercased.) Others are usually lowercased, though a few (e.g., Cynic, Scholastic) are capitalized to distinguish them from the generic words used in everyday speech. Terms lowercased below may appropriately be capitalized in certain works if done consistently. (If, for example, *impressionism* is capitalized in a work about art, all other art movements must *also* be capitalized. But a profusion of capitals can then result.) For religious movements, see 8.105. See also 8.64.

abstract expressionism
Aristotelian
art deco
art nouveau
Beaux-Arts (derived from École des
  Beaux-Arts)
baroque
camp
Cartesian
Chicago school (of architecture,
  of economics)

classicism, classical
conceptualism
cubism mysticism, mystic
Cynicism, Cynic naturalism
Dadaism, Dada
deconstruction
Doric
Epicurean (see text below)
existentialism
fauvism
formalism

Gothic (*but* gothic fiction)
Gregorian chant
Hellenism
Hudson River school
humanism
idealism
imagism
impressionism
Keynesianism
mannerism
miracle plays
modernism
neoclassicism, neoclassical
Neoplatonism
New Criticism
nominalism
op art
Peripatetic (see text below)
philosophe (French)
Platonism

pop art
postimpressionism
postmodernism
Pre-Raphaelite
Reaganomics
realism
rococo
Romanesque
romanticism, romantic (sometimes
   capitalized to avoid ambiguity)
Scholasticism, Scholastic, Schoolmen
scientific rationalism
Sophist (see text below)
Stoicism, Stoic (see text below)
structuralism
Sturm und Drang (*but* storm and stress)
surrealism
symbolism
theater of the absurd
transcendentalism

Some words capitalized when used of a school of thought are lowercased when used metaphorically.

epicurean tastes
peripatetic families

she's a sophist, not a logician
a stoic attitude

ACTS, TREATIES, AND GOVERNMENT PROGRAMS

8.86   *Formal names.* Formal or accepted titles of pacts, plans, policies, treaties, acts, programs, and similar documents or agreements are capitalized. Incomplete or generic forms are usually lowercased. For citing the published text of a bill or law, see 17.309–10.

the Fifteenth Amendment (to the U.S. Constitution); the Smith Amendment; the amendment
the Articles of Confederation
the Bill of Rights
the Brady law
the Constitution of the United States; the United States (*or* U.S.) Constitution; the Constitution (usually capitalized in reference to the U.S. Constitution); Article VI; the article (see also 9.32)

the Illinois Constitution; the constitution
the Constitution Act, 1982 (Canada; for punctuation, see 6.43)
the Corn Laws (Great Britain)
the Declaration of Independence
the due process clause
the equal rights amendment (not ratified); ERA
the Family and Medical Leave Act; FMLA; the 1993 act
the Food Stamps Act of 1964; food stamps
the Hawley-Smoot Tariff Act; the tariff act
Head Start
impeachment; the first and second articles of impeachment
the Marshall Plan
the Mayflower Compact; the compact
Medicare; Medicaid
the Monroe Doctrine; the doctrine
the Munich agreement; Munich
the New Economic Policy; NEP (Soviet Union)
the Open Door policy
the Pact of Paris (*or, less correctly,* the Kellogg-Briand Pact); the pact
the Peace of Utrecht
the Reform Bills; the Reform Bill of 1832 (Great Britain)
Social Security
Temporary Assistance to Needy Families; TANF
Title VII *or* Title 7
the Treaty of Versailles; the treaty
the Wilmot Proviso
the Treaty on European Union (official name); the Maastricht treaty (informal name)

8.87 *Generic terms.* Informal, purely descriptive references to pending legislation are lowercased.

The anti-injunction bill was introduced on Tuesday.

LEGAL CASES

8.88 *Italics and abbreviations.* The names of legal cases are italicized when mentioned in text. The abbreviation *v.* (versus) occasionally appears in roman, but Chicago recommends italics. In footnotes, legal dictionaries, and contexts where numerous legal cases appear, they are usually set in roman. For legal citation style, see 17.275–79.

Bloomfield Village Drain Dist. v. Keefe
Miranda v. Arizona

In discussion, a case name may be shortened.

the *Miranda* case (or simply *Miranda*)

AWARDS

8.89   *What to capitalize.* Names of awards and prizes are capitalized, but some generic terms used with the names are lowercased. For military awards, see 8.123.

the 1998 Nobel Prize in Physiology or Medicine; a Nobel Prize winner; a Nobel Prize–
    winning physiologist; a Nobel Peace Prize; the Nobel Prize in Literature
the 1998 Pulitzer Prize for Commentary; a Pulitzer in journalism
an Academy Award; an Oscar
an Emmy Award; she has three Emmys
the Presidential Medal of Freedom
a Guggenheim Fellowship (*but* a Guggenheim grant)
an International Music Scholarship
National Merit scholarships

OATHS AND PLEDGES

8.90   *Capitalization.* Formal oaths and pledges are usually lowercased.

the presidential oath of office
the oath of citizenship
marriage vows
but
the Pledge of Allegiance

ACADEMIC SUBJECTS, COURSES OF STUDY, AND LECTURE SERIES

8.91   *Disciplines.* Academic subjects are not capitalized unless they form part of a department name or an official course name or are themselves proper nouns (e.g., English, Latin).

She has published widely in the history of religions.
They have introduced a course in gender studies.
He is majoring in comparative literature.

She is pursuing graduate studies in philosophy of science.
but
Jones is chair of the Committee on Comparative Literature.

8.92   *Courses.* Official names of courses of study are capitalized.

I am signing up for Beginning Archaeology.
A popular course is Basic Manuscript Editing.
but
His ballroom dancing classes have failed to civilize him.

8.93   *Lectures.* Names of lecture series are capitalized. Individual lectures are capitalized and usually enclosed in quotation marks.

This year's Robinson Memorial Lectures were devoted to the nursing profession. The first lecture, "How Nightingale Got Her Way," was a sellout.

Calendar and Time Designations

8.94   *Days of the week, months, and seasons.* Names of days and months are capitalized. The four seasons are lowercased (except when used to denote an issue of a journal; see 17.164). For centuries and decades, see 8.77.

Tuesday	spring	the vernal (*or* spring) equinox
November	fall	the winter solstice

8.95   *Holidays.* The names of secular and religious holidays or specially designated days or seasons are capitalized.

All Fools' Day	Lincoln's Birthday
Christmas Day	Martin Luther King Jr. Day
Father's Day	Memorial Day
the Fourth of July, the Fourth	Mother's Day
Good Friday	National Poetry Month
Halloween	New Year's Day
Hanukkah	New Year's Eve
Holy Week	Passover
Independence Day	Presidents' Day
Kwanzaa	Ramadan
Labor Day	Remembrance Day (Canada)
Lent	Rosh Hashanah

Saint Patrick's Day	*but*
Thanksgiving Day	D day
Yom Kippur	election day
Yuletide	inauguration day

8.96   *Time and time zones.* When spelled out, time and time zones are lower-cased (except for proper nouns). Abbreviations are capitalized.

eastern standard time; EST	Pacific daylight time; PDT
central daylight time; CDT	Greenwich mean time; GMT
mountain standard time; MST	daylight saving time

Religious Names and Terms

8.97   *"Down" style.* Chicago urges a spare, *"down"* style in the field of religion as elsewhere. Lowercasing rarely gives offense. Understanding is best served by capitalizing only what are clearly proper nouns and adjectives in the context under discussion.

DEITIES AND REVERED PERSONS

8.98   *Deities.* Names of deities, whether in monotheistic or polytheistic religions, are capitalized.

Allah	Itzamna	Satan (*but* the devil)
Astarte	Jehovah	Serapis
Freyja	Mithra	Yahweh
God		

8.99   *Alternative names.* Alternative or descriptive names for God as supreme being are capitalized. See also 8.100.

Adonai	the Lord
the Almighty	Providence
the Deity	the Supreme Being
the Holy Ghost *or* the Holy Spirit	the Trinity
or the Paraclete	

8.100   *Prophets and the like.* Designations of prophets, apostles, saints, and other revered persons are often capitalized.

the Buddha	Saint John; the Beloved Apostle
the prophet Isaiah	the Virgin Mary; the Blessed
Jesus; Christ; the Good Shepherd;	Virgin; Mother of God
the Son of man	*but*
John the Baptist	the apostles
the Messiah	the patriarchs
Muhammad; the Prophet	the psalmist

8.101   *Platonic ideas.* Words for transcendent ideas in the Platonic sense, especially when used in a religious context, are often capitalized.

Good; Beauty; Truth; the One

8.102   *Pronouns.* Pronouns referring to God or Jesus are not capitalized. (Note that they are lowercased in most English translations of the Bible.)

They prayed to God that he would deliver them.
Jesus and his disciples

RELIGIOUS GROUPS

8.103   *What to capitalize.* Names of religions, denominations, communions, and sects are capitalized, as are their adherents and adjectives derived from them.

8.104   *Major religions*

Buddhism; Buddhist	Judaism; Jew; Jewry; Jewish
Christianity; Christian; Christendom	Shinto; Shintoism; Shintoist
(see also 8.106)	Taoism; Taoist; Taoistic
Confucianism; Confucian	*but*
Hinduism; Hindu	atheism
Islam; Islamic; Muslim	agnosticism

8.105   *Denominations, sects, orders, and religious movements*

the Amish; Amish communities
Anglicanism; the Anglican Communion (see also Episcopal Church)
Baptists; a Baptist church; the Baptist General Convention; the Southern Baptist Convention
Christian Science; Church of Christ, Scientist; Christian Scientist
the Church of England (*but* an Anglican church)

the Church of Ireland

Conservative Judaism; a Conservative Jew

Dissenter (lowercased when used in a nonsectarian context)

Druidism; Druid (sometimes lowercased)

Eastern Orthodox churches; the Eastern Church (*but* an Eastern Orthodox church)

the Episcopal Church; an Episcopal church; an Episcopalian

the Episcopal Church of Scotland

Essenes; an Essene

Gnosticism; Gnostic

Hasidism; Hasid (singular); Hasidim (plural); Hasidic

Jehovah's Witnesses

Jesuit(s); the Society of Jesus; jesuitic(al) (lowercased when used pejoratively)

Methodism; the United Methodist Church (*but* a United Methodist church); Wesleyan

Mormonism; Mormon; the Church of Jesus Christ of Latter-day Saints (Utah); Community of Christ (Missouri)

Nonconformism; Nonconformist (lowercased when used in a nonsectarian context)

the Order of Preachers; the Dominican order; a Dominican

Old Catholics; an Old Catholic church

Orthodox Judaism; an Orthodox Jew

Orthodoxy; the (Greek, Serbian, etc.) Orthodox Church (*but* a Greek Orthodox church)

Protestantism; Protestant (lowercased when used in a nonsectarian context)

Puritanism; Puritan (lowercased when used in a nonsectarian context)

Quakerism; Quaker; the Religious Society of Friends; a Friend

Reform Judaism; a Reform Jew

Roman Catholicism; the Roman Catholic Church (*but* a Roman Catholic church)

Satanism; Satanist

Shiism; Shia; Shiite

Sufism; Sufi

Sunnism; Sunni; Sunnite

Theosophy; Theosophist; the Theosophical Society

Vedanta

Wicca; Wiccan

Zen; Zen Buddhism

8.106 *Church.* When used alone to denote organized Christianity as an institution, *the church* is usually lowercased.

church and state	the church in the twenty-first century
the early church	the church fathers

Church is capitalized when part of the formal name of a denomination (e.g., the United Methodist Church; see other examples in 8.105) or congregation (e.g., the Church of St. Thomas the Apostle).

8.107 *Generic versus religious terms.* Many terms lowercased when used generically, such as *animism, fundamentalism,* or *spiritualism,* may be capitalized when used as the name of a specific religion or a sect. Similarly, many of the terms listed in 8.105 may be lowercased in certain contexts.

a popular medium in Spiritualist circles
but
liberal versus fundamentalist Christians

8.108 *Religious jurisdictions.* The names of official divisions within organized religions are capitalized. The generic terms used alone are lowercased.

the Archdiocese of Chicago; the archdiocese
the Eastern Diocese of the Armenian Church
the Fifty-seventh Street Meeting; the (Quaker) meeting
the Holy See
the Missouri Synod; the synod

8.109 *Buildings.* The names of the buildings in which religious congregations meet are capitalized. The generic terms used alone are lowercased.

Babri Mosque; the mosque
Bethany Evangelical Lutheran Church; the church
Temple Emmanuel; the temple; the synagogue
Nichiren Buddhist Temple; the temple

8.110 *Councils, synods, and the like.* The accepted names of historic councils and the official names of modern counterparts are capitalized.

the Council of Chalcedon; the Fourth General Council
the General Convention (Episcopal)
the Second Vatican Council; Vatican II
the Synod of Whitby

RELIGIOUS WRITINGS

8.111 *Scriptures.* Names of scriptures and other highly revered works are capitalized but not italicized.

the Bible; biblical   Bhagavad Gita
the Hebrew Bible   the Book of Common Prayer

the Dead Sea Scrolls
Mishnah; Mishnaic
Qur'an; Qur'anic (*or* Koran, Koranic)
Rig-Veda
Sunnah

Sutra
Talmud; Talmudic
Tripitaka
the Upanishads
the Vedas; Vedic

8.112   *Other terms.* Other names and versions of the Hebrew and Christian bibles are capitalized but not italicized.

the Authorized Version *or* the King James
   Version
the Breeches Bible
Codex Sinaiticus
Complutensian Polyglot Bible
the Douay (*or* Rheims-Douay) Version
the Holy Bible
Holy Writ (sometimes used satirically)
the New English Bible

the New Jerusalem Bible
the New Revised Standard Version
Peshitta
the Psalter (*but* a psalter)
the Septuagint
the Vulgate
but
scripture(s); scriptural

8.113   *Books of the Bible.* The names of books of the Bible are not italicized. The word *book* is usually lowercased, and the words *gospel* and *epistle* are usually capitalized. But in a work in which all three terms are used with some frequency, they may all be treated alike, either lowercased or capitalized. See also 9.30, 15.47–54.

Genesis; the book of Genesis
Job; the book of Job
2 Chronicles; Second Chronicles; the second book of the Chronicles
the Psalms; a psalm
John; the Gospel according to John
Acts; the Acts of the Apostles
1 Corinthians; the First Epistle to the Corinthians

8.114   *Sections of the Bible.* Names of sections of the Bible are not italicized.

the Hebrew scriptures *or* the Old Testament
the Christian scriptures *or* the New Testament
the Apocrypha; apocryphal
the Epistles; the pastoral Epistles
the Gospels; the synoptic Gospels
the Pentateuch *or* the Torah; Pentateuchal
Hagiographa *or* Ketuvim; hagiographic

8.115 *Prayers, creeds, and such.* Named prayers, canticles, creeds, and such, as well as scriptural terms of special importance, are usually capitalized. Parables and miracles are usually lowercased.

the Decalogue; the Ten Commandments; the first commandment	the Sermon on the Mount
	the Shema
Kaddish; to say Kaddish	*but*
the Lord's Prayer; the Our Father	the doxology
Luther's Ninety-five Theses	the parable of the prodigal son
the Nicene Creed; the creed	the miracle of the loaves and fishes
Salat al-fajr	the star of Bethlehem

RELIGIOUS EVENTS, CONCEPTS, SERVICES, AND OBJECTS

8.116 *Events and concepts.* Religious events and concepts of major theological importance are often capitalized. Used generically, such terms are lowercased.

the Creation	the Second Coming
the Crucifixion	*but*
the Diaspora	Most religions have creation myths.
the Exodus	For the Romans, crucifixion was a
the Fall	common form of execution.
the Hegira	

Doctrines are usually lowercased.

atonement	original sin	transubstantiation

8.117 *Heaven, hell, and so on.* Terms for divine dwelling places, ideal states, places of divine punishment, and the like are usually lowercased.

heaven	paradise	*but*
hell	the pearly gates	Eden
limbo	purgatory	Elysium
nirvana		Hades
outer darkness		Olympus

8.118 *Services and rites.* Names of services and rites are usually lowercased.

baptism	morning prayer; matins (*or* mattins)
bar mitzvah	the seder
bas mitzvah	the sun dance
confirmation	vespers

Terms denoting the eucharistic sacrament, however, are traditionally capitalized, though they may be lowercased in nonreligious contexts.

the Eucharist
Holy Communion
Mass; to attend Mass; *but* three masses are offered daily
High Mass; Low Mass

8.119 *Objects.* Objects of religious use or significance are usually lowercased.

altar	mandala	sacred pipe
ark	mezuzah	sanctuary
chalice and paten	rosary	stations of the cross

Military Terms

FORCES AND TROOPS

8.120 *Armies, battalions, and such.* Titles of armies, navies, air forces, fleets, regiments, battalions, companies, corps, and so forth are capitalized. Unofficial but well-known names, such as Green Berets, are also capitalized. Words such as *army* and *navy* are lowercased when standing alone, when used collectively in the plural, or when not part of an official title.

Allied Expeditionary Force; the AEF
the Allies (World Wars I and II); the Allied forces
Army Corps of Engineers; the corps
Army of Northern Virginia; the army
Army of the Potomac
Army Special Forces
the Axis powers (World War II)
Canadian Forces (unified in 1968)
the Central powers (World War I)
Combined Chiefs of Staff (World War II)
Confederate army (American Civil War)

Continental navy (American Revolution)
Eighth Air Force; the air force
Fifth Army; the army
First Battalion, 178th Infantry; the battalion; the 178th
French foreign legion
Green Berets
Joint Chiefs of Staff
the Luftwaffe; the German air force
National Guard
Pacific Fleet (U.S., World War II)
Red Army (Russian, World War II); Russian army
the Resistance; the French Resistance; a resistance movement
Rough Riders
Royal Air Force; RAF; British air force
Royal Canadian Air Force (until 1968; *see* Canadian Forces above)
Royal Canadian Mounted Police; the Mounties
Royal Canadian Navy (until 1968; *see* Canadian Forces above)
Royal Navy; the British navy
Royal Scots Fusiliers; the fusiliers
Seventh Fleet; the fleet
Thirty-third Infantry Division; the division; infantry
Union army (American Civil War)
United States (*or* U.S.) Army; the army
United States Coast Guard; the Coast Guard *or* the coast guard
United States Marine Corps; the Marine Corps; the U.S. Marines; a marine
United States Navy; the navy
United States Signal Corps; the Signal Corps *or* the signal corps

WARS, REVOLUTIONS, BATTLES, AND CAMPAIGNS

8.121   *Wars and revolutions.* Names of most major wars and revolutions are capitalized. The generic terms are usually lowercased when used alone.

American Civil War; the War between the States
American Revolution; American War of Independence; the Revolution (traditionally capitalized); the Revolutionary War
Conquest of Mexico; the conquest
Crusades; the Sixth Crusade; a crusader
French Revolution; the Revolution (traditionally capitalized); revolutionary France
Great Sioux War; the Sioux war
Gulf War
Korean War; the war

Mexican Revolution; the revolution
Napoleonic Wars
Norman Conquest; the conquest of England
the revolution(s) of 1848
Russian Revolution; the revolution
Seven Years' War
Shays's Rebellion
Six Days' War
Spanish-American War
Spanish civil war
Vietnam War
War of 1812
Whiskey Rebellion
World War I; the First World War; the Great War; the war
World War II; the Second World War; World Wars I and II; the two world wars

8.122 *Battles and campaigns.* In names of major battles, campaigns, and theaters of war, generic terms are capitalized only when part of an accepted name.

Battle of Britain	European theater of operations; ETO
Battle of the Bulge	Mexican border campaign
battle of Bunker Hill; Bunker Hill; the battle	Operation Overlord
	third battle of Ypres
battle of Vimy Ridge	Vicksburg campaign
the Blitz	western front (World War I)

MILITARY AWARDS

8.123 *Medals and awards.* Specific names of medals and awards are capitalized. For civil awards, see 8.89.

Distinguished Flying Cross; DFC	Silver Star
Distinguished Service Order; DSO	Victoria Cross; VC
Medal of Honor; congressional medal	Croix de Guerre (sometimes lowercased)
Purple Heart	

Ships, Trains, Aircraft, and Spacecraft

8.124 *Ships.* Names of specific ships and other vessels are both capitalized and italicized. Note that when such abbreviations as USS (United States ship) or HMS (Her [or His] Majesty's ship) precede a name, the word *ship* or other vessel type should not be used. The abbreviations themselves are not italicized. For much useful information, consult A. D. Baker III, *The Naval Institute Guide to Combat Fleets of the World, 2002–2003* (bibliog. 5).

Apollo 11	HMS *Frolic*; the British ship *Frolic*
the *Spirit of Saint Louis*	SS *United States*; the *United States*
USS *SC-530*; the U.S. ship *SC-530*	

Every U.S. Navy ship built after 1885 is assigned a hull number, consisting of a combination of letters (indicating the type of ship) and a serial number. Where necessary to avoid confusion between vessels of the same name—in a work on naval history, for example—the numbers should be included at first mention. Smaller ships such as landing craft and submarine chasers are individually numbered but not named.

USS *Enterprise* (CVN-65) was already on its way to the Red Sea.

8.125 *Aircraft, automobiles, trains, and the like.* Names of makes and classes of aircraft, models of automobiles and other vehicles, names of trains or train runs, and names of space programs are capitalized but not italicized.

Boeing 747	Dodge Caravan	Metroliner
Concorde	Superchief	Project Apollo

8.126 *Pronouns.* When a pronoun is used to refer to a vessel, the neuter *it* or *its* (rather than *she* or *her*) is generally preferred. See also 5.49, 8.83.

Scientific Terminology

SCIENTIFIC NAMES OF PLANTS AND ANIMALS

8.127 *Overview.* The following paragraphs offer only general guidelines. Writers or editors requiring detailed guidance should consult *Scientific Style and Format* (bibliog. 1.1). The ultimate authorities are the *International Code of Botanical Nomenclature* (*ICBN*), whose guidelines are followed in the botanical examples below, and the *International Code of Zoological Nomenclature* (*ICZN*) (see bibliog. 5). Note that some fields, such as virology, have slightly different rules. Writers and editors should try to follow the standards established within those fields.

8.128 *Genus and specific epithet.* Whether in lists or in running text, the binomial Latin species names of plants and animals are italicized. The genus name is capitalized, and the specific epithet (even if it is a proper adjective) is lowercased. Do not confuse species names with phyla, orders, and such, which are not italicized; see 8.134.

> The Pleistocene saber-toothed cats all belonged to the genus *Smilodon*.
>
> Many species names, such as *Rosa caroliniana* and *Styrax californica*, reflect the locale of the first specimens described.
>
> The pike, *Esox lucius*, is valued for food as well as sport.
>
> For the grass snake *Natrix natrix*, longevity in captivity is ten years.
>
> Certain lizard taxa such as *Basiliscus* and *Crotaphytus* are bipedal specialists.

8.129 *Abbreviation of genus name.* After the first use the genus name may be abbreviated to a single capital letter. If two or more species of the same genus are listed together, the abbreviation may be doubled (to indicate the plural) before the first species, though repeating the abbreviation with each species is more common. But if species of different genera beginning with the same letter are discussed in the same context, different abbreviations must be used.

> Two methods allow us to estimate the maximum speeds obtained by *Callisaurus draconoides* in the field. Irschick and Jayne (1998) found that stride durations of both *C. draconoides* and *Uma scoparia* do not change dramatically after the fifth stride during accelerations from a standstill.
>
> The "quaking" of the aspen, *Populus tremuloides*, is due to the construction of the petiole; an analogous phenomenon has been noted in the cottonwood, *P. deltoides*.
>
> Among popular species of the genus *Cyclamen* are *CC. coum*, *hederifolium*, and *persicum* (or, more commonly, *C. coum*, *C. hederifolium*, and *C. persicum*)
>
> Studies of *Corylus avellana* and *Corokia cotoneaster* . . . ; in further studies it was noted that *C. avellana* and *Cor. cotoneaster* . . .

8.130 *Subspecies and varieties.* Subspecific epithets, when used, follow the binomial species name and are also italicized.

> *Trogon collaris puella*
> *Noctilio labialis labialis* (or *Noctilio l. labialis*)

In horticultural usage, the abbreviations "subsp.," "var.," and "f." (none of them italicized) are inserted before the subspecific epithet or variety or form name. See also 8.131.

Hydrangea anomala subsp. *petiolaris*
Buxus microphylla var. *japonica*
Rhododendron arboreum f. *album*

8.131 *Unspecified species and varieties.* The abbreviations "sp." and "var.", when used without a following element, indicate that the species or variety is unknown or unspecified. The plural "spp." is used to refer to a group of species. The abbreviations are *not* italicized.

Viola sp.   *Rosa rugosa* var.   *Rhododendron* spp.

8.132 *Author names.* The name of the person who proposed a specific epithet is sometimes added, often abbreviated, and never italicized. A capital *L.* stands for Linnaeus.

Molossus coibensis J. A. Allen   *Quercus alba* L.
Diaemus youngii cypselinus Thomas   *Euchistenes hartii* (Thomas)
Felis leo Scop.

The parentheses in the last example mean that Thomas described the species *E. hartii* but referred it to a different genus.

8.133 *Plant hybrids.* The crossing of two species is indicated by a multiplication sign (×; *not* the letter *x*), between the two species names, with space on each side. Many older primary plant hybrids are indicated by a multiplication sign immediately before the specific epithet of the hybrid, with space only before it.

Magnolia denudata × *M. liliiflora* (crossing of species)
Magnolia ×*soulangeana* (hybrid name)

8.134 *Higher divisions.* Divisions higher than genus—phylum, class, order, and family—are capitalized but *not* italicized. (The terms *order, family,* and so on are not capitalized.) Intermediate groupings are treated similarly.

Chordata (phylum)
Chondrichthyes (class)
Monotremata (order)
Hominidae (family)
Ruminantia (suborder)
Felinae (subfamily)
Selachii (term used of various groups of cartilaginous fishes)
The new species *Gleichenia glauca* provides further details about the history of Gleicheniaceae.

8.135 *English derivatives.* English names, though sometimes identical with the scientific names, are lowercased and treated as English words.

carnivore(s) (from the order Carnivora)	feline(s) (from subfamily Felinae)
hominid(s) (from the family Hominidae)	mastodon(s) (from the genus *Mastodon*)
irid(s) (from the family Iridaceae)	astilbe(s) (from the genus *Astilbe*)

VERNACULAR NAMES OF PLANTS AND ANIMALS

8.136 *Common names.* For the correct capitalization and spelling of common names of plants and animals, consult a dictionary or the authoritative guides to nomenclature, the *ICBN* and the *ICZN*, mentioned in 8.127. In any one work, a single source should be followed. In general, Chicago recommends capitalizing only proper nouns and adjectives, as in the following examples, which conform to *Merriam-Webster's Collegiate Dictionary*.

Dutchman's-breeches	jack-in-the-pulpit	Rocky Mountain sheep
mayapple	rhesus monkey	Cooper's hawk

8.137 *Domestic animals and horticultural categories.* Either a dictionary or the guides to nomenclature *ICZN* and *ICBN* should be consulted for the proper spelling of breeds of domestic animals and broad horticultural categories.

Rhode Island Red	boysenberry
Hereford	rambler rose
German shorthaired pointer	Thoroughbred horse
Maine coon *or* coon cat	

8.138 *Horticultural cultivars.* Many horticultural cultivars (cultivated varieties) have fanciful names that must be respected since they may be registered trademarks. Such names should be enclosed in single quotation marks; any following punctuation is placed *after* the closing quotation mark. If the English name follows the Latin name, there is no intervening punctuation.

a 'Queen of the Market' aster

the 'Peace' rose

The hybrid *Agastache* 'Apricot Sunrise', best grown in zone 6, mingles with sheaves of cape fuchsia (*Phygelius* 'Salmon Leap')

For impeccable usage, consult any issue of the magazine *Horticulture* (bibliog. 5).

359

GENETIC TERMS

8.139 *Overview.* Only the most basic guidelines can be offered here. Writers or editors working in the field of genetics should consult the *American Medical Association Manual of Style* or *Scientific Style and Format* (both in bibliog. 1.1) and online databases including the Human Gene Nomenclature Committee Database and the Mouse Genome Database (both in bibliog. 5).

8.140 *Genes.* Names of genes, or gene symbols, including any arabic numerals that form a part of such names, are usually italicized. (They were originally italicized because they were only inferred to exist.) Gene names contain no Greek characters or roman numerals. Human gene symbols are set in full capitals, as are the genes for other primates. Mouse gene symbols are usually spelled with an initial capital; rat gene symbols are treated similarly. Gene nomenclature systems for other organisms (yeast, fruit flies, nematodes, plants, fish) vary. Protein names, also called gene products and often derived from the symbol of the corresponding genes, are set in roman.

Human genes

BRCA1
SNRPN
GPC3
IGH@ (the symbol @ indicates a family or cluster)

Mouse genes

Wnt1
Cmv1
Rom1
Fgf12
NLP3 (gene symbol); NLP3p (encoded protein; note *p* suffix)
GIF (gene symbol); GIF (gastric intrinsic factor)

Only a very few gene names contain hyphens.

HLA-DRB1, for human leukocyte antigen D-related β chain 1

8.141 *Enzymes.* Enzyme names consist of a string of italic and roman characters. The first three letters, which represent the name of the organism (usually a bacterium) from which the enzyme has been isolated, are italicized. The roman letter that sometimes follows (see fifth example below) represents the strain of bacterium, and the roman numeral represents the series number.

*Ava*I   *Bam*HI   *Cla*I   *Eco*R   *Hind*III

GEOLOGICAL TERMS

8.142   *Overview.* The following paragraphs offer only the most general guidelines. Writers or editors working in the geological studies should consult U.S. Geological Survey, *Suggestions to Authors of the Reports of the United States Geological Survey*, and *Scientific Style and Format* (both listed in bibliog. 1.1).

8.143   *What to capitalize.* Formal geological terms are capitalized; informal terms are not. The generic terms *eon*, *era*, and the like are lowercased or omitted immediately following a formal name. Eons are divided into eras, eras into periods, periods into epochs, and epochs into stages.

the Archean (eon)   the Tertiary period of the Cenozoic
the Mesoproterozoic (era)   the Paleocene (epoch)
the Paleozoic (period)

The modifiers *early*, *middle*, or *late* are capitalized when used formally but lowercased when used informally.

Early Archean   *but*
Late Quaternary   early Middle Cambrian
Middle Cambrian   in late Pleistocene times

8.144   *Ice age.* The term *ice age* is best lowercased because of the uncertainty surrounding any formal use of the term. As with other geological terms, formal names are capitalized, informal ones are not.

Pleistocene
Holocene
Illinoian glaciation
the second interglacial stage *or* II interglacial

8.145   *Stratigraphy.* Formal stratigraphic names are capitalized. For prehistoric cultural terms, see 8.80.

Morrison Formation   Dykwa Supergroup
Niobrara Member   Ramey Ridge Complex

ASTRONOMICAL TERMS

8.146 *Overview.* The following paragraphs offer only the most general guidelines. Writers or editors working in astronomy or astrophysics should consult *Scientific Style and Format* (bibliog. 1.1) and the *Astrophysical Journal* (published by the University of Chicago Press; see bibliog. 5).

8.147 *Celestial bodies.* The names of galaxies, constellations, stars, planets, and such are capitalized. For *earth, sun,* and *moon,* see 8.149, 8.150.

Aldebaran	the Magellanic Clouds
Alpha Centauri *or* α Centauri	the North Star *or* the Pole Star
the Big Dipper *or* Ursa Major	85 Pegasi
or the Great Bear	Saturn
Cassiopeia's Chair	*but*
the Crab Nebula	Halley's comet
the Milky Way	the solar system

The *Astrophysical Journal* always capitalizes *galaxy* when it means the Milky Way; hence "the Galaxy," "our Galaxy." In a nontechnical work, however, the word would be lowercased.

8.148 *Catalog names.* Celestial objects listed in well-known catalogs are designated by the catalog name, usually abbreviated, and a number.

NGC 6165   Bond 619   Lalande 5761   Lynds 1251 *or* L1251

8.149 *Earth.* In nontechnical contexts the word *earth,* in the sense of our planet, is usually lowercased when preceded by *the* or in such idioms as "down to earth" or "move heaven and earth." When used as the proper name of our planet, especially in context with other planets, it is capitalized, and *the* is usually omitted.

Some still believe the earth is flat.
The gender accorded to the moon, the sun, and the earth varies in different mythologies.
Where on earth have you been?
The astronauts have returned successfully to Earth.
Mars, unlike Earth, has no atmosphere.

(The *Astrophysical Journal* always capitalizes *Earth,* whether or not preceded by *the.*)

8.150 *Sun and moon.* The words *sun* and *moon* are usually lowercased in nontechnical contexts and always lowercased in the plural.

The moon circles the earth, as the earth circles the sun.
Some planets have several moons.

In specialized contexts these words may be capitalized.

Gravitational interaction between our Galaxy's dark matter and the ordinary matter in
Earth and the Moon might not fulfill the equivalence principle.
Solar neutrino experiments provide unique information about the interior of the Sun.

8.151   *Descriptive terms.* Merely descriptive terms applied to celestial objects or
phenomena are not capitalized.

aurora borealis *or* northern lights   the rings of Saturn
gegenschein   interstellar dust

MEDICAL TERMS

8.152   *Overview.* The following paragraphs offer only the most general guidelines. Medical writers or editors should consult the *American Medical Association Manual of Style* or *Scientific Style and Format* (both in bibliog. 1.1).

8.153   *Diseases, procedures, and such.* Names of diseases, syndromes, diagnos-
tic procedures, anatomical parts, and the like are lowercased, except for
proper names forming part of the term. Acronyms and initialisms are capitalized.

acquired immunodeficiency syndrome   finger-nose test
  or AIDS   islets of Langerhans
Alzheimer disease (see below)   non-Hodgkin lymphoma (see below)
computed tomography *or* CT   ultrasound; ultrasonography
Down syndrome (see below)

The possessive forms *Alzheimer's, Down's, Hodgkin's,* and the like, though
rarely used in medical literature, may be preferred in a general context.
For x-rays and radiation, see 8.160.

8.154   *Infections.* Names of infectious organisms are treated like other specific
names (see 8.128–30). Names of conditions based on such names are neither italicized nor capitalized.

Microorganisms of the genus *Streptococcus* are present in the blood of persons with
streptococcal infection.
The larvae of *Trichinella spiralis* are responsible for the disease trichinosis.

8.155 *Drugs.* Generic names of drugs, which should be used wherever possible in preference to brand names, are lowercased. Brand names must be capitalized; they are often enclosed in parentheses after the first use of the generic name. For guidance, consult the *American Medical Association Manual of Style* and *Scientific Style and Format* (bibliog. 1.1) and *USP Dictionary of USAN and International Drug Names* (bibliog. 5). For brand names and trademarks, see 8.162.

> The patient takes weekly injections of interferon beta-1a (Avonex) to control his multiple sclerosis.

PHYSICAL AND CHEMICAL TERMS

8.156 *Overview.* The following paragraphs offer only the most general guidelines for nontechnical editors. Writers or editors working in physics should consult *The AIP Style Manual* (bibliog. 1.1) or, among other journals, *Physical Review Letters* and *Astrophysical Journal* (both in bibliog. 5); those working in chemistry should consult *The ACS Style Guide* (bibliog. 1.1).

8.157 *Laws and theories.* Names of laws, theories, and the like are lowercased, except for proper names attached to them.

Avogadro's hypothesis	(Einstein's) general theory of relativity
the big bang theory	Newton's first law
Boyle's law	

8.158 *Chemical names and symbols.* Names of chemical elements and compounds are lowercased when written out. Symbols, however, are capitalized and set without periods; the number of atoms in a molecule appears as a subscript. For a list of symbols for the elements, see 15.70.

sulfuric acid; H_2SO_4	tungsten carbide; WC
sodium chloride; NaCl	ozone; O_3

8.159 *Mass number.* In formal chemical literature, the mass number appears as a superscript to the left of the symbol. In work intended for a general audience, however, it may follow the symbol, after a hyphen, in full size.

> ^{238}U (formal style); U-238 *or* uranium-238 (informal style)
> ^{14}C (formal style); C-14 *or* carbon-14 (informal style)

8.160 *Radiations.* Terms for electromagnetic radiations may be spelled as follows.

x-ray (noun, verb, or adjective)
β-ray (noun or adjective)
beta ray (in nonscientific contexts, noun or adjective)
γ-ray (noun or adjective)
gamma ray (in nonscientific contexts, noun or adjective)
cosmic ray (noun); cosmic-ray (adjective)
ultraviolet rays (noun); ultraviolet-ray (adjective)

Note that the verb *to x-ray,* though acceptable in a general context, is not normally used in medical literature, where writers would more likely speak of obtaining an x-ray film, or a radiograph, of something. *To irradiate* refers to radiation therapy.

8.161 *Metric units.* Although the spellings *meter, liter,* and so on are widely used in the United States, some American business, government, or professional organizations have adopted the European spellings (*metre, litre,* etc.). Chicago accepts either as long as consistency is maintained within a work. For abbreviations used in the International System of Units, see 15.58–64.

Brand Names and Trademarks

8.162 *Trademarks.* Brand names that are registered trademarks—often so indicated in dictionaries—should be capitalized if they must be used. A better choice is to substitute a generic term when available. Although the symbols ® and ™ often accompany trademark names on product packaging and in promotional material, there is no legal requirement to use these symbols, and they should be omitted wherever possible. Note also that some companies want people to use both the proper and the generic terms in reference to their products ("Kleenex facial tissue," not just "Kleenex"), but here again there is no legal requirement. For computer names, see 7.81.

Bufferin; buffered aspirin	Ping-Pong; table tennis
Coca-Cola; cola	Pyrex; heat-resistant glassware
Jacuzzi; whirlpool bath	Scrabble
Kleenex; (facial) tissue	Vaseline; petroleum jelly
Levi's; jeans	Xerox; photocopier
Monopoly	

Registered trademarks may be found on the Web sites of the U.S. Patent and Trademark Office and the International Trademark Association.

8.163 *Lowercase initial letter.* Brand names or names of companies that are spelled with a lowercase initial letter (eBay, iMac, etc.) pose a problem if they begin a sentence in normal prose. Chicago recommends either capitalizing the first letter in that position or, better, recasting the sentence so the name does not appear at the beginning. Company or product names with an internal capital immediately following, and followed by, a lowercase letter ("midcap") should be left unchanged (WordPerfect, HarperCollins, SmithKline Beecham). See also 8.6.

Titles of Works

CAPITALIZATION, HYPHENATION, AND PUNCTUATION

8.164 *Overview.* The following guidelines apply to titles as they appear on title pages; in tables of contents; at chapter, article, or section openings; and cited in text or notes. They apply to titles of books, journals, newspapers, and other freestanding publications as well as to shorter works (stories, poems, articles, etc.), divisions of longer works (parts, chapters, sections), unpublished works (lectures, etc.), plays and films, radio and television programs, musical works, and artworks. For details on citing titles in notes and bibliographies, see chapters 16 and 17.

8.165 *Capitalization.* In their original form (on title pages or at the head of articles or chapters) most titles appear either in capitals and lowercase, "clc" (Like This), or in caps and small caps, "csc" (Like This). Regardless of their original appearance, quoted titles may be capitalized either in sentence style (see 8.166) or, more commonly, in headline style (see 8.167). For capitalization of foreign titles, see 10.3.

8.166 *Sentence style.* In sentence-style capitalization only the first word in a title, the first word in a subtitle, and any proper names are capitalized. This style is commonly used in reference lists (see chapter 16) and library catalogs. It is also useful in works whose section headings are very long or in works whose headings include terms (such as species names) that require their own internal capitalization. For quotations as titles, see 8.171.

Crossing *Magnolia denudata* with *M. liliiflora* to create a new hybrid: A success story

8.167 *Headline style.* The conventions of headline style, admittedly arbitrary, are governed by a mixture of aesthetics (the appearance of a title on a printed page), emphasis, and grammar. Some words are always capitalized; some are always lowercased (unless used as the first or last word in a title); others require a decision. Chicago recommends the following rules, pragmatic rather than logically rigorous but generally accepted: (1) Always capitalize the first and last words both in titles and in subtitles and all other major words (nouns, pronouns, verbs, adjectives, adverbs, and some conjunctions—but see rule 4). (2) Lowercase the articles *the, a,* and *an.* (3) Lowercase prepositions, regardless of length, except when they are stressed (*through* in *A River Runs Through It*), are used adverbially or adjectivally (*up* in *Look Up, down* in *Turn Down, on* in *The On Button,* etc.), are used as conjunctions (*before* in *Look Before You Leap,* etc.), or are part of a Latin expression used adjectivally or adverbially (*De Facto, In Vitro,* etc.). (4) Lowercase the conjunctions *and, but, for, or, nor.* (5) Lowercase the words *to* and *as* in any grammatical function, for simplicity's sake. (6) Lowercase the second part of a species name, such as *lucius* in *Esox lucius,* or the part of a proper name that would be lowercased in text, such as *de* or *von.* For hyphenated terms, see 8.168–70. For words that can be used as prepositions, as adverbs, or as adjectives, consult Webster. All the following examples illustrate rule 1; the numbers in parentheses refer to rules 2–6.

Mnemonics That Work Are Better Than Rules That Don't

Singing While You Work

A Little Learning Is a Dangerous Thing (2)

Four Theories concerning the Gospel according to Matthew (3)

Taking Down Names, Spelling Them Out, and Typing Them Up (3, 4)

Tired but Happy (4)

The Editor as Anonymous Assistant (5)

From *Homo erectus* to *Homo sapiens*: A Brief History (3, 5, 6)

Sitting on the Floor in an Empty Room, *but* Turn On, Tune In, and Enjoy (3)

Traveling with Fido, *but* A Good Dog to Travel With (3, 5)

Voting for the Bond Issue, *but* Voting For and Against the Bond Issue (3)

Ten Hectares per Capita, *but* Landownership and Per Capita Income (3)

Progress in In Vitro Fertilization (3)

If you are not sure what grammatical function a word is performing (or even if you are), try reading the title aloud: if you would stress the word, capitalize it; if not, lowercase it. See also 5.170.

8.168 *Hyphenated compounds in titles.* Two options for capitalizing a hyphenated compound in headline style are offered here—first, a simple rule (see 8.169), beloved of some but disdained by others, and, second, a complex but more traditional set of rules (see 8.170). Contrary to practice elsewhere in this manual, the first option, requiring a single paragraph, precedes the one generally preferred by Chicago.

8.169 *Hyphenation: the simple rule.* Capitalize only the first element unless any subsequent element is a proper noun or adjective.

Death-defying Feats by Nineteenth-century Tightrope Walkers
An All-American Girl: How a Non-English-speaking Immigrant Made Good

8.170 *Hyphenation: the more traditional rules.* (1) Always capitalize the first element. (2) Capitalize any subsequent elements unless they are articles, prepositions, coordinating conjunctions (*and, but, for, or, nor*) or such modifiers as *flat* or *sharp* following musical key symbols. (3) If the first element is merely a prefix or combining form that could not stand by itself as a word (*anti, pre*, etc.), do not capitalize the second element unless it is a proper noun or proper adjective. (4) Do not capitalize the second element in a hyphenated spelled-out number (*twenty-one*, etc.). (5) Break a rule when it doesn't work (see the last three examples below).

Under-the-Counter Transactions and Out-of-Fashion Initiatives
Sugar-and-Spice Stories for Girls or Boys
Record-Breaking Borrowings from Medium-Sized Libraries
Cross-Stitching for Beginners
The E-flat Concerto
Self-Sustaining Reactions
A Two-thirds Majority of Non-English-Speaking Representatives
Anti-intellectual Pursuits
Does E-mail Alter Speech Patterns?
Lolita's Twenty-first Birthday
A History of the Chicago Lying-In Hospital
but
Twenty-First-Century History (*first*, if lowercased, would look inconsistent here)
Hand-me-downs and Forget-me-nots (lowercase short and unstressed elements)
Run-ins and Take-offs (lowercase short and unstressed elements)

8.171 *Quotations as titles.* When a quoted sentence, or at least a full clause, is used as a title, sentence-style capitalization is often appropriate. A following subtitle—or, if the quotation is the subtitle, a preceding title—may be in headline style.

"We all live more like brutes than like humans": Labor and Capital in the Gold Rush
but
My Kingdom for a Horse: Memoirs of a Disappointed Car Owner

8.172   *Quoted titles: font and capitalization.* When quoted in text or listed in a bibliography, titles of books, journals, plays, and other freestanding works are italicized (see 8.178–81); titles of articles, chapters, and other shorter works are set in roman and enclosed in quotation marks (see 8.187). Only initialisms or acronyms should be set in full capitals. For foreign titles, see 10.3–7.

> Many editors use *The Chicago Manual of Style.*
> Refer to the article titled "A Comparison of the MLA and the APA Style Manuals."

8.173   *Subtitles.* A subtitle, whether in sentence-style or headline-style capitalization, always begins with a capital letter. Although on a title page or in a chapter heading a subtitle is often distinguished from a title by a different typeface, when quoted in text or listed in a bibliography it is separated from the title by a colon. When an em dash rather than a colon is used, what follows the em dash is not normally considered to be a subtitle, and the first word is not necessarily capitalized. See also 17.54.

> "Manuals of Style: Guidelines, Not Strangleholds" (headline style)
> Tapetum character states: Analytical keys (sentence style)
> *but*
> *Chicago—a Good Town*

8.174   *Permissible changes to quoted titles.* When a title is quoted, its original spelling (including non-Latin letters such as π or γ), hyphenation, and punctuation should be preserved, regardless of the style used in the surrounding text (but see 8.175). Capitalization should also be preserved, except that words in full capitals on the original title page should be set in upper and lower case (see 8.172). As a matter of editorial discretion, an ampersand (&) may be changed to *and,* or, more rarely, a numeral may be spelled out. See also 17.52.

8.175   *Punctuation in quoted titles.* On title pages, where the title often appears in very large type, commas are sometimes omitted from the ends of lines. When a title is quoted, such commas should be added. (Serial commas need be added only if it is clear that they are used in the work itself.) A date at the end of a title or subtitle sometimes appears on a line by itself; when quoted, it should be preceded by a comma. If title and subtitle on a title page are distinguished by typeface, a colon must be added when the subtitle is quoted. A dash in the original should be retained. (For two subtitles in the original, see 17.54.) The following examples illustrate the way quoted titles and subtitles are normally punctuated and capitalized in running text, notes, and bibliographies using headline capitalization. The first three are books, the fourth is an article.

Disease, Pain, and Sacrifice: Toward a Psychology of Suffering
Melodrama Unveiled: American Theater and Culture, 1800–1850
Browning's Roman Murder Story: A Reading of "The Ring and the Book"
"Milton Friedman's *Capitalism and Freedom*—a Best-Seller for Chicago"

For more on titles within titles (as in the third and fourth examples above), see 8.184, 8.187.

8.176 *Punctuation vis-à-vis surrounding text.* Since a title is a noun form, any punctuation within it should not affect the punctuation of the surrounding text. See also 6.43, 8.185.

His role in *Play It Again, Sam* confirmed his stature. (No comma after *Sam*)

8.177 *Double titles.* Old-fashioned double titles (or titles and subtitles) connected by *or* are traditionally quoted as in the first example, less traditionally but more simply as in the second. In both forms, the second title begins with a capital. Either form is acceptable if used consistently.

England's Monitor; or, The History of the Separation
England's Monitor, or The History of the Separation

BOOKS AND PERIODICALS

8.178 *Freestanding publications.* Titles and subtitles of books, pamphlets, periodicals, newspapers, and sections of newspapers that are published separately in either print or electronic form are italicized when mentioned in text, notes, or bibliography. In text and notes they are capitalized headline style (see 8.167), though sentence style may be used in a bibliography or reference list (see 8.166).

8.179 *Full and shortened titles.* A title cited in full in the notes or bibliography may be shortened in the text. A subtitle may be omitted, or an initial *a, an,* or *the* may be dropped if it does not fit the surrounding syntax. For short titles in notes, see 16.42.

Hawking, in *A Brief History of Time*, opens up the universe.
Hawking's *Brief History of Time* explains black holes with alarming lucidity.
That dreadful *Old Curiosity Shop* character, Quilp . . .
but
In *The Old Curiosity Shop*, Dickens . . .

8.180 *Initial "the" in periodical titles.* When newspapers and periodicals are mentioned in text, an initial *the*, even if part of the official title, is lowercased (unless it begins a sentence) and not italicized. Foreign-language titles, however, retain the article in the original language—but only if it is an official part of the title. (For notes and bibliography, see 17.195–96.)

> She reads the *Chicago Tribune* on the train.
> We read *Le Monde* and *Die Zeit* while traveling in Europe.
> Did you see the review in the *Frankfurter Allgemeine*?

8.181 *What to italicize.* Only the official name of a periodical should be italicized. An added descriptive term is lowercased and set in roman.

> She subscribes to *Newsweek* and the *Economist*.
> I read it both in *Time* magazine and in the *Washington Post*.
> but
> His article was reprinted in the *New York Times Magazine*.

8.182 *When not to italicize.* When the name of a newspaper or periodical is part of the name of a building, organization, prize, or the like, it is not italicized.

> Los Angeles Times Book Award
> Chicago Defender Charities
> Tribune Tower

8.183 *Titles as singular nouns.* A title, being a singular noun, always takes a singular verb.

> *Coconuts and Coquinas* describes island life on Fort Myers Beach.

8.184 *Terms within titles.* A term in a quoted title that is itself normally italicized, such as a foreign word, a genus name, or the name of a ship, is set in roman type ("reverse italics"). A title within a title, however, should remain in italics and be enclosed in quotation marks. See also 8.175, 17.60.

> From Tyrannosaurus rex to *King Kong: Large Creatures in Fact and Fiction*
> *A Key to Whitehead's "Process and Reality"*

8.185 *Title not interchangeable with subject.* The title of a work should not be used to stand for the subject of a work.

Dostoevsky wrote a book about crime and punishment. (*Not* . . . about *Crime and Punishment*)

Edward Wasiolek's book on *Crime and Punishment* is titled *"Crime and Punishment" and the Critics*.

In their book *The Craft of Translation*, Biguenet and Schulte . . . (*Not* In discussing *The Craft of Translation*, Biguenet and Schulte . . .)

8.186   *Series and editions.* Quoted titles of book series and editions are capitalized but not italicized. The words *series* and *edition* are capitalized only if part of the title.

the Loeb Classics

a Modern Library edition

Late Editions: Cultural Studies for the End of the Century

the Crime and Justice series

a book in the Heritage of Sociology Series

ARTICLES IN PERIODICALS AND PARTS OF A BOOK

8.187   *Articles.* Quoted titles of articles and features in periodicals and newspapers, chapter and part titles, titles of short stories or essays, and individual selections in books are set in roman type and enclosed in quotation marks. (If there are quotation marks in the original title, single quotation marks must be used, as in the fourth example.)

John S. Ellis's article "Reconciling the Celt" appeared in the *Journal of British Studies*.

In chapter 3 of *The Footnote*, "How the Historian Found His Muse," Anthony Grafton . . .

"Tom Outland's Story," by Willa Cather, . . .

The article "Schiller's 'Ode to Joy' in Beethoven's Ninth Symphony" received unexpected attention.

8.188   *Collected works.* When two or more works, originally published as separate books, are included in a single volume, often as part of an author's collected works, they are best italicized when quoted.

The editor's introduction to the *Critique of Pure Reason* in Kant's *Collected Works*, . . .

8.189   *Parts of a book.* Such generic terms as *foreword, preface, acknowledgments, introduction, appendix, bibliography, glossary,* and *index,* whether used in cross-references or in reference to another work, are lowercased and set in roman type.

The author states in her preface that . . .

For further documentation, see the appendix.

Full details are given in the bibliography.

The book contains a glossary, a subject index, and an index of names.

8.190 *Numbered chapters, parts, and so on.* The words *chapter, part, appendix, table, figure,* and the like are lowercased and spelled out in text (though sometimes abbreviated in parenthetical references). Numbers are given in arabic numerals, regardless of how they appear in the original. If letters are used, they may be upper- or lowercase and are sometimes put in parentheses. See also 9.30–31.

This matter is discussed in chapters 4 and 5.

The Latin text appears in appendix B.

The range is presented numerically in table 4.2 and diagrammed in figure 4.1.

These connections are illustrated in table A3.

Turn to section 5(a) for further examples.

POEMS AND PLAYS

8.191 *Titles of poems.* Quoted titles of most poems are set in roman type and enclosed in quotation marks. A very long poetic work, especially one constituting a book, is italicized and not enclosed in quotation marks.

Robert Frost's poem "The Housekeeper" in his collection *A Boy's Will*

Dante's *Inferno*

In literary studies where many poems, short and long, are mentioned, it is usually better to set all their titles in italics.

8.192 *First lines.* Poems referred to by first line rather than by title are capitalized sentence style (but according to the capitalization used in the poem itself). See also 18.149.

"Shall I compare thee to a Summer's day?"

8.193 *Titles of plays.* Quoted titles of plays, regardless of the length of the play, are italicized.

Shaw's *Arms and the Man*, in volume 2 of his *Plays: Pleasant and Unpleasant*

8.194 *Divisions of plays or poems.* Words denoting parts of long poems or acts and scenes of plays are usually lowercased, neither italicized nor enclosed in quotation marks.

canto 2   stanza 5   act 3, scene 2

UNPUBLISHED WORKS

8.195 *Written works.* Titles of unpublished works—theses, dissertations, manuscripts in collections, printouts of speeches, and so on—are set in roman type, capitalized as titles, and enclosed in quotation marks. Names of manuscript collections take no quotation marks. The title of a not-yet-published book that is under contract may be italicized, but the word *forthcoming* (or *in press* or some other equivalent term), in parentheses, must follow the title. For speeches, see 8.82. See also 17.122.

In a master's thesis, "Charles Valentin Alkan and His Pianoforte Works," . . .

"A Canal Boat Journey, 1857," an anonymous manuscript in the Library of Congress Manuscripts Division, describes . . .

Letters and other material may be found in the Collis P. Huntington Papers at the George Arents Library of Syracuse University.

Giangreco's *Third Millennium* (forthcoming) continues this line of research.

MOVIES, TELEVISION, AND RADIO

8.196 *What to italicize.* Titles of movies and of television and radio programs are italicized. A single episode in a television series is set in roman and enclosed in quotation marks.

the classic movie *Gone with the Wind*
The Godfather II
PBS's *Sesame Street*
WFMT's *From the Recording Horn*
"Casualties," an episode in *The Fortunes of War*, a *Masterpiece Theater* series
but
the ten o'clock news

Formal names of broadcast networks, channels, and the like are set in roman.

Voice of America
the Discovery Channel
the Sundance and Disney channels

ELECTRONIC SOURCES

8.197 *Analogy to print.* Any work available on the Internet or as a CD-ROM (or part of a CD-ROM), whether or not it also exists in print form, is treated the same way as the works described in 8.164–95. In other words, periodicals or complete works are italicized; articles or sections of works are set in roman and, where appropriate, enclosed in quotation marks. For citing electronic works (including such works as databases or DVDs) in notes or bibliography, see chapter 17.

8.198 *Online sources.* Works available online are treated much the same as printed matter: books or book-length works are italicized; articles, poems, short stories, and the like are set in roman and enclosed in quotation marks. For citing online material, see chapter 17.

> An excerpt from Albert Borgmann's 1999 book *Holding On to Reality* can be found on the University of Chicago Press Web site.
>
> For help with style matters, visit the regularly updated feature "The Chicago Manual of Style Q&A" on our Web site.

8.199 *Web sites.* Web sites, if titled, should be set in roman, headline style, without quotation marks. For typographic treatment of URLs, see 6.17, 6.82, 6.110, 6.119, 7.44.

8.200 *Electronic files.* File names may be italicized or set in roman, capitalized or lowercased. See 7.79.

MUSICAL WORKS

8.201 *Overview.* The following paragraphs are intended only as general guidance for citing musical works. Writers or editors working with highly musicological material should consult D. Kern Holoman, *Writing about Music* (bibliog. 1.1). For typographic conventions used in musicology, see 7.70–75. See also fig. 16.16.

8.202 *Operas, songs, and the like.* Titles of operas, oratorios, tone poems, and other long musical compositions are italicized. Titles of songs are set in roman and enclosed in quotation marks, capitalized in the same way as poems (see 8.191–92).

> Handel's *Messiah*
> *Rhapsody in Blue*

Finlandia
"All You Need Is Love"
"The Star-Spangled Banner"
"Oh, What a Beautiful Mornin'" from *Oklahoma* (a title as much as a first line, so head-
  line style)
"Wohin" from *Die schöne Müllerin*
"La vendetta, oh, la vendetta" from *The Marriage of Figaro*
the "Anvil Chorus" from Verdi's *Il Trovatore*

8.203   *Instrumental works.* Many instrumental works are known by their generic
names—*symphony, quartet, nocturne,* and so on—and often a number or
key or both. Such names are capitalized but not italicized. A descriptive
title, however, is usually italicized if referring to a full work, set in roman
and in quotation marks if referring to a section of a work. The abbreviation *no.* (number; plural *nos.*) is set in roman and usually lowercased. (For
letters indicating keys, see 7.71.)

B-flat Nocturne; Chopin's nocturnes
the Menuetto from the First Symphony; the third movement
Concerto no. 2 for Piano and Orchestra; the second movement, Allegro appassionato,
  from Brahms's Second Piano Concerto; two piano concertos
Bartók's Concerto for Orchestra (or *Concerto for Orchestra*)
Bach's Mass in B Minor
Hungarian Rhapsody no. 12; the Twelfth Hungarian Rhapsody.
Piano Sonata no. 2 (*Concord, Mass., 1840–60*); Charles Ives's *Concord* Sonata
Symphony no. 6 in F Major; the Sixth Symphony; the *Pastoral* Symphony
Air with Variations ("The Harmonious Blacksmith") from Handel's Suite no. 5 in E
Elliott Carter's String Quartet no. 5 and his *Figment* for cello
Augusta Read Thomas's Triple Concerto (*Night's Midsummer Blaze*)

8.204   *Opus.* The abbreviation *op.* (opus; plural *opp.* or *opera*) is set in roman
and usually lowercased. An abbreviation designating a catalog of a particular composer's works is always capitalized (e.g., BWV [Bach-Werke-
Verzeichnis]; D. [Deutsch] for Schubert; K. [Köchel] for Mozart). When *op.*
or a catalog number is used restrictively (see 6.31), no comma precedes it.

Sonata in E-flat, op. 31, no. 3; Sonata op. 31
Fantasy in C Minor, K. 475; Fantasy K. 475

8.205   *Recordings.* The name of an album is italicized, that of the performer or ensemble set in roman. Individual items in the album—songs, movements,
and the like—are treated as illustrated in the paragraphs above. See also
17.269–72.

In a CD titled *The Art of the Trumpet*, the New York Trumpet Ensemble plays . . .

Lennon and McCartney's song "I Will" appeared in the Beatles' famous *White Album* (so called because the cover was white and bore no title).

Miles Davis, *Kind of Blue*, is one of the most influential jazz records ever made.

The Pink Floyd album *Dark Side of the Moon* is a favorite of hers.

His Majestie's Clerkes' 1998 CD, *Hear My Prayer: Choral Music of the English Romantics*, includes Vaughan Williams's Mass in G Minor.

She obtained a video of Verdi's *Falstaff* presented by the Metropolitan Opera.

PAINTINGS, GRAPHIC ART, AND SCULPTURE

8.206 *Paintings, statues, and such.* Titles of paintings, drawings, statues, and other works of art are italicized, whether the titles are original, added by someone other than the artist, or translated. The names of works of antiquity (whose creators are often unknown) are usually set in roman. Titles of photographs are set in roman and enclosed in quotation marks.

Rothko's *Orange Yellow Orange*
Leonardo da Vinci's *Mona Lisa* and *The Last Supper*
Hogarth's series of drawings *The Rake's Progress*
There are several copies of Michelangelo's *David*.
the Winged Victory
the Venus de Milo
"North Dome," one of Ansel Adams's photographs of Kings River Canyon

8.207 *Cartoons.* Titles of regularly appearing cartoons or comic strips are italicized.

The Far Side   *Doonesbury*   *Willy 'n Ethel*   *Dilbert*

8.208 *Exhibitions and such.* Titles of exhibitions and fairs are not italicized, but catalog titles are.

the World's Columbian Exposition
the Century-of-Progress Expositions (included more than one fair)
the New York World's Fair
A remarkable exhibition, Motor Cycles, was mounted at the Guggenheim Museum.
We saw the show Mary Cassatt: Modern Woman when visiting the Art Institute of Chicago.
In her introduction to *Mary Cassatt: Modern Woman* (the catalog of the show), Judith A. Barter writes . . .

Notices and Mottoes

8.209 *Signs and notices.* Specific wording of common short signs or notices is capitalized headline style in running text. A longer notice is better treated as a quotation.

> The door was marked Authorized Personnel Only.
> She encountered the usual Thank You for Not Smoking signs.
> We were puzzled by the notice "Anyone entering this store with no intention of making a purchase will leave disappointed."

8.210 *Mottoes.* Mottoes may be treated the same way as signs. If the wording is in another language, it is usually italicized and only the first word capitalized. See also 6.54.

> The flag bore the motto Don't Tread on Me.
> *Souvent me souviens* is the motto of my old college.
> The motto "All for one and one for all" appears over the door.

Numbers

Introduction

9.1   *Consistency and readability.* This chapter summarizes some of the conventions Chicago observes in handling numbers, especially in making the choice between spelling them out and using numerals. Consistency must sometimes give way to readability. Even in scientific and financial contexts, where numerals are used far more widely than in the humanities, they can never totally replace spelled-out numbers, and few readers would want them to. The following guidelines apply mainly to general works and to scholarly works in the humanities and social sciences.

Numerals or Words

9.2   *Principles.* Among the factors governing the choice between spelling out numbers and using numerals are whether the number is large or small, whether it is an approximation or an exact quantity, what kind of entity it stands for, and what context it appears in.

9.3   *Chicago's general rule.* In nontechnical contexts, the following are spelled out: whole numbers from one through one hundred, round numbers, and any number beginning a sentence. For other numbers, numerals are used. For the numerous exceptions and special cases, see throughout this chapter and consult the index. For hyphens used with numbers, see 7.90, section 1.

Thirty-two children from eleven families were packed into three vans.
The property is held on a ninety-nine-year lease.
The building is three hundred years old.
The three new parking lots will provide space for 540 more cars.
The population of our village now stands at 5,893.

9.4   *Round numbers.* Round numbers—hundreds, thousands, hundred thousands, and millions—are usually spelled out (except in the sciences), whether used exactly or as approximations. See also 9.7, 9.10.

A millennium is a period of one thousand years.
Some forty-seven thousand persons attended the fair.
The population of our city is more than two hundred thousand.
An estimated thirty million Americans lacked health insurance in 1998.

9.5   *Number beginning a sentence.* When a number begins a sentence, it is always spelled out. To avoid awkwardness, a sentence should be recast.

One hundred and ten candidates were accepted. (*And* may be omitted.)
or
In all, 110 candidates were accepted.

Nineteen ninety-nine was marked, among other things, by the war in Yugoslavia.
or
The year 1999 . . .

9.6   *An alternative rule.* Many publications, including those in scientific and financial contexts, follow the simple rule of spelling out only single-digit numbers and using numerals for all others. This system should be used with flexibility so as to avoid such awkward locutions as "12 eggs, of which nine were laid yesterday."

9.7   *Consistency and flexibility.* Where many numbers occur within a paragraph or a series of paragraphs, maintain consistency in the immediate context. If according to rule you must use numerals for one of the numbers in a given category, use them for all in that category. In the same sentence or paragraph, however, items in one category may be given as numerals and items in another spelled out.

A mixture of buildings—one of 103 stories, five of more than 50, and a dozen of only 3 or 4—has been suggested for the area.
The population grew from an initial 15,000 in 1960 to 21,000 by 1970 and 34,000 by 1980.
Between 1,950 and 2,000 persons attended the concert.

9.8   *Ordinals.* The general rule applies to ordinal as well as cardinal numbers.

Robert stole second base in the top half of the eighth inning.
The restaurant on the forty-fifth floor has a splendid view of the city.
She found herself in 125th position out of 360.
The 122nd and 123rd days of the strike were marked by renewed violence.
The thousandth child to be born in Mercy Hospital was named Mercy.

Note that although the forms *2nd* and *3rd* (with an *n* and an *r*) are more common and are appropriate in most contexts, *2d* and *3d*, formerly Chicago's preferred style, are fully acceptable, especially in legal style. Consistency should be maintained within any one work.

9.9   *Ordinals with letters.* When a letter is used in place of a numeral, the letter is italicized (as it would be if used as a cardinal) but the suffix is roman.

the *n*th degree

9.10 *Very large numbers.* A mixture of numerals and spelled-out numbers is sometimes used to express very large numbers (in the millions or more), especially when they are fractional. For monetary amounts, see 9.24–28; for the use of superscripts in scientific contexts, see 9.11. See also 9.59–60.

> By the end of the fourteenth century the population of Britain had probably reached 2.3 million.
> A figure of 4.5 billion years is often given as the age of the solar system.
> They were speaking in the order of 25 billion (*or* twenty-five billion).

Note that *billion* in traditional British usage means a million million, not, as in American usage, a thousand million. Editors working with material by British writers may need to query the use of this term. See 5.202 under *billion; trillion.*

9.11 *Use of the superscript.* Large round numbers may also be expressed in powers of 10, especially in scientific writing. This system is known as scientific notation. For further examples, consult *Scientific Style and Format* (bibliog. 1.1).

$10^2 = 100$
$10^3 = 1,000$
$10^6 = 1,000,000$

$10^9 = 1,000,000,000$
$10^{12} = 1,000,000,000,000$
$5.34 \times 10^8 = 534,000,000$

Inversely, very small numbers may be expressed in powers of –10.

$10^{-2} = 0.01$
$10^{-3} = 0.001$
$10^{-6} = 0.000001$

$10^{-9} = 0.000000001$
$10^{-12} = 0.000000000001$

9.12 *Use of "MYR" and "GYR."* In astrophysical contexts, the abbreviations *MYR* and *GYR*, standing for megayear (one million years) and gigayear (one billion years) are sometimes used.

3MYR = 3,000,000 years
7GYR = 7,000,000,000 years

9.13 *Use of "dex."* The term *dex* is sometimes used in scientific notation as shorthand for differential exponent.

Errors of 3dex (i.e., 10^3) can lead to dangerous misconceptions.

Physical Quantities

9.14 *General contexts.* In nontechnical material, physical quantities such as distances, lengths, areas, and so on are treated according to the general rule (see 9.3).

> Within fifteen minutes the temperature dropped twenty degrees.
> The train approached at seventy-five miles an hour.
> Some students live more than fifteen kilometers from the school.
> Three-by-five-inch index cards are now seldom used in index preparation.
> She is five feet nine (*or, more colloquially,* five foot nine). (See also 9.16.)

In certain contexts, however, tradition and common sense clearly recommend the use of numerals.

> an 8-point table with 6-point footnotes
> a 40-watt bulb
> 120 square feet is equal to 11.15 square meters
> a size 6 dress
> a fuel efficiency of 80 miles per gallon (*or* 3 liters per 100 kilometers)
> The reading jumped to almost 5 volts.

9.15 *Simple fractions.* Simple fractions are spelled out. When, as in the first four examples below, a fraction is considered a single quantity, it is hyphenated. When, less commonly, individual parts of a quantity are in question, as in the last example, the fraction is spelled open. See also 7.90, section 1, under *fractions, simple.*

> She has read three-quarters of the book.
> Four-fifths of the students are boycotting the class.
> I do not want all of your material; two-thirds is quite enough.
> A two-thirds majority is required.
> *but*
> We cut the cake into four quarters; John took three quarters, and Susan one.

9.16 *Whole numbers plus fractions.* Quantities consisting of whole numbers and simple fractions may be spelled out if short but are often better expressed in numerals. (For typesetting mathematical material, see chapter 14.)

> We walked for three and one-quarter miles.
> Page proofs are usually issued on $8\frac{1}{2} \times 11$ inch paper.
> I need $6\frac{7}{8}$ yards.
> Susan is exactly 3 feet $5\frac{1}{4}$ inches tall.

9.17 *Scientific contexts.* In mathematical, statistical, technical, or scientific text, physical quantities and units of time are expressed in numerals, whether whole numbers or fractions, almost always followed by an abbreviated form of the unit (see also 15.55–66). Any writer or editor working with highly technical material should consult *Scientific Style and Format* or the *American Medical Association Manual of Style* (bibliog. 1.1).

50 km (kilometers)	4.5 L (liters)	240 V (volts)
21 ha (hectares)	85 g (grams)	10°C, 10.5°C

Note that a unit of measurement used *without* a numeral should always be spelled out, even in scientific contexts.

We took the measurements in kilojoules. (*not* . . . in kJ)

9.18 *Abbreviations and symbols.* If an abbreviation or a symbol is used for the unit of measure, the quantity is always expressed by a numeral. See also 15.65.

3 mi	7 h	35 mm film
55 mph	3 g	3′6″

For two or more quantities, the abbreviation or symbol is repeated if it is closed up to the number but not if it is separated.

35%–50%	10°C–15°C	6⅝″ × 9″	2 × 5 cm

Percentages and Decimal Fractions

9.19 *Percentages.* Percentages are always given in numerals. In humanistic copy the word *percent* is used; in scientific and statistical copy, or in humanistic copy that includes numerous percentage figures, the symbol % is more appropriate.

Only 45 percent of the electorate voted.
With 90–95 percent of the work complete, we can relax.
A 75 percent likelihood of winning is worth the effort.
Her five-year certificate of deposit carries an interest rate of 5.9 percent.
Only 20% of the ants were observed to react to the stimulus.
The treatment resulted in a 10%–15% reduction in discomfort.

Note that *percent* is not interchangeable with the noun *percentage* (1 percent is a very small percentage). Note also that no space appears between the numeral and the symbol %.

9.20   *Decimal fractions: use of the zero.* When a quantity equals less than 1.00, a zero normally appears before the decimal point, especially if quantities greater than 1.00 appear in the same context.

a mean of 0.73
the ratio 0.85
The average number of children born to college graduates dropped from 2.3 to 0.95 per
   couple

9.21   *Decimal fractions: omission of the zero.* If the quantity is always less than 1.00, as in probabilities, correlation coefficients, and the like, a zero is typically omitted before the decimal point. For tables, see 13.39.

$p < .05$ $R = .10$

The zero is routinely omitted in baseball batting averages and firearm caliber.

Ty Cobb's average was .367.
They found and confiscated a .38 police special and a .22-caliber single-shot rifle.

9.22   *European practice.* In European countries, except for Great Britain, the decimal point is represented by a comma. A space, not a comma, separates groups of three digits, whether to the left or to the right of the decimal point. The Canadians retain the decimal point but often use a space to separate groups of three digits. In U.S. publications, U.S. style should be followed, except in direct quotations. See also 9.60, 15.65.

36 333,333 (European style)
36 333.333 (Canadian style)
36,333.333 (U.S. and British style)

Money

9.23   *Words versus symbols and numerals.* Isolated references to amounts of money are spelled out or expressed with currency symbols and numerals in accord with the general rules presented above.

fifteen dollars = $15   seventy-five pounds = £75

9.24   *U.S. currency.* If a number expressing an amount of money is spelled out, so are the words *dollar(s)* or *cent(s)*; if numerals are used, they are accompanied by the symbol $ or ¢ (see previous paragraph).

> Children can ride for seventy-five cents.
> The instructor charged fifty dollars a lesson.
> The twenty million dollars was quickly invested.
> Last year they paid $2 each for admission; this year they may have to pay $3 or $4.
> Geoffrey found 5¢, Miranda 12¢, Nathan 26¢, and Maria 35¢.
> Prices ranged from $0.95 or $1.00 up to $9.95 or $10.00.

Note the singular verb in the third example above. Note also, in the last example, that zeros are included after the decimal point only when they appear in the same context with fractional amounts.

9.25   *Other currencies using the dollar symbol.* In contexts where the symbol $ may refer to non-U.S. currencies, these currencies should be clearly identified.

> Three hundred Canadian dollars = C$300 *or* Can$300
> $749 in New Zealand dollars = NZ$749
> If you subtract A$15.69 from US$25, . . .
> Ninety-eight Mexican pesos = Mex$98

For further abbreviations, consult *Scientific Style and Format* or the *United States Government Printing Office Style Manual 2000* (bibliog. 1.1). Where the context makes clear what currency is meant, the dollar sign alone is enough.

9.26   *British currency.* The basic unit of British currency is the pound, or pound sterling, for which the symbol is £. One-hundredth of a pound is a penny (plural *pence*), abbreviated as *P* (no period).

> fifteen pounds = £15   fifty pence = 50P   £4.75, £5.00, and £5.25

Until the decimalization of British currency in 1971, the pound was divided into shillings (s.) and pence (d.).

> Ten pounds, fifteen shillings, and sixpence = £10 15s. 6d.
> twopence halfpenny = 2¹/₂d.

9.27   *Other currencies.* Most other currencies are handled the same way as U.S. currency, with a decimal point between the main unit and subunits (e.g.,

EUR 10.75). When one or more letters are used, a space separates the letter(s) from the numeral.

65 Israeli pounds = I£65
forty euros (*or, in European Union documents*, 40 euro) = EUR 40 (*or* 40)
95 (euro) cents (*or, in European Union documents*, 95 cent)
725 yen = ¥725
65.50 Swiss francs = SF 65.50

Before adoption of the euro, monetary symbols included *F* (French franc), *DM* (deutsche mark), and *Lit* (Italian lira), among others.

9.28   *Very large monetary amounts.* Like other very large round numbers, sums of money may be expressed by a mixture of numerals and spelled-out numbers. For *billion*, see 9.10.

A price of $3 million was agreed on.
The military requested an additional $7.3 billion.
The marquess sold his ancestral home for £25.5 million.

In a financial context, thousands are sometimes represented by *K*.

Three-bedroom condominiums are priced at $350K.

9.29   *Currency with dates.* Where the value of a currency in any particular year is in question, the date may be inserted in parentheses, without intervening space, after the currency symbol.

US$(1992)2.47   £(2002)15,050

Divisions in Publications and Other Documents

9.30   *Books.* Numbers referring to pages, chapters, parts, volumes, and other divisions of a book, as well as numbers referring to illustrations or tables, are set as numerals. Pages of the front matter are usually in lowercase roman numerals, those for the rest of the book in arabic numerals. For documentation style, see chapters 16–17. See also 8.190.

The preface will be found on pages vii–xiv and the introduction on pages 1–35.
See part 3, especially chapters 9 and 10, for further discussion; see also volume 2, table 15 and figures 7–9.

Biblical references are given in numerals only; chapter and verse are separated by a colon with no space following it. For abbreviations to be used in notes or parenthetical references, see 15.50–54. For use of abbreviations versus spelled-out forms, see 15.48–49. See also 8.113.

Acts 27:1
Exodus 20:3–17
Psalm 121; Psalms 146–50
2 Corinthians 11:29–30
Gen. 47:12

9.31 *Periodicals.* References to volumes, issues, and pages of a journal are usually made, in that order, with arabic numerals; the words *volume* and *page* are omitted. See also chapters 16–17.

His article appeared in the *Journal of Religion* 79, no. 1 (1999): 19–53.

9.32 *Legal instruments.* Arabic or roman numerals are sometimes used to distinguish divisions within legal instruments and other documents. When in doubt, prefer arabic. A mixture of arabic and roman sometimes distinguishes smaller from larger divisions. For bibliographic forms, see the sections "Legal Citation" and "Public Documents" in chapter 17. For legal and nonlegal references to the U.S. Constitution, see 17.288, 17.321.

They have filed for Chapter 11 protection from creditors.
Proposition XII (*or* Proposition 12) will be voted on next week.
Title IX (*or* Title 9) is a gender equity law.
Do you have a 401(k)?
In paragraph 14(vi) of the bylaws, . . .
According to the Constitution of the United States, article 2, section 4, . . . (*or* . . . Article II, Section 4)
but
the Fifth Amendment (*or* Amendment V)

Dates

9.33 *The year alone.* Years are expressed in numerals unless they stand at the beginning of a sentence (see 9.12). See also 9.38.

We all know what happened in 1776.
Twenty twenty-one should be an interesting year.

9.34 *The year abbreviated.* In informal contexts the first two digits of a particular year are often replaced by an apostrophe (not an opening single quotation mark).

the spirit of '76   the class of '06

9.35 *The day of the month.* When specific dates are expressed, cardinal numbers are used, although these may be pronounced as ordinals. For the month-day-year date form versus the day-month-year form, see 6.46.

April 5, 2001, was just a working day for the crew.
The *Seafarer's Clarion* (5 April 2001) praised the crew's heroism.

When a day is mentioned without the month or year, the number, an ordinal, is usually spelled out.

On November 5, McManus declared victory. By the twenty-fifth, most of his supporters had deserted him.

9.36 *Centuries.* Particular centuries are spelled out and lowercased. See also 9.38.

the twenty-first century
the eighth and ninth centuries
the eighteen hundreds (the nineteenth century)

9.37 *Decades.* Decades are either spelled out (as long as the century is clear) and lowercased or expressed in numerals. No apostrophe appears between the year and the *s*.

the nineties
the 1980s and 1990s (*or, less formally*, the 1980s and '90s)

Note that the first two decades of any century cannot be treated in the same way as other decades. "The 1900s," for example, would be taken to refer to the whole of the twentieth century, and "the 1910s" would be thoroughly confusing. (To refer to the second decade as "the teens," as is occasionally done, seems contrived.) Note also that some consider the first decade of, for example, the twenty-first century to consist of the years 2001–10; the second, 2011–20; and so on. Chicago defers to the preference of its authors in this matter.

the first decade of the twenty-first century (*or* the years 2000–2009)
the second decade of the twenty-first century (*or* the years 2010–2019)

9.38   *Eras.* Era designations, at least in the Western world, are usually expressed in one of two ways: either CE ("of the common era") and BCE ("before the common era"), or AD (*anno Domini,* "in the year of the Lord") and BC ("before Christ"). Other forms include AH (*anno Hegirae,* "in the year of [Muhammad's] Hegira," or *anno Hebraico,* "in the Hebrew year"), AUC (*ab urbe condita,* "from the founding of the city [Rome]"), and—for archaeological purposes—BP ("before the present"). Note that the Latin forms AD and AH precede the year number, whereas the others follow it. Choice of the era designation depends on tradition, academic discipline, or personal preference. These abbreviations traditionally appeared in small capitals with periods following each letter (e.g., 3000 B.C.). For simplicity and consistency with the guidelines in chapter 15, Chicago now recommends full capitals and no periods. Small capitals with or without periods, however, are fully acceptable. See also 15.41.

> Herod Antipas (21 BCE–39 CE) was tetrarch of Galilee from 4 BCE until his death.
> Britain was invaded successfully in 55 BC and AD 1066.
> The First Dynasty appears to have lasted from 4400 BP to 4250 BP in radiocarbon years.
> Mubarak published his survey at Cairo in 1886 (AH 1306).
> The campsite seems to have been in use by about 13,500 BP.
> Rome, from its founding in the eighth century BCE, . . .

Note that inclusive dates used with BCE or BC, where the higher number comes first, should be given in full to avoid confusion (e.g., "350–345 BCE"). See also 9.67.

9.39   *All-numeral dates and other brief forms.* The all-numeral style of writing dates (5/10/99, etc.) should not be used in formal writing for practical as well as aesthetic reasons. Whereas in American usage the first numeral refers to the month and the second to the day, in the usage of other English-speaking countries and of most European languages it is the other way around. When quoting letters or other material dated, say, 5/10/03, a writer must first ascertain and then make it clear to readers whether May 10 or October 5 is meant. In text, therefore, the full date should always be spelled out (see 9.35). In documentation and in tables, if numerous dates occur, months may be abbreviated, and the day-month-year form, requiring no punctuation, may be neater (e.g., 5 Oct 2003). See also 15.42.

9.40   *ISO style.* The International Organization for Standardization (ISO) recommends an all-numeral style consisting of year-month-day, hyphenated. The year is given in full, and the month or day, if one digit only, is preceded by a zero. Thus October 5, 2003, appears as 2003-10-05 (sometimes without the hyphens, 20031005). This style has the advantage of allowing dates to be sorted correctly by computer in a spreadsheet.

Time of Day

9.41 *Spelled-out forms.* Times of day in even, half, and quarter hours are usually spelled out in text. With *o'clock*, the number is always spelled out.

> Her day begins at five o'clock in the morning.
> The meeting continued until half past three.
> He left the office at quarter of four.
> We will resume at ten thirty.
> Cinderella almost forgot that she should leave the ball before midnight. (See also 9.43.)

9.42 *Numerals.* Numerals are used (with zeros for even hours) when exact times are emphasized. The abbreviations a.m. (*ante meridiem*) and p.m. (*post meridiem*) often appear in small capitals (AM and PM), in which case periods are unnecessary.

> The first train leaves at 5:22 a.m. and the last at 11:00 p.m.
> She caught the 6:20 flight.
> Please attend a meeting in Grand Rapids, Michigan, on December 5 at 10:30 a.m. (EST).

For more on time zones, see 15.44.

9.43 *Noon and midnight.* Except in the twenty-four-hour system (see 9.44), numerals should never be used to express noon or midnight. Although noon can be expressed as 12:00 m. (m. = *meridies*), very few use that form. And the term 12:00 p.m. is ambiguous, if not nonsensical. In the second example below, note the double date for clarity.

> The meeting began at 9:45 a.m. and was adjourned by noon.
> Rodriguez was born at midnight, August 21–22.

9.44 *The twenty-four-hour system.* In the twenty-four-hour system of expressing time (used in Europe and in the military), four digits always appear, with no punctuation between hours and minutes.

> 1200 = noon
> 2400 *or* 0000 = midnight
> 0001 = 12:01 a.m.
> 1438 = 2:38 p.m.

At 1500 hours (*or* 1500h) we started off on our mission.
General quarters sounded at 0415.

9.45 *Seconds and dates included.* A variation of the twenty-four-hour system shows hours, minutes, and seconds separated by colons; it also shows fractions of a second following a period. This format may be preceded by an ISO-style date (see 9.40).

09:27:08.6 = 27 minutes, 8.6 seconds after 9:00 a.m.
1999-05-10-16:09:41.3 = May 10, 1999, at 9 minutes, 41.3 seconds after 4:00 p.m.

For further details, consult *Scientific Style and Format* (bibliog. 1.1).

Names

9.46 *Monarchs and such.* Sovereigns, emperors, popes, and Orthodox patriarchs with the same name are differentiated by numerals, traditionally roman.

Elizabeth II   John XXIII

In continental European practice the numeral is sometimes followed by a period (e.g., Wilhelm II.) or a superscript (e.g., François Ier) indicating that the number is an ordinal. In an English context the roman numeral alone should appear.

9.47 *Personal names.* Some personal names are followed by a roman numeral or an arabic ordinal numeral. No punctuation precedes the numeral. For *Jr.* see 6.49.

Adlai E. Stevenson III   Michael F. Johnson 2nd

9.48 *Titles of works.* Roman numerals are used to designate the sequel to a novel or a movie or to differentiate two chapter titles dealing with the same subject matter.

The Godfather II
Chapter 9. Alligator Studies in the Everglades—I
Chapter 10. Alligator Studies in the Everglades—II

The em dash in the second and third examples is used to avoid ambiguity.

9.49   *Vehicles and vessels.* Boats and the like differentiated by a number usually take a roman numeral, spacecraft an arabic numeral. See also 8.124–26.

Bluebird III   *Mariner 9*

9.50   *Governments.* Ordinal numbers designating successive dynasties, governments, and other governing bodies are spelled out if one hundred or less.

Eighteenth Dynasty   Second International
Fifth Republic   Ninety-seventh Congress
Second Continental Congress   107th Congress

9.51   *Political and judicial divisions.* Ordinal numbers of one hundred or less designating political or judicial divisions are spelled out.

Fourteenth Precinct   Twelfth Congressional District
Fifth Ward   Tenth Circuit

9.52   *Military units.* Ordinal numbers designating military units are spelled out if one hundred or less.

Fifth Army   First Corps Support Command
Fourth Infantry Division   101st Airborne Division

9.53   *Places of worship.* Ordinal numbers that are part of the names of places of worship are spelled out.

Fourth Presbyterian Church   Twenty-first Church of Christ, Scientist

9.54   *Unions and lodges.* Numbers designating local branches of labor unions and fraternal lodges are usually expressed in arabic numerals after the name.

Typographical Union no. 16
American Legion, Department of Illinois, Crispus Attucks Post no. 1268
United Auto Workers, Local 890

Addresses and Thoroughfares

9.55   *Highways.* State, federal, and interstate highways are designated by arabic numerals. See also 8.60.

U.S. Route 41 (*or* U.S. 41)   Interstate 90 (*or* I-90)   Illinois 12

9.56   *Numbered streets.* Names of numbered streets, avenues, and so forth are usually spelled out if one hundred or less. For the use of *N, E, SW*, and the like, see 15.35. See also 8.60.

First Avenue   Ninety-fifth Street   122nd Street

9.57   *Building and apartment numbers.* Building numbers, in arabic numerals, precede the street name. For readability, text usage may differ slightly from an address on an envelope.

They lived in Oak Park, at 1155 South Euclid Avenue, for almost ten years.
She now lives in unit 114A, 150 Ninth Avenue, with an unrivaled view of the city.
Our office is at 1427 East Sixtieth Street, Chicago, Illinois.
Please return your proof to 1427 E. 60th St., Chicago IL 60637.

When a building's name is its address, the number is often spelled out.

One Thousand Lake Shore Drive   One IBM Plaza

Plurals and Punctuation of Numbers

9.58   *Plurals.* Spelled-out numbers form their plurals as other nouns do (see 7.6).

The contestants were in their twenties and thirties.
The family was at sixes and sevens.

Numerals form their plurals by adding *s*. No apostrophe is needed.

Among the scores were two 240s and three 238s.
Jazz forms developed in the 1920s became popular in the 1930s.

9.59   *Comma between digits.* In most numerals of one thousand or more, commas are used between groups of three digits, counting from the right. (In scientific writing, commas are often omitted from four-digit numbers.)

1,512   32,987   4,000,500

No commas are used in page numbers, addresses, and years (though years of five digits or more do include the comma.)

Punctuation conventions can be found on page 1535 of the tenth edition.

Our business office is at 11030 South Langley Avenue.

Human artifacts dating from between 35,000 BP and 5000 BP have been found there.

9.60 *Space between digits.* In the International System of Units, half-spaces rather than commas are used to mark off groups of three digits, both to the left and to the right of the decimal point. In numbers of only four digits either to the left or the right of the decimal point, no space is used (except in table columns with numbers having five or more digits). This system is far more common in Europe than in the United States. Chicago's *Astrophysical Journal*, for example, uses commas, not spaces (see bibliog. 5). See also 9.22, 9.59.

3 426 869

0.000 007

2501.4865 (four-digit numbers require no space)

See B. N. Taylor, *Guide for the Use of the International System of Units (SI)* (bibliog. 2.4).

9.61 *Lists and outline style.* For the use of numerals (arabic and roman) and letters to distinguish items in lists, see 6.126–30.

Inclusive Numbers

9.62 *When to use the en dash.* An en dash used between two numbers implies *up to and including,* or *through.* For more on the use of the en dash, see 6.83.

Please refer to pages 75–110.

Here are the figures for 1999–2000

Campers were divided into age groups 5–7, 8–10, 11–13, and 14–16.

9.63 *When not to use the en dash.* If *from* or *between* is used before the first of a pair of numbers, the en dash should not be used; instead, *from* should be followed by *to* or *through, between* by *and.* The wording or context should indicate the degree of inclusiveness. Avoid *between . . . and* where precision is required.

from 75 to 110

from 1898 to 1903

from January 1, 1898, through December 31, 1903
between 150 and 200

Inclusive spelled-out numbers should not be joined by an en dash.

women aged forty-five to forty-nine years
sixty- to seventy-year-olds

9.64   *Abbreviating, or condensing, inclusive numbers.* Inclusive numbers are abbreviated according to the principles illustrated below (examples are page
or serial numbers, which do not require commas). This system, used by
Chicago since the first edition of this manual, generally reflects the way
the numbers would be read aloud and is both easy on the eye and unambiguous (but see 9.65).

FIRST NUMBER	SECOND NUMBER	EXAMPLES
1–99	Use all digits	3–10, 71–72, 96–117
100 or multiples of 100	Use all digits	100–104, 1100–1113
101 through 109, 201 through 209, etc.	Use changed part only	101–8, 1103–4
110 through 199, 210 through 299, etc.	Use two or more digits as needed	321–28, 498–532, 1087–89, 11564–615, 12991–13001
	But if three digits change in a four-digit number, use all four	1496–1504, 2787–2816

To avoid ambiguity, inclusive roman numerals are always given in full.

xxv–xxviii   cvi–cix

9.65   *Alternative systems.* A foolproof system is to give the full form of numbers
everywhere (e.g., 234–245, 25000–25001). This is the only form to use for
vote tallies, sports scores, and the like, where the en dash does not imply
a range. Another practice, more economical, is to include in the second
number only the changed part of the first (e.g., 234–5, 25000–1). Chicago,
however, prefers the system presented in 9.64.

9.66 *Inclusive numbers with commas.* When inclusive numbers with commas are abbreviated, numbers to the right of the comma should be repeated as necessary. Ease of reading should be the guide.

6,000–6,018	12,473–479	1,247,689–690

9.67 *Inclusive years.* Inclusive years follow the pattern illustrated in 9.64. When the century changes, or when the sequence is BCE, BC, or BP (diminishing numbers), all digits change. See also 9.38.

the war of 1914–18	327–321 BCE (a six-year span)
fiscal year 1997–98 (*or* 1997/98; see 6.114)	327–21 BCE (a 306-year span)
the winter of 2000–2001	115 BC–AD 10
in 1504–5	15,000–14,000 BP

9.68 *Inclusive years in titles.* Where inclusive dates occur in book titles, it is customary to repeat all digits. In chapter titles, subheads, table titles, and figure captions, however, the abbreviated form is usually more appropriate.

An English Mission to Muscovy, 1589–1591
In chapter 4, "From Meeting to Marriage, 1932–38,". . .
Table 12. Profitability, risks, and returns of investment strategies, 1978–93

Roman Numerals

9.69 *General principles.* Table 9.1 shows the formation of roman numerals with their arabic equivalents. The general principle is that a smaller letter before a larger one subtracts from its value, and a smaller letter after a larger one adds to it; a bar over a letter multiplies its value by one thousand. Roman numerals may also be written in lowercase letters (i, ii, iii, iv, etc.).

9.70 *A historical note.* The use of subtrahends (back counters) was introduced during the Renaissance. Note that IIII, not IV, still appears on some clock faces. The Romans would have expressed the year 1999, for example, as MDCCCCLXXXXVIIII. A more modern form, approved by the U.S. government and accepted (if reluctantly) by classical scholars, is MCMXCIX (*not* MIM, considered a barbarism).

9.71 *Use of roman numerals.* Chicago uses arabic numerals in many situations where roman numerals were formerly common, as in references to vol-

TABLE 9.1 Roman and arabic numerals

Arabic	Roman	Arabic	Roman	Arabic	Roman
1	I	16	XVI	90	XC
2	II	17	XVII	100	C
3	III	18	XVIII	200	CC
4	IV	19	XIX	300	CCC
5	V	20	XX	400	CD
6	VI	21	XXI	500	D
7	VII	22	XXII	600	DC
8	VIII	23	XXIII	700	DCC
9	IX	24	XXIV	800	DCCC
10	X	30	XXX	900	CM
11	XI	40	XL	1,000	M
12	XII	50	L	2,000	MM
13	XIII	60	LX	3,000	MMM
14	XIV	70	LXX	4,000	$M\bar{V}$
15	XV	80	LXXX	5,000	$\bar{V}$

ume numbers of books and journals or chapters of books (see 9.31). For the use of roman numerals in the front matter of books, see 1.4, 1.101, 9.30; with the names of monarchs, prelates, and such, 9.46; with personal names, 9.47; with names of boats and the like, 8.124, 9.49; in titles of works, 9.48; in legal instruments, 9.32; and in outline style, 6.130.

IO

Foreign Languages

~~~~~~

~~~~~~

Introduction

10.1   *Scope and organization.* This chapter addresses some of the problems—largely typographic—that arise in publishing copy in languages other than modern written English. Only the languages likely to be met in general and scholarly writing are dealt with. The level of coverage varies widely; languages that commonly appear in English-language publications and those that present complex problems are treated most fully. The general paragraphs 10.3–8, 10.9–15, and 10.89–93, however, apply equally to all. The chapter begins with some typographic matters—capitalization, italics, and so forth—that apply to most of the languages discussed. It then deals with languages using the Latin alphabet; transliterated (or romanized) languages; classical Greek; Old English and Middle English; and (new to this edition and not really "foreign") American Sign Language. Individual languages or groups of languages are presented in alphabetical order within their particular sections. A note of warning: authors who include words or sentences in a language they do not know well should seek help from someone who does, since they cannot count on a publisher's manuscript editor to know a wide variety of foreign languages.

10.2 *Alphabets and accents.* The problems encountered with foreign-language copy differ according to whether the language uses the Latin alphabet (most European languages, including English, and some others), whether the language uses a different alphabet but copy is to appear in transliterated (or romanized) form, or whether copy is to appear in the alphabet of the original. Table 10.1 lists accented letters of the Latin alphabet. Tables 10.3 and 10.4 give the original alphabets with corresponding Latin-alphabet letters for Russian (Cyrillic) and Greek.

Titles and Other Proper Names

10.3 *Capitalization of foreign titles.* For foreign titles of works, whether these appear in text, notes, or bibliographies, Chicago recommends a simple rule: capitalize only the words that would be capitalized in normal prose—first word of title and subtitle and all proper nouns. In other words, use *sentence style* (see 8.166). This rule applies equally to transliterated titles. For examples, see 17.51, 17.64, 17.159. For exceptions, see 10.24, 10.43. For variations in French, see 10.30.

10.4 *Punctuation of foreign titles.* When a foreign title is included in an English-language context, the following changes are permissible: a period (or, more rarely, a semicolon) between title and subtitle may be changed to a colon, and guillemets (see 10.32) may be changed to quotation marks. No other marks of punctuation should be tampered with. Commas should not be inserted or deleted. See also 8.174–75.

10.5 *Italic versus roman type.* Titles of works in languages that use the Latin alphabet are set in italic or roman type according to the principles set forth in 8.178–208—for example, books and periodicals italic; poems and other short works roman.

> Stendhal's *Le rouge et le noir* was required reading in my senior year.
> We picked up a copy of the *Neue Zürcher Zeitung* to read on the train.
> She published her article in the *Annales de démographie historique*.
> Strains of the German carol "Es ist ein' Ros' entsprungen" reached our ears.
> Miguel Hernández's poem "Casida del sediento" has been translated as "Lament of the Thirsting Man."

Titles transliterated from non-Latin alphabets are always italicized, regardless of the kind of work.

10.6   *Foreign titles with English translation.* When the title of a foreign work is mentioned in text, an English gloss often follows (see 6.99). If the translation has not been published, the English is not italicized and appears in sentence style (as in the first example below). A published translation, however, is both italicized and capitalized headline style (as in the second example; see 8.167). For foreign titles in notes and bibliographies, see 17.66.

> Leonardo Fioravanti's *Compendio de i secreti rationali* (Compendium of rational secrets) became a best-seller.
> Proust's *À la recherche du temps perdu* (*Remembrance of Things Past*) was the subject of her dissertation.

10.7   *Translated titles.* Whether to use the original title of a foreign work or the translated title when discussing a work in text depends on context and readership. In a general work, the English title of Proust's novel could be cited first, with the French following in parentheses (see also 17.65), or the French could be omitted entirely. For celebrated Russian novels, the original title is rarely needed. Some authors prefer to cite all foreign titles in an English form, whether or not they have appeared in English translation. As long as the documentation makes clear what has been published in English and what has not, translated titles appearing in text may be capitalized headline style and treated like other English-language titles (see 8.167, 8.172).

> A Chinese textbook, *Elementary Learning* (*Xiao xue*), has gained a wide following.
> Molière's comedy *The Miser* may have drawn on an obscure, late-medieval French treatise, *The Evils of Greed*, recently discovered in an abandoned château.

10.8   *Foreign institutions.* If given in the original language, names of foreign institutions and businesses are capitalized according to the usage of the country concerned. Unless transliterated from a non-Latin alphabet, they are not italicized. If translated, such names are capitalized according to English usage.

> He is a member of the Société d'entraide des membres de l'ordre national de la Légion d'honneur.
> He was comforted to learn of the Mutual Aid Society for Members of the National Order of the Legion of Honor.

Transliterated names of institutions are usually italicized and lowercased. But if used instead of an English equivalent, they may be treated as English proper names.

The number of cases adjudicated by People's Court (*renmin fayuan*) has increased
sharply.

but

The number of cases adjudicated by Renmin Fayuan has increased sharply.

Languages Using the Latin Alphabet

10.9 *Capitalization.* In English, capitalization is applied to more classes of
words than in any other Western language. The remarks under "Capitalization" in the sections that follow suggest some of the ways other languages differ from English in their use of capitals. Except where stated to
the contrary, the language in question is assumed to lowercase all adjectives (except those used as proper nouns), all pronouns, months, and days
of the week. In addition, capitals are used more sparingly than in English
for names of offices, institutions, and so on. For foreign personal names,
see 8.10–20.

10.10 *Capitalization in translations.* No translator of a German work would capitalize all nouns, as German does. Translators from the French, however,
are sometimes tempted to reproduce the French capitalization of certain
terms that do not require such treatment in English. The French, for example, often capitalize *Histoire* meaning history but lowercase *histoire*
meaning story. Similarly, they often distinguish *État* from *état*, using the
capitalized form to refer to the state, nation, or country as a whole. To capitalize *history* or *state* in English may imply a status not intended or, worse,
look pompous. Chicago's preferred "down" style may be followed in translated text as well as in original English text (see 8.2).

10.11 *Punctuation.* The remarks in this chapter about punctuation point out the
more obvious departures from what is familiar to English speakers. They
apply to foreign-language contexts—books, articles, or lengthy quotations
wholly in a foreign language (as in the examples in 10.34)—rather than to
snippets from a foreign language incorporated into an English text (for example, "L'état, c'est moi," where English-style quotation marks would be
used).

10.12 *Punctuation in translations.* In English translations of foreign-language
works, English-style punctuation should be used. For example, the tightly
spaced suspension points (to indicate omissions or breaks in thought) favored by French, Italian, and Spanish typesetters should be converted to
spaced periods. If the original work uses both bracketed and unbracketed

TABLE 10.1 Special characters used with the Latin alphabet

Á	á	Ḥ	ḥ	Œ	œ
À	à	Í	í	Ŗ	ŗ
Ä	ä	Ì	ì	R̥̄	ṝ
Â	â	Ï	ï	Ř	ř
Ã	ã	Î	î	Ś	ś
Ā	ā	Ī	ī	Ṣ	ṣ
Ă	ă	Ỵ	ỵ	Š	š
Å	å	ị	ı	Ș	ș
Ą	ą	Ḳ	ḳ		ß
Æ	æ	Ł	ł	Ț	ţ
Ǣ	ǣ	Ḷ	ḷ	Ť	t'
Ć	ć	Ḹ	ḹ	Ṭ	ṭ
Ç	ç	M̥	ṃ	Þ	þ
Č	č	Ń	ń	Ù	ù
Ḍ	ḍ	Ñ	ñ	Ü	ü
Ď	d'	Ň	ň	Ű	ű
Đ	đ	Ṇ	ṇ	Û	û
Ð	ð	Ṅ	ṅ	Ū	ū
É	é	Ŋ	ŋ	Ŭ	ŭ
È	è	Ó	ó	Ú	ú
Ë	ë	Ò	ò	Ų	ų
Ê	ê	Ö	ö	Ů	ů
Ē	ē	Ő	ő	Ý	ý
Ĕ	ĕ	Ô	ô	Ź	ź
Ě	ě	Õ	õ	Ż	ż
Ė	ė	Ō	ō	Ž	ž
Ę	ę	Ǒ	ǒ	Ʒ	ʒ
Ǧ	ǧ	Ø	ø		
Ġ	ǧ	Ǫ	ǫ		

suspension points to distinguish omissions from breaks in thought, the translator (or editor) may convert the unbracketed ones to dashes (see 6.90); or else brackets can be used around English-style spaced ellipses to preserve the distinction (see 10.36, 11.51). English-style quotation marks will replace the guillemets or whatever is used in the original. And the upside-down question mark used at the beginning of a Spanish question will be omitted when the question is translated.

10.13 *Word division.* Anyone who has ever read a book in English that was composed and printed in a non-English-speaking country knows how easy it is to err in word division when working with a language not one's own. The following general rules, however, apply to foreign languages as well as to English: (1) Single-syllable words should never be broken. (2) No words should be broken after one letter, nor should a single letter be carried over to another line. (3) Hyphenated words and solid compounds should be broken at the hyphen or between elements, if at all possible (see 7.34). For proper names, see 7.40. Specific rules for some of the languages covered in this chapter appear in the relevant sections.

10.14 *Special characters.* Any foreign words, phrases, or titles that occur in an English-language work should be checked for special characters—that is, letters with accents (diacritical marks), diphthongs, ligatures, and other alphabetical forms that do not normally occur in English. Most accented letters used in European languages—for example, acute accent (é), grave accent (è), circumflex (ê), cedilla (ç), diaeresis or umlaut (ü), tilde (ñ), macron (ē), and breve (ĕ)—can easily be reproduced in print from an author's software and need no coding. (For coding, see 2.89.) WordPerfect and Microsoft Word, for example, include numerous special characters as well as several non-Latin alphabets. If type is to be set from an author's hard copy, marginal clarifications may be needed for handwritten accents or special characters (e.g., "oh with grave accent" or "Polish crossed el"). Or a copy of table 10.1 with the relevant characters circled may provide helpful illustration. If a file is being prepared for an automated typesetting system or for presentation in electronic form (or both), special characters must exist or be "enabled" in the typesetting and conversion programs, and output must be carefully checked to ensure that the characters appear correctly. For diacritical marks used in transliteration, see 10.92.

10.15 *Phonetic symbols.* Phonetic symbols are always set in roman. For details, consult Geoffrey K. Pullum and William A. Ladusaw, *Phonetic Symbol Guide* (bibliog. 5).

AFRICAN LANGUAGES

10.16 *Capitalization and punctuation.* Most African languages, other than Arabic (10.94–99), use the Latin alphabet and follow English capitalization and punctuation. The most widespread is Swahili, spoken by many ethnic groups in eastern and central Africa. Hausa too is spoken by millions, largely in western Africa.

10.17 *Special characters.* Swahili uses no additional letters or diacritics. Among the more than two thousand other African languages, however, many rely on diacritics and phonetic symbols to stand for sounds that cannot be represented by letters or combinations of letters. Hausa, which provides the phonetic base for transcribing other African languages, such as Kriol, requires the following special characters.

Ŋ ŋ, Ɓ ʻƁ ɓ, Ɗ ʻƊ ɗ ɗ, Ƙ ƙ, Ọ ọ

Additional diacritics, too numerous to be listed here, are used in African languages. Other languages used in Africa (such as French, Portuguese, and Arabic) are dealt with in separate sections in this chapter.

CROATIAN

10.18 *Capitalization.* See 10.3, 10.9.

10.19 *Special characters.* Although Serbo-Croatian used either the Cyrillic or (if the speakers were Catholic) the Latin alphabet, Croatian has used only the Latin alphabet since the 1991 Balkan war. The following special characters are needed for Croatian. See also 10.73–74.

Č č, Ć ć, Đ đ, Š š, Ž ž

CZECH

10.20 *Capitalization.* See 10.3, 10.9.

10.21 *Special characters.* Czech, a Slavic language written in the Latin alphabet, uses many diacritical marks to indicate sounds not represented by this alphabet.

Á á, Č č, Ď ď, É é, Ě ě, Í í, Ň ň, Ó ó, Ř ř, Š š, Ť ť, Ů ů, Ú ú, Ý ý, Ž ž

DANISH

10.22 *Capitalization.* See 10.3, 10.9. The polite personal pronouns *De, Dem,* and *Deres* (now used ever more rarely) and the familiar *I* are capitalized in Danish. Until the mid-twentieth century, common nouns were capitalized, as in German, but they no longer are.

10.23 *Special characters.* Danish has three additional alphabetic letters, which require special characters.

Å å, Æ æ, Ø ø

DUTCH

10.24   *Capitalization.* See 10.3, 10.9. For the capitalization of particles with personal names, see 8.13. In personal correspondence, the pronouns *U, Uw,* and *Gij* are capitalized. Proper adjectives (as well as nouns) are capitalized as in English. When a word beginning with the diphthong *ij* is capitalized, both letters are capitals: *IJsland.* When a single letter begins a sentence, it is lowercased, but the next word is capitalized: *'k Heb niet . . .*

10.25   *Special characters.* Dutch requires no special characters.

FINNISH

10.26   *Capitalization.* See 10.3, 10.9.

10.27   *Special characters.* Finnish requires two umlauted vowels.

Ä ä, Ö ö

Because Swedish is the second official language in Finland, the Finnish alphabet taught in schools and the standard keyboard used in Finland include the Swedish *a* with an overcircle.

Å å

FRENCH

10.28   *Variation.* There is considerable variation in French publications with respect to capitalization and punctuation. For elegant advice, with frequent reference to the Académie française and numerous examples from literature, consult Maurice Grevisse, *Le bon usage* (bibliog. 5).

10.29   *Capitalization.* See 10.3, 10.9. Generic words denoting roadways, squares, and the like are lowercased, whether used alone or with a specific name as part of an address. Only the proper name is capitalized.

le boulevard Saint-Germain   la place de l'Opéra   13, rue des Beaux-Arts

In most geographical names, the generic word is lowercased and the modifying word capitalized.

la mer Rouge   le pic du Midi

Names of buildings are usually capitalized.

l'Hôtel des Invalides   le Palais du Louvre

In names of organizations and institutions, only the first substantive is capitalized, not the preceding article.

l'Académie française
la Légion d'honneur
le Conservatoire de musique

In hyphenated names, both elements are capitalized.

la Comédie-Française   la Haute-Loire

Names of religious groups are usually lowercased.

un chrétien   des juifs

In names of saints, the word *saint* is lowercased. But when a saint's name is used as part of a place-name or the name of a church or other institution, *saint* is capitalized and hyphenated to the following element.

le supplice de saint Pierre
but
l'église de Saint-Pierre

Adjectives formed from proper nouns are usually lowercased.

une imagination baudelairienne

10.30 *Capitalization of titles.* French publications vary in the way they capitalize titles of works. Chicago recommends the simple rule followed by Grevisse, *Le bon usage* (see 10.3, 10.28): capitalize only the first word of a title (of a book, an article, etc.) and anything that would be capitalized in ordinary text. (An exception may be made for titles of journals, which are often capitalized headline style; see 17.176.) For another practice, more difficult to apply and not covered in this manual, consult *French Review, PMLA*, or *Romanic Review* (bibliog. 5). For punctuation in titles, see 10.4.

10.31 *Spacing in punctuation.* In French typeset material, thin spaces sometimes occur before colons, semicolons, question marks, and exclamation marks. In an English context, such spacing need not be observed.

10.32   *Guillemets.* For quotation marks, the French use guillemets (« »), often with a thin space between each pair of guillemets and the quoted matter (but see 10.12). Such tags as *écrit-il* or *dit-elle* are often inserted within the quoted matter without additional guillemets. Only punctuation belonging to the quoted matter is placed within the closing guillemets; other punctuation follows them.

> « Mission accomplie? » a-t-il demandé.
> En ce sens, « avec » signifie « au moyen de ».
> À vrai dire, Abélard n'avoue pas un tel rationalisme: « je ne veux pas être si philosophe, écrit-il, que je résiste à Paul, ni si aristotélicien que je me sépare du Christ ».

As in English, when a quotation (other than a block quotation) continues for more than one paragraph, opening guillemets appear at the beginning of each additional paragraph. Closing guillemets appear only at the end of the last paragraph.

10.33   *Quotation marks.* For quotations within quotations, single (or sometimes double) quotation marks are now used. Formerly, additional guillemets were used, with opening guillemets repeated on each runover line.

> « Comment peux-tu dire, "Montre-nous le père"? » (current style)
> Raoul suggéra à sa sœur: « Tu connais sans doute la parole « De l'abondance du cœur la « bouche parle » (former style)

Note that when guillemets are used, if the two quotations end simultaneously, only one set of closing guillemets appears.

10.34   *Dialogue.* In dialogue, guillemets are often replaced by em dashes. The dash, followed by a thin space, is used before each successive speech but is not repeated at the end of the speech. To set off a quotation within a speech, guillemets may be used.

> — Vous viendrez aussitôt que possible? a-t-il demandé.
> — Tout de suite.
> — Bien. Bonne chance!

> — Tu connais sans doute la parole « De l'abondance du cœur la bouche parle ».
> — Non, je ne la connais pas.

10.35   *Suspension points.* The French often use suspension points (three unspaced dots followed by a word space) to indicate interruptions or breaks in thought. They also use them in lieu of *and so forth.* See also 10.12.

« Ce n'est pas que je n'aime plus l'Algérie... mon Dieu! un ciel! des arbres!... et le reste!...
Toutefois, sept ans de discipline...»

10.36 *Ellipses.* To indicate omissions, the French use unspaced dots enclosed in brackets, with thin spaces between the brackets and the dots. See also 10.12.

« Oh, dit-elle avec un mépris écrasant, des changements intellectuels! [...] »
Les deux amis se réunissaient souvent chez Luc [...].

10.37 *Word division: vowels.* In French, division is made after a vowel wherever possible. One-letter syllables at the ends or beginnings of lines should be avoided if a word can be broken elsewhere (see 10.13).

ache-ter (*or, less desirable*) a-cheter
in-di-vi-si-bi-li-té
tri-age

Two or more vowels forming a single sound, or diphthong, are never broken.

écri-vain   fouet-ter   Gau-guin   éloi-gner   vieux

10.38 *Word division: consonants.* Two adjacent consonants, whether the same or different, are normally divided between them.

der-riè-re   Mal-raux   *but*
feuil-le-ter   ob-jet   qua-tre
ba-lan-cer   par-ler   ta-bleau

Groups of three adjacent consonants are normally divided after the first.

es-prit   res-plen-dir

10.39 *Words containing apostrophes.* Division should never be made immediately after an apostrophe.

jus-qu'au   au-jour-d'hui

10.40 *Words best left undivided.* Since there are as many syllables in French as there are vowels or diphthongs (even if some are unsounded except in poetry), the French break words that appear to English speakers to be of only one syllable (e.g., *fui-te, guer-re, sor-tent*). French practice also permits division after one letter (e.g., *é-tait*). In English-language publications, however, such breaks should be avoided, since they may confuse readers not fluent in French. Words of four or fewer letters should in any case be left undivided. See 7.34.

10.41 *Special characters.* French employs the following special characters.

À à, Â â, Ç ç, É é, È è, Ê ê, Ë ë, Î î, Ï ï, Ô ô, Œ œ, Ù ù, Û û, Ü ü

Although French publishers often omit accents on capital letters (especially *A*) and may set the ligature *Œ* as two separate letters (OE), accented capitals are available in most software and in most fonts, and they should appear where needed in English works, especially in works whose readers may not be familiar with French typographic usage.

GERMAN

10.42 *The new orthography.* A more logical spelling of certain German words or terms became official in 1998—for example, *Rad fahren* (instead of *radfahren*), *rau* (instead of *rauh*), *heute Abend* (instead of *heute abend*). For principles and details, consult the latest edition of *Duden Rechtschreibung der deutschen Sprache* or Hertha Beuschel-Menze and Frohmut Menze, *Die neue Rechtschreibung* (bibliog. 5). Quoted material published before 1998 should reflect the old spelling, except for word division.

10.43 *Capitalization.* In German, all nouns and words used as nouns are capitalized, whether in ordinary sentences or in titles of works (see 10.3).

ein Haus	Deutsch (the German language)
die Weltanschauung	eine Deutsche (a German woman)
das Sein	etwas Schönes

Proper adjectives are generally lowercased. Exceptions include invariable adjectives ending in *er* (often referring to a city or region) and adjectives that themselves are part of a proper name. For further exceptions, consult Duden (see 10.42).

die deutsche Literatur
nordamerikanische Sprachen
die platonischen Dialoge
but
eine berühmte Berliner Straße
der Nahe Osten
der Deutsch-Französische Krieg

The pronouns *Sie*, *Ihr*, and *Ihnen*, as polite second-person forms, are capitalized. As third-person pronouns they are lowercased. The familiar second-person forms *du*, *dich*, *dein*, *ihr*, *euch*, and so on are lowercased. Until the change in 1998 (see 10.42) they were traditionally capitalized in correspondence; capitals should therefore be retained in quoted material published before that date.

10.44 *Punctuation: apostrophe.* An apostrophe is used to denote the colloquial omission of *e*.

wie geht's   was gibt's   hab' ich

Although an apostrophe rarely appears before a genitive *s*, an apostrophe is used to denote the omission of the *s* after proper names ending in *s*, *ß*, *x*, or *z*.

Jaspers' Philosophie   Leibniz' Meinung

10.45 *Punctuation: quotation marks.* In German, quotations usually take reversed guillemets (» «); split-level inverted quotation marks („ "); or, in Switzerland, regular guillemets (see 10.32). Other punctuation is placed outside the closing quotation marks unless it belongs to the quoted matter.

Eros bedeutet für sie primär »zusammen-sein mit« und nicht »anschauen«.
Denn: „An die Pferde", hieß es: „Aufgesessen!"

10.46 *Word division: vowels.* In German, division is made after a vowel wherever possible.

Fa-brik   hü-ten   Bu-ße

Two vowels forming a single sound, or diphthong, are never broken.

Lau-ne   blei-ben

10.47 *Word division: consonants.* Two or more adjacent consonants, whether the same or different, are divided before the last one unless they belong to different parts of a compound (see 10.13).

klir-ren   Verwand-te   Morgen-stern
Was-ser   Meis-ter

The consonant combinations *ch, sch, th,* and *ck* are never divided unless they belong to separate syllables. (Until the 1998 spelling change, *st* was subject to this rule. The combination *ck,* on the other hand, was changed to *kk* and divided between the *k's.*)

Mäd-chen	Philo-so-phie	rau-schen
Klapp-hut	Zu-cker	Häus-chen

In non-German words, combinations of *b, d, g, k, p,* and *t* with *l* or *r* are not divided.

Hy-drant	Me-trum	Pu-bli-kum

10.48 *Word division: compound words.* Compound words should be divided between their component elements whenever possible.

Meeres-ufer	mit-einander	Rasier-apparat	Tür-angel

10.49 *Special characters.* For setting German in roman type (the old gothic or Fraktur type having long been out of use), one special character, the eszett (ß), and three umlauted vowels are needed.

ß, Ä ä, Ö ö, Ü ü

Although umlauted vowels are occasionally represented by omitting the accent and adding an *e (ae, Oe,* etc.), the availability of umlauted characters in text-editing software makes such a practice unnecessary. The eszett (ß), also easily available, must not be confused with, or replaced by, the Greek beta (β). In the new spelling it is replaced by *ss* in certain words. Consult a German dictionary published after 1998.

HUNGARIAN

10.50 *Capitalization.* See 10.3, 10.9.

10.51 *Special characters.* Hungarian requires several varieties of accented vowels.

Á á, É é, Í í, Ó ó, Ö ö, Ő ő, Ú ú, Ü ü, Ű ű

ITALIAN

10.52 *Capitalization.* See 10.3, 10.9. In Italian, a title preceding a proper name is normally lowercased.

il commandatore Ugo Emiliano   la signora Rossi

In commercial correspondence, the formal second-person pronouns are capitalized in both their nominative forms, *Lei* (singular) and *Voi* (plural), and their objective forms, *La* (accusative singular), *Le* (dative singular), and *Vi* (accusative and dative plural). The older singular and plural forms *Ella* (*Le, La*) and *Loro* (*Loro, Loro*) are handled the same way. These pronouns are capitalized even in combined forms.

Posso pregarLa di farmi una cortesia?
Vorrei darLe una spiegazione.

10.53 *Quoted matter.* Italian uses guillemets (*virgolette a caporale*) to denote quoted matter, but usually without the space between guillemets and quoted text that appears in many French publications. It also uses regular quotation marks—sometimes as scare quotes (see 7.58) in the same text in which guillemets are used for quotations.

«Cosa pensi del fatto che io posso diventare "un qualcosa di imperial regio"? Questo non è proprio possibile».

In dialogue, em dashes are sometimes used, as in French. The dash, followed by a thin space, is used before each successive speech. Unlike French, however, another dash is used at the end of the speech if other matter follows in the same paragraph.

— Avremo la neve, — annunziò la vecchia.
— E domani? — chiese Alfredo, voltandosi di scatto della finestra.

10.54 *Apostrophe.* An apostrophe is used to indicate the omission of a letter. A word space should appear after an apostrophe that follows a vowel; after an apostrophe that follows a consonant, however, *no* space should appear.

po' duro   de' malevoli   l'onda   all'aura

10.55 *Suspension points and ellipses.* Italian, like French, uses suspension points (three unspaced dots followed by a space) to indicate interruptions or breaks in thought. To indicate omitted material, the unspaced dots are enclosed in brackets, with thin spaces between the brackets and the dots. See also 10.12.

Voglio... quattro milioni.
Davvero? [...] Non ci avevo pensato.

10.56 *Word division: vowels.* In Italian, division is made after a vowel wherever possible. One-letter syllables at the ends or beginnings of lines should be avoided if a word can be broken elsewhere (see 10.13).

a-cro-po-li   mi-se-ra-bi-le   ta-vo-li-no

Consecutive vowels are rarely divided, and two vowels forming a single sound, or diphthong, are never divided.

miei   Gio-van-ni   pau-sa
pia-ga   Giu-sep-pe   gio-iel-lo

10.57 *Word division: consonants.* Certain consonant groups must never be broken: *ch, gh, gli, gn, qu, sc,* and *r* or *l* preceded by any consonant other than itself.

aqua-rio   la-ghi   pa-dre   ri-flet-te-re
fi-glio   na-sce   rau-che   so-gna-re

Three groups of consonants, however, may be divided: double consonants; the group *cqu*; and any group beginning with *l, m, n,* or *r.*

bab-bo   ac-qua   cam-po   den-tro
af-fre-schi   cal-do   com-pra   par-te

10.58 *Words containing apostrophes.* Division should never be made immediately after an apostrophe (but see 10.54).

dal-l'accusa   quel-l'uomo   l'i-dea
del-l'or-ga-no   un'ar-te

10.59 *Special characters.* In Italian, the following special characters are required.

À à, È è, É é, Ì ì, Ò ò, Ù ù

Although the grave accent on capitalized vowels is optional, in stressed final syllables it must be retained to avoid confusion.

CANTÒ (he sang)
CANTO (I sing)

PAPÀ (daddy)
PAPA (pope)

If an accented capital is not available, an apostrophe may be used in place of the accent on stressed final vowels.

E' (it is)   E (and)

LATIN

10.60   *Capitalization.* In English-speaking countries, titles of ancient and medieval Latin works are capitalized in sentence style—that is, only the first word in the title or subtitle, proper nouns, and proper adjectives are capitalized.

De bello Gallico   *De viris illustribus*   *Cur Deus homo?*

Renaissance and modern works with Latin titles are usually capitalized in the English fashion.

Novum Organum   *Religio Medici*

10.61   *Word division: syllables.* A Latin word has as many syllables as it has vowels or diphthongs (*ae, au, ei, eu, oe, ui* and, in archaic Latin, *ai, oi, ou*) and should be divided between syllables.

na-tu-ra   cae-li-co-la   in-no-cu-us

10.62   *Word division: single consonants.* When a single consonant occurs between two vowels, the word is divided before the consonant except for *x*. Note that *i* and *u* sometimes act as consonants (and, when they do, are sometimes written as *j* and *v*).

Cae-sar   me-ri-di-es   in-iu-ri-or   lex-is

10.63   *Word division: multiple consonants.* When two or more consonants come together, the word is divided before the last consonant, except for the combinations noted below.

om-nis   cunc-tus

416

The combinations *ch, ph, th, gu,* and *qu* are treated as single consonants and thus never separated.

co-phi-nus   lin-gua   ae-qua-lis

The following consonant groups are never broken: *chl, chr, phl, phr, thl, thr, bl, br, cl, cr, dl, dr, gl, gr, pl, pr, tl,* and *tr.*

pan-chres-tus   in-scrip-ti-ones   ex-em-pla   pa-tris

10.64 *Compound words.* Compound words are first separated into their component elements; within each element the foregoing rules apply.

ab-rum-po   ad-est   red-eo   trans-igo

10.65 *Special characters.* Latin requires no special characters for setting ordinary copy. Elementary texts, however, usually mark the long vowels with a macron and, occasionally, the short vowels with a breve, as follows.

Ā ā, Ă ă, Ē ē, Ĕ ĕ, Ī ī, Ĭ ĭ, Ō ō, Ŏ ŏ, Ū ū, Ŭ ŭ

NORWEGIAN

10.66 *Capitalization.* See 10.3, 10.9. The polite personal pronouns *De, Dem,* and *Deres* (now used ever more rarely) are capitalized in Norwegian. Until the mid-twentieth century, common nouns were capitalized (as in German), but they no longer are.

10.67 *Special characters.* Norwegian requires the same special characters as Danish.

Å å, Æ æ, Ø ø

POLISH

10.68 *Capitalization.* See 10.3, 10.9. In formal address the second-person plural pronoun *Państwo* (you) is capitalized, as are related forms.

Czekam na Twój przyjazd. (I await your arrival.)
Pozdrawiam Cię! (Greetings to you!)

10.69 *Word division.* Division of Polish words is similar to that of transliterated Russian (see 10.123–28). Division normally follows syllabic structure.

kom-pli-ka-cja   sta-ro-pol-ski

Note that the conjunction *i* (and) should never appear at the end of a line but must be carried over to the beginning of the next.

10.70 *Special characters.* Polish requires the following special characters.

Ą ą, Ć ć, Ę ę, Ł ł, Ń ń, Ó ó, Ś ś, Ź ź, Ż ż

Since Ą, Ę, and Ń never occur at the beginning of a word, these capitalized forms would be needed only if an entire word were capitalized.

PORTUGUESE

10.71 *Capitalization.* See 10.3, 10.9.

10.72 *Special characters.* Portuguese requires the following special characters (except that European Portuguese does not use *ü*)

À à, Á á, Â â, Ã ã, È è, É é, Ê ê, Ì ì, Í í, Ï ï, Ò ò, Ó ó, Ô ô, Õ õ, Ù ù, Ú ú, Ü ü, Ç ç

If display lines are to be set in full or small capitals, accented characters must be available. But in running text (upper- and lowercase), accented capitals may be dispensed with.

SERBIAN

10.73 *Capitalization.* See 10.3, 10.9.

10.74 *Special characters.* Serbian (as of 1999) uses either the Cyrillic or the Latin alphabet. The following special characters are needed when the Latin alphabet is used. See also 10.18–19.

Ĉ ĉ, Ć ć, Đ đ, Š š, Ž ž

Đ and *đ* may be replaced by *Dj* and *dj*.

SPANISH

10.75 *Capitalization.* See 10.3, 10.9. In Spanish, a title preceding a proper name is normally lowercased.

el señor Jaime López
la señora Lucía Moyado de Barba
doña Perfecta

Nouns as well as adjectives denoting membership in nations are lowercased, but names of countries are capitalized.

los mexicanos   la lengua española   Inglaterra

10.76 *Question marks and exclamation points.* A question or an exclamation in Spanish is preceded by an upside-down question mark or exclamation point and followed by a regular mark. A question or an exclamation included in a sentence begins with a lowercase letter (see second example).

¿Qué pasa, amigo?
Por favor, señor ¿dónde está la biblioteca municipal?
Alguien viene. ¡Vámonos!

Because the opening marks are so integral to Spanish punctuation, they should be retained even when Spanish is being quoted in an English context (but see 10.12). Since an upside-down question mark looks odd when immediately following English-style opening quotation marks, a writer may prefer to begin a quotation a little earlier or to set it off typographically (see 11.11).

10.77 *Guillemets.* For quotation marks, Spanish uses guillemets (« ») Only punctuation belonging to the quoted matter is placed within the closing guillemets; other punctuation follows them. Within a quotation, em dashes may be used to set off words identifying the speaker. The opening dash is *preceded* by a space; the closing dash is *followed* by a space unless immediately followed by punctuation (but see 10.12).

El demonio, el activo demonio cuyo poder había quebrantado Hernán Cortés con espada y con lanza, gozaba utilizando al hijo como instrumento de sus infernales designios. «Vino el negocio a tanto —comenta Suárez—, que ya andaban muchos tomados por el diablo».

10.78 *Dialogue.* In dialogue, em dashes introduce each successive speech. Any other matter that follows the quoted speech in the same paragraph should be preceded by a dash or a comma.

—Esto es el arca de Noé, afirmó el estanciero.
—¿Por qué estas aquí todavía? —preguntó Juana alarmada.

10.79 *Suspension points and ellipses.* Spanish, like French, uses suspension points (three unspaced dots followed by a space) to indicate interruptions or breaks in thought. To indicate omitted material (that is, to serve as ellipses), the unspaced dots are enclosed in brackets, with thin spaces between the brackets and the dots. See also 10.35–36.

Hemos comenzado la vida juntos... quizá la terminaremos juntos también...
La personalidad más importante del siglo XIX es Domingo Faustino Sarmiento [...], llamado el hombre representante del intelecto sudamericano. [...] El gaucho [...] servía de tema para poemas, novelas, cuentos y dramas.

10.80 *Word division: vowels.* In Spanish, division is made after a vowel whenever possible.

ca-ra-co-les   mu-jer   re-cla-mo   se-ño-ri-ta

Two or more vowels that form a single syllable (a diphthong or a triphthong) may not be divided.

cam-bias   fue-go   tie-ne   viu-da

If adjacent vowels belong to separate syllables, however, they are divided between syllables.

ba-úl   cre-er   pa-ís   cam-biá-is

10.81 *Word division: consonants.* If two adjacent consonants cannot occur together at the beginning of a word, the break must be made between them.

ac-cio-nis-ta   al-cal-de   efec-to
ad-ver-ten-cia   an-cho   is-leño

The consonant groups *bl, cl, fl, gl, pl, br, cr, dr, fr, gr, pr,* and *tr*—all pairs that can occur at the beginning of Spanish words—are inseparable (unless each belongs to a different element of a compound; see 10.13).

ci-fra	li-bro	no-ble	re-gla
co-pla	ma-dre	pa-tria	se-cre-to
im-po-si-ble	ne-gro	re-fle-jo	te-cla
le-pra			

Groups of three consonants not ending with one of the inseparable pairs listed above always have an *s* in the middle. They are divided after the *s*.

cons-pi-rar	cons-ta	ins-tan-te	obs-cu-ro	obs-tan-te

Spanish *ch* and *ll* were long considered single characters, alphabetized as such, and never divided. The Spanish Royal Academy has now declared that these combinations are to be alphabetized as two-letter groups, and new publications have adopted this convention. Along with *rr*, however, they still cannot be divided, since they represent single sounds. For details, consult Real Academia Española, *Ortografía de la lengua española* (bibliog. 5).

ci-ga-rri-llo	mu-cha-cho

10.82 *Dividing compound words.* Compound words are usually divided between their component parts.

des-igual	mal-es-tar	semi-es-fe-ra	sub-lu-nar
in-útil	nos-otros	bien-aven-tu-ra-do	sub-ra-yar

10.83 *Special characters.* Spanish employs the following special characters.

Á á, É é, Í í, Ó ó, Ú ú, Ü ü, Ñ ñ

SWEDISH

10.84 *Capitalization.* See 10.3, 10.9. In Swedish the second-person pronouns *Ni* and *Er*, traditionally capitalized in correspondence, are now lowercased in all contexts.

10.85 *Special characters.* Swedish requires the following special characters.

Å å, Ä ä, Ö ö

TURKISH

10.86 *Capitalization.* See 10.3, 10.9. In Turkish, as in English, the names of months and days of the week are capitalized.

10.87 *Spelling.* Modern Turkish suffers from a lack of standardization in spelling. Different but not necessarily erroneous spellings of the same word or name are often encountered. Writers or editors can therefore achieve only limited consistency.

10.88 *Special characters.* Turkish requires the following special characters.

Â â, Ç ç, Ğ ğ (or Ǧ ǧ), İ, ı, Ö ö, Ş ş, Û û, Ü ü

Note that there are dotted and undotted varieties of both the capital and the lowercase *i*. A dotted lowercase *i* retains its dot when capitalized.

Languages Usually Transliterated (or Romanized)

10.89 *Transliteration.* In nonspecialized works it is customary to transliterate—that is, convert to the Latin alphabet, or romanize—words or phrases from languages that do not use the Latin alphabet. These languages include Arabic, Chinese, Hebrew, Japanese, Russian, and other living languages as well as ancient languages such as Greek and Sanskrit. For discussion and illustration of scores of alphabets, see Peter T. Daniels and William Bright, eds., *The World's Writing Systems* (bibliog. 5). For alphabetic conversion, the most comprehensive resource is the Library of Congress publication *ALA-LC Romanization Tables* (bibliog. 5). Do not attempt to transliterate from a language unfamiliar to you.

10.90 *Typesetting non-Latin alphabets.* Some word-processing software allows users to key in words in several of the non-Latin alphabets mentioned in the previous paragraph—for example, Cyrillic, Greek, and Hebrew. Authors who want to include such copy should check with their publishers to ensure that it is easily convertible to print. See also 2.18.

10.91 *Proofreading copy in non-Latin alphabets: a warning.* Anyone unfamiliar with a language that uses a non-Latin alphabet should exercise extreme caution in proofreading even single words set in that alphabet. Grave errors can occur when similar characters are mistaken for each other.

10.92   *Diacritics.* Nearly all systems of transliteration require diacritics—most commonly, in the languages discussed below, macrons, underdots, ʿayns, and hamzas, though there are many more. Except in linguistic studies or other highly specialized works, a system using as few diacritics as are needed to aid pronunciation is easier on readers, publisher, and author. Most readers of a nonspecialized work on Hindu mythology, for example, will be more comfortable with Shiva than Śiva or with Vishnu than Viṣṇu, though specialists would want to know that the *Sh* in Shiva and the *sh* in Vishnu actually represent different Sanskrit letters. Transliterated forms without diacritics that are listed in any of the Merriam-Webster dictionaries are acceptable in most contexts.

10.93   *Italics versus roman.* Transliterated terms (other than proper names) that have not become part of the English language are italicized (see 7.51–52). If used throughout a work, a transliterated term may be italicized on first appearance and then set in roman (see 7.55). Words listed in the dictionary are usually set in roman (see 7.54).

The preacher pointed out the distinction between agape and eros.

but

Once the Greek words *erōs* and *agapē* had been absorbed into the English language, it became unnecessary to italicize them or to use the macrons.

ARABIC

10.94   *Transliteration.* There is no universally accepted form for transliterating Arabic. One very detailed system may be found in the *ALA-LC Romanization Tables* (bibliog. 5). Another system is followed by the *International Journal of Middle East Studies* (bibliog. 5). Having selected a system, an author should stick to it with as few exceptions as possible. In the following examples, only the hamza (ʾ) and the ʿayn (ʿ) are used (see next paragraph). Letters with underdots and some of the other special characters used in transliteration from Arabic are included in table 10.1. (The Arabic alphabet may be found in the alphabet table in *Merriam-Webster's Collegiate Dictionary* [bibliog. 3.1], among other sources.)

10.95   *The hamza and the ʿayn.* The hamza (ʾ) and the ʿayn (ʿ) frequently appear in transliterated Arabic words and names. Writers using hamzas or ʿayns must on every occurrence make it clear, by coding or by careful instructions to the editor or typesetter, which of the two marks is intended. Inserting the marks by hand on a computer printout is not a good option unless the entire manuscript is to be rekeyed from the printout. If necessary, the typesetter can use a Greek smooth breathing (ʼ) for the hamza and a rough breathing (ʿ) for the ʿayn. The hamza is sometimes represented—especially in nonspecialized works—by an apostrophe, as in Qurʾan, and the ʿayn by a single opening quotation mark (ʿayn). (Since an ʿayn often occurs at the beginning of a word, a quotation mark must be used with caution.)

10.96 *Spelling.* Isolated references in text to well-known persons or places should employ the forms familiar to English-speaking readers.

Avicenna (*not* Ibn Sina)   Damascus (*not* Dimashq)   Mecca (*not* Makkah)

10.97 *The definite article.* The definite article, *al*, is usually joined to a noun with a hyphen.

al-Islam   *but*
al-Nafud   al Qaeda (*or* al-Qaida)
Bahr al-Safi

In speech the sound of the *l* in *al* is assimilated into the sounds *d*, *n*, *r*, *s*, *sh*, *t*, and *z*. Where rendering the *sound* of the Arabic is important (for example, when transliterating poetry), the assimilations are often shown, as in the examples below. In most other situations, the article-noun combination is written without indication of the elision, as above.

an-Nafud   Bahr as-Safi

10.98 *Capitalization.* Since the Arabic alphabet does not distinguish between capital and lowercase letter forms, practice in capitalizing transliterated Arabic varies widely. Chicago recommends the practice outlined in 10.3: capitalize only the first word and any proper nouns. This practice applies to titles of works as well as to names of journals and organizations. Note that *al*, like *the*, is capitalized only at the beginning of a sentence or a title.

ʿAbd al-Rahman al-Jabarti, ʿAjaʾib al-athar fi al-tarajim wa al-akhbar [The marvelous remains in biography and history]

For citing and alphabetizing Arabic personal names, see 8.17, 18.74.

10.99 *Word division.* Breaking transliterated Arabic words or names at the end of lines should be avoided wherever possible. If necessary, a break may be made after *al* or *Ibn*. A break may be made after two letters if the second has an underdot (e.g., *iṭ-baq*). Breaks must never be made between the digraphs *dh*, *th*, *sh*, or *kh* unless both letters have underdots. Nor should breaks be made before or after a hamza. Aside from these niceties, the rules governing English word division may be followed (see 7.33–40).

CHINESE AND JAPANESE

10.100 *Chinese romanization.* The pinyin romanization system, introduced by the Chinese in the 1950s, has largely supplanted both the older Wade-Giles system and the place-name spellings of the *Postal Atlas of China*, making pinyin the standard system for romanizing Chinese. Representing sounds of Chinese more explicitly, pinyin has been widely accepted as the system for teaching Chinese as a second language. In 1998, the Library of Congress issued new romanization guidelines with a view to converting its entire online catalog records for the Chinese collection to comply with pinyin. Although a few scholars, long familiar with Wade-Giles or other older systems, have not switched to pinyin in their writings, Chicago joins librarians in urging that pinyin now be used in all scholarly writing about China or the Chinese language. (In some contexts it may be helpful to the reader to add the Wade-Giles spelling of a name or term in parentheses following the first use of the pinyin spelling.) Table 10.2 is included as an aid for conversion of Wade-Giles to pinyin but should be used with caution by anyone unfamiliar with Chinese.

10.101 *Exceptions and modifications.* Even where pinyin is adopted, certain place-names, personal names, and other proper nouns long familiar in the Western world may retain their old spellings. Or, for greater consistency, the old spelling may be added in parentheses after the pinyin version. Copyeditors must be wary, however, of altering spellings without the advice of an expert.

10.102 *Apostrophes and hyphens.* Pinyin spellings often differ markedly from the older ones. Personal names are usually spelled without apostrophes or hyphens, but an apostrophe is sometimes used to avoid ambiguity when syllables are run together (as in Xi'an to distinguish it from Xian).

10.103 *Common names.* Some names frequently encountered are listed below.

Dynasties

WADE-GILES	PINYIN
Chou	Zhou
Ch'in	Qin
Ch'ing	Qing
Sung	Song
T'ang	Tang
Yüan	Yuan

TABLE 10.2 Conversion of Chinese romanization, Wade-Giles to pinyin and pinyin to Wade-Giles

					Wade-Giles to Pinyin						
Wade-Giles	Pinyin	Wade-Giles	Pinyin	Wade-Giles	Pinyin	Wade-Giles	Pinyin	Wade-Giles	Pinyin	Wade-Giles	Pinyin
a	a	ch'ün	qun	ka	ga	mao	mao	po	bo	tou	dou
ai	ai	chung	zhong	k'a	ka	mei	mei	p'o	po	t'ou	tou
an	an	ch'ung	chong	kai	gai	men	men	p'ou	pou	tsa	za
ang	ang	en	en	k'ai	kai	meng	meng	pu	bu	ts'a	ca
ao	ao	erh	er	kan	gan	mi	mi	p'u	pu	tsai	zai
cha	zha	fa	fa	k'an	kan	miao	miao	sa	sa	ts'ai	cai
ch'a	cha	fan	fan	kang	gang	mieh	mie	sai	sai	tsan	zan
chai	zhai	fang	fang	k'ang	kang	mien	mian	san	san	ts'an	can
ch'ai	chai	fei	fei	kao	gao	min	min	sang	sang	tsang	zang
chan	zhan	fen	fen	k'ao	kao	ming	ming	sao	sao	ts'ang	cang
ch'an	chan	feng	feng	kei	gei	miu	miu	se	se	tsao	zao
chang	zhang	fo	fo	ken	gen	mo	mo	sen	sen	ts'ao	cao
ch'ang	chang	fou	fou	k'en	ken	mou	mou	seng	seng	tse	ze
chao	zhao	fu	fu	keng	geng	mu	mu	sha	sha	ts'e	ce
ch'ao	chao	ha	ha	k'eng	keng	na	na	shai	shai	tsei	zei
che	zhe	hai	hai	ko	ge	nai	nai	shan	shan	tsen	zen
ch'e	che	han	han	k'o	ke	nan	nan	shang	shang	ts'en	cen
chen	zhen	hang	hang	kou	gou	nang	nang	shao	shao	tseng	zeng
ch'en	chen	hao	hao	k'ou	kou	nao	nao	she	she	ts'eng	ceng
cheng	zheng	hei	hei	ku	gu	nei	nei	shen	shen	tso	zuo
ch'eng	cheng	hen	hen	k'u	ku	nen	nen	sheng	sheng	ts'o	cuo
chi	ji	heng	heng	kua	gua	neng	neng	shih	shi	tsou	zou
ch'i	qi	ho	he	k'ua	kua	ni	ni	shou	shou	ts'ou	cou
chia	jia	hou	hou	kuai	guai	niang	niang	shu	shu	tsu	zu
ch'ia	qia	hsi	xi	k'uai	kuai	niao	niao	shua	shua	ts'u	cu
chiang	jiang	hsia	xia	kuan	guan	nieh	nie	shuai	shuai	tsuan	zuan
ch'iang	qiang	hsiang	xiang	k'uan	kuan	nien	nian	shuan	shuan	ts'uan	cuan
chiao	jiao	hsiao	xiao	kuang	guang	nin	nin	shuang	shuang	tsui	zui
ch'iao	qiao	hsieh	xie	k'uang	kuang	ning	ning	shui	shui	ts'ui	cui
chieh	jie	hsien	xian	kuei	gui	niu	niu	shun	shun	tsun	zun
ch'ieh	qie	hsin	xin	k'uei	kui	no	nuo	shuo	shuo	ts'un	cun
chien	jian	hsing	xing	kun	gun	nou	nou	so	suo	tsung	zong
ch'ien	qian	hsiu	xiu	k'un	kun	nu	nu	sou	sou	ts'ung	cong
chih	zhi	hsiung	xiong	kung	gong	nü	nü	ssu	si	tu	du
ch'ih	chi	hsü	xu	k'ung	kong	nuan	nuan	su	su	t'u	tu
chin	jin	hsüan	xuan	kuo	guo	nüeh	nüe	suan	suan	tuan	duan
ch'in	qin	hsüeh	xue	k'uo	kuo	nung	nong	sui	sui	t'uan	tuan
ching	jing	hsün	xun	la	la	o	e	sun	sun	tui	dui
ch'ing	qing	hu	hu	lai	lai	ou	ou	sung	song	t'ui	tui
chiu	jiu	hua	hua	lan	lan	pa	ba	ta	da	tun	dun
ch'iu	qiu	huai	huai	lang	lang	p'a	pa	t'a	ta	t'un	tun
chiung	jiong	huan	huan	lao	lao	pai	bai	tai	dai	tung	dong
ch'iung	qiong	huang	huang	le	le	p'ai	pai	t'ai	tai	t'ung	tong
cho	zhuo	hui	hui	lei	lei	pan	ban	tan	dan	tzu	zi
ch'o	chuo	hun	hun	leng	leng	p'an	pan	t'an	tan	tz'u	ci
chou	zhou	hung	hong	li	li	pang	bang	tang	dang	wa	wa
ch'ou	chou	huo	huo	lia	lia	p'ang	pang	t'ang	tang	wai	wai
chu	zhu	i	yi	liang	liang	pao	bao	tao	dao	wan	wan
ch'u	chu	jan	ran	liao	liao	p'ao	pao	t'ao	tao	wang	wang
chü	ju	jang	rang	lieh	lie	pei	bei	te	de	wei	wei
ch'ü	qu	jao	rao	lien	lian	p'ei	pei	t'e	te	wen	wen
chua	zhua	je	re	lin	lin	pen	ben	teng	deng	weng	weng
ch'ua	chua	jen	ren	ling	ling	p'en	pen	t'eng	teng	wo	wo
chuai	zhuai	jeng	reng	liu	liu	peng	beng	ti	di	wu	wu
ch'uai	chuai	jih	ri	lo	luo	p'eng	peng	t'i	ti	ya	ya
chuan	zhuan	jo	ruo	lou	lou	pi	bi	tiao	diao	yang	yang
ch'uan	chuan	jou	rou	lu	lu	p'i	pi	t'iao	tiao	yao	yao
chüan	juan	ju	ru	lü	lü	piao	biao	tieh	die	yeh	ye
ch'üan	quan	juan	ruan	luan	luan	p'iao	piao	t'ieh	tie	yen	yan
chuang	zhuang	jui	rui	lüeh	lüe	pieh	bie	tien	dian	yin	yin
ch'uang	chuang	jun	run	lun	lun	p'ieh	pie	t'ien	tian	ying	ying
chüeh	jue	jung	rong	lung	long	pien	bian	ting	ding	yu	you
ch'üeh	que			ma	ma	p'ien	pian	t'ing	ting	yü	yu
chui	zhui			mai	mai	pin	bin	tiu	diu	yüan	yuan
ch'ui	chui			man	man	p'in	pin	to	duo	yüeh	yue
chun	zhun			mang	mang	ping	bing	t'o	tuo	yün	yun
ch'un	chun					p'ing	ping			yung	yong
chün	jun										

TABLE 10.2 (continued)

Pinyin to Wade-Giles

Pinyin	Wade-Giles
a	a
ai	ai
an	an
ang	ang
ao	ao
ba	pa
bai	pai
ban	pan
bang	pang
bao	pao
bei	pei
ben	pen
beng	peng
bi	pi
bian	pien
biao	piao
bie	pieh
bin	pin
bing	ping
bo	po
bu	pu
ca	ts'a
cai	ts'ai
can	ts'an
cang	ts'ang
cao	ts'ao
ce	ts'e
cen	ts'en
ceng	ts'eng
cha	ch'a
chai	ch'ai
chan	ch'an
chang	ch'ang
chao	ch'ao
che	ch'e
chen	ch'en
cheng	ch'eng
chi	ch'ih
chong	ch'ung
chou	ch'ou
chu	ch'u
chua	ch'ua
chuai	ch'uai
chuan	ch'uan
chuang	ch'uang
chui	ch'ui
chun	ch'un
chuo	ch'o
ci	tz'u
cong	ts'ung
cou	ts'ou
cu	ts'u
cuan	ts'uan
cui	ts'ui
cun	ts'un
cuo	ts'o
da	ta
dai	tai
dan	tan
dang	tang
dao	tao
de	te
deng	teng
di	ti
dian	tien
diao	tiao
die	tieh
ding	ting
diu	tiu
dong	tung
dou	tou
du	tu
duan	tuan
dui	tui
dun	tun
duo	to
e	o
en	en
er	erh
fa	fa
fan	fan
fang	fang
fei	fei
fen	fen
feng	feng
fo	fo
fou	fou
fu	fu
ga	ka
gai	kai
gan	kan
gang	kang
gao	kao
ge	ko
gei	kei
gen	ken
geng	keng
gong	kung
gou	kou
gu	ku
gua	kua
guai	kuai
guan	kuan
guang	kuang
gui	kuei
gun	kun
guo	kuo
ha	ha
hai	hai
han	han
hang	hang
hao	hao
he	ho
hei	hei
hen	hen
heng	heng
hong	hung
hou	hou
hu	hu
hua	hua
huai	huai
huan	huan
huang	huang
hui	hui
hun	hun
huo	huo
ji	chi
jia	chia
jian	chien
jiang	chiang
jiao	chiao
jie	chieh
jin	chin
jing	ching
jiong	chiung
jiu	chiu
ju	chü
juan	chüan
jue	chüeh
jun	chün
ka	k'a
kai	k'ai
kan	k'an
kang	k'ang
kao	k'ao
ke	k'o
ken	k'en
keng	k'eng
kong	k'ung
kou	k'ou
ku	k'u
kua	k'ua
kuai	k'uai
kuan	k'uan
kuang	k'uang
kui	k'uei
kun	k'un
kuo	k'uo
la	la
lai	lai
lan	lan
lang	lang
lao	lao
le	le
lei	lei
leng	leng
li	li
lia	lia
lian	lien
liang	liang
liao	liao
lie	lieh
lin	lin
ling	ling
liu	liu
long	lung
lou	lou
lu	lu
lü	lü
luan	luan
lüe	lüeh
lun	lun
luo	lo
ma	ma
mai	mai
man	man
mang	mang
mao	mao
mei	mei
men	men
meng	meng
mi	mi
mian	mien
miao	miao
mie	mieh
min	min
ming	ming
miu	miu
mo	mo
mou	mou
mu	mu
na	na
nai	nai
nan	nan
nang	nang
nao	nao
nei	nei
nen	nen
neng	neng
ni	ni
nian	nien
niang	niang
niao	niao
nie	nieh
nin	nin
ning	ning
niu	niu
nong	nung
nou	nou
nu	nu
nü	nü
nuan	nuan
nüe	nüeh
nuo	no
ou	ou
pa	p'a
pai	p'ai
pan	p'an
pang	p'ang
pao	p'ao
pei	p'ei
pen	p'en
peng	p'eng
pi	p'i
pian	p'ien
piao	p'iao
pie	p'ieh
pin	p'in
ping	p'ing
po	p'o
pou	p'ou
pu	p'u
qi	ch'i
qia	ch'ia
qian	ch'ien
qiang	ch'iang
qiao	ch'iao
qie	ch'ieh
qin	ch'in
qing	ch'ing
qiong	ch'iung
qiu	ch'iu
qu	ch'ü
quan	ch'üan
que	ch'üeh
qun	ch'ün
ran	jan
rang	jang
rao	jao
re	je
ren	jen
reng	jeng
ri	jih
rong	jung
rou	jou
ru	ju
ruan	juan
rui	jui
run	jun
ruo	jo
sa	sa
sai	sai
san	san
sang	sang
sao	sao
se	se
sen	sen
seng	seng
sha	sha
shai	shai
shan	shan
shang	shang
shao	shao
she	she
shen	shen
sheng	sheng
shi	shih
shou	shou
shu	shu
shua	shua
shuai	shuai
shuan	shuan
shuang	shuang
shui	shui
shun	shun
shuo	shuo
si	ssu
song	sung
sou	sou
su	su
suan	suan
sui	sui
sun	sun
suo	so
ta	t'a
tai	t'ai
tan	t'an
tang	t'ang
tao	t'ao
te	t'e
teng	t'eng
ti	t'i
tian	t'ien
tiao	t'iao
tie	t'ieh
ting	t'ing
tong	t'ung
tou	t'ou
tu	t'u
tuan	t'uan
tui	t'ui
tun	t'un
tuo	t'o
wa	wa
wai	wai
wan	wan
wang	wang
wei	wei
wen	wen
weng	weng
wo	wo
wu	wu
xi	hsi
xia	hsia
xian	hsien
xiang	hsiang
xiao	hsiao
xie	hsieh
xin	hsin
xing	hsing
xiong	hsiung
xiu	hsiu
xu	hsü
xuan	hsüan
xue	hsüeh
xun	hsün
ya	ya
yan	yen
yang	yang
yao	yao
ye	yeh
yi	i
yin	yin
ying	ying
yong	yung
you	yu
yu	yü
yuan	yüan
yue	yüeh
yun	yün
za	tsa
zai	tsai
zan	tsan
zang	tsang
zao	tsao
ze	tse
zei	tsei
zen	tsen
zeng	tseng
zha	cha
zhai	chai
zhan	chan
zhang	chang
zhao	chao
zhe	che
zhen	chen
zheng	cheng
zhi	chih
zhong	chung
zhou	chou
zhu	chu
zhua	chua
zhuai	chuai
zhuan	chuan
zhuang	chuang
zhui	chui
zhun	chun
zhuo	cho
zi	tzu
zong	tsung
zou	tsou
zu	tsu
zuan	tsuan
zui	tsui
zun	tsun
zuo	tso

Personal names

WADE-GILES	PINYIN
Fang Li-chih	Fang Lizhi
Hua Kuo-feng	Hua Guofeng
Lin Piao	Lin Biao
Lu Hsün	Lu Xun
Mao Tse-tung	Mao Zedong
Teng Hsiao-p'ing	Deng Xiaoping

Sun Yat-sen and Chiang Kai-shek, among a few others, usually retain the old spellings.

Geographical names

WADE-GILES	POSTAL ATLAS	PINYIN
Kuang-tung	Kwangtung	Guangdong
Pei-ching (Pei-p'ing)	Peking (Peiping)	Beijing
Shang-hai	Shanghai	Shanghai
Su-chou	Soochow	Suzhou
Ta-lien	Dairen	Dalian

10.104 *Japanese romanization.* The Japanese language in its usual written form is a mixture of Chinese characters (called *kanji* in Japanese) and two *kana* syllabaries. (A syllabary is a series of written characters, each used to represent a syllable.) Since romanized Japanese, *rōmaji,* was introduced into Japan in the sixteenth century, a number of systems of romanization have been developed. The one in most common use since the early part of the Meiji period (1868–1912) is the modified Hepburn (or *hyōjun*) system. This system is used in *Kenkyūsha's New English–Japanese Dictionary* (bibliog. 3.2) and most other Japanese-English dictionaries; it is also used almost exclusively outside Japan, notably in Asian collections in libraries throughout the world.

10.105 *Modified Hepburn system.* In the modified Hepburn system,[1] an apostrophe is placed at the end of a syllable that is followed by a vowel or *y: Gen'e, San'yo.* A macron is used over a long vowel in all Japanese words except well-known place-names (e.g., Tokyo, Hokkaido, Kobe) and words such as "shogun" and "daimyo" that have entered the English language and are thus not italicized. (When the pronunciation of such names or words is

---

1. James Curtis Hepburn (1815–1911) was an American missionary, physician, and publisher of Japanese-English dictionaries.

important to readers, however, macrons may be used: Tōkyō, Hokkaidō, Kōbe, *shōgun, daimyō*.) Hyphens should be used sparingly: *Meiji jidai-shi* (or *jidaishi*) *no shinkenkyū*. *Shinjuku-ku* (or *Shinjukuku*) *no meisho*.

10.106 *Chinese and Japanese: capitalization and italics*. Although capital letters do not exist in Japanese or Chinese, they are introduced in romanized versions of these languages where they would normally be used in English (see 8.2–4). Personal names and place-names are capitalized. In hyphenated names, only the first element is capitalized in romanized Chinese, though not in Japanese. Common nouns and other words used in an English sentence are lowercased and italicized (see 7.51–52). Names of institutions, schools of thought, religions, and so forth are capitalized if set in roman, lowercased if set in italics.

> Donglin Academy; the Donglin movement
> Buddhism, Taoism, *fengshui*, and other forms . . .
> Under the Ming dynasty the postal service was administered by the Board of War (*bingbu*) through a central office in Beijing (*huitong guan*).
> The heirs of the Seiyūkai and Minseitō are the Liberal and Progressive parties of Japan.
> It was Genrō Saionji (the *genrō* were the elder statesmen of Japan) who said . . . (note that *genrō* is both singular and plural)

10.107 *Titles of works*. As in English, titles of books and periodicals are italicized, and titles of articles are set in roman and enclosed in quotation marks. The first word of a romanized title is always capitalized, and proper nouns (especially in Japanese) often are.

> Chen Shiqi, *Mingdai guan shougongye de yanjiu* [Studies on government-operated handicrafts during the Ming dynasty], . . .
> Hua Linfu, "Qingdai yilai Sanxia diqu shuihan zaihai de chubu yanjiu" [A preliminary study of floods and droughts in the Three Gorges region since the Qing dynasty], *Zhongguo shehui kexue* . . .
> Okamoto Yoshitomo, *Jūrokuseiki Nichi-Ō kōtsūshi no kenkyū* [Study of the intercourse between Japan and Europe during the sixteenth century] . . .
> Akiyama Kenzō, "Goresu wa Ryūkyūjin de aru" [The Gores and the Ryūkyūans], *Shigaku-Zasshi* (or *Shigaku Zasshi*) . . .

10.108 *Inclusion of original characters*. Chinese and Japanese characters, immediately following the romanized version of the item they represent, are sometimes necessary to help readers identify references cited or terms used. They are largely confined to bibliographies and glossaries. Where needed in running text, they may be enclosed in parentheses. Computer technology has made it much easier than it used to be to typeset words in non-Latin alphabets.

Hua Linfu 華林甫, "Qingdai yilai Sanxia diqu shuihan zaihai de chubu yanjiu" 清代以來三峽地區水旱災害的初步研究 [A preliminary study of floods and droughts in the Three Gorges region since the Qing dynasty], *Zhongguo shehui kexue* 中國社會科學 1 (1999): 168–79 . . .

Harry Harootunian and Sakai Naoki, "Nihon kenkyū to bunka kenkyū 日本研究と文化研究, *Shisō* 思想 7 (July 1997): 4–53.

That year the first assembly of the national Diet was held and the Imperial Rescript on Education (*kyōiku chokugo* 教育勅語) issued.

HEBREW

10.109 *Transliteration systems.* There are several acceptable romanization systems for Hebrew, including that in the *ALA-LC Romanization Tables* (see bibliog. 5). Any such system may be used, but it is the author's responsibility to use it consistently in a given work. (The Hebrew alphabet may be found in the alphabet table in *Merriam-Webster's Collegiate Dictionary* [bibliog. 3.1], among other sources.)

10.110 *Diacritics.* In transliterated Hebrew, the following accents and characters are sometimes needed: underdots (ḥ, ṭ), macrons (ā, ē, ī, ō, ū), acute accents (ś), hačeks (ǎ, ě), and superscript ə (ᵊ). The ʾalef and the ʿayin may be represented in the same ways as the Arabic hamza and ʿayn (see 10.95).

10.111 *Spelling.* In Hebrew, several prepositions, conjunctions, and articles appear as prefixes. Some authors use apostrophes or hyphens after these prefixes in romanized text and some do not. (In Hebrew, no such marker is used.) Either approach is acceptable if used consistently.

10.112 *Capitalization and italics.* The Hebrew alphabet has no capital letters, and there is no universally used system for capitalizing romanized Hebrew. Writers may follow normal English usage—capitalizing proper names, book titles, and so forth (see 10.3, 10.9). Some writers eschew capitalization altogether. As always, the author must ensure internal consistency. For italics in romanized Hebrew, the normal English usage may also be followed (see 10.5).

10.113 *Word division.* For romanized Hebrew, or Hebrew words incorporated into English, the principles set forth in 7.33–45 may be followed. When a double consonant occurs at the point of division, one consonant goes with each division.

Rosh Ha-shana   Yom Kip-pur

10.114 *Unromanized phrases.* Hebrew is read from right to left. In English sentences that contain an unromanized Hebrew phrase, the Hebrew order is maintained within the sentence.

The first phrase in Lamentations is איכה ישבה בדד (How she sits in solitude!).

If a line break occurs within a Hebrew phrase, the words must still be read right to left on each line. Thus, if the Hebrew phrase in the example above had to be broken, the Hebrew words would appear to be in a different order.

The first phrase in Lamentations is איכה ישבה

בדד (How she sits in solitude!).

or

The first phrase in Lamentations is איכה

ישבה בדד (How she sits in solitude!).

Hebrew-language word-processing software will automatically make correct line breaks in this sort of mixed text. In the more likely event that the Hebrew will appear as a special font in English software, the author should hand number on the hard copy (or number code in the electronic file) all the words in Hebrew phrases and should furnish detailed instructions on dealing with line breaks.

10.115 *A note on vowels.* Most Hebrew vowels are not letters; they are marks attached to the letters, most of which are consonants. In Hebrew texts the vowel marks (as well as dots that modify the pronunciation of consonants) rarely appear. Among texts in which the marks do appear are prayer books, printed Bibles, and poetry.

RUSSIAN

10.116 *Transliteration.* Of the many systems for transliterating Russian, the most important are summarized in table 10.3. Journals of Slavic studies generally prefer a "linguistic" system that makes free use of diacritics and ligatures, reflecting the nature of the Cyrillic alphabet (one symbol to one

TABLE 10.3 Russian alphabet and romanization

Cyrillic Alphabet				U.S. Board on Geographic Names	Library of Congress	"Linguistic" System
Upright		Cursive				
А	а	*А*	*а*	a		
Б	б	*Б*	*б*	b		
В	в	*В*	*в*	v		
Г	г	*Г*	*г*	g		
Д	д	*Д*	*д*	d		
Е	е	*Е*	*е*	ye,[1] e	e	e
Ё	ё[2]	*Ё*	*ё*	yë,[1] ë	ë	e, ë
Ж	ж	*Ж*	*ж*	zh		ž
З	з	*З*	*з*	z		
И	и	*И*	*и*	i		
Й	й	*Й*	*й*	y	ĭ	j
К	к	*К*	*к*	k		
Л	л	*Л*	*л*	l		
М	м	*М*	*м*	m		
Н	н	*Н*	*н*	n		
О	о	*О*	*о*	o		
П	п	*П*	*п*	p		
Р	р	*Р*	*р*	r		
С	с	*С*	*с*	s		
Т	т	*Т*	*m*	t		
У	у	*У*	*у*	u		
Ф	ф	*Ф*	*ф*	f		
Х	х	*Х*	*х*	kh	x̄	x
Ц	ц	*Ц*	*ц*	ts	t͡s	c
Ч	ч	*Ч*	*ч*	ch		č
Ш	ш	*Ш*	*ш*	sh		š
Щ	щ	*Щ*	*щ*	shch		šč
Ъ	ъ[3]	*Ъ*	*ъ*	"	"	"
Ы	ы[3]	*Ы*	*ы*	y		
Ь	ь[3]	*Ь*	*ь*	'	'	'
Э	э	*Э*	*э*	e	ė	è
Ю	ю	*Ю*	*ю*	yu	i͡u	ju
Я	я	*Я*	*я*	ya	i͡a	ja

NOTE: The Library of Congress and "linguistic" systems employ the same characters as the U.S. Board system except where noted.

[1] Initially and after a vowel or ъ or ь.

[2] Not considered a separate letter; usually represented in Russian by *e*.

[3] Does not occur initially.

sound). In works intended for a general audience, however, diacritics and ligatures should be avoided. For general use, Chicago recommends the system of the United States Board on Geographic Names. Regardless of the system followed, the name spellings in *Merriam-Webster's Biographical Dictionary* (bibliog. 4.1) and *Merriam-Webster's Geographical Dictionary* (bibliog. 4.2) should prevail.

| Catherine the Great | Dnieper | Nizhniy Novgorod |
| Chekhov | Moscow | Tchaikovsky |

10.117 *Capitalization.* Capitalization conventions in Cyrillic are much like those of French and should be preserved in transliteration. Pronouns, days of the week, months, and most proper adjectives are lowercased. Geographical designations are capitalized when they apply to formal institutions or political units but otherwise lowercased.

| Tverskaya guberniya | Moskovskiy universitet |
| tverskoye zemstvo | russkiy kompositor |

10.118 *Titles of works.* Only the first word and any proper nouns are capitalized in titles.

N. A. Kurakin, *Lenin i Trotskiy*

O. I. Skorokhodova, *Kak ya vosprinimayu i predstavlyayu okruzhayushchiy mir* [How I perceive and imagine the external world]

10.119 *Titles in Cyrillic.* In the Cyrillic originals, titles are set in ordinary type; the Cyrillic *kursiv* is used more sparingly than our italic and never for book titles. In transliterations, however, italic should be used.

10.120 *Dialogue and quotations.* Russian generally resembles French in its use of guillemets for dialogue and quoted material and of dashes for dialogue (see 10.32, 10.34).

« Bozhe, bozhe, bozhe! » govorit Boris.

— S kem ya rabotayu?
— S tovarishchem.
— Kak my rabotayem?
— S interesom.

To set off a quotation within a speech, guillemets may be used, as in French. For an example, see 10.34.

10.121 *Suspension points.* Suspension points (three unspaced dots followed by a space) are used as in French (see 10.35) to indicate interruptions or breaks in thought.

Ya... vy... my tol'ko chto priyekhali.

In Russian, however, an exclamation point or a question mark takes the place of one of the dots.

Mitya!.. Gde vy byli?..

10.122 *Uses of the dash.* A dash is sometimes inserted, without space, between subject and complement when the equivalent of *is* or *are* is omitted.

Moskva—stolitsa Rossii.

A dash, preceded and followed by a word space, is used in place of a verb omitted because it would be identical to the preceding verb.

Ivan i Sonya poyedut v Moskvu poyezdom, Lev i Lyuba — avtobusom.

10.123 *Word division: general.* Transliterated Russian should be divided according to the rules governing word division in the Cyrillic original. The following rules are adapted from the transliteration system of the United States Board on Geographic Names.

10.124 *Combinations not to be divided.* Combinations representing single Cyrillic letters—*ye, yë, zh, kh, ts, ch, sh, shch, yu, ya*—should never be divided, nor should combinations of a vowel plus short *i* (transliterated *y*)—*ay, ey, yey,* and so on.

10.125 *Division between consonants.* Words may be divided between single consonants or between consonants and consonant combinations.

ubor-ku	chudes-nym	mol-cha	sred-stvo	mor-skoy

10.126 *Consonant combinations.* The following consonant combinations are not normally divided: *bl, pl, gl, kl, fl, vl, br, pr, gr, kr, fr, vr, dv, dr, tv, tr, sk, skv, skr, st, stv, str, zhd, ml.* They may, however, be divided if they fall across the boundary of a prefix and a root or other such units (e.g., *ob-lech, ras-kol*).

10.127 *Division after prefixes or between parts.* Words may be divided after a prefix, but generally the prefix itself should not be divided.

bes-poryadok	za-dat'	pro-vesti
pere-stroika	pred-lozhit'	obo-gnat'

Compound words should be divided between parts.

radio-priyëmnik	gor-sovet	kino-teatr

10.128 *Division after vowel or diphthong.* Words may be divided after a vowel or a diphthong before a single (Cyrillic) consonant.

Si-bir'	voy-na	Gorba-chev	da-zhe

Division may also be made before a consonant combination.

puteshe-stvennik	khi-trit'	pro-stak	ru-brika

SOUTH ASIAN LANGUAGES

10.129 *Special characters.* Transliteration of the principal South Asian languages requires some or all of the following special characters:

Ā ā, Æ æ, Ǣ ǣ, Ē ē, Ī ī, Ō ō, Ū ū, Ḍ ḍ, Ḥ ḥ, Ḷ ḷ, Ḹ ḹ, Ṃ ṃ, Ṇ ṇ, Ṅ ṅ, Ñ ñ, Ṛ ṛ, Ṝ ṝ, Ṣ ṣ, Ś ś

Classical Greek

10.130 *Overview.* The following information is intended mainly for editors, proof-readers, or typesetters who do not read classical Greek.

10.131 *Transliterating Greek.* Isolated Greek words and phrases in works not dealing with ancient Greece are usually transliterated. Table 10.4 shows the Greek alphabet with corresponding Latin-alphabet letters. In transliteration, all Greek accents are omitted. The macron is used to distinguish the long vowels eta (*ē*) and omega (*ō*) from the short vowels epsilon (*e*) and omicron (*o*). The iota subscript is transliterated by an *i* on the line, following the vowel it is associated with (ἀνθρώπῳ, *anthrōpōi*). The rough breathing is transliterated by *h*, which precedes a vowel or diphthong and follows the letter *rho* (as in the English word *rhythm*). The smooth breathing is ignored, since it represents merely the absence of the *h* sound. If a diaeresis appears in the Greek, it also appears in transliteration. Transliterated Greek words or phrases are usually italicized unless the same words occur frequently, in which case they may be italicized at first mention and then set in roman.

10.132 *Typesetting Greek.* If, as sometimes happens, an author has handwritten Greek-alphabet words into the hard copy, the electronic file must carry a note directing the typesetter to the relevant page of that copy. More com-

TABLE 10.4 Greek alphabet and romanization

Name of Letter	Greek Alphabet		Transliteration
Alpha	A	α	a
Beta	B	β	b
Gamma	Γ	γ¹	g
Delta	Δ	δ ∂²	d
Epsilon	E	ε	e
Zeta	Z	ζ	z
Eta	H	η	ē
Theta	Θ	θ ϑ²	th
Iota	I	ι	i
Kappa	K	κ	k
Lambda	Λ	λ	l
Mu	M	μ	m
Nu	N	ν	n
Xi	Ξ	ξ	x
Omicron	O	o	o
Pi	Π	π	p
Rho	P	ρ	r; *initially*, rh; *double*, rrh
Sigma	Σ	σ ς³	s
Tau	T	τ	t
Upsilon	Υ	υ	u; *often* y, *exc. after* a, e, ē, i
Phi	Φ	φ φ²	ph
Chi	X	χ	kh, ch
Psi	Ψ	ψ	ps
Omega	Ω	ω	ō

¹Note that γγ becomes ng, and γκ becomes nk.

²Old-style character. Usually used in mathematical formulas.

³Final letter.

monly, the author or editor has typed in the Greek, in which case the publisher should make sure that the Greek in the author's software is usable for typesetting, since word-processing and typesetting strategies are not always compatible. Greek may need to be set in a slightly different size to make it visually match the surrounding type. Extra white space must occasionally be added where more than one diacritic appears over a vowel.

BREATHINGS AND ACCENTS

10.133 *Breathings.* When Greek is set in the Greek alphabet, every initial vowel or diphthong or rho must be marked with a breathing, either rough (') or smooth ('). The breathing mark is placed over the initial lowercase vowel (or the second vowel of a diphthong). It is placed to the left of capital letters. Note that a single quotation mark cannot function as a breathing because it is the wrong size and does not sit close enough to the letter.

αὖτε, ἕτεραι, ῞Ελλην, ἥβη, ᾿Ιρις, ὑπέχω, ὠκυς, ῥᾴδιος

10.134 *Accents*. There are three Greek accent marks: acute (´); circumflex, either tilde shaped or rounded (˜, ˆ); and grave (`). Accents in Greek occur only over vowels. The circumflex occurs only on the two final syllables of a word. The grave accent occurs only on the last syllable. Like breathings, accents are placed over lowercase vowels, over the second vowel of a diphthong, and to the left of capital vowels. A diaeresis is used to indicate that two successive vowels do not form a diphthong but are voiced separately (as in French *naïf*).

10.135 *Unaccented words*. With two exceptions, all Greek words are marked with accents—usually one, occasionally two (see below). The first exception is a group of monosyllabic words called proclitics, which are closely connected with the words following them. The proclitics are the forms of the definite article ὁ, ἡ, οἱ, αἱ; the prepositions εἰς, ἐν, ἐκ [ἐξ]; the conjunctions εἰ, ὡς; and the adverb οὐ [οὐκ, οὐχ]. The second exception is a group called enclitics, short words pronounced as if part of the word preceding them. Enclitics usually lose their accents (’αρταξερξής τε), and in certain circumstances the word preceding them gains a second accent (φοβεῖταί τις).

10.136 *Vowels*. Vowels complete with breathing marks and accents, in all combinations, are an integral part of every Greek font used in publishing. Each font, for example, should be able to provide, for lowercase eta, η, ή, ῆ, ὴ, ἠ, ἤ, ἦ, ᾔ, ῄ, ῂ, ᾖ, ᾑ, and, for uppercase eta, Η, Ἡ, Ἧ, Ἤ, Ἦ, Ἧ, Ἧ, Ἧ, Ἧ. Additional symbols are needed for scholarly works dealing with ancient manuscripts or papyri.

PUNCTUATION AND NUMBERS

10.137 *Punctuation*. In Greek the period and comma are the same as in English; the colon and semicolon are both represented by a raised dot (·); the question mark is represented by a semicolon. The apostrophe is used as an elision mark when the final vowel of one word is elided before a second word beginning with a vowel. With some fonts it may be preferable to use an English apostrophe in place of the Greek one. In English texts, quoted words or passages in the Greek alphabet, of whatever length, should not be enclosed in quotation marks.

10.138 *Numbers*. Numbers, when not written out, are represented in ordinary Greek text by the letters of the alphabet, supplemented by three obsolete Greek letters, ϛ´ = 6, ϟ´ = 90, ϡ´ = 900. The diacritical mark resembling a prime distinguishes the letters as numerals and is added to a sign stand-

TABLE 10.5 Greek numerals

1	α´	13	ιγ´	30	λ´	600	χ´
2	β´	14	ιδ´	40	μ´	700	ψ´
3	γ´	15	ιε´	50	ν´	800	ω´
4	δ´	16	ιϛ´	60	ξ´	900	ϡ´
5	ε´	17	ιζ´	70	ο´	1,000	͵α
6	ϛ´	18	ιη´	80	π´	2,000	͵β
7	ζ´	19	ιθ´	90	ϟ´	3,000	͵γ
8	η´	20	κ´	100	ρ´	4,000	͵δ
9	θ´	21	κα´	200	σ´	10,000	͵ι
10	ι´	22	κβ´	300	τ´	100,000	͵ρ
11	ια´	23	κγ´	400	υ´		
12	ιβ´	24	κδ´	500	φ´		

ing alone or to the last sign in a series, 111 = ρια´. For thousands, the foregoing signs are used with a different diacritical mark: ͵α = 1,000, ͵αρια´ = 1,111, ͵βσκβ´ = 2,222. See table 10.5.

WORD DIVISION

10.139   *Consecutive vowels.* Diphthongs (αι, ει, οι, υι, αυ, ευ, ηυ, ου, ωυ) are never divided. But two consecutive vowels that do not form a diphthong are divided.

θε-ά-ο-μαι   υἱ-ός   παύ-ε-τε   νε-ώς

10.140   *Single consonants.* When a single consonant occurs between two vowels, the word is divided before the consonant.

φω-νή   κε-φα-λις   μέ-γα   δέ-δω-κεν   μή-τηρ

10.141   *Two or more consonants.* If a consonant is doubled, or if a mute is followed by its corresponding aspirate (πφ, βφ, κχ, γχ, τθ, δθ), the word is divided after the first consonant.

θά-λασ-σα

If the combination of two or more consonants begins with a liquid (λ, ρ) or a nasal (μ, ν), division is made after the liquid or nasal.

ἔμ-προ-σθεν
(But before μν: μέ-μνημαι)

All other combinations of two or more consonants *follow* the division.

πρᾶ-γμα	τέ-χνη	βα-θμός	αἰ-σχρός
βι-βλί-ον	δά-κτυ-λος	σκῆ-πτρον	βά-κτρον

10.142 *Compound words.* Compound words are divided between parts; within each part the above rules apply. The commonest type of compound word begins with a preposition or a prefix.

ἀμφ-	ἀν-	ἀπ-	ὑπ-	ἐξ-έβαλον	δύσ-μορφος
ἀφ-	ἐφ-	ὑφ-	κατ-	καπ-ίστημι	

Old English and Middle English

10.143 *Special characters.* Several Old English or Middle English letters not used in modern English occur in both lowercase and capital forms.

ð   Ð   Called edh or eth
þ   Þ   Called thorn

Both edh and thorn are used to represent voiced or unvoiced *th*, as in *them* or *three.*

ȝ   Ȝ   Called yogh; occurs in Middle English sometimes for *y* as in
year, sometimes for *gh* as in *light.*
æ   Æ   Ligature; should not be printed as two letters in Old English
names and text (Ælfric).

Edh, thorn, and the ligature are available in most text-editing software and thus require no special coding. Yogh, if unavailable, will require coding (see 2.89). In any case, consult your publisher.

10.144 *Substitutions.* Two characters occasionally found in Old English texts are ⁊ for *and* (or ampersand) and ƿ (wyn) for *w*; but the modern ampersand and *w* may be substituted for these.

American Sign Language

10.145 *Signed languages.* The visual/gestural languages used by deaf people all over the world are called signed languages. Most countries have their own distinct sign language—American Sign Language (ASL), British Sign Language, Thai Sign Language, and so on. The individual elements of these languages are known as *signs*. Although they are not spoken languages, as are the other languages in this chapter, signed languages nonetheless have unique grammatical structures that are different from those of the spoken languages used in their respective countries. See also 8.45.

10.146 *Writing ASL.* No formal system yet exists for writing ASL. Since more and more linguists and anthropologists are studying and writing about signed languages, this section offers just a few of the typographic conventions for transferring signed communication to a written medium. For a fuller discussion, see Clayton Valli and Ceil Lucas, *The Linguistics of American Sign Language* (bibliog. 5). As research into the structure of ASL continues to grow and evolve, more transcription conventions will be necessary.

10.147 *Glosses.* The English representation of a sign is called a *gloss*. Glosses are written in small capital letters: WOMAN, SCHOOL, CAT. When two or more English words are needed to express a single sign, the glosses are separated by hyphens. When the English words are referred to in text, they are enclosed in double quotation marks.

The sign for "a car drove by" is written as VEHICLE-DRIVE-BY.

10.148 *Components of signs.* Signs have five major components—handshape, location, orientation, movement, and nonmanual signals. A description of a sign will normally include all five elements.

10.149 *Fingerspelling.* Not all English words have a sign equivalent. This is especially true for proper nouns and new words in the lexicon. When no sign exists, or when a signer does not know a particular sign or wants to clarify or emphasize a word, the signer fingerspells the word, using the American Manual Alphabet. Each letter is a distinct sign. When represented in type, fingerspelled words appear in small capital letters, with the letters separated by hyphens: B-O-W-I-E, I-N-T-E-R-N-E-T.

10.150 *Lexicalized signs.* Over time, some fingerspelled words have taken on the quality of distinct signs either by the omission of some of the individual letter signs or by a change in the orientation or movement of the letter signs. These *lexicalized signs* are represented by the "pound" symbol (#): #WHAT, #BACK, #DO.

10.151 *Handshape.* The handshapes of American Sign Language come from the American Manual Alphabet and the manual numbers. A single capital letter or an arabic numeral is used to describe the handshape:

APPLE is made with an X handshape; CREATE is made with a 4 handshape.

Some letters and numbers, however, have variants that have become distinct handshapes. Note the capitalization in the following example.

ANY is made with an Open A handshape; YELL is made with a Bent 5 handshape.

10.152 *Compound signs.* Some combinations of signs have taken on a meaning separate from the meaning of the individual signs. These compound signs are represented typographically with an eyebrow-shaped mark (or close-up mark) between them.

MOTHER⁀FATHER = PARENTS
THINK⁀MARRY = BELIEVE

10.153 *Sentence transcriptions.* Signed sentences are written in small capital letters with the English translation in upper- and lowercase italics underneath. In signed sentences, pronouns sometimes are written as PRO.1 (first person), PRO.2 (second person), and PRO.3 (third person), regardless of gender or whether the pronoun is the subject or object of the sentence. Punctuation is generally omitted from sentence transcriptions (though not from the translations). Some writers add question marks and exclamation points, but interior punctuation and periods are rarely used.

YESTERDAY STORE PRO.1 GO
Yesterday I went to the store.

BOY THERE FACE⁀STRONG SAME FATHER
That boy looks just like his father.

10.154 *Nonmanual signals.* Additional grammatical information is added to signs through nonmanual signals such as raising the eyebrows or shifting eye gaze. Such signals, indicated by various abbreviations and terms, are typeset in a smaller font followed by a half-point rule above the ASL sentence. Correct alignment is critical to an accurate transcription. The first sentence below is an example of a yes-no question, which is indicated by raising the eyebrows; the second sentence is an example of shifting eye gaze.

q
———————————————
FINISH SEE MOVIE YOU
Have you seen that movie?

gaze left   gaze to addressee
————————————————————————————
PRO.1 LOOK-AT-THEM TALK NO A-C-T HIT NOTHING TALK
I looked at my two friends, but they were all talk and no action.

Quotations and Dialogue

Introduction

11.1 *Scope of this chapter—and where else to look.* This chapter offers guidelines for dealing with quoted matter and, to a lesser degree, dialogue. For the use of quotation marks for purposes other than direct quotation, see chapter 7. For citing the sources of quotations, discussed only peripherally here, see chapters 16–17. For typing quotations, see 2.25–26; for the manuscript editor's responsibilities regarding quoted material, see 2.60.

11.2 *Quoting and citing.* "Quoting other writers and citing the places where their words are to be found," Jacques Barzun and Henry F. Graff point out, "are by now such common practices that it is pardonable to look upon the habit as natural, not to say instinctive. It is of course nothing of the kind, but a very sophisticated act, peculiar to a civilization that uses printed books, believes in evidence, and makes a point of assigning credit or blame in a detailed, verifiable way."[1]

11.3 *Giving credit and seeking permission.* Authors drawing on the work of others to illustrate their arguments should first decide whether direct quotation or paraphrase will be more effective. Will a reader who chooses to skip over long or frequent quotations miss any significant point? Whether quoting, paraphrasing, or using others' ideas to advance their own argument, authors should give credit to the source of those words or ideas. A note or a parenthetical reference often suffices. (Throughout this chapter the word *note* refers to a note wherever it appears—at the foot of a page; at the back of a printed book; at the end of an article or a chapter; or somewhere on an electronic page, linked to the primary document by means of hypertext. For documentation forms, see chapters 16–17.) Written permission is probably needed for more than a line or two of a poem or a song

---

1. *The Modern Researcher,* 5th ed. (Boston: Houghton Mifflin, 1992), 273.

lyric in copyright; for prose quotations of, say, more than three paragraphs or for many short passages from a work in copyright; or for any excerpt from certain unpublished materials (letters, e-mail messages, and so forth). For more information about permissions, consult chapter 4, especially 4.67–79.

11.4   *What not to quote.* A verbally accurate quotation that contains minor factual or grammatical errors not noted by the author using the quotation does a disservice to readers and embarrasses the publisher. Authors who notice an error in a passage they wish to quote should paraphrase the original, eliminating the error. For "silent correction," see 11.8(5); for *sic*, see 11.69.

11.5   *When source citation is unneeded.* Commonly known facts, proverbs, and other familiar expressions require no source citation unless the wording is taken directly from another work. See also 6.54. No source need be cited for such statements as the following.

> On April 14, 1865, a few days after Lee's surrender, Lincoln was assassinated.
> No one can convince the young that practice makes perfect.
> If reading maketh a full man, Henry is half-empty.

11.6   *Accuracy.* It is impossible to overemphasize the importance of meticulous accuracy in quoting from the works of others. Authors should check every direct quotation against the original or, if the original is unavailable, against a careful transcription of the passage. (Authors who transcribe carelessly or illegibly are in for trouble later if they no longer have access to their sources.)

11.7   *Checking.* Quotations must be checked at manuscript stage, preferably before the manuscript is submitted to the publisher and certainly before it is typeset. Corrections in proof are expensive (and often chargeable to the author) as well as time consuming. See 2.36, 3.15.

Permissible Changes

11.8   *Syntactic and typographic considerations.* Although in a direct quotation the wording, spelling, capitalization, and internal punctuation of the original should be reproduced exactly, the following changes are generally permissible to make the passage fit into the syntax and typography of the surrounding text. See also 11.13–14.

1. Single quotation marks may be changed to double, and double to single (see 11.33, 11.35).
2. The initial letter may be changed to a capital or a lowercase letter (see 11.16–18, 11.63).
3. The final period may be omitted or changed to a comma as required, and punctuation may be omitted where ellipsis points are used (see 11.51, 11.55–58, 11.60–61, 11.64–65).
4. Original notes and note reference marks may be omitted unless omission would affect the meaning of the quotation. If an original note is included, the quotation should be set off as a block quotation (see 11.11, 11.17), with the note in smaller type at the end, or the note may be summarized in the accompanying text. Authors may, on the other hand, add note references of their own within quotations.
5. Obvious typographic errors may be corrected silently (without comment or *sic*; see 11.69) unless the passage quoted is from an older work or a manuscript source where idiosyncrasies of spelling are generally preserved. If spelling and punctuation are modernized or altered for clarity, readers must be so informed in a note, in a preface, or elsewhere.
6. In quoting from early printed documents, the archaic ſ, used at the beginning or in the middle but never at the end of a lowercase word ("Such goodneſs of your juſtice, that our ſoul . . ."), may be changed to a modern *s*. Similarly, *Vanitie and Vncertaintie* (in a quoted title) may be changed to *Vanitie and Uncertaintie*, but writers or editors without a strong background in classical or Renaissance studies should generally be wary of changing *u* to *v*, *i* to *j*, or vice versa. See also 10.62.

11.9 *Typographic style.* Elements of typography that were imposed not by the original author but by the original publisher or typesetter need not, and often should not, be reproduced exactly, as long as the intent and emphasis of the original style are maintained. For example, the typeface or font should be changed to agree with the surrounding text. Words in full capitals in the original may be set in small caps. In dialogue, names of speakers may be moved from a centered position to flush left. For citing titles of books, articles, poems, and other works, see 8.164–210.

11.10 *Manuscript versus print style.* Underlined words in a quoted manuscript are printed as italics (although underlining can be reproduced typographically where relevant). In quoting correspondence, such matters as paragraph indention and the position of the salutation and signature may be adjusted. Capital letters, if used arbitrarily, should be lowercased (for example, "When I get Home" should be reproduced as "When I get home" unless the capital *H* has some significance).

Relation to Text

RUN IN OR SET OFF

11.11 *The two styles.* In typeset form, quotations may be either run in—that is, integrated into the text in the same type size as the text and enclosed in quotation marks—or set off from the text as block quotations, or extracts. Block quotations are not enclosed in quotation marks and always start a new line. They may be indented or set in smaller type or a different font from the text; they may have unjustified right-hand margins or less space between lines. These matters are normally decided by the publisher's designer or by journal style. Authors preparing block quotations should avoid such devices (unless otherwise advised by their publishers) and simply use the indention feature of their word processors. For placement of quotation marks, double and single, in relation to other punctuation, see 6.8–10, 7.52, 7.58, 11.33–34.

11.12 *Choosing between the styles.* Whether to run in or set off a quotation is commonly determined by its length. In general, a short quotation, especially one that is not a full sentence, is run in. A hundred words or more— or at least eight lines—are set off as a block quotation. Other criteria apply, however: the nature of the material, the number of quotations, and the appearance of the printed page. A quotation of two or more paragraphs is best set off (see 11.23–25), as are quoted letters (if salutations, signatures, and such are included), lists, and any material that requires special formatting. If many quotations of varying length occur close together, running them all in may make for easier reading. But where quotations are being compared or otherwise used as entities in themselves, it may be better to set them all as block quotations, however short. Poetry is nearly always set off (see 11.28–32).

11.13 *Syntax.* In incorporating fragmentary quotations into a text, phrase the surrounding sentence in such a way that the quoted words fit into it logically and grammatically, quoting only as much of the original as is necessary. Ronald S. Crane's two-volume *The Idea of the Humanities* (Chicago: University of Chicago Press, 1967) provides many excellent illustrations of this principle. The following example may be used as a model.

> In short, there has been "almost a continual improvement" in all branches of human knowledge; and since this improvement has taken place not merely in the speculative sciences but likewise in those other forms of learning, such as politics, morality, and religion, "which apparently have a more immediate influence upon the welfare of civil life,

447

and man's comfortable subsistence in it," it seems to follow, "as a corollary, plainly deducible from a proposition already demonstrated," that human happiness has also increased. (1:281)

11.14 *Tenses and pronouns.* In quoting verbatim, writers need to integrate tenses and pronouns into the new context.

[*Original*] Mr. Moll took particular pains to say to you, gentlemen, that these eleven people here are guilty of murder; he calls this a cold-blooded, deliberate and premeditated murder.

[*As quoted*] According to Darrow, Moll had told the jury that the eleven defendants were "guilty of murder" and had described the murder as "cold-blooded, deliberate and premeditated."

Occasional adjustments to the original may be bracketed. This device should be used sparingly, however.

Mr. Graham has resolutely ducked the issue, saying he won't play the game of rumor-mongering, even though he has "learned from [his] mistakes."

INITIAL CAPITAL OR LOWERCASE LETTER

11.15 *General versus specialized works.* The guidelines in 11.16–18 are recommended for general works, including most scholarly studies. For more rigorous usage, appropriate to legal writing and textual commentary, see 11.19, 11.63.

11.16 *Capital to lowercase initial letter: run-in quotations.* When a quotation is used as a syntactical part of a sentence, it begins with a lowercase letter even if the original is a complete sentence or a fragment of poetry beginning with a capital. For use of brackets in legal works and textual commentary, see 11.63.

Benjamin Franklin admonishes us to "plough deep while sluggards sleep."

With another aphorism he reminded his readers that "experience keeps a dear school, but fools will learn in no other"—an observation as true today as then.

Whether "to be, or not to be" was a major consideration or not, Sir Thomas hastily put away his sword.

When the quotation has a more remote syntactic relation to the rest of the sentence, the initial letter remains capitalized.

As Franklin advised, "Plough deep while sluggards sleep."

His aphorism "Experience keeps a dear school, but fools will learn in no other" is a cogent warning to people of all ages.

11.17   *Capital to lowercase letter: block quotations.* The initial letter of a block quotation may be lowercased if the syntax demands it—for example, if a phrase such as "So-and-so maintains that" precedes the quotation. In the following example, the quotation from Aristotle in the Jowett translation (Modern Library) begins in the original with a capital letter and a paragraph indention. See also 11.24.

> In discussing the reasons for political disturbances Aristotle observes that
>
> > revolutions also break out when opposite parties, e.g. the rich and the people, are equally balanced, and there is little or no middle class; for, if either party were manifestly superior, the other would not risk an attack upon them. And, for this reason, those who are eminent in virtue usually do not stir up insurrections, always a minority. Such are the beginnings and causes of the disturbances and revolutions to which every form of government is liable. (*Politics* 5.4)

11.18   *Lowercase to capital letter.* Similarly, if a quotation that is only a part of a sentence in the original forms a complete sentence as quoted, a lowercase letter may be changed to a capital if appropriate. To use the second sentence in the Aristotle quotation in the example above,

> Aristotle put it this way: "Those who are eminent in virtue usually do not stir up insurrections, always a minority."

11.19   *Brackets to indicate a change in capitalization.* In legal writing, textual commentary, and other contexts where silently changing from capital to lowercase or vice versa might mislead readers or make reference to the original text more difficult, any change in capitalization should be indicated by brackets.

> According to article 6, section 6, she is given the power "[t]o extend or renew any existing indebtedness."

> "[R]eal estates may be conveyed by lease and release, or bargain and sale," according to section 2 of the Northwest Ordinance.

> Let us compare Aristotle's contention that "[i]nferiors revolt in order that they may be equal, and equals that they may be superior" (*Politics* 5.2) with his later observation that

449

"[r]evolutions also break out when opposite parties, e.g. the rich and the people, are equally balanced" (5.4).

INTRODUCTORY PHRASES AND PUNCTUATION

11.20 *Use of the colon.* A formal introductory phrase, such as *thus* or *the following*, is usually followed by a colon.

> The role of the author has been variously described. Henry Fielding, at the beginning of his *History of Tom Jones*, defines it thus: "An author ought to consider himself, not as a gentleman who gives a private or eleemosynary treat, but rather as one who keeps a public ordinary, at which all persons are welcome for their money."

Such perfunctory phrases as "Jacqueline Jones writes:" or "The defendant stated:" are often awkward, and sensitive writers avoid them.

11.21 *Use of the comma.* A comma rather than a colon is often used after *said, replied, asked,* and similar verbs.

> Garrett replied, "I hope you are not referring to me."

> Fish says, "What [the students] did was move the words out of a context (the faculty club door) in which they had a literal and obvious meaning into another context (my classroom) in which the meaning was no less obvious and literal and yet was different."

11.22 *Use of the period.* Unless introduced by *thus, as follows,* or other wording that requires a colon, a block quotation may be preceded by a period, though a colon is quite acceptable. Either usage should be followed consistently.

> He then took a clearly hostile position toward Poland, having characterized it as a Fascist state that oppressed the Ukrainians, the Belorussians, and others.

> > Under present conditions, suppression of that state will mean that there will be one less Fascist state. It will not be a bad thing if Poland suffers a defeat and thus enables us to include new territories and new populations in the socialist system.

PARAGRAPHING

11.23 *Block quotations.* Quoted material of more than a paragraph, even if very brief, is best set off as a block quotation. For a less desirable alternative, see 11.36.

11.24 *Paragraph indention.* A block quotation should generally reflect the paragraphing of the original. If the first paragraph quoted includes the beginning of that paragraph, however, it need not start with a paragraph indention except in contexts where strict adherence to the original text is required (such as those mentioned in 11.19 in connection with brackets). If the first part of the opening paragraph is omitted, the opening line always begins flush left. Any subsequent paragraphs in the quotation are indented. For ellipsis points at the beginning of paragraphs, see 11.56, 11.60.

11.25 *Quoting unindented paragraphs.* The opening paragraph of a chapter, or any paragraph in a typed letter, often appears flush left in the original. When quoted, such paragraphs may be flush left or indented according to the needs of the surrounding text.

11.26 *Block quotations beginning in text.* A long quotation may begin with a few words run into the text. This device should be used only when text intervenes between the quoted matter in the text and its continuation.

"There is no safe trusting to dictionaries and definitions," observed Charles Lamb.

> We should more willingly fall in with this popular language, if we did not find *brutality* sometimes awkwardly coupled with *valour* in the same vocabulary. The comic writers . . . have contributed not a little to mislead us upon this point. To see a hectoring fellow exposed and beaten upon the stage, has something in it wonderfully diverting. ("Popular Fallacies," *Essays of Elia*)

"In short," says Crane, summarizing Gordon's philosophy,

> there has been "almost a continual improvement" in all branches of human knowledge; . . .

A permissible alternative is to set off the entire quotation, enclosing the intervening words of text in brackets.

> There is no safe trusting to dictionaries and definitions [observed Charles Lamb]. We should more willingly . . .

11.27 *Text following a block quotation.* If the text following a block quotation is a continuation of the paragraph that introduces the quotation, it begins flush left. If the resuming text begins a new paragraph, it receives a paragraph indention.

POETRY

11.28 *Setting off poetry.* Two or more lines of verse are best set off as a block quotation. A poetry quotation, if isolated, is often centered on the page, but if two or more stanzas of the same poem appear on the same page, a uniform indention from the left may work better (see 11.29). A half line to a full line of space should appear between stanzas. Within each piece or stanza, the indention pattern of the original should be reproduced (but indention should be distinguished from runover lines; see 11.30).

> Sure there was wine
> Before my sighs did drie it: there was corn
> Before my tears did drown it.
> Is the yeare onely lost to me?
> Have I no bayes to crown it?
> No flowers, no garlands gay? all blasted?
> All wasted?
> (George Herbert, "The Collar")

If the quotation does not begin with a full line, space approximating the omitted part should be left.

> there was corn
> Before my tears did drown it.

11.29 *Uniform indention.* Where all or most poetic quotations consist of blank verse (as in studies of Shakespeare) or are very long, uniform indention usually works best.

> I have full cause of weeping, but this heart
> Shall break into a hundred thousand flaws
> Or ere I'll weep. O fool! I shall go mad.

11.30 *Long lines and runovers.* Runover lines (the remainder of lines too long to appear as a single line) are usually indented one em from the line above, as in the following quotation from Walt Whitman's "Song of Myself":

> My tongue, every atom of my blood, form'd from this
>   soil, this air,
> Born here of parents born here from parents the same,
>   and their parents the same,
> I, now thirty-seven years old in perfect health begin,
> Hoping to cease not till death.

Runover lines, although indented, should be distinct from new lines deliberately indented by the poet (as in the Herbert poem quoted in 11.28).

11.31 *Quotation marks in poems.* Quotation marks at the beginning of a line of poetry are preferably "cleared," that is, placed outside the alignment of the poem, as in the first example below. This practice is easier with computer typesetting; in the days of hot metal it required considerable handwork.

> He holds him with his skinny hand.
> "There was a ship," quoth he.
> "Hold off! unhand me, grey-beard loon!"
> Eftsoons his hand dropt he.

An acceptable alternative is to align opening quotation marks with the line above.

> He holds him with his skinny hand.
> "There was a ship," quoth he.

11.32 *Run-in poetry quotations.* If space or context requires that two lines be run in, the lines are separated by a slash, with equal space on either side (a thin space to an en space). For running in full stanzas (to be avoided if at all possible), see 11.38.

> Andrew Marvell's praise of John Milton, "Thou has not missed one thought that could be fit, / And all that was improper does omit" ("On *Paradise Lost*") might well serve as our motto.

Quotation Marks

DOUBLE OR SINGLE

11.33 *Quotations and "quotes within quotes."* Quoted words, phrases, and sentences run into the text are enclosed in double quotation marks. Single quotation marks enclose quotations within quotations; double marks, quotations within these; and so on. For permissible changes from single to double quotation marks and vice versa, see 11.8(1). For dialogue, see 11.43. For technical uses of single quotation marks, see 7.52, 8.138.

> "Don't be absurd!" said Henry. "To say that 'I mean what I say' is the same as 'I say what I mean' is to be as confused as Alice at the Mad Hatter's tea party. You remember what

the Hatter said to her: 'Not the same thing a bit! Why you might just as well say that "I see what I eat" is the same thing as "I eat what I see"!'"

The practice in other English-speaking countries is often the reverse: single marks are used first, then double, and so on.

11.34 *Placement of closing quotation marks.* Note carefully not only the placement of the single and double closing quotation marks but also that of the exclamation points in relation to those marks in the example above. Question marks and exclamation points are placed just within the set of quotation marks ending the element to which such terminal punctuation belongs. For the placement of other punctuation—commas, periods, question marks, and so on—in relation to closing quotation marks, see 6.8–10.

11.35 *Quotation marks in block quotations.* Although material set off as a block quotation is not enclosed in quotation marks, quoted matter *within* the block quotation is enclosed in double quotation marks—in other words, treated as it would be in text (see 11.33). An author or editor who changes a run-in quotation to a block quotation must delete the opening and closing quotation marks and change any internal ones. The following examples illustrate the same material first in run-in form and then as a block quotation.

The narrator then breaks in: "Imagine Bart's surprise, dear reader, when Emma turned to him and said, contemptuously, 'What "promise"?'"

The narrator then breaks in:

> Imagine Bart's surprise, dear reader, when Emma turned to him and said, contemptuously, "What 'promise'?"

Similarly, converting a block quotation to a run-in quotation requires adding and altering quotation marks. For interpolations that include quoted matter, see 11.71.

RUN-IN QUOTATIONS OF MORE THAN ONE PARAGRAPH

11.36 *Quotation marks.* If quoted material of more than one paragraph cannot be set as a block quotation (which is normally much preferred; see 11.23), quotation marks are needed at the beginning of *each* paragraph but at the end of only the *final* paragraph. The same practice is followed in dialogue when one speaker's remarks extend over more than one paragraph.

11.37   *Quotations within quotations.* If a run-in quoted passage contains an interior quotation that runs for more than one paragraph, a single quotation mark appears at the beginning and end of the interior quotation, and both double and single quotation marks appear before each new paragraph belonging to it. If the interior quotation concludes at the same point as the including one, the single closing quotation mark precedes the double one.

11.38   *Poetry.* If a poem cannot be set off as a block quotation (which is greatly to be preferred; see 11.28), quotation marks should appear at the beginning of each stanza and at the end of only the final one.

11.39   *Letters.* A letter quoted in its entirety should be set off as a block quotation. In the undesirable event that it must be run in, it should carry opening quotation marks before the first line (including the salutation) and before each paragraph. Closing marks appear only after the last line (often the signature).

QUOTATION MARKS OMITTED

11.40   *Epigraphs.* Quotation marks are not used around epigraphs (quotations used as ornaments preceding a text rather than as illustration or documentation). Though sometimes set as block quotations, epigraphs usually receive distinctive typographic treatment. The first example below by no means suggests that all poetry epigraphs should be set italic. Treatment of sources varies also. For more on sources, see 11.72, 11.83. See also 1.38–39.

> *Oh, what a tangled web we weave,*
> *When first we practice to deceive!*
> —Sir Walter Scott

> It is a truth universally acknowledged, that a single man in possession of a good fortune must be in want of a wife.
> Jane Austen, *Pride and Prejudice*

11.41   *Decorative initials ("drop caps" and raised initials).* When the first word of a chapter or section opens with a large raised or dropped initial letter, and the first words of the chapter or section consist of a run-in quotation, the opening quotation mark is traditionally omitted. The absence of what would be an oversize (and often ugly) mark is unlikely to confuse readers. If there is any danger of confusion, the opening quotation mark may be set in regular text size.

O F THE MAKING OF MANY BOOKS there is no end," declared an ancient Hebrew sage, who had himself magnificently aggravated the situation he was decrying.

11.42   *Maxims, questions, and the like.* Maxims, mottoes, rules, and other familiar expressions, sometimes enclosed in quotation marks, are discussed in 6.54 and 8.210. Questions that do not require quotation marks are discussed in 6.55 and 6.71.

SPEECH, DIALOGUE, AND CONVERSATION

11.43   *Direct discourse.* Direct discourse or dialogue is traditionally enclosed in quotation marks. A change in speaker is usually indicated by a new paragraph, as in the following excerpt from *Huckleberry Finn*. If one speech occupies more than a paragraph, the rule for repeating opening quotation marks at the beginning of succeeding paragraphs applies (see 11.36).

> "Ransomed? What's that?"
>
> "I don't know. But that's what they do. I've seen it in books; and so of course that's what we've got to do."
>
> "But how can we do it if we don't know what it is?"
>
> "Why, blame it all, we've got to do it. Don't I tell you it's in the books? Do you want to go to doing different from what's in the books, and get things all muddled up?"

Paragraphing does not have to depend on a change of speaker. Different speeches may sometimes be run into a single paragraph (thus saving space), as in this excerpt from Anthony Yu's translation of *Journey to the West.*

> The king lighted incense in the hall, and the various officials bowed down before the steps. "It was most kind of you to show us your precious forms," said the king. "Please go back, and we shall say a special mass another day to thank you." "All of you deities may now retire," said Pilgrim, "for the king has promised to thank you with a special mass on another day." The Dragon Kings returned to the oceans, while the other deities all went back to Heaven.

11.44   *Single-word speech.* Words such as *yes, no, where, how,* and *why,* when used singly, are not enclosed in quotation marks except in direct discourse. See also 6.73.

> Ezra always answered yes; he could never say no to a friend.
> Please stop asking why.

but
"Yes," he replied weakly.
Again she repeated, "Why?"

11.45 *Faltering or interrupted speech.* Ellipsis points may be used to suggest faltering or fragmented speech accompanied by confusion or insecurity. In the examples below, note the relative positions of the ellipsis points and other punctuation. (For ellipsis points used to represent omitted text, see 11.51–65.)

"I . . . I . . . that is, we . . . yes, *we* have made an awful blunder!"
"The ship . . . oh my God! . . . it's sinking!" cried Henrietta.
"But . . . but . . . ," said Tom.

Interruptions or abrupt changes in thought are usually indicated by em dashes. See 6.90.

11.46 *Alternatives to quotation marks.* In presenting dialogue, continental Europeans often use em dashes. For examples, see 10.34, 10.53, 10.78, 10.120. For guillemets (« »), see 10.32.

11.47 *Unspoken discourse.* Thought, imagined dialogue, and other interior discourse may be enclosed in quotation marks or not, according to the context or the writer's preference.

"I don't care if we have offended Morgenstern," thought Vera. "Besides," she told herself, "they're all fools."

Why, we wondered, did we choose this route?

The following passage from James Joyce's *Ulysses* illustrates interior monologue and stream of consciousness without need of quotation marks.

Reading two pages apiece of seven books every night, eh? I was young. You bowed to yourself in the mirror, stepping forward to applause earnestly, striking face. Hurray for the God-damned idiot! Hray! No-one saw: tell no-one. Books you were going to write with letters for titles. Have you read his F?

11.48 *Indirect discourse.* Indirect discourse, which paraphrases dialogue, takes no quotation marks.

Tom told Huck they had to do it that way because the books said so.
Very well, you say, but is there no choice?

DRAMA, DISCUSSION, AND INTERVIEWS

11.49 *Drama.* The speaker's name is usually set in a font distinct from the dialogue—caps and small caps, for example, or all small caps. The dialogue is not enclosed in quotation marks and is usually set in flush-and-hang style, or hanging indention (the style most often used in bibliographies and indexes and illustrated in the following examples).

> R. ROISTER DOISTER. Except I have her to my wife, I shall run mad.
> M. MERYGREEKE. Nay, "unwise" perhaps, but I warrant you for "mad."

Stage directions are usually italicized.

> HECTOR, *breaking loose.* Wait a minute! It's freezing over here!
> EMMA. Here, take my coat. (*She envelops him in her fur.*) There!
>   Now please, it's getting late.

11.50 *Discussion and interviews.* The transcription of a discussion or an interview is treated in much the same way as drama (see 11.49). The speaker's name is often followed by a colon, and interjections such as "laughter" are italicized and enclosed in brackets. Paragraph indention is usually preferred to flush-and-hang style, to avoid the appearance of an excerpt from a drama and also because respondents' comments may be lengthy. Flush-and-hang style, however, which allows easier identification of the speaker, may work better if many speakers' names appear and the comments are relatively brief.

> INTERVIEWER: You weren't thinking that this technology would be something you could use to connect to the Office of Tibet in New York or to different Tibet support groups in Europe?
> RESPONDENT: No. Nobody seemed to have anything to do with GreenNet in the Tibet world at that time. That came much later. That's not really right. I specifically wasn't interested in connecting to the community of Tibet martyrs and fellow sufferers [*laughs*] and the emotional pathological there-but-for-the-grace-of-god-go-I people.

Ellipses

11.51 *Definition and form.* An *ellipsis*—the omission of a word, phrase, line, paragraph, or more from a quoted passage—is indicated by ellipsis points (or dots), not by asterisks. Ellipsis points are three spaced periods (. . .), sometimes preceded or followed by other punctuation. They must always appear together on the same line, but any preceding punctuation may appear at the end of the line above (see also 11.64).

11.52 *Three methods.* Three methods of using ellipsis points are described here: the three-dot method (11.55–56); the three-or-four-dot method (11.57–61); and a refinement of the latter, here called the rigorous method (11.62–65). The choice between the three is usually made by the author, sometimes by the editor. The three-dot method is presented first only because it is the simplest. The second, which requires more care, is preferred by many authors and editors. The third allows maximum fidelity to the original material. Elements from each can be combined to suit the needs of a particular work or the preference of an author, as long as a consistent pattern is maintained throughout the work. For a European practice sometimes adopted by English-speaking scholars, see 10.36. For capitalizing or lowercasing initial letters, see 11.15–19.

11.53 *Danger of skewing meaning.* More important than the number of ellipsis points used is the duty not to misrepresent the original. Part of one sentence or paragraph may be syntactically joined to part of another yet result in a statement alien to the material quoted. Accuracy of sense and emphasis must accompany accuracy of transcription.

11.54 *When not to use ellipsis points.* Ellipsis points are normally *not* used (1) before the first word of a quotation, even if the beginning of the original sentence has been omitted; or (2) after the last word of a quotation, even if the end of the original sentence has been omitted, unless the sentence as quoted is deliberately incomplete (see 11.59). For exceptions, see 11.65.

THE THREE-DOT METHOD

11.55 *The method explained.* The three-dot method is appropriate for most general works and many scholarly ones. No more than three points are used, whether the omission occurs in the middle of a sentence or between sentences. Where necessary for fidelity to the original and ease of reading, these three may be preceded or followed—depending on where the omission occurs—by a comma, a colon, a semicolon, a question mark, or an exclamation point.

> To address the insulated understanding is to lay aside the Prospero's robe of poetry . . . If the true purpose of a man's writing a didactic poem were to teach, by what suggestion of idiocy should he choose to begin by putting on fetters? . . . Now this collision between two purposes . . . shows by the uniformity of its solution, which of the two is the true purpose, and which the merely ostensible purpose.

> The lightning flashes through my skull; mine eye-balls ache and ache; . . . my whole beaten brain seems as beheaded . . . Oh, thou foundling fire, . . . thou too hast thy incommunicable riddle, thy unparticipated grief.

> It is not, gentlemen, that from the time I commenced this case until I shall speak my last word I ever had one single moment of doubt about the verdict of this jury . . . ; for I do not believe . . . that anywhere on the face of the earth a jury could be found today that would send men to jail for the crime of loving their fellow-men.

The first word after ellipsis points is capitalized if it begins a grammatically complete sentence, even if it was lowercased in the original. But see also 11.63.

11.56 *Paragraphs or beginnings of paragraphs omitted.* In the three-dot method, the omission of one or more paragraphs within a quotation is indicated by three ellipsis points at the end of the paragraph preceding the omitted part. If the first part of a paragraph is omitted within a quotation, a paragraph indention and three ellipsis points appear before the first quoted word (as before the third paragraph of the example in 11.60).

THE THREE-OR-FOUR-DOT METHOD

11.57 *The method explained.* The three-or-four-dot method is appropriate for poetry and most scholarly works other than legal writings or textual commentary (see 11.62). Three dots indicate an omission within a quoted sentence. Four mark the omission of one or more sentences (but see 11.58). When three are used, space occurs both before the first dot and after the final dot. When four are used, the first dot is a true period—that is, there is no space between it and the preceding word. What precedes and, normally, what follows the four dots should be grammatically complete sentences as quoted, even if part of either sentence has been omitted. A complete passage from Emerson's essay "Politics" reads:

> The spirit of our American radicalism is destructive and aimless: it is not loving, it has no ulterior and divine ends; but is destructive only out of hatred and selfishness. On the other side, the conservative party, composed of the most moderate, able, and cultivated part of the population, is timid, and merely defensive of property. It vindicates no right, it aspires to no real good, it brands no crime, it proposes no generous policy, it does not build, nor write, nor cherish the arts, nor foster religion, nor establish schools, nor encourage science, nor emancipate the slave, nor befriend the poor, or the Indian, or the immigrant. From neither party, when in power, has the world any benefit to expect in science, art, or humanity, at all commensurate with the resources of the nation.

The passage might be shortened as follows:

> The spirit of our American radicalism is destructive and aimless. . . . On the other side, the conservative party . . . is timid, and merely defensive of property. . . . It does not build, nor write, nor cherish the arts, nor foster religion, nor establish schools.

Note that the first word after an ellipsis is capitalized if it begins a new grammatical sentence. Compare 11.63.

11.58 *The three-or-four-dot method with other punctuation.* Other punctuation—a comma, a colon, a semicolon, a question mark, or an exclamation point—may precede or follow three (but never four) ellipsis points. Placement of the other punctuation depends on whether the omission precedes or follows the mark. See also 11.55.

> It does not build, . . . nor cherish the arts, nor foster religion.

> As to *Endymion*, was it a poem to be treated contemptuously by those who had celebrated, with various degrees of complacency and panegyric, *Paris*, and *Woman*, and a *Syrian Tale* . . . ? Are these the men who . . .

11.59 *Deliberately incomplete sentence.* Three dots are used at the end of a quoted sentence that is deliberately left grammatically incomplete (as in the last sentence in the example above).

> Everyone knows that the Declaration of Independence begins with the sentence "When, in the course of human events . . ." But how many people can recite more than the first few lines of the document?

> Please look at the example beginning "The spirit of our American radicalism . . ." and tell me how you would shorten it.

11.60 *Whole or partial paragraphs omitted.* The omission of one or more paragraphs within a quotation is indicated by four ellipsis points at the end of the paragraph preceding the omitted part. (If that paragraph ends with an incomplete sentence, only three points are used; see 11.59.) If the first part of a paragraph is omitted within a quotation, a paragraph indention and three ellipsis points appear before the first quoted word. It is thus possible to use ellipsis points both at the end of one paragraph and at the beginning of the next, as illustrated in the following excerpt from Alexander Pope's "Letter to a Noble Lord."

Missing

I should indeed be obliged to lessen this respect, if all the nobility . . . are but so many hereditary fools, if the privilege of lords be to want brains, if noblemen can hardly write or read. . . .

Were it the mere excess of your Lordship's wit, that carried you thus triumphantly over all the bounds of decency, I might consider your Lordship on your Pegasus, as a sprightly hunter on a mettled horse. . . .

. . . Unrivalled as you are, in making a figure, and in making a speech, methinks, my Lord, may you well give up the poor talent of making a distich.

11.61 *Ellipsis points in poetry.* Omission of the end of a line of poetry is indicated by four ellipsis points if what precedes them is a complete grammatical sentence, otherwise by three. The omission of a full line or of several consecutive lines within a quoted poem is indicated by one line of widely spaced dots (see second example) approximately the length of the line above (or of the missing line, if that is determinable). See also 11.28–32, 11.38.

> The shadows of his fellows ring him round
> In the high night. . . .
>   (Wallace Stevens, "Dutch Graves")

> She would dwell on such dead themes, not as one who remembers,
>   But rather as one who sees.
> . . . .
> Past things retold were to her as things existent,
>   Things present but as a tale
>   (Thomas Hardy, "One We Knew")

THE RIGOROUS METHOD

11.62 *Legal works and such.* In legal works, textual commentary, and other works that require frequent reference to the quoted material, the three-or-four-dot method (see 11.57–61) should be followed, with the refinements noted in the following three paragraphs (11.63–65).

11.63 *Capitalization.* In the rigorous method, any change in capitalization of the original must be indicated by bracketing the letter concerned, whether in a run-in or a block quotation. For the original from which the following excerpt is drawn, see 11.57. See also 11.19.

> [T]he conservative party . . . is timid, and merely defensive of property. . . . [I]t does not build, nor write, nor cherish the arts, nor foster religion, nor establish schools.

Outside the law, some writers or editors prefer to retain the original case of all letters, letting ellipsis points do the work (". . . the conservative party is . . . merely defensive of property. . . . it does not . . ."). But brackets, though unlovely, usually make for easier reading.

11.64 *Placement of first dot.* Where the last part of a quoted sentence is omitted, the rigorous method logically requires a space before the first dot; the last rather than the first dot thus serves as the true period. For the original from which the following excerpt is drawn, see 11.57.

> The spirit of our American radicalism is destructive and aimless . . . . On the other side, the conservative party . . . is timid, and merely defensive of property. . . . It does not build, nor write, nor cherish the arts, nor foster religion, nor establish schools.

Where space is needed before the first of four dots, all four must appear on the same line. Where the first dot is closed up with the preceding text, the following three may appear on the next line.

11.65 *Ellipsis points at beginning and end of quotations.* Unlike the three-dot and the three-and-four-dot methods (see 11.54), the rigorous method sometimes requires ellipsis points at the beginning or end of a quotation (see 11.63). Should a quotation begin with a capitalized word (such as a proper name) that did not appear at the beginning of a sentence in the original, three ellipsis points must be used. Should the last part of the last sentence quoted be omitted, four dots—all spaced, including the first—will alert readers to that omission.

> . . . Dimitrov and Manouilski were at his bidding; Litvinov served this function in the Ministry of Foreign Affairs.

> It vindicates no right, it aspires to no real good, it brands no crime, it proposes no generous policy, it does not build, nor write, nor cherish the arts, nor foster religion . . . .

MISSING OR ILLEGIBLE WORDS

11.66 *Ellipsis points and brackets.* In reproducing a document in which certain words are missing or illegible, an author may use ellipsis points (see above), a bracketed comment or guess (sometimes followed by a question mark), or both. For brackets, see 6.104. See also 11.68.

> If you will assure me of your . . . [illegible], I shall dedicate my life to your endeavor.
> She marched out of the door, headed for the [president's?] office.

11.67 *Brackets and 2-em dashes.* A 2-em dash (see 6.95), sometimes in combination with an interpolated guess (see 11.66), may also be used for missing material.

> I have great marvel that ye will so soon incline to every man his device and [counsel and ——] specially in matters of small impor[tance ——] yea, and as [it is] reported [unto me——] causes as meseemeth th[a——] nothing to [——]ne gentlewomen.

Whatever device is chosen should be explained (in the prefatory material or a note) and used consistently.

INTERPOLATIONS

11.68 *Use of brackets.* Insertions may be made in quoted material to clarify an ambiguity, to provide a missing word or letters, or, in a translation, to give the original word or phrase where the English fails to convey the exact sense. Such interpolations, which should be kept to a minimum lest they irritate or distract readers, are enclosed in brackets (not parentheses). See also 6.104, 11.14 (third example), 11.66–67.

> Marcellus, doubtless in anxious suspense, asks Barnardo, "What, has this thing [the ghost of Hamlet's father] appear'd again tonight?"

> "Well," said she, "if Mr. L[owell] won't go, then neither will I."

11.69 *Use of "sic."* Literally meaning "so," "thus," "in this manner" and traditionally set in italics, *sic* may be inserted in brackets following a word misspelled or wrongly used in the original. This device should be used only where it is relevant to call attention to such matters or where paraphrase or silent correction is inappropriate (see 11.4, 11.8[5]). *Sic* would be permissible in the following quoted sentence from Thoreau's *Walden* because readers might think *cronching* is a misprint for *crunching*:

> Or on a Sunday afternoon. if I chanced to be at home, I heard the cronching [sic] of the snow made by the step of a long-headed farmer, who from far through the woods sought my house, to have a social "crack."

Where material with many errors and variant spellings (such as a collection of informal letters) is reproduced as written, a prefatory comment or a note to that effect will make a succession of *sics* unnecessary.

11.70 *Italics added.* An author wishing to call particular attention to a word or phrase in quoted material may italicize it but must tell readers what has been done, by means of such formulas as "italics mine," "italics added," "emphasis added," or "emphasis mine." This information appears either in parentheses following the quotation or in a source note to the quotation. If there are italics in the original of the passage quoted, the information is best enclosed in brackets and placed directly after the added italics. Consistency in usage throughout a work is essential.

> You have watched the conduct of Ireland in the difficult circumstances of the last nine months, and that conduct I do not hesitate to risk saying on your behalf has evoked in every breast a responsive voice of sympathy, and an increased conviction that we may deal freely *and yet deal prudently* with our fellow-subjects beyond the Channel. Such is your conviction. (William Ewart Gladstone, October 1891; italics added)

> In reality not one didactic poet has ever yet attempted to use any parts or processes of the particular art which he made his theme, unless in so far as they seemed susceptible of poetic treatment, and only *because* they seemed so. Look at the poem of *Cyder* by Philips, of the *Fleece* by Dyer, or (which is a still weightier example) at the *Georgics* of Virgil,—does any of these poets show the least anxiety for the *correctness of your principles* [my italics], or the delicacy of your manipulations, in the worshipful arts they affect to teach? (Thomas De Quincey, "Essay on Pope")

Occasionally it may be important to point out that italics in a quotation were indeed in the original. Here the usual phrase is "italics in the original" or, for example, "De Quincey's italics."

11.71 *Interpolations requiring quotation marks.* Occasionally a bracketed interpolation that includes quotation marks appears in material already enclosed in quotation marks. In such cases, the double/single rule (see 11.33) does not apply; the quotation marks within the brackets may remain double.

> "Do you mean that a double-headed calf ["two-headed calf" in an earlier version] has greater value than two normal calves? That a freak of nature, even though it cannot survive, is to be more highly treasured for its rarity than run-of-the mill creatures are for their potential use?"

Citing Sources in Text

11.72 *Placement of a citation.* Although the source of a direct quotation is usually given in a note, it may sometimes appear parenthetically in the text, especially in a work containing no notes or bibliography and only a few quoted passages. Although the source normally follows a quotation, it may come earlier if it fits more smoothly into the introductory text (as in the second example in 11.73). The following paragraphs focus on sources in general or humanistic works.

11.73 *Full source given.* An entire source may be given in parentheses immediately following a quotation, or some of the data may be worked into the text, with details confined to parentheses.

"If an astronaut falls into a black hole, its mass will increase, but eventually the energy equivalent of that extra mass will be returned to the universe in the form of radiation. Thus, in a sense, the astronaut will be 'recycled'" (Stephen W. Hawking, *A Brief History of Time: From the Big Bang to Black Holes* [New York: Bantam Books, 1988], 112).

In the preface to their revision of *The Complete Plain Words* by Sir Ernest Gowers (Penguin Books, 1986), Sidney Greenbaum and Janet Whitcut admit that "Gowers' frequent use of the first person pronoun 'I' presents a difficulty for revisers," since Fraser, having decided to retain the "I," tried "to distinguish the 'I' of Gowers from the 'I' of Fraser by listing in his preface the parts of the book that were wholly or mainly written by each of the authors."

11.74 *Ibid.* If a second passage from the same source is quoted close to the first and there is no intervening quotation from a different source, "ibid." (set in roman) may be used in the second parenthetical reference (e.g., "ibid., 114"). If a quotation from another source has intervened, a shortened reference may be given (e.g., "Hawking, *Brief History of Time*, 114").

11.75 *Parenthetical citations supplementing annotation.* In a work containing notes, the full citation of a source may be given in a note at first mention. The note may include such wording as "hereafter cited in text." Subsequent quotations from that source can use a shortened reference (e.g., "Hawking, 114").

11.76 *Frequent reference to a single source.* The method described in 11.75 works well in literary studies that use frequent quotations from a single source. In a study of *Much Ado about Nothing*, for example, the note would list the edition and include wording such as "Text references are to act, scene, and line of this edition." A parenthetical reference to act 2, scene 4, lines 46–47, would then appear as in the example below. ("Ibid." is not used in such references.)

"Ye light o' love with your heels! then, if your husband have stables enough, you'll see he shall lack no barns," says Beatrice (2.4.46–47).

Line numbers can be omitted when reference is, for example, to part, chapter, and section, or to canto and stanza. In references to a work of fiction, page numbers alone may be given.

11.77   *Abbreviations.* Where a number of such sources are used in the same work, it is well to devise an abbreviation for each and to include a list of the abbreviations at the beginning or end of the work (see 16.40). The reference at the end of the example in 11.76 might then read *Much Ado* 3.4.46–47 (or, perhaps, *MAN* 3.4.46–47).

11.78   *Different editions.* If more than one edition of the same work has been cited, each text reference must mention the edition quoted.

(*Canterbury Tales*, ed. Furnivall, 49)

SOURCES FOLLOWING RUN-IN QUOTATIONS

11.79   *No period preceding source.* After a run-in quotation, the source is usually given after the closing quotation mark, followed by the rest of the surrounding sentence or the final punctuation of that sentence.

With his "Nothing will come of nothing; speak again" (1.1.92), Lear tries to draw from his youngest daughter an expression of filial devotion.

It has been three-quarters of a century since Henry Adams said: "Fifty years ago, science took for granted that the rate of acceleration could not last. The world forgets quickly, but even today the habit remains of founding statistics on the faith that consumption will continue nearly stationary" (*Education*, 493).

A parenthetical reference need not immediately follow the quotation as long as it is clear what it belongs to. For an example, see 11.76.

11.80   *Question mark or exclamation point.* When a quotation comes at the end of a sentence and is itself a question or an exclamation, that punctuation is retained within the quotation marks, and a period is still added after the closing parentheses.

And finally, in the frenzy of grief that kills him, Lear rails, "Why should a dog, a horse, a rat, have life, / And thou no breath at all?" (5.3.306).

SOURCES FOLLOWING BLOCK QUOTATIONS

11.81   *Placement and punctuation.* The source of a block quotation is given in parentheses at the end of the quotation and in the same type size. The opening parenthesis appears *after* the final punctuation mark of the quoted material. No period either precedes or follows the closing parenthesis.

> If you happen to be fishing, and you get a strike, and whatever it is starts off with the preliminaries of a vigorous fight; and by and by, looking down over the side through the glassy water, you see a rosy golden gleam, the mere specter of a fish, shining below in the clear depths; and when you look again a sort of glory of golden light flashes and dazzles as it circles nearer beneath and around and under the boat; . . . and you land a slim and graceful and impossibly beautiful three-foot goldfish, whose fierce and vivid yellow is touched around the edges with a violent red—when all these things happen to you, fortunate but bewildered fisherman, then you may know you have been fishing in the Galapagos Islands and have taken a Golden Grouper. (Gifford Pinchot, *To the South Seas* [Philadelphia: John Winston, 1930], 123)

11.82   *Shortened references.* Shortened references are treated in the same way as full ones. *Line, vol.,* and so on, lowercased after run-in quotations, are capitalized after block quotations. If the abbreviation *p.* for page is required, it may be lowercased for visual reasons, defying logic, though a capital *P.* is an acceptable alternative. If the page number alone is clear to readers, so much the better, as long as consistency is preserved.

> Then the fish swam straight below the boat, back and forth and back again, and that was worse then ever, for the pull was straight up and down. But still the rod, like the fish, held on.
>
> At last the fish came into sight—at first a mere gleam in the water, and then his full side. This was not even a distant cousin to the fish I thought I was fighting, but something else again entirely. (p. 142)

11.83   *Poetry.* Citations following poetry quotations are dropped to the line below the last line of the quotation. They may be centered on the last letter of the longest line of the quotation (as in the first example below) or set flush with the right margin (as in the first example in 11.40). Other locations are also possible, as long as consistency and clarity are preserved.

> Now more than ever seems it rich to die,
> To cease upon the midnight with no pain,
> While thou art pouring forth thy soul abroad
>   In such an ecstasy
>   (Keats, "Ode to a Nightingale," stanza 6)

11.84   *Shortened references.* Shortened references to poetry are treated the same way as full ones. A quotation from Edmund Spenser's *The Faerie Queene,* once the reader knows that reference is to book, canto, and stanza, might appear thus:

Who will not mercie unto others shew,
How can he mercy ever hope to have?
(6.1.42)

Foreign-Language Quotations

11.85 *Typographic style.* Quotations in a foreign language that are incorporated into an English text are normally treated like quotations in English, set in roman type and run in or set off as block quotations according to their length. They are punctuated as in the original except that quotation marks replace guillemets (or their equivalents) and ellipsis points are spaced. For isolated words and phrases, see 7.51. For excerpts from the original language following an English translation, see 11.87.

"Wo weilst du, weilst du denn, mein milder Schein?" asked Droste-Hülshoff, waiting for the moon.

If em dashes are used in the original (see 10.34), they should be retained in a block quotation but may be replaced by quotation marks if only a phrase or sentence is quoted.

11.86 *Whether translation is needed.* Whether to provide translations of quoted passages depends on the linguistic abilities of the likely readers. For example, in a work to be read by classicists, Latin or Greek sources may be quoted freely in the original. Or in a literary study of, say, Goethe, quotations from Goethe's work may be given in the original German only. For a wider readership, translations should probably be furnished. See also 6.99, 7.52.

11.87 *Where to place translations.* A translation may follow the original—or, as in the third example, the original may follow a translation—in parentheses if following a run-in quotation or (usually) in brackets if following a block quotation. No quotation marks are needed other than those required internally. If a long sentence or more than one sentence appears in parentheses or brackets, as in the second example (a block quotation) and the third (which includes a run-in quotation), closing punctuation of both the original and the translation should remain distinct.

A line from Goethe, "Wer nie sein Brot mit Tränen aß" (Who never ate his bread with tears), comes to mind.

À vrai dire, Abélard n'avoue pas un tel rationalisme: "je ne veux pas être si philosophe, écrit-il, que je résiste à Paul, ni si aristotélicien que je me sépare du Christ."
[As a matter of fact, Abelard admits no such rationalism. "I do not wish to be so much of a philosopher," he writes, "that I resist Paul, nor so much of an Aristotelian that I separate myself from Christ."]

When both a source and a translation are required in text, the source may be enclosed in parentheses and the translation in brackets (as in the following example, quoting a thirteenth-century author writing in Middle Dutch). For punctuation following the source, see 11.79.

Hadewijch insists that the most perfect faith is "unfaith," which endlessly stokes desire and endlessly demands love from God. "Unfaith never allows desire to rest in any faith but always distrusts her, [feeling] that she is not loved enough" (letter 8:39). [Ende ontrowe en laet gegherten niewers ghedueren in gheenre trowen, sine mestrout hare altoes, datse niet ghenoech ghemint en es.]

If adding a translation or the original in text creates too much clutter, it may be placed in a note, in which case it is enclosed in quotation marks but not in parentheses or brackets.

11.88 *Quoting in translation.* In many works, quotations from a foreign-language source need appear only in translation. Should the original be necessary, it can be placed in a note. If the bracketed passage in the second example in 11.87 were to appear in text unbracketed, without the French, as either a run-in or a block quotation, a note could read as follows:

> 4. "À vrai dire, Abélard n'avoue pas un tel rationalisme: 'je ne veux pas être si philosophe, écrit-il, que je résiste à Paul, ni si aristotélicien que je me sépare du Christ.'"

11.89 *Crediting the translation.* When quoting a passage from a foreign language that requires a translation, authors should use a published English translation if one is available and give credit to the source of that translation, including the title of the translation, the translator's name, relevant bibliographic details, and page number (see 17.66). Authors providing their own translations should so state, in parentheses following the translation, in a note, or in the prefatory material—for example, "My translation" or "Unless otherwise noted, all translations are my own."

11.90 *Adjusting translations.* An author using a published translation may occasionally need to adjust a word or two. "Translation modified" or some such wording must then be added in brackets or in a note. This device should be used very sparingly. If a published translation is unsuitable for the author's purpose, it should be abandoned and all quoted passages should be newly translated.

11.91 *Editing a translation.* Published translations can be copyedited only with respect to the permissible changes described in 11.8. In new translations furnished by the author, however, capitalization, punctuation, spelling, and idiom may be adjusted for consistency with the surrounding text.

11.92 *The sin of retranslation.* Never should a passage from a work originally published in English (or any other language, for that matter) be retranslated from a foreign-language version. For example, in quoting from a German study of Blackstone's Commentaries that quotes from Blackstone in German, the author must track down the original passages and reproduce them. If unable to locate the original, one must resort to paraphrase.

11.93 *Titles in translation.* For citing titles in English translation, see 10.6–7.

12

Illustrations and Captions

Introduction

12.1   *Range of examples.* This chapter offers guidelines on preparation, placement, numbering, and captioning of illustrations in published works and presents some examples, all drawn from University of Chicago Press journals and books. The examples show different typographic and editorial treatment, reflecting various journal styles and book design decisions. Since the way illustrations are prepared by authors and handled by publishers is changing rapidly, authors who wish to include illustrations in their works should consult their publishers early in the game. For definitions of many of the terms used throughout this chapter, see the list of key terms in appendix A. For general guidelines on the preparation of electronic files containing illustrations, see 12.25–27. For checking illustrations in proofs, see 3.10, 3.40–41. See also 2.30, 2.33–35.

Definitions

12.2 *Artwork.* Artwork, or simply *art*, is the term used by publishers, type-setters, and printers for illustrative material prepared for reproduction, whether in the form of photographs, laser prints, electronic files, or other media. A questionnaire, for example, if reproduced photographically rather than typeset, would be considered artwork. Special characters not readily available in the typeface used for the text, such as a line of Sanskrit, may be treated as artwork.

12.3 *Illustrations, figures, charts.* The terms *illustration* and *figure*, virtually interchangeable, refer to a variety of materials including (among other things) paintings, photographs, line drawings, maps, charts, videos, animations, and musical examples furnished as line art (see 12.5). The term *chart*, as used in this chapter, refers to graphs, diagrams, flow charts, bar charts, and the like. Charts are not to be confused with tables, which, though a kind of illustration, are handled rather differently and are dealt with in chapter 13. Some criteria for an effective chart are offered in 12.56–61.

12.4 *Continuous tone versus halftones.* Continuous-tone art is any image that contains gradations of shading, such as a painting or a photograph, that can be duplicated in offset printing only by the creation of a halftone reproduction (see fig. 12.1). A halftone breaks the image into patterns of dots that vary in size, creating the illusion of continuous tone. For black-and-white halftone reproduction, authors should submit glossy prints of original art. For illustrations to be reproduced in color, which involves a four-color process, color transparencies are usually required. For submitting art in an electronic file, see 12.26.

12.5 *Line art.* Artwork containing only black and white, with no shading—such as a pen-and-ink drawing, a graph, or a bar chart—is known as line art (or,

The World's Columbian Exposition of 1893. Planning for the Exposition was coordinated by Daniel H. Burnham. (Detail of a photo by C. D. Arnold, courtesy of the Chicago Historical Society; ICHi–02520.)

Fig. 12.1. A halftone.

less commonly, line copy). Publishers can reproduce computer-generated line art, if properly prepared, directly from an author's disk; all authors, however, should first obtain guidelines from the publisher. For avoidance of shading, see 12.30. See figures 12.2 and 12.3.

12.6   *Text figures and plates.* In printed works, illustrations—whether halftones or line art—that are interspersed in the text (as are the illustrations in this chapter) are known as text figures. The term *plate*, strictly speaking, is a

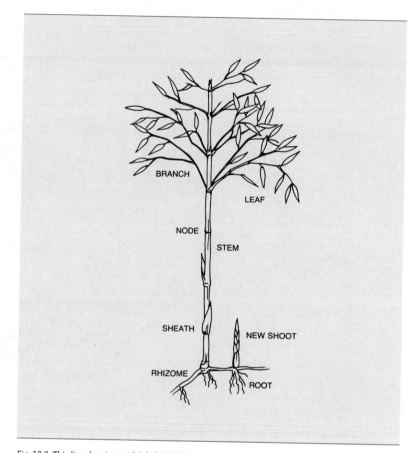

Fig. 12.2. This line drawing, with labels, appears without a caption in the original. The surrounding text clearly identifies the plant as a *Sinarundinaria* stem. Other illustrations in the same book are numbered as "figures" (graphs, maps, and the like) and "plates" (photographs).

full-page illustration that is printed separately, typically on coated paper; plates can appear individually between certain pages of text but are more often gathered into *galleries*. (In a work that contains both photographs and line art, *plate* is sometimes used—a little loosely—for the former and *figure* for the latter. See fig. 1.9.)

12.7   *Galleries.* A gallery is a section of a printed work devoted to illustrations— usually halftones. It can consist of four, eight, twelve, or more pages (for purposes of printing and binding, always a number that can be divided by four). If printed on stock different from that used for the text, a gallery is not paginated; for example, an eight-page gallery could appear between

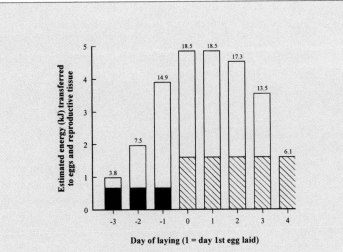

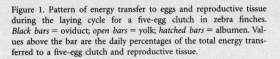

Figure 1. Pattern of energy transfer to eggs and reproductive tissue during the laying cycle for a five-egg clutch in zebra finches. *Black bars* = oviduct; *open bars* = yolk; *hatched bars* = albumen. Values above the bar are the daily percentages of the total energy transferred to a five-egg clutch and reproductive tissue.

Fig. 12.3. A bar chart (also called a bar graph).

pages 134 and 135. If the gallery is printed along with the text, on the same paper, its pages may be included in the numbering, even if the numbers do not actually appear (see 1.45). A gallery always begins on a recto (a right-hand page).

12.8   *Captions, legends, and keys.* The terms *caption* and *legend* are sometimes used interchangeably for the explanatory material that appears immediately below an illustration, or sometimes above it or to the side. A caption (as used in this chapter) is not necessarily a full sentence but can consist of two or more sentences or of a title followed by one or more full sentences. A key (also sometimes called a legend) appears within the illustration itself and not as part of the caption; it identifies the symbols used in a map or a chart. (Previous editions of this manual defined a caption as a title or headline that is never a grammatical sentence, and a legend as an explanation consisting of one or more sentences immediately following the caption. That distinction is rarely made nowadays.) For more on captions, see 12.31–51.

12.9   *Labels.* Labels are the descriptive terms that appear within an illustration (e.g., "branch," "leaf," etc., in fig. 12.2 and "Estimated energy . . ." and "Day of laying . . ." in fig. 12.3). They may also be symbols (often letters) used to indicate an illustration's parts (e.g., "A," "B," and "C" in fig. 12.6). For more on labels, see 12.60.

Placement and Numbering

12.10   *Placement.* In a printed work, an illustration should appear as soon as possible after the first text reference to it (unless in a gallery; see 12.7, 12.16). It may precede the reference only if it appears on the same page or same two-page spread as the reference or if the text is too short to permit placing all figures and tables after their references. If illustrations are interspersed in the text, the author or (if the author has not done so) the editor must indicate *in the manuscript* approximately where each is to appear—in other words, provide callouts (see 2.30, 2.33). Note that a callout (e.g., "fig. 5 about here") is an instruction for typesetting or production; it is not the same as a text reference (see 12.11), which is addressed to readers. In the printed version, most illustrations will appear at either the top or the bottom of a page. No callouts are needed for illustrations that appear in a gallery. In an electronic work, a callout may take the form of markup that surrounds text references to an illustration. It may contain information that is used to enable a hypertext link between the text reference and the illustration.

12.11   *Text references and numbering.* If there are more than a handful of illustrations in a printed work (or any at all in an online work), they normally bear numbers (but see 12.15), and all text references to them should be by the numbers: "as figure 1 shows, . . ." "compare figures 4 and 5." If the work will be published in print and electronic versions that will vary in the number of figures included, the text references and numbering may have to be adjusted for each version. In some cases it may be preferable not to number the figures at all but to refer to them by title or description, as long as, in the electronic version, the text references can be linked gracefully to the figures. But an illustration should never be referred to in the text as "the photograph opposite" or "the graph on this page," for such placement may not be possible when print pages are made up and is likely to be erroneous in an electronic version (see 12.35). In text, the word *figure* is typically set roman, lowercased, and spelled out except in parenthetical references ("fig. 10"). *Plate,* however, should not be abbreviated to *pl.* unless saving space is crucial. For various treatments of these terms in the captions (roman, boldface, small caps, abbreviated or spelled out), see 12.34 and the illustrations in this chapter.

12.12 *Continuous versus separate numbering.* Halftones, charts, maps, and the like—in other words, all illustrations—may be numbered in one continuous sequence throughout a work. Maps are sometimes numbered separately if that is more convenient for readers. And in a work published in both print and electronic versions, illustrations that appear only in the electronic or the print version must be numbered separately so that numbering in each version is logical and sequential. For double numeration, see 12.13. For illustrations in a gallery, see 12.7, 12.16.

12.13 *Double numeration.* In scientific and technical books, heavily illustrated books, and books with chapters by different authors double numeration may be employed. Each illustration carries the number of the chapter followed by the illustration number, usually separated by a period. Thus, for example, figure 9.6 is the sixth figure in chapter 9. Should a chapter contain only one illustration, a double number would still be used (e.g., figure 10.1). Appendix figures may be numbered A.1, A.2, and so on or, if there are several appendixes and each bears a letter, A.1, A.2, B.1, B.2, and so on. At the editing stage, double numeration makes it easier to handle multiple illustrations and, should any be added or removed, involves far less renumbering. It also makes it easier for readers to find a particular illustration. This manual uses double numeration for illustrations as well as for text paragraphs. See also 1.76.

12.14 *Numerals and letters.* Chicago recommends the use of arabic numerals for illustrations of all kinds: "figure 12," "fig. 10.7." Where a figure consists of several parts, the parts may carry letters (A, B, C, etc.); a single caption, keying the letters to the parts, suffices (see figs. 12.4, 12.6). Text references may then refer, for example, to "fig. 10.7C"—or, if lowercase letters are used, "10.7c." Parts may also be described according to their relative positions on a printed page (see 12.36); the relative positions must be maintained in an electronic version if the same description is to be used. (In the highly undesirable event that a figure has to be added at a late stage, when it is no longer feasible to renumber all the other figures, "fig. 10.7A" might refer to a figure inserted between figures 10.7 and 10.8. In that case, the editor must ensure that readers are not misled.)

12.15 *Unnumbered illustrations.* In some printed works, where illustrations are neither integral to the text nor specifically referred to, numbers are

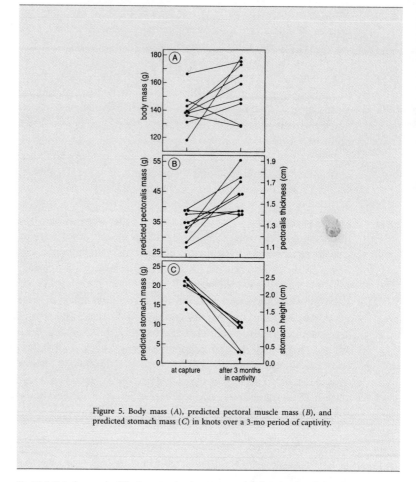

Figure 5. Body mass (*A*), predicted pectoral muscle mass (*B*), and predicted stomach mass (*C*) in knots over a 3-mo period of captivity.

Fig. 12.4. Note how each of the three graphs that compose this figure is identified and described.

unnecessary. In the editing and production stages, however, all illustrations should carry working numbers, as should their captions, to ensure that they are correctly placed. After final page proof has been approved and before the work goes to press, the artwork should be labeled with page numbers (if it is to appear on text pages) and other relevant information (e.g., "page 47, top"). For a work that will be published electronically, an alternative scheme must be used to differentiate illustrations and to facilitate navigation, both between text and illustrations and from one illustration to another (see 12.11).

12.16   *Illustrations in a gallery.* When illustrations are gathered in a gallery, they need not be numbered unless referred to in text, although in the editing and production stages they should carry working numbers to ensure the correct order. If numbers are required, however, and the work also contains illustrations interspersed in the text, two number sequences must be adopted. For example, text illustrations may be referred to as "figure 1" and so on and gallery illustrations, if halftones, as "plate 1" and so on.

Physical Handling of Artwork

ARTWORK TO BE REPRODUCED PHOTOGRAPHICALLY

12.17   *Identifying artwork.* All artwork that is to be reproduced photographically must be clearly identified by the author or, failing that, by the publisher. Here are some dos and don'ts: Number each item on the back in pencil, very gently, making sure no mark is visible on the other side. If the paper does not accept lead pencil, use a self-sticking label. Do *not* use a ballpoint pen, a grease pencil, a felt-tip marker, staples, or paper clips on any piece of artwork. For numbering, see 12.10–14; for captions, see 12.31–39. For artwork delivered in electronic form, see 12.25–26.

12.18   *Alterations to artwork.* Make no marks on the front of the artwork. If a photograph is to be cropped (see 12.21), if a piece of artwork adjusted in any way, or if there might be doubt as to which is the top and which the bottom, make such annotation on a tissue overlay or a self-adhesive label that will not damage the artwork. Leave the actual alterations to a professional.

12.19   *Author's inventory.* Along with artwork, the author should supply a complete list of illustrations, noting any that are to appear in color, any duplicates or extras, and any that are still to come. (Note, however, that for both books and journals it is always expected and often mandatory that all illustrations be supplied at the time a manuscript is submitted; see 2.3–4.) If the work is to be published in print and electronic versions that will vary in the number of illustrations or in the use of color, that information must be noted in the inventory.

12.20   *Publisher's inventory.* As soon as the illustrations arrive from the author, they should be dealt with as follows: Check each piece against the author's list. Make sure that no illustration is damaged and that each is indeed reproducible; request better copies for any that are not. Turn each illustration over to be sure it is numbered. If captions are attached to illustrations, detach them (making sure they are numbered) and attach them to separate sheets for later editing. (Authors should supply captions as a separate file, however; see 2.33.) If any illustrations are missing, find out where they are and when they will arrive. Make a photocopy of each piece, including all numbering and other information. (Beware, however, of using photocopies to prepare or check caption or credit information unless the copies reproduce the original with total clarity. For these purposes, use originals or high-resolution digital prints.) Check for any necessary permissions (see 4.67–74, 4.91–94).

12.21 *Cropping.* Any adjustment to artwork, including cropping (cutting down an illustration to remove extraneous parts), should be done by a professional—often a member of the publisher's design or production staff—or at least with the guidance of a designer, printer, or professional photographer. Suggested cropping should be marked on a tissue overlay.

12.22 *Scaling.* When a piece of artwork is to be reduced or enlarged to fit a particular space, it must be scaled; that is, finished dimensions must be computed from the dimensions of the original or those of the cropped material. This task too should be done by a professional. Authors preparing line art must bear in mind that black lines and any words or symbols become fainter when reduced. (Using a photocopying machine to scale line art down will give an idea of what the printed version will look like.) The publisher should be consulted before any camera-ready art is prepared.

12.23 *Editorial changes to artwork.* Any labels (words or symbols) to be altered on or added to a line drawing or a chart should be typed as a separate document, keyed to the illustration, since the labels may be typeset separately. Where possible, wording, abbreviations, and symbols should be consistent with those used in the text. Capitalization should be minimized; labels should not be treated as formal titles.

12.24 *Maps.* All names on a map that is to be redrawn should be typed as a separate list, in which countries, provinces, cities, rivers, and so forth are divided into separate groups, each group arranged alphabetically.

ARTWORK TO BE REPRODUCED ELECTRONICALLY

12.25 *Changing technology.* Authors preparing illustrations electronically must consult their publishers before submitting the files. The guidelines given above in the section "Placement and Numbering" apply equally to electronic and paper images.

12.26   *What to furnish and how.* Artwork prepared in electronic (or digital) form should be placed in files separate from the text files and named for easy identification. The files should be accompanied by hard copies, usually laser printouts, of each piece of artwork. Consult the publisher early about any special fonts used in the construction of drawings, diagrams, and so forth; the publisher may need the fonts themselves. Any illustrations that cannot be printed (such as a computer animation to be published electronically) must be noted and described in the author's cover letter or inventory; simply including the file on the disk is not sufficient (see 12.19). A list of the software programs used to create the digital artwork should also be furnished. For further guidance, consult the publisher; note that any of these procedures may be modified according to the requirements of particular publishers. See also 2.4, 2.19.

12.27   *Scans.* All scans must be made in accordance with the publisher's guidelines, preferably by a professional graphic arts service (see fig. A.9 in appendix A for an example of such guidelines). Some printers prefer to scan illustrations themselves, to ensure consistent quality and to facilitate subsequent stages in the publication process. Color scans for black-and-white reproduction are unacceptable. For color art, transparencies should be furnished.

12.28   *Proportion.* The relations between font size, line weight (thickness, measured in points), and final printed size should be considered when drawings are created. As a general guideline, art with an intended final size of 4 × 7 inches should have a font size of 8 points and a line weight of 0.5 point; art with an intended final size of 5 × 7 inches should have a font size of 10 points and a line weight of 1 point; and art with an intended final size of 8 × 10 inches should have a font size of 14 points and a line weight of 1.5 points. Hairline rules and other figure elements must be heavy enough that they will not disappear when reduced. (Note that the "hairline" rules specified by computer drawing programs, being inconsistent in weight, are especially susceptible to disappearing.)

12.29   *Appearance.* For aesthetic purposes, there should be no more than a 20 percent difference between the smallest and the largest point sizes used for labels (written copy) within a drawing or chart. Visual distinctions may be made with capitals, italics, and boldface. Variations should be kept to a minimum. See also 12.56–61.

12.30   *Shading.* Avoid shading, since it may print out poorly when reduced. Stripes (as illustrated in fig. 12.3) or spots are preferable in a bar chart to distinguish areas from plain black or white.

Captions

12.31 *Definition.* A caption (see 12.8) is the explanatory material that appears outside (usually below) an illustration. It is distinct from a key (see 12.8) and from a label (see 12.9, 12.60), which appear within an illustration.

EDITORIAL CONVENTIONS

12.32 *Syntax, punctuation, and capitalization.* A caption may consist of a word or two, an incomplete or a complete sentence, several sentences, or a combination (see 12.8). No punctuation is needed after a caption consisting solely of an incomplete sentence. If one or more full sentences follow it, each (including the opening phrase) has closing punctuation. In a work in which most captions consist of full sentences, even incomplete ones may be followed by a period for consistency. Sentence capitalization (see 8.166) is recommended in all cases except for the formal titles of works of art (see 12.33).

Milton at the Nobel ceremony, 1976

The White Garden, reduced to its bare bones in early spring. The box hedges, which are still cut by hand, have to be carefully kept in scale with the small and complex garden as well as in keeping with the plants inside the "boxes."

12.33 *Formal titles.* Titles of works of art are capitalized headline style (see 8.167) and italicized, whether standing alone or incorporated into a caption. See also 8.206.

Leonardo da Vinci, *Madonna of the Rocks.* Oil on canvas (original panel), 78 × 48$\frac{1}{2}$ in. Louvre, Paris.

The head of Venus—a detail from Botticelli's *Birth of Venus.*

Francis Bedford, *Stratford on Avon Church from the Avon*, 1860s. Albumen print of collodion negative, 18.8 × 28.0 cm. Rochester, International Museum of Photography at George Eastman House.

12.34 *Caption with number.* An illustration number may be separated from the caption by a period or, if the number is typographically distinct, by a space. The style used is often the designer's choice. Whether *figure* is spelled out or abbreviated as *fig.* may be specified by journal style or, for books, may be up to the designer or editor or both.

Fig. 7. Idealized random distribution curve

FIGURE 4.7 A 5.5 day route of the male Wei, based on tracking in snow. All rest sites, drinking places, and scent-marked trees were tallied.

Plate 3 Venice in winter

The word *figure* or *plate* is sometimes omitted; the number alone may be sufficient if all the illustrations (maps, photographs, etc.) are numbered in a single series.

96. Aerial photograph of Galena from the south, April 1988

12.35 *Identifying placement.* In a print publication, a caption may not fit on the same printed page as a large illustration. In such a case, explanatory wording (usually in italics) is needed. The caption appears at the foot (or, sometimes, the head) of the nearest text page. Note that placement-related wording added for the printed version is likely to be irrelevant in any non-printed versions of the work and should be omitted in those versions.

Opposite: The tall trees of the valley, planted by Russell Page, are reflected among the water lilies, *Nymphaea*, and pickerelweed, *Pontederia cordata*.

Overleaf: The zebra-striped leaves of the miscanthus, *Miscanthus sinensis 'Zebrinus'*, are light and almost transparent in the strong rays of the August sun.

12.36 *Identifying parts of an illustration.* Such terms as *top, bottom, left, right, above, below, left to right,* or *clockwise from left* are frequently used in captions to identify subjects within a single illustration or parts of a composite. The term, usually italicized, is followed by a comma or, if a list follows, a colon.

Fig. 4. *Above left,* William Livingston; *above right,* Henry Brockholst Livingston; *below left,* John Jay; *below right,* Sarah Livingston Jay

Left to right: Madeleine K. Albright, Dennis Ross, Ehud Barak, and Yassir Arafat

For electronic works in which illustration parts will be presented in a way that differs from the printed version, captions must be modified accordingly. If the same wording is to be used in both print and electronic forms, the illustration parts must be configured identically in both.

12.37 *Letters as identifiers.* If the various parts of a figure have been assigned letters, these are used in a similar way, sometimes italicized. See also 12.14.

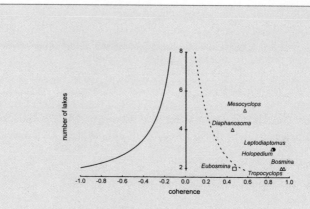

Figure 5: Homogeneous subsets of common zooplankton species plotted in coherence space. Both the open triangles and solid circle identify species for which a significant correlation was observed, but only the latter was unaffected by influential years. The open square identifies a species that was not significantly coherent. The critical values of r_i used to explore coherence in species subsets were obtained from the test of H_{04}; the grand mean of the matrix equals 0 (Brien et al. 1984) at $P = .05$.

Fig. 12.5. Compare figure 12.3 for a slightly different way of defining the symbols used in the chart. Parenthetical citations may be used in captions as in text, as long as the full reference appears in a list at the end of the work.

Figure 3 DNA sequence from a small region within the PC gene, showing the G→T transition at nucleotide 2229. The partial sequence of intron 13 is also shown. A, wild-type sequence; B, sequence from a PC-deficient Micmac homozygous for the mutation.

Fig. 5. Three types of Hawaiian fishhooks: *a*, barbed hook of tortoise shell; *b*, trolling hook with pearl shell lure and point of human bone; *c*, octopus lure with cowrie shell, stone sinker, and large bone hook.

12.38   *Identifying symbols used in figures.* When symbols are used in a map or chart, the symbols must be identified either in a key within the figure or, more commonly, in the caption. See figures 12.5, 12.6.

Fig. 9.4. Photosynthetic light response. Data are presented from shade-grown (■) and open-grown (□) culms of the current year.
or
Fig. 9.4. Photosynthetic light response. Data are presented from shade-grown (solid symbols) and open-grown (open symbols) culms of the current year.

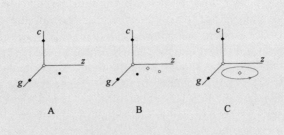

Figure 2: Attractors (*black circles, limit cycles*), saddles (*black squares, white squares*), and repellors (*white circles*) in the state space. *A, B,* and *C* refer to subregions [a], [b], and [c] of figure 1.

Fig. 12.6. The creator of this three-part diagram uses yet another device to define the symbols; compare figures 12.3 and 12.5 and examples at 12.38.

12.39   *Dimensions of the original.* When a caption provides the dimensions of an original work of art, these follow the medium and are listed in order of height, width, and (if applicable) depth. This information need appear only if relevant to the text, unless the rights holder requests that it be included (see 12.48).

Oil on canvas, 45 × 38 cm
Bronze, 49 × 22 × 16 in.

See also examples in 12.33. Photomicrographs, in scientific publications, may include in their captions information about the degree of magnification (original magnification, ×400; *bar,* 100 μm).

CREDIT LINES

12.40   *Source.* A brief statement of the source of an illustration, known as a credit line, is usually appropriate and sometimes mandatory. The major exception is an illustration (a drawing, a chart, a photograph, etc.) created by the author. See also 12.44.

12.41   *Permissions.* Illustrative material under copyright, whether published or unpublished, usually requires permission from the copyright owner before it can be reproduced. You cannot simply take a photo of your favorite Monet and use it to illustrate your history of the haystack; before attempting to reproduce the painting you must write to obtain written permission, as well as a print of the work, from the museum, or person, that owns it. Nor may you use a photograph or other portrayal of an identifiable human subject without the consent of that person or someone acting on his or her behalf. Although it is the author's responsibility, not the publisher's, to obtain permissions, consult your publisher about what needs permission and the best way to obtain it. For a fuller discussion, see 4.81–82, 4.90–93. For a work that will be published in electronic as well as printed form, see 4.60.

12.42 *Placement.* A credit line usually appears at the end of a caption, sometimes in parentheses or in different type (or both). A photographer's name occasionally appears in small type parallel to the bottom or side of a photograph.

37.1 The myth that all children love dinosaurs is contradicted by this nineteenth-century scene of a visit to the monsters at Crystal Palace. (Cartoon by John Leech. "Punch's Almanac for 1855," *Punch* 28 [1855]: 8. Photo courtesy of The Newberry Library, Chicago.)

If most or all of the illustrations in a work are from a single source, that fact may be stated in a note or, in the case of a book, in the preface or acknowledgments or on the copyright page. In a heavily illustrated book, all credits are sometimes listed together in the end matter or, more rarely, the front matter. (Note, however, that some permissions grantors stipulate placement of the credit with the illustration itself; others may charge a higher fee if the credit appears elsewhere.) See also 12.52.

12.43 *Form.* The form, or language, of a credit line varies according to its placement and to the type and copyright status of the illustration. For material under copyright, the copyright owner may demand particular language. Otherwise, credit lines should follow a consistent pattern within any one work. In the examples that follow, it is assumed that the credit line will run below the illustration or at the end of the caption. In the latter case it will require final punctuation.

12.44 *Author's own material.* Although illustrations created by the author do not need credit lines, such wording as "Photo by author" may be appropriate if other illustrations in the same work require credit.

12.45 *Commissioned material.* Work commissioned by the author—such as maps, photographs, drawings, or charts—is usually produced under a "work made for hire" contract (see 4.9–12). Even if no credit is required under such an arrangement, professional courtesy dictates mentioning the creator (unless the illustration is signed and the signature reproduced).

Map by Kevin Hand   Photograph by Ted Lacey   Drawing by Barbara Smith

12.46   *Material obtained free of charge.* For material that the author has obtained free and without restrictions on its use, the credit line may use the word *courtesy*.

Photograph courtesy of Ford Motor Company

Mies at the groundbreaking ceremony of the National Gallery, September 1965. Courtesy of Reinhard Friedrich.

12.47   *Material requiring permission.* Unless fair use applies (see 4.75, 4.80–83), an illustration reproduced from a published work under copyright always requires formal permission. In addition to author, title, publication details, and (occasionally) copyright date, the credit line should include a page or figure number. If the work being credited is in the bibliography or reference list, only a shortened form need appear in the credit line (see fourth example). See also 12.41, 12.43, 12.48.

Reproduced by permission from Mark Girouard, *Life in the English Country House: A Social and Architectural History* (New Haven, CT: Yale University Press, 1978), 162.

Reproduced by permission from George B. Schaller et al., *The Giant Pandas of Wolong* (Chicago: University of Chicago Press, 1985), 52. © 1985 by The University of Chicago.

Reproduced by permission of the publisher from William Shakespeare, *Comedies, Histories, and Tragedies*, CD-ROM edition (Oakland, CA: Octavo, 2001), Provenance essay, fig. 5, © 2001 by Octavo.

Reprinted by permission from Duncan 1999, fig. 2.

12.48   *Specific language versus consistency.* Some permission grantors request specific language in the credit line. In a work with many illustrations, such language in one or two credit lines may conflict with consistent usage in the rest. Editorial discretion should then be exercised: in giving full credit to the source, an editor may follow the spirit rather than the letter. Where the specific language requested does not create a problem of consistency, syntax, spelling, or punctuation—or where the grantor is intractable—it may be simpler to use the language requested. For source notes, see 16.68.

12.49   *Material in the public domain.* Illustrations from works in the public domain (see 4.19–22) may be reproduced without permission. For readers'
information, however, a credit line is appropriate.

> Illustration by Joseph Pennell for Henry James, *English Hours* (Boston, 1905), facing
> p. 82.

> Reprinted from John D. Shortridge, *Italian Harpsichord Building in the Sixteenth and Sev-
> enteenth Centuries,* U.S. National Museum Bulletin 225 (Washington, DC, n.d.).

12.50   *Agency material.* Photographs of prints, drawings, paintings, and the like
obtained from a commercial agency usually require a credit line.

> Woodcut from Historical Pictures Service, Chicago
> Photograph from Wide World Photos

12.51   *Adapted material.* An author creating an illustration adjusted from, or using data from, another source should credit that source for reasons of professional courtesy and readers' information.

> Figure 1.2. Weight increase of captive pandas during the first years of life. (Data from New
> York Zoological Park; National Zoological Park; Giron 1980.)

> Adapted from Pauly 2001, fig. 5.5

List of Illustrations

12.52   *When to include a list.* Not every illustrated work requires a list of illustrations. A journal issue rarely uses one. The criterion is whether the illustrations are of intrinsic interest apart from the text they illustrate. The illustrations in this manual, for example, do not fit that criterion. But a book
on Roman architecture, illustrated by photographs of ancient buildings,
would benefit from a list. A list of illustrations may occasionally double as
a list of credits if these do not appear with the illustrations themselves (see
12.42).

12.53   *Location and form of list.* In a printed work, a list of illustrations, if
included, usually follows the table of contents. For guidelines and examples, see 1.43–47 and figures 1.8 and 1.9. In an electronic work, a small
number of illustrations may be listed as part of a menu incorporated in the

design for each page, or readers may follow a link to a complete list of illustrations. The list may include thumbnails that help readers identify illustrations and navigate among them.

12.54   *Illustrations in galleries.* Illustrations that are to appear in galleries are not always listed separately. For example, in a printed book containing interspersed line art and two photo galleries, a line reading "Photographs follow pages 228 and 332" might be inserted after the detailed list of figures. If all the illustrations were in galleries, that line could appear at the end of the table of contents (see fig. 1.7). (All illustrations, including those in galleries, should be listed if integral to the text.)

12.55   *Editing the list.* In the list of illustrations, long captions should be shortened to a single line (or two at the most).

[*Caption*] The White Garden, reduced to its bare bones in early spring. The box hedges, which are still cut by hand, have to be carefully kept in scale with the small and complex garden as well as in keeping with the plants inside the "boxes."

[*Entry in list*] The White Garden in early spring 43

[*Caption*] The tall trees of the valley, planted by Russell Page, are reflected among the water lilies, *Nymphaea*, and pickerelweed, *Pontederia cordata.*

[*Entry in list*] Page's tall trees reflected among water lilies 75

Charts: Some Guidelines

12.56   *Essential properties.* A chart should present data in a simple, comprehensible graphic form. It should be used only if it summarizes the data more effectively than words can. While integral to the text, it should, like a table (see 13.1), make sense on its own terms. For guidance in chart design, consult Edward R. Tufte, *The Visual Display of Quantitative Information* (bibliog. 2.3). For electronic (or digital) preparation, see 12.25–30.

12.57   *Consistency.* Where two or more charts are used within a work, especially if they deal with comparable material, they must follow a consistent style in graphics and typography. Whatever graphic device is used, elements of the same kind must always be represented in the same way. Different visual effects should be used only to distinguish one element from another, never just for variety.

12.58   *Graphs: the axes.* Both the *x* (horizontal) and the *y* (vertical) axis should be labeled (see, e.g., fig. 12.5); the axes serve a function similar to that of column heads and stubs in a table (see 13.25). The label on the *y* axis is read from the bottom up (the opposite of copy on the spine of books or journals, which is read from the top down).

12.59   *Graphs: the curves.* Curves should be presented in graphically distinct forms—for example, one may be a continuous line, another a broken line. The elements in a bar chart or a pie chart that correspond to curves—the bars or the wedges—should similarly be graphically distinct. All such elements should be labeled or else identified in a key or in the caption (see 12.8).

12.60   *Labels in relation to captions.* In printed works, the title of a chart appears in the caption below the chart, not as a label above it. Labels, the descriptive items within a chart (see 12.9), are normally lowercased (unless they are species names or other terms capitalized in the text); if phrases, they may be capitalized sentence style (see 8.166). Although labels may be explained or discussed in a caption (see, e.g., fig. 12.5), they should never duplicate the caption.

12.61   *Abbreviations.* Abbreviations and symbols may be used in labels as long as they are easily recognizable or explained in a key or in the caption. A form such as *US\$millions* may be more appropriate for nonspecialized (or non-English-speaking) readers than *US\$M*, but the shorter form is acceptable if readers will find it clear and it is used consistently. Numbers and abbreviations are covered in chapters 9 and 15.

Musical Examples

12.62   *Treatment.* Works in musicology nearly always include *musical examples*—often excerpted from existing musical scores but sometimes newly created by the author. The author may furnish artwork to be reproduced photographically or digitally; such material is treated in much the same way as artwork for a graph or line drawing. Or the music may have to be typeset, in which case a typesetter specializing in music should be used. Like other kinds of artwork, musical examples require captions and text callouts, are often numbered, and must be carefully scaled to ensure readability.

12.63   *Editorial concerns.* An editor unfamiliar with the conventions of printed music must seek guidance from an expert before attempting to edit or

EXAMPLE 7.6 *Daliso e Delmita*, act 2, "Nel lasciarti, oh Dio! mi sento," mm. 86–97

Fig. 12.7. Musical examples, like tables, carry their captions above the illustration rather than below. Although often reproduced photographically, musical examples can be typeset by specialists.

proofread musical examples. For example, verbal instructions such as *forte* or *pianissimo* are usually italicized and often abbreviated (*f*, *pp*); line breaks and page breaks can be made only at points where such breaks are acceptable in musical scores; and in transcriptions of vocal music the words must appear exactly below the notes they are sung to (see fig. 12.7). For an authoritative reference, see D. Kern Holoman, *Writing about Music* (bibliog. 1.1). See also 7.70–75.

Tables

Introduction

13.1   *Virtues of tables.* A table offers an excellent means of presenting a large number of individual, similar facts so that they are easy to scan and compare. A simple table can give information that would require several paragraphs to present textually, and it can do so more clearly. An electronic table allows presentation of even more data, well beyond what may be practical in print. A table should be as simple as the material allows and understandable on its own; even a reader unfamiliar with the material presented should be able to make general sense of a table. The text may highlight the main points in a table and summarize its message but should not duplicate the details. This chapter describes and illustrates the basic elements of a table and accepted ways of editing, arranging, and typesetting these elements. No one table in this chapter should be taken as a prototype; all merely illustrate workable patterns and may be adapted according to the data and the potential users of the tables. For excellent advice on table preparation, consult the *Publication Manual of the American Psychological Association* (bibliog. 1.1). For specific instructions on preparing electronic table files, consult your publisher. (Some publishers, including the University of Chicago Press, Journals Division, give instructions for table preparation on their Web sites.)

13.2   *Consistency.* Because a prime virtue of tables is easy comparison, consistency in style is indispensable both within one table and among several. Whatever style is chosen for titles, column heads, abbreviations, and the like for one table must be followed in all others in the same work. Similarly, the choice between horizontal rules and extra space or between indention and font variation to distinguish between elements within a table must be made uniformly for all tables in a work. Certain tables, however, may require rules or other devices not needed in other tables in the same work.

13.3   *Column heads and rows.* A table has elements analogous to the horizontal and vertical axes of a graph. The horizontal axis consists of the *column heads*, which are read across. The vertical axis consists of the stub column, which is read down.

13.4   *The variables.* The data in most tables include two sets of variables, dependent and independent. One set (traditionally the independent variables) appears in the first column, or stub (see 13.24–25), and the other appears in the column heads (see 13.19–23). In the printed work, the choice of location is sometimes limited by the physical dimensions of the table (see 13.54–59). If the same set of variables is included in two or more tables in the same work, it must appear in the same location in each.

TABLE 13.1 Characteristics of SDF, CPS, and WECD workers

Characteristic	SDF workers	1988 May CPS workers, manufacturing	WECD workers	WECD workers weighted
	(1)	(2)	(3)	(4)
Male (%)	66.9	65.4	70.1	66.9
Non-Hispanic white (%)	85.2	88.8	89.6	88.3
Now married (%)	67.3	66.7	71.0	67.7
In occupation (%)				
Manager and professional	18.2	18.6	16.4	19.2
Technical, clerical, and sales	21.6	20.8	19.7	21.4
Production worker	60.2	60.6	64.0	59.4
Region (%)				
Northeast	20.8	27.6	27.9	19.9
Midwest	33.0	28.4	44.5	33.3
South	31.7	32.5	21.8	33.8
West	14.5	11.5	5.9	11.8
Age (mean years)	38.9	38.3	39.9	38.8
	(37)	(37)	(39)	(39)
Weeks worked (mean number)[a]	47.5	—	48.9	48.2
	(52)		(52)	(52)
Usual hours worked per week	41.2	41.0	41.7	41.3
(mean number)[a]	(40)	(40)	(40)	(40)
Wage or salary income (mean	25,558.1	—	28,106.7	25,676.8
dollars)[a]	(21,000)		(25,000)	(25,000)
Hourly wage (mean dollars)[a,b]	13.25	10.30	13.87	12.90
	(10.58)	(9.08)	(11.96)	(11.96)
N	3,176,986	4,757	199,558	1,639,556.2

NOTE: Numbers in parentheses are the medians of the distribution.

[a]Reference period is the previous year (1989) for SDF and WECD workers and the previous week for the CPS workers.

[b]For the SDF and WECD workers, hourly wage is estimated as (wage or salary income / number of weeks worked) / usual hours worked per week.

13.5   *The population and the sample: "N" vs. "n."* An italic capital *N* is used in many statistical tables to stand for the total group, or "population," from which data are drawn (see table 13.1). An italic lowercase *n* stands for a portion of the total group, or a "sample." For example, if *N* refers to the total number of subjects (of both sexes) in a study, lowercase *n* might refer to the number of females in the study.

13.6   *"Percent" vs. "percentage."* Despite changing usage, Chicago continues to regard *percent* as an adverb ("of each hundred") (or, less commonly, an adjective) and to use *percentage* as the noun form. The symbol %, however, may stand for either word. See also 13.42, 13.69.

13.7   *Number ranges.* Anyone preparing or editing a table must ensure that number ranges do not overlap, that there are no gaps between them, and that they are as precise as the data require. It must be clear whether "up to" or "up to and including" is meant. Dollar amounts, for example, might be given as "less than $5, $5–$9, $10–$14, and $15–$19" (*not* "$1–$5, $5–$10," etc.). If greater precision is needed, they might be given as "$1.00–$4.99, $5.00–$9.99," and so forth. The symbols < and > must be used only to mean *less than* and *more than*. In a table including age ranges, >60 means "more than 60 years old" (not "60 and up," which would be typeset as ≥60).

13.8 *Journals and series.* Every journal that accepts tables has its own style for them, as for other editorial and typographic elements. Tables in a book that is part of a series may also follow a specific style. Authors should therefore consult their editors on how closely to adhere to the guidelines offered in this chapter.

13.9 *Appropriate use of tables.* In scientific, statistical, financial, and other technical material, tables are familiar and appropriate tools for conveying data. In general works, they may be more daunting to readers. It is wise to consult the publisher on the appropriate number, size, and physical form of any tables to be included in a work. In certain contexts—if, for example, exact values are not essential to an author's argument—a graph or a bar chart, or plain text, may more effectively present the data. Because tables are expensive both to typeset and to correct in proof, they must be designed and constructed with care. Software makes it easier to construct tables but does not guarantee that they will be logical or clear.

The Main Parts of a Table

TABLE NUMBER

13.10 *Form.* Every table should be given a number (arabic numerals are used) and should be cited in the text by the number, either directly or parenthetically. For table titles, see 13.14–18.

The wide-ranging nature of the committee's discussions can be judged from the topics listed in table 14.

Topics covered by the worker-management committee in three years of deliberations fell into five general categories (table 14).

Note that the word *table* is lowercased in text references.

13.11 *Tabular matter not requiring a number.* A simple list or other tabular matter that requires only two columns can usually be left unnumbered and untitled.

The prospective mountaineers were asked to bring the following equipment, in addition to toiletries:

ITEM	QUANTITY
Backpack	1
Boots	3 pairs
Down jackets	2
Pants	3 pairs
Sweaters	5
Underwear	5 sets
Socks	12 pairs
Bedroll	1

13.12 *Number sequence.* Table numbers follow the order in which the tables are to appear in the text, and first mentions should follow that order as well. (In the rare instances where context demands a reference to a table in a subsequent chapter of a book, such wording as "A different set of variables is presented in chapter 5, table 10" may be appropriate.) Each table, even in a closely related set, should be given its own number (tables 14, 15, and 16, *rather than* tables 14A–C).

13.13 *Double numeration.* In a book with many tables, or with chapters by different authors, double numeration is often used, as it is for illustrations (see 1.76, 12.13). All examples in this chapter use double numeration.

TABLE TITLE

13.14 *Length.* The title should identify the table as briefly as possible. It should not furnish background information, repeat the column heads, or describe the results illustrated by the table. For example, a lengthy title such as "Effect of DMSO on arthritic rats and nonarthritic rats after 20, 60, and 90 days of treatment" should be pared down to "Effect of DMSO on arthritic and nonarthritic rats." From a title such as "High degree of recidivism among reform school parolees," eliminate "high degree of." Let the table give the facts; commentary can be offered in the text.

13.15 *Syntax.* The title should be a noun form. Use participles rather than relative clauses—for example, "Families subscribing to weekly news magazines" (rather than "Families that subscribe to weekly news magazines").

13.16 *Capitalization.* Like illustration captions, table titles may be capitalized sentence style (see 8.166), as are all the examples in this chapter. This style is particularly appropriate in works that include both tables and charts dealing with similar material. Nonetheless, some authors and editors prefer—and certain journals and series require—the more traditional headline style (see 8.167) for table titles.

13.17 *Parenthetical information.* Important explanatory or statistical information is often included in parentheses in a title (as in table 13.4). It is set in sentence style even if the main title is in headline style. More detailed information should go in a note to the table (see 13.46–47).

Federal employees in the Progressive Era (total plus selected agencies)
Scan statistics S_L of varying lengths L for sib-pair data (broad diagnosis)
Gender as a factor in successful business transactions ($N = 4,400$)

13.18 *Number plus title.* In a printed table, the title usually follows the number on the same line, separated by punctuation or by space and typographic distinction. Less commonly, the number appears on a line by itself, the title starting a new line. The number is always preceded by the word *table.*

Table 2. Description of species pools used in the simulations

Table 6.4
Likelihood of poor weather for centennial parades (percentages)

COLUMN HEADS

13.19 *Treatment.* Like table titles, column heads should be as brief as possible and, space being at a premium, are best capitalized sentence style (as in all examples in this chapter). As long as their meaning is clear to readers, abbreviations may be used as needed. The first column (the stub) does not always require a head (see 13.24). In a work that includes a number of tables, column heads should be treated consistently.

13.20 *Explanatory tags.* Like table titles, a column head sometimes requires an explanatory tag (or subheading) indicating the unit of measurement employed in the column below. (*Tag* as used here is not be confused with the tags used in SGML, HTML, or XML.) The tag, which may consist of a symbol or an abbreviation ($, %, km, *n*, and so on), is usually in parentheses (see table 13.2). Parentheses may also be used in column heads when some of the data in the cells are in parentheses. For example, a column

TABLE 13.2 Yen versus dollar invoice ratios in Japan's export and imports, 1970–91

Year	Export contracts (%)		Import contracts (%)	
	In yen	In dollars	In yen	In dollars
1970	0.9	90.4	0.3	80.0
1975	17.5	78.0	0.9	89.9
1980	28.9	66.3	2.4	93.1
1981	31.8	62.8	—	—
1982	33.8	60.9	—	—
1983	42.0	50.2	3.0	—
1984	39.5	53.1	—	—
1985	39.3	52.2	7.3[a]	—
1986	36.5	53.5	9.7[a]	—
1987	33.4	55.2	10.6	81.7
1988	34.3	53.2	13.3	78.5
1989	34.7	52.4	14.1	77.3
1990	37.5	48.8	14.5	75.5
1991	39.4	46.7	15.6	75.4

Source: Tavlas and Ozeki 1992. Original data on exports until 1982 from BOJ, *Yushutsu Shinyojyo Toukei;* after 1982, MITI, Export Confirmation Statistics. Original data on imports until 1980 from MITI, Yushutsu Shyonin, Todokede Houkokusho; 1981–85, MOF, Houkokushyorei ni Motoduku Houkoku; after 1986, MITI, Import Reporting Statistics.

Note: Entries are percentages of Japanese trade contracts denominated in yen and dollars. Percentages are the average over the calendar year, except where otherwise noted.

[a]Fiscal year average.

head might read "Children with positive results, % (no. positive/no. tested)" and a cell under this head contain "27.3 (6/22)."

13.21 *Numbered columns.* If columns must be numbered for text reference, use arabic numerals in parentheses, centered immediately below the column head, above the rule separating the head from the column (as in table 13.1). See also 13.59.

13.22 *Spanner heads.* When a table demands column heads of two or more levels—when related columns require both a collective head and individual heads—spanner heads, or spanners (sometimes called decked heads), are used. A horizontal rule, called a spanner rule, appears between the spanner and the column heads to show which columns the spanner applies to (see table 13.2). For ease of reading, spanner heads should seldom exceed two levels.

13.23 *Cut-in heads.* Cut-in heads, spanning all columns but the first, may be used as subheads within a table. They usually appear between horizontal rules (see table 13.3), though space may be used instead (see table 13.4). Since they interfere with downward scanning, they should be used with caution.

TABLE 13.3 Elections in Gotefrith Province, 1900–1910

Party	1900 % of vote	1900 Seats won	1906 % of vote	1906 Seats won	1910 % of vote	1910 Seats won
	Provincial Assembly					
Conservative	35.5	47	26.0	37	30.9	52
Socialist	12.4	18	27.1	44	24.8	39
Christian Democrat	49.2	85	41.2	68	39.2	59
Other	2.8	0	5.7	1[a]	5.1	0
Total	100.0	150	100.0	150	100.0	150
	National Assembly					
Conservative	32.6	4	23.8	3	28.3	3
Socialist	13.5	1	27.3	3	24.1	2
Christian Democrat	52.1	7	42.8	6	46.4	8
Other	1.8	0	6.1	0	1.2	0
Total	100.0	12	100.0	12	100.0	13[b]

Source: Erewhon National Yearbooks for the years cited.

[a]This seat was won by a Radical Socialist, who became a member of the Conservative coalition.

[b]Reapportionment in 1910 gave Gotefrith an additional seat in the National Assembly.

TABLE 13.4 Monthly returns in developed equity market (percent)

Market	Annualized mean[a]	Risk[b]	Sharpe ratio[c]
	A. Sample period: 1985:02–1989:12		
Canada	16.0	17.8	0.9
France	37.1	27.0	1.4
Germany	32.9	27.0	1.2
Italy	35.3	28.0	1.3
Japan	38.5	23.4	1.6
United Kingdom	27.6	24.5	1.1
United States	18.5	17.6	1.1
World	25.9	15.4	1.7
	B. Sample period: 1990:01–1997:06		
Canada	8.3	13.6	0.6
France	9.9	16.9	0.6
Germany	10.9	17.8	0.6
Italy	5.5	25.7	0.2
Japan	0.2	26.8	0.0
United Kingdom	13.8	16.1	0.9
United States	16.4	11.9	1.4
World	9.7	13.2	0.7

Source: Morgan Stanley Capital International.

Note: End-of-month total returns are in U.S. dollars.

[a]The annualized mean is the monthly percentage change times twelve.

[b]The annualized standard deviation is the monthly standard deviation times the square root of twelve.

[c]The Sharpe ratio is the annualized mean divided by the annualized standard deviation.

TABLE 13.5 Factors affecting arithmetic instruction among Arabs and Jews

Variable	Arabs		Jews	
	Mean	SD	Mean	SD
Town characteristics				
Socioeconomic index	−1.773	.38	.21	.44
School inputs				
Expenditure per student ($)	523.25	166.7	1,288.94	464.6
Hours per student	1.15	.15	1.54	.20
Percentage of noncertified teachers	8.10	5.46	7.49	2.92
Computers for arithmetic instruction	.19	.40	.68	.47
Hours of arithmetic instruction	4.46	.58	4.82	1.58
Arithmetic instruction by arithmetic teacher	.81	.33	.38	.42
Number of observations	126		747	

THE STUB

13.24 *Definition.* The left-hand column of a table, known as the stub, is usually a vertical listing of categories about which information is given in the following columns. If all the entries are of like kind, the stub usually carries a column head: even a general head such as "Characteristic" (as in table 13.1) aids readers. If the entries are too unlike (as in table 13.5), a head may be omitted. If the entries are words, they are capitalized sentence style. Unless they are questions, they carry no end punctuation. They should be consistent in syntax: Authors, Publishers, Printers (*not* Authors, Publishing concerns, Operates printshop). In the stub, entries are aligned on the left. For alignment in other columns, see 13.36–39.

13.25 *Stub entries and subentries.* Items in the stub may form a straight sequential list (for example, all the states in the Union listed alphabetically) or a classified list (the states listed by geographic region, with a subhead above each region). The first word in a subentry as well as in a main entry is capitalized, as in table 13.5, to avoid confusion with runover lines. There is generally no need for colons following main entries (unless a particular journal style requires them). See also 13.27.

13.26 *Typographic treatment of subentries.* It is essential to clearly distinguish subentries both from main entries and from runover lines (see 13.27). Subentries are often indented (as in tables 13.1 and 13.5), or italics may be used for the main entries and roman for the subentries. A combination of italics and indention may also be used, especially if sub-subentries are required (as in table 13.6). The choice may be governed by the amount of horizontal or vertical space available or by journal or series style.

13.27 *Runover lines.* If there are no subentries, runover lines should be indented one em. Only if there is extra space between rows should runovers be set

TABLE 13.6 Best-fitting multiple regression models assuming instantaneous and sequential island separations

Variable	Squamates and turtles		Squamates only	
	Coefficient	P	Coefficient	P
Uncorrected regressions[a]				
Instantaneous separation				
Constant	.356	<.001	.356	<.001
Abundance	−.059	<.001	−.058	<.001
HSI^2	−.001	.067	−.001	.009
Sequential separation				
Constant	.276	<.001	.271	<.001
Abundance	−.036	<.001	−.033	<.001
HSI^2	−.001	.004	−.001	.001
Phylogeny-independent regressions[b]				
Instantaneous separation				
Abundance	−.070	.002	−.056	<.001
HSI	−.004	.709	−.018	.014
Sequential separation				
Abundance	−.049	<.001	−.035	<.001
HSI	−.003	.677	−.015	.011

[a]Phylogenetic relationships not taken into account. Models include all species for which both abundance and HSI are available. Instantaneous separation: squamates and turtles, $R^2 = 0.734$, $N = 28$; squamates only, $R^2 = 0.826$, $N = 23$. Sequential separation: squamates and turtles, $R^2 = 0.753$, $N = 28$; squamates only, $R^2 = 0.803$, $N = 23$.

[b]Models for phylogeny-independent contrasts for all species with a full set of available data. Instantaneous separation: squamates and turtles, $R^2 = 0.538$, $N = 20$; squamates only, $R^2 = 0.836$, $N = 17$. Sequential separation: squamates and turtles, $R^2 = 0.559$, $N = 20$; squamates only, $R^2 = 0.802$, $N = 17$.

flush left. If there are indented subentries (as in table 13.5), any runover lines must be more deeply indented than the lowest level of subentry, as in an indented-style (or stacked) index (see 18.25). Runovers from main entries and subentries carry the same indention from the left margin (not from the line above).

13.28 *Abbreviations and the like.* Where space is at a premium, symbols or abbreviations ($, %, km, *n*, and so on) are acceptable in the stub. Ditto marks are not, however, since they save no space and make work for readers. Any nonstandard abbreviations must be defined in a table footnote.

13.29 *Totals.* When the word *total* appears at the foot of the stub, it is often indented more deeply than the greatest indention above (see tables 13.3, 13.9, 13.13) or distinguished typographically (see table 13.8). See also 13.40–41.

13.30 *Leaders.* Leaders—several spaced periods following a stub entry—are sometimes used in a table where the connection between the stub entries

TABLE 13.7 Correlations between adult/adolescent parenting inventory (dysfunctional parenting attitudes) and parental control and supervision of children's television viewing

PARENTAL CONTROL OR SUPERVISION OF TV	ADULT/ADOLESCENT PARENTING INVENTORY		
	All subjects	Males	Females
Overall control or supervision			
Year 1	−.10	−.17	−.03
Year 2	.15	.05	.28*
Use of TV privileges as punishment			
Year 1	.07	−.04	.19
Year 2	.22*	.16	.31*
Use of TV privileges as reward			
Year 1	.12	.17	.04
Year 2	.19*	.12	.28*
*N*s			
Year 1	162–165	85–86	77–79
Year 2	119	66	53
Of parents who reported setting limits on amount of time spent viewing			
Time restrictions on weekdays			
Year 1	−.02	.13	−.23
Year 2	.02	.32*	−.41*
Time restrictions on weekends			
Year 1	.20	.42**	−.09
Year 2	.16	.24	.03
*N*s			
Year 1	94	50–51	43–44
Year 2	70–74	42	28–32

*p < .05   **p < .01

and the rows they apply to would otherwise be unclear. Some journals routinely use leaders in stubs (see table 13.7); books use them more rarely.

THE BODY AND THE CELLS

13.31   *Table body.* The body of a table consists of the columns to the right of the stub and below the column headings—the real substance of the table. The *cells* are the individual spaces within those columns, usually occupied by data but occasionally empty (see 13.33). For example, the third cell in the second column of table 13.7 contains the datum ".07."

13.32   *Column data.* Whenever possible, columns should carry the same kinds of information. For instance, amounts of money should appear in one column, percentages in another, and information expressed in words in another (but see 13.34). No column should contain identical information in all the cells; such information is better handled in a footnote.

TABLE 13.8 State expansion in the Progressive Era: Number of federal employees (total plus selected agencies)

Selected agencies	1909	1917	Increase (%)
Dept. of Agriculture	11,279	20,269	79.7
Interstate Commerce Commission	560	2,370	323.2
Dept. of Justice	3,198	4,512	41.1
Dept. of Commerce and Labor[a]	11,999	14,993	25.0
Dept. of the Navy[b]	3,390	6,420	89.4
Dept. of War[c]	22,292	30,870	38.5
Dept. of the Interior[d]	17,900	22,478	25.6
Federal Reserve Board	...	75	
Civil Service Commission	193	276	43.0
Federal Trade Commission	...	244	
Shipping Board	...	22	
Total			
DC and non-DC	342,159	497,867[e]	45.5
Excluding Post Office	136,799	198,199	44.9

SOURCE: *Reports of the United States Civil Service Commission* (Washington, DC: GPO): 1910, table 19; 1917, tables 9–10; 1919, p. vi; U.S. Department of Commerce, Bureau of the Census, *Statistical Abstract of the United States, 1917* (Washington, DC: GPO, 1918), table 392.

[a]The Departments of Commerce and Labor were combined until 1913. The Civil Service Commission continued to combine their employees in its subsequent reports through 1917. Separate employment figures for the Labor Department, taken from *The Anvil and the Plow: A History of the Department of Labor* (Washington, DC: GPO, 1963), appendix, table 6, show an essentially stable personnel level (2,000 in 1913, 2,037 in 1917). The bulk of employees (1,740) were attached to the Bureau of Immigration and Naturalization in 1917. The Bureau of Labor Statistics was second in importance, with 104. The Children's Bureau had 103, an increase of 88 from 1913; and the Conciliation Service had only 12, taken from the secretary's personal allotment. In the next two years of wartime, given new labor-market and conciliation functions, the departments' personnel would almost triple; however, the number fell back sharply in 1920.

[b]Exclusive of trade and labor employees.

[c]Excludes "ordinance and miscellaneous" categories.

[d]Includes Land, Pension, Indian, and Reclamation Services.

[e]Excludes Panama Canal workforce.

13.33 *Empty cells.* If a column head does not apply to one of the entries in the stub, the cell should either be left blank or be filled in by an em dash or three unspaced ellipsis dots. If a distinction is needed between "not applicable" and "no data available," a blank cell may be used for the former and an em dash or ellipsis dots for "no data" (see table 13.8). This distinction must be made clear in a note or elsewhere. (Alternatively, the abbreviations n.a. and n.d. may be used, with definitions given in a note.) A zero means literally that the quantity in a cell is zero (see table 13.3).

13.34 *Parentheses.* To avoid multiple columns, actual numbers sometimes share a column with some other value, with one of the figures in parentheses. An explanatory note may be needed (see tables 13.1, 13.9).

TABLE 13.9 Summary of income data from five-year panel survey in rural Pakistan

Source of income	Mean annual household income* in rupees†				
	Year 1 (1986–87)	Year 2 (1987–88)	Year 3 (1988–89)	Year 4 (1989–90)	Year 5 (1990–91)
Nonfarm	937.64	1,117.16	906.26	955.79	922.26
	(1,090.32)	(1,257.51)	(1,043.21)	(1,053.29)	(1,026.50)
Agriculture	661.26	807.46	699.00	436.25	597.62
	(1,559.87)	(2,072.42)	(1,611.23)	(738.12)	(1,221.20)
Livestock	465.73	416.98	417.53	330.93	256.25
	(578.69)	(688.41)	(533.98)	(409.73)	(482.75)
Rental	465.01	299.26	315.75	176.65	282.42
	(1,829.74)	(2,229.84)	(1,903.84)	(654.41)	(1,042.25)
External remittances	247.22	269.74	127.53	178.89	293.74
	(951.95)	(1,262.82)	(674.55)	(772.28)	(1,576.49)
Internal remittances	276.89	139.23	59.39	54.13	129.01
	(551.53)	(380.17)	(189.88)	(223.18)	(450.45)
Other‡	−15.44	99.22	106.72	23.70	28.76
	(256.58)	(507.32)	(365.78)	(101.14)	(125.93)
Total	3,038.31	3,149.04	2,632.19	2,156.35	2,510.07
	(2,416.42)	(2,872.57)	(2,282.39)	(1,651.62)	(2,506.84)

NOTE: *N* = 469 households. Standard deviations are given in parentheses.

*Mean income figures include negative source incomes recorded for some households in various years.

† In 1986, 1 Pakistan rupee = US$0.062. All rupee figures in constant 1986 terms.

‡ Other income includes government pensions, cash, and zakat (payments to the poor).

13.35 *Horizontal alignment.* Horizontally, each cell aligns with the stub entry it applies to. If the stub entry occupies more than one line, the cell entry is normally aligned on the last line of the stub entry (see table 13.8). But if both the stub and one or more cells contain more than one line, the first lines are aligned throughout the body of the table (see table 13.10). First lines are also aligned in a table where the content of each column is of the same sort—in other words, where the first column is not a stub as described in 13.24 (see table 13.11).

13.36 *Vertical alignment: with column head.* The column head is normally centered on the longest cell entry. If the latter is unusually long, adjustment may be necessary; the heads should *look* right. If centering does not work, align column heads and cells on the left. The stub head and entries are always aligned on the left.

13.37 *Vertical alignment: numerals.* A column consisting of numerals without commas or decimal points is usually aligned on the last number, "ranged right" (see table 13.13). If the numerals have decimal points, the column is typically aligned on the decimal point (see tables 13.1–4). If the numer-

TABLE 13.10 Description of species pools used in the simulations: Pools that combine the four basic types in table 1

Species pool effect	Principal biodiversity component responsible for effect(s) as variable increases		Description
	From small values	To large values	
Varying functional compensation	Number of species	Number of groups	If any species are present from group, the contribution of that group to the response is equal to the fraction of species of the group that are present plus some compensation amount that is determined by the variable "degree of compensation."
Varying difference among groups	Number of species	Number of species	Similar to strong group effect, except that the difference among the groups is determined by the variable "group multiplying factor" in the following manner: group 1 effect = multiplying factor; group 2 effect = (multiplying factor + 1)/2; group 3 effect = 1.0 (constant throughout).
Varying single species effect	Number of species	Composition	The response is the sum of the effect of each species present. One species in group 1, if present, has an effect on the response that is determined by the variable "keystone strength." This variable is scaled relative to the effect size of each other species.

NOTE: See appendix A for quantitative descriptions. For each species pool effect there are two pools: single-factor designs (nested, randomized, and factorial) are tested with pools that consist of 24 total species, arbitrarily divided into three functional groups of 8, 7, and 9 species. The multiple-factor designs are tested with pools that consist of 54 species, divided into three functional groups of 18 species.

als have commas but no decimal points, alignment is made on the comma—the last comma if more than one (see table 13.8). Where spaces rather than commas are used to separate groups of digits (see 9.22), alignment is made on the implicit comma. A column including different kinds of numerals is best aligned on the ones that occur most frequently (as in tables 13.1 and 13.7, in which most numerals are aligned on the decimal point, with larger quantities centered). Ellipses and em dashes are centered. Where a column includes many figures in the thousands (or millions), "in thousands" (or "in millions") may be added to the column head, and the numbers in the column shortened accordingly. For more on dec-

TABLE 13.11 Role-style differentiae in the Lewin, Lippitt, and White "group atmosphere" studies

Authoritarian	Democratic	Laissez-faire
All determination of policy by leader	All policies a matter of group discussion and decision, encouraged and assisted by the leader	Complete freedom for group or individual decision, with a minimum of leader participation
Techniques and activity steps dictated by the authority, one at a time, so that future steps were uncertain to a large degree	Activity perspective gained during discussion period. General steps to group goal sketched; when advice was needed, the leader suggested two or more alternative procedures from which choice could be made	Various materials supplied by leader, who made clear a willingness to supply technical information when asked. He took no other part in work discussion
Leader usually dictated the task and companion of each member	Members were free to work with whomever they chose, and division of tasks was left to the group	Complete nonparticipation of the leader
Leader tended to be "personal" in praise and criticism of each member's work; remained aloof from active group participation except when demonstrating	Leader was "objective" in praise and criticism and tried to be a regular group member in spirit without doing too much work	Leader did not comment on member activities unless questioned, did not attempt to appraise or regulate the course of events

imal points, see 13.39. For the different alignment of numerals in the stub and in the other columns, see tables 13.12 and 13.13.

13.38 *Vertical alignment: words.* When a column consists of words, phrases, or sentences, appearance governs vertical alignment. If no runover lines are required, entries may be centered. Longer entries usually look better if they begin flush left. Runover lines may be indented (as in table 13.10) or, if enough space is left between entries, set flush with the first line (as in table 13.11).

13.39 *Zeros before decimal points.* Although, in text, zeros are usually added before the decimal point in quantities less than 1.00, in tables they may be omitted unless prescribed by a journal or series style. For inclusion, see table 13.2; for omission, see table 13.12. See also 9.20–22.

13.40 *Totals, averages, means: typographic treatment.* Extra vertical space or short rules sometimes appear above totals at the foot of columns but may equally well be omitted (see table 13.13). Consistency must be maintained and, where applicable, journal or series style followed. The word *total* in

TABLE 13.12 The net effect of hyperthermia on the water balance (in g) of hypothetical 10-, 100-, and 1,000-g birds that were hyperthermic during periods of 1 h and 5 h

Period and bird mass (g)	Improved thermal gradient[a]	Heat storage[b]	Increased REWL[c]	Net savings	TEWL[d]
1h					
10	.28	.04	−.05	.27	.49
100	.83	.42	−.46	.79	1.78
1,000	2.45	4.16	−3.63	2.98	6.46
5h					
10	1.41	.04	−.27	1.18	2.45
100	4.16	.42	−2.31	2.27	8.89
1,000	12.27	4.16	−18.18	−1.75	32.28

NOTE: Calculations are based on an increase in T_b from 41°C–44°C at T_a of 45°C.

[a]Savings by improved thermal gradient calculated from equation (5).

[b]Savings by heat storage calculated from equation (7).

[c]Costs of increased REWL gradient calculated from equation (12).

[d]Total evaporative water loss at 45°C calculated from equation (6).

TABLE 13.13 Correlation of Dir 1 expansion size with RED score in individuals with RED scores of ≥180 nucleotides

Dir I repeat size (bp)	RED score (nucleotides)					Total
	180	210	240	270	300	
≤150	2	7	5	4	1	19
151–180	20	1	1	0	0	22
181–210	14	23	3	0	1	41
211–240	0	6	10	0	0	16
>240	0	0	0	1	0	1
Total	36	37	19	5	2	99

the stub is often indented. Subtotals are similarly treated. No rules, however, should appear above averages or means.

13.41   *When to use totals.* Totals and subtotals may be included or not, according to how useful they are to the presentation. When the percentages in a column are based on different *n*'s, a final percentage based on the total *N* may be informative and, if so, should be included. Note that rounding often causes a percentage total to be slightly more or less than 100. In such cases the actual figure (e.g., 99% or 101%) should be given, with a footnote explaining the apparent discrepancy.

13.42   *Signs and symbols.* In a column consisting exclusively of, for example, dollar amounts or percentages, the signs should be omitted from the cells and included in the column head (see 13.20 and table 13.2). Mathematical operational signs preceding quantities in a column of figures are not necessarily aligned with other such signs but should appear immediately to the left of the figures they belong to (see tables 13.5, 13.6, and 13.13).

FOOTNOTES

13.43 *Four kinds of footnotes.* Footnotes to a table are of four general kinds and, where two or more kinds are needed, should appear in this order: (1) source notes, (2) other notes applying to the whole table, (3) notes applying to specific parts of the table, and (4) notes on significance levels. Table footnotes always appear immediately below the table they belong to and must be numbered separately from the text notes.

13.44 *Source notes: acknowledgment of data.* If data for a table are not the author's own but are taken from another source or other sources, professional courtesy requires that full acknowledgment be made in an unnumbered footnote. The note is introduced by *Source* or *Sources* (often in italics and followed by a colon; see tables 13.2, 13.3, 13.4).

Sources: Data from Richard H. Adams Jr., "Remittances, Investment, and Rural Asset Accumulation in Pakistan," *Economic Development and Cultural Change* 47, no. 1 (1998): 155–73; David Bevan, Paul Collier, and Jan Gunning, *Peasants and Government: An Economic Analysis* (Oxford: Clarendon Press, 1989), 125–28.

If the sources are listed in the bibliography or reference list, a shortened form may be used:

Sources: Data from Adams 1998; Bevan, Collier, and Gunning 1989.

13.45 *Source notes: credit lines.* Unless *fair use* applies (see 4.75, 4.80–83), a table reproduced without change from a published work under copyright requires formal permission. Credit should be given in an unnumbered footnote, introduced by *Source*: (often in italics). See 12.48 for more information about styling credit lines.

Source: Reprinted by permission from *Scientific Style and Format: The CBE Manual for Authors, Editors, and Publishers*, 6th edition (Cambridge: Cambridge University Press, 1994), 202, table 11.3.

For further examples, which may be adjusted for use with tables, see 12.42, 12.47.

13.46   *General notes.* A note applying to the table as a whole follows any source note, is also unnumbered, and is introduced by *Note:* (often in italics; see tables 13.1, 13.2, 13.4).

Note: Since data were not available for all items on all individuals, there is some disparity in the totals. See also table 14, which presents similar data for Cincinnati, Ohio.

If the substance of a general note can be expressed as a brief phrase, it may be added parenthetically to the title (see also 13.17).

Net private capital flows to emerging markets (billions of U.S. dollars)

13.47   *Specific notes.* For notes on specific parts of a table, superior letters, beginning with *a* in each table, are most commonly used as reference marks. In an electronic table, these letter designators are linked to the notes below the table. At the beginning of the note itself, the letter remains superior and is not followed by a period. The sequence runs from left to right, top to bottom, as in text. Unlike note reference numbers in text, however, the same letter is used on two or more elements if the corresponding note applies to them. A footnote letter attached to a column head applies to the items in the column below it. See tables 13.1, 13.2, 13.4. For asterisks and other marks, see 13.50.

13.48   *Avoiding conflation.* Using letters rather than numbers not only eliminates the danger that a superior numeral will be mistaken for an exponent (see, e.g., table 13.6) but clearly distinguishes table notes from text notes. If, for some reason, numbers rather than letters have to be used, each table has its own series, starting with note 1. Note numbers must never be continuous with or conflated with text notes.

13.49   *Notes on significance levels.* If a table contains notes on significance levels (also called probability notes), asterisks may be used as reference marks. If two or three standard significance levels are noted, a single asterisk is used for the lowest level of significance, two for the next higher, and so on. If values other than these three are given, however, footnote letters are preferable to asterisks, to avoid misleading the reader. In the note, the letter p (probability) is usually lowercase and in italic. Zeros are generally omitted before the decimal point. Probability notes follow all other notes. (Since p stands for the probability of a Type I error, that of rejecting the null hypothesis when in fact it is true, the level of significance increases as the probability of this error decreases.)

$*p < .05$ $**p < .01$ $***p < .001$

These short notes may be set on the same line; if they are spaced, no intervening punctuation is needed (see table 13.7), but if they are run together they should be separated by semicolons. For more on *p* values, consult the *Publication Manual of the American Psychological Association* (bibliog. 1.1). Some journals capitalize *p*, and some give probability values in regular table footnotes.

13.50 *Other reference marks.* For a table that includes mathematical or chemical equations, where superior letters or numerals might be mistaken for exponents, a series of arbitrary symbols may be used (see table 13.9), as follows:

* (asterisk; but do not use if *p* values occur in the table), † (dagger), ‡ (double dagger), § (section mark), ‖ (parallels), # (number sign, or pound)

When more symbols are needed, these may be doubled and tripled in the same sequence:

*, †, ‡, etc., **, ††, ‡‡, etc., ***, †††, ‡‡‡, and so on

These symbols have become less common in electronic publications because not all are rendered reliably by all Web browsers.

RULES

13.51 *Function.* The rules in a table should be functional. Almost every table requires horizontal rules; very few require vertical ones. The table-creating feature in some word processors, which encloses every cell in a rectangle, results in an unsightly checkerboard; omit unnecessary rules.

13.52 *Horizontal rules.* The most frequently used horizontal rules separate title from column heads, column heads from cells, spanner heads from column heads (see 13.22), and the body of the table from the table footnotes. Cut-in heads are usually enclosed in a pair of horizontal rules (see 13.23). A rule above a row of totals is traditional but inessential (unless required by a journal or series style). A rule always closes the body of the table, but no rule follows the notes. See also 13.29. The double rule traditionally used between title and column heads is rarely seen nowadays.

13.53 *Vertical rules.* Vertical rules should be used only to avoid confusion—for example, when a table is doubled up (see 13.57 and table 13.14). Their use between all columns has long been abandoned.

TABLE 13.14 Relative contents of odd isotopes for heavy elements

Element	Z	γ	Element	Z	γ
Sm	62	1.48	W	74	0.505
Gd	64	0.691	Os	76	0.811
Dy	66	0.930	Pt	78	1.160
Eb	68	0.759	Hg	80	0.500
Yb	70	0.601	Pb	82	0.550
Hf	72	0.440			

Shape and Dimensions

13.54 *Vertical versus broadside tables.* In a printed work, a vertical table is one that can be read down the page. If longer than one page, it can continue onto subsequent pages (see table 13.15). A broadside table, such as table 13.19, requires that the open book or journal be turned around; it should therefore be resorted to only if a table is too wide to fit across the page. (Note that the book or journal is turned *clockwise*, whether the table appears on a verso or a recto.) If possible, such a table should be recast as vertical (see 13.57). Both vertical and broadside tables, if too long for one page, can continue onto following pages. If only two pages are required, these should face each other. See also 13.58. Tables to be published electroni-

TABLE 13.15 Type of private capital flow (millions of U.S. dollars)

	1992	1993	1994	1995	1996
			Asia		
China					
GDP	469,003	598,765	546,610	711,315	834,311
Current account	6,401	−11,609	6,908	1,618	7,243
Capital inflows	−250	23,474	32,645	38,674	39,966
Equity	7,922	24,266	34,208	36,185	39,981
Bank credits	4,008	2,146	3,786	8,405	10,625
Indonesia					
GDP	139,116	158,007	176,892	202,131	227,370
Current account	−2,780	−2,106	−2,792	−6,431	−7,663
Capital inflows	6,129	5,632	3,839	10,259	10,847
Equity	1,947	2,692	2,573	4,285	5,195
Bank credits	663	1,573	2,030	8,021	12,602
			Latin America		
Argentina					
GDP	228,990	257,842	281,925	279,613	297,460
Current account	−5,462	−7,672	−10,117	−2,768	−3,787
Capital inflows	7,373	9,827	9,279	574	7,033
Equity	4,630	4,038	3,954	4,589	7,375
Bank credits	1,152	9,945	1,139	2,587	959

TABLE 13.15 *(continued)*

	1992	1993	1994	1995	1996
			Latin America		
Brazil					
GDP	446,580	438,300	546,230	704,167	774,868
Current account	6,089	20	−1,153	−18,136	−23,602
Capital inflows	5,889	7,604	8,020	29,306	33,984
Equity	3,147	4,062	5,333	8,169	15,788
Bank credits	11,077	4,375	9,162	11,443	14,462
Chile					
GDP	41,882	44,474	50,920	65,215	69,218
Current account	−958	−2,554	−1,585	−1,398	−3,744
Capital inflows	3,134	2,996	5,294	2,488	6,781
Equity	876	1,326	2,580	1,959	4,090
Bank credits	2,192	804	1,108	1,100	1,808

. . . .

cally may not be bound by the same considerations discussed in paragraphs 13.55–63.

13.55 *Dimensions.* Let us assume that a vertical table is to appear in 8-point type, with a maximum width of about 4^1/$_2$ inches and a length of about half a page, in a printed book or journal with pages measuring 6 × 9 inches. In *manuscript* form, this table should print out in 12-point type, double-spaced, on one full sheet of 8^1/$_2$ × 11-inch paper, with one-inch margins. Since many tables are copyedited by hand rather than online, and typesetters often prefer to reset rather than to use the electronic files for tables, the author's printout must be in an editable form, that is, clearly printed and double-spaced. (Editors working with electronic tables typically depend on the author's printout as well, since the on-screen version may become increasingly cluttered with codes, tags, or redlining and since electronic files occasionally become garbled.)

13.56 *Very large tables.* Authors of works to be printed should consult their publishers early about tables that cannot easily be printed out on 8^1/$_2$ × 11-inch paper (see 13.55). Huge tables may be impossible to reproduce in printable form. Foldouts are extremely expensive and are thus rarely used. In a printed work, a series of manageable tables rather than one massive one will make things easier for both publisher and readers. In a work published electronically, hypertext links make navigation easy, and large tables present fewer problems.

13.57 *Awkward shapes.* When drafting a table for print publication, an author should consider its shape as well as its size. Neither a long, narrow table with few columns but many rows nor a wide, shallow one with many columns and few rows looks good in print, and both waste paper. The remedy for a long, skinny table is to double it up—run the table in two halves, side by side, with the column heads repeated over the second half (see table 13.14). For a wide, shallow table, the remedy is to turn it around, making column heads of the stub items and stub items of the column heads; if the table turns out to be too narrow that way, it can then be doubled up. See also 13.4.

13.58 *Copyfitting large tables.* If an oversize table cannot be accommodated in a printed work by the methods suggested in 13.54–55 and 13.57, further editorial or typographic adjustments will be needed. Wording may be shortened or abbreviations used. Omitting the running head when a table takes a full page (see 1.99) allows more space for the table itself. A wide table may extend a little into the left margin if on a verso or the right margin if on a recto or, if it looks better, equally on both sides. For a particularly large table, the publisher may decide to reduce the type size or to publish the table in electronic form only, if that is an option.

13.59 *Very wide tables.* To reduce excessive width, two other measures (neither very convenient for readers) are worth considering: numbers are used for column heads, and the text of the heads is relegated to footnotes, as illustrated in table 13.16; or column heads are turned on their sides so that they read up the printed page rather than across; this device is expensive to typeset.

13.60 *A dangerous option.* It can be dangerous to set a wide table horizontally across a double-page spread. While the columns will not suffer, the rows—unless there is ample vertical space between them—are likely to experience a jog between the two pages once the book or journal is bound, thus losing their essential alignment with the stub. A long vertical table that continues ("downward") onto a second page, however, is an acceptable arrangement (see 13.15).

13.61 *"Continued" lines.* In a vertical table that requires two or more pages, a "continued" line, usually in italics, is used at the top of each page but the first (see table 13.15). In a broadside table, it is used only on a verso. It will read, for example, *"Table 14 continued."* (Using *"Continued on next page"* is unnecessary unless the foot of the previous page looks like the end of the table.)

13.62 *Repeating column heads.* For a vertical table of more than one page, the column heads are repeated on each page (see table 13.15). For a broadside table, they are repeated only on each verso.

TABLE 13.16 Timing of socialist entry into elections and of suffrage reforms

Country	(1)	(2)	(3)	(4)	(5)	(6)	(7)
Austria	1889	1897	1907	—	1919	—	—
Belgium	1885[a]	1894	1894	45.7	1948	38.4	22.2
Denmark	1878[a]	1884	1849	28.1[b]	1915	24.6	23.9
Finland	1899	1907	1906	22.0	1906	—	22.0
France	1879	1893	1876	36.5[c]	1946	33.9	24.9
Germany	1867	1871	1871	25.5	1919	34.2[d]	34.0[d]
Italy	1892[a]	—	1913	—	1945	—	—
Netherlands	1878	1888	1917	—	1917	—	—
Norway	1887	1903	1898	34.1	1913	27.7	28.8
Spain	1879	1910	1907	—	1933	—	—
Sweden	1889	1896	1907	28.9	1921	35.0	37.0
Switzerland	1887	1897	1848	—	—	—	—
United Kingdom	1893[a]	1892[e]	1918	—	1928	—	—

NOTE: Column headings are as follows: (1) Socialist Party formed; (2) first candidates elected to Parliament; (3) universal male suffrage; (4) workers as a proportion of the electorate in the first elections after universal male suffrage; (5) universal suffrage; (6) workers as a proportion of the electorate in the last election before extension of franchise to women; and (7) workers as a proportion of the electorate in the first election after the extension.

[a]Major socialist or workers' parties existed earlier and dissolved or were repressed.

[b]In 1884, approximate.

[c]In 1902.

[d]Under different borders.

[e]Keir Hardie elected.

13.63 *Footnotes to a multipage table.* In a printed work, both general and specific footnotes in a table that continues beyond one printed page are usually gathered at the end of the table. But if a table contains no general notes and any specific notes pertain only to a single page, these notes may appear at the foot of the printed pages they apply to. In an electronic version that includes hypertext links, all footnotes are grouped at the bottom of the table.

Special Types of Tables

13.64 *Matrix.* A matrix is a tabular structure designed to show reciprocal relationships within a group of individuals, concepts, or whatever. In a matrix, the column heads and stub items are identical (see table 13.17). If there is no value for the cells that represent the meeting of the row and column that have the same name, such cells may be marked by ellipsis dots, as in table 13.18, or by an em dash, or they may be left blank, as in table 13.17. For matrices in mathematical notation, see 14.49–50.

TABLE 13.17 Innovations in measures of Amgen operating performance and stock market returns: Correlation matrix for the variables

	Revenue	Net income	Operating cash flow	Free cash flow	S&P 500 return	CRSP return
Revenue	1.00					
Net income	.03	1.00				
Operating cash flow	−.07	.91	1.00			
Free cash flow	.09	.12	.04	1.00		
S&P 500 return	.05	.04	.22	.16	1.00	
CRSP return	.08	.00	.19	.16	.99	1.00

NOTE: For revenue, the innovation is defined as the log-first difference. For all the other operating variables, it is the arithmetic-first difference.

TABLE 13.18 Average Euclidean distances between populations, calculated from morphological data

Population	Chunliao	Lona	Yunshanchau	Tunchiu	Tenchu	Hohuanshan	Tatachia
Chunliao	...						
Lona	0.57	...					
Yunshanchau	0.75	1.25	...				
Tunchiu	0.71	1.03	0.78	...			
Tenchu	1.15	1.10	1.59	0.97	...		
Hohuanshan	1.51	1.43	2.00	1.65	1.16	...	
Tatachia	1.85	2.03	2.17	1.69	1.24	1.55	...

13.65 *Genealogical table.* A genealogical table (traditionally so called, though it may be prepared and treated as line art; see 12.5) attempts to show important relationships within a family or several families by means of branching and connecting lines. Equals signs often indicate marriages or alliances producing offspring. Some, all, or no children may be listed, as needed. These tables require careful planning to illustrate relationships with minimal crossing of lines or extraneous data and, for a printed work, to remain within a reproducible shape and size. Table 13.19, for instance, shows that Galla Placidia was the daughter of Galla, whose half-brother Gratian married Constancia, granddaughter of Constantine the Great. This effectively designed table succinctly illustrates the complicated connection of Constantine to Hilderic, King of the Vandals.

13.66 *Pedigree table.* In works mainly genealogical in approach and concentration, pedigree tables may be used. These fan-shaped tables (not shown here) illustrate the ancestry of a given person, typically detailing the two parents, four grandparents, eight great-grandparents, and sixteen great-great-grandparents. They may also show several generations of offspring from a single pair of ancestors and can be used to trace the inheritance of a trait or disorder.

TABLE 13·19 The family of Galla Placidia Augusta

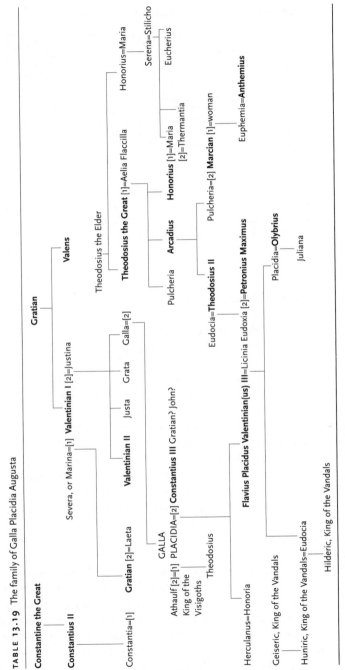

NOTE: Stemmata are simplified. Emperors are shown in boldface type.

TABLE 13.20 Mendelian cross: Cocker spaniel and basenji

CS ♀, cocker spaniel × BA ♂, basenji CS ♂, cocker spaniel, × BA ♀, basenji

× − BCSF₁ ♂ × BCSF₁ ♀	CSB ♀ × CSB ♂ − ×
BCS × CS BCSF₂	CSBF₂ CSB × BA
BACKCROSS TO COCKER	BACKCROSS TO BASENJI
BCS CROSS	*CSB CROSS*

NOTE: The basic plan was to repeat each of the two crosses with four matings and obtain two litters from each mating. Because of deaths among the cocker spaniel females, replication was completed only three times in the BCS cross.

13.67   *Genetic table.* Genetic tables are designed to show the results of cross-breeding in plants or animals according to Mendelian principles (see table 13.20). Multiplication signs show the crosses, and various symbols and abbreviations show the genetic makeup of the individual.

Editing Tables

13.68   *Content.* Tables should be edited with the same care as the text. They should be checked for relevance and for freedom from duplication. Totals should be checked and any discrepancies referred to the author for resolution. A lay reader or a nontechnical editor should be able to make logical sense of a table, even if the material is highly technical.

13.69   *Consistency.* However neat and orderly a table may appear, it must be checked not only for internal consistency but for conformity to the text and to other tables in the same work. Column heads and stubs must match one another in style across a series of tables. Spelling, capitalization, punctuation, abbreviations, and symbols must likewise be regularized. As in the text, footnote references must be checked against the footnotes, and the correct sequence of letters or symbols must be verified. See also 13.47.

13.70   *Format.* The editor should ensure that rules appear as needed, that spanner rules are the right length and are distinct from underlining (so that a rule and not italicized text appears in the typeset version), and that subentries in the stub are distinct from runover lines. If every entry in a column is preceded by a dollar sign or followed by a percent sign, the editor should add the sign to the column head and delete the signs in the column. In some instances the editor may have to recast a table to improve its shape or its logic or to make it consistent with other tables in the work (see 13.57–58).

13.71   *Instructions for typesetting.* Both vertical and horizontal alignment (see 13.35–38) must be clearly specified so as to avoid expensive changes in proof. (In a printed work with many tables, the tables are best checked in galley proof before pages are made up; see 3.16.) For long tables, the editor should make it clear whether and where "continued" lines and repeated column heads are needed and where footnotes should appear (see 13.63). The editor should also be sure that running heads are omitted on full-page and multipage tables (see 1.99, 3.10).

Typographic Considerations

13.72   *Books.* In a publication that is not part of a series, the designer will set the typographic style for tables, as for the text and other elements. Authors should therefore keep their style as simple as possible, avoiding full capitals, italics (except where these would be used in text, as for a species name), boldface, and the like. They should also avoid different font sizes, leaving it to the publisher to impose the variations. (Many tables are set in 8-point type, with their footnotes in 7- or 6-point type.) For a useful discussion of table design, see Richard Eckersley et al., *Glossary of Typesetting Terms* (bibliog. 2.6).

13.73   *Journals.* Simplicity of preparation also applies to tables to be published in journals. They will be set according to the journal's established typographic style.

13.74   *Table numbers, titles, and column heads.* The table number and title may be set in the same size as the body of the table or in a larger size. The number may be in a different font from the title (see 13.18). All column heads, including spanners and cut-in heads, are usually treated alike as to type size and style, usually 8-point roman, as in the body of the table. (Some publications use caps and small caps for first-level heads, including spanner heads, and upper- and lowercase for second-level heads, as in table 13.7.) Italics must be used for terms italicized in text (see table 13.21), and the expressions N and n should be italicized regardless of the style of other heads.

13.75   *Stub entries.* For indention versus other ways of distinguishing subentries from main entries and runover lines from subentries, see 13.25–26.

13.76   *Alignment.* For vertical and horizontal alignment, see 13.35–38.

TABLE 13.21 A comparison of the cost of carrying a 20 mg load 1 m for several ant species

Ant species	Mass (mg)	Energy cost (mJ)	Reference
Messor capitatus	2–21	7.1	Nielsen and Baroni-Urbani 1990
Camponotus herculeanus	41.2	9.2	Nielsen and Baroni-Urbani 1990
Pogonomyrmex rugosus	14.0	2.74	Lighton et al. 1993
Pogonomyrmex maricopa	8.7	2.58	Weier et al. 1995
Myrmecocystus mendax	6.2	3.3	Duncan and Lighton 1994
Pachycondyla analis			
Minor workers	15	2.82	Duncan 1995
Major workers	40	2.32	Duncan 1995
Pachycondyla berthoudi	25.5	2.26	Present study

13.77 *Footnotes.* Footnotes are normally set one point smaller than the body of a table. They may be paragraph indented or begin flush left; if they are set flush left, a little extra space should be left between them. Notes of a full line or more run the full width of the table. Short notes, if a flush-left format is used, are occasionally set two or more to a line. Such words as *Source* or *Note* at the beginning of a note may be set in italics, boldface, or caps and small caps. See also 13.43–50.

13.78 *Numerals.* Old-style figures (like this: 1938), though elegant as page numbers or in text that contains few numerals, should be avoided in tabular matter. To avoid any ambiguity that might be caused by old-style 1, for example, as well as for purposes of alignment, lining figures (like this: 1938) should be used in all tables.

14

Mathematics in Type

Introduction

14.1 *The role of the author and the editor.* The advent of sophisticated computer typesetting software has revolutionized the setting of mathematical copy. Many mathematical expressions and arrangements of expressions that formerly were very difficult to reproduce in print are now relatively easy to achieve. As a result, the role of the specialized typographer has increasingly been occupied by the author and editor, who now may have access to tools such as TeX that allow them to typeset complex mathematical copy during writing and editing. What used to be a two-step process, with the author and editor marking typescript, has become a one-step procedure in which they compose mathematical copy in its final form even if it has to be typeset again. When this is not the case, authors and editors must communicate to the typesetter exactly how the mathematical content should be typeset (see 14.59–66). Regardless of which method is used to prepare and typeset mathematical copy, the following general guidelines apply.[1]

Style of Mathematical Expressions

GENERAL USAGE

14.2 *Standards for mathematical copy.* The author and editor should give careful attention to matters of style, usage, sense, meaning, clarity, accuracy, and consistency. Authors should use correct terminology and notation and should carefully follow the conventions of their special fields, and editors should query any apparent violations of typographical or grammatical conventions. As a general rule, mathematical copy, including displayed equations, should "read" as clearly and grammatically as any other kind of copy. The signs for simple mathematical operations and relations have direct verbal translations: $a < b$ reads "a is less than b"; $a > b$ reads "a is greater than b"; $a + b = c$ reads "a plus b equals c." The translation is not always straightforward, however, as is the case with $df(x)/dx$, which means "the derivative of the function f of x with respect to x" and is not the quotient of two numbers $df(x)$ and dx. Moreover, mathematical notation is often abbreviated: the two inequalities $a < b$ and $b < c$ are usually written $a < b < c$.

14.3 *Consistency of notation.* Notation should be consistent and unambiguous: the same symbol should denote the same thing whenever it occurs and

---

1. The requirements of mathematical copy have prompted a different typographical treatment of the examples and tables in this chapter from that used in other chapters.

not be used for more than one thing. Typographical distinctions should also be made consistently; for example, if uppercase italic letters A, B, and C are used to denote sets and lowercase italic letters x, y, and z to denote the elements of sets, then a, b, and c should not be used for sets at another place without good reason.

14.4 *Words versus symbols in text.* Mathematical symbols should not be used as shorthand for words:

> $\exists$ a minimum value of the function f on the interval $[a, b]$

should be replaced by

> there exists a minimum value of the function f on the interval $[a, b]$

or

> the function f has a minimum value on the interval $[a, b]$.

In the phrase

> the vectors $r_1, \ldots, r_n, \neq 0$,

the condition "$\neq 0$" should be expressed in words:

> the nonzero vectors $r_1, \ldots, r_n$

or

> the vectors $r_1, \ldots, r_n$, all nonzero,

depending on the emphasis desired.

14.5 *Concise expression.* Mathematical symbols should not be used superfluously. For example, the symbol n is extraneous in the statement

> There is no integer n between 0 and 1.

As a general rule, no letter standing for a mathematical object should be used only once. Symbols that appear to be redundant may be qualified later in the same discussion, however, and editors should never delete a symbol without explicit instruction from the author.

14.6 *Sentence beginning with a mathematical symbol.* Mathematical symbols should not begin a sentence, especially if the preceding sentence ended with a symbol, since it may be difficult to tell where one sentence ends and another begins. For example, it is difficult to read

Assume that $x \in S$. S is countable.

If a sentence starting with a symbol cannot easily be rephrased, the appropriate term for the symbol can be inserted in apposition at the beginning of the sentence:

Assume that $x \in S$. The set S is countable.

If the sentences are closely related, a semicolon may be used to connect them:

A function f is even if $f(x) = f(-x)$; f is odd if $f(x) = -f(-x)$.

14.7   *Adjacent mathematical symbols.* Mathematical symbols in adjacent mathematical expressions should be separated by words or punctuation, for the same reason:

Suppose that $a = bq + r$, where $0 \leq r < b$.

SIGNS AND SYMBOLS

14.8   *Mathematical characters.* The smallest units of mathematical writing are mathematical signs and symbols, which include letters and numbers. Table 14.1 lists some of the standard mathematical characters and their verbal translations.

14.9   *Letters and accents.* Ordinary italic letters are used to represent various kinds of mathematical objects. The set of letters can be greatly extended by the use of accents, including, for example, $\hat{a}$, $\tilde{a}$, $\bar{a}$, $\breve{a}$, $\dot{a}$, $\ddot{a}$, $\check{a}$, and $\vec{a}$. Double accents may also be used; for example, $\bar{\bar{a}}$ and $\dot{\dot{a}}$. They can, however, sometimes be difficult to center over a letter and, in combination with capital letters, may interfere with descenders from the line above, so they should be avoided if possible. Accents over several letters or groups of letters (for example, $\widehat{1-x}$ and $\widetilde{1-x}$) are difficult to produce in some typesetting systems, as are some accent marks placed under a symbol, and they may require special treatment during composition.

14.10   *Letters and fonts.* The number of symbols can also be extended by using letters from other alphabets, most often the Greek alphabet, and by representing letters from the Latin alphabet in other fonts and typefaces. Examples of characters from four fonts and typefaces commonly used in mathematics are

GREEK	SCRIPT	BOLDFACE ITALIC	BOLDFACE GREEK
ΑΒΓΔαβγδ	𝒜ℬ𝒞𝒟	**ABCDabcd**	**ΑΒΓΔαβγδ**

Lowercase script characters are often not available. See also 14.64 for marking fonts on paper manuscripts.

14.11 *List of unusual characters.* Before editing begins, it may be advisable, depending on the typesetter and the publisher's knowledge of the typesetter's resources, to prepare a list of unusual mathematical signs, symbols, and special characters used in the manuscript. This is preferably done by the author but may be done by the editor. In preparing an electronic manuscript, the author should make a list of any special, nonstandard fonts. A copy should be given to the publisher, who will check with the typesetter to make sure the necessary characters are available. If some are not, the author may be asked to use more accessible forms; if that is impossible, the typesetter must be asked to obtain or generate the characters needed.

14.12 *Special mathematical symbols.* Many mathematical symbols have a reserved meaning: π stands for the number $3.14159265\ldots$, e for the number $2.71828183\ldots$, and i for the square root of -1. The symbols $\forall$, $\exists$, $\in$, $\subset$, and $\varnothing$ are used in all mathematical disciplines. Open-faced (blackboard) symbols are reserved for familiar systems of numbers: $\mathbb{N}$ for the natural numbers, $\mathbb{Z}$ for the integers ($\mathbb{Z}^+$ is the same as $\mathbb{N}$), $\mathbb{Q}$ for the rational numbers, $\mathbb{R}$ for the real numbers, and $\mathbb{C}$ for the complex numbers.

14.13 *Signs for binary operations and relations.* Binary operations combine two mathematical expressions. Examples of binary operation signs are $+$ (plus sign), $-$ (minus sign), $\cdot$ (multiplication dot), $\times$ (multiplication cross), $\div$ (division sign), $/$ (solidus or slash), and $\circ$ (composition sign). Binary relations express a relationship between two mathematical expressions. Examples of relation signs are $=$, $\neq$, $<$, $>$, and $|$.

14.14 *Basic spacing in mathematics.* An em space (or "quad") is approximately the width of an em (or, again approximately, a capital M) in the font in use. In mathematical typesetting, a thick space is $5/18$ of an em, a medium space is $2/9$ of an em, and a thin space is $1/6$ of an em. Signs for binary operations are preceded and followed by medium spaces, and signs for binary relations are preceded and followed by thick spaces:

TABLE 14.1 Mathematics signs and symbols

Sign	Definition	Sign	Definition
	Operations		*Operators*
+	Addition	Σ	Summation
−	Subtraction	Π	Product
×	Multiplication	$\int$	Integral
·	Multiplication	$\oint$	Contour integral
÷	Division		*Logic*
/	Division	$\wedge$	And, conjunction
∘	Composition	$\vee$	Or, disjunction
∪	Union	¬	Negation
∩	Intersection	$\Rightarrow$	Implies
±	Plus or minus	$\rightarrow$	Implies
∓	Minus or plus	$\Leftrightarrow$	If and only if
*, ⊛	Convolution	$\leftrightarrow$	If and only if
⊕	Direct sum, various	$\exists$	Existential quantifier
⊖	Various	$\forall$	Universal quantifier
⊗	Various	$\in$	A member of
⊙	Various	$\notin$	Not a member of
:	Ratio	⊢	Assertion
⨿	Amalgamation	$\therefore$	Hence, therefore
	Relations	$\because$	Because
=	Equal to		*Radial units*
≠	Not equal to	′	Minute
≈	Nearly equal to	″	Second
≅	Equals approximately, isomorphic to	°	Degree
<	Less than		*Constants*
≪	Much less than	π	Pi (≈3.14159265)
>	Greater than	e	Base of natural logarithms
≫	Much greater than		(≈2.71828183)
≤	Less than or equal to		*Geometry*
≦	Less than or equal to	⊥	Perpendicular
≦	Less than or equal to	‖	Parallel
≥	Greater than or equal to	∦	Not parallel
≧	Greater than or equal to	∠	Angle
≧	Greater than or equal to	⊀	Spherical angle
≡	Equivalent to, congruent to	⋎	Equal angles
≢	Not equivalent to, not congruent to		*Miscellaneous*
|	Divides, divisible by	i	Square root of −1
∼	Similar to, asymptotically equal to	′	Prime
:=	Assignment	″	Double prime
∈	A member of	‴	Triple prime
∉	Not a member of	$\sqrt{}$	Square root, radical
⊂	Subset of	$\sqrt[3]{}$	Cube root
⊆	Subset of or equal to	$\sqrt[n]{}$	nth root
⊃	Superset of	!	Factorial
⊇	Superset of or equal to	!!	Double factorial
∝	Varies as, proportional to	∅	Empty set, null set
≐	Approaches a limit, definition	∞	Infinity
→	Tends to, maps to	∂	Partial differential
←	Maps from	Δ	Delta
↦	Maps to	∇	Nabla, del
↪	Maps into	∇^2, Δ	Laplacian operator
↩	Maps into	$\square^2$	d'Alembertian operator

$$x^n + y^n = z^n, \qquad X \cup \varnothing = X, \qquad (a \circ b) \circ c = a \circ (b \circ c).$$

Signs for binary operations are not followed by a space when they are used to modify a symbol rather than combine two mathematical symbols or expressions:

$$-1, \quad +\infty, \quad \times 5.$$

No space is inserted before or after operation or relation signs in subscripts and superscripts (see 14.35–37).

14.15 *Functions.* The concept of a function is one of the most common and important ideas in mathematics. A function is an assignment that associates an element of a set, called the domain, with a unique element of a set, called the codomain. Functions are specified in several different ways. For example, if f is a function from a domain X into a codomain Y, this relationship can be written

$$f : X \rightarrow Y,$$

where the function symbol stands to the left of the colon and the symbols for the domain and codomain, connected by an arrow that means "maps," are to the right of the colon. Functions are often expressed as mathematical formulas. For example,

$$f(x) = x^2$$

describes the function that associates every number x in a given domain with its square. In this notation, the variable x is the argument of the function f. Some functions are so common that special names have been assigned to them, and the abbreviations for these functions, set in roman, are frequently used in mathematical expressions. Examples are log (logarithm), ln (natural logarithm), exp (exponential function), max (maximum), min (minimum), lim (limit), sin (sine), cos (cosine), tan (tangent), arg (argument), and mod (modulo):

$$\ln 2\pi \qquad \sin(x + y) \qquad \min(x_1, x_2).$$

These abbreviations are followed by a thin space unless the argument is enclosed in delimiters (see 14.25), in which case they are usually closed up to the opening delimiter. For a more complete list of abbreviated functions, see table 14.2.

TABLE 14.2 Standard abbreviations in mathematical copy

sin	Sine	sn	Elliptic function, sn
cos	Cosine	cn	Elliptic function, cn
		dn	Elliptic function, dn
tan	Tangent	tg	Tangent[a]
cot	Cotangent	ctg	Cotangent[a]
sec	Secant	csc	Cosecant
sinh	Hyperbolic sine	cosh	Hyperbolic cosine
tanh	Hyperbolic tangent	coth	Hyperbolic cotangent
$\sin^{-1}$	Inverse sine	arcsin	Inverse sine
log	Common logarithm ($\log_{10}$)	ln	Natural logarithm
lg	Binary logarithm ($\log_2$)	$\log_e$	Natural logarithm, alternate form
sgn	Sign	arg	Argument
det or Det	Determinant	Tr	Trace (also Sp, or *spur*)
Re, $\Re$	Real part	Im, $\Im$	Imaginary part
curl	Curl; vector operator, same as $\nabla \times$	div	Divergence; vector operator, same as $\nabla \cdot$
prob or Pr	Probability	mod	Modulo (as in a mod β)
inf	Infimum; greatest lower bound	sup	Supremum; least upper bound
isom	Isomorphism	hom	Homeomorphism
min	Minimum	max	Maximum
gcd	Greatest common divisor	lcm	Least common multiple
dex	Decimal exponent; from $10^{-1.5}$ to 10^{-3} is 1.5 dex	norm	Norm; norm $(a) = \|a\|$
dim or Dim	Dimension	ker	Kernel
wrt	With respect to	iff	If and only if
Var	Variance	Cov	Covariance

[a]Frequently used by non–North American authors.

14.16 *Functions that take limits.* Some standard functions can take limits. The limits are set as subscripts to the right of the abbreviation in text and below the abbreviation in display:

$$\lim_{x \to a} f(x) \qquad \lim_{x \to a} f(x)$$

$$\max_{a_i, b_i \in S}(a_i, b_i) \qquad \max_{a_i, b_i \in S}(a_i, b_i)$$

MATHEMATICAL EXPRESSIONS IN DISPLAY

14.17 *Displaying mathematical expressions.* Mathematical expressions should be displayed, that is, set on a separate line clear of text and centered, if they are important to the exposition, if they are referenced, or if they are difficult to read or typeset in the body of the text. If different mathematical expressions are displayed on the same line, the expressions should be separated by spacing, together with words or punctuation:

If $a = b$, then for all real numbers x,

$$a + x = b + x, \qquad ax = bx, \qquad -a = -b.$$

If different mathematical expressions are displayed on separate consecutive lines, each expression should be centered on the line:

If $a = b$, then for all real numbers x,

$$a + x = b + x,$$
$$ax = bx,$$
$$-a = -b.$$

14.18 *Qualifying clauses for displayed expressions.* Qualifying clauses may be presented in several ways. If the main expression is displayed, the qualifying clause may also be displayed:

If f is a constant function, then

$$f'(a) = 0 \quad \text{for all real numbers } a.$$

The qualifying clause may appear in the text, following the displayed main expression:

Suppose that the prime factorization of the integer a is given by

$$a_n = p_1^{k_1} \cdots p_r^{k_r},$$

where the p_i are distinct prime numbers and $k_i > 0$.

The qualifying clause may appear in the text, preceding the displayed main expression:

For all real numbers a and b,

$$|a + b| \le |a| + |b|.$$

14.19 *Breaking displayed expressions.* When long mathematical expressions occur in the body of the text, they may need to be displayed if they break badly at the end of a line. Even in displayed form, however, some long expressions may not fit on one line. If necessary, displayed expressions may be broken before a relation or operation sign. Examples of several such signs follow:

Operation signs: $+ - \times \div \pm \cup \cap$
Relation signs: $= \ne > < \ge \le \to \supset \subset \in \approx \equiv$

See table 14.1 for a more complete list. If displayed expressions are centered, runover lines are aligned on the relation signs, which should be followed by thick spaces:

$$h(x) = (x - a)(x - \beta)(x - \gamma)$$
$$= x^3 - (a + \beta + \gamma)x^2 + (a\beta + a\gamma + \beta\gamma)x - a\beta\gamma.$$

If a runover line begins with an operation sign, the operation sign should be lined up with the first character to the right of the relation sign in the line above it, followed by a medium space:

$$\frac{\pi}{4} = \frac{1}{2} - \frac{1}{3 \times 2^3} + \frac{1}{5 \times 2^5} - \frac{1}{7 \times 2^7} + \frac{1}{9 \times 2^9} - \frac{1}{11 \times 2^{11}} + \cdots$$
$$+ \frac{1}{3} - \frac{1}{3 \times 3^3} + \frac{1}{5 \times 3^5} - \frac{1}{7 \times 3^7} + \frac{1}{9 \times 3^9} - \cdots$$
$$+ \frac{1}{4} - \frac{1}{3 \times 4^3} + \frac{1}{5 \times 4^5} - \frac{1}{7 \times 4^7} + \cdots.$$

For additional rules on breaking expressions, consult Ellen Swanson, *Mathematics into Type* (bibliog. 2.4).

NUMERATION

14.20 *Methods of numeration.* Displayed mathematical expressions may be numbered or labeled, as may definitions, theorems, lemmas, and other formal parts of the exposition. If the numbering system is not too cumbersome, this offers a convenient and space-saving method of cross-reference. A double-numeration system is often used in texts with many displays and several chapters or sections (see 1.76); in this system, displays are labeled with the chapter or section number first, followed by the equation number, starting with number 1 for the displayed expressions in each chapter or section. If a single-numeration system is used in a text with several chapters or sections, the displays are also often numbered starting with 1 in each chapter or section.

14.21 *Numbering displayed mathematical expressions.* Mathematical expressions that are referenced later in the text should be numbered or otherwise labeled. Displayed mathematical expressions that present important results are often numbered or labeled, as are important steps in a calculation or proof. All numbered mathematical expressions must be displayed. For example:

Hence it is apparent that $1^3 + 2^3 + \cdots + n^3 = (1 + 2 + \cdots + n)^2.$ (1.1)

Hence it is apparent that

$$1^3 + 2^3 + \cdots + n^3 = (1 + 2 + \cdots + n)^2.$$ (1.1)

Displays are centered on the line (without regard to the equation number or label). The number or label, enclosed in parentheses to prevent misreading, is usually put at the right margin, but it may be placed at the left margin. In cross-references, display numbers or labels are enclosed in parentheses to match the marginal enumerations:

Recalling equation (1.1), we may conclude that . . .

A range of equations is referred to by giving the first and last equation numbers, joined by an en dash:

From equations (2)–(5) we obtain . . .

PUNCTUATION

14.22   *Mathematical expressions and punctuation.* Mathematical expressions are sentences or parts of sentences, and they should be punctuated accordingly. Punctuation of displayed expressions requires special attention. In general, if several expressions appear in a single display, they should be separated by commas or semicolons. For example,

$$x_1 + x_2 + x_3 = 3,$$
$$x_1 x_2 + x_2 x_3 + x_3 x_1 = 6,$$
$$x_1 x_2 x_3 = -1.$$

Consecutive lines of a single multiline expression should not be punctuated:

$$\begin{aligned}
(|a + b|)^2 = (a + b)^2 &= a^2 + 2ab + b^2 \\
&\leq a^2 + 2|a||b| + b^2 \\
&= |a|^2 + 2|a||b| + |b|^2 \\
&= (|a| + |b|)^2.
\end{aligned}$$

Displayed equations must carry ending punctuation if they end a sentence. All ending punctuation and the commas and semicolons separating expressions should be aligned horizontally on the baseline, even when preceded by constructs such as subscripts, superscripts, or fractions.

14.23   *Elided lists.* In elided lists, commas should come after each term in the list and after the ellipsis points if the list has a final term. For example,

$$y = 0, 1, 2, \ldots \quad \text{not} \quad y = 0, 1, 2 \ldots$$
$$x_1, x_2, \ldots, x_n \quad \text{not} \quad x_1, x_2, \ldots x_n.$$

The ellipsis points should be on the baseline when the terms of the list are separated by commas.

14.24   *Elided operations and relations.* In elided sums or elided relations, the ellipsis points should be centered between the operation or relation signs. For example,

$$x_1 + x_2 + \cdots + x_n, \quad \text{not} \quad x_1 + x_2 + \ldots + x_n$$
$$a_1 < a_2 < \cdots < a_n, \quad \text{not} \quad a_1 < a_2 < \ldots < a_n.$$

Multiplication is often signified by the juxtaposition of the factors without a multiplication sign between them. That is,

$$abc \qquad \text{means} \qquad a \cdot b \cdot c.$$

When the multiplication sign is not explicit, the elided product may be denoted with ellipsis points either on the baseline or vertically centered:

$$a_1 a_2 \ldots a_n \qquad \text{or} \qquad a_1 a_2 \cdots a_n.$$

The second alternative is commonly used in displays with built-up factors:

$$\phi(n) = n\left(1 - \frac{1}{p_1}\right)\left(1 - \frac{1}{p_2}\right) \cdots \left(1 - \frac{1}{p_k}\right).$$

If the multiplication dot is present, then ellipsis points should be on the baseline and not centered. For example,

$$a_1 \cdot a_2 \cdot \ldots \cdot a_n, \quad \text{not} \quad a_1 \cdot a_2 \cdot \cdots \cdot a_n.$$

If the multiplication cross is present, then ellipsis points should be centered. For example,

$$a_1 \times a_2 \times \cdots \times a_n.$$

Multiplication signs are always used when the factors need to be separated:

$$1 \times 2 \times \cdots \times 10.$$

Often the use of the multiplication cross rather than dot is merely a matter of preference, but in some cases the cross is standard notation. For example, the Cartesian product of n sets $S_1, S_2, \ldots, S_n$ is denoted

$$S_1 \times S_2 \times \cdots \times S_n, \quad \text{not} \quad S_1 \times S_2 \times \ldots \times S_n.$$

DELIMITERS

14.25   *Common delimiters or fences.* Three sorts of symbols are commonly used to group mathematical expressions: parentheses ( ), brackets [ ], and braces { }. They are used in pairs, and their normal order is $\{[( )]\}$. When necessary, the sequence of fences can be extended by large parentheses, brackets, and braces as follows:

$$\Big\{\big[\big(\{[(\quad)]\}\big)\big]\Big\}$$

In text, the braces are sometimes omitted from this sequence. Angle brackets, vertical bars, and double vertical bars carry special mathematical significance and should not be used to supplement the sequence of common delimiters.

14.26   *Functional notation.* In functional notation, nested pairs of parentheses are used instead of brackets or braces to indicate grouping:

$$(f \circ g \circ h)(x) = f(g(h(x))).$$

14.27   *Set notation.* Braces are used to delimit the elements of a set, and other delimiters should not be substituted. For example,

$$\{a_1, a_2, \ldots, a_n\}$$

denotes the set consisting of n objects $a_1, a_2, \ldots, a_n$, and

$$\{x : x \in D\}$$

denotes the set of all elements x in a domain D. In the second example (called "set-builder" notation), the condition that defines the set follows the colon. A vertical bar is sometimes used instead of the colon to delimit the condition.

14.28 *Ordered set notation.* Parentheses are used to delimit an ordered set of objects. For example,

$$(a, b)$$

denotes the ordered pair of objects a and b, where a is the first element in the pair and b is the second element. More generally,

$$(a_1, a_2, \ldots, a_n)$$

denotes the ordered n-tuple of objects $a_1, a_2, \ldots, a_n$. This notation is standard, and other delimiters should not be substituted.

14.29 *Intervals.* Parentheses are used to delimit an open interval, that is, one that does not include its endpoints; for example, (a, b) denotes the set of all real numbers between a and b, not including either a or b. Brackets are used to delimit a closed interval, that is, an open interval together with a and b. The notation $(a, b]$ signifies the interval not including a but including b, while $[a, b)$ denotes the interval including a but not including b. Parentheses and brackets in interval notation should not be replaced with other delimiters.

14.30 *Delimiters denoting inner product.* Parentheses are sometimes used to denote the inner product of two vectors: (u, w). Angle brackets are also used as notation for the inner product: $\langle u, w \rangle$. See also 14.51–52.

14.31 *Binomial coefficients.* The notation $\binom{n}{k}$, "n choose k," is called the binomial coefficient and stands for the number of ways k objects can be chosen from among a collection of n objects. It is defined by

$$\binom{n}{k} = \frac{n!}{k!(n-k)!},$$

where n and k are positive integers and the notation ! stands for the factorial function,

$$n! = n \times (n-1) \times \cdots \times 1.$$

14.32   *Vertical bars.* Vertical bars serve several special purposes. The modulus or absolute value of x is denoted $|x|$. The notation $|\mathbf{u}|$ is used for the "length" of a vector $\mathbf{u}$ in a Euclidean vector space; this is sometimes called the norm of $\mathbf{u}$ and is written with a double vertical bar, $||\mathbf{u}||$. Vertical bars are used to denote the cardinal number of a set. The notation $|A|$ can signify the determinant of a matrix A, which is also denoted det A.

14.33   *Single vertical bar.* A single vertical bar with limits is used to denote the evaluation of a formula at a particular value of one of its variables. For example,

$$\int_0^{\pi/2} \sin x \, dx = -\cos x \Big|_{x=0}^{x=\pi/2} = 1 .$$

14.34   *Cases.* Displayed mathematical expressions that present a choice between alternatives may be grouped using a single brace and are punctuated as follows:

$$|a| = \begin{cases} a, & a \geq 0 ; \\ -a, & a < 0 . \end{cases}$$

Another acceptable style is

$$f(x) = \begin{cases} 1 & \text{if } x \geq 0 , \\ 0 & \text{otherwise} . \end{cases}$$

As a general rule, each alternative is equivalent to a clause in ordinary language and should be punctuated as such. If the alternatives are very long, they may be stated as separate equations:

$$I(t) = Ae^{\Gamma_1(t-t_p)}\{1 + \varepsilon_1 \cos[2\pi f(t - t_p)]\} \\ + B\{1 + \varepsilon_2 \cos[2\pi f(t - t_p)]\} , \quad t \leq t_p , \tag{1a}$$

$$I(t) = Ae^{-\Gamma_2(t-t_p)}\{1 + \varepsilon_1 \cos[2\pi f(t - t_p)]\} \\ + B\{1 + \varepsilon_2 \cos[2\pi f(t - t_p)]\} , \quad t > t_p . \tag{1b}$$

SUBSCRIPTS AND SUPERSCRIPTS

14.35   *Simple subscripts and superscripts.* Inferior and superior indices, exponents, and other superscript symbols such as primes occur very frequently in mathematical copy and are indispensable for concise expression in mathematics. Examples are

$$x_1,\ x^2,\ 2^x,\ x',\ x_{ij}y_{jk},\ x^{ab},\ a^x b^y,\ x''_{12}.$$

Multiple indices are written without commas between them unless there is a possibility of confusion: x_{ij} instead of $x_{i,j}$, but $x_{1,2}$ if there is a possibility of confusing the subscripts "1, 2" and "12." Abbreviations or words that serve as labels in subscripts or superscripts are usually set in roman type:

$$x_{\mathrm{min}},\ u_{\mathrm{av}}.$$

14.36 *Complex subscripts and superscripts.* Subscripts and superscripts may themselves have subscripts and superscripts. For example,

$$x_{a_k},\quad x_{a_k^2},\quad 2^{x^2},\quad 2^{x_i^2}.$$

Mathematical expressions may occur as subformulas in the superior or inferior positions. For example,

$$x^{a+b},\quad a^{-x}b^{(y-z)^2},\quad a^{x'y'}_{2n},\quad 2^{\sqrt{n}}.$$

14.37 *Alignment of subscripts and superscripts.* Subscripts and superscripts may be stacked

$$x_i^n,\quad x_{ij}^{mn}$$

or staggered

$$X^{ab}{}_{cd},\quad X_{ij}{}^{kl}.$$

Because there are standard conventions for raising and lowering indices in some branches of mathematics, most especially in tensor calculus, the relative position between superior and inferior indices must be respected. For example,

$$T^i{}_j$$

(the tensor arising from T^{ij} by lowering its second index) and

$$T_i{}^j$$

(the tensor arising from T^{ij} by lowering its first index) are different and must be clearly distinguished. Neither should be written T_j^i. Ordinary punctuation marks carrying special meaning may occur in subscripted or superscripted expressions. For instance,

$$T^i{}_{,j} \quad \text{and} \quad T^i{}_{;j}$$

have a precise mathematical meaning and should not be changed. In tensor expressions, the symbol $R_{[i,j]}$ is not the same as $R_{(i,j)}$, and they should not be interchanged.

SUMMATIONS AND INTEGRALS

14.38   *Summation sign.* The summation sign $\sum$ is used to stand for a sum, finite or infinite, of terms. For example, the sums

$$a_1 + a_2 + \cdots + a_n \quad \text{and} \quad a_1 + a_2 + \cdots$$

may be written

$$\sum_{i=1}^{n} a_i \quad \text{and} \quad \sum_{i=1}^{\infty} a_i,$$

respectively. The variable i in the expressions above is called the index of summation. The subformulas below and above the summation sign are called the limits of summation and indicate where the summation begins and, if it is finite, ends. Summation limits are sometimes omitted if it is clear from the context what the limits are; for example, if all vectors are stated to be of size n and all matrices are of size $n \times n$, it is acceptable to write

$$y_i = \sum_j a_{ij} x_j.$$

When a summation sign occurs in text, its limits are placed to the right of the summation sign to avoid spreading the lines of text: $\sum_{i=1}^{n} a_i$.

14.39   *Product sign.* Product notation follows similar conventions. The products

$$a_1 \cdot a_2 \cdot \ldots \cdot a_n \quad \text{and} \quad a_1 \cdot a_2 \cdot \ldots$$

may be written

$$\prod_{i=1}^{n} a_i \quad \text{and} \quad \prod_{i=1}^{\infty} a_i,$$

respectively, and in text the limits are placed to the right of the product symbol to avoid spreading lines: $\prod_{i=1}^{n} a_i$.

14.40 *Integral sign.* The integral sign $\int$ is used to denote two sorts of integrals, called *definite* and *indefinite.* The definite integral is the integral of a function f on an interval $[a, b]$. This integral is denoted

$$\int_a^b f(x)\,dx.$$

The numbers a and b are called the lower and upper limits of integration, and dx is called the element of integration or the differential. The limits of integration are often placed to the right of the integral sign in both text and display. The indefinite integral is denoted

$$\int f \quad \text{or} \quad \int f(x)\,dx\,,$$

without limits of integration. In more advanced texts the definite integral is written

$$\int_D f(x)\,dx\,,$$

where D is the set of integration. If the function has two variables, it is common to have a double integral sign; double integrals can appear in iterated notation, in which case one of the differentials may be placed between the integral signs:

$$\iint_{[a,b]\times[c,d]} f(x)\,dx\,dy = \int_a^b dx \int_c^d f(x, y)\,dy\,.$$

Triple integrals are also used if the integration is performed in three variables; this occurs most commonly in engineering books. In text, the set of integration is placed to the right of the integral sign: $\int_D f(x)dx$.

14.41 *Spacing around differentials.* Thin spaces are placed before and after differentials:

$$r^2 = dr\,d\theta\,a^2\cos 2\theta.$$

Differentials should be closed up to the slash:

$$dx/dt.$$

RADICALS

14.42 *Radical signs.* The radical sign $\sqrt{}$ is used to denote the square root. A horizontal bar extends from the top of the radical sign to the end of the radicand:

$$\sqrt{2} \quad \sqrt{\sin^2 x + \cos^2 x}\,.$$

In display, the radical sign extends vertically to accommodate a built-up radicand:

$$\sqrt{\dfrac{\ln n}{n}}\,.$$

The radical sign may be used to denote cube and higher-order roots. For these roots, a superscript-sized number or letter is set above the radical sign:

$$\sqrt[3]{5} \quad \sqrt[n]{n!}\,.$$

14.43 *Radical signs in text.* Radical signs can be used in text if the radicand is a simple expression: $a = m + n\sqrt{3}$. If the radicand is more complex or if the text design uses tight leading, radical signs can give the page a crowded look or interfere with descending letters in the line above. One remedy is to substitute the appropriate exponent, using delimiters to indicate the extent of the radicand. For example,

$$\sqrt{a^2 + b^2}$$

may be replaced by

$$(a^2 + b^2)^{1/2}.$$

FRACTIONS

14.44 *Fractions in text.* Fractions are set in text with a slash to separate the numerator and denominator:

$$1/2, \quad 2/3, \quad 1/10, \quad 97/100, \quad \pi/2, \quad 11/5, \quad a/b.$$

Some common numerical fractions may be set as case fractions (text-sized fractions with a horizontal bar):

$$\tfrac{1}{2}, \quad \tfrac{2}{3}, \quad \tfrac{1}{10}\,.$$

Fractions should be enclosed in parentheses if they are followed by a mathematical symbol or expression:

$(a/b)x.$

For simple algebraic fractions in text, the slash should be used rather than the horizontal fraction bar. For example,

$$(ax + b)/(cx + d), \quad \text{not} \quad \tfrac{ax+b}{cx+d}.$$

The slash connects only the two groups of symbols immediately adjacent to it. Thus, $a + b/cd$ means

$$a + \frac{b}{cd},$$

not

$$\frac{a + b}{cd},$$

which should be written $(a + b)/cd$.

14.45 *Fractions in display.* In displayed mathematical expressions, all fractions should be built up unless they are part of a numerator or denominator or in a subscript or superscript:

$$\left| x^2 \sin \frac{1}{x} \right| < \frac{1}{10}, \quad \text{not} \quad |x^2 \sin \tfrac{1}{x}| < \tfrac{1}{10}.$$

Fractions that include summation, product, or integral signs should always be displayed. For example:

$$\frac{\int_0^{\pi/2} \sin^{2n} x \, dx}{\int_0^{\pi/2} \sin^{2n+1} x \, dx}.$$

If there are no built-up fractions in the display, common numerical fractions may be set as case fractions:

$$|a - b| < \tfrac{1}{10}.$$

14.46 *Fractions in subscripts and superscripts.* Fractions in subscripts and superscripts should always use the slash, both in text and in display:

$$x^{a/b}, \, y_{3/2}.$$

14.47   *Multiple and multilevel fractions.* If a mathematical expression contains more than one fraction, it should be displayed, and the horizontal bar should be used for the principal fraction sign:

$$\frac{ax + b}{cx + d} = \frac{px + q}{rx + s}.$$

Fractions should preferably be limited to two levels:

$$\frac{a/b + c}{p/q + r} \quad \text{not} \quad \frac{\frac{a}{b} + c}{\frac{p}{q} + r}.$$

Continued fractions, that is, expressions of the form $a_1 + 1/b_1$, where $b_1 = a_2 + 1/b_2$, $b_2 = a_3 + 1/b_3$, and so on, are set display size:

$$a_1 + \cfrac{1}{a_2 + \cfrac{1}{a_3 + \cfrac{1}{a_4 + \cdots}}}.$$

14.48   *Rewriting fractions using exponents.* There are times when it is desirable to represent the denominator of a fraction without using a fraction rule or a slash. This may be done by using delimiters followed by the exponent –1:

$$ab(cd)^{-1} \quad \text{instead of} \quad \frac{ab}{cd}.$$

If there is already an exponent in the denominator, it can be changed to its negative:

$$ab(cd)^{-2} \quad \text{instead of} \quad \frac{ab}{(cd)^2}.$$

If an exponential expression, particularly in text, is very complex, it may be rewritten in a simpler form. An exponential term such as

$$e^{(2\pi i \sum n_j)/\sqrt{x^2 + y^2}}$$

can be rewritten using the abbreviation exp:

$$\exp[(2\pi i \sum n_j)/(x^2 + y^2)^{1/2}].$$

MATRICES AND DETERMINANTS

14.49   *Matrices.* Matrices are arrays of terms displayed in rectangular arrangements of rows and columns and enclosed on the left and right by large brackets or parentheses. Matrices may be written

$$\begin{bmatrix} a_{11} & a_{12} & \cdots & a_{1n} \\ a_{21} & a_{22} & \cdots & a_{2n} \\ \vdots & \vdots & & \vdots \\ a_{m1} & a_{m2} & \cdots & a_{mn} \end{bmatrix} \quad \text{or} \quad \begin{pmatrix} a_{11} & a_{12} & \cdots & a_{1n} \\ a_{21} & a_{22} & \cdots & a_{2n} \\ \vdots & \vdots & & \vdots \\ a_{m1} & a_{m2} & \cdots & a_{mn} \end{pmatrix}$$

The notation should be consistent. The horizontal lists of entries are called the rows of the matrix, and the vertical lists the columns. A matrix with m rows and n columns is called an $m \times n$ matrix. A matrix consisting of a single row is called a row matrix or a row vector; a matrix consisting of a single column is a column matrix or a column vector. For example,

$$\begin{bmatrix} a & b & c \end{bmatrix} \quad \text{and} \quad \begin{bmatrix} a \\ b \\ c \end{bmatrix}$$

are row and column matrices, respectively. The transpose of a matrix A, denoted A^T, is the matrix obtained by interchanging the rows and columns of A. For example,

$$\begin{pmatrix} a_{11} & a_{21} & \cdots & a_{m1} \\ a_{12} & a_{12} & \cdots & a_{m2} \\ \vdots & \vdots & & \vdots \\ a_{1n} & a_{2n} & \cdots & a_{mn} \end{pmatrix}$$

is the transpose of the $m \times n$ matrix given above. Column matrices such as

$$\begin{bmatrix} a \\ b \\ c \end{bmatrix}$$

may be represented in text as $(a, b, c)^T$, col. (a, b, c), or the column vector (a, b, c), and a $2 \times n$ (for small n) matrix may be set, for example, as $\left(\begin{smallmatrix} a & c \\ b & d \end{smallmatrix} \right)$. Most matrices and determinants are displayed, however. In-line matrices cannot be broken on the line, and display matrices cannot be broken across the column or page.

14.50 *Determinants.* If A is a square matrix, the determinant of A, denoted $|A|$ or det A, is a function that assigns a specific number to the matrix A. If A is an $n \times n$ matrix, the determinant of A is represented by

$$\begin{vmatrix} a_{11} & a_{12} & \cdots & a_{1n} \\ a_{21} & a_{22} & \cdots & a_{2n} \\ \vdots & \vdots & & \vdots \\ a_{n1} & a_{2n} & \cdots & a_{nn} \end{vmatrix}.$$

Vertical bars are used to distinguish the determinant of A from the matrix A. The Jacobian has a reserved notation:

$$J = \left| \frac{\partial(A, B)}{\partial(x, y)} \right|.$$

This is sometimes generalized:

$$J = \left| \frac{\partial(f_1, f_2, \ldots, f_n)}{\partial(x_1, x_2, \ldots, x_n)} \right|.$$

SCALARS, VECTORS, AND TENSORS

14.51 *Definitions.* Three basic quantities often encountered in scientific mathematical material are scalars, vectors, and tensors. Scalars, usually denoted by lowercase italic or Greek letters, are ordinary numbers and are treated as such. Vectors are quantities that have direction as well as magnitude, and they are often denoted by boldface letters or by an arrow accent to distinguish them from scalars:

r or $\vec{r}$.

A vector may be written as the sum of its components:

$$r = \sum_i r_i \hat{e}^i.$$

The circumflex over the e is used to denote a vector of length 1, called a "unit vector." Tensors are multidimensional quantities that extend the vector concept. A scalar is a tensor of rank zero, and a vector is a tensor of rank one.

14.52 *Vector and tensor multiplication.* Vector and tensor multiplication employs a special notation that is relatively easy to identify in text. The inner or dot product of two vectors $\boldsymbol{u}$ and $\boldsymbol{w}$ is denoted $\boldsymbol{u} \cdot \boldsymbol{w}$; the dot product is signified by the boldface multiplication dot. The vector or cross product of two vectors $\boldsymbol{u}$ and $\boldsymbol{w}$ is denoted $\boldsymbol{u} \times \boldsymbol{w}$; the cross product is signified by the boldface multiplication cross. The multiplication dot and multiplication cross are not interchangeable for vectors as they are for ordinary multiplication. The standard notation for the tensor product of tensors T and S is $T \otimes S$. Index notation for vectors and tensors usually takes the following form:

$$S = S_{jk}\boldsymbol{e}^j\boldsymbol{e}^k \,,$$
$$T^{i \cdots m}_{k \cdots l} = A^{i \cdots m}_{k \cdots n} B^n_{ml} \,,$$
$$b^i = a^i_j c^j \,.$$

Note the correspondence of the indices in these expressions (see 14.37 for discussion of index positioning). The Einstein convention has been used here, which implies summation over the repeated index. Thus

$$c_k = \sum_j a^j b_{jk} \quad \text{is the same as} \quad c_k = a^j b_{jk}$$

unless otherwise stated.

14.53   *Additional tensor notation.* Two additional special notations are used to differentiate tensors. One is denoted $A^i_{,j}$, where the comma indicates a coordinate (or "ordinary") derivative. The other is denoted $A^i_{;j}$, where the semicolon indicates the covariant derivative. These are not mistakes and should not be interchanged.

14.54   *Dirac notation.* A special form of the inner product, used especially in physics, is the Dirac bracket notation,

$$\langle a|b \rangle,$$

which can also be used in combination with operators, as in $\langle a|T|b \rangle$ (which is not the same as $\langle aTb \rangle$) or $\langle Ta|b \rangle$. The combinations $\langle a|$ and $|b \rangle$ are also used to denote dual vectors and vectors, respectively.

DEFINITIONS, THEOREMS, AND OTHER FORMAL STATEMENTS

14.55   *Formal statements in text.* For definitions, theorems, propositions, corollaries, lemmas, axioms, and rules, it is common practice to set the head in caps and small caps and the text—including symbolic expressions except for numerals—in italic, sometimes indented from the left margin. Numbers for these statements, unlike those for equations, are not enclosed in parentheses, and in cross-references the numbers are also not enclosed.

DEFINITION. *A permutation is a one-to-one transformation of a finite set into itself.*

(In a definition, the term defined is set in roman type in order to distinguish it from the rest of the text.)

THEOREM 1. *The order of a finite subgroup is a multiple of the order of every one of its subgroups.*

COROLLARY. *If p and q are distinct prime numbers and a is an integer not divisible by either p or q, then*

$$a^{(p-1)(q-1)} \equiv 1 \ (\mathrm{mod} \ pq).$$

LEMMA 2. *The product of any two primitive polynomials is itself primitive.*

AXIOM. *Every set of nonnegative integers that contains at least one element contains a smallest element.*

RULE 4.4. *The length of a vertical segment joining two points is given by the difference of the ordinates of the upper and the lower points.*

The text of proofs, examples, remarks, demonstrations, and solutions is usually set in roman, with only variables in italic. The heads, however, are set in caps and small caps.

PROOF. Let $A = B$. Hence $C = D$.
SOLUTION. If $y = 0$, then $x = 5$.

Proofs of theorems often end with the abbreviation "QED" or a special symbol, □ or ■.

PROBABILITY AND STATISTICS

14.56   *Probability.* The notation $\mathrm{Pr}(A)$ or $P(A)$ is used to denote the probability of an event A. The sample space, that is, the set of all possible outcomes of a given experiment, is usually denoted Ω. An event A is a subset of the sample space: $A \subseteq \Omega$. The elements of the sample space are usually denoted ω. The conditional probability of event A relative to event B—that is, the probability that event A occurs once event B has occurred—is written

$$\mathrm{Pr}(A|B) \qquad \text{or} \qquad P(A|B).$$

Variance is denoted Var(X) and covariance is denoted Cov(X, Y). Both the variance and the covariance functions may be expressed with lowercase letters.

14.57   *Means and standard deviations.* The population mean is often given a special symbol in statistics denoted $\mu(X)$. The sample mean is denoted by $\overline{X}$. In evaluating an expression, be careful not to substitute angle brackets, $\langle X \rangle$, for an overbar, $\overline{X}$. They can mean very different things. The dispersion is often written as σ. The population standard deviation (the most common measure of dispersion) is denoted by σ, and the sample standard deviation is more commonly denoted as s; sd or SD may be used to distinguish it from se or SE, for standard error. The mean is most frequently written in physical sciences literature as $\langle A \rangle$, the average as $\overline{A}$, and the cumulant as $\langle\langle A \rangle\rangle$. Several abbreviations are used in stochastic theory and probability theory without special definition: a.e., almost everywhere; a.c., almost certainly; a.s., almost surely. See table 14.3 for statistical notation.

14.58   *Uncertainties.* Uncertainties in quantities are usually written in the form 2.501 ± 0.002 or, if there is an exponent, $(6.157 \pm 0.07) \times 10^5$ or $10^{4.3 \pm 0.3}$. However, there are cases in which the bounds rather than the range are given, and these may be unequal; hence,

$$\ldots \text{where } D/H = 1.65^{+0.11}_{-0.08} \times 10^{-5}. \ldots$$

Uncertainties may also be specified as se for standard error, $1\,\sigma$ (or a larger multiple) or sd for standard deviation. Finally, separation into random and systematic uncertainties is written as

$$71.0 \pm 5.0 \text{ (random)} \pm 2.5 \text{ (sys)}$$

or $71.0^{+5.0}_{-4.8}$ (random) $^{+2.1}_{-1.8}$ (sys) for asymmetric bounds. When such expressions occur in an exponent, it is preferable to write a separate expression for the exponent (see 14.48).

Preparation of Paper Manuscripts

14.59   *Format of paper manuscripts.* Manuscripts for mathematical articles and books should be printed out one-sided and double-spaced, on $8^1/_2 \times 11$-inch white paper, with $1^1/_4$-inch margins for text and 2-inch margins for display work. The print quality should be 300 dots per inch or better. If

TABLE 14.3 Statistical notation

Greek alphabet			
α	Probability of rejecting a true null hypothesis (Type I error)	Σ	Sum of
β	Probability of accepting a false null hypothesis (Type II error)	σ	Standard deviation of the population
κ	Cumulant	σ^2	Population variance
$\mu(X)$	Mean of the population	χ^2	Value for the chi-squared distribution
Latin alphabet			
df, DF, dof	Degrees of freedom	s, sd, SD	Standard deviation
F	F-ratio	se, SE	Standard error
H	Value from the Kruskal-Wallis test	sem, SEM	Standard error of the mean
H_0	Null hypothesis	t	Value from Student's t-test
mse, MSE	Mean squared error	T	Value from the Wilcoxon matched-pairs signed-rank test
p, P, Pr	Probability	U	Value from the Mann-Whitney test
r_p	Pearson correlation coefficient	W_s	Value from the Wilcoxon rank-sum test
r_s	Value from the Spearman rank-order test	z	Value from the normal distribution

handwritten equations or symbols are to be inserted in the printout, allow generous space for them. Since the editor will need to provide instructions to the typesetter, there should be ample margins.

EDITING MATHEMATICS ON PAPER

14.60 *Mathematical copy.* Paper manuscripts in mathematics are now most often prepared with specialized software, notably LaTeX, that can typeset not only italic and boldface material but most mathematical symbols and signs as well. To the extent that a manuscript shows such characters, symbols, and signs as they should appear, the typesetter may simply be instructed to follow the author's copy. Any unusual characters not achieved in the manuscript must be marked or identified. Authors should supply the highest quality printout possible.

14.61 *Italic type.* The editor of a mathematical text should either underline all copy that is to be set in italic or give general instructions to the typesetter to set all letters used in mathematical terms in italic unless they are marked otherwise. The general instructions to the typesetter should also specify italic type for letters used in subscripts or superscripts. If italics have been used in the manuscript, the editor can instruct the typesetter to follow the copy.

14.62 *Abbreviations.* Abbreviations for common functions, geometric points, units of measurement, and chemical elements, which are set in roman type, should be marked by the editor only where ambiguity could occur. For a list of some frequently used abbreviations, see table 14.2.

14.63 *Marking single letters in other type styles.* Special marking must be used when single letters used as variables are to be set in any typeface other than italic. A mathematical text may require the use of some roman letters, usually to indicate properties different from those expressed by the same letters in italic. Underlining is the standard method of indicating italic, but it can be used instead, with instructions to the typesetter, to indicate letters that are to be in roman. If, however, the editor does not use general instructions but underlines all letters to be set italic, then letters not underlined will be set, as implied, in roman type. Double underlining is used to indicate small capitals. Wavy underlining is used for boldface. Color codes are often used to indicate other typefaces. For example, red underlining or circling can be used for Fraktur, blue for script, green for sans serif, and so forth. The general instructions to the typesetter must clearly explain the marking and coding system used. If a photocopy must be made of the edited manuscript for estimating by the typesetter or for querying the author, avoid color coding.

14.64 *Mathematics fonts.* Boldface, script, Fraktur, and sans serif are frequently used in mathematical expressions. Examples of each are shown below:

FRAKTUR	SCRIPT	BOLDFACE	SANS SERIF
$\mathfrak{ABCD}$	$\mathcal{ABCD}$	**ABCD**	ABCD

Open face, or blackboard, characters are often used for special mathematical symbols, for example, $\mathbb{N}, \mathbb{Z}, \mathbb{Q}, \mathbb{R}, \mathbb{C}$ (see 14.12).

14.65 *Marking subscripts and superscripts.* As long as inferior and superior characters have been marked in a few places by the symbols $\vee$ and $\wedge$ (see examples below), and new characters or symbols identified when they first appear, a typesetter should have no difficulty interpreting the manuscript. If the spatial relationship of terms is not clearly shown in typed or handwritten expression, the terms should be marked to avoid ambiguity. For example, given the copy

$$X_{t1}^{k},$$

it may not be clear from the manuscript whether this means

$$X^k_{t_1} \quad \text{or} \quad X^k_{t^1} \quad \text{or} \quad X^k_{t_1}.$$

The expression should therefore be marked in one of the following ways for complete clarity:

$$X \quad \text{or} \quad X \quad \text{or} \quad X$$

The examples above show the subscripts and superscripts aligned or stacked. See 14.37 for discussion and examples of staggered subscripts and superscripts.

14.66   *Examples of marked copy.* Figure 14.1 shows a page of a paper manuscript as marked initially by the author and then by the editor before being sent to the typesetter. The author's marks merely identify ambiguous symbols. Figure 14.2 shows that same page set in type. Figure 14.3 shows the La-TeX source code that would generate the first part of figure 14.2. Signs and symbols that could be misread by the typesetter should be clearly identified on a paper manuscript by marginal notations or in a separate list. For lists of symbols and special characters commonly used in mathematics, see table 14.1. Illegible handwriting and unidentifiable signs and symbols can reduce composition speed and result in time-consuming and costly corrections. Certain letters, numbers, and symbols can easily be misread, especially when Greek, Fraktur, script, and sans serif letters are handwritten rather than typed. Some of the characters that cause the most difficulty are shown in table 14.4.

Therefore $F_x^n \subset G \cap B_n$ and $F_x^n \cap B_m = \emptyset$ for $n \neq m$, since $b \in G$.

The temperature function is *(null set)* *("element of")*

$$u(x,\ t) = \frac{2}{L} \sum_1^\infty \exp\left(-\frac{u^2 \pi^2 kt}{L^2}\right) \sin\frac{n\pi x}{L} \int_0^L f(x') \sin\frac{n\pi x'}{L}\,dx'. \qquad (3.1)$$

An $m \times n$ matrix $\underset{\sim}{A}$ over a field F is a rectangular array of mn elements a_j^i in F, arranged in m rows and n columns:

$$\underset{\sim}{A} = \begin{bmatrix} a_1^1 & a_2^1 & \cdots & a_n^1 \\ a_1^2 & a_2^2 & \cdots & a_n^2 \\ \cdot & \cdot & \cdots & \cdot \\ a_1^m & a_2^m & \cdots & a_n^m \end{bmatrix}.$$

The modulus of the correlation coefficient of X_1 and X_2 is *"greater than"*

(rho) $\rho = |\langle x_1,\ x_2 \rangle| / \|x_1\| \|x_2\|$ for $\|x_1\| > 0$, $1 = 1,\ 2.$ *(all)* *(all)*

(angle brackets)

Hence

$$\frac{\partial F}{\partial x} = \lim_{\Delta x \to 0} \frac{\Delta F}{\Delta x} = \lim_{\Delta x \to 0} \frac{1}{\Delta x} \left\{ \int_{a,b}^{x+\Delta x, y} P\,dx + Q\,dy \right.$$

$$\left. - \int_{a,b}^{x,y} P\,dx + Q\,dy \right\} + P + Q.$$

From equation (2.4), where $M = [(a + b - 1)/(k + 1)]$, we obtain

(alpha)

$$\alpha_{\nu}(a + b) = (-1)^\nu \sum' \frac{(i_1 + \cdots + i_M)!}{i_1! \cdots i_M!} \prod_{h=1}^M (-1)^{\nu} \left(\frac{a + b - kh - 1}{h}\right)^{i_h},$$

(lc Gr. mu)

the sum being extended over all sets $(i_1,\ \ldots,\ i_M)$.

To summarize our findings:

(lc Gr. eta)

$$v^*(z,\ t_n) \gtrless H_{\delta_1} [v(x) + o(1)] - 2\eta \gtrless v(z) + o(1) + \eta^{1/2} o(1).$$

(lc oh) *(lc oh)* *(cap oh)*

Therefore $F_{x^n} \subseteq G \cap B_n$ and $F_{x^n} \cap B_m = \emptyset$ for $n \neq m$, since $b \in G$. The temperature function is

$$u(x,\, t) = \frac{2}{L} \sum_{1}^{\infty} \exp\left(-\frac{u^2\pi^2 kt}{L^2}\right) \sin\frac{n\pi x}{L}$$

$$\times \int_{o}^{L} f(x') \sin\frac{n\pi x'}{L}\, dx' . \quad (3.1)$$

An $m \times n$ matrix $\mathbf{A}$ over a field F is a rectangular array of mn elements $a_j{}^i$ in F, arranged in m rows and n columns:

$$\mathbf{A} = \begin{bmatrix} a_1{}^1 & a_2{}^1 & \ldots & a_n{}^1 \\ a_1{}^2 & a_2{}^2 & \ldots & a_n{}^2 \\ . & . & \ldots & . \\ a_1{}^m & a_2{}^m & \ldots & a_n{}^m \end{bmatrix}.$$

The modulus of the correlation coefficient of X_1 and X_2 is

$$\rho \,=\, |\langle X_1,\, X_2\rangle|/\|X_1\|\, \|X_2\| \quad \text{for} \quad \|X_l\| > 0 , \quad l = 1,\, 2 .$$

Hence

$$\frac{\partial F}{\partial x} = \lim_{\Delta x \to 0} \frac{\Delta F}{\Delta x} = \lim_{\Delta x \to 0} \frac{1}{\Delta x} \left\{ \int_{a,b}^{x+\Delta x, y} P\, dx + Q\, dy \right.$$

$$\left. - \int_{a,b}^{x,y} P\, dx + Q\, dy \right\} + P + Q .$$

From equation (2.4), where $M = [(a + b - 1)/(k + 1)]$, we obtain

$$a_\nu(a + b) = (-1)^\nu \sum{}' \frac{(i_1 + \ldots + i_M)!}{i_1! \ldots i_M!}$$

$$\times \prod_{h=1}^{M} (-1)^{i_h} \left(\frac{a + b - kh - 1}{h}\right)^{i_h},$$

the sum being extended over all sets $(i_1, \ldots, i_M)$.

To summarize our findings:

$$v^*(z,\, t_n) \geq H_{\delta_1}[v(x) + o(1)] - 2\eta \geq v(z) + o(1) + \eta^{1/2} O(1).$$

Fig. 14.2. The page of manuscript shown in figure 14.1 set in type.

```
\renewcommand{\theequation}{3.\arabic{equation}}

Therefore $F_x{}^n \subset G \cap B_n$ and $F_x{}^n \cap B_m = \emptyset$
for $n \ne m$, since $b \in G$. The temperature function is
\begin{eqnarray}
\lefteqn{u(x,t) = \frac{2}{L} \sum_1^\infty \exp \left( -
        \frac{u^2\pi^2kt}{L^2} \right) \sin \frac{n\pi x}{L}} \nonumber
        \hspace{7.5pc} \\
  & & \times\int_0^L f(x^\prime)\sin\frac{n\pi x^\prime}{L}dx^\prime .
\end{eqnarray}
An $m \times n$ matrix {\bf A} over a field $F$ is a rectangular array
of $mn$ elements $a_j{}^i$ in $F$, arranged in $m$ rows and $n$
columns:
\begin{displaymath}
{\bf A} = \left[ \begin{array}{cccc}
                a_1{}^1 & a_2{}^1 & \ldots & a_n{}^1 \\
                a_1{}^2 & a_2{}^2 & \ldots & a_n{}^2 \\
                .      & .      & \ldots & .       \\
                a_1{}^m & a_2{}^m & \ldots & a_n{}^m
             \end{array} \right] .
\end{displaymath}
The modulus of the correlation coefficient of $X_1$ and $X_2$ is
\begin{displaymath}
\rho = \left| \langle X_1,X_2 \rangle \right| / \left\| X_1\right\|
       \, \left\| X_2 \right\| \hspace{10pt} \mbox{for} \hspace{10pt}
       \left\| X_1 \right\| > 0, \hspace{10pt} 1 = 1,2 .
\end{displaymath}
```

Fig. 14.3. LaTeX source listing that would generate a portion of the mathematical copy shown in figure 14.2.

TABLE 14.4 Potentially ambiguous mathematical symbols

Symbols set in type[a]	Marginal notation to operator[b]	Remarks and suggestions for manuscript preparation
a	lc "aye"	Leave medium space before and after $\propto$ and all binary
α	lc Gr. alpha	operation signs (=, $\leq$, $\in$, $\cap$, $\subset$, etc.)
$\propto$	proportional to	
∞	infinity	
B	cap "bee"	
β	lc Gr. beta	
χ	lc Gr. chi	
X	cap "ex"	
x	lc "ex"	
$\times$	"times" or "mult"	Leave medium space before and after $\times$ and all other operation signs (+, −, ÷, etc.). Do not add space when such signs as −, +, or ± are used to modify symbols or expressions (−3, ±1, etc.)
δ	lc Gr. delta	
∂	partial differential	Simpler to use printer's term "round dee"
d	lc "dee"	
ϵ	lc Gr. epsilon	
$\in$	"element of"	
η	lc Gr. eta	
n	lc "en"	
γ	lc Gr. gamma	
τ	lc Gr. tau	
r	lc "are"	
t	lc "tee"	
ι	lc Gr. iota	Avoid using ι and i together because of similarity in print
i	lc "eye"	
κ	lc Gr. kappa	
k	lc "kay"	
$\Kappa$	cap Gr. kappa	
K	cap "kay"	
l	lc "ell"	In some fonts, l and 1 look identical; note "ell" but leave numeral unmarked; ℓ should not be used if l is available
ℓ	script "ell"	
1	numeral 1	
ν	lc Gr. nu	
v	lc "vee"	Avoid using ν and v together because of similarity in print
O	cap "oh"	Asymptotic upper bounds $O(x)$ and $o(x)$ may occur together
o	lc "oh"	
0	zero	
O	cap Gr. omicron	
o	lc Gr. omicron	
$\circ$	degree sign	
Λ	cap Gr. lambda	
$\wedge$	wedge	
ϕ, φ	lc Gr. phi	
$\varnothing$	empty or null set	

TABLE **14.4** *(continued)*

Symbols set in type[a]	Marginal notation to operator[b]	Remarks and suggestions for manuscript preparation
Π	product	
Π	cap Gr. pi	
π	lc Gr. pi	
ρ	lc Gr. rho	
p	lc "pee"	
Σ	summation	
Σ	cap Gr. sigma	
θ, ϑ	lc Gr. theta	Preference for form ϑ should be specified by author;
Θ	cap Gr. theta	θ more commonly used
U	cap "you"	
$\cup, \cup$	union symbol	
υ	lc Gr. upsilon	
μ	lc Gr. mu	
ν	lc Gr. nu	
u	lc "you"	
ω	lc Gr. omega	
ϖ	round lc Gr. pi	
w	lc "doubleyou"	
Z	cap "zee"	
z	lc "zee"	
2	numeral 2	
$'$	prime	Use apostrophe for prime if no prime available
$_1$	superscript 1	In handwritten formulas, take care to distinguish comma from subscript 1 and prime from superscript 1
$,$	comma	
$_1$	subscript 1	
—	em dash	Use two hyphens for em dash; no space on either side
–	minus sign	To indicate subtraction, leave medium space on each side of
–	en dash	sign; omit space after sign if negative quantity is represented
·	multiplication dot	Use centered period for multiplication dot, allowing medium space on each side; do *not* show space around a center dot in a chemical formula ($CO_3 \cdot H_2$)

NOTE: Symbols and letters that are commonly mistaken for each other are arranged in groups.

[a]Letters in mathematical expressions will automatically be set in italics unless marked otherwise.

[b]Only if symbols, letters, or numbers are badly written or rendered in the manuscript is it necessary to identify them for the typesetter.

15

Abbreviations

Introduction

15.1 *Overview.* This chapter is concerned mainly with abbreviations and symbols used in general and scholarly writing. It also offers some guidance in technical work, especially for the generalist editor confronted with unfamiliar terms. The abbreviations listed are unavoidably incomplete; for many more examples, consult *Merriam-Webster's Collegiate Dictionary* (bibliog. 3.1); Dean Stahl and Karen Kerchelich, *Abbreviations Dictionary* (bibliog. 4.7); or, if you have access to a large library, the multivolume *Acronyms, Initialisms, and Abbreviations Dictionary* (bibliog. 4.7). Authors and editors of technical material will need to refer to more specialized manuals.

15.2 *When to use abbreviations.* Outside the area of science and technology, abbreviations and symbols appear most frequently in tabular matter, notes, bibliographies, and parenthetical references. Abbreviations should be used only in contexts where they are clear to readers. Some are almost never used in their spelled-out form (IQ, GOP, DNA) and may be used without explanation. Others, though in common use (HMO, UPS, AT&T), are normally spelled out at first occurrence—at least in formal text—as a courtesy to those readers who might not easily recognize them. Less familiar ones, however, should be used only if they occur, say, five times or more within an article or chapter, and the terms must be spelled out on their first occurrence. (The abbreviation usually follows immediately, in parentheses, but it may be introduced in other ways; see example.) Writers and editors should monitor the number of different abbreviations used in a document; readers trying to keep track of a large number of abbreviations, especially unfamiliar ones, will lose their way (for lists of abbreviations, see 1.55, 2.28). For rules concerning the plural form of various abbreviations, see 7.15. For abbreviations preceded by *a* or *an*, see 7.46, 15.9.

Among recent recommendations of the Federal Aviation Administration (FAA) are . . .
The National Aeronautics and Space Administration was founded in 1958. Since its inception, NASA has . . .
The benefits of ERISA (Employee Retirement Income Security Act) are familiar to many.

15.3 *Some definitions.* In precise usage, the word *acronym* refers only to terms based on the initial letters of their various elements and read as single words (NATO, AIDS); *initialism* refers to terms read as a series of letters (BBC, ATM); and *contraction* refers to abbreviations that include the first and last letters of the full word (Mr., amt.). In this chapter the umbrella term *abbreviation* will be used for all three, as well as for lowercase shortened forms (ibid., vol., prof., etc.), except where greater precision is required.

15.4 *Periods: general guidelines.* To avoid unnecessary periods in abbreviations, Chicago recommends the following general guidelines: use periods with abbreviations that appear in lowercase letters; use no periods with abbreviations that appear in full capitals or small capitals, whether two letters or more. For feasible exceptions, see 15.5. For a mixture of lowercase and capital letters, see 15.6. For the omission of periods in scientific usage, see 15.55, 15.58.

p. e.g. a.k.a. etc. p.m. vol. et al. (*et* is not an abbreviation; *al.* is)
VP CEO USA AAUP BCE

15.5 *Periods: exceptions and options.* Obviously, Chicago's guidelines are subject to modification. For example, periods are used after initials standing for given names (E. B. White, G. K. Chesterton); strict scientific style omits all periods (m, cm, kg [see 15.55]); traditionalists may draw the line at "PhD" or "US" (Chicago bows to tradition on the latter); the British and the French (among others) omit periods from contractions (Dr, assn, Mme). A slash is occasionally used instead of a period (as in *c/o*) but more often denotes *per* (see 6.116).

15.6 *Space or no space between elements.* No space is left between the letters of initialisms and acronyms, whether lowercase or in capitals. Space is usually left between abbreviated words. For personal names, see 15.12. See also 15.25.

RN NBC YMCA Nafta
Gov. Gen. Mng. Ed. Dist. Atty.

Where part of an abbreviation is a shortened word or contraction and part a single letter, no space is left.

DLitt (*or, if periods are used*, D.Litt.)   S.Dak.   SSgt (*or, if periods are used*, S.Sgt.)

15.7 *Capitals versus lowercase.* Usage rather than logic determines whether abbreviations other than those standing for proper names are given in upper- or lowercase letters. Noun forms are usually uppercase (HIV, VP), adverbial forms lowercase (rpm, mpg). Note also that acronyms, especially those of five or more letters, tend to become lowercase with frequent use (NAFTA/Nafta, WASP/Wasp).

15.8   *Italics versus roman type.* Abbreviations are italicized only if they stand for a term that would be italicized if spelled out—the title of a book or periodical, for example. Common Latin abbreviations are set in roman.

OED (*Oxford English Dictionary*)
JAMA (*Journal of the American Medical Association*)
ibid.   etc.   e.g.   i.e.

15.9   *"A" or "an" preceding an abbreviation.* When an abbreviation follows an indefinite article, the choice of *a* or *an* is determined by the way the abbreviation would be read aloud. Acronyms are read as words and, except when used adjectivally, are rarely preceded by *a, an,* or *the* ("member nations of NATO"). Initialisms are read as a series of letters and are often preceded by an article ("member nations of the EU"). See 15.3; see also 7.46.

an HMO
a UFO
a NATO member
a LOOM parade
an NAACP convention
an NBA coach
an HIV test
an MS symptom (a symptom of multiple sclerosis)
but
a MS by . . . (would be read as "a manuscript by . . .")

An initialism such as *AAA*, normally pronounced "Triple A," should not follow an indefinite article; resort to rewording (e.g., "a map from AAA," *not* "a AAA map").

15.10   *Ampersands.* No space is left on either side of an ampersand used within an initialism.

R&D   Texas A&M

Names and Titles

15.11   *Personal names.* Normally, abbreviations should not be used for given names. A signature, however, should be transcribed as the person wrote it.

Benj. Franklin   Geo. D. Fuller   Ch. Virolleaud

15.12 *Initials in personal names.* Initials standing for given names are followed by a period and a word space. A period is normally used even if the middle initial does not stand for a name (as in Harry S. Truman).

Roger W. Shugg   P. D. James   M. F. K. Fisher

If an entire name is abbreviated, space and periods are omitted.

FDR (Franklin Delano Roosevelt)   MJ (Michael Jordan)

15.13 *Titles before names.* A civil or military title preceding a full name may be abbreviated. Preceding a surname alone, however, it is spelled out.

Rep. Mark Kirk; Representative Kirk
Lt. Col. Mary Pierce; Lieutenant Colonel Pierce
but
Senator Susan Collins ("Sen.," though used in journalism, is better avoided in formal prose)

15.14 *Civil titles.* The following abbreviations, among others, may precede a full name where space is tight.

Ald.	Gov.	Prof.
Assoc. Prof.	Insp. Gen.	Rep.
Asst. Prof.	Judge Adv. Gen.	Sr. (sister)
Atty. Gen.	Pres.	Supt.
Fr. (father)		

15.15 *Military titles.* The military omits periods and now uses full capitals for the abbreviated forms of ranks. Such forms should be used with discretion, however, since they may be unfamiliar to readers. In general or historical contexts, including military history, traditional abbreviations are usually preferred, especially when preceding a name ("Adj. Gen. John Jones" rather than "AG John Jones"). The following very selective list merely illustrates the difference between current military usage and traditional forms. Where no traditional abbreviation is appropriate before a name, use the full form.

ADM	*or*	Adm.	COL	*or*	Col.
A1C	*or*	Airman First Class	CDR	*or*	Cdr.
BG	*or*	Brig. Gen.	CWO	*or*	Chief Warrant Officer
CPT	*or*	Capt.	GEN	*or*	Gen.

LT	or	Lt.		MG	or	Maj. Gen.
1LT	or	1st Lt.		MSG	or	M.Sgt. (master sergeant)
2LT	or	2nd Lt.		PO	or	Petty Officer
LTC	or	Lt. Col.		SGT	or	Sgt.
LG	or	Lt. Gen.		SSG	or	S.Sgt. (staff sergeant)
MAJ	or	Maj.		WO	or	Warrant Officer

Many reference books containing more detailed lists of abbreviations and terms are published regularly. See, for example, John V. Noel Jr. and Edward L. Beach, *Naval Terms Dictionary*, and Timothy Zurick, *Army Dictionary and Desk Reference* (both in bibliog. 5). While each branch of the armed forces has its own style, the latest edition of Norman Polmar, Bruce Warren, and Eric Wertheim's *Dictionary of Military Abbreviations* (bibliog. 4.7) provides a general cross-service list.

15.16 *Social titles.* Always abbreviated, whether preceding the full name or the surname only, are such social titles as the following. See also 15.20.

Ms. Mrs. Messrs. Mr. Dr.

When *Mister* or *Doctor* is used without a name, in direct address, it is spelled out.

15.17 *French social titles.* Note the presence or absence of periods after the following French forms used with either a full name or a surname only.

M. MM. Mme Mlle

When *Monsieur, Messieurs, Madame,* or *Mademoiselle* is used without a name, in direct address, it is spelled out.

15.18 *"Reverend" and "Honorable."* The abbreviations *Rev.* and *Hon.* are used before a name when no *the* precedes the title. With *the*, such titles should be spelled out.

Rev. Jane Schaefer; the Reverend Jane Schaefer
Rt. Rev. Msgr. Thomas L. Bennett; the Right Reverend Monsignor Thomas L. Bennett
Hon. Henry M. Brown; the Honorable Henry M. Brown

With a last name only, *Rev., the Reverend, Hon., the Honorable,* and so forth are normally omitted.

Rev. Sam Portaro; Portaro
the Honorable Patricia Birkholz; Birkholz

15.19 *"Jr.," "Sr.," and the like.* The abbreviations *Jr.* and *Sr.*, as well as roman or arabic numerals such as *II* or *3rd,* after a person's name are part of the name and so are retained in connection with any titles or honorifics. Note that these abbreviations are used only with the full name, never with the surname only. See also 6.49, 9.47.

> Mrs. James Jefferson Sr. spoke first. After Mrs. Jefferson had sat down, . . .
> Dexter Harrison III, MD, spoke last. In closing, Dr. Harrison reiterated . . .

15.20 *Omission of "Mr." and the like.* Social titles such as Mr., Mrs., Ms., and Dr. may be omitted in most contexts with no loss of respect. When an academic degree or professional designation follows a name, such titles are always omitted.

> André Beauvois, PhD, was appointed principal. The faculty welcomed Beauvois by . . .
> It is my pleasure to introduce Jennifer James, MD. Dr. James has shown . . .

Similarly, the now somewhat archaic abbreviation *Esq.* (Esquire) is used only after a full name and never when *Mr., Dr.,* or the like precedes the name.

> Anthony White, Esq., led the parade. Mr. White was carrying . . .

15.21 *Some academic degrees.* In conservative practice, periods are added to abbreviations of all academic degrees (B.A., D.D.S., etc.). Chicago now recommends omitting them unless they are required for tradition or consistency. In the following list, periods are shown only where uncertainty might arise as to their placement.

AB	Artium Baccalaureus (Bachelor of Arts)
AM	Artium Magister (Master of Arts)
BA	Bachelor of Arts
BD	Bachelor of Divinity
BFA	Bachelor of Fine Arts
BM	Bachelor of Music
BS	Bachelor of Science; Bachelor of Surgery
DB	Divinitatis Baccalaureus (Bachelor of Divinity)
DD	Divinitatis Doctor (Doctor of Divinity)
DDS	Doctor of Dental Surgery
DMD	Doctor of Dental Medicine
DMin (D.Min.)	Doctor of Ministry
DO	Doctor of Osteopathy
DVM	Doctor of Veterinary Medicine

EdD	Doctor of Education
JD	Juris Doctor (Doctor of Law)
LHD	Litterarum Humaniorum Doctor (Doctor of Humanities)
LittD (Litt.D.)	Litterarum Doctor (Doctor of Letters)
LLB (LL.B.)	Legum Baccalaureus (Bachelor of Laws)
LLD (LL.D.)	Legum Doctor (Doctor of Laws)
MA	Master of Arts
MBA	Master of Business Administration
MD	Medicinae Doctor (Doctor of Medicine)
MFA	Master of Fine Arts
MS	Master of Science
MSN	Master of Science in Nursing
MSW	Master of Social Welfare *or* Master of Social Work
PhB (Ph.B.)	Philosophiae Baccalaureus (Bachelor of Philosophy)
PhD (Ph.D.)	Philosophiae Doctor (Doctor of Philosophy)
PhG (Ph.G.)	Graduate in Pharmacy
SB	Scientiae Baccalaureus (Bachelor of Science)
SM	Scientiae Magister (Master of Science)
STB	Sacrae Theologiae Baccalaureus (Bachelor of Sacred Theology)

These designations are set off by commas when they follow a personal name.

David H. Pauker, JD, attended Northwestern University Law School.

15.22   *Some professional, religious, and other designations*

CNM	Certified Nurse Midwife
FAIA	Fellow of the American Institute of Architects
FRS	Fellow of the Royal Society
JP	Justice of the Peace
MP	Member of Parliament
LPN	Licensed Practical Nurse
OFM	Order of Friars Minor
OP	Ordo praedicatorum
RN	Registered Nurse
SJ	Society of Jesus

These designations, like academic degrees, are set off by commas when they follow a personal name.

Joan Hotimlanska, LPN, will be working on the second floor.

FIRMS AND COMPANIES

15.23   *Some commonly used generic abbreviations.* See also 15.76.

Assoc.	Ltd.
Bros.	Mfg.
Co.	PLC (public limited company)
Corp.	RR (railroad)
Inc.	Ry. (railway)
LP (limited partnership)	

Abbreviations of foreign-language terms omit the period if they are contractions.

Cia (Sp. *compañia*)	Cie (Fr. *compagnie*)

15.24   *Company names.* Abbreviations and ampersands are appropriate in notes, bibliographies, tabular matter, and the like. See also 17.106.

Ginn & Co.	Moss Bros.	Rand Corp.

In running text, company names are best given in their full forms, though such tags as *Inc.* and *PLC*, which are rarely spelled out, may be omitted unless relevant to the context.

Brooks Brothers was purchased and later resold by Marks and Spencer.
The Shoreline Financial Corporation reported an excellent fourth quarter.

AGENCIES AND ORGANIZATIONS

15.25   *Associations and the like.* Both in running text (preferably after being spelled out on first occurrence) and in tabular matter, notes, and so forth the names of many agencies and organizations, governmental and fraternal, are commonly abbreviated. Whether acronyms or initialisms (see 15.3), such abbreviations appear in full capitals and without periods. Acronyms of five letters or more may be spelled with only an initial capital (see also 15.7). For *a* or *an* with abbreviations, see 15.9.

AAUP	EU (European Union)	WTO (*formerly* GATT)
AFL-CIO	HMO (*pl.* HMOs)	
ERISA *or* Erisa	WHO	

15.26 *Broadcasting companies.* Periods are never used after call letters of radio stations and TV channels.

ABC	HBO	MTV	WFMT
CBS	KFTV	NBC	WTTW

SAINTS AND PERSONAL NAMES WITH *SAINT* OR *ST.*

15.27 *Saints.* The word *Saint* is often abbreviated (*St.*, pl. *SS.*) before the name of a Christian saint, but many prefer to spell the word out, abbreviating only where space is at a premium.

Saint (*or* St.) Teresa
Saints (*or* SS.) Francis of Paola and Francis of Sales

15.28 *Personal names.* When *Saint* or *St.* forms part of a personal name, the bearer's usage is followed. See also 15.32.

Augustus Saint-Gaudens   Muriel St. Clare Byrne

Geographical Terms

15.29 *U.S. states and territories.* In running text, the names of states, territories, and possessions of the United States should always be spelled out when standing alone and preferably (except for DC) when following the name of a city: for example, "Lake Bluff, Illinois, was incorporated in 1895." In bibliographies, tabular matter, lists, and mailing addresses they are usually abbreviated. The two-letter, no-period state abbreviations preferred by the U.S. Postal Service should always be used where a zip code follows, and they may appear in any context where abbreviations are appropriate (see 17.100). Many writers and editors, however, prefer the older forms, included here (names of some states and territories have traditionally not been abbreviated).

AK	Alaska	CO	Colo.	GU	Guam
AL	Ala.	CT	Conn.	HI	Hawaii
AR	Ark.	DC	D.C.	IA	Iowa
AS	American Samoa	DE	Del.	ID	Idaho
AZ	Ariz.	FL	Fla.	IL	Ill.
CA	Calif.	GA	Ga.	IN	Ind.

KS	Kans.	NE	Neb. or Nebr.	SC	S.C.
KY	Ky.	NH	N.H.	SD	S.Dak.
LA	La.	NJ	N.J.	TN	Tenn.
MA	Mass.	NM	N.Mex.	TX	Tex.
MD	Md.	NV	Nev.	UT	Utah
ME	Maine	NY	N.Y.	VA	Va.
MI	Mich.	OH	Ohio	VI	V.I. *or* Virgin Islands
MN	Minn.	OK	Okla.	VT	Vt.
MO	Mo.	OR	Ore. *or* Oreg.	WA	Wash.
MS	Miss.	PA	Pa.	WI	Wis. or Wisc.
MT	Mont.	PR	P.R. *or* Puerto Rico	WV	W.Va.
NC	N.C.	RI	R.I.	WY	Wyo.
ND	N.Dak.				

15.30 *Canadian provinces and territories.* Canadian provinces and territories are normally spelled out in text (e.g., "Kingston, Ontario, is worth a visit") but may be abbreviated in bibliographies and the like.

AB	Alberta	NU	Nunavut
BC	British Columbia	ON	Ontario
MB	Manitoba	PE	Prince Edward Island
NB	New Brunswick	QC	Quebec *or* Québec
NL	Newfoundland and Labrador	SK	Saskatchewan
NS	Nova Scotia	YT	Yukon
NT	Northwest Territories		

15.31 *Punctuation.* When following the name of a city, abbreviations of states, provinces, and territories are enclosed in commas when the older forms are used. Commas may be omitted with the newer forms.

Delegates came from Bedford, Pa., and Jamestown, N.Y.
Ms. Spiegel has lived in Washington, D.C., all her life.
or
Ms. Spiegel has lived in Washington DC all her life.

A hyphen separates such abbreviations from political party designations accompanying the names of senators or other elected officials.

Among politicians seen at the gathering were Kent Conrad (D-ND), Conrad Burns (R-MT), and Dianne Feinstein (D-CA).

15.32 *Place-names with "Fort," "Mount," and the like.* Generic terms as elements of geographic names should be abbreviated only where space is at a premium. *San* and *Santa* (e.g., San Diego, Santa Barbara) are never abbreviated.

Fort (Ft.) Myers   Mount (Mt.) Airy   Port (Pt.) Arthur

Place-names with *Saint*, however, may be abbreviated or spelled out in text. For French place-names with *Saint*, see 10.29.

St. Louis *or* Saint Louis   St. Lawrence *or* Saint Lawrence
St. Paul *or* Saint Paul

NAMES OF COUNTRIES

15.33 *When to abbreviate.* Names of countries are spelled out in text but may be abbreviated in tabular matter, lists, and the like. In the absence of any universal standards for such abbreviations, use discretion in forming the abbreviations and make sure they are defined below the table (or in some fashion) if there is any possibility of confusion.

Fr.   Ger.   Isr.   It.   Neth.   Swed.   Russ.   UAE (United Arab Emirates)   UK

Note that before reunification (in 1990) East Germany was generally known as the GDR (German Democratic Republic) or DDR (Deutsche Demokratische Republik), and West Germany as the FRG (Federal Republic of Germany) or BRD (Bundesrepublik Deutschland). The former Soviet Union was abbreviated USSR (Union of Soviet Socialist Republics).

15.34 *"U.S." or "US."* Except in scientific style, *U.S.* traditionally appears with periods. Periods may nonetheless be omitted in most contexts. Writers and editors need to weigh tradition against consistency. In running text, the abbreviation (in either form) is permissible when used as an adjective, but *United States* as a noun should be spelled out.

U.S. (*or* US) dollars   U.S. (*or* US) involvement in Asia

ADDRESSES

15.35 *Abbreviations used.* In mailing addresses, tabular matter, and the like, the following abbreviations (among others) are used:

Ave. Bldg. Blvd. Ct. Dr. Expy. Hwy. La. Pkwy. Pl. POB (*or* PO Box)
Rd. Rm. RR Rt. (*or* Rte.) Sq. St. Ste. Terr.

Single-letter compass points accompanying a street name are normally followed by a period; two-letter ones are not. Note that when used in an address the abbreviations *NE, NW, SE,* and *SW* remain abbreviated even in text (there is no comma before them when they follow a street name).

1060 E. Prospect Ave.
456 NW Lane St.
I stayed in a building on N Street SW, close to the city center.

A compass point that is the name (or part of the name) of a street or a place-name must never be abbreviated (e.g., South Ave., Northwest Hwy., South Shore Dr., West Bend, East Orange). For the use of numerals in addresses, see 9.56–57.

15.36   *When not to abbreviate.* Abbreviations fully acceptable on envelopes and mailing labels should rarely be used in addresses in running text.

Chicago's new Symphony Center is at 221 South Michigan Avenue.
Take the Eisenhower Expressway west to Interstate 294.

COMPASS POINTS, LATITUDE, AND LONGITUDE

15.37   *Compass points.* Points of the compass (other than in mailing addresses) may be abbreviated as follows, without periods. These abbreviations are seldom appropriate in formal, nontechnical text. See also 15.35.

N, E, S, W, NE, SE, SW, NW, NNE, ENE, ESE, etc.
N by NE, NE by N, NE by E, etc.

15.38   *When not to abbreviate.* The words *latitude* and *longitude* are never abbreviated in nontechnical running text or when standing alone.

longitude 90° west   the polar latitudes

15.39   *When to abbreviate.* In technical work, the abbreviations *lat* and *long,* usually without periods, may be used when part of a coordinate. They can sometimes be dropped, since the compass point identifies the coordinate.

lat 42°15′09″ N, long 89°17′45″ W
lat 45°16′17″ S, long 116°40′18″ E
The chart showed shoal water at 19°29′65″ N, 107°45′36″ W

Note that primes (′) and double primes (″), *not* quotation marks, are used. For greater detail, consult *Scientific Style and Format* (bibliog. 1.1).

Designations of Time

15.40   *Other discussions.* For units of time (seconds, minutes, etc.), see 15.75. For numerical designations of dates and times of day, see 9.34, 9.37, 9.39, 9.42–45.

15.41   *Systems of chronology.* The following abbreviations are used in text and elsewhere. Although these have traditionally appeared in small capitals with periods, Chicago now recommends full capitals without periods, in keeping with the general guidelines in this chapter. (Small capitals with or without periods, however, are still quite acceptable.) The first four precede the year number; the others follow it. See also 9.38.

AD	*anno Domini* (in the year of [our] Lord)
AH	*anno Hegirae* (in the year of the Hegira); *anno Hebraico* (in the Hebrew year)
AM	*anno mundi* (in the year of the world) (not to be confused with *ante meridiem*; see 15.44)
AS	*anno salutis* (in the year of salvation)
AUC	*ab urbe condita* (from the founding of the city [Rome, in 753 BCE])
BC	before Christ
BCE	before the common era
BP	before the present
CE	common era
MYA (*or* mya)	million years ago
YBP (*or* ybp)	years before the present

15.42   *Months.* Where space restrictions require that the names of months be abbreviated, one of the following systems may be used. The second and third, which take no periods, are used respectively in computer systems and indexes of periodical literature.

Jan.	*or*	Jan	*or*	Ja		Mar.	*or*	Mar	*or*	Mr
Feb.	*or*	Feb	*or*	F		Apr.	*or*	Apr	*or*	Ap

May	*or* May	*or* My		Sept.	*or* Sep	*or* S
June	*or* Jun	*or* Je		Oct.	*or* Oct	*or* O
July	*or* Jul	*or* Jl		Nov.	*or* Nov	*or* N
Aug.	*or* Aug	*or* Ag		Dec.	*or* Dec	*or* D

15.43 *Days of the week.* Where space restrictions require that days of the week be abbreviated, one of the following systems may be used. The second uses no periods.

Sun.	*or* Su		Thurs.	*or* Th
Mon.	*or* M		Fri.	*or* F
Tues.	*or* Tu		Sat.	*or* Sa
Wed.	*or* W			

15.44 *Time of day.* The following abbreviations are used in text and elsewhere; they may also be set in small capitals, in which case periods are unnecessary. For further explanation and examples, see 9.42, 9.44.

a.m. *or* AM	*ante meridiem* (before noon)
m. *or* M	*meridies* (noon [rarely used])
p.m. *or* PM	*post meridiem* (after noon)

The abbreviations a.m. and p.m. should not be used with *morning, afternoon, evening, night,* or *o'clock.* See also 7.90 (section 1), under *time.*

10:30 a.m. *or* ten thirty in the morning   11:00 P.M. *or* eleven o'clock at night

Time zones, where needed, are usually given in parentheses—for example, 4:45 p.m. (CST).

EST	eastern standard time		MST	mountain standard time
EDT	eastern daylight time		MDT	mountain daylight time
CST	central standard time		PST	Pacific standard time
CDT	central daylight time		PDT	Pacific daylight time

Scholarly Abbreviations

15.45 *Overview.* Abbreviations and symbols such as those listed in the following two paragraphs rarely appear in running text. They are normally confined to bibliographic references, glossaries, and other scholarly apparatus. Some can stand for several terms; only the terms likely to be met in scholarly works (mainly in the humanities) and serious nonfiction are included here. The choice between different abbreviations for one term (e.g., *L.* and *Lat.* for *Latin*) depends on the writer's preference, context, readership, and other factors. Note that Latin abbreviations are normally set in roman. Note also that *ab, ad, et,* and other Latin terms that are complete words take no periods. See also 7.56. For terms used more commonly in science and technology, see 15.55.

abbr.	abbreviated, -ion
ab init.	*ab initio*, from the beginning
abl.	ablative
abr.	abridged; abridgment
acc.	accusative
act.	active
add.	addendum
ad inf.	*ad infinitum*
ad init.	*ad initium*, at the beginning
ad int.	*ad interim*, in the intervening time
adj.	adjective
ad lib.	*ad libitum*, at will
ad loc.	*ad locum*, at the place
adv.	adverb
aet.	*aetatis*, aged
AFr.	Anglo-French
AN	Anglo-Norman
anon.	anonymous (see 17.32–34)
app.	appendix
art.	article
AS	Anglo-Saxon
b.	born; brother
bib.	Bible, biblical
bibl.	*bibliotheca*, library
bibliog.	bibliography, -er, -ical
biog.	biography, -er, -ical
biol.	biology, -ist, -ical
bk.	book
c.	century; chapter (in law citations)
ca. *or* c.	*circa*, about, approximately (*ca.* preferred for greater clarity)
Cantab.	*Cantabrigiensis*, of Cambridge
cet. par.	*ceteris paribus*, other things being equal
cf.	*confer*, compare ("see, by way of comparison"; should not be used when *see* alone is meant)
chap.	chapter

col.	column
colloq.	colloquial, -ly, -ism
comp.	compiler (*pl.* comps.), compiled by
compar.	comparative
con.	*contra*, against
conj.	conjunction; conjugation
cons.	consonant
constr.	construction
cont.	continued
contr.	contraction
cp.	compare (rarely used; *cf.* is far more common)
d.	died; daughter
dat.	dative
def.	definite, definition
dept.	department
deriv.	derivative
d.h.	*das heißt*, namely (used only in German text)
d.i.	*das ist*, that is (used only in German text)
dial.	dialect
dict.	dictionary
dim.	diminutive
dist.	district
div.	division; divorced
do.	ditto
dram. pers.	*dramatis personae*
Dr. u. Vrl.	*Druck und Verlag*, printer and publisher
D.V.	*Deo volente*, God willing
ea.	each
ed.	editor (*pl.* eds.), edition, edited by (never add *by* after *ed.*: either "ed. Jane Doe" or "edited by Jane Doe"; use *eds.* only after, never before, the names of two or more editors; see examples throughout chapter 17)
EE	Early English
e.g.	*exempli gratia*, for example (not to be confused with *i.e.*)
encyc.	encyclopedia
Eng.	English
eng.	engineer, -ing
engr.	engraved, -ing
eq.	equation (*pl.* eqq. *or* eqs.)
esp.	especially
et al.	*et alii* (or *et alia*), and others (normally used of persons; no period after *et*)
etc.	*et cetera*, and so forth (normally used of things)

et seq.	*et sequentes*, and the following (no period after *et*)
ex.	example (*pl.* exx. *or* exs.)
f. *or* fem.	feminine; female
fasc.	fascicle
ff.	and following (see 17.131)
fig.	figure
fl.	*floruit*, flourished (used with a date to indicate the productive years of a historical figure whose birth and death dates are unknown)
fol.	folio
Fr.	French
fr.	from
fut.	future
f.v.	*folio verso*, on the back of the page
Gael.	Gaelic
gen.	genitive; genus
geog.	geography, -er, -ical
geol.	geology, -er, -ical
geom.	geometry, -ical
Ger. *or* G.	German
ger.	gerund
Gk.	Greek
hist.	history, -ian, -ical
HQ	headquarters
ibid.	*ibidem*, in the same place (see 16.47–48)
id.	*idem*, the same (see 16.49)
IE	Indo-European
i.e.	*id est*, that is (not to be confused with *e.g.*)
imper.	imperative
incl.	including
indef.	indefinite
indic.	indicative
inf.	*infra*, below
infin.	infinitive
infra dig.	*infra dignitatem*, undignified
in pr.	*in principio*, in the beginning
inst.	instant, this month; institute, institution
instr.	instrumental
interj.	interjection
intrans.	intransitive
introd. *or* intro.	introduction
irreg.	irregular
It.	Italian
L.	Latin; left (in stage directions)

l.	left; line (*pl.* ll. but best spelled out to avoid confusion with numerals 1 and 11)
lang.	language
Lat.	Latin
lit.	literally
loc.	locative
loc. cit.	*loco citato*, in the place cited (best avoided; see 16.50)
loq.	*loquitur*, he or she speaks
m.	male; married; measure (*pl.* mm.)
m. *or* masc.	masculine
marg.	margin, -al
math.	mathematics, -ical
MHG	Middle High German
mimeo.	mimeograph, -ed
misc.	miscellaneous
MM	Maelzel's metronome
m.m.	*mutatis mutandis*, necessary changes being made
Mod.E.	Modern English
MS (*pl.* MSS)	*manuscriptum* (pl. *manuscripta*), manuscript
mus.	museum; music, -al
n.	*natus*, born; note, footnote (*pl.* nn.); noun
nat.	national; natural
NB, n.b.	*nota bene*, take careful note (capitals are illogical but often used for emphasis)
n.d.	no date; not determined
neg.	negative
neut.	neuter
no. (*pl.* nos.)	number
nom.	nominative
non obs.	*non obstante*, notwithstanding
non seq.	*non sequitur*, it does not follow
n.p.	no place; no publisher; no page
NS	New Style (dates)
n.s.	new series
ob.	*obiit*, died
obs.	obsolete
OE	Old English
OFr.	Old French
OHG	Old High German
ON	Old Norse
op. cit.	*opere citato*, in the work cited (best avoided; see 16.50)
OS	Old Style (dates)
o.s.	old series

Oxon.	*Oxoniensis*, of Oxford
p.	page (*pl.* pp.); past
par.	paragraph
part.	participle
pass.	passive
path.	pathology, -ist, -ical
perf.	perfect
perh.	perhaps
pers.	person, personal
pl.	plate; plural
p.p.	past participle
PPS	*post postscriptum*, a later postscript
prep.	preposition
pres.	present
pron.	pronoun
pro tem.	*pro tempore*, for the time being (often used without a period)
prox.	*proximo*, next month
PS	*postscriptum*, postscript
pt.	part
pub.	publication, publisher, published by
QED	*quod erat demonstrandum*, which was to be demonstrated
quar., quart.	quarter, quarterly
q.v.	*quod vide*, which see (used only in a cross-reference *after* the term referred to; cf. *s.v.*)
R.	*rex*, king; *regina*, queen; right (in stage directions)
r.	right; recto; reigned
refl.	reflexive
repr.	reprint
rev.	review; revised, revised by, revision (never add *by* after *rev.*: either "rev. Jane Doe" or "revised by Jane Doe")
RIP	*requiescat in pace*, may he or she rest in peace
s.	son; substantive, -ival
s.a.	*sine anno*, without year; *sub anno*, under the year
sc.	scene; *scilicet*, namely; *sculpsit*, carved by
s.d.	*sine die*, without setting a day for reconvening
sec.	section; *secundum*, according to
ser.	series
sing. *or* sg.	singular
s.l.	*sine loco*, without place
sociol.	sociology, -ist, -ical
Sp.	Spanish
st.	stanza
subj.	subject; subjective; subjunctive

subst. *or* s.	substantive, -al
sup.	*supra*, above
superl.	superlative
supp. *or* suppl.	supplement
s.v. (*pl.* s.vv.)	*sub verbo, sub voce*, under the word (used in a cross-reference *before* the term referred to; cf. *q.v.*)
syn.	synonym, -ous
theol.	theology, -ian, -ical
trans.	translated by, translator(s) (never add *by* after *trans.*: either "trans. Jane Doe" or "translated by Jane Doe"); transitive
treas.	treasurer
TS	typescript
ult.	*ultimatus*, ultimate, last; *ultimo*, last month
univ.	university
usw.	*und so weiter*, and so forth (equivalent to *etc.*; used only in German text)
ut sup.	*ut supra*, as above
v.	verse (*pl.* vv.); verso; versus; *vide*, see
v. *or* vb.	verb
v.i.	*verbum intransitivum*, intransitive verb
viz.	*videlicet*, namely
voc.	vocative
vol.	volume
vs. *or* v.	versus (in legal contexts use *v.*)
v.t.	*verbum transitivum*, transitive verb
yr.	year; your

15.46 *Some symbols used in scholarship and elsewhere*

§ (*pl.* §§)	section
¶ (*pl.* ¶¶)	paragraph
©	copyright
@	at
=	the same as (for examples, see 15.52)
#	number; pound (weight)
/	per (see 6.116)
$	dollar
¢	cent
£	pound sterling
	euro

Bible

15.47   *Other discussions.* For authoritative guidance in many biblical areas not covered here, consult *The SBL Handbook of Style* (bibliog. 1.1). For citing scriptural references in notes or text references, see 17.246–49.

15.48   *When not to abbreviate.* In running text, books of the Bible are spelled out. See also 9.30.

> The opening chapters of Ephesians constitute a sermon on love.
> Jeremiah, chapters 42–44, records the flight of the Jews to Egypt.
> According to Genesis 1:27, God created man in his own image.
> The Twenty-third Psalm is probably the best known of all the psalms.

15.49   *When to abbreviate.* In parenthetical citations or in notes, references to specific scriptural passages use abbreviations for most books of the Bible. Where many such references occur in text, abbreviations may be used there also.

> My concordance lists five instances of the word *nourish*: Gen. 47:12, Ruth 4:15, Isa. 44:14, Acts 7:21, and 1 Tim. 4:6.

15.50   *Abbreviations used.* The following three paragraphs give traditional abbreviations and commonly used shorter forms for books of the Bible. (Note that the shorter forms have no periods.) The listing is alphabetical, both for easier reference and because the order varies slightly in the Jewish, Protestant, and Roman Catholic versions of the Bible. Alternative names for the same books are indicated by an equals sign.

15.51   *The Jewish Bible/the Old Testament*

Amos *or* Am	Amos	Hag. *or* Hg	Haggai
1 Chron. *or* 1 Chr	1 Chronicles	Hosea *or* Hos	Hosea
2 Chron. *or* 2 Chr	2 Chronicles	Isa. *or* Is	Isaiah
Dan. *or* Dn	Daniel	Jer. *or* Jer	Jeremiah
Deut. *or* Dt	Deuteronomy	Job *or* Jb	Job
Eccles. *or* Eccl	Ecclesiastes	Joel *or* Jl	Joel
Esther *or* Est	Esther	Jon. *or* Jon	Jonah
Exod. *or* Ex	Exodus	Josh. *or* Jo	Joshua
Ezek. *or* Ez	Ezekiel	Judg. *or* Jgs	Judges
Ezra *or* Ezr	Ezra	1 Kings *or* 1 Kgs	1 Kings
Gen. *or* Gn	Genesis	2 Kings *or* 2 Kgs	2 Kings
Hab. *or* Hb	Habakkuk	Lam. *or* Lam	Lamentations

Lev. *or* Lv	Leviticus	Ruth *or* Ru	Ruth
Mal. *or* Mal	Malachi	1 Sam. *or* 1 Sm	1 Samuel
Mic. *or* Mi	Micah	2 Sam. *or* 2 Sm	2 Samuel
Nah. *or* Na	Nahum	Song of Sol. *or* Sg	Song of Solomon
Neh. *or* Neh	Nehemiah		(= Song of Songs)
Num. *or* Nm	Numbers	Zech. *or* Zec	Zechariah
Obad. *or* Ob	Obadiah	Zeph. *or* Zep	Zephaniah
Prov. *or* Prv	Proverbs		
Ps. (*pl.* Pss.)	Psalms		
or Ps (*pl.* Pss)			

15.52   *The Apocrypha.* The books of the Apocrypha are accepted in Roman Catholic versions of the Bible, though not in Jewish and Protestant versions. Some are not complete in themselves but are continuations of books listed in 15.51. For example, a Roman Catholic scholar would likely refer not to Bel and the Dragon but to Daniel. Where no abbreviation is given, the full form should be used.

Additions to Esther	(= The Rest of Esther)
Bar. *or* Bar	Baruch
Bel and Dragon	Bel and the Dragon
Ecclus.	Ecclesiasticus (= Sirac)
1 Esd.	1 Esdras
2 Esd.	2 Esdras
Jth. *or* Jdt	Judith
1 Macc. *or* 1 Mc	1 Maccabees
2 Macc. *or* 2 Mc	2 Maccabees
Pr. of Man.	Prayer of Manasses (= Manasseh)
Sir	Sirach (= Ecclesiasticus)
Song of Three Children	Song of the Three Holy Children
Sus.	Susanna
Rest of Esther	(= Additions to Esther)
Tob. *or* Tb	Tobit
Ws	Wisdom (= Wisdom of Solomon)
Wisd. of Sol.	Wisdom of Solomon (= Wisdom)

15.53   *The New Testament*

Acts	Acts of the	Eph. *or* Eph	Ephesians
	Apostles	Gal. *or* Gal	Galatians
Apoc. (= Revelation)	Apocalypse	Heb. *or* Heb	Hebrews
Col. *or* Col	Colossians	James *or* Jas	James
1 Cor. *or* 1 Cor	1 Corinthians	John *or* Jn	John (Gospel)
2 Cor. *or* 2 Cor	2 Corinthians	1 John *or* 1 Jn	1 John (Epistle)

2 John *or* 2 Jn	2 John (Epistle)	Phil. *or* Phil	Philippians
3 John *or* 3 Jn	3 John (Epistle)	Rev. *or* Rv	Revelation
Jude	Jude	(= Apocalypse)	
Luke *or* Lk	Luke	Rom. *or* Rom	Romans
Mark *or* Mk	Mark	1 Thess. *or* 1 Thes	1 Thessalonians
Matt. *or* Mt	Matthew	2 Thess. *or* 2 Thes	2 Thessalonians
1 Pet. *or* 1 Pt	1 Peter	1 Tim. *or* 1 Tm	1 Timothy
2 Pet. *or* 2 Pt	2 Peter	2 Tim. *or* 2 Tm	2 Timothy
Philem. *or* Phlm	Philemon	Titus *or* Ti	Titus

15.54 *Versions and sections of the Bible*

Apoc.	Apocrypha
ARV	American Revised Version
ASV	American Standard Version
AT	American Translation
AV	Authorized (King James) Version
CEV	Contemporary English Version
DV	Douay Version
ERV	English Revised Version
EV	English version(s)
HB	Hebrew Bible
JB	Jerusalem Bible
LXX	Septuagint
MT	Masoretic Text
NAB	New American Bible
NEB	New English Bible
NJB	New Jerusalem Bible
NRSV	New Revised Standard Version
NT	New Testament
OT	Old Testament
RV	Revised Version
RSV	Revised Standard Version
Syr.	Syriac
Vulg.	Vulgate

Technology and Science

15.55 *Miscellaneous abbreviations.* The following list, which cannot aim to be comprehensive, includes some abbreviations used in various branches of the physical and biological sciences and in technical writing. Some, such as *CD* and *DVD*, are also in wide general use. Abbreviations used in highly specialized areas have generally been omitted, as have all adjectival forms. Many of the abbreviations for units are identical to or compatible with those used in the International System of Units, or SI (see 15.57–66). Periods are omitted, even with one-letter abbreviations. In nonscientific contexts, however, or where the international system is not being followed, editorial discretion is in order. The capitalization given below, based largely on current usage, sometimes departs from that used in *Merriam-Webster's Collegiate Dictionary* (see bibliog. 3.1). Plurals do not add an *s* (10 A, 5 ha). For statistical abbreviations, see 15.56. For traditional English units of measure, see 15.71–75. See also 9.17–18.

A	ampere; adenine (in genetic code)
Å	angstrom
ac	alternating current
AF	audiofrequency
Ah	ampere-hour
AM	amplitude modulation
ASCII	American Standard Code for Information Interchange
atm	atmosphere, -ic
av *or* avdp	avoirdupois
bar	bar (no abbreviation)
Bé *or* °Bé	degree Baumé (symbol immediately precedes letter)
bhp	brake horsepower
BMI	body mass index
bp	boiling point; base pair
bps	bits per second
Bq	becquerel
Btu	British thermal unit
°C	degree Celsius (symbol immediately precedes letter)
C	coulomb; cytidine (in genetic code)
cal	calorie
Cal	kilocalorie (in nonscientific contexts; see also kcal)
cc	cubic centimeter (in clinical contexts; see also cm^3)
CD	compact disc
cgs	centimeter-gram-second system (SI)
Ci	curie
cm	centimeter
cm^3	cubic centimeter (in scientific contexts; see also cc)
cM	centimorgan
cp	candlepower
CP	chemically pure
cps *or* c/s	cycles per second

CPU	central processing unit
cu	cubic
d	day; deuteron
Da	dalton
dB	decibel
dc	direct current
DNS	domain name system
DOI	digital object identifier
dpi	dots per inch
DVD	digital versatile (or video) disc
dyn	dyne
emf	electromotive force
erg	erg
eV	electron volt
°F	degree Fahrenheit (symbol immediately precedes letter)
F	farad
fp	freezing point
FM	frequency modulation
FTP	file transfer protocol
g	gram; gas
GeV	10^9 electron volts
GIF	graphic interchange format
GIS	geographic information system
GPS	global positioning system
Gy	gigayear; gray (joule per kilogram)
h	hour; helion
H	henry (*pl.* henries)
ha	hectare
hp	horsepower
HTML	hypertext markup language
HTTP	hypertext transfer protocol
Hz	hertz
IR	infrared
IP	Internet protocol
IU	international unit
J	joule
K	kelvin (no degree symbol used); kilobyte (in commercial contexts)
kB	kilobyte (in scientific contexts)
kb	kilobar (DNA); kilobase (RNA)
kc	kilocycle
kcal	kilocalorie (in scientific contexts; see also Cal)
KE	kinetic energy
kg	kilogram

kHz	kilohertz
kJ	kilojoule
km	kilometer
km/h	kilometers per hour
kn	knot (nautical mph)
kW	kilowatt
kWh	kilowatt-hour
L	liter (capitalized to avoid confusion with numeral 1)
m	meter
M	molar; metal
Mb	megabase
Mc	megacycle
mCi	millicurie
MeV	million electron volts
mg	milligram
MIDI	musical instrument digital interface
mks	meter-kilogram-second system (SI)
mL	milliliter
mp	melting point
mpg	miles per gallon
mph	miles per hour
N	newton; number (see also 15.56)
neg	negative
nm	nanometer; nautical mile
OCR	optical character recognition
ohm	ohm
OS	operating system
Pa	pascal
pc	parsec
PC	personal computer
PE	potential energy
pF	picofarad
pH	negative log of hydrogen ion concentration (measure of acidity)
pos	positive
ppb	parts per billion
ppm	parts per million
ppt	parts per trillion
R	electrical resistance (*R* is italicized)
°R	degree Réaumur (symbol immediately precedes letter)
RAM	random access memory
RF	radio frequency
ROM	read-only memory
rpm *or* r/min	revolutions per minute

S	siemens
SGML	standard generalized markup language
soln	solution
sp gr	specific gravity
sq	square
std	standard
STP	standard temperature and pressure
Sv	sievert
t	metric ton (10^3 kg); triton (nucleus of tritium)
temp	temperature
URL	uniform resource locator
UV	ultraviolet
V	volt
W	watt
Wb	weber
wt	weight
w/v	weight per volume
w/w	weight per weight
XML	extensible markup language
y	year
Z	atomic number

A word space usually appears between a numeral and an abbreviation.

4 L
13 Mc
but
512K (when K = kilobytes)
36°C

15.56 *Statistics.* The following abbreviations are used in statistical material, especially in tables. They are often italicized. See also 14.56–57, table 14.3.

ANCOVA	analysis of covariance
ANOVA	analysis of variance
CI	confidence interval
CL	confidence limit
CLT	central limit theorem
df, DF, *or* dof	degrees of freedom
GLIM	generalized linear model
IQR	interquartile range
LS	least squares
MLE	maximum likelihood estimate

MS	mean square
N	number (of population)
n	number (of sample)
ns	not (statistically) significant
OLS	ordinary least squares
OR	odds ratio
p	probability
r	bivariate correlation coefficient
R	multivariate correlation coefficient
RMS	root mean square
sd *or* SD	standard deviation
se *or* SE	standard error
sem *or* SEM	standard error of the mean
SS	sum of squares
SSE	error sum of squares
SST	total sum of squares
WLLN	weak law of large numbers
$\bar{x}$ or $\bar{X}$	mean value

THE INTERNATIONAL SYSTEM OF UNITS

15.57   *SI.* The International System of Units (*Système international d'unités*, abbreviated internationally as SI) is an expanded version of the metric system. It is in general use among the world's scientists and in many other areas. The following paragraphs discuss only the basics. For further guidance and more abbreviations, see B. N. Taylor, *Guide for the Use of the International System of Units* (bibliog. 2.4) and *Scientific Style and Format* (bibliog. 1.1).

15.58   *Absence of periods.* No periods are used after any of the SI symbols for units, and the same symbols are used for both the singular and the plural. Most symbols are lowercased; exceptions are those that stand for units derived from proper names (*A* for *ampere*, etc.) and those that must be distinguished from similar lowercased forms. All units are lowercased in their spelled-out form except for degree (°*C*).

15.59   *Base units.* There are seven fundamental SI units.

Quantity	*Unit*	*Symbol*
length	meter	m
mass	kilogram	kg
time	second	s

electric current	ampere	A
thermodynamic temperature	kelvin	K
amount of substance	mole	mol
luminous intensity	candela	cd

Note that although *weight* and *mass* are usually measured in the same units, they are not interchangeable. Weight is a force due to gravity that depends on an object's mass. Note also that no degree sign is used with the symbol *K*.

15.60 *Prefixes.* Prefixes, representing a power of ten, are added to the name of a base unit to allow notation of very large or very small numerical values. The units so formed are called multiples and submultiples of SI units. For example, a kilometer, or km, is equal to a thousand meters (or 10^3 m), and a millisecond, or ms, is equal to one-thousandth of a second (or 10^{-3} s). The following prefixes, with their symbols, are used in the international system.

Factor	Prefix	Symbol	Factor	Prefix	Symbol
10^{24}	yotta	Y	10^{-1}	deci	d
10^{21}	zetta	Z	10^{-2}	centi	c
10^{18}	exa	E	10^{-3}	milli	m
10^{15}	peta	P	10^{-6}	micro	μ
10^{12}	tera	T	10^{-9}	nano	n
10^{9}	giga	G	10^{-12}	pico	p
10^{6}	mega	M (megabyte	10^{-15}	femto	f
		but megohm)	10^{-18}	atto	a
10^{3}	kilo	k	10^{-21}	zepto	z
10^{2}	hecto	h (hectogram	10^{-24}	yocto	y
		but hectare)			
10^{1}	deka	da			

15.61 *Grams.* Although for historical reasons the kilogram rather than the gram was chosen as the base unit, prefixes are applied to the term *gram*—megagram (Mg), milligram (mg), nanogram (ng), and so forth.

15.62 *Derived units.* Derived units are expressed algebraically in terms of base units or other derived units.

Derived unit	Symbol
square meter	m^2
cubic meter	m^3

meter per second	m/s
meter per second, squared	m/s²
kilogram per cubic meter	kg/m³

15.63 *Special names.* Certain derived units have special names and symbols. Several of the most common—hertz (Hz), volt (V), watt (W), and so forth—are listed in 15.55. These are used in algebraic expressions to denote further derived units. A few are listed below. Note the raised dot in the second expression.

Derived unit	*Symbol*
joule per kelvin	J/K
newton meter	N·m
newton per meter	N/m

15.64 *Alternative expressions.* A derived unit can often be expressed in different ways. For example, the weber may be expressed either as Wb or, in another context, in terms of the volt second (V·s).

15.65 *Numerals with SI units.* Only numbers between 0.1 and 1,000 should be used to express the quantity of any SI unit. Thus 12,000 meters is expressed as 12 km (not 12 000 m), and 0.003 cubic centimeter as 3 mm³ (not 0.003 cm³). SI does not use commas in numbers; in numbers of five or more digits, insert a thin, fixed space between groups of three digits, counting from the decimal point toward the left and right. A word space appears between the numeral and the abbreviation or symbol (see 15.55) *except for* the percent sign (%).

| 8015 | 43 279 522 | 0.491 722 3 |

15.66 *Non-SI units accepted for use.* Certain widely used units such as liter (L, capitalized to avoid confusion with the numeral 1), metric ton (t), and hour (h) are not officially part of the international system but are accepted for use within the system.

ASTRONOMY

15.67 *Overview.* Astronomers and astrophysicists employ the international system of measure supplemented with special terminology and abbreviations. The following two paragraphs offer a minimum of examples for the generalist. Anyone working in the field should become familiar with the conventions followed in Chicago's *Astronomical Journal* or *Astrophysical Journal* (see bibliog. 5).

15.68   *Celestial coordinates.* Right ascension, abbreviated RA or α, is given in hours, minutes, and seconds (abbreviations set as superscripts) of sidereal time. Declination, abbreviated δ, is given in degrees, minutes, and seconds (using the degree symbol, prime, and double prime) of arc north (marked + or left unmarked) or south (marked –) of the celestial equator. Note the abbreviations (set as superscripts) and symbols used.

$14^h6^m7^s$ $-49°8'22''$

Decimal fractions of the basic units are indicated as shown.

$14^h6^m7^s.2$ $+34°.26$

15.69   *Some other abbreviations*

AU	astronomical unit (mean earth-sun distance)
lt-yr	light-year (9.46×10^{12} km)
pc	parsec (parallax second: 3.084×10^{13} km)
kpc	1,000 pc
Mpc	10^6 pc
UT *or* UTC	universal time

CHEMICAL ELEMENTS

15.70   *Naming conventions.* The International Union of Pure and Applied Chemistry (IUPAC) is the recognized body in charge of approving element names. Each element bears a number (reflecting the number of protons in its nucleus) as well as a name—as in "element 106," also known as seaborgium. This number is an important identifier in cases where formal names are in dispute; between 1995 and 1997, for example, the American Chemical Society and IUPAC adopted different names for some of the same elements. The differences were reconciled, and the list that follows reflects names and symbols approved by IUPAC. It is arranged in alphabetical order by common name. If the symbol is based on a term other than the common name—for example, Sb (*stibium*) for antimony—the term is added in parentheses. Although the names of elements are always lowercased, the symbols all have an initial capital. No periods are used. In specialized works, the abbreviations commonly appear in text as well as in tables, notes, and so forth. See also 8.158–59.

89	Ac	actinium
13	Al	aluminum (U.S.), aluminium (IUPAC)
95	Am	americium
51	Sb	antimony (*stibium*)
18	Ar	argon
33	As	arsenic
85	At	astatine
56	Ba	barium
97	Bk	berkelium
4	Be	beryllium
83	Bi	bismuth
107	Bh	bohrium
5	B	boron
35	Br	bromine
48	Cd	cadmium
20	Ca	calcium
98	Cf	californium
6	C	carbon
58	Ce	cerium
55	Cs	cesium
17	Cl	chlorine
24	Cr	chromium
27	Co	cobalt
29	Cu	copper
96	Cm	curium
105	Db	dubnium
66	Dy	dysprosium
99	Es	einsteinium
68	Er	erbium
63	Eu	europium
100	Fm	fermium
9	F	fluorine
87	Fr	francium
64	Gd	gadolinium
31	Ga	gallium
32	Ge	germanium
79	Au	gold (*aurum*)
72	Hf	hafnium
108	Hs	hassium
2	He	helium
67	Ho	holmium
1	H	hydrogen
49	In	indium
53	I	iodine
77	Ir	iridium
26	Fe	iron (*ferrum*)
36	Kr	krypton
57	La	lanthanum
103	Lr	lawrencium
82	Pb	lead (*plumbum*)
3	Li	lithium
71	Lu	lutetium
12	Mg	magnesium
25	Mn	manganese
109	Mt	meitnerium
101	Md	mendelevium
80	Hg	mercury (hydrargyrum)
42	Mo	molybdenum
60	Nd	neodymium
10	Ne	neon
93	Np	neptunium
28	Ni	nickel
41	Nb	niobium
7	N	nitrogen
102	No	nobelium
76	Os	osmium
8	O	oxygen
46	Pd	palladium
15	P	phosphorus
78	Pt	platinum
94	Pu	plutonium
84	Po	polonium
19	K	potassium (*kalium*)
59	Pr	praseodymium
61	Pm	promethium
91	Pa	protactinium
88	Ra	radium
86	Rn	radon
75	Re	rhenium
45	Rh	rhodium
37	Rb	rubidium
44	Ru	ruthenium
104	Rf	rutherfordium
62	Sm	samarium

21	Sc	scandium	50	Sn	tin (*stannum*)
106	Sg	seaborgium	43	Tc	technetium
34	Se	selenium	22	Ti	titanium
14	Si	silicon	74	W	tungsten (*wolfram*)
47	Ag	silver (*argentum*)	112	Uub	ununbium
11	Na	sodium (*natrium*)	110	Uun	ununnilium
38	Sr	strontium	114	Uuq	ununquadium
16	S	sulfur	111	Uuu	unununium
73	Ta	tantalum	92	U	uranium
43	Tc	technetium	23	V	vanadium
52	Te	tellurium	54	Xe	xenon
65	Tb	terbium	70	Yb	ytterbium
81	Tl	thallium	39	Y	yttrium
90	Th	thorium	30	Zn	zinc
69	Tm	thulium	40	Zr	zirconium

ENGLISH MEASURE

15.71 *Periods.* In the rare instances in which abbreviations for English units of measure are used in scientific copy, they are usually set without periods; in nonscientific contexts, periods are customary.

15.72 *Plurals.* Abbreviations of units of measure are identical in the singular and the plural. See also 15.75.

10 yd.   5 lb.   8 sq. mi.

15.73 *Length, area, and volume*

Length		Area		Volume	
in. *or* "	inch	sq. in.	square inch	cu. in.	cubic inch
ft. *or* '	foot	sq. ft.	square foot	cu. ft.	cubic foot
yd.	yard	sq. yd.	square yard	cu. yd.	cubic yard
rd.	rod	sq. rd.	square rod		
mi.	mile	sq. mi.	square mile		

Note that *in.* can mean *inch* or *inches, ft.* can mean *foot* or *feet*, and so forth (see 15.72).

8 sq. in.   6 cu. yd.

Exponents are sometimes used with abbreviations to designate area or volume, but only when no ambiguity can occur.

The area of the floor to be covered is 425 ft.^{2} (= 425 sq. ft., *not* 425 ft. by 425 ft.).

A tank 638 ft.^{3} is required (= 638 cu. ft.).

15.74 *Weight and capacity.* The English system comprises three systems of weight and mass: avoirdupois (the common system), troy (used mainly by jewelers), and apothecaries' measure. Although confusion is unlikely, an abbreviation can, if necessary, be referred to the appropriate system thus: lb. av., lb. t., lb. ap. Also, the systems of capacity measure used in the United States and the British Commonwealth differ (an American pint being four ounces smaller than a British pint, for example), but the same abbreviations are used.

Weight or mass		Dry measure		Liquid measure	
gr.	grain	pt.	pint	min. or ℟	minim
s.	scruple	qt.	quart	fl. Dr. or f. ʒ	fluid dram
dr.	dram	pk.	peck	fl. oz. or f. ℥	fluid ounce
dwt.	pennyweight	bu.	bushel	gi.	gill
oz.	ounce			pt.	pint
lb. or #	pound			qt.	quart
cwt.	hundredweight			gal.	gallon
tn.	ton			bbl.	barrel

As with length and so forth, abbreviations do not change in the plural.

12 gal. gas   3 pt. milk

15.75 *Time*

sec.	second	d. or day	day
min.	minute	mo.	month
h. or hr.	hour	yr.	year

In nontechnical writing, plurals of these abbreviations, unlike those of length, area, weight, and the like, are often formed by adding an *s*.

5 secs.   12 hrs. *or* 12 h.   15 yrs.

Business and Commerce

15.76 *Some conventions.* Periods are normally used in lowercased forms. See also 15.71–75. For company names, see 15.23.

acct.	account	ea.	each
agt.	agent	f.o.b. *or* FOB	free on board
a.v. *or* AV	ad valorem	FY	fiscal year
bal.	balance	gro.	gross
bdl.	bundle	inst.	instant (this month)
bu.	bushel	mdse.	merchandise
c. *or* ct.	cent	mfg.	manufacturing
c.l.	carload	mfr.	manufacturer
c/o	in care of	mgmt.	management
COD	cash on delivery	mgr.	manager
cr.	credit, creditor	pd.	paid
cttee.	committee	pkg.	package
d/b/a	doing business as	std.	standard
doz.	dozen	ult.	ultimo (last month)

16

Documentation I: Basic Patterns

Introduction

16.1 *Two basic systems.* Ethics, copyright laws, and courtesy to readers require authors to identify the sources of direct quotations and of any facts or opinions not generally known or easily checked. Conventions for documentation vary according to scholarly discipline, the preferences of publishers and authors, and the needs of a particular work. This chapter describes, compares, and illustrates the two basic systems preferred by Chicago—notes and bibliography on the one hand and the author-date system on the other. Chapter 17 deals with the specific components and style of individual bibliographic entries, notes, and parenthetical citations.

16.2 *The essentials.* Whichever system is chosen, the primary criterion is sufficient information to lead readers to the sources used, whether these are published or unpublished materials, in printed or electronic form. For journals, the choice between systems is likely to have been made long ago; anyone writing for a journal should consult the specific journal's instructions to authors.

16.3 *Notes and bibliography: overview.* In the system favored by many writers in literature, history, and the arts, bibliographic citations are provided in notes (whether footnotes or endnotes), preferably supplemented by a bibliography. If the bibliography includes all works cited in the notes, the note citations—even the first citation to a particular work—can be quite concise, since readers can turn to the bibliography for publication details and other information. Chicago recommends this practice as user-friendly and economical—duplication of information is minimized. In works with no bibliography or only a selected list, full details must be given in a note at first mention of any work cited. For discussion of the difference in format between note citations and bibliographic entries, see 16.8–18. For a detailed discussion of notes, see 16.19–70. For shortened references, see 16.41–49. For a detailed discussion of bibliographies, see 16.71–90. See also figures 16.1–16 at the end of this chapter.

Bibliographic entry:

Doniger, Wendy. *Splitting the Difference: Gender and Myth in Ancient Greece and India.* Chicago: University of Chicago Press, 1999.

First note citation in a work *with* full bibliography:

1. Doniger, *Splitting the Difference,* 23.

First note citation in a work *without* full bibliography:

1. Wendy Doniger, *Splitting the Difference: Gender and Myth in Ancient Greece and India* (Chicago: University of Chicago Press, 1999), 23.

16.4 *The author-date system: overview.* The system used by many in the physical, natural, and social sciences, and recommended by Chicago for works in those areas, is known as the author-date system. Sources are cited in the text, usually in parentheses, by the author's last (family) name, the publication date of the work cited, and a page number if needed. Full details appear in the bibliography—usually titled "References" or "Works Cited"—in which the year of publication appears immediately after the author's name. Initials often replace authors' given names, and subtitles are sometimes omitted. This system works best where all or most of the sources are easily convertible to author-date references. Anonymous works, manuscript collections, or other sources less easily converted are better dealt with in notes. For a detailed discussion of the author-date system, see 16.90–120; for comparison with notes and bibliography, see 16.8–18; for more examples, see figure 16.5.

Text citations:

All of Eurasia was affected by climatic oscillations during Pleistocene glacials and interglacials (Frenzel 1968). . . . Behavioral observations can provide useful insights into evolutionary relationships, as Morris and Morris (1966, 1–24) first tried to show for the giant panda.

Reference-list entries:

Frenzel, B. 1968. The Pleistocene vegetation of northern Eurasia. *Science* 161:637–49.
Morris, R., and D. Morris. 1966. *Men and pandas.* New York: McGraw-Hill.

16.5 *Other systems.* Among other well-known systems are those of the Modern Language Association, the American Psychological Association, and the American Medical Association. Guidelines and examples are to be found in the manuals of those associations. *Scientific Style and Format* also furnishes useful guidelines on both the author-date system and numbered references (see bibliog. 1.1 for these and other style manuals). Many journals and serials—including some of those published by the University of Chicago Press—either follow one of these styles or have their own styles, often based on or similar to the systems mentioned here and in the previous two paragraphs.

16.6   *Numbered references.* A system that saves considerable space but does not allow for changes or corrections without renumbering employs a numbered list of references cited in the text by number. The text numbers may be enclosed in parentheses or brackets or may appear as superior figures like note reference numbers. The list of references is arranged in order of the first appearance of each source in text or, sometimes, alphabetically. Examples may be found in the *American Medical Association Manual of Style, Scientific Style and Format,* and such journals as Chicago's *Journal of Infectious Diseases.*

16.7   *Flexibility.* Elements of different systems can be combined or adjusted as appropriate to the subject matter and readership or to follow an established journal or series style. For example, a work using the author-date method may include footnotes or endnotes in which parenthetical references appear (see figs. 16.6, 16.9). Or a work in which most citations are made in the notes may include a few parenthetical text citations, as illustrated in 11.72–84. Headline-style capitalization (see 8.167), usually preferred in the notes-and-bibliography system, is not out of place in a work using the author-date system (see fig. 16.15).

Source Citation: Basic Elements, Different Formats

16.8   *Overview.* In order to compare the two main styles illustrated in this manual—notes and bibliography versus text citations and reference list— the following paragraphs deal with the bare bones of citing books and journal articles. For more on each system, see paragraphs later in this chapter under the main headings "Notes," "Bibliographies," and "The Author-Date System." Detailed discussion of many kinds of sources and supplementary elements is given in chapter 17.

16.9   *Common elements.* Citations of books, articles, and other materials in notes, bibliographies, and reference lists all include the following elements: author (or editor, compiler, or translator standing in place of the author), title (and usually subtitle), and date of publication. For books, the place and publisher are also given; for articles, the journal name, volume number, year of publication, page number(s), and, often, the issue number. For other than printed sources—electronic works or audiovisual material, for example—the medium is indicated. For online works, retrieval information and sometimes the date of access are included. Certain elements are omitted in shortened citations (see 16.41–49). For fuller treatment of all the elements, including those for electronic sources, see chapter 17.

16.10 *Examples.* Key: N = note; B = bibliography; T = parenthetical text citation in author-date style; R = reference list in author-date style. See also 16.11–18.

N: 1. Douglas D. Heckathorn, "Collective Sanctions and Compliance Norms: A Formal Theory of Group-Mediated Social Control," *American Sociological Review* 55 (1990): 370.

   2. Lynne Rossetto Kasper, *The Italian Country Table: Home Cooking from Italy's Farmhouse Kitchens* (New York: Scribner, 1999), 10–11.

   3. Philip B. Kurland and Ralph Lerner, eds., *The Founders' Constitution* (Chicago: University of Chicago Press, 2000), chap. 9, doc. 3, http://press-pubs.uchicago.edu/founders/.

B: Heckathorn, Douglas D. "Collective Sanctions and Compliance Norms: A Formal Theory of Group-Mediated Social Control." *American Sociological Review* 55 (1990): 366–84.

   Kasper, Lynne Rossetto. *The Italian Country Table: Home Cooking from Italy's Farmhouse Kitchens.* New York: Scribner, 1999.

   Kurland, Philip B., and Ralph Lerner, eds. *The Founders' Constitution.* Chicago: University of Chicago Press, 2000. http://press-pubs.uchicago.edu/founders/.

T: (Heckathorn 1990, 370)

   (Kasper 1999, 10–11)

   (Kurland and Lerner 2000, chap. 9, doc. 3)

R: Heckathorn, D. D. 1990. Collective sanctions and compliance norms: A formal theory of group-mediated social control. *American Sociological Review* 55:366–84.

   Kasper, L. R. 1999. *The Italian country table: Home cooking from Italy's farmhouse kitchens.* New York: Scribner.

   Kurland, P. B., and R. Lerner, eds. 2000. *The founders' Constitution.* Chicago: University of Chicago Press. http://press-pubs.uchicago.edu/founders/.

The formats illustrated above may be modified as long as consistency is preserved within a work (see 16.7). For more examples, see figures 16.1–16 at the end of this chapter.

16.11 *Authors' names.* ("Author" is used here to include editors, compilers, and translators standing in place of authors.) In bibliographies and reference lists, arranged alphabetically, authors' names are inverted to put the family name first (but only for the first of two or more authors). In notes, names are given in the normal order. To avoid conflation of similar names, it is helpful to use authors' given names (at least the first) where known or generally used. For the use of initials, see 8.6, 17.20–24. For more on al-phabetizing, see chapter 18.

16.12   *Year of publication.* In notes and bibliographies, the year of publication ap-pears after the publisher or the journal name. In reference lists, it imme-diately follows the name(s) of the author(s).

16.13   *Page numbers.* In notes or parenthetical citations, where reference is usu-ally to a particular passage in a book or journal, only the page numbers pertaining to that passage are given. In bibliographies and reference lists, no page numbers are given for books. For easier location of journal ar-ticles, the beginning and ending page numbers of the entire article are given. For citing a chapter in a book, see 17.68–69. For citing passages from unpaginated print material, see 17.136–37.

16.14   *Locators for unpaginated electronic sources.* Electronic sources often do not use page numbers. Readers may be able to perform a search for a quota-tion from an electronic source. When possible, however, a subhead, a chapter or paragraph number, or a descriptive phrase that follows the or-ganizational divisions of the work cited is used in notes or parenthetical citations (such locators are analogous to the "other specific references" discussed at 16.109).

16.15   *Punctuation.* In bibliographies and reference lists the main elements are separated by periods. In notes they are separated by commas. A colon al-ways separates title from subtitle. For a book, the place, publisher, and year of publication are enclosed in parentheses in a note but not in a bib-liography or a reference list. For an article, the year of publication appears in parentheses in a note or a bibliography (unless it is used in place of a volume number; see 17.166), but in a reference list it is not enclosed in parentheses.

16.16   *Font.* Italics are used for titles of books and names of journals. Titles of ar-ticles (as well as chapters, poems, etc.; see 8.187, 8.191) are set in roman; in notes and bibliographies they are put in quotation marks, but in refer-ence lists they are not.

16.17   *Capitalization.* In notes and bibliographies, titles of books, articles, and journal names are usually capitalized headline style (see 8.167). In refer-ence lists, only journal names are headline style; titles and subtitles of books and articles are usually sentence style (see 8.166). The first word of the subtitle is always capitalized.

16.18   *Styling electronic source titles.* The style used for citing print source titles is easily adapted to most electronic source titles. The name of a complete work is italicized, and that of an item within a work is set in roman. Quotation marks, parentheses, and headline- versus sentence-style capitalization should be used as in the surrounding documentation. When in doubt, avoid italics and quotation marks and give as much information as may be useful; too much is better than too little. For examples, see chapter 17.

Notes

16.19   *Footnotes versus endnotes in printed works.* Footnotes are properly so called when they appear at the foot of a page. In a journal, endnotes appear at the end of an article; in a book, at the end of a chapter or, more commonly because easier to locate, at the back of the book. (In multiauthor books, where the notes may differ in kind and length, and where chapters may be reprinted separately, they are usually placed at the end of the chapter to which they pertain.)

16.20   *Creating notes.* Notes should be created by use of the footnote or endnote function of the word processor. In manuscript they may appear either as footnotes or as endnotes to an article or chapter, regardless of how they will appear in the published version. Keeping the notes embedded rather than placing them in a separate file makes it easier to add, delete, or renumber notes. For footnotes to tables, see 2.32, 13.43–50. For notes in previously published material, see 2.43.

16.21   *Footnotes: virtues.* Readers of scholarly works usually prefer footnotes for ease of reference. Where the notes are closely integrated into the text and make interesting reading, they belong at the foot of the page. They also belong there if immediate knowledge of the sources is essential to readers.

16.22   *Footnotes: vices.* In a work containing many long footnotes, it may be difficult to fit them onto the pages they pertain to, especially in an illustrated work. A basic requirement for all footnotes is that they at least begin on the page on which they are referenced. Several long footnotes with their references falling close together toward the end of a page present a major problem in page makeup. There is also the matter of appearance; a page consisting almost exclusively of footnotes is daunting. For some remedies, see 16.36–40.

16.23   *Endnotes: virtues.* Endnotes obviate many of the disadvantages of footnotes (see 16.22). Tables, quoted poetry, and other matter that requires special typography are best handled in endnotes. Publishers' marketing and sales staff often recommend endnotes in books directed to general as well as scholarly or professional readers. Since general readers may be disappointed to find a third or more of a book devoted to endnotes, authors should aim for a healthy balance between text and notes. For more on endnotes, see 16.59–62.

16.24   *Endnotes: vices.* The difficulty of finding a particular note is the main problem with endnotes. The difficulty can be reduced, however, by informative running heads (see 16.60–61). For minor differences in citation form between footnotes and endnotes, see 16.62.

NOTE NUMBERS

16.25   *Position of numbers.* Note reference numbers in text are set as superior (superscript) numbers. In the notes themselves, they are normally full size, not raised, and followed by a period.

"Nonrestrictive relative clauses are parenthetic, as are similar clauses introduced by conjunctions indicating time or place."[1]

1. William Strunk Jr. and E. B. White, *The Elements of Style*, 4th ed. (New York: Allyn and Bacon, 2000), 3.

16.26   *Numbering.* Notes, whether footnotes or endnotes, should be numbered consecutively, beginning with 1, throughout each article or chapter—not throughout an entire book unless the text has no internal divisions. If a work contains only a handful of footnotes, they may be referenced by asterisks rather than numbers.

16.27   *Footnotes plus endnotes.* Some works require both footnotes and endnotes. In such a case, the footnotes are usually referenced by asterisks, daggers, and so on (see 16.63) and the endnotes by numbers.

16.28   *Nontextual notes.* Notes to tables or other nontextual matter are numbered independently of the text notes. See 2.32, 13.47–48, 13.50.

16.29   *Renumbering.* If any notes are added or deleted, all following notes must be renumbered. At the proof stage, however, renumbering is expensive and time consuming. Only essential changes should be made, and any necessary additions should be put at the end of an existing note.

16.30   *Placement of number.* A note number should be placed at the end of a sentence or at the end of a clause. The number follows any punctuation mark except for the dash, which it precedes. It follows a closing parenthesis.

"This," wrote George Templeton Strong, "is what our tailors can do." (In an earlier book he had said quite the opposite.)[2]

The bias was apparent in the Shotwell series[3]—and it must be remembered that Shotwell was a student of Robinson's.

For a parenthetical phrase within a sentence, it may occasionally be appropriate to place the note number before the closing parenthesis.

Men and their unions, as they entered industrial work, negotiated two things: young women would be laid off once they married (the commonly acknowledged "marriage bar"[1]), and men would be paid a "family wage."

16.31   *Note number with quotation.* A note number normally follows a quotation, whether the quotation is run into the text or set off as an extract (see 16.30, first example).

16.32   *Headings.* For aesthetic reasons, a note number should never appear within or at the end of a chapter or article title or a subhead. A note that applies to an entire chapter or article should be unnumbered and is usually placed at the foot of the first page of the piece, preceding any numbered notes (see 16.66–70). A note that applies to a section following a subhead should be placed in an appropriate place in the text—perhaps after the first sentence in the section.

16.33   *Multiple citation.* A note that applies to more than one location should be cross-referenced; a note number cannot reappear out of sequence.

18. See note 3 above.

16.34   *Multiple references.* Using more than one note reference at a single location (such as [5,6]) should be rigorously avoided. A single note can contain more than one citation or comment (see 16.37).

16.35   *Asterisks, daggers, and the like.* Where only a handful of footnotes appear in an entire book or, perhaps, just one in an article, symbols may be used instead of numbers. Usually an asterisk is enough, but if more than one note is needed on the same page, the sequence is * † ‡ §. See figure 16.10. Because the sequence of symbols starts over for each page, this system may not be appropriate for electronic works. See also 16.65.

REMEDIES FOR EXCESSIVE ANNOTATION

16.36 *Avoiding overlong footnotes.* Lengthy, discursive notes should be reduced or integrated into the text. Complicated tabular material, lists, and other entities not part of the text should be put in an appendix rather than in the footnotes. A parenthetical note in the text might read, for example, "For a list of institutions involved, see appendix A."

16.37 *Several citations in one note.* The number of note references in a sentence or a paragraph can sometimes be reduced by grouping several citations in a single note. The citations are separated by semicolons and must appear in the same order as the text material (whether works, quotations, or whatever) to which they pertain. Take care to avoid any ambiguity as to what is documenting what.

Text:

Only when we gather the work of several scholars—Walter Sutton's explications of some of Whitman's shorter poems; Paul Fussell's careful study of structure in "Cradle"; S. K. Coffman's close readings of "Crossing Brooklyn Ferry" and "Passage to India"; and the attempts of Thomas I. Rountree and John Lovell, dealing with "Song of Myself" and "Passage to India," respectively, to elucidate the strategy in "indirection"—do we begin to get a sense of both the extent and the specificity of Whitman's forms.[1]

Note:

1. Sutton, "The Analysis of Free Verse Form, Illustrated by a Reading of Whitman," *Journal of Aesthetics and Art Criticism* 18 (December 1959): 241–54; Fussell, "Whitman's Curious Warble: Reminiscence and Reconciliation," in *The Presence of Whitman*, ed. R. W. B. Lewis, 28–51; Coffman, "'Crossing Brooklyn Ferry': Note on the Catalog Technique in Whitman's Poetry," *Modern Philology* 51 (May 1954): 225–32; Coffman, "Form and Meaning in Whitman's 'Passage to India,'" *PMLA* 70 (June 1955): 337–49; Rountree, "Whitman's Indirect Expression and Its Application to 'Song of Myself,'" *PMLA* 73 (December 1958): 549–55; and Lovell, "Appreciating Whitman: 'Passage to India,'" *Modern Language Quarterly* 21 (June 1960): 131–41.

In the example above, authors' given names are omitted in the note because they appear in text. For inclusion of names in endnotes, see 16.62.

16.38 *Parenthetical text references.* Another way to reduce the number of notes is to cite sources (usually in parentheses) in text. *Ibid.* may be dealt with in the same way. For discussion and examples, see 11.72–84.

16.39 *Abbreviations.* A frequently mentioned work may be cited either parenthetically in text or in subsequent notes by means of an abbreviation, with full citation provided in a note at first mention. See also 11.76–77, 16.40, 16.41–49.

> 2. François Furet, *The Passing of an Illusion: The Idea of Communism in the Twentieth Century*, trans. Deborah Furet (Chicago: University of Chicago Press, 1999), 368 (hereafter cited in text as *PI*).

> (Subsequent text references) "In this sense, the Second World War completed what the First had begun—the domination of the great political religions over European public opinion," Furet points out (*PI*, 360). But he goes on to argue . . .

An abbreviation differs from a short title (see 16.45) in that words may be abbreviated and the word order changed.

> 3. Nathaniel B. Shurtleff, ed., *Records of the Governor and Company of the Massachusetts Bay in New England (1628–86)*, 5 vols. (Boston, 1853–54), 1:126 (hereafter cited as *Mass. Records*).
> 4. *Mass. Records*, 2:330.

16.40 *List of abbreviations.* Where many abbreviations of titles, manuscript collections, personal names, or other entities are used in a work—say, ten or more—they are best listed alphabetically in a separate section (see fig. 16.7). In a book, the list may appear in the front matter (if footnotes are used) or in the end matter preceding the endnotes (if these are used). It is usually headed "Abbreviations" and should be included in the table of contents (see 1.4). Where only a few abbreviations are used, these are occasionally listed as the first section of the endnotes (see fig. 16.8) or at the head of the bibliography. Titles that are italicized in the notes or bibliography should be italicized in the list of abbreviations.

SHORTENED CITATIONS

16.41 *Purpose.* To reduce the bulk of documentation in scholarly works that use footnotes or endnotes, subsequent citations to sources already given in full should be shortened whenever possible. The short form, as distinct from an abbreviation, should include enough information to remind readers of the full title or to lead them to the appropriate entry in the bibliography (for the relation of notes to bibliography, see 16.3). For guidance on shortened references to certain materials, see the relevant sections in chapter 17.

16.42 *The basic short form.* The most common short form consists of the last name of the author and the main title of the work cited, usually shortened if more than four words, as in examples 4–6 below. For more on author's name, see 16.44. For more on short titles, see 16.45. For more on journal articles, see 17.179.

> 1. Samuel A. Morley, *Poverty and Inequality in Latin America: The Impact of Adjustment and Recovery* (Baltimore: Johns Hopkins University Press, 1995), 24–25.
>
> 2. Regina M. Schwartz, "Nationals and Nationalism: Adultery in the House of David," *Critical Inquiry* 19, no. 1 (1992): 131–32.
>
> 3. Ernest Kaiser, "The Literature of Harlem," in *Harlem: A Community in Transition*, ed. J. H. Clarke (New York: Citadel Press, 1964).
>
> 4. Morley, *Poverty and Inequality*, 43.
>
> 5. Schwartz, "Nationals and Nationalism," 138.
>
> 6. Kaiser, "Literature of Harlem," 189, 140.

16.43 *Cross-reference to full citation.* When references to a particular source are far apart, readers encountering the short form may be helped by a cross-reference to the original note (especially in the absence of a full bibliography). Repeating the full details in each new chapter, formerly a common practice in scholarly works, is seldom necessary.

> 95. Miller, *Quest*, 81 (see chap. 1, n. 4).

16.44 *Author's name.* Only the last name of the author, or of the editor or translator if given first in the full reference, is needed in the short form. Full names or initials are included only when two or more authors with the same last name have been cited. Such abbreviations as *ed.* or *trans.* following a name in the full reference are omitted in subsequent references. If a work has two or three authors, give the last name of each; for more than three, the last name of the first author followed by *et al.* or *and others.*

> Kathryn Petras and Ross Petras, eds., *Very Bad Poetry*
> (Short form) Petras and Petras, *Very Bad Poetry*

> Joseph A. Belizzi, H. F. Kruckeberg, J. R. Hamilton, and W. S. Martin, "Consumer Perceptions of National, Private, and Generic Brands"
> (Short form) Belizzi et al., "Consumer Perceptions"

16.45   *Title.* The short title contains the key word or words from the main title. An initial *A* or *The* is omitted. The order of the words should not be changed (for example, *Daily Notes of a Trip around the World* should be shortened not to *World Trip* but to *Daily Notes* or *Around the World*). Titles of four words or fewer are seldom shortened. The short title is italicized or set in roman according to the way the full title appears.

The War Journal of Major Damon "Rocky" Gause
(Short title) *War Journal*

"A Brief Account of the Reconstruction of Aristotle's *Protrepticus*"
(Short title) "Aristotle's *Protrepticus*"

Kriegstagebuch des Oberkommandos der Wehrmacht, 1940–1945
(Short title) *Kriegstagebuch*

In short titles in languages other than English, no word should be omitted that governs the case ending of a word included in the short title. If in doubt, ask someone who knows the language.

16.46   *Other short forms.* For citing different chapters in the same work, see 17.70; for letters, see 17.76–77; for legal citations, see 17.287. Other short forms may be patterned on the examples above or as illustrated by the examples in chapter 17.

16.47   *"Ibid."* The abbreviation *ibid.* (from *ibidem,* "in the same place") refers to a single work cited in the note immediately preceding (but see also 16.48). It must never be used if the preceding note contains more than one citation. It takes the place of the name(s) of the author(s) or editor(s), the title of the work, and as much of the succeeding material as is identical. If the entire reference, including page number(s) or other particulars, is identical, the word *ibid.* alone is used (as in example 7 below). The word *ibid.* (italicized in this paragraph only because it is a word used as a word—see 7.62) is set in roman and followed by a period.

5. Farmwinkle, *Humor of the Midwest,* 241.
6. Ibid., 258–59.
7. Ibid.
8. Ibid., 333–34.
9. Losh, *Diaries and Correspondence,* 1:150.
10. Ibid., 2:35–36.
11. Ibid., 2:37–40.

To avoid a succession of *ibid.* notes, the page numbers in examples 6–8, 10, and 11 above might be run into the text in parentheses (see 11.74).

16.48   *Within one note. Ibid.* may also be used within one note in successive references to the same work.

> 8. Morris Birkbeck, "The Illinois Prairies and Settlers," in *Prairie State: Impressions of Illinois, 1673–1967, by Travelers and Other Observers*, ed. Paul M. Angle (Chicago: University of Chicago Press, 1968), 62. "The soil of the Big-prairie, which is of no great extent notwithstanding its name, is a rich, cool sand; that is to say, one of the most desirable description" (ibid., 63).

16.49   *"Idem."* When several works by the same person are cited successively in the same note, *idem* ("the same," sometimes abbreviated to *id.*), may be used in place of the author's name. Except in legal references, where the abbreviation *id.* is used in place of *ibid.*, the term is rarely used nowadays. It is safer to repeat the author's last name.

16.50   *"Op. cit." and "loc. cit." Op. cit.* (*opere citato*, "in the work cited") and *loc. cit.* (*loco citato*, "in the place cited"), used with an author's last name and standing in place of a previously cited title, are rightly falling into disuse. Since they can refer to works cited many pages or even chapters earlier, they are exceptionally unhelpful. Consider a reader's frustration on meeting, for example, "Wells, op. cit., 10" in note 95 and having to search back to note 2 for the full source or, worse still, finding that *two* works by Wells have been cited. Chicago disallows both *op. cit.* and *loc. cit.* and instead uses the short-title form described in 16.45.

NOTE STRUCTURE

16.51   *Separating citations.* Several references documenting a single fact in the text are normally separated by semicolons, with the last reference (often preceded by *and*) followed by a period. See example in 16.37.

16.52   *Citations plus commentary.* When a note contains not only the source of a fact or quotation in the text but related substantive material as well, the source comes first. A period usually separates the citation from the commentary. Such comments as "emphasis mine" are usually put in parentheses. See also 11.70.

> 11. Shakespeare, *Julius Caesar*, act 3, sc. 1. Caesar's claim of constancy should be taken with a grain of salt.
> 12. Little, "Norms of Collegiality," 330 (my italics).

16.53   *Quotation within a note.* When a note includes a quotation, the source normally follows the terminal punctuation of the quotation. The entire source need not be put in parentheses, which involves changing existing parentheses to brackets and creating unnecessary clutter.

> 14. One estimate of the size of the reading public at this time was that of Sydney Smith: "Readers are fourfold in number compared with what they were before the beginning of the French war. . . . There are four or five hundred thousand readers more than there were thirty years ago, among the lower orders." *Letters*, ed. Nowell C. Smith (New York: Oxford University Press, 1953), 1:341, 343.

16.54   *Substantive notes.* Substantive, or discursive, notes may merely amplify the text and include no sources. When a source is needed, it is treated as in the example in 16.53 or, if brief and already cited in full, may appear parenthetically, as in the following example.

> 1. Ernst Cassirer takes important notice of this in *Language and Myth* (59–62) and offers a searching analysis of man's regard for things on which his power of inspirited action may crucially depend.

16.55   *Long quotations in notes.* Long quotations, which might be set off as extracts in the text, are best run in (enclosed in quotation marks) when they appear in footnotes or endnotes, since changes in type size, indention, and vertical space can be awkward to deal with in notes. More than three lines of poetry must be set off (see 11.28, 11.32).

16.56   *Long notes and paragraphing.* Paragraph indents should be avoided in notes wherever possible, since a new paragraph may be confused with a new note and thus disregarded. This holds for endnotes as well as footnotes.

16.57   *Continuation footnotes.* When a footnote begins on one page and continues on the next, the break must be made in midsentence, or readers may miss the end of the note. A short rule appears above the continued part (see fig. 16.1).

16.58   *"See" and "cf."* Authors should keep in mind the distinction between *see* and *cf.*, using *cf.* only to mean "compare" or "see, by way of comparison." Neither term is italicized in notes (though *see* is italicized in indexes; see 18.21).

> 22. For further discussion of this problem, see Jones, *Conflict*, 49.
> 23. Others disagree with my position; cf. Jones, *Conflict*, 101–3.

ENDNOTES

16.59   *Placement.* Endnotes to each chapter of a book are best grouped in the end matter, following the text and any appendixes and preceding the bibliography if there is one (see 1.4). The main heading is simply "Notes," and the group of notes to each chapter is introduced by a subhead bearing the chapter number or title or both (see fig. 16.2). In a book that has a different author for each chapter (such as a symposium volume), endnotes normally appear at the end of each chapter. (This location is essential when offprints are to be supplied for each chapter.) In a journal, they appear at the end of each article. In the latter two cases, a subhead "Notes" usually appears between text and notes (see fig. 16.9).

16.60   *Running heads for notes sections.* Where endnotes are gathered at the back of a printed book and occupy more than two or three pages, running heads (both verso and recto) carrying the page numbers to which the notes pertain are a boon to readers (see 1.86, 1.98). To determine what text page numbers to use on a particular page of notes, find the numbers of the first and last notes beginning on that page (disregarding a runover from a previous page) and locate the references to these notes in the text. The numbers of the first and last pages on which these references appear in text are the numbers to use in the running head: for example, "Notes to Pages 9–16." Since these running heads can be completed only when page proof is available, the corrections are considered "alterations" (see 3.14), and the cost may be charged to the publisher. When notes appear at the ends of chapters, such running heads are rarely necessary.

16.61   *Running heads: another system.* Less useful for readers but cheaper for the publisher are running heads in the notes section that simply read "Notes to Chapter One," "Notes to Chapter Two," and so on. (If notes to more than one chapter appear on the same page, the running head will read, for example, "Notes to Chapters Two and Three.") Since readers are often unaware of the number of the chapter they are reading, chapter numbers must also appear in either the verso or the recto running heads of the text itself.

16.62   *Special needs of endnotes.* Whereas footnote citations, because they appear so close to the text, can omit certain elements mentioned in the text, omitting them in endnotes risks irritating readers, who have to go back and forth. For example, an author or title mentioned in the text need not be repeated in the footnote citation, though it is often helpful to do so. In an endnote, however, the author (or at least the author's last name) and title should be repeated, since at least some readers may have forgotten whether the note number was 93 or 94 by the time they find it at the back of the work. It is particularly annoying to arrive at the right place in the endnotes only to find another "ibid." Such frustration can be prevented by the devices illustrated in the examples below. See also 11.73–76.

> 34. This and the preceding four quotations are all from *Hamlet*, act 1, sc. 4.
>
> 87. Barbara Wallraff, *Word Court: Wherein Verbal Virtue Is Rewarded, Crimes against the Language Are Punished, and Poetic Justice Is Done* (New York: Harcourt, 2000), 34. Further citations to this work are given in the text.

TWO SETS OF NOTES

16.63   *Endnotes plus footnotes.* In a heavily documented work it is occasionally helpful to separate substantive notes from source citations. In such a case, the citation notes should be numbered and appear as endnotes. The substantive notes, indicated by asterisks and other symbols, appear as footnotes. The first footnote on each printed page is referenced by an asterisk. If more than one footnote begins on a page, the sequence of symbols is * † ‡ §. Should more than four such notes appear on the same page, the symbols are doubled for the fifth to the eighth notes: ** †† ‡‡ §§. See also 13.50.

16.64   *Footnotes plus author-date citations.* The rather cumbersome practice described in 16.63 may be avoided by the use of author-date citations for sources (see 16.4) and numbered footnotes or endnotes for the substantive comments.

16.65   *Editor's or translator's notes plus author's notes.* In an edited or translated work that includes notes by the original author, any additional notes furnished by the editor or translator must be distinguished from the others. Most commonly, the added notes are interspersed and consecutively numbered with the original notes but distinguished from them either by appending "—Ed." or "—Trans." (following a period) at the end of the note or by enclosing the entire note, except the number, in square brackets.

> 14. Millicent Cliff was Norton Westermont's first cousin, although to the very last she denied it.—Ed.
>
> 21. [The original reads *gesungen*; presumably *gesunken* is meant.]

Alternatively, if there are only a few added notes, these can be referenced by asterisks and other symbols and appear as footnotes; the original notes, numbered, then appear below them, as footnotes (see fig. 16.10), or are treated as endnotes (see 16.19, 16.27). See also 16.67.

UNNUMBERED NOTES

16.66 *Placement.* Unnumbered footnotes always precede any numbered notes on the same printed page. They most often appear on the opening page of a chapter or other main division of a work. They may be used even when the numbered notes are endnotes. Unnumbered endnotes—to be used with caution because they are easily missed—should appear immediately before note 1 for each chapter. A note applying to a *book* epigraph may precede the endnotes to the first chapter and appear under a heading "Epigraph" (analogous to "Chapter Eight" in fig. 16.2). If the book has footnotes, the author will have to work in a reference to the epigraph somewhere in the prefatory material or in a numbered note. A footnote or endnote applying to a *chapter* epigraph may begin either with the word *Epigraph* in italics, followed by a period, or with such wording as "The epigraph to this chapter is drawn from . . ." Source notes, biographical notes, and other notes pertaining to an entire chapter or section are treated in 16.68–70.

16.67 *Notes keyed to text by line or page numbers.* In some works—translations and editions of the classics, for example—it may be desirable to omit note numbers in the text. Any necessary notes may then be keyed to the text by line or page number, or both, usually followed by the word or phrase being annotated. (Line numbers are used as locators only if line numbers appear in the text.) Such notes may appear at the foot of the page or at the back of the work. Such typographic devices as brackets and italics are used to distinguish the keywords from the annotation. See figures 16.11, 16.12.

16.68 *Source notes.* In anthologies and other collections of previously published material, or in largely new publications that contain one or more previously published chapters, the source of each reprinted piece may be given in an unnumbered footnote on the first printed page of the chapter, preceding any numbered footnotes. If the other notes are endnotes, the source note should remain a footnote (see 16.66), and it must do so if it carries a copyright notice. For material still in copyright, the note should include the original title, publisher or journal, publication date, page numbers or other locators, and—very important—mention of permission from the copyright owner to reprint. It may also include a copyright notice if requested. Some permissions grantors demand particular language in the source note. For exercising discretion versus acceding literally to the grantor's request, see 12.48, which deals with illustrations but applies equally to text. In many cases, wording can be adjusted for consistency as long as proper credit is given. The following examples show various acceptable forms. See also 4.95.

Reprinted with permission from Steven Shapin, *The Scientific Revolution* (Chicago: University of Chicago Press, 1996), 15–64.

If an article or chapter is reprinted under a different title:

Originally published as "Manet in His Generation: The Face of Painting in the 1860s," *Critical Inquiry* 19, no. 1 (1992): 22–69, © 1992 by The University of Chicago. All rights reserved. Reprinted by permission.

If an article or chapter has been revised:

Originally published in a slightly different form in *The Metropolis in Modern Life*, ed. Robert Moore Fisher (New York: Doubleday, 1955), 125–48. Reprinted by permission of the author and the publisher.

If a work is in the public domain (such as government publications):

Reprinted from B. N. Taylor, *Guide for the Use of the International System of Units (SI)* (Washington, DC: U.S. Department of Commerce, Technology Administration, National Institute of Standards and Technology, 1995), 38–39.

For source notes with tables, see 13.44–45.

16.69 *Biographical notes.* In journals or multiauthor works, a brief biographical note on the author or authors may appear as an unnumbered note on the first page of each article or chapter. Such identifying notes are unnecessary when the work includes a list of contributors with their affiliations. For acknowledgment notes, see 16.70.

Alice Y. Kaplan teaches in the Department of Romance Studies at Duke University. She is the author of *Reproductions of Banality: Fascism, Literature, and French Intellectual Life* (1986); *Relevé des sources et citations dans "Bagatelles pour un massacre"* (1987); a memoir, *French Lessons* (1993); and *The Collaborator: The Trial and Execution of Robert Brasillach* (2000).

16.70 *Acknowledgment notes.* In journals or multiauthor works, special acknowledgments may be given in an unnumbered footnote on the first page of an article or chapter, sometimes appended to the biographical information.

The authors gratefully acknowledge the assistance of Oscar J. Blunk of the National Cyanide Laboratory in the preparation of this chapter.

Michael Saler is assistant professor of history at the University of California, Davis. For their comments and assistance the author would like to thank T. W. Heyck, Norma Landau, D. L. LeMahieu, Fred Leventhal, Chun Li, Dianne Macleod, Peter Mandler, Paul Robinson, Peter Stansky, Meredith Veldman, Chris Waters, and the Mabel Macleod Lewis Memorial Foundation.

Bibliographies

16.71   *Need for a bibliography.* Although not all annotated works require a bibliography, since full details can be given in the notes, an alphabetical bibliography serves a number of purposes. It provides an overview of all the sources the author used and easy reference to individual sources cited. Citations in the notes can be shortened (see 16.3, 16.41–45), thus reducing both duplication and clutter.

16.72   *One alphabetical list.* A bibliography arranged in a single alphabetical list is the most common and usually the most reader-friendly form for a work with or without notes to the text. All sources to be included—books, articles, dissertations, papers—are alphabetically arranged in a single list by the last names of the authors (or, if no author or editor is given, by the title or a keyword readers are most likely to seek). For an illustration, see figure 16.3; for the arrangement of entries, see 16.81–83. For division into sections, see 16.80.

16.73   *Placement.* In a printed work, a bibliography is normally placed at the end, preceding the index. In a multiauthor book or a textbook, each chapter may be followed by a brief bibliography.

16.74   *Kinds of bibliographies.* "Bibliography" is used here to denote the list of books, articles, and other references that often appears in a work using notes for citation. (It is similar but not identical to a reference list, used in the author-date system, discussed in 16.91–106.) A full bibliography includes all cited works and sometimes other relevant ones (see 16.75). A selected bibliography includes only the most important works cited (see 16.76). In a work with few or no notes, the bibliography may merely list recommended works that have not been cited in the text, sometimes with annotations (see 16.77), or it may take the form of a discursive essay on relevant literature (see 16.78). Occasionally a bibliography may list the works of a single author—the subject of a biography or a critical essay, for example (see 16.79).

16.75   *Full bibliography.* A full bibliography includes all works cited, whether in text or in the notes, other than personal communications (see 17.208–9).

Some particularly relevant works the author has consulted may also be listed, even if not mentioned earlier. The usual heading is Bibliography, though Works Cited or Literature Cited may be used if no additional works are included.

16.76 *Selected bibliography.* If, for whatever reason, the author does not wish to list all works cited, the title must so indicate: either Selected Bibliography or (less frequently) Select Bibliography may be used or, if the list is quite short, Suggested Readings or Further Readings. A headnote should explain the principles of selection. See figure 16.4.

16.77 *Annotated bibliography.* Generally more convenient for readers than a bibliographic essay is an annotated bibliography. Annotations may simply follow the publication details (sometimes in brackets if only a few entries are annotated) or may start a new line, often with a paragraph indention.

16.78 *Bibliographic essay.* An informal vehicle occasionally used to provide information is a bibliographic essay, in which the author treats the literature discursively, giving the facts of publication in parentheses following each title. Since works are not alphabetized, subject divisions may freely be made. Such an essay is sometimes called Suggested Reading. It may be used in addition to a bibliography or a reference list, in which case—in a printed work—it should come first. If works discussed in the essay are listed in the bibliography or references, they may be given in shortened form (as in notes) or in author-date style. If there is no bibliography or reference list, the essay must include facts of publication, whether or not the titles also appear in the notes. For an illustration, see figure 16.13.

16.79 *Writings of one person.* A list of works by one person, usually titled Published Works [of So-and-So] or Writings [of So-and-So], is most often arranged chronologically. If several titles are listed for each year, the dates may appear as subheads (see fig. 16.14).

16.80 *Division into sections.* A bibliography may occasionally be divided into sections—but only if that makes things easier for readers. Where readers need to refer frequently from notes to bibliography, a continuous alphabetical list is far preferable, since in a subdivided bibliography the alphabetizing starts over with each section. Rarely should books be separated from articles, since a book and an article by the same author are best listed close together. It may be appropriate to subdivide a bibliography (1) when it includes manuscript sources, archival collections, or other materials that do not fit into a straight alphabetical list (see fig. 16.15); (2) when readers need to see at a glance the distinction between different kinds of works—for example, in a study of one writer, between works by the writer and those about him or her; or (3) when the bibliography is intended primarily as a guide to further reading (as in this manual, pp. 863–79). When divisions are necessary, a headnote should appear at the beginning of the bibliography, and each section should be introduced by an explanatory subhead. No source should be listed in more than one section. For alphabetizing, see 16.81–89.

ARRANGEMENT OF ENTRIES

16.81 *Alphabetizing.* Rules for alphabetizing an index (see 18.55–91) apply also to a bibliography, with the modifications described in 16.82–89.

16.82 *Single author versus several authors.* A single-author entry precedes a multi-author entry beginning with the same name. Only the name of the first author is inverted.

> Kogan, Herman. *The First Century: The Chicago Bar Association, 1874–1974.* Chicago: Rand McNally, 1974.
> Kogan, Herman, and Lloyd Wendt. *Chicago: A Pictorial History.* New York: Dutton, 1958.

16.83 *Author with different coauthors.* Successive entries by two or more authors in which only the first author's name is the same are alphabetized according to the coauthors' last names.

> Brooks, Daniel R., and Deborah A. McLennan. *The Nature of Diversity: An Evolutionary Voyage of Discovery.* Chicago: University of Chicago Press, 2002.
> Brooks, Daniel R., and E. O. Wiley. *Evolution as Entropy.* 2nd ed. Chicago: University of Chicago Press, 1986.

THE 3-EM DASH FOR REPEATED NAMES IN A BIBLIOGRAPHY

16.84 *One repeated name.* For successive entries by the same author(s), editor(s), translator(s), or compiler(s), a 3-em dash (followed by a period or comma, as in the previous entry) replaces the name(s) after the first appearance. For more than one repeated name, see 16.85.

> Squire, Larry R. "The Hippocampus and the Neuropsychology of Memory." In *Neurobiology of the Hippocampus,* edited by W. Seifert, 491–511. New York: Oxford University Press, 1983.
> ———. *Memory and Brain.* New York: Oxford University Press, 1987.

Krueger, Anne O., ed. *Trade and Employment in Developing Countries.* Vol. 3, *Synthesis and Conclusions.* Chicago: University of Chicago Press, 1983.

————, ed. *The WTO as an International Organization.* Chicago: University of Chicago Press, 1998.

16.85 *More than one repeated name.* The dash can stand for the same two or more authors (or editors or translators, etc.) as in the previous entry, provided they are listed in the same order.

Marty, Martin E., and R. Scott Appleby. *The Glory and the Power: The Fundamentalist Challenge to the Modern World.* Boston: Beacon Press, 1992.

————, eds. *Fundamentalisms Comprehended.* Chicago: University of Chicago Press, 1995.

but

Comaroff, Jean, and John Comaroff, eds. *Modernity and Its Malcontents: Ritual and Power in Postcolonial Africa.* Chicago: University of Chicago Press, 1993.

Comaroff, John, and Jean Comaroff. *Of Revelation and Revolution.* 2 vols. Chicago: University of Chicago Press, 1991–97.

16.86 *An institutional name.* The dash may be used for institutional or corporate authors.

U.S. Senate. Committee on Foreign Relations. *The Security Assistance Act of 2000.* 106th Cong., 2nd sess., 2000, ftp://ftp.loc.gov/pub/thomas/cp106/sr351.txt.

————. Committee on Public Lands. *Leasing of Oil Lands.* 65th Cong., 1st sess., 1917.

————. Committee on Public Lands. *Leases upon Naval Oil Reserves.* 68th Cong., 1st sess., 1924.

In the third example above, note the repetition of "Committee on Public Lands" (because a different committee is cited in the first example). Only where no ambiguity could occur (as in the second example below) should the em dash stand for two parts of an institutional name that are separated by a period in the preceding entry.

U.S. Senate. Committee on Public Lands. *Leasing of Oil Lands.* 65th Cong., 1st sess., 1917.

————. *Leases upon Naval Oil Reserves.* 68th Cong., 1st sess., 1924.

16.87 *Titles: alphabetical versus chronological order.* In a bibliography, as opposed to a reference list (see 16.103), titles by the same author are normally listed alphabetically. An initial *the* or *an* is ignored in the alphabetizing.

Ginger, Ray. *The Bending Cross: A Biography of Eugene Victor Debs.* New Brunswick, NJ: Rutgers University Press, 1949.

———. *Six Days or Forever? Tennessee v. John Thomas Scopes.* Chicago: Quadrangle Books, 1969.

16.88   *Single-author bibliography.* A bibliography of works by a single author (Writings of So-and-So) is usually arranged chronologically. Two or more titles published in any one year are arranged alphabetically. See figure 16.14.

16.89   *Edited, translated, or compiled works.* For works edited, translated, or compiled by a person, the name is followed by an abbreviation (ed., trans., comp., etc.), and alphabetization by title of work is maintained, regardless of the added abbreviation. This practice represents a change from earlier Chicago style.

Mulvany, Nancy C. "Copyright for Indexes, Revisited." *ASI Newsletter* 107 (November–December 1991): 11–13.

———, ed. *Indexing, Providing Access to Information—Looking Back, Looking Ahead: Proceedings of the 25th Annual Meeting of the American Society of Indexers.* Port Aransas, TX: American Society of Indexers, 1993.

———. "Software Tools for Indexing: What We Need." *Indexer* 17 (October 1990): 108–13.

The Author-Date System: Reference Lists and Text Citations

16.90   *Overview.* The author-date system of documentation comprises two indispensable parts: a complete list of sources cited, often called a reference list (the term used in this chapter), and very brief text citations, usually enclosed in parentheses. For the principal advantages of this system, see 16.4.

REFERENCE LISTS

16.91   *Function.* In the author-date system, the reference list is the prime vehicle for documentation. The text citations (see 16.107–19) are merely pointers to the full list.

16.92   *Placement.* A reference list, like a bibliography, is normally placed at the end of a work, preceding the index, if there is one. In a multiauthor book, a textbook, or a journal article, each chapter or article may be followed by its own reference list, in which case the list is preceded by a subhead such as References or Literature Cited.

16.93   *Alphabetical arrangement.* A reference list is always arranged alphabetically (except in a numbered reference system) and is rarely divided into sections. (Division is appropriate only where very different kinds of materials are listed, as in fig. 16.15.) All sources are listed by the last names of the authors (or, if no author or editor is given, by the title or by a keyword readers are most likely to seek). For an illustration, see figure 16.5.

16.94   *Alphabetizing.* Rules for alphabetizing an index (see 18.55–91) apply also to a reference list, with the modifications described in 16.82–89.

16.95   *Dates: an essential component.* Because the text citations consist of the last name of the author or authors (or that of the editor or translator) and the date of publication, the date in the reference list appears directly after the name, not with the publication details. See also 16.103.

> Cox, T. F., ed. 1967. *Risk taking and information handling in consumer behavior.* Cambridge, MA: Harvard Univ. Press.

16.96   *Titles: capitalization.* Titles and subtitles of books and articles in reference lists, especially in the sciences, are usually capitalized sentence style (see 8.166; see also 16.7). Note that the first word of the subtitle is capitalized.

> The fifth miracle: The search for the origin of life.

Names of journals, however, are capitalized headline style, whether spelled out or abbreviated. When names are abbreviated, periods are usually omitted, especially in the sciences.

> *Economic Development and Cultural Change*
> *Am J Bot*
> *Psychiatr Genet*

16.97   *Titles: italics and quotation marks.* Titles of books and journals are usually italicized just as they would be in text or in a bibliography. Articles or chapters, however, are not enclosed in quotation marks. (Where quotation marks have been used consistently, however, they need not be deleted, except to conform to the needs of a particular journal or series.)

> Sturkin, Marita. 1997. *Tangled memories.* Berkeley and Los Angeles: Univ. of California Press.
> Swidler, Ann. 1986. Culture in action. *American Sociological Review* 51:273–86.

16.98   *Subtitles.* Where space is at a premium, subtitles are occasionally omitted from reference lists. Chicago strongly recommends including them, since subtitles are (or are meant to be) informative.

16.99   *Authors' names.* In a reference list, especially in the natural sciences, initials rather than full given names are often given. Where this practice is followed, an exception should be made where two authors share the same initials and last name. For initials without periods, see 17.24.

Richards, A. A.   Richards, Alfred E.
Richards, A. Ethel   Richards, B. Y.

For text citations, see 16.108.

16.100 *Abbreviations.* In reference lists, such phrases as *edited by* or *translated by* are usually abbreviated to *ed.* or *trans.*, capitalized if following a period. *University* may be abbreviated to *Univ.* Months given with journal citations may be abbreviated. In the sciences, journal titles are usually abbreviated (often with periods omitted) unless they consist of only one word. Standard abbreviations for scientific journals may be found in *BIOSIS Serial Sources* (bibliog. 5) and *Index Medicus* (bibliog. 4.5), among other reference works. Both are published annually in print form and are also available online. For a partial list of standard abbreviations of frequently used journal title words, see *Scientific Style and Format* or the *American Medical Association Manual of Style* (bibliog. 1.1). For more examples, see 16.101–2 and figure 16.5.

Fritzsch, Harald. 1994. *An equation that changed the world.* Trans. Karin Heusch. Chicago: Univ. of Chicago Press.
Ikeuchi, T. 1984. Inhibiting effect of ethidium bromide on mitotic chromosome condensation and its application to high-resolution chromosome banding. *Cytogenet Cell Genet* 38:56–61.

16.101 *Single author versus several authors.* As in a bibliography, a single-author entry precedes a multiauthor entry beginning with the same name. Only the first author's name is inverted.

Pacini, E. 1997. Tapetum character states: Analytical keys for tapetum types and activities. *Can J Bot* 75:1448–59.
Pacini, E., G. G. Franchi, and M. Hesse. 1985. The tapetum: Its form, function, and possible phylogeny in embryophyta. *Plant Syst Evol* 149:155–85.

16.102 *Author with different coauthors.* As in a bibliography, successive entries by two or more authors in which only the first author's name is the same are alphabetized according to the coauthors' last names (regardless of how many coauthors there are).

Pacini, E., G. G. Franchi, and M. Hesse. 1985. The tapetum: Its form, function, and possible phylogeny in embryophyta. *Plant Syst Evol* 149:155–85.

Pacini, E., and B. E. Juniper. 1983. The ultrastructure of the formation and development of the amoeboid tapetum in *Arum italicum* Miller. *Protoplasma* 117:116–29.

For using *et al.* for works by more than three authors, see 17.29–30.

THE 3-EM DASH FOR REPEATED NAMES IN A REFERENCE LIST

16.103 *Chronological arrangement.* For successive entries by the same author(s), translator(s), editor(s), or compiler(s), a 3-em dash replaces the name(s) after the first appearance. The entries, however, are arranged chronologically by year of publication, *not* (as in a bibliography) alphabetized by title (but see 16.104). Undated works designated *n.d.* or *forthcoming* follow all dated works (see 17.121–22).

Schuman, Howard, and Jacqueline Scott. 1987. Problems in the use of survey questions to measure public opinion. *Science* 236:957–59.

———. 1989. Generations and collective memories. *American Sociological Review* 54:359–81.

16.104 *Edited, translated, or compiled works.* The 3-em dash replaces the preceding name or names only, not an added *ed., trans., comp.,* or whatever. The chronological order is maintained, regardless of the added abbreviation. This practice represents a change from earlier Chicago style.

Woodward, David. 1977. *All American map: Wax engraving and its influence on cartography.* Chicago: Univ. of Chicago Press.

———, ed. 1987. *Art and cartography: Six historical essays.* Chicago: Univ. of Chicago Press.

———. 1996. *Catalogue of watermarks in Italian printed maps, ca. 1540–1600.* Chicago: Univ. of Chicago Press.

Woodward is the author of the first and third items, editor of the second. Compare 16.89.

16.105 *Same author(s), same year.* Two or more works by the same author or authors published in the same year are distinguished by *a, b, c,* and so forth (set in roman, not italic), following the date. These entries are alphabet-ized by title.

> Beijing Zoo. 1974a. Observations on the breeding of the giant panda and the raising of its young [in Chinese]. *Acta Zoologica Sinica* 20:139–47.
> ———. 1974b. On the diseases of the giant panda and their preventive and curative measures [in Chinese]. *Acta Zoologica Sinica* 20:154–61.

When two or more authors, even though the same, are listed in a different order, *a*, *b*, and so forth cannot be used. See 16.85, 17.30.

16.106   *Institutional authors.* As in bibliographies, the dash may be used for insti-tutional or corporate authors.

> U.S. Senate. 1917. Committee on Public Lands. *Leasing of oil lands.* 65th Cong., 1st sess.
> ———. 1919–20. Committee on Foreign Relations. *Investigations of Mexican affairs.* 2 vols. 66th Cong., 2nd sess.
> ———. 1924. Committee on Public Lands. *Leases upon naval oil reserves.* 68th Cong., 1st sess.

Although the committees listed in the examples above are, strictly speak-ing, authors, placing the date after "U.S. Senate" allows for more conven-ient text citation—"U.S. Senate 1917," and the like. If context suggests otherwise, exercise editorial discretion.

TEXT CITATIONS

16.107   *Agreement of citation and reference.* Author-date citations in the text *must* agree exactly, in both name and date, with the corresponding entries in the reference list, and there must be an entry for every text citation. It is the author's responsibility to ensure such agreement as well as the accuracy of the reference. Also, a specific page reference, when given in text, must fall within the range of pages given for the article in the complete citation. Manuscript editors cross-check text citations and reference lists. Any dis-crepancies or omissions should be rectified during the editorial process, not in proof.

16.108   *Basic form.* An author-date citation in running text or at the end of a block quotation consists of the last (family) name of the author, followed by the year of publication of the work in question. In this context, "author" may refer not only to one or more authors or an institution but also to one or more editors, translators, or compilers. No punctuation appears between author and date. Abbreviations such as *ed.* or *trans.* are omitted (unless an original and an edited work by the same person appeared in the same year, in which case *ed.* would be added to the text citation where appropriate). For more specific citations, see 16.109–10.

Text citations:

(Pacini 1997)
(Woodward 1987)

References:

Pacini, E. 1997. Tapetum character states: Analytical keys for tapetum types and activities. *Can J Bot* 75:1448–59.
Woodward, David, ed. 1987. *Art and cartography: Six historical essays.* Chicago: Univ. of Chicago Press.

Where two or more works by different authors with the same last name are listed in a reference list, the text citation must include an initial (or two initials or even a given name if necessary).

T: (C. Doershuk 2000)
      (J. Doershuk 2001)

R: Doershuk, Carl. 2000. . . .
      Doershuk, John. 2001. . . .

16.109 *Page numbers or other specific references.* When a specific page, section, equation, or other division of the work is cited, it follows the date, preceded by a comma.

(Piaget 1980, 74)
(Johnson 1979, sec. 24)
(Fowler and Hoyle 1965, eq. 87)
(Barnes 1998, 2:354–55, 3:29)
(Fischer and Siple 1990, 212n3)
(Hellman 1998, under "The Battleground") [an unpaginated electronic work]

Page numbers are sometimes omitted in citations to journal articles except with direct quotations.

16.110 *Volume numbers.* When a volume as a whole is referred to, without a page number, *vol.* is used. For volume plus page, only a colon is needed.

(García 1987, vol. 2)
(García 1987, 2:345)

16.111 *Additional material in parentheses.* The parentheses that enclose a text citation may also include a comment, separated from the citation by a semicolon.

(Doe 1999; *t*-tests are used here)

16.112 *Placement of text citations.* Author-date citations are usually placed just before a mark of punctuation. (For citations following block quotations, see
11.81–82.)

Recent literature has examined long-run price drifts following initial public offerings (Ritter 1991; Loughran and Ritter 1995), stock splits (Ikenberry, Rankine, and Stice 1996),
seasoned equity offerings (Loughran and Ritter 1995), and equity repurchases (Ikenberry,
Lakonishok, and Vermaelen 1995).

Where the author's name appears in the text, it need not be repeated in the
parenthetical citation.

Litman (1983) finds that Academy Award nominations or winnings are significantly related to revenues.

Tufte's excellent book on chart design (2001) warns against a common error.

16.113 *Placement of citation vis-à-vis direct quotations.* Although citation of a source
normally follows a direct quotation, it may precede the quotation if syntax
permits.

As Edward Tufte points out (2001, 139), "a graphical element may carry data information
and also perform a design function usually left to non-data-ink."

16.114 *Several references to same source.* When the same page or pages in the same
source are cited more than once in one paragraph, the parenthetical citation can be placed after the last reference or at the end of the paragraph (as
a note number would be; see 16.31), but preceding the final period. If the
page numbers change, the citation should occur at the first reference; the
following citations need include only the page.

16.115 *Syntactic considerations.* An author-date citation, like any other bibliographic citation, is a noun form; it denotes a work, not a person. Note
how, in the examples in 16.112–13, the wording distinguishes between

authors and works. A locution such as "in Smith 1999," though technically proper, is awkward and best avoided. Reword—for example, "Smith's study (1999) indicates that . . ."

16.116 *Same author(s), same year.* When a reference list includes two or more works published in the same year by the same author or authors (see 16.105), the text citations as well as the reference list must use the letters *a*, *b*, and so on (set in roman).

(Beijing Zoo 1974a)
(Hollingsworth and Sockett 1994b)

16.117 *Two or three authors.* For works by two or three authors, all names are included. The word *and* is preferable to an ampersand (which should be confined to corporate names). For examples, see 16.112.

16.118 *More than three authors.* For more than three authors (or in some science publications, more than two), only the name of the first author is used, followed by *et al.* or *and others.* Note that *et al.* is *not* italicized in text citations.

(Zipursky et al. 1997)
In a study by Zipursky and others (1997), . . .

If a reference list includes another work *of the same date* that would also be abbreviated as "Zipursky et al." but whose coauthors are different persons or listed in a different order, the text citations must distinguish between them. In such cases, the first two (or the first three) authors should be cited, followed by *et al.* or *and others.*

(Zipursky, Jones, et al. 1997)
(Zipursky, Smith, et al. 1997)

If necessary a shortened title, enclosed in commas, may be added. In the following examples, "et al." refers to different coauthors, so *a*, *b*, and so on cannot be used (see 16.116). For treatment of multiple authors in a reference list, see 17.27–30.

(Zipursky, Smith, et al., "Giant snails," 1997)
(Zipursky, Smith, et al., "Seed attackers," 1997)

16.119 *Multiple references.* Two or more references in a single parenthetical citation are separated by semicolons. The order in which they are given may depend on what is being cited, and in what order, or it may reflect the relative importance of the items cited. If neither criterion applies, alphabetical or chronological order may be appropriate. Unless the order is prescribed by a particular journal style, the decision is the author's.

(Armstrong and Malacinski 1989; Beigl 1989; Pickett and White 1985)

Additional works by the same author(s) are given by date only, separated by commas except where page numbers are required.

(Whittaker 1967, 1975; Wiens 1989a, 1989b)
(Wong 1999, 328; 2000, 475; García 1998, 67)

16.120 *Author-date system with notes.* Where footnotes or endnotes are used to supplement the author-date system, source citations within notes are treated in the same way as in text (see fig. 16.9).

10. James Wilson has noted that "no politician ever lost votes by denouncing the bureaucracy" (1989, 235). Yet little is actually ever done to bring major reforms to the system.

CHAPTER TWO

It would thus be too simplistic to suggest that book dealers could be found only in the major areas of trade concentration. Nonetheless, for the most part someone searching for learned works would not need to look much further than the vicinities of Saint Paul's, Little Britain, the Fleet Street and Cornhill thoroughfare, and perhaps Moorfields. Anyone wanting to *produce* such a work would similarly go first to one of these few precincts. In particular, it was to these districts, and especially to Saint Paul's Churchyard, that the men of the Royal Society went when they wanted to purchase, borrow, read, and respond to the books of their Continental counterparts. And it was here that they went when they wanted to spread the word of their new experimental philosophy.[27]

Printing houses were of rather more immediate concern to the authorities than bookshops, largely because they seemed to offer greater opportunities for regulation. Their numbers were therefore relatively closely monitored, and as a result can now be stated with greater confidence. Repeated attempts were made to limit the number of printing houses to twenty, besides the King's Printers and those for Oxford and Cambridge Universities. These efforts were especially intense in the early years of the Restoration, when those keen to display their loyalty to the crown chose to blame the "miserable confusions and Calamities" of the previous two decades on printers' "monstrous excess and exorbitant disorder." Samuel Parker, for one, praised the 1662 Press Act for suppressing "the very engine of rebellion."[28] But, as was so often the case with early modern governance, such attempts met with only partial and qualified success. There were at least 53 houses in 1661–2, as the Restoration's printing regime was being constructed and put into effect. Some 40 were still operating by the time of the Fire, and a list made in 1675 mentioned 23. This was the lowest point. By 1705, ten years after the end of the Press Act, numbers had risen again, and there were about 62, not including the royal printers. Two decades later Samuel Negus could count a dozen more still, and by this time a provincial trade was also thriving.[29]

---

was being printed for four Stationers: "1st Mr Thomas at ye Adam & Eve in litle-Brittaine. 2ly Mr Thomson in Smith-Field. 3 Fisher on Tower-hill. 4 Hurlock at London-Bridge." The sequence of names, and the declining use of titles, suggests something of the standard topographical hierarchy. Oldenburg, *Correspondence*, 4:424–27, esp. 426.

27. E.g., Gunther, *Early Science in Oxford*, 12:398.

28. *London Printers Lamentation*, 2–3; Parker, *Bishop Parker's History of His Own Time*, 22–23; 14 Car. II, c. 33, § 10. The Restoration regime also tried to delimit even more closely the number of typefounders to just four masters, since this offered a still more auspicious opportunity for restriction. It was also hoped that with few sources of type available, the producers of illicit books could be identified by comparing their typography to specimen sheets stored centrally.

29. Hetet, "Literary Underground," 37–38, 104–5, 244–257; SCB D, fol. 82ʳ (mentioning fifty-nine masters in 1663); Maslen and Lancaster, *Bowyer Ledgers*, xxiii.

Fig. 16.1. A page of text with footnotes; the first note is continued from the previous page (with a short rule above it).

273. Feuer, "Lawless Sensations," 107.

274. The conversion of Haller's disciple Johann Blumenbach to epigenesis in 1780 signaled a major turn in German natural history, the emergence of what Timothy Lenoir has called the "Göttingen school." See Timothy Lenoir, "Kant, Blumenbach, and Vital Materialism in German Biology," *Isis* 71 (1980): 77–108; Lenoir, "The Göttingen School and the Development of Transcendental Naturphilosophie in the Romantic Era" (Baltimore: Johns Hopkins University Press, 1981), 111–205. On Blumenbach, see also Georgette Legée, "Johann Friedrich Blumenbach (1752–1840), La naissance de l'anthropologie à l'époque de la Révolution française," in *Scientifiques et sociétés pendant la Révolution et l'Empire* (Paris: Editions du CTHS, 1990), 395–420; Peter McLaughlin, "Blumenbach und der Bildungstrieb," *Medizinhistorisches Journal* 17 (1982): 357–72; Frank Dougherty, "Johann Friedrich Blumenbach und Samuel Thomas Soemmerring," in *Samuel Thomas Soemmerring und die Gelehrten der Goethezeit*, ed. Gunter Mann and Franz Dumont (Stuttgart: G. Fischer, 1985), 35–56.

CHAPTER EIGHT

1. There is a sense in which one could almost refer the reader to Wolfgang Pross, "Herder und die Anthropologie seiner Zeit," "Nachwort" to *Herder und die Anthropologie der Aufklärung*, vol. 2 of Herder's *Werke* (Darmstadt: Wissenschaftliche Buchgesellschaft, 1987), 1128–1216, and be done with things. Pross offers a massive case for the centrality of anthropology in the work of Herder and implicitly of Herder in the emergence of anthropology. I am deeply in the debt of this interpretation, but I resolve to offer a variant reconstruction.

2. "Herder followed Schaftesbury, Hume and Rousseau; the genre of the essay is utilized not simply as a form of education or edification, as an emancipation from purely metaphysical discourse and useless theoretical controversy, but as a medium of a particular kind of philosophical self-reflection that has become conscious of its own rhetoricity, its own constitution within language and history." Robert Leventhal, *The Disciplines of Interpretation* (New York: De Gruyter, 1994), 170. This passage is a rare point of agreement I can find with this drastic imposition of De Man and Derrida upon Herder.

3. "His fundamental thought . . . is: by enlightenment of all the members of a people, through the cultivation of the specific spatio-temporal possibilities and through the nationalization of civilizational reform projects to foster at one and the same time the freedom of the individual person and the culture of nations, societies and states without recourse to violence, and thus to bring about the perfection of mankind in general and of the revelation of God's providence." Wisbert, commentary on *Journal meiner Reise im Jahre 1769*, DKV 9:880.

4. Herder, *Journal meiner Reise im Jahre 1769*, DKV 9:36.

5. Herder, *Viertes Kritischen Wäldchen*, DKV 2:304.

6. Herder, *Journal meiner Reise im Jahre 1769*, DKV 9:118.

7. Herder, *Viertes Kritischen Wäldchen*, DKV 2:303–5.

Fig. 16.2. A page of endnotes, with a subhead introducing the notes to a new chapter and a running head showing the text pages on which the notes are referenced.

Bibliography

Abrams, M. H. *Natural Supernaturalism*. New York: W. W. Norton, 1971.

Augustine. *Confessions*. Translated by R. S. Pine-Coffin. Harmondsworth, UK: Penguin Books, 1971.

Ayer, A. J. "Can There Be a Private Language?" In *Wittgenstein: The Philosophical Investigations*, edited by George Pitcher. Garden City, NY: Doubleday, 1966.

Baker, G. P., and P. M. S. Hacker. *Language, Sense, and Nonsense*. Oxford, Basil Blackwell, 1984.

———. *Scepticism, Rules, and Language*. Oxford: Basil Blackwell, 1984.

———. *Wittgenstein: Rules, Grammar, and Necessity*. Oxford: Basil Blackwell, 1985.

———. *Wittgenstein: Understanding and Meaning*. Oxford: Basil Blackwell, 1980.

Baynes, Kenneth, James Bohmann, and Thomas McCarthy, eds. *After Philosophy*. Cambridge, MA: MIT Press, 1987.

Beck, J. S. "Letter to Kant, June 24, 1797." In Kant, *Philosophical Correspondence*, edited and translated by Arnulf Zweig. Chicago: University of Chicago Press, 1967.

Beiser, Frederick C. *The Fate of Reason: German Philosophy from Kant to Fichte*. Cambridge, MA: Harvard University Press, 1987.

Bernstein, J. M. *The Fate of Art: Aesthetic Alienation from Kant to Derrida and Adorno*. University Park: Pennsylvania State University Press, 1992.

Bloor, David. *Wittgenstein: A Social Theory of Knowledge*. New York: Columbia University Press, 1983.

Bourdieu, Pierre. *Le sens pratique*. Paris: Minuit, 1980. Cited in Charles Taylor, "To Follow a Rule," in *Rules and Conventions: Literature, Philosophy, Social Theory*, edited by Mette Hjort. Baltimore: Johns Hopkins University Press, 1992.

Bouveresse, Jacques. "'The Darkness of This Time': Wittgenstein and the Modern World." In *Wittgenstein: Centenary Essays*, edited by A. Phillips Griffith. Cambridge, : Cambridge University Press, 1991.

Breazale, Daniel. "Fichte's *Aenesidemus* Review and the Transformation of German Idealism." *Review of Metaphysics* 34 (1981): 545–68.

Cavell, Stanley. *The Claim of Reason*. New York: Oxford University Press, 1979.

———. *Conditions Handsome and Unhandsome: The Constitution of Emersonian Perfectionism*. Chicago: University of Chicago Press, 1990.

———. *In Quest of the Ordinary: Lines of Skepticism and Romanticism*. Chicago: University of Chicago Press, 1988.

———. *Must We Mean What We Say?* New York: Charles Scribner's Sons, 1969.

———. "'The *Philosophical Investigations*' Everyday Aesthetics of Itself." Lecture at the University of Pennsylvania, October 23, 1995.

291

Fig. 16.3. The first page of a humanities bibliography.

SELECTED BIBLIOGRAPHY

I list here only the writings that have been of use in the making of this book. This bibliography is by no means a complete record of all the works and sources I have consulted. It indicates the substance and range of reading upon which I have formed my ideas, and I intend it to serve as a convenience for those who wish to pursue the study of humor, comic literature, the history of comic processes, the British novel, and the particular writers and fictions that are the subjects of this inquiry. (Unless there is a standard edition or only one widely available edition of the complete works of the novelists I study, I have not listed their complete works.)

1. THE THEORY, PSYCHOLOGY, AND HISTORY OF THE COMIC

Auden, W. H. "Notes on the Comic." In *Comedy: Meaning and Form,* edited by Robert Corrigan, 61–72. San Francisco: Chandler, 1965.
Bakhtin, Mikhail. *Rabelais and His World.* Translated from the Russian by Helene Iswolsky. Cambridge, MA: MIT Press, 1968.

. . . .

2. JANE AUSTEN AND *EMMA*

Austen, Jane. *The Novels of Jane Austen.* Edited by R. W. Chapman. 5 vols. 3rd ed. London: Oxford University Press, 1932–34.
———. *Jane Austen's Letters to Her Sister Cassandra and Others.* Edited by R. W. Chapman. 2nd ed. London: Oxford University Press, 1952.
———. *Minor Works.* Edited by R. W. Chapman. Vol. 6 of *The Novels of Jane Austen.* London: Oxford University Press, 1954.
———. *"Emma": An Authoritative Text, Backgrounds, Reviews, and Criticism.* Edited by Stephen M. Parrish. Includes commentary and criticism by Sir Walter Scott, George Henry Lewes, Richard Simpson, Henry James, A. C. Bradley, Reginald Ferrar, Virginia Woolf, E. M. Forster, Mary Lascelles, Arnold Kettle, Wayne Booth, G. Armour Craig, A. Walton Litz, W. A. Craik, and W. J. Harvey. New York: W. W. Norton, 1972.

Fig. 16.4. The opening page of a bibliography divided into sections, with an author's note explaining the principle of selection.

Anholt, B., S. Negovetic, C. Som, and R. Mulheim. 1998b. Marking tadpoles with VIE. http://www.mp1pwrc.usgs/gov/marking/anholt.html.

Anholt, B. R., D. K. Skelly, and E. E. Werner. 1996. Factors modifying antipredator behavior in larval toads. *Herpetologica* 52:301–13.

Anholt, B. R., and E. E. Werner. 1995. Interaction between food availability and predation mortality mediated by adaptive behavior. *Ecology* 76:2230–34.

Annandale, N. 1912. Biological results of the Abor expedition, 1911–12. I. *Batrachia. Rec. Indian Mus.* 8:7–36, plates 2–4.

———. 1917. The occurrence of *Rana pleskei* Günther in Kashmir. *Rec. Indian Mus.* 13:417–18.

———. 1918. Some undescribed tadpoles from the hills of southern India. *Rec. Indian Mus.* 15:17–23, place 1.

———. 1919. The tadpoles of *Nyctibatrachus pygmaeus* and *Ixalus variabilis:* A correction. *Rec. Indian Mus.* 16:303.

Annandale, N., and S. L. Hora. 1922. Parallel evolution in the fish and tadpoles of mountain torrents. *Rec. Indian Mus.* 24:505–10.

Annandale, N., and C. R. N. Rao. 1918. The tadpoles of the families Ranidae and Bufonidae found in the plains of India. *Rec. Indian Mus.* 15:25–40, plate 4.

Antal, M., R. Kraftsik, G. Székely, and H. Van Der Loos. 1986. Distal dendrites of frog motor neurons: A computer aided electron microscopic study of cobalt-filled cells. *J. Neurocytol.* 15:303–10.

Fig. 16.5. Part of a reference list for a scientific work. Note the sentence-style capitalization and the abbreviated journal titles.

Turning to the econometric evidence, I present some estimates of changes in expected retirement ages drawn from the Bank of Italy panel of household-level data. The methodology adopted is a "difference-in-difference" estimator and draws heavily on the work of Attanasio and Brugiavini (1997) described above. In particular, the basic identifying assumption is that the 1992 reform is the only relevant change (as far as differential labor supply decisions are concerned), and I therefore exploit the reform to measure behavioral responses before and after the event. The first difference is the time difference, the second that between groups. Groups in the population are assumed to be exogenously determined, and, given the availability of panel data, I can control for individuals' characteristics throughout (Venti and Wise 1995). . . . It is worth recalling at this stage that the Amato reform of 1992 has gradually postponed the normal retirement age but has not tackled the early retirement option, apart from restricting eligibility requirements in the public sector.[47]

47. The normal retirement age gradually moves from sixty to sixty-five for men. The early retirement option is available (Hoy 1996), but public-sector employees need thirty-five years of constitutions to become eligible in place of the previous twenty years (fifteen for married women). In the public sector, normal retirement age has been sixty-five throughout.

Fig. 16.6. A sample of text with both parenthetical text citations and a footnote.

Abbreviations

AAS	*Acta Apostolicae Sedis*
ACA	Archivo de la Corona de Aragón, Barcelona
AKKR	*Archiv für katholisches Kirchenrecht*
Annales: É.s.c.	*Annales: Économies, sociétés, civilisations*
Auth.	*Authenticum*, in *Corpus iuris civilis* (Lyon: Apud Iuntas, 1584).
Berkeley Proceedings	*Proceedings of the Sixth International Congress of Medieval Canon Law*, ed. Stephan Kuttner and Kenneth Pennington (Vatican City: Biblioteca Apostolica Vaticana, 1985)
Bieler	*The Irish Penitentials*, ed. Ludwig Bieler (Dublin: Dublin Institute for Advanced Studies, 1963)
BL	British Library, London
BMCL	*Bulletin of Medieval Canon Law*
BN	Bibliothèque nationale, Paris
Boston Proceedings	*Proceedings of the Second International Congress of Medieval Canon Law*, ed. Stephan Kuttner and J. Joseph Ryan (Vatican City: S. Congregatio de Seminariis et Studiorum Universitatibus, 1965)

Fig. 16.7. Part of a list of abbreviations.

Notes

In citing works in the notes, short titles have generally been used. Works frequently cited have been identified by the following abbreviations:

Ac. Sc.	Archives de l'Académie des sciences.
A.P.	*Archives parlementaires de 1787 à 1860, première série (1787 à 1799)*. Edited by M. J. Mavidal and M. E. Laurent. 2nd ed. 82 vols. Paris, 1879–1913.
Best.	Theodore Besterman, ed. *Voltaire's Correspondence*. 107 vols. Geneva, 1953–65.
B. Inst.	Bibliothèque de l'Institut de France.
B.N., nouv. acqu.	Bibliothèque nationale. Fonds français, nouvelles acquisitions.
Corresp. inéd.	Charles Henry, ed. *Correspondance inédite de Condorcet et de Turgot (1770–1779)*. Paris, 1883.
HMAS	*Histoire de l'Académie royale des sciences. Avec les mémoires de mathématique et de physique . . . tirés des registres de cette académie (1699–1790)*. 92 vols. Paris, 1702–97. Each volume comprises two separately paginated parts, referred to as *Hist.* and *Mém.*, respectively.
Inéd. Lespinasse	Charles Henry, ed. *Lettres inédites de Mlle de Lespinasse*. Paris, 1887.
O.C.	A. Condorcet-O'Connor and F. Arago, eds. *Oeuvres de Condorcet*. 12 vols. Paris, 1847–49.

Preface

1. Peter Gay. *The Enlightenment: An Interpretation*, 2 vols. (New York, 1966–69), 2:319. I have suggested some criticisms of Gay's treatment of this theme in a review of the second volume of his work, *American Historical Review* 85 (1970): 1410–14.

2. Georges Gusdorf, *Introduction aux sciences humaines: Essai critique sur leurs origines et leur développement* (Strasbourg, 1960), 105–331.

Fig. 16.8. A short list of abbreviations preceding endnotes.

Since 1883, piecemeal adjustments in the civil service system have been made in response to the objectives of the president and the Congress, as they competed for control of the bureaucracy, and in response to the demands of federal employee unions. Through this process, attributes have been incorporated into the civil service rules that have had long-term consequences for the governance and performance of the federal bureaucracy. As this book makes clear, the bureaucratic structure put into place at the behest of these three parties has created the "problem of bureaucracy," and changes in this system will occur at best incrementally.

Notes

1. See, e.g., Sayre (1965), Heclo (1977), Mosher (1979, 1982), Kaufman (1981), Seidman and Gilmour (1986), Knott and Miller (1987), Wilson (1989), and Osborne and Gaebler (1992). These discussions cover nearly thirty years, and it is striking how little the problems have changed. More recent discussions include U.S. House of Representatives (1993) and Dilulio, Garvey, and Kettl (1993). The report of the U.S. House of Representatives' Committee on Government Operations states, "In general, we found that public perceptions—those that waste and abuse are rampant throughout the Federal Government—to be generally accurate. It pervades every agency and hundreds of important programs" (1993, v–vii). The committee had examined nineteen departments and agencies. Similarly, Dilulio, Garvey, and Kettl (1993, 62–65) claim that federal programs and bureaucrats have a reputation for cumbersome or unresponsive administration, excessive complexity, and rudeness. In this book, we do not attempt a broad comparison of the performance of the federal government relative to corporations, private nonprofit organizations, or state and local governments. Our concern is with how the institutional structure of the civil service system came to be and its implications for the performance and accountability of the federal bureaucracy. We examine aspects of the efficiency of the civil service system in chapter 8.

2. The Clinton administration's plan for reforming the federal bureaucracy, submitted to the president by Vice President Gore, hopes to remove "useless bureaucracy and waste" and free workers "from red tape and senseless rules" (see Gore 1993).

Fig. 16.9. Chapter endnotes (first two notes only), including parenthetical citations. Endnotes like these are often used in journals and multiauthor works. A list of references will follow the notes in each chapter.

Each county has a court of justice,[10] a sheriff to execute the decrees of tribunals, a prison to hold criminals.

There are needs that are felt in a nearly equal manner by all the townships of the county; it was natural that a central authority be charged with providing for them. In Massachusetts this authority resides in the hands of a certain number of magistrates whom the governor of the state designates with the advice[11] of his council.[12]

The administrators of the county have only a limited and exceptional power that applies only to a very few cases that are foreseen in advance. The state and the township suffice in the ordinary course of things. These administrators do nothing but prepare the budget of the county; the legislature votes it.[13] There is no assembly that directly or indirectly represents the county.

The county therefore has, to tell the truth, no political existence.

In most of the American constitutions one remarks a double tendency that brings legislators to divide executive power and concentrate legislative power. The New England township by itself has a principle of existence that they do not strip from it; but one would have to create that life fictitiously in the county, and the utility of doing so has not been felt: all the townships united have only one single representation, the state, center of all national* powers; outside township and national action one can say that there are only individual forces.

*Here "national" refers to the states.

10. See the law of February 14, 1821, *Laws of Massachusetts*, 1:551 [2:551–56].

11. See the law of February 20, 1819, *Laws of Massachusetts*, 2:494.

12. The governor's council is an elected body.

13. See the law of November 2, 1791 [November 2, 1781]. *Laws of Massachusetts*, 1:61.

Fig. 16.10. Translator's footnote referenced by an asterisk, followed by author's numbered notes. Notes referenced by symbols always precede numbered notes, regardless of the order in which the symbols and numbers appear in the text.

O sweete soule Phillis w'haue liu'd and lou'd for a great while,   45
(If that a man may keepe any mortal ioy for a great while)
Like louing Turtles and Turtledoues for a great while:
One loue, one liking, one sence, one soule for a great while,
Therfore one deaths wound, one graue, one funeral only
Should haue ioyned in one both loue and louer Amintas.   50
   O good God what a griefe is this that death to remember?
For such grace, gesture, face, feature, beautie, behauiour,
Neuer afore was seene, is neuer againe to be lookt for.
O frowning fortune, ô death and desteny dismal:
Thus be the poplar trees that spred their tops to the heauens,   55
Of their flouring leaues despoil'd in an houre, in a moment:
Thus be the sweete violets that gaue such grace to the garden,
Of their purpled roabe despoyld in an houre, in a moment.
   O how oft did I roare and crie with an horrible howling,
When for want of breath Phillis lay feintily gasping?   60
O how oft did I wish that Phœbus would fro my Phillis
Driue this feuer away: or send his sonne from Olympus,
Who, when lady Venus by a chaunce was prickt with a
   bramble,
Healed her hand with his oyles, and fine knacks kept for a
   purpose.
Or that I could perceiue Podalyrius order in healing,   65
Or that I could obtaine Medæas exquisite ointments,
And baths most precious, which old men freshly renewed.
Or that I were as wise, as was that craftie Prometheus,
Who made pictures liue with fire that he stole from Olympus.
Thus did I cal and crie, but no body came to Amintas,   70
Then did I raile and raue, but nought did I get by my railing,   [C₄ᵛ]
Whilst that I cald and cry'd, and rag'd, and rau'd as a mad
   man,

45 for] *omit* C E
49 Therfore] Thefore A
58 roabe] roabes B C D E
59 roare and crie] cry, and
roare D

62 this] that D
64 his] *omit* E   purpose.] purpose:
C E; purpose? D
70 Amintas,] Amintas. C E;
Amintas: D

Fig. 16.11. Footnotes keyed to line numbers—a device best used with verse. (With prose, the notes cannot be numbered until the text has been typeset.)

cusses Rilke's complex use of "Nacht" as a possible mediator between immanent and transcendent being.

166 *orthodox view of revelation* Rilke suppresses two crucial details of Michelangelo's Cumaean Sibyl: her prominent breasts, which suggest the "celestial milk" that is "the future food of salvation" (Wind, "Michelangelo's Prophets and Sibyls," 68), and the massive book from which she is reading, which suggests the conversion of Sibylline leaves into Christian doctrine. Hence the poem deliberately empties the prophecy of its content. Rilke's early effort to make a Christ of his own may be studied in *Visions of Christ,* ed. Siegfried Mandel, trans. Aaron Kramer (Boulder: University of Colorado Press, 1967).

sibyls and prophets "Tenth Elegy," line 72.

167 *an ideal profession* It may be worth noting that in the most authoritative study of the *Elegies,* Jacob Steiner, *Rilkes Duineser Elegien* (Bern: Francke, 1969), the index entry for "Frau" directs the reader to "Mutter, Mädchen, Liebende"—a fair commentary on Rilke's priorities.

far more complex The relations between the two artists are the subject of a full-length study by Heinrich Wigand Petzet, *Das Bildnis des Dichters* (Frankfurt am Main: Societäts-Verlag, 1957).

self-justification Paula Modersohn-Becker in Briefen und Tagebüchern, ed. Günter Busch and Liselotte von Reinken (Frankfurt am Main: S. Fischer, 1979), 307–11.

to lay a ghost Robert Hass discusses the raw and morbid emotions of the "Requiem" in his introduction to *The Selected Poetry of Rainer Maria Rilke,* trans. Stephen Mitchell (New York: Random House, 1982), xxvii–xxxiv.

168 *auf Besitz* Rilke, *Sämtliche Werke* 1:653, 654.

in mir Ibid., 656.

169 *a countertruth* "Paula Becker to Clara Westhoff" was reprinted in an epilogue to *The Letters and Journals of Paula Modersohn-Becker,* ed. J. Diane Radycki (Metuchen, NJ: Scarecrow Press, 1980), 328–30. The epilogue also contains a translation of Rilke's "Requiem" by Lilly Engler and Rich, 319–27.

lonelier than solitude Adrienne Rich, *The Dream of a Common Language* (New York: Norton, 1978), 43.

her voice will go on Ovid, *Metamorphoses* 14:129–53.

Chapter Six

170 *dass ich wurde wie sie* Duino Elegies, "First Elegy," lines 45–48.

Rilke supplies some answers In *Three Women Poets* (Lewisburg, PA: Bucknell University Press, 1987), which offers translations of poems by Stampa, Louise Labé, and Sor Juana Inés de la Cruz, Frank J. Warnke concludes that "Rilke has commented on what is truly in the text"—the transcendent divinity of the woman who loves (55).

171 *other lovers* Duino Elegies, trans. C. F. MacIntyre (Berkeley: University of California Press, 1961), 7n.

Fig. 16.12. Endnotes keyed to page numbers, with key phrases italicized.

1. The "Great Tradition" in the History of Science

Those setting out to acquaint themselves with the identity of the Scientific Revolution, and with its major actors, themes, problems, achievements, and conceptual resources, can draw on a distinguished body of what now is commonly called "traditional" scholarship. If indeed it *is* traditional, that is because this literature typically manifested robust confidence that there was a coherent and specifiable body of early modern culture rightly called revolutionary, that this culture marked a clear break between "old" and "new," that it had an "essence," and that this essence could be captured through accounts of the rise of mechanism and materialism, the mathematization of natural philosophy, the emergence of a full-blooded experimentalism, and for many, though not all, traditional writers, the identification of an effective "method" for producing authentic science.

Among the outstanding achievements of this type of scholarship are the early work of E. A. Burtt, *The Metaphysical Foundations of Modern Physical Science* (New York: Doubleday Anchor, 1954; orig. publ. 1924); A. C. Crombie, *Augustine to Galileo: The History of Science, A.D. 400–1650* (London: Falcon, 1952); A. Rupert Hall, *The Scientific Revolution, 1500–1800: The Formation of the Modern Scientific Attitude,* 2nd ed. (Boston: Beacon Press, 1966; orig. publ. 1954); Hall, *From Galileo to Newton, 1630–1720* (London: Collins, 1963); Marie Boas [Hall], *The Scientific Renaissance, 1450–1630*

Fig. 16.13. Part of the first section of a bibliographic essay.

1973

[1962] "The Algerian Subproletariate." In *Man, State, and Society in the Contemporary Maghrib,* edited by I. W. Zartman, 83–89. London: Pall Mall Press.

[1971] "Cultural Reproduction and Social Reproduction." In *Knowledge, Education, and Cultural Change,* edited by Richard Brown, 71–112. London: Tavistock.

"The Three Forms of Theoretical Knowledge." *Social Science Information* 12: 53–80.

[1970] "The Berber House." In *Rules and Meanings,* edited by Mary Douglas, 98–110. Harmondsworth: Penguin.

with Jean-Claude Chamboredon, and Jean-Claude Passeron. [1968]. *Le métier de sociologue. Préalables épistémologiques.* 2nd ed. Paris and The Hague: Mouton. Translated as *The Craft of Sociology: Epistemological Preliminaries.* Berlin and New York: Walter de Gruyter. 1991.

1974

"Avenir de classe et causalité du probable." *Revue française de socologie* 15, no. 1 (January–March): 3–42.

[1966] "The School as a Conservative Force: Scholastic and Cultural Inequalities." In *Contemporary Research in the Sociology of Education,* edited by John Eggleston, 32–46. London: Metheun.

Fig. 16.14. A sample from a bibliography of the writings of a single author, grouped by year of (English) publication. Brackets denote original publication dates.

*W*orks Cited

MANUSCRIPTS

Bodleian MS Mus.e.1–5. Compilation of part songs, made for and probably by John Sadler, 1585. Bodleian Library, Oxford.

Folger MS V.a.311. Thomas Fella, visual commonplace book, 1585–98. Folger Shakespeare Library, Washington, DC.

Folger MS V.b.232. Thomas Trevelyon, visual commonplace book, 1608. Folger Shakespeare Library, Washington, DC.

Folger MS V.a.345. Verse miscellany in several hands, associated with Christ Church, Oxford, 1630 and later. Folger Shakespeare Library, Washington, DC.

Folger MS V.a.381. Commonplace book compiled ca. 1600–ca. 1650. Folger Shakespeare Library, Washington, DC.

PRINTED MUSIC

Brett, Philip, ed. 1967. *Consort Songs*. Musica Britannica, vol. 22. London: The Royal Musical Association.

Bronson, Bertrand Harris, ed. 1976. *The Singing Tradition of Child's Popular Ballads*. Princeton: Princeton University Press.

Campion, Thomas. 1601. *A Booke of Ayres, Set foorth to be song to the Lute, Orpherian, and Base Violl*. London: Philip Rosseter.

Morley, Thomas. 1962. *Madrigalls to Foure Voyces . . . The First Booke*. Edited by Edmund H. Fellowes. Revised by Thurston Dart. London: Stainer & Bell.

Ravenscroft, Tomas. 1611. *Melismata: Musicall Phansies. Fitting the Court, Citie, and Countrey*. London: Thomas Adams.

Sharp, Cecil J., and Maud Karpeles. 1968. *Eighty English Folk Songs from the Southern Appalachians*. London: Faber, 1968.

PRINTED BROADSIDES

Anon. 1569. "A newe Ballade intytuled, Good Fellowes must go learne to daunce." London: William Griffith.

———. ca. 1590. "A ditty delightfull of mother watkins ale." [London: publisher unspecified.]

———. 1598. "Luke Huttons lamentation: Which he wrote the day before his death, being condemned to be hanged at Yorke this last assises

Fig. 16.15. The first page of a reference list in a work in the humanities—an example of a hybrid style, with headline capitalization and sections for different kinds of works.

DISCOGRAPHY

This list provides the recording session dates and names of the original companies associated with selected recordings cited in this work, emphasizing those that provide the basis for its original transcriptions. In some cases in which the original albums are no longer in print or are difficult for readers to obtain, it mentions reissues. Part 1 arranges compositions chronologically by session date under the names of featured artists. Part 2 follows the same basic scheme but lists those albums or CDs whose citation in this work does not include reference to specific compositions. For further information, see comprehensive jazz discographies by Bruyninckx (1980), Kraner (1979), Lord (1992), and Rust (1978).

1. Listing by Artist and Composition Titles

ADDERLEY, JULIAN "CANNONBALL"
"Somethin' Else," March 9, 1958. *Somethin' Else,* Blue Note BST-81595.

ARMSTRONG, LOUIS
"Big Butter and Egg Man from the West," Nov. 16, 1926. *The Smithsonian Collection of Classic Jazz* (compilation), CBS, Inc., CD Edition RD 033 A5 19477.
"S.O.L. Blues" and "Gully Low Blues," May 13 and 14, 1927; "Struttin' with Some Barbecue," Dec. 9, 1927. *The Louis Armstrong Story,* Columbia CBS 66427.
"Weather Bird," Dec. 5, 1928a. *The Smithsonian Collection of Classic Jazz* (compilation), CBS, Inc., CD Edition RD 033 A5 19477.
"Muggles" and "Tight Like This," Dec. 12, 1928b. *The Louis Armstrong Story.* Columbia CBS 66427.

BAKER, CHET
"Like Someone in Love," July 30, 1956. *Let's Get Lost,* Capital/Pacific Jazz CDP 7 92932 2.

BLAKEY, ART
"Soft Winds," Nov. 11, 1955. *The Jazz Messengers at the Cafe Bohemia. Volume 1,* Blue Note CDP 7 46521 2.
"Moanin'" (original and alternate take), Oct. 30, 1958a. *Moanin',* Blue Note CDP 7 46516 2.
"I Remember Clifford," Nov. 22, 1958b. "Moanin'," Dec. 17, 1958b. *Jazz Messengers 1958—Paris Olympia.* Fontana 832 659-2.
"Like Someone in Love," Aug. 7, 1960. *Like Someone in Love,* Blue Note CDP 7 84245 2.

BROWN, CLIFFORD
"I Can Dream, Can't I?" (takes 1–3), Oct. 15, 1953. *The Clifford Brown Quartet in Paris,* Prestige OJCCD-357-2.
"Parisian Thoroughfare," Aug. 2 and 14, 1954a. *The Immortal,* Limelight LM2-8201.
"Jordu," Aug. 2, 1954b. *Jordu,* EmArcy MG 36036.

Fig. 16.16. The first page of a discography.

17

Documentation II: Specific Content

Introduction

17.1   *Range of examples.* This chapter offers rules for and examples of individual note forms, text citations, and bibliography or reference-list entries. It deals with the various elements included in citations of books, periodicals, electronic media, unpublished materials, audiovisual materials, legal cases, and public documents. For a general discussion and illustration of two basic methods of documentation, see chapter 16.

17.2   *Finding solutions.* Writers or editors who fail to find solutions here for rare or unique problems in documentation—and no manual can cover every kind of citation—are advised to consult the notes and bibliographies of works in the field they are dealing with. If no model can be found, an inventive solution is quite acceptable as long as readers understand what is being cited and how they might track it down.

17.3   *Four formats.* Many of the examples in this chapter will be presented in four formats—those appropriate to notes, bibliographies, text citations, and reference lists. To conserve space, others are presented in only one or two formats. Since all four are illustrated and compared in chapter 16 (see especially 16.8–18) and, more briefly, below, users should have little trouble converting the examples to whatever format is required. The following abbreviations are used here to indicate the various formats: N = note; B = bibliography; T = parenthetical text citation in author-date style; R = reference list in author-date style. Where two or more bibliography or reference-list entries appear together as examples, they are listed alphabetically as if in an actual bibliography, so their order may vary from that of the notes.

N: 1. Paul Davies, *The Fifth Miracle: The Search for the Origin of Life* (New York: Simon & Schuster, 1999), 23.

        2. Kathleen Burnett and Eliza T. Dresang, "Rhizomorphic Reading: The Emergence of a New Aesthetic in Literature for Youth," *Library Journal* 69 (October 1999): 439.

B: Burnett, Kathleen, and Eliza T. Dresang. "Rhizomorphic Reading: The Emergence of a New Aesthetic in Literature for Youth." *Library Journal* 69 (October 1999): 421–45.

        Davies, Paul. *The Fifth Miracle: The Search for the Origin of Life.* New York: Simon & Schuster, 1999.

T: (Davies 1999, 23) (Burnett and Dresang 1999, 439)

R: Burnett, K., and E. T. Dresang. 1999. Rhizomorphic reading: The emergence of a
        new aesthetic in literature for youth. *Library J* 69 (Oct.): 421–45.
        Davies, Paul. 1999. *The fifth miracle: The search for the origin of life*. New York: Si-
        mon & Schuster.

THE ADVENT OF ELECTRONIC SOURCES

17.4   *Introduction.* In recent years, electronic content and the online environment have become major components of academic work. The nature of
electronic media, however, requires that authors keep the following characteristics in mind when consulting them in the course of their research.
See 17.15 for a list of the paragraphs in this chapter that deal specifically
with electronic citations.

17.5   *Permanence.* Whatever archiving, retrieval, and linking techniques may be
in place in the future, electronic content by its very nature will continue to
be impermanent and manipulable. If a source changes or becomes unavailable, citations to that source may need to be adjusted; authors and
publishers should therefore verify the accuracy of citations to electronic
content as close to the publication date as possible.

17.6   *Authority.* As for any other medium, authors should consider the publisher or sponsoring body when assessing electronic content. Content presented without formal ties to a publisher or sponsoring body has authority equivalent to that of unpublished or self-published material in other
media. Authors should note, however, that *anything* posted on the Internet is "published" in the sense of copyright (see 4.2, 4.61–62) and must be
treated as such for the purposes of complete citation and clearance of permissions, if relevant.

17.7   *Content available from multiple online sources.* When content is available
from more than one online source, authors should consider whether, on
the basis of the nature and practices of the publisher or sponsoring body,
they have consulted the most permanent.

17.8   *Publications available in both print and electronic forms.* In many cases the
content of the print and electronic forms of the same publication is identical, but the potential for differences, intentional or otherwise, requires
that authors cite the form consulted. Other forms of the same publication
may be mentioned in the citation when helpful to readers so long as the
language makes it clear that the author did not in fact consult these other
forms (see 17.144).

17.9 *Uniform resource locators (URLs).* A URL, sometimes referred to as an "address," is an expression of the location of a file. Every URL begins with an abbreviation of the protocol used to deliver electronic material to readers. The most common are *http* (hypertext transfer protocol) and *ftp* (file transfer protocol). This abbreviation is invariably followed by a colon and a double slash, after which appears the publisher's domain name, followed by the path to the resource. Components following the domain name are separated from the domain name and from each other by single slashes.

http://www.journals.uchicago.edu/JMH/journal/issues/v72n4/002401/002401.html

The URL above refers to an article—file name 002401.html, in volume 72, issue 4, of the *Journal of Modern History*—published by the University of Chicago Press. Authors and editors are encouraged to pursue at least a basic understanding of the typical components of URLs, if only to help them spot typos.[1]

17.10 *URLs and punctuation.* Even if it follows a period, the first letter of the protocol (e.g., the *h* in *http*) is not capitalized. The capitalization of the remaining components varies; because some URLs are case sensitive, they should not be edited for style. A "trailing slash," the last character in a URL pointing to a directory, is part of the URL. Other punctuation marks used following a URL will readily be perceived as belonging to the surrounding text. It is therefore unnecessary to omit appropriate punctuation after the URL or to bracket the URL as a matter of course. Any logically parenthetical reference to a URL should be put in parentheses; angle brackets (< >), which have specific meaning within some markup languages, including html, should never be used to enclose a URL.

17.11 *URLs and line breaks.* In a printed work, if a URL has to be broken at the end of a line, the break should be made *after* a double slash (//) or a single slash (/); *before* a tilde (~), a period, a comma, a hyphen, an underline (_), a question mark, a number sign, or a percent symbol; or *before or after* an equals sign or an ampersand. A hyphen should never be added to a URL to denote a line break, nor should a hyphen that is part of a URL appear at the end of a line. See also 6.17, 7.44.

http://press-pubs.uchicago
.edu/founders/

---

1. For more information about URLs, consult the Web site of the World Wide Web Consortium (http://www.w3.org).

http://www.uiowa.edu/
~vpr/research/organize/humalink.htm

http://www.pubmedcentral.nih.gov/b.cgi
?artid=19161

http://www.internetnews.com/ec
-news/article/0,,4_353451,00.html

17.12 *Access dates.* Access dates in online source citations are of limited value, since previous versions will often be unavailable to readers (not to mention that an author may have consulted several revisions across any number of days in the course of research). Chicago therefore does not generally recommend including them in a published citation. For sources likely to have substantive updates, however, or in time-sensitive fields such as medicine or law where even small corrections may be significant, the date of the author's last visit to the site may usefully be added. For examples, see 17.187, 17.237.

17.13 *Revision dates.* Though some Internet sites may state the date of the last revision, this practice is neither universal nor necessarily reliable. The revision date therefore should *not* be given in addition to or in lieu of the access date.

17.14 *Permanent source identifiers.* Chicago anticipates a simpler and more reliable electronic source citation method following the development of standards for assigning permanent identifiers to sources and of methods for providing access to sources using those identifiers. The University of Chicago Press now (2003) considers one such scheme—digital object identifiers—promising.[2] (See 17.181, final example, for an example of one setting in which DOIs are already in use.)

17.15 *Specific examples.* Chicago's recommendations for electronic source citation fit easily within the two systems described in chapter 16. Discussion and examples appear throughout this chapter under the relevant source types: books, 17.47, 17.142–47; journals, 17.180–81; magazines, 17.187; newspapers, 17.198; informally published materials, 17.211, 17.234–37; reference works, 17.239; multimedia, 17.270; CD-ROMs and DVD-ROMs, 17.271; public documents, 17.356; databases, 17.357–59.

---

2. A digital object identifier is a serial number for electronic content. Like an ISSN or an ISBN, the DOI is a unique identifier assigned by publishers. The DOI, however, can be assigned to a single article or chapter of a book or even a single illustration—any unit of intellectual content. For an example of how to record a DOI, see 17.181.

Books

INFORMATION TO BE INCLUDED

17.16 *Basic versus supplementary information.* A full reference must include enough information to enable an interested reader to find the book. Some references contain supplementary information not strictly needed for that purpose but enlightening nonetheless.

17.17 *Elements of the information.* The elements listed below are included, where applicable, in full documentary notes and bibliography and reference-list entries. The order in which they appear varies slightly (see 16.9–18) according to type of publication, and certain elements are sometimes omitted; such variation will be discussed and illustrated in the course of this chapter.

1. Author: full name of author or authors; full name of editor or editors or, if no author is listed, name of institution standing in place of author
2. Title: full title of the book, including subtitle if there is one
3. Editor, compiler, or translator, if any, if listed on title page in addition to author
4. Edition, if not the first
5. Volume: total number of volumes if multivolume work is referred to as a whole; individual number if single volume of multivolume work is cited, and title of individual volume if applicable
6. Series title if applicable, and volume number within series if series is numbered
7. Facts of publication: city, publisher, and date
8. Page number or numbers if applicable
9. A URL for Internet sources or, for other electronic sources, an indication of the medium consulted (e.g., DVD, CD-ROM)

17.18 *Flexibility and consistency.* As long as a consistent style is maintained within any one work, logical variations on the style illustrated here are quite acceptable if agreed to by author and publisher. Such flexibility, however, is rarely possible in journal publication, which calls for adherence to the established style of the journal in question.

17.19 *Foreign terms.* When books in a language other than English are cited in an English-language work, terms used for volume, edition, and so on may be translated—but only if the author or editor has a firm grasp of bibliographic terms in the foreign language. It is often wiser to leave them in the original. "Ausgabe in einem Band," for example, may be rendered as "one-volume edition" or simply left untranslated. See also 17.64–66.

AUTHOR'S NAME

17.20 *Form of name.* Authors' names are normally given as they appear on the title pages of their books. Certain adjustments, however, may be made to assist correct identification (unless they conflict with the style of a particular journal or series). First names may be given in full in place of initials. If an author uses his or her given name in one cited book and initials in another (e.g., "Mary L. Jones" versus "M. L. Jones"), the same form, preferably the fuller one, should be used in all references to that author. To assist alphabetization, middle initials should be given wherever known. Degrees and affiliations following names on a title page are omitted. See also 16.99, 17.22–24.

17.21 *Author's name in text citation.* For the form of names in reference lists and text citations, see 16.108.

17.22 *Given name supplied.* A portion of an author's given name omitted on the title page is occasionally supplied in brackets in a bibliographic entry—for example, R. S. Crane may be listed as R[onald] S. Crane. The brackets are an unnecessary refinement for most scholarly purposes.

17.23 *Authors preferring initials.* Full names should not be supplied for authors who always use initials only, for example, T. S. Eliot, M. F. K. Fisher, O. Henry (pseud.), P. D. James, C. S. Lewis, J. D. Salinger, H. G. Wells. Note that space is added between initials (see 8.6).

17.24 *Publications preferring initials.* The reference lists in some journals (especially in the natural sciences) always use initials instead of given names. When periods are used, space appears between them (Wells, H. G.); when periods are omitted, as in some journals' styles, no comma intervenes between last name and initials, and no space appears between the initials (Wells HG). See also 16.99.

17.25 *Monarchs, saints, and the like.* Authors known only by their given names are listed and alphabetized by those names. Such titles as "King" or "Saint" are omitted.

B: Augustine. *On Christian Doctrine.* Translated by D. W. Robertson Jr. Indianapolis: Bobbs-Merrill, 1958.

648

Elizabeth I. *Collected Works.* Edited by Leah S. Marcus, Janel Mueller, and Mary Beth Rose. Chicago: University of Chicago Press, 2000.

17.26 *One author.* In a note, the author's name is given in the normal order. In a bibliography or reference list, where names are arranged alphabetically, it is inverted (last name first). See also 16.11.

N: 1. Salman Rushdie, *The Ground beneath Her Feet* (New York: Henry Holt, 1999).
2. Roger Martin du Gard, *Lieutenant-Colonel de Maumort,* trans. Luc Brébion and Timothy Crouse (New York: Alfred A. Knopf, 2000).

B: Martin du Gard, Roger. *Lieutenant-Colonel de Maumort.* Translated by Luc Brébion and Timothy Crouse. New York: Alfred A. Knopf, 2000.
Rushdie, Salman. *The Ground beneath Her Feet.* New York: Henry Holt, 1999.

Note that Martin du Gard is a surname, so it is alphabetized under *M* (see 18.70). For alphabetizing names with particles (*de, van,* etc.), see 18.69. For Chinese, Hungarian, and other non-English names where the given name follows the family name in normal use, see 18.75–80, 18.83–85.

17.27 *Two authors.* Two authors (or editors) of the same work are listed in the order used on the title page. In a bibliography or reference list, only the first author's name is inverted, and a comma must appear both before and after the first author's given name or initials. Use the conjunction *and* (not an ampersand).

N: 2. Kurt Johnson and Steve Coates, *Nabokov's Blues: The Scientific Odyssey of a Literary Genius* (Cambridge, MA: Zoland Books, 1999).

B: Harnack, Andrew, and Eugene Kleppinger. *Online! A Reference Guide to Using Internet Sources.* 3rd ed. New York: St. Martin's Press, 2000.

T: (Walker and Taylor 1998)

R: Walker, J. R., and T. Taylor. 1998. *The Columbia guide to online style.* New York: Columbia Univ. Press.

When both authors have the same family name, the name is repeated.

N: 3. Milton Friedman and Rose Friedman, *Two Lucky People: Memoirs* (Chicago: University of Chicago Press, 1998).

17.28 *Three authors.* Three authors (or editors) of the same work are listed in the order shown on the title page. In a bibliography or reference list, only the first author's name is inverted, and a comma must appear both before and after the first author's given name or initials. In a text citation or a short form in a note, all three last names are given. The conjunction *and,* following a comma, is used before the last name.

T: (Schellinger, Hudson, and Rijsberman 1998)

R: Schellinger, Paul, Christopher Hudson, and Marijk Rijsberman, eds. 1998. *Ency-
       clopedia of the novel.* Chicago: Fitzroy Dearborn.

17.29   *More than three authors.* For works by or edited by four to ten persons, all names are usually given in a bibliography or reference list. Word order and punctuation are the same as for three authors. In a note or a text citation, only the name of the first author is included, followed by "and others" or, especially in science, "et al.," with no intervening comma. For works by eleven or more authors, see 17.30.

N: 4. Jeri A. Sechzer and others, eds., *Women and Mental Health* (Baltimore: Johns
       Hopkins University Press, 1996), 243.
       7. Sechzer and others, *Women and Mental Health,* 276.

T: (Sechzer et al. 1996, 243)

R: Sechzer, J. A., S. M. Pfaffilin, F. L. Denmark, A. Griffin, and S. J. Blumenthal, eds.
       1996. *Women and mental health.* Baltimore: Johns Hopkins University Press.

17.30   *Multiple authors.* Reference lists in the natural sciences sometimes include works by numerous authors (occasionally a score or more). Furthermore, many of the authors in successive entries may be the same, though in a different order. To avoid an unwieldy string of names, and with apologies to those authors whose names are sacrificed, Chicago recommends the policy followed by the *American Naturalist* (see bibliog. 5): for references with ten authors or fewer, all should be listed; for references with eleven or more, only the first seven should be listed, followed by "et al." (Where space is limited, the policy of the American Medical Association may be followed: up to six authors' names are listed; if there are more than six, only the first three are listed, followed by "et al.")

17.31   *Author's name in title.* When the author's name appears in the title or subtitle of a cited work (such as an autobiography), the note citation may begin with the title. The bibliography or reference-list entry, however, should begin with the author's name, even though it is repeated in the title. See also 17.41.

N: 5. *One More Time: The Best of Mike Royko* (Chicago: University of Chicago Press, 1999).
        6. *The Letters of George Meredith*, ed. C. L. Cline, 3 vols. (Oxford: Clarendon Press, 1970), 1:125.
        7. *Illumination and Night Glare: The Unfinished Autobiography of Carson McCullers*, ed. Carlos L. Dews (Madison: University of Wisconsin Press, 1999).

B: McCullers, Carson. *Illumination and Night Glare: The Unfinished Autobiography of Carson McCullers*. Edited by Carlos L. Dews. Madison: University of Wisconsin Press, 1999.
        Meredith, George. *The Letters of George Meredith*. Edited by C. L. Cline. 3 vols. Oxford: Clarendon Press, 1970.
        Royko, Mike. *One More Time: The Best of Mike Royko*. Chicago: University of Chicago Press, 1999.

T: (Michelangelo 1999)

R: Michelangelo. 1999. *The complete poems of Michelangelo*. Trans. J. F. Nims. Chicago: Univ. of Chicago Press.

17.32   *Anonymous works: unknown authorship.* If the author or editor is unknown, the note or bibliographic entry begins with the title (but see 17.33). An initial article is ignored in alphabetizing.

N: 8. *A True and Sincere Declaration of the Purpose and Ends of the Plantation Begun in Virginia, of the Degrees Which It Hath Received, and Means by Which It Hath Been Advanced* (1610).
        9. *Stanze in lode della donna brutta* (Florence, 1547).

B: *Stanze in lode della donna brutta*. Florence, 1547.
        A True and Sincere Declaration of the Purpose and Ends of the Plantation Begun in Virginia, of the Degrees Which It Hath Received, and Means by Which It Hath Been Advanced. 1610.

17.33   *"Anonymous" as author.* Although the use of "Anonymous" is generally to be avoided, it may stand in place of the author's name in a reference list or in a bibliography in which several anonymous works need to be grouped. In such an instance, *Anonymous* or *Anon.* (set in roman) appears at the first entry, and 3-em dashes (see 16.84) are used thereafter.

B: Anonymous. *Stanze in lode della donna brutta*. Florence, 1547.
        ———. *A True and Sincere Declaration of the Purpose and Ends of the Plantation Begun in Virginia, . . .* 1610.

T: (Anon. 1547)

R: Anon. 1547. *Stanze in lode della donna brutta*. Florence.

17.34 *Anonymous works: known authorship.* If the authorship is known or guessed at but was omitted on the title page, the name is included in brackets.

N: 10. [Samuel Horsley], *On the Prosodies of the Greek and Latin Languages* (1796).
11. [Ebenezer Cook?], *Sotweed Redivivus, or The Planter's Looking-Glass*, by "E. C. Gent" (Annapolis, 1730).

B: [Cook, Ebenezer?]. *Sotweed Redivivus, or The Planter's Looking-Glass*. By "E. C. Gent." Annapolis, 1730.
[Horsley, Samuel]. *On the Prosodies of the Greek and Latin Languages*. 1796.

17.35 *Pseudonyms: unknown authorship.* If an author's real name is not known, *pseud.* (roman, in brackets) may follow the name. (In a text citation, *pseud.* is omitted.)

B: Centinel [pseud.]. Letters. In *The Complete Anti-Federalist*, edited by Herbert J. Storing. Chicago: University of Chicago Press, 1981.

17.36 *Pseudonyms: known authorship.* A widely used pseudonym is generally treated as if it were the author's real name.

B: Eliot, George. *Middlemarch*. Norton Critical Editions. New York: Norton, 1977.
Twain, Mark. *The Prince and the Pauper: A Tale for Young People of All Ages*. New York: Harper & Brothers, 1899.

The real name, if of interest to readers, may follow the pseudonym in brackets.

R: Le Carré, John [David John Moore Cornwell]. 1982. *The quest for Karla*. New York: Knopf.
Stendhal [Marie Henri Beyle]. 1925. *The charterhouse of Parma*. Trans. C. K. Scott-Moncrieff. New York: Boni and Liveright.

17.37 *Pseudonyms rarely used.* If the author's real name is better known than the pseudonym, the real name should be used. If needed, the pseudonym may be included in brackets, followed by *pseud.*

B: Brontë, Charlotte. *Jane Eyre*. London, 1847.
or
Brontë, Charlotte [Currer Bell, pseud.]. *Jane Eyre*. London, 1847.

17.38 *Descriptive phrase as "author."* A descriptive phrase standing in place of the author is treated in much the same way as a pseudonym (see 17.35). *The* or *A* may be omitted in a bibliography or reference list.

> N: 11. A Cotton Manufacturer, *An Inquiry into the Causes of the Present Long-Continued Depression in the Cotton Trade, with Suggestions for Its Improvement* (Bury, UK, 1869).

> B: Cotton Manufacturer. *An Inquiry . . .*

17.39 *Cross-references for pseudonyms.* If a bibliography or reference list includes two or more works published by the same author but under different pseudonyms, all may be listed under the real name followed by the appropriate pseudonym in brackets, with cross-references under the pseudonyms. Alternatively, they may be listed under the pseudonyms, with a cross-reference at the real name to each pseudonym.

> Creasey, John [Gordon Ashe, pseud.]. *A Blast of Trumpets.* New York: Holt, Rinehart and Winston, 1976.
> ——— [Anthony Morton, pseud.]. *Hide the Baron.* New York: Walker, 1978.
> ——— [Jeremy York, pseud.]. *Death to My Killer.* New York: Macmillan, 1966.

or

> Ashe, Gordon [John Creasey]. *A Blast of Trumpets.* New York: Holt, Rinehart and Winston, 1976.
> Creasey, John. *See* Ashe, Gordon; Morton, Anthony; York, Jeremy.

17.40 *Alternative real names.* When a writer has published under different forms of his or her name, the works should be listed under the name used on the title page—unless the difference is merely the use of initials versus full names (see 17.20). Cross-references are occasionally used.

> B: Doniger, Wendy. *The Bedtrick: Telling the Difference.* Chicago: University of Chicago Press, 2000.
> ———. *See also* O'Flaherty, Wendy Doniger.

If a person discussed in the text publishes under a name not used in the text, a cross-reference may be useful.

> Overstone, Lord. *See* Lloyd, Samuel Jones.

17.41 *Editor in place of author.* When no author appears on the title page, a work is listed by the name(s) of the editor(s), compiler(s), or translator(s). In full note citations and in bibliographies and reference lists, the abbreviation *ed.* or *eds., comp.* or *comps.,* or *trans.* follows the name, preceded by a comma. In shortened note citations and text citations, the abbreviation is omitted.

N: 3. Ori Z. Soltes, ed., *Georgia: Art and Civilization through the Ages* (London: Philip Wilson, 1999), 280.

        4. Theodore Silverstein, trans., *Sir Gawain and the Green Knight* (Chicago: University of Chicago Press, 1974), 34.

        5. Soltes, *Georgia,* 285; Silverstein, *Sir Gawain,* 38.

B: Silverstein, Theodore, trans. *Sir Gawain and the Green Knight.* Chicago: University of Chicago Press, 1974.

    Soltes, Ori Z., ed. *Georgia: Art and Civilization through the Ages.* London: Philip Wilson, 1999.

T: (Kamrany and Day 1980)

R: Kamrany, Nake M., and Richard H. Day, eds. 1980. *Economic issues of the eighties.* Baltimore: Johns Hopkins Univ. Press.

17.42   *Editor or translator in addition to author.* The edited, compiled, or translated work of one author is normally listed with the author's name appearing first and the name(s) of the editor(s), compiler(s), or translator(s) appearing after the title, preceded by *edited by* or *ed., compiled by* or *comp.,* or *translated by* or *trans.* Note that the plural forms *eds.* and *comps.* are never used in this position. Note also that *edited by* and the like are usually spelled out in bibliographies but abbreviated in notes and reference lists. If a translator as well as an editor is listed, the names should appear in the same order as on the title page of the original. See also 17.31, 17.69.

N: 6. Yves Bonnefoy, *New and Selected Poems,* ed. John Naughton and Anthony Rudolf (Chicago: University of Chicago Press, 1995).

        7. Rigoberta Menchú, *Crossing Borders,* trans. and ed. Ann Wright (New York: Verso, 1999).

        8. *Four Farces by Georges Feydeau,* trans. Norman R. Shapiro (Chicago: University of Chicago Press, 1970).

        10. Theodor W. Adorno and Walter Benjamin, *The Complete Correspondence, 1928–1940,* ed. Henri Lonitz, trans. Nicholas Walker (Cambridge, MA: Harvard University Press, 1999).

B: Adorno, Theodor W., and Walter Benjamin. *The Complete Correspondence, 1928–1940.* Edited by Henri Lonitz. Translated by Nicholas Walker. Cambridge, MA: Harvard University Press, 1999.

Bonnefoy, Yves. *New and Selected Poems.* Edited by John Naughton and Anthony Rudolf. Chicago: University of Chicago Press, 1995.

Feydeau, Georges. *Four Farces by Georges Feydeau.* Translated by Norman R. Shapiro. Chicago: University of Chicago Press, 1970.

Menchú, Rigoberta. *Crossing Borders.* Translated and edited by Ann Wright. New York: Verso, 1999.

T: (Menchú 1999)

R: Menchú, Rigoberta. 1999. *Crossing borders.* Trans. and ed. Ann Wright. New York: Verso.

17.43 *Supplementary information.* When the title page carries such phrases as "Edited with an Introduction and Notes by" or "Translated with a Foreword by," the bibliographic or note reference can usually be simplified to "Edited by" or "Translated by."

17.44 *"With the assistance of" and the like.* The title page of some edited books carries information that must be dealt with ad hoc. The usual formats, phrases, and abbreviations may not work. For ghostwritten books, *with* is usually sufficient.

B: *Chaucer Life-Records.* Edited by Martin M. Crow and Clair C. Olson from materials compiled by John M. Manly and Edith Richert, with the assistance of Lilian J. Redstone and others. London: Oxford University Press, 1966.

Cullen, John B. *Old Times in the Faulkner Country.* In collaboration with Floyd C. Watkins. Chapel Hill: University of North Carolina Press, 1961.

Prather, Marla. *Alexander Calder, 1898–1976.* With contributions by Arnauld Pierre and Alexander S. C. Rower. New Haven, CT: Yale University Press, 1998.

Rodman, Dennis. *Walk on the Wild Side.* With Michael Silver. New York: Delacorte Press, 1997.

Williams, Joseph M. *Style: Toward Clarity and Grace.* With two chapters co-authored by Gregory G. Colomb. Chicago: University of Chicago Press, 1990.

If a title page lists, for example, two editors, followed in smaller type by "Associate Editor So-and-So" and "Assistant Editor So-and-So," the secondary names may be included with such wording as "With the assistance of So-and-So and So-and-So" (or simply omitted).

17.45 *Editor versus author.* Occasionally, when an editor or a translator is more important to a discussion than the original author, a book may be listed under the editor's name.

B: Eliot, T. S., ed. *Literary Essays,* by Ezra Pound. New York: New Directions, 1953.

17.46 *Authors of forewords and the like.* Authors of forewords or introductions to books by other authors are included in notes and bibliographic entries only if the foreword or introduction is of major significance.

B: Hayek, F. A. *The Road to Serfdom.* Anniversary edition, with a new introduction by Milton Friedman. Chicago: University of Chicago Press, 1994.

For specific citation of a foreword or an introduction, see 17.74–75.

17.47 *Organization as author.* If a publication issued by an organization, association, or corporation carries no personal author's name on the title page, the organization is listed as author in a bibliography or reference list, even if it is also given as publisher. If long names are cited several times, abbreviations may be used, clarified by a cross-reference.

B: University of Chicago Press. *The Chicago Manual of Style.* 15th ed. Chicago: University of Chicago Press, 2003.
World Health Organization. *WHO Editorial Style Manual.* Geneva: World Health Organization, 1993.

T: (British Standards Institute 1985)
(ISO 2001)

R: British Standards Institute. 1985. *Specification for abbreviation of title words and titles of publications.* Linford Woods, Milton Keynes, UK: British Standards Institute.
ISO. *See* International Organization for Standardization.
International Organization for Standardization. 2001. *Information and documentation: Bibliographic references.* Part 2, *Electronic documents or parts thereof. Excerpts from International Standard ISO 690-2.* Ottawa: National Library of Canada. http://www.nlc-bnc.ca/iso/tc46sc9/standard/690-2e.htm.

TITLE

17.48 *Additional discussion.* The section "Titles of Works" in chapter 8 (8.164–200), though focusing on the way quoted titles of books as well as other materials are treated in running text, is obviously relevant to documentation and provides additional discussion and examples.

17.49 *Italics.* Book titles and subtitles are italicized. For titles within titles, see 17.58.

B: Hibbert, Christopher. *George III: A Personal History.* New York: Basic Books, 1999.

17.50   *Headline-style capitalization.* In headline style, the first and last words of title and subtitle and all other major words are capitalized. For a more detailed definition and more examples, see 8.167. English-language book titles and subtitles are usually capitalized headline style in notes and bibliographies. For hyphenated compounds in headline style, see 8.168–70. For headlines in newspapers, see 17.189.

> *The Fifth Miracle: The Search for the Origin of Life*
> *How to Do It: Guides to Good Living for Renaissance Italians*

17.51   *Sentence-style capitalization.* In sentence style, more commonly used in reference lists (and exemplified in the *R* examples in this chapter), only the first word in a title or a subtitle and any proper names are capitalized (see 8.166). Latin titles—except for works in English with Latin titles—are capitalized sentence style, whether in reference lists, bibliographies, or notes. For foreign-language book titles and subtitles, see 17.64–67.

> *The house of Rothschild: The world's banker, 1849–1999*
> *De sermone amatorio apud elegiarum scriptores*
> *Quo Vadis*

17.52   *Spelling and such.* The spelling, hyphenation, capitalization, and punctuation in the original title should be preserved, with the following exceptions: capitalization may be adjusted in sentence-style reference-list entries; words in full capitals on the original title page (except for initialisms or acronyms) should be set in upper- and lowercase; and an ampersand should be changed to *and*. Numbers should remain spelled out or given as numerals according to the original (*Twelfth Century* or *12th Century*) unless there is a good reason to make them consistent (but *12th* may be changed to *12th*). For the addition of commas (including serial commas), see 8.175–76. For older titles, see 17.63. See also 17.53.

17.53   *Subtitles: the colon.* A colon, also italicized, is used to separate the main title from the subtitle. A regular word space follows the colon. The subtitle, like the title, begins with a capital in both headline and sentence style. (In the author-date style, subtitles are sometimes omitted.) See also 8.173.

> B: Hazzard, Shirley. *Greene on Capri: A Memoir.* New York: Farrar, Straus & Giroux, 2000.

> R: Lynch, Patrick J., and Sarah Horton. 1999. *Web style guide: Basic design principles for creating Web sites.* New Haven, CT: Yale Univ. Press.

Although in European bibliographic style a period often separates title from subtitle, English-language publications need not follow that convention.

Fausts Himmelfahrt: Zur letzten Szene der Tragödie

17.54 *Two subtitles.* If, as occasionally happens, there are two subtitles in the original (an awkward contingency), a colon normally precedes the first and a semicolon the second. The second subtitle also begins with a capital.

B: Ahmed, Leila. *A Border Passage: From Cairo to America; A Woman's Journey.* New York: Farrar, Straus & Giroux, 1999.

Sereny, Gitta. *Cries Unheard: Why Children Kill; The Story of Mary Bell.* New York: Metropolitan Books / Henry Holt, 1999.

17.55 *Use of "or."* Old-fashioned double titles (or titles and subtitles) connected by *or* are traditionally separated by a semicolon, with a comma following *or*, and less traditionally but more simply by a single comma preceding *or*. In both forms, the second title begins with a capital. Either form is acceptable if used consistently.

England's Monitor; or, The History of the Separation
or
England's Monitor, or The History of the Separation

17.56 *"And other stories" and such.* Such tags as *and other stories* or *and other poems* are treated as part of the main title but usually separated from the title story, poem, essay, or whatever by a comma (but see also 17.61). The first part of the title is *not* enclosed in quotation marks.

N: 34. Norman Maclean, *A River Runs Through It, and Other Stories* (Chicago: University of Chicago Press, 1976), 104.

35. Emily Hiestand, *Angela the Upside-down Girl, and Other Domestic Travels* (Boston: Beacon, 1999), 7.

17.57 *Dates in titles.* When not introduced by a preposition (e.g., "from 1920 to 1945"), dates in a title or subtitle are set off by commas, even if differentiated only by type style on the title page. If a colon has been used in the original, it should be retained.

B: Ferguson, Niall. *The House of Rothschild: The World's Banker, 1849–1999.* New York: Viking, 1999.

R: Roberts, J. M. 1999. *The history of the world, 1901 to 2000.* New York: Viking.

17.58 *Titles within titles.* Titles of long or short works appearing within an italicized title are enclosed in quotation marks. For a title within an article or a chapter title, see 17.157.

N: 22. Allen Forte, *The Harmonistic Organization of "The Rite of Spring"* (New Haven, CT: Yale University Press, 1978).
23. Roland McHugh, *Annotations to "Finnegans Wake"* (Baltimore: Johns Hopkins University Press, 1980).

R: McHugh, Roland. 1980. *Annotations to "Finnegans wake."* Baltimore: Johns Hopkins Univ. Press.

Quotation marks within a book title do not always denote another title. But confusion is unlikely.

N: 24. *"Race," Writing, and Difference,* ed. Henry Louis Gates Jr. and Kwame Anthony Appiah (Chicago: University of Chicago Press, 1986).

17.59 *Italicized terms within titles.* When terms normally italicized in running text, such as species names or names of ships, appear within an italicized title, they are set roman ("reverse italics"; see 8.184). For an italicized term within an article or a chapter title, see 17.157.

R: Suangtho, V., and E. B. Lauridsen. 1990. *Flowering and seed production in* Tectona grandis *L.f.: Report on the DANIDA Training Course on Tree Improvement Program.* Chiang Mai, Thailand.

17.60 *Quotations as titles.* A quotation used as a book title is not enclosed in quotation marks. See also 8.171.

B: Whitaker, Agnes, ed. *All in the End Is Harvest: An Anthology for Those Who Grieve.* London: Darton, Longman and Todd, 1984.

17.61 *Question marks or exclamation points.* When a title or a subtitle ends with a question mark or an exclamation point, no other punctuation follows. See also 6.123.

N: 25. Peter Glen, *It's Not My Department! How to Get the Service You Want, Exactly the Way You Want It!* (New York: William Morrow, 1990), 63.
26. Herrlee Glessner Creel, *What Is Taoism? and Other Studies in Chinese Cultural History* (Chicago: University of Chicago Press, 1970), 34.

B: Aaron, Henry. 1973. *Why Is Welfare So Hard to Reform?* Washington, DC: Brookings Institution Press, 1973.

17.62 *Very long titles.* An extremely long title or subtitle may be shortened in a bibliography or note. Enough information should be given to allow readers to find the full title in a library or a publisher's catalog. For examples, see 17.63.

17.63 *Older titles.* Titles of works published in the eighteenth century or earlier may retain their original punctuation, spelling, and capitalization (except for whole words in capital letters, which should be given an initial capital only). Very long titles may be shortened, omissions being indicated by three ellipsis dots within a title and four at the end (see 11.57).

B: Escalante, Bernardino. *A Discourse of the Navigation which the Portugales doe make to the Realmes and Provinces of the East Partes of the Worlde. . . .* Translated by John Frampton. London, 1579.

Ray, John. *Observations Topographical, Moral, and Physiological: Made in a Journey Through part of the Low-Countries, Germany, Italy, and France: with A Catalogue of Plants not Native of England . . . Whereunto is added A Brief Account of Francis Willughby, Esq., his Voyage through a great part of Spain.* [London], 1673.

17.64 *Non-English titles.* Sentence-style capitalization is strongly recommended for non-English titles (see 10.3). Still, writers or editors unfamiliar with the usages of the language concerned should not attempt to alter capitalization without expert help. For more on French titles, see 10.30; for more on German, see 10.43; for romanized titles originally in a non-Latin alphabet, see 10.3; for English forms of foreign cities, see 17.101.

N: 3. Danielle Maisonneuve, Jean-François Lamarche, and Yves St-Amand, *Les relations publiques: Dans une société en mouvance* (Sainte-Foy, QC: Presses de l'Université de Québec, 1998).

4. Gabriele Krone-Schmalz, *In Wahrheit sind wir stärker: Frauenalltag in der Sowjetunion* (Frankfurt am Main: Fischer Taschenbuch Verlag, 1992).

5. G. Martellotti et al., *La letteratura italiana: Storia e testi*, vol. 7 (Milan: Riccardo Ricciardi, 1955).

6. Ljiljana Piletic Stojanovic, ed. *Gutfreund i ceški kubizam* (Belgrade: Muzej savremene umetnosti, 1971).

17.65 *Translation added.* If an English translation of a title is needed, it follows the original title and is enclosed in brackets, without italics or quotation marks. It is capitalized sentence style regardless of the bibliographic style followed. Parentheses may be used instead of brackets, as in running text (see 10.6–7), but brackets more clearly distinguish the translation from publishing information in parentheses.

N: 7. Henryk Wereszycki, *Koniec sojuszu trzech cesarzy* [The end of the Three Emperors' League] (Warsaw: PWN, 1977); includes a summary in German.

B: *Zhongguo renkou tongji nianjian 1996* [China population statistics yearbook 1996]. Beijing: Zhongguo tongji chubanshe, 1996.

R: Pirumova, N. M. 1977. *Zemskoe liberal'noe dvizhenie: Sotsial'nye korni i evoliutsiia do nachala XX veka* [The zemstvo liberal movement: Its social roots and evolution to the beginning of the twentieth century]. Moscow: Izdatel'stvo "Nauka."

17.66 *Original plus published translation.* A published translation is normally treated as illustrated in 17.42. If, for some reason, both the original and the translation need to be cited, either of the following forms may be used, depending on whether the original or the translation is of greater interest to readers.

B: Furet, François. *Le passé d'une illusion.* Paris: Éditions Robert Laffont, 1995. Translated by Deborah Furet as *The Passing of an Illusion* (Chicago: University of Chicago Press, 1999).

or

Furet, François. *The Passing of an Illusion.* Translated by Deborah Furet. Chicago: University of Chicago Press, 1999. Originally published as *Le passé d'une illusion* (Paris: Éditions Robert Laffont, 1995).

17.67 *Unpublished translation.* In those rare instances when a title is given only in translation but no published translation of the work is listed, the original language must be specified.

N: 8. N. M. Pirumova, *The Zemstvo Liberal Movement: Its Social Roots and Evolution to the Beginning of the Twentieth Century* [in Russian] (Moscow: Izdatel'stvo "Nauka," 1977).

CHAPTERS OR OTHER TITLED PARTS OF A BOOK

17.68 *Chapter in a single-author book.* When a specific chapter (or other titled part of a book) is cited, the author's name is followed by the title of the chapter (or other part) in roman, followed by *in* (also roman), followed by the title of the book in italics. Either the inclusive page numbers (see 9.62, 9.64) or the chapter or part number is usually given also. In notes and bibliographies, but not in reference lists, the chapter is enclosed in quotation marks. For a multiauthor work, see 17.69. See also 17.135.

N: 1. Brendan Phibbs, "Herrlisheim: Diary of a Battle," in *The Other Side of Time: A Combat Surgeon in World War II* (Boston: Little, Brown, 1987), 117–63.

B: Ashbrook, James B., and Carol Rausch Albright. "The Frontal Lobes, Intending, and a Purposeful God." Chap. 7 in *The Humanizing Brain*. Cleveland, OH: Pilgrim Press, 1997.

       or

       Ashbrook, James B., and Carol Rausch Albright. *The Humanizing Brain*. Cleveland, OH: Pilgrim Press, 1997. See esp. chap. 7, "The Frontal Lobes, Intending, and a Purposeful God."

T: (Phibbs 1987, 122–24)

R: Phibbs, Brendan. 1987. Herrlisheim: Diary of a battle. In *The other side of time: A combat surgeon in World War II*, 117–63. Boston: Little, Brown.

17.69 *Contribution to a multiauthor book.* When one contribution to a multiauthor book is cited, the contributor's name comes first, followed by the title of the contribution in roman, followed by *in* (also roman), followed by the title of the book in italics, followed by the name(s) of the editor(s). The inclusive page numbers are usually given also. In notes and bibliographies, but not in reference lists, the contribution title is enclosed in quotation marks. For several contributions to the same book, see 17.70.

N: 3. Anne Carr and Douglas J. Schuurman, "Religion and Feminism: A Reformist Christian Analysis," in *Religion, Feminism, and the Family*, ed. Anne Carr and Mary Stewart Van Leeuwen (Louisville, KY: Westminster John Knox Press, 1996), 11–32.

B: Ellet, Elizabeth F. L. "By Rail and Stage to Galena." In *Prairie State: Impressions of Illinois, 1673–1967, by Travelers and Other Observers*, edited by Paul M. Angle, 271–79. Chicago: University of Chicago Press, 1968.

T: (Wiens 1983)

R: Wiens, J. A. 1983. Avian community ecology: An iconoclastic view. In *Perspectives in ornithology*, ed. A. H. Brush and G. A. Clark Jr., 355–403. Cambridge: Cambridge Univ. Press.

17.70 *Several contributions to the same book.* If two or more contributions to the same multiauthor book are cited, the book itself, as well as the specific contributions, may be listed in the bibliography. The entries for the individual contributions may then cross-refer to the book's editor, thus avoiding clutter. In notes, details of the book may be given only once, with subsequent cross-references.

N: 4. William H. Keating, "Fort Dearborn and Chicago," in *Prairie State: Impressions of Illinois, 1673–1967, by Travelers and Other Observers*, ed. Paul M. Angle (Chicago: University of Chicago Press, 1967), 84–87.

27. Sara Clarke Lippincott, "Chicago," in *Prairie State* (see note 4), 362–70.

or

. . . in Angle, *Prairie State*, 362–70.

B: Draper, Joan E. "Paris by the Lake: Sources of Burnham's Plan of Chicago." In Zukowsky, *Chicago Architecture*, 107–19.

Harrington, Elaine. "International Influences on Henry Hobson Richardson's Glessner House." In Zukowsky, *Chicago Architecture*, 189–207.

Zukowsky, John, ed. *Chicago Architecture, 1872–1922: Birth of a Metropolis*. Munich: Prestel-Verlag in association with the Art Institute of Chicago, 1987.

T: (Brush and Clark 1983)

(Wiens 1983)

R: Brush, A. H., and G. A. Clark Jr., eds. 1983. *Perspectives in ornithology*. Cambridge: Cambridge Univ. Press.

Wiens, J. A. 1983. Avian community ecology: An iconoclastic view. In Brush and Clark 1983, 355–403.

17.71 *Conference proceedings.* Individual contributions to conference proceedings may be treated like chapters in multiauthor books (see 17.69).

17.72 *Book-length work within a book.* If the cited part of a book is a large enough entity in itself (see 8.172, 8.193), it too may be italicized.

N: 3. Thomas Bernard, *A Party for Boris*, in *Histrionics: Three Plays*, trans. Peter K. Jansen and Kenneth Northcott (Chicago: University of Chicago Press, 1990).

17.73 *Chapter originally published elsewhere.* When a chapter is cited that was originally published as an article in a journal, only the book version need be cited. If the original publication is of particular interest, details may be added to the entry in the bibliography after such wording as "originally published as" (see 17.66, second example).

17.74 *Author's introduction and the like.* If the reference is to a generic title such as *introduction, preface,* or *afterword,* that term (lowercased unless following a period) is added before the title of the book. See also 8.189.

N: 1. Valerie Polakow, afterword to *Lives on the Edge: Single Mothers and Their Children in the Other America* (Chicago: University of Chicago Press, 1993).

17.75 *Introductions or chapters by someone other than the author.* If reference is to an introduction, foreword, or chapter written by someone other than the main author of a book, the other person's name comes first, and the author's name follows the title. See also 17.46.

N: 6. Francine Prose, introduction to *Word Court: Wherein Verbal Virtue Is Rewarded, Crimes against the Language Are Punished, and Poetic Justice Is Done,* by Barbara Wallraff (New York: Harcourt, 2000).

B: Williams, Joseph M., and Gregory G. Colomb. "Coherence II." In *Style: Toward Clarity and Grace,* by Joseph M. Williams, 81–95. Chicago: University of Chicago Press, 1990.

T: (Friedman 1994)

R: Friedman, Milton. 1994. Introd. to *The road to serfdom,* by F. A. Hayek. Anniversary ed. Chicago: Univ. of Chicago Press.

LETTERS AND OTHER COMMUNICATIONS IN PUBLISHED COLLECTIONS

17.76 *Writers' names.* A reference to a letter, memorandum, or similar communication in a published collection begins with the names of the sender and the recipient, in that order, followed by a date and sometimes the place where the communication was prepared. The word *letter* is unnecessary, but other forms, such as reports or memoranda, should be specified. The title of the collection is given in the usual form for a book. For date forms, see 6.46, 9.33–35. For unpublished communications, see 17.208–9, 17.211, 17.234–37.

N: 1. Adams to Charles Milnes Gaskell, London, 30 March 1868, in *Letters of Henry Adams, 1858–1891,* ed. Worthington Chauncey Ford (Boston: Houghton Mifflin, 1930), 141.
 2. EBW to Harold Ross, memorandum, 2 May 1946, in *Letters of E. B. White,* ed. Dorothy Lobrano Guth (New York: Harper & Row, 1976), 273.
 3. Adams to Gaskell, 142.

B: Jackson, Paulina. Paulina Jackson to John Pepys Junior, 3 October 1676. In *The Letters of Samuel Pepys and His Family Circle*, ed. Helen Truesdell Heath, no. 42. Oxford: Clarendon Press, 1955.

17.77   *Citing letters and such in the author-date system.* In the author-date system, the material in the examples to 17.76 could be cited as follows:

T: In a letter to Charles Milnes Gaskell from London, March 30, 1868 (Adams 1930, 141), Adams wrote . . .
        White (1976, 273) sent Ross an interoffice memo on May 2, 1946, pointing out that . . .

R: Adams, Henry. 1930. *Letters of Henry Adams, 1858–1891.* Ed. Worthington Chauncey Ford. Boston: Houghton Mifflin.
        White, E. B. 1976. *Letters of E. B. White.* Ed. Dorothy Lobrano Guth. New York: Harper & Row.

17.78   *Several citations to same published collection.* If several letters or other communications are cited from a single source, the source itself rather than the individual pieces should be listed in a bibliography or reference list.

T: (Churchill and Eisenhower 1990)

R: Churchill, Winston, and Dwight D. Eisenhower. 1990. *The Churchill-Eisenhower correspondence, 1953–1955.* Ed. Peter G. Boyle. Chapel Hill: Univ. of North Carolina Press.

EDITION

17.79   *Editions other than the first.* When an edition other than the first is used or cited, the number or description of the edition follows the title in the listing. An edition number usually appears on the title page and is repeated, along with the date of the edition, on the copyright page. Such wording as "Second Edition, Revised and Enlarged" is abbreviated in notes, bibliographies, and reference lists simply as "2nd ed."; "Revised Edition" (with no number) is abbreviated as "rev. ed." Other terms are similarly abbreviated. Any volume number mentioned follows the edition number. For the use of the word *edition* and Chicago's preferences, see 1.22. For inclusion of the original date of an older work cited in a modern edition, see 17.123–27.

N: 1. Karen V. Harper-Dorton and Martin Herbert, *Working with Children, Adolescents, and Their Families,* 3rd ed. (Chicago: Lyceum Books, 2002), 43.

2. Florence Babb, *Between Field and Cooking Pot: The Political Economy of Marketwomen in Peru*, rev. ed. (Austin: University of Texas Press, 1989), 199.

3. Elizabeth Barrett Browning, *Aurora Leigh: Authoritative Text, Backgrounds and Contexts, Criticism*, ed. Margaret Reynolds, Norton Critical Editions (New York: Norton, 1996). All subsequent citations are to this edition.

B: Strunk, William, Jr., and E. B. White. *The Elements of Style*. 4th ed. New York: Allyn and Bacon, 2000.

T: (Anderson and Richie 1982)
      (Weber, Burlet, and Abel 1928)

R: Anderson, J. L., and D. Richie. 1982. *The Japanese film art and industry*. Exp. ed. Princeton, NJ: Princeton Univ. Press.
      Weber, M., H. M. de Burlet, and O. Abel. 1928. *Die Säugetiere*. 2nd ed. 2 vols. Jena: Gustav Fischer.

17.80   *Modern editions of the classics.* Modern editions of Greek, Latin, and medieval classics are discussed in 17.251–61; modern editions of English classics in 17.261–62.

17.81   *Reprint editions.* Reprint editions, facsimile editions, and the like are discussed in 17.123–27.

17.82   *Online editions.* Online editions of books are discussed in 17.142–47.

MULTIVOLUME WORKS

17.83   *Volume numbers.* In documentation, volume numbers are always given in arabic numerals, even if in the original work they appear in roman numerals or are spelled out. The word *vol.* is omitted if the volume number is immediately followed by a page number (see the following paragraphs for examples).

17.84   *Citing the work as a whole.* When a multivolume work is cited as a whole, the total number of volumes is given after the title of the work (or, if an editor as well as an author is mentioned, after the editor's name). If the volumes have been published over several years, the range of years is given. See also 17.117.

B: Aristotle. *Complete Works of Aristotle: The Revised Oxford Translation*. Edited by J. Barnes. 2 vols. Bollingen Series. Princeton, NJ: Princeton University Press, 1983.

> Byrne, Muriel St. Clare, ed. *The Lisle Letters*. 6 vols. Chicago: University of Chicago Press, 1981.

T: (Wright 1968–78, 2:341)

R: Wright, Sewell. 1968–78. *Evolution and the genetics of populations*. 4 vols. Chicago: Univ. of Chicago Press.

17.85 *Citing a particular volume in a note.* If a particular volume of a multivolume work is cited, the volume number and the individual volume title, if there is one, are given in addition to the general title. If volumes have been published in different years, only the date of the cited volume is given.

N: 36. Muriel St. Clare Byrne, ed., *The Lisle Letters* (Chicago: University of Chicago Press, 1981), 4:243.
      37. Sewell Wright, *Evolution and the Genetics of Populations*, vol. 2, *Theory of Gene Frequencies* (Chicago: University of Chicago Press, 1969), 129.

The different treatment of the volume numbers in the examples above is prescribed by logic: all six volumes of the Byrne work appeared in 1981, whereas only volume 2 of the Wright work appeared in 1969.

17.86 *Citing a particular volume in a bibliography or reference list.* If only one volume of a multivolume work is of interest to readers, it may be listed alone in a bibliography or reference list in either of the following ways.

B: Pelikan, Jaroslav. *The Christian Tradition: A History of the Development of Doctrine*. Vol. 1, *The Emergence of the Catholic Tradition*. Chicago: University of Chicago Press, 1971.

T: (Wright 1969, 129)

R: Wright, Sewell. 1969. *Theory of gene frequencies*. Vol. 2 of *Evolution and the genetics of populations*. Chicago: Univ. of Chicago Press.

17.87 *Chapters and other parts of individual volumes.* Specific parts of individual volumes of multivolume books are cited in the same way as parts of single-volume books.

N: 38. "Buddhist Mythology," in *Mythologies*, ed. Yves Bonnefoy (Chicago: University of Chicago Press, 1991), 2:893–95.

A chapter number, if available, may replace page numbers; for example, "vol. 2, chap. 6."

17.88 *One volume in two or more books.* Occasionally, if it is very long, a single volume of a multivolume work may be published as two or more physical books. The reference must then include book as well as volume number.

N: 39. Donald Lach, *Asia in the Making of Europe*, vol. 2, bk. 3, *The Scholarly Disciplines* (Chicago: University of Chicago Press, 1977), 351.

B: Harley, J. B., and David Woodward, eds. *The History of Cartography*. Vol. 2, bk. 2, *Cartography in the Traditional East and Southeast Asian Societies*. Chicago: University of Chicago Press, 1994.

    or

    Harley, J. B., and David Woodward, eds. *Cartography in the Traditional East and Southeast Asian Societies*. Vol. 2, bk. 2, of *The History of Cartography*. Chicago: University of Chicago Press, 1994.

17.89 *Authors and editors of multivolume works.* Some multivolume works have both a general editor and individual editors or authors for each volume. When individual volumes are cited, the editor's or author's name follows that part for which he or she is responsible.

N: 40. Herbert Barrows, *Reading the Short Story*, vol. 1 of *An Introduction to Literature*, ed. Gordon N. Ray (Boston: Houghton Mifflin, 1959).
    41. *The Variorum Edition of the Poetry of John Donne*, ed. Gary A. Stringer, vol. 6, *The "Anniversaries" and the "Epicedes and Obsequies,"* ed. Gary A. Stringer and Ted-Larry Pebworth (Bloomington: Indiana University Press, 1995).
    42. *Orestes*, trans. William Arrowsmith, in *Euripides*, vol. 4 of *The Complete Greek Tragedies*, ed. David Grene and Richmond Lattimore (Chicago: University of Chicago Press, 1958), 185–288.

In a bibliography or reference list, the first name(s) or title listed should be the one most relevant to the work in which the entry appears. Note the different capitalization and punctuation of *edited by* in the following alternative versions, analogous to the treatment of a chapter in a multiauthor book (see 17.69). (Certain multivolume works may, for bibliographical purposes, more conveniently be treated as series; see 17.93.)

B: Donne, John. *The Variorum Edition of the Poetry of John Donne*. Edited by Gary A. Stringer. Vol. 6, *"The Anniversaries" and the "Epicedes and Obsequies,"* edited by Gary A. Stringer and Ted-Larry Pebworth. Bloomington: Indiana University Press, 1995.

    or

    Donne, John. *The "Anniversaries" and the "Epicedes and Obsequies."* Edited by Gary

A. Stringer and Ted-Larry Pebworth. Vol. 6 of *The Variorum Edition of the Poetry of John Donne*, edited by Gary A. Stringer. Bloomington: Indiana University Press, 1995.

T: (Ray 1959) *or* (Barrows 1959)

R: Ray, Gordon N., ed. 1959. *An introduction to literature.* Vol. 1, *Reading the short story*, by Herbert Barrows. Boston: Houghton Mifflin.

or

Barrows, Herbert. 1959. *Reading the short story.* Vol. 1 of *An introduction to literature*, ed. Gordon N. Ray. Boston: Houghton Mifflin.

SERIES

17.90 *Series titles, numbers, and editors.* The title of a series is capitalized headline style even in a reference list, but it is neither italicized nor put in quotation marks or parentheses. The series editor is usually omitted, but see 17.92–93. Some series are numbered; many are not. The number (if any) follows the series title with no intervening comma unless *vol.* or *no.* is used. These abbreviations may be omitted, however, unless both are needed in a single reference (see last example below). For a foreign-language series, use sentence style (see 10.3 and third example below).

N: 1. Gershon David Hundert, *The Jews in a Polish Private Town: The Case of Opatów in the Eighteenth Century*, Johns Hopkins Jewish Studies (Baltimore: Johns Hopkins University Press, 1992).

B: *The Cahokia Atlas: A Historical Atlas of Cahokia Archaeology.* Studies in Illinois Archaeology 6. Springfield: Illinois Historic Preservation Agency, 1989.
       Grenier, Roger. *Les larmes d'Ulysse.* Collection l'un et l'autre. Paris: Gallimard, 1998.

T: (Tulchin and Garland 2000)
       (Hopp 1977)
       (Wauchope 1950)

R: Hopp, Joachim. 1977. *Untersuchungen zur Geschichte der letzten Attaliden.* Vestigia: Beiträge zur alten Geschichte 25. Munich: C. H. Beck'sche Verlagsbuchhandlung.
       Tulchin, J. S., and A. M. Garland, eds. 2000. *Social development in Latin America: The politics of reform.* Woodrow Wilson Center Current Studies on Latin America. Boulder, CO: Lynne Rienner.

> Wauchope, Robert. 1950. *A tentative sequence of pre-Classic ceramics in Middle America*. Middle American Research Records, vol. 1, no. 14. New Orleans, LA: Tulane University.

17.91 *Whether to include series titles.* Including a series title in a citation often helps readers decide whether to pursue a reference. But if books belonging to a series can be located without the series title, it may be omitted to save space (especially in a footnote).

17.92 *Series editor.* The name of the series editor is usually omitted (see 17.90). When included, it follows the series title.

> R: Howell, M. C. 1998. *The marriage exchange: Property, social place, and gender in the cities of the Low Countries*. Women in Culture and Society, ed. C. R. Stimpson. Chicago: Univ. of Chicago Press.

17.93 *Series or multivolume work?* Certain works may be treated bibliographically either as multivolume works or as series of volumes, depending on whether the emphasis is on the group of books as a whole (as in the first two examples) or on single volumes (as in the second two).

> B: Boyer, John W., and Julius Kirshner, eds. *Readings in Western Civilization*. 9 vols. Chicago: University of Chicago Press, 1986–87.
> Grene, David, and Richmond Lattimore, eds. *The Complete Greek Tragedies*. Chicago: University of Chicago Press, 1942–58. Nine unnumbered volumes.
> Cochrane, Eric W., Charles K. Gray, and Mark Kishlansky. *Early Modern Europe: Crisis of Authority*. Readings in Western Civilization, edited by John W. Boyer and Julius Kirshner, 6. Chicago: University of Chicago Press, 1987.
> Euripides. *Orestes*. Translated by William Arrowsmith. In *Euripides IV*, edited by David Grene and Richmond Lattimore. The Complete Greek Tragedies. Chicago: University of Chicago Press, 1958.

17.94 *Multivolume work within a series.* If a book within a series consists of more than one volume, the number of volumes or the volume number (if reference is to a particular volume) follows the book title.

> B: Ferrer Benimeli, José Antonio. *Masonería, iglesia e illustración*. Vol. 1, *Las bases de un conflito (1700–1739)*. Vol. 2, *Inquisición: Procesos históricos (1739–1750)*. Publicaciones de la Fundación Universitaria Española, Monografías 17. Madrid, 1976.

17.95 *"Old series," "new series," and such.* Some numbered series have gone on so long that, as with certain long-lived journals, numbering has started over again, preceded by *n.s. (new series), 2nd ser. (second series),* or some similar notation, usually enclosed in commas. Books in the old series are identified by *o.s., 1st ser.,* or whatever fits.

N: 3. Charles R. Boxer, ed. *South China in the Sixteenth Century,* Hakluyt Society Publications, 2nd ser., 106 (London, 1953).

B: Palmatary, Helen C. *The Pottery of Marajó Island, Brazil.* Transactions of the American Philosophical Society, n.s., 39, pt. 3. Philadelphia, 1950.

FACTS OF PUBLICATION

17.96 *Place, publisher, and date.* Traditionally the facts of publication include the place (city), the publisher, and the date (year). These elements are put in parentheses in a note but not in a bibliography or reference list. A colon appears between place and publisher. In a note or a bibliography, the date follows the publisher, preceded by a comma. In a reference list, the date follows the author's name, preceded by a period. See also 16.10, 16.12.

N: 1. Ted Heller, *Slab Rat* (New York: Scribner, 2000).

B: Youngblood, Shay. *Black Girl in Paris.* New York: Riverhead Books, 2000.

R: Wilson, E. O. 1992. *The diversity of life.* New York: Norton.

17.97 *Place and date only.* Omitting the publisher's name is an acceptable practice, followed by many journals and preferred by many authors. It spares authors and editors the task of verifying publishers' past and present names and spellings, but it may deprive some readers of useful information. A comma, not a colon, follows the place. Even where publishers' names are given in most references, they may be omitted in books published in the nineteenth century or earlier, or where the publisher is not known. For more on place, see 17.99–102.

N: 2. Colin Harrison, *Afterburn* (New York, 2000).

B: Pittman, Philip. *The Present State of the European Settlements on the Mississippi; with a Geographical Description of That River.* London, 1770.

17.98 *Date only.* A less common practice (except in legal style; see 17.280) is to include only the date. This bare-bones practice is acceptable if neither place nor publisher is ascertainable or of particular value to readers. It is most commonly used for books published in the nineteenth century or earlier.

N: 3. Margaret Mitchell, *Gone with the Wind* (1936).

        4. Winston Churchill, *History of the English-Speaking Peoples* (1956–58).

B: Lamb, Charles. *Essays of Elia.* 1823.

17.99   *Place: city.* The place to be included is the one that usually appears on the title page but sometimes on the copyright page of the book cited—the city where the publisher's main editorial offices are located. Where two or more cities are given ("Chicago and London," for example, appears on the title page of this manual), only the first is normally included in the documentation.

New York: Macmillan, 1980

Los Angeles: J. Paul Getty Trust Publications

Oxford: Clarendon Press

New York: Oxford University Press

but

Berkeley and Los Angeles: University of California Press

17.100   *When to specify state, province, or country.* If the city of publication may be unknown to readers or may be confused with another city of the same name, the abbreviation of the state, province, or (sometimes) country is added. *Washington* is traditionally followed by *DC*, but other major cities, such as Los Angeles and Baltimore, need no state abbreviation. (For countries not easily abbreviated, spell out the name.) For the relevant abbreviations, including the older forms of state abbreviations (Ill., Mass., etc.), see 15.29–30.

Cheshire, CT: Graphics Press

Reading, MA: Perseus Books

Harmondsworth, UK: Penguin Books

Waterloo, ON: Wilfrid Laurier University Press

Washington, DC: Smithsonian Institution Press

Englewood Cliffs, NJ: Prentice Hall

Ithaca, NY: Cornell University Press

New Haven, CT: Yale University Press

Princeton, NJ: Princeton University Press

Cambridge, MA: MIT Press

Cambridge, MA: Harvard University Press

but

Cambridge: Cambridge University Press

Although the abbreviations may be unnecessary for some readers, they are useful for others and therefore worth including. When the publisher's name includes the state name, the abbreviation is not needed.

Chapel Hill: University of North Carolina Press

17.101 *Foreign city names.* Current, commonly used English names for foreign cities should be used.

Belgrade (not Beograd)	Munich (not München)	The Hague (not den Haag)
Cologne (not Köln)	Prague (not Praha)	Turin (not Torino)
Mexico City (not México)	Rome (not Roma)	Vienna (not Wien)
Milan (not Milano)		

17.102 *"No place."* When the place of publication is not known, the abbreviation *n.p.* (or *N.p.* if following a period) may be used before the publisher's name. If the place can be surmised, it may be given with a question mark, in brackets. See also 17.98.

(n.p.: Windsor, 1910)   ([Lake Bluff, IL?]: Vliet & Edwards, 1890)

A place of publication that is known but does not appear in the book may be given in the normal way or—though usually an unnecessary precaution—in brackets. When neither place nor date is known, *n.p., n.d.* may be used. See also 17.119.

17.103 *Publisher's name.* The publisher's name may be given either in full, as printed on the title page of the book, or in a somewhat abbreviated form. The shorter forms are preferred in most reference lists and many bibliographies. Publishers' names and the usual abbreviations for them are listed in such reference works as *Books in Print, Whitaker's Books in Print* (British publications), *Canadian Books in Print*, and *Australian Books in Print*, which can be found in many large libraries (see bibliog. 4.5). The use of full or shorter forms must be consistent throughout a bibliography, reference list, or set of notes.

17.104 *Abbreviations and omissible parts of a publisher's name.* Even when the full publisher's name is given, an initial *The* is omitted, as are such abbreviations as *Inc., Ltd*, or *S.A.* following a name. *Co., & Co., Publishing Co.*, and the like are often omitted. A given name or initials preceding a family name may be omitted. *Books* is usually retained (Basic Books, Riverhead Books). The word *Press* can sometimes be omitted (for example, Pergamon Press and Ecco Press can be abbreviated to Pergamon and Ecco, but

Free Press and New Press must be given in full). *Press* should not be omitted from the name of a university press because the university itself may issue publications independent of its press. The word *University* may be abbreviated to *Univ.* (especially in reference lists).

Houghton Mifflin *or* Houghton Mifflin Co.
Little, Brown *or* Little, Brown & Co.
Macmillan *or* Macmillan Publishing Co. (New York)
Macmillan *or* Macmillan Publishers (London)
Wiley or John Wiley

17.105 *Punctuation and spelling.* In the examples in 17.104, note that there is no comma in Houghton Mifflin, but there is one in Little, Brown. Harcourt, Brace has a comma, but Harcourt Brace Jovanovich does not. Macmillan has a lowercase *m* after the *Mac.* To ensure the correct form of publishers' names, past and present, writers and editors may search the Internet or refer to current and earlier editions of *Books in Print, Whitaker's Books in Print,* or *LMP (Literary Market Place)* (see bibliog. 4.5, 2.7).

17.106 *"And" or ampersand.* Either *and* or & may be used in a publisher's name, regardless of how it is rendered on the title page. It is advisable to stick to one or the other throughout a bibliography. Unless an ampersand is used in a foreign publisher's name, the foreign word for *and* must be used.

Harper and Row *or* Harper & Row
Duncker und Humblot *or* Duncker & Humblot

17.107 *Changes in publishers' names.* If the name of the publisher has changed since the book was published, the name on the title page is the one to use, not the current name. For reprint editions, see 17.123–27.

17.108 *Foreign publishers' names.* No part of a foreign publisher's name should be translated, even though the city has been given in its English form.

Paris: Presses Universitaires de France, 1982
Mexico City: Fondo de Cultura Económica, 1981
Munich: Delphin Verlag, 1983

Note that abbreviations corresponding to *Inc.* or *Ltd.* (German *GmbH,* for example) are omitted (see 17.104). Capitalization of a publisher's name should follow the original unless the name appears in full capitals there; in that case, it should be capitalized headline style.

17.109 *Publisher unknown.* When the publisher is unknown, use just the place (if known) and date (see 17.97). Privately printed works should be cited with as much information as is known (e.g., Topeka, KS: privately printed, 1890).

17.110 *Parent companies and such.* When a parent company's name appears on the title page in addition to the publisher's name, only the latter need be used in a bibliographical listing. For example, the title page of *The New York Times Manual of Style and Usage* (1999 edition) bears the imprint "Times Books"; below, in smaller type, appears "Random House." The spine carries "Times Books" (but not Random House), and the copyright page gives a New York address for Times Books. The work may therefore be listed as follows:

B: Siegal, Allan M., and William G. Connolly, eds. *The New York Times Manual of Style and Usage.* Rev. ed. New York: Times Books, 1999.

If it is not clear which name to list, both may appear in a bibliographic entry, separated by a slash (with a thin space either side). The smaller entity often precedes the larger, but either order is acceptable.

N: 12. Jorie Graham, *Swarm: Poems* (New York: Ecco Press / HarperCollins, 1999).

B: Dunn, Susan. *Sister Revolutions: French Lightning, American Light.* New York: Faber & Faber / Farrar, Straus & Giroux, 1999.

17.111 *Joint imprint.* For books published by a consortium, the name of the consortium may be followed by that of an individual member, the two names separated by a slash (with space either side).

B: Cohen, Naomi W. *Jacob H. Schiff: A Study in American Leadership.* Hanover, NH: University Press of New England / Brandeis University Press, 1999.

If the consortium as a whole rather than a partner is the publisher, its name stands alone.

Gaspar, Frank X. *Leaving Tico.* Hanover, NH: University Press of New England, 1999.

17.112 *Special imprint.* Some publishers issue certain books through a special publishing division or under a special imprint. In such instances the imprint may be given after the publisher's name, preceded by a comma.

B: Bonney, Orrin H., and Lorraine G. Bonney. *Guide to the Wyoming Mountains and Wilderness Areas*. 3rd ed. Athens: Ohio University Press, Swallow Press, 1977.

17.113   *Copublication.* When books are published simultaneously (or almost so) by two publishers, usually in different countries, only one publisher need be listed—the one that is more relevant to the users of the citation. For example, if a book copublished by a British and an American publisher is listed in the bibliography of an American publication, only the American publication details need be given. In certain contexts, however, both sets of details may be of interest to readers. For reprints, see 17.123–27.

N: 1. Marc Bloch, *Feudal Society*, trans. L. A. Manyon (Chicago: University of Chicago Press; London: Routledge and Kegan Paul, 1961).

B: Lévi-Strauss, Claude. *The Savage Mind*. Chicago: University of Chicago Press; London: Weidenfeld and Nicolson, 1962.

17.114   *Distributed books.* For a book published by one company and distributed by another, the name on the title page should be used. Since distribution agreements are sometimes impermanent, the distributor's name is best omitted unless essential to users of a bibliography.

B: Cane, Peter. *Atiyah's Accidents, Compensation and the Law*. 6th ed. Law-in-Context, 1999. Distributed by Northwestern University Press.

Wording on the title page such as "Published by arrangement with . . . ," if it is of particular interest, may be included in a similar manner.

17.115   *Publication date: general.* For books, only the year, not the month or day, is included in the publication date. The date is found on the title page or, more commonly, on the copyright page. It is usually identical to the copyright date. If two or more copyright dates appear in a book (as in this manual), the first being those of earlier editions or versions, the most recent indicates the publication date. Chicago's books normally carry both copyright date and publication date on the copyright page. For any edition other than the first, both the edition and the date of that edition must be included in a listing.

N: 56. *The Chicago Manual of Style*, 14th ed. (Chicago: University of Chicago Press, 1993), 15.170; cf. 13th ed. (1982), 16.88.

R: Turabian, Kate L. 1996. *A manual for writers of term papers, theses, and dissertations*. 6th ed. Rev. John Grossman and Alice Bennett. Chicago: Univ. of Chicago Press.

17.116 *New impressions and renewal of copyright.* The publication date must not be confused with the date of a subsequent printing or a renewal of copyright. Such statements on the copyright page as "53rd impression" or "Copyright renewed 1980 by ————" should be disregarded. For new editions as opposed to new impressions, see 1.19–22; for reprints, see 17.123–27.

17.117 *Two dates.* Copublished books occasionally appear in different calendar years—when, for example, a book published in Great Britain in November appears in the United States in February of the following year. Only if both dates are of interest to readers need both be included. See also 17.113, 17.126–27.

> N: 13. E. P. Thompson, *The Making of the English Working Class* (1963; New York: Pantheon, 1964), 12–13.

> R: Thompson, E. P. 1964. *The making of the English working class.* New York: Pantheon. (Published in UK in 1963.)

17.118 *Multivolume works published over several years.* When an entire multivolume work is cited, the range of dates is given. If the work has not yet been completed, the date of the first volume is followed by an en dash. If a single volume is cited, only the date of that volume need appear. See also 17.83–89.

> N: 78. *The Collected Works of F. A. Hayek* (Chicago: University of Chicago Press, 1988–).

> B: Tillich, Paul. *Systematic Theology.* 3 vols. Chicago: University of Chicago Press, 1951–63.

> R: Freeman, D. S. 1951. *George Washington,* vol. 3, *Planter and patriot.* New York: Scribner.

17.119 *"No date."* When the publication date of a printed work cannot be ascertained, the abbreviation *n.d.* takes the place of the year in the publication details. A guessed-at date may either be substituted (in brackets) or added. See also 17.102.

> Boston, n.d.   Edinburgh, [1750?] *or* Edinburgh, n.d., ca. 1750

In the author-date system, the bracketed date appears in the normal position.

> T: (Author [1750?])

R: Author, E. R. [1750?] *Title of work* . . .
  ——. n.d. *Title of another work* . . .

17.120 *No ascertainable information.* A work for which neither publisher, nor place, nor date can be determined or reasonably guessed at should be included in a bibliography only if accompanied by the location where a copy can be found (e.g., "Two copies in the Special Collections department of the University of Chicago Library"). See also 17.102.

17.121 *"Forthcoming."* When a book is under contract with a publisher and is already titled, but the date of publication is not yet known, *forthcoming* is used in place of the date. Although *in press* is sometimes used (strictly speaking for a printed work that has already been typeset and paginated), Chicago recommends the more inclusive term, which can also be used for nonprint media, for any work under contract. If page numbers are available, they should be given. Books not under contract are treated as unpublished manuscripts (see 17.211, 17.214).

N: 91. Jane Q. Author, *Book Title* (Place: Publisher, forthcoming).
  92. John J. Writer, *Another Book Title* (Place: Publisher, forthcoming), 345–46.

B: Contributor, Anna. "Contribution." In *Edited Volume*, ed. Ellen Editor. Place: Publisher, forthcoming.

T: (Researcher, forthcoming, 230)

R: Researcher, J. J. Forthcoming. New findings. In *Major symposium*, ed. F. F. Editor, 223–37. Place: Publisher.

Note that *forthcoming* is capitalized only in a reference list, where it follows a period. For forthcoming journal articles, see 17.167. Works cited as *forthcoming* follow other works by the same author.

17.122 *Use of "n.d." for forthcoming works.* In certain works documented by reference lists and text citations, it may sometimes be convenient—though the practice is frowned on by some—to use *n.d.* in place of a date that is not yet known. *Forthcoming* should then be added to the end of the reference-list entry. (Without this apparent redundancy, *n.d.* could be taken in its traditional sense; see 17.119.) If the source being cited is published while the new work is in manuscript or proof, the date can be substituted for *n.d.* and *forthcoming* can be dropped. To avoid conflation with an author's name, *n.d.* is lowercased.

T: (Author n.d.)

R: Author, Jane. n.d. *Book title.* Place: Publisher. Forthcoming.

        Author, J. Q. n.d. *Another book title.* Place: Publisher. Forthcoming.

REPRINT EDITIONS AND MODERN EDITIONS

17.123   *Citing in notes and bibliographies.* Books may be reissued in paperback by the original publisher or in paper or hardcover by another company. In bibliographic listings the original publication details—at least the date— are often the more relevant. If page numbers are mentioned, give the date of the edition cited unless pagination is the same. The availability of a paperback or an electronic version (see 17.144), the addition of new material, or other such matters can be added as needed. The examples below indicate various ways to present the data in notes and bibliographies. For the author-date system, see 17.124–27.

N: 22. Ernest Gowers, *The Complete Plain Words*, 3rd ed. (London: H.M. Stationery Office, 1986; Harmondsworth, UK: Penguin Books, 1987), 26. Citations are to the Penguin edition.

        23. Jacques Barzun, *Simple and Direct: A Rhetoric for Writers*, rev. ed. (1985; repr., Chicago: University of Chicago Press, 1994), 152–53.

B: Emerson, Ralph Waldo. *Nature.* 1836. A facsimile of the first edition with an introduction by Jaroslav Pelikan. Boston: Beacon, 1985.

        Fitzgerald, F. Scott. *The Great Gatsby.* New York: Scribner, 1925. Reprinted with preface and notes by Matthew J. Bruccoli. New York: Collier Books, 1992. Page references are to the 1992 edition.

        Bernhardt, Peter. *The Rose's Kiss: A Natural History of Flowers.* Chicago: University of Chicago Press, 2002. First published 1999 by Island Press.

        Schweitzer, Albert. *J. S. Bach.* Translated by Ernest Newman. 1911. Reprint, New York: Dover, 1966.

        National Reconnaissance Office. *The KH-4B Camera System.* Washington, DC: National Photographic Interpretation Center, 1967. Now declassified and also available online, http://www.fas.org/spp/military/program/imint/kh-4%20camera%20system.htm.

17.124   *Citing in the author-date system.* When citing a reprint or modern edition in the author-date system, the writer (or editor) must decide whether text citations should give the original date (see 17.125), the later date (see 17.126), or both (see 17.127). Context usually determines the choice, but as long as the reference list gives full details, most readers will be comfortable with any of the following practices.

17.125   *Author-date system: original date.* When the original date is of prime importance, it is given in the text citation and follows the author's name in the reference list. Any later dates appear with the publication details of the edition cited.

T: (Darwin 1859)

(Maitland 1898)

R: Darwin, Charles. 1859. *On the origin of species.* Facsimile of the 1st ed., with introd. by Ernest Mayr. Cambridge, MA: Harvard University Press, 1964.

Maitland, Frederic W. 1898. *Roman canon law in the Church of England.* Repr., Union, NJ: Lawbook Exchange, 1998.

17.126   *Author-date system: later date.* When the more recent date is of greater interest in a particular context, it is given in the text citation, follows the author's name in the reference-list entry, and determines placement in the list regardless of the original date (which may be added if needed).

T: (Trollope 1977)

(Trollope 1983)

R: Trollope, Anthony. 1977. *The Claverings.* New introd. by Norman Donaldson. New York: Dover. (Orig. pub. 1866–67.)

————. 1983. *He knew he was right.* 2 vols. in one. New York: Dover. (Orig. pub. 1869.)

17.127   *Author-date system: both dates.* If both the original date and the later date are required in the text citation, the two may be separated by a slash. The first date determines placement in the reference list.

T: (Maitland 1898/1998)

(Maitland 1909/1926)

R: Maitland, Frederic W. 1898/1998. *Roman canon law in the Church of England.* Repr. Union, NJ: Lawbook Exchange.

————. 1909/1926. *Equity, also the forms of action at common law: Two courses of lectures.* Ed. A. H. Chaytor et al. Repr. Cambridge: Cambridge Univ. Press.

More traditionally, the earlier date may be enclosed in brackets and still, as with the slash, determines placement in the reference list.

T: (Emerson [1836] 1985)

R: Emerson, Ralph Waldo. [1836] 1985. *Nature*. A facsimile of the first ed. with an introd. by Jaroslav Pelikan. Boston: Beacon.

PAGE, VOLUME, AND OTHER LOCATING INFORMATION

17.128   *General.* Further examples of the points discussed in this section may be found throughout this chapter and chapter 16.

17.129   *Arabic versus roman numerals.* Arabic numerals should be used wherever possible in documentation—for volumes, chapters, and other divisions— regardless of the way the numerals appear in the works cited, with the following exceptions: pages numbered with roman numerals in the original (usually in the front matter of a book) are given in lowercase roman numerals; and references to works with many and complex divisions may be easier to disentangle if a mixture of roman and arabic numerals is used.

N: 21. See the article "Feathers," in *Johnson's Universal Cyclopaedia*, rev. ed. (New York: A. J. Johnson, 1886), vol. 3.
       22. Jerome Kagan, "Introduction to the Tenth-Anniversary Edition," in *The Nature of the Child* (New York: Basic Books, 1994), xxii–xxiv.

17.130   *Ranges, or inclusive numbers.* For Chicago's preferred style in expressing a range of pages, paragraphs, or similar divisions, see 9.64. First and last numbers should be used rather than first number plus *ff.* (but see 17.131).

Chicago Manual of Style, 14th ed., 15.248–56.

17.131   *Using or avoiding "ff." and "passim."* Only when referring to a section for which no final number can usefully be given should *ff.* ("and the following pages, paragraphs, etc.") be resorted to. Instead of the singular *f.*, the subsequent number should be used (e.g., "140–41," *not* "140f."). Similarly, *passim* ("here and there") is to be discouraged unless there are more than three or four precise references. When used, *ff.* has no space between it and the preceding number and is followed by a period. *Passim*, being a complete word, takes no period. Neither is italicized in notes. (For *passim*, see 18.12.)

17.132   *Abbreviations.* In citations, the words *page*, *volume*, and the like are usually abbreviated and often simply omitted (see 17.133). The most commonly used abbreviations are *p.* (pl. *pp.*), *vol.*, *pt.*, *chap.*, *bk.*, *sec.*, *n.* (pl. *nn.*), *no.*, *app.*, and *fig.*; for others, see chapter 15. All are set in roman and, unless following a period, lowercased. None is italicized unless an integral part of an italicized book title. All the abbreviations mentioned in this paragraph, except for *p.* and *n.*, form their plurals by adding *s*.

A Cry of Absence, chap. 6   *A Dance to the Music of Time*, 4 vols.

17.133 *When to omit "p." and "pp."* When a number or a range of numbers clearly denotes the pages in a book, *p.* or *pp.* may be omitted (unless ambiguity would result); the numbers alone, preceded by a comma, are sufficient. (If an author has used *p.* and *pp.* consistently, however, there is no need to delete them.) See also 17.134.

Charlotte's Web, 75–76
but
Complete Poems of Michelangelo, p. 89, nos. 135–36

17.134 *When to omit "vol."* When a volume number is followed immediately by a page number, neither *vol.* nor *p.* or *pp.* is needed. The numbers alone are used, separated by a colon. No comma precedes the volume number unless required syntactically (as in the second example below). For usage in citing articles, see 7.162, 17.165. For more on volume numbers, see 17.83–88. For citing a particular volume, with and without the abbreviation *vol.*, see 17.85.

Bonnefoy, *Mythologies* 2:345
Grene and Lattimore, *Complete Greek Tragedies*, 4-vol. ed., 3:453

17.135 *Page and chapter numbers.* Page numbers, needed for specific references in notes and text citations, are usually unnecessary in bibliographies and reference lists except when the piece cited is a part within a whole (see 17.68–75) or a journal article (see 17.161, 17.168). If the chapter or other section number is given, page numbers may be omitted. The total page count of a book is not included in documentation. (Total page counts do, however, appear in headings to book reviews, catalog entries, and elsewhere. For book-review headings, see 1.156.)

N: 14. Claire Kehrwald Cook, "Mismanaged Numbers and References," in *Line by Line: How to Improve Your Own Writing* (Boston: Houghton Mifflin, 1985), 75–107.
      15. Nuala O'Faolain, *Are You Somebody? The Accidental Memoir of a Dublin Woman* (New York: Holt, 1996), chap. 17.

17.136 *Signatures.* Some books printed before 1800 did not carry page numbers, but each signature (a group of consecutive pages) bore a letter, numeral, or other symbol (its "signature") to help the binder gather them in correct sequence. In citing pages in books of this kind, the signature symbol is given first, then the number of the leaf within the signature, and finally *r* (*recto*, the front of the leaf) or *v* (*verso*, the back of the leaf). Thus, for example, G6v identifies one page, G6r–7v a range of four pages.

17.137 *Folios.* In some early books the signatures consisted of folios—one large sheet folded once. Each folio thus had two sheets, or four pages. The sheets were numbered only on the front, or recto, side. Page citation therefore consists of sheet number plus *r* (*recto*) or *v* (*verso*)—for example, 176r, 231v, 232r–v; or, if entire folios are cited, fol. 49, fols. 50–53. See also 17.136, 17.226.

17.138 *Lines.* The abbreviations *l.* (line) and *ll.* (lines) can too easily be confused with the numerals 1 and 11 and so should be avoided. *Line* or *lines* should be used or, where it has been made clear that reference is to lines, simply omitted (see 11.76).

N: 44. Ogden Nash, "Song for Ditherers," lines 1–4.

17.139 *Citing notes: form 1.* Notes are cited with the abbreviation *n* or *nn*. Form 1, the usage recommended for indexes (see 18.111–12), works equally well in citations. If the note cited is the only footnote on a particular page or is an unnumbered footnote, the page number is followed by *n* alone.

N: 45. Anthony Grafton, *The Footnote: A Curious History* (Cambridge, MA: Harvard University Press, 1997), 72n, 80n.

If there are other notes on the same page as the note cited, a number must be added. In this case the page number is followed by *n* or (if two or more consecutive notes are cited) *nn*, followed by the note number (or numbers or, in rare cases, an asterisk or other symbol). No intervening space or punctuation is required.

N: 46. Dwight Bolinger, *Language: The Loaded Weapon* (London: Longman, 1980), 192n23, 192n30, 199n14, 201nn16–17.
47. Richard Rorty, *Philosophical Papers* (New York: Cambridge University Press, 1991), 1:15n29.

17.140 *Citing notes: form 2.* In form 2 (more traditional but requiring more space) *n* alone, without a period, is used when no number follows, as in form 1 (see 17.139, first example). When followed by a number, however, the abbreviation *n.* or *nn.* is used (with a period), a word space intervening.

N: 48. Bolinger, *Language*, 200 n. 16, 201 nn. 12, 17.

          49. Rorty, *Philosophical Papers* 1:15 n. 29.

17.141   *Citing illustrations and tables.* The abbreviation *fig.* may be used for *figure*, but *table, map, plate*, and other illustration forms are spelled out. The page number, if given, precedes the illustration number, with a comma between them.

N: 50. Richard Sobel, *Public Opinion in U.S. Foreign Policy: The Controversy over Contra Aid* (Boston: Rowman and Littlefield, 1993), 87, table 5.3.

ELECTRONIC BOOKS

17.142   *General principles.* Many of the rules above for citing printed books apply to references to electronic books. Such information (about author, title, chapters or other titled parts of a book, edition, multivolume works, and so on), to the extent it can be determined, constitutes the permanent basis of any citation, whatever the medium. Electronic books, however, are more dynamic than printed works; their content and availability to readers may vary according to data format, and it is therefore important to indicate the medium consulted. At least for the time being, there is no need to indicate "paper" in a citation to a traditional bound book, but all other media should be indicated. A URL is sufficient to show that a book may be obtained from the Internet in a format compatible with standard browsers; in other cases, the name of the medium (e.g., CD-ROM, DVD) should be included.

17.143   *Books published online.* When citing a book that is available online—one that resides on the Internet and is intended to be read by standard browsers—include the URL as part of the citation. If the publisher or discipline requires it, or for especially time-sensitive data, also record in parentheses the date the material was last retrieved (see 17.12).

N: 1. J. Sirosh, R. Miikkulainen, and J. A. Bednar, "Self-Organization of Orientation Maps, Lateral Connections, and Dynamic Receptive Fields in the Primary Visual Cortex," in *Lateral Interactions in the Cortex: Structure and Function*, ed. J. Sirosh, R. Miikkulainen, and Y. Choe (Austin, TX: UTCS Neural Networks Research Group, 1996), http://www.cs.utexas.edu/users/nn/web-pubs/htmlbook96/ (accessed August 27, 2001).

          27. Sirosh, Miikkulainen, and Bednar, "Self-Organization of Orientation Maps."

B: Sirosh, J., R. Miikkulainen, and J. A. Bednar, "Self-Organization of Orientation Maps, Lateral Connections, and Dynamic Receptive Fields in the Primary

Visual Cortex." In *Lateral Interactions in the Cortex: Structure and Function*, ed. J. Sirosh, R. Miikkulainen, and Y. Choe. Austin, TX: UTCS Neural Networks Research Group, 1996. http://www.cs.utexas.edu/users/nn/web-pubs/ htmlbook96/ (accessed August 27, 2001).

T: (Sirosh, Miikkulainen, and Bednar 1996)

R: Sirosh, J., R. Miikkulainen, and J. A. Bednar. 1996. Self-organization of orientation maps, lateral connections, and dynamic receptive fields in the primary visual cortex. In *Lateral interactions in the cortex: Structure and function*, ed. J. Sirosh, R. Miikkulainen, and Y. Choe. Austin, TX: UTCS Neural Networks Research Group. http://www.cs.utexas.edu/users/nn/web-pubs/htmlbook96/ (accessed August 27, 2001).

Note that it is not sufficient simply to provide the URL; as far as they can be determined, the full facts of publication should be recorded. The URL is the fastest way to get a reader to the source; it is also the most vulnerable element of a citation. If the URL in the example above should become invalid, readers could presumably find the electronic text by conducting a search for the stated title and author—information that the syntax of a URL may not reveal.

17.144   *Books published in printed and electronic forms.* Always cite the source consulted (see 17.8). It is acceptable, however, to point out that a work is available in another form when doing so would be helpful to readers. In the example that follows, the print edition is cited and the book's availability in other media is noted.

B: Kurland, Philip B., and Ralph Lerner, eds. *The Founders' Constitution*. Chicago: University of Chicago Press, 1987. Also available online at http://press-pubs .uchicago.edu/founders/ and as a CD-ROM.

17.145   *Other electronic formats.* Non-Internet sources, typically those available for download or other delivery from a bookseller or library, should include an indication of the format (e.g., CD-ROM, Microsoft Reader e-book).

N: 1. Thomas H. Davenport and John C. Beck, *The Attention Economy: Understanding the New Currency of Business* (Harvard Business School Press, 2001), TK3 Reader e-book.

B: Hellman, Hal. *Great Feuds in Science: Ten of the Liveliest Disputes Ever*. New York: John Wiley, 1998. Rocket e-book.

R: Hicks, R. J. 1996. *Nuclear medicine, from the center of our universe*. Victoria, Austl.: ICE T Multimedia. CD-ROM.

17.146   *Electronic editions of older works.* Books that have fallen out of copyright are often available online. When citing these sources, authors should give as much of the standard publication information as they can, as discussed elsewhere in this chapter. Many of these works do not have traditional title and copyright pages, making it more difficult to determine publishers and dates. Keep in mind that it may not be possible to tell which edition was used to prepare the online text.

N: 1. Henry James, *The Ambassadors* (Project Gutenberg, 1996), bk. 6, chap. 1, ftp://ibiblio.org/pub/docs/books/gutenberg/etext96/ambas10.txt.

B: James, Henry. *The Ambassadors*. Project Gutenberg, 1996. ftp://ibiblio.org/pub/docs/books/gutenberg/etext96/ambas10.txt.

T: (James 1996, bk. 6, chap. 1)

R: James, Henry. 1996. *The ambassadors*. Project Gutenberg. ftp://ibiblio.org/pub/docs/books/gutenberg/etext96/ambas10.txt.

Note that there is no place of publication in this example. Such information is less likely to accompany online works, and it may be dispensed with without the use of "n.p." (for "no place") when it cannot be easily determined.

17.147   *Including older print publication date in citation.* Whenever possible, include the original facts of publication, or at least the date, when citing electronic editions of older works (see 17.124–27). In the example in 17.146, Project Gutenberg notes that their text is based on the 1909 New York edition of *The Ambassadors*. (When such information about a text is not available, consider consulting a different, more authoritative version.)

N: 1. Henry James, *The Ambassadors* (1909; Project Gutenberg, 1996), ftp://ibiblio.org/pub/docs/books/gutenberg/etext96/ambas10.txt.

It may make more sense to use the original date of publication as the primary date in author-date citations (see 17.125):

T: (James 1909) *or* (James 1909/1996) *or* (James [1909] 1996)

R: James, Henry. 1909. *The ambassadors*. Project Gutenberg, 1996. ftp://ibiblio.org/pub/docs/books/gutenberg/etext96/ambas10.txt.

or

James, Henry. 1909/1996. . . . *or* James, Henry. [1909] 1996. . . .

Periodicals

17.148 *Definition.* The word *periodical* is used here to include scholarly and professional journals, popular magazines, and newspapers—whether printed or online. Except for the addition of a URL, the form of citation to an online periodical is the same as that recommended for printed periodicals. Some publishers may also require access dates for sources consulted online; see examples of such information, and special considerations, under specific types of periodicals.

17.149 *Information to be included.* Citations to periodicals require some or all of the following data:

1. Author's or authors' name(s)
2. Title and subtitle of article or column
3. Title of periodical
4. Issue information (volume, issue number, date, etc.)
5. Page reference (where appropriate)
6. For online periodicals, a URL

Enough data must be furnished to allow readers to track down articles in libraries or other archives or databases. Indispensable for newspapers and most magazines is the specific date (month, day, and year). For journals, the volume or year and the month or issue number are required. Additional data make location easier.

17.150 *Journals versus magazines.* In this manual, *journal* is used for scholarly or professional periodicals available mainly by subscription (e.g., *Library Quarterly, Journal of the American Medical Association*). Journals are normally cited by volume and date (see 17.161). *Magazine* is used here for the kind of weekly or monthly periodical—professionally produced, sometimes specialized, but more accessible to general readers—that is available either by subscription or in individual issues at bookstores or newsstands (e.g., *Scientific American, Horticulture*). Magazines are normally cited by date alone (see 17.183). If in doubt whether a particular periodical is better treated as a journal or as a magazine, use journal form if the volume number is easily located, magazine form if it is not.

17.151 *Punctuation.* In notes, commas appear between author, title of article, and title of magazine, newspaper, or journal. In bibliographies and reference lists, periods replace these commas. For more examples, see 17.3 and elsewhere in this chapter. Note that *in* is *not* used between the article title and the journal title. (*In* is used only with chapters or other parts of books; see 17.68–69.)

> N: 1. Philip Kitcher, "Essence and Perfection," *Ethics* 110, no. 1 (1999): 60.

> B: Cook, Alison. "Phoenix Rising." *Gourmet*, April 2000, 62–64. A review of Restaurant Hapa.

> R: Calabrese, E. J., and L. A. Baldwin. 1999. Reevaluation of the fundamental dose-response relationship. *BioScience* 49:725–32.

17.152 *Page numbers.* In bibliographic and reference-list entries, the first and last pages of an article are given (for inclusive numbers, see 9.62, 9.64). In notes and text citations, only specific pages need be cited (unless the article as a whole is referred to).

17.153 *Flexibility and consistency.* On acceptable style variations, see 17.18.

JOURNALS

17.154 *Author's name.* Authors' names are normally given as they appear at the heads of their articles. Adjustments can be made, however, as indicated in 17.20. Most of the guidelines offered in 17.20–47 apply equally to authors of journal articles.

17.155 *Many authors.* For the treatment of four or more authors, see 17.29; for seven or more, see 17.30.

17.156 *Article title.* Titles of articles are set in roman (except for words or phrases that require italics, such as species names or book titles; see 17.157). In notes and bibliographies they are usually capitalized headline style and put in quotation marks; in reference lists they are usually capitalized sentence style, without quotation marks. As with a book, title and subtitle are separated by a colon, and the first word of the subtitle is always capitalized. (Subtitles and even titles of articles are omitted in some publications. This practice, though space saving, may deprive readers of useful information. But see 16.42–49. See also 8.164–87. For examples, see 17.3 and the paragraphs below.)

B: Morris, Romma Heillig. "Woman as Shaman: Reclaiming the Power to Heal." *Women's Studies: An Interdisciplinary Journal* 24 (September 1995): 573–84.

R: Terborgh, J. 1974. Preservation of natural diversity: The problem of extinction-prone species. *BioScience* 24:715–22.

17.157 *Italics and quotation marks within article titles.* Book titles and other normally italicized terms remain italicized within an article title. A term normally quoted is enclosed in single quotation marks in a note or a bibliography (since it is already within double quotation marks) but remains in double quotation marks in a reference list. See also 8.175, 8.187.

N: 23. Judith Lewis, "'Tis a Misfortune to Be a Great Ladie': Maternal Mortality in the British Aristocracy, 1558–1959," *Journal of British Studies* 37 (1998): 26–53.

B: Loften, Peter. "Reverberations between Wordplay and Swordplay in *Hamlet*." *Aeolian Studies* 2 (1989): 12–29.

R: Connell, A. D., and D. D. Airey. 1982. The chronic effects of fluoride on the estuarine amphipods *Grandidierella lutosa* and *G. lignorum*. *Water Research* 16:1313–17.
Loomis, C. C., Jr. 1960. Structure and sympathy in Joyce's "The dead." *PMLA* 75:149–51.

17.158 *Question marks or exclamation points.* As with book titles (see 17.61), an article title or subtitle ending with a question mark or an exclamation point is not followed by a comma or a period. See also 6.123.

R: Batson, C. Daniel. 1990. How social is the animal? The human capacity for caring. *American Psychologist* 45 (March): 336–46.

17.159 *Journal title.* Titles of journals are italicized and capitalized headline style in notes, bibliographies, and reference lists. They are usually given in full—except for the omission of an initial *The*—in notes and bibliographies (e.g., *Journal of Business*). With foreign-language journals and magazines, an initial article should be retained (e.g., *Der Spiegel*). Occasionally an initialism, such as *PMLA*, is the official title and is never spelled out. In reference lists, especially in scientific works, journal titles are often abbreviated (e.g., *Plant Syst Evol*), unless they consist of only one word (e.g., *Science, Mind*). Except for reference lists in journals, which prescribe their own style, it is never incorrect to spell out all journal titles.

17.160 *Standard abbreviations.* Any abbreviations used should follow the standard conventions, often without periods (e.g., *J* = *Journal*; *Assoc* = *Association*;

Psychol = *Psychology*), and should be understandable to the readers who use the bibliographic entries. *Periodical Title Abbreviations* (bibliog. 4.5) provides an authoritative list. Useful lists of standard abbreviations of frequently used words in journal names appear in *Scientific Style and Format* and the *American Medical Association Manual of Style* (bibliog. 1.1).

17.161 *Issue information: elements required.* Most journal citations include volume (see 17.162); issue number or month (see 17.163, 17.165); year (see 17.164, 17.166); and page numbers (see 17.168). Although not all these elements may be required to locate an article, furnishing them all provides a hedge against possible error in one or another of them. For example, if the year is incorrect or missing, the volume number will serve as a locator; if the issue number is incorrect, the page number(s) will locate the article, provided the pagination is continuous throughout a volume. Whether the data are inclusive or spare, consistency must be maintained.

17.162 *Volume.* The volume number follows the journal title without intervening punctuation and is not in italics. Arabic numerals are used even if the journal itself uses roman numerals. For space versus no space following a colon, see 17.169.

N: 2. Christopher S. Mackay, "Lactantius and the Succession to Diocletian," *Classical Philology* 94, no. 2 (1999): 205.

R: Emlen, S. T. 1997. When mothers prefer daughters over sons. *Trends in Ecology and Evolution* 12:291–92.

17.163 *Issue.* When the issue number is given, it follows the volume number, separated by a comma and preceded by *no.*

B: McMillen, Sally G. "Antebellum Southern Fathers and the Health Care of Children." *Journal of Southern History* 60, no. 3 (1994): 513–32.

In reference-list style, the issue number is often in parentheses. The issue number may be omitted, however, if pagination is continuous throughout a volume (but see 17.161). It is also unnecessary when a month or season precedes the year (see 17.164). See also 17.168.

R: Allison, G. W. 1999. The implications of experimental design for biodiversity manipulations. *American Naturalist* 153 (1): 26–45.
       Giraudeau, B., A. Mallet, and C. Chastang. 1996. Case influence on the intraclass correlation coefficient estimate. *Biometrics* 52:1492–97.

17.164 *Date.* The year, sometimes preceded by an exact date, a month, or a season, appears in parentheses after the volume number (or issue number, if given). Seasons, though not capitalized in running text (see 8.94), are traditionally capitalized when standing in lieu of a month or an issue number. Neither month nor season is necessary (though it is not incorrect to include one or the other) when the issue number is given (see 17.161).

B: White, Stephen A. "Callimachus Battiades (*Epigr.* 35)." *Classical Philology* 94 (April 1999): 168–81.
Wilson, George. "Again, Theory: On Speaker's Meaning, Linguistic Meaning, and the Meaning of a Text." *Critical Inquiry* 19 (Autumn 1992): 1–21.

R: Muldoon, D. D. 1987. Daily life of the mountain rapper. *Journal of the West* 26 (October): 14–20.

Where a span of months is given, use an en dash (e.g., March–April).

17.165 *No volume number.* When a journal uses issue numbers only, without volume numbers, a comma follows the journal title. See also 17.166.

B: Beattie, J. M. "The Pattern of Crime in England, 1660–1800." *Past and Present*, no. 62 (1974): 47–95.

R: Meyerovitch, Eva. 1959. The Gnostic manuscripts of Upper Egypt. *Diogenes*, no. 25:84–117.

17.166 *Year as volume number.* When the year itself serves as volume number, it is an indispensable element and should therefore not be enclosed in parentheses. A comma follows the journal title.

N: 3. I. G. Rozner, "The War of Liberation of the Ukrainian People in 1648–1654 and Russia" [in Russian], *Voprosy istorii*, 1979, no. 4:51–64.

B: Myers, N., and R. Tucker. "Deforestation in Central America: Spanish Legacy and North American Consumers." *Environmental Review*, Spring 1987, 55–71.

17.167 *Forthcoming works.* If an article has been accepted for publication by a journal but has not yet appeared, *forthcoming* stands in place of the year and the page numbers. Any article not yet accepted should be treated as an unpublished manuscript. See also 17.121–22.

N: 4. Margaret M. Author, "Article Title," *Journal Name* 98 (forthcoming).

B: Author, Margaret M. "Article Title." *Journal Name* 98 (forthcoming).

T: (Researcher and Assistant, forthcoming)

R: Researcher, A. A., and B. B. Assistant. Forthcoming. Article title. *Journal Name* 103.

17.168   *Page references.* In citations to a particular passage in a journal article, only the pages concerned are given. In references to the article as a whole (as in a bibliography or reference list), first and last pages are given.

N: 4. Paul Thompson, "Democracy and Popular Power in Beijing," *Radical America* 22 (September–October 1988): 22.

B: Gold, Ann Grodzins. "Grains of Truth: Shifting Hierarchies of Food and Grace in Three Rajasthani Tales." *History of Religions* 38, no. 2 (1998): 150–71.

T: (Ryan 1988, 890) *or* (Ryan 1988)

R: Ryan, M. J. 1988. Energy, calling, and selection. *Am Zool* 28:885–98.

Except with direct quotations, text citations in the natural and physical sciences often omit specific page numbers of journal articles. See also 17.181.

17.169   *Space versus no space after a colon.* When page numbers immediately follow a volume number (or occasionally an issue number), separated only by a colon, no space follows the colon. But when parenthetical information intervenes, a word space follows the colon. Compare the spacing in the examples below.

Social Networks 14:213–29   *Critical Inquiry* 19 (Autumn): 164–85
Diogenes, no. 25:84–117.   *American Naturalist* 153 (1): 59–72.

17.170   *Special issues.* A journal issue (occasionally a double issue) devoted to a single theme is known as a *special issue*. It carries the normal volume and issue number (or numbers if a double issue). Such an issue may have an editor and a title of its own. A special issue as a whole may be cited as in the second and third examples below; an article within the issue is cited as in the first example.

N: 67. Alice Conley, "Fifth-Grade Boys' Decisions about Participation in Sports Activities," in "Non-subject-matter Outcomes of Schooling," ed. Thomas L. Good, special issue, *Elementary School Journal* 99, no. 5 (1999): 131–46.

B: Good, Thomas L., ed. "Non-subject-matter Outcomes of Schooling." Special is-
     sue, *Elementary School Journal* 99, no. 5 (1999).

R: Whittington, D., et al., eds. 1991. A study of water vending and willingness to pay
     for water in Onitsha, Nigeria. Special issue, *World Development* 19, nos. 2–3.

17.171 *Supplements.* A journal supplement, unlike a special issue, is numbered
separately from the regular issues of the journal. Like a special issue, however, it may have a title and author or editor of its own.

B: Card, David. "Changes in Labor Force Attachment." *Journal of Political Economy*
     92, no. 3 (1999): S174–S199.

R: Wall, J. V. 1971. 2700 MHz observations of 4C radio sources in the declination
     zone +4 to –4. *Australian J. Phys. Astrophys.* Suppl. no. 20.

17.172 *Articles published in installments.* Articles published in parts over two or
more issues may be listed separately or in the same entry, depending on
whether the part or the whole is cited.

N: 68. George C. Brown, ed., "A Swedish Traveler in Early Wisconsin: The Obser-
     vations of Frederika Bremer," pt. 1, *Wisconsin Magazine of History* 61 (Summer
     1978): 312.
     69. Ibid., pt. 2, *Wisconsin Magazine of History* 62 (Autumn 1978): 50.

B: Brown, George C., ed. "A Swedish Traveler in Early Wisconsin: The Observations
     of Frederika Bremer." Pts. 1 and 2. *Wisconsin Magazine of History* 61 (Summer
     1978): 300–318; 62 (Autumn 1978): 41–56.

If installments appear in different years, a reference-list entry will require
a range of dates (e.g., 1978–79).

17.173 *Article appearing in two publications.* Chapters in books have sometimes begun their lives as journal articles, or vice versa. Revisions are often made
along the way. The version actually consulted should be cited in a note or
text citation, but annotation such as the following, if of specific interest to
readers, may follow the citation. See also 16.68.

Previously published in *Journal Title* 20, no. 3 (2005): 345–62.

A slightly revised version appears in *Book Title*, ed. E. Editor (Place: Publisher, 2004),
15–30.

17.174 *Place where journal is published.* If a journal might be confused with another with a similar title, or if it might not be known to the users of a bibliography, add the name of the place or institution where it is published in parentheses after the journal title.

N: 87. Diane-Dinh Kim Luu, "Diethylstilbestrol and Media Coverage of the 'Morning After' Pill," *Lost in Thought: Undergraduate Research Journal* (Indiana University South Bend) 2 (1999): 65–70.

B: Garrett, Marvin P. "Language and Design in *Pippa Passes.*" *Victorian Poetry* (West Virginia University) 13, no. 1 (1975): 47–60.

R: Bullock, D. J., H. M. Bury, and P. G. H. Evans. 1993. Foraging ecology in the lizard *Anolis oculatus* (Iguanidae) from Dominica, West Indies. *Journal of Zoology* (London) 230:19–30.

17.175 *Translated or edited article.* A translated or edited article follows essentially the same style as a translated or edited book (see 17.41–42).

N: . . . "Article Title," trans. So-and-So, *Journal Title* . . .

B: . . . "Article Title." Edited by So-and-So. *Journal Title* . . .

17.176 *Foreign-language articles and journals.* Titles of foreign-language articles, like book titles, are usually capitalized sentence style (see 8.166) but according to the conventions of the particular language (see 17.64). German, for example, capitalizes common nouns in running text as well as in titles (see 10.43). Journal titles may either be treated the same way or, if an author has done so consistently, be capitalized headline style. An initial definite article (*Le, Der,* etc.) should be retained, since it may govern the inflection of the following word. Months and the equivalents of such abbreviations as *no.* or *pt.* are given in English (but see 17.19).

N: 22. Gérard Bouchard, "Un essai d'anthropologie régionale: L'histoire sociale du Saguenay aux XIXe et XXe siècles," *Annales: Économies, sociétés, civilisations* 34 (January 1979): 118. (*or . . . Annales: Économies, Sociétés, Civilisations . . .*)
       23. Marcel Garaud, "Recherches sur les défrichements dans la Gâtine poitevine aux XIe et XIIe siècles," *Bulletin de la Société des antiquaires de l'Ouest*, 4th ser., 9 (1967): 11–27. (Note capitalization of *Société* [the first word of an organization name] and *Ouest* [the West].)

B: Broszat, Martin. "'Holocaust' und die Geschichtswissenschaft." *Vierteljahrshefte der Zeitgeschichte* 27 (April 1979): 285–98.

R: Alerić, Danijel. 1969. Ime zagrebačkoga biskupa u zadarskoj ispravi kralja Kolo-
    mana. *Slovo* 18–19:155–70.

    Schneider, B. 1975. Eine mittelpleistozäne Herpetofauna von der Insel Chios,
    Ägäis. *Senckenbergiana Biologica* 56:191–98.

17.177   *Translated article titles.* If an English translation is added to a foreign-
language article title, it is enclosed in brackets, without quotation marks,
and capitalized sentence style. If a title is given only in English translation,
however, the original language must be specified. See also 17.65, 17.67.

B: Kern, W. "Waar verzamelde Pigafetta zijn Maleise woorden?" [Where did Pigafetta
    collect his Malaysian words?] *Tijdschrift voor Indische taal-, land- en volkenkunde*
    78 (1938): 271–73.

R: Chu Ching and Long Zhi. 1983. The vicissitudes of the giant panda, *Ailuropoda
    melanoleuca* (David). [In Chinese.] *Acta Zoologica Sinica* 20 (1): 191–200.

17.178   *Volume series.* New series in journal volumes are identified by *n.s. (new series), 2nd ser.,* and so forth, as for books (see 17.95). Note the comma between the series identifier and the volume number.

N: 23. "Letter of Jonathan Sewall," *Proceedings of the Massachusetts Historical Soci-
    ety,* 2nd ser., 10 (January 1896): 414.

B: Moraes, G. M. "St. Francis Xavier, Apostolic Nuncio, 1542–52." *Journal of the Bom-
    bay Branch of the Royal Asiatic Society,* n.s., 26 (1950): 279–313.

Some institutions publish transactions in series representing different
subject areas. In the following example, *B* (not italicized) denotes Biological Series.

R: Conway, M. S. 1998. The evolution of diversity in ancient ecosystems: A review.
    Philosophical Transactions of the Royal Society B 353:327–45.

17.179   *Short titles.* In subsequent references to journal articles, the author's last
name and the main title of the article (often shortened) are most com-
monly used. In the absence of a full bibliography, however, the journal
title, volume number, and page number(s) may prove more helpful guides
to the source.

N: 24. Russell W. Belk and Janeen Arnold Costa, "The Mountain Man Myth: A Con-
    temporary Consuming Fantasy," *Journal of Consumer Research* 25, no. 3 (1998):
    218–40.

26. Belk and Costa, "Mountain Man Myth," 220.

or

26. Belk and Costa, *Journal of Consumer Research* 25:220.

ELECTRONIC JOURNALS

17.180 *General.* To cite electronic journals, follow the relevant examples presented above. In addition, add the URL and, if the publisher or discipline requires it, or for especially time-sensitive data, the date the material was last accessed (see 17.12).

17.181 *Pagination and examples.* The number ranges that appear in some of the following examples are those usually provided for articles in online journals that have parallel print versions. Many scholarly journals also make images of the printed page available online, so that citations to individual pages are possible. When citing an article, always include the page range, if it is available, in the bibliography or reference list. If individual page numbers are not available, add a descriptive locator (such as the subhead "The Consequences of Fear" in the examples below) to citations in text or in the notes if doing so will be helpful to readers. Page ranges generally should not be included in a note unless reference is to the article as a whole.

N: 1. M. Tornikoski and others, "Radio Spectra and Variability of Gigahertz-Peaked Spectrum Radio Sources and Candidates," *Astronomical Journal* 121, no. 3 (2001), http://www.journals.uchicago.edu/AJ/journal/issues/v121n3/200486/200486 .html.

5. Mark Warr and Christopher G. Ellison, "Rethinking Social Reactions to Crime: Personal and Altruistic Fear in Family Households," *American Journal of Sociology* 106, no. 3 (2000), under "The Consequences of Fear," http://www.journals .uchicago.edu/AJS/journal/issues/v106n3/050125/050125.html.

14. Bernard Testa and Lamont B. Kier, "Emergence and Dissolvence in the Self-Organisation of Complex Systems," *Entropy* 2, no. 1 (2000): 17, http://www.mdpi .org/entropy/papers/e2010001.pdf.

If an access date is required, include it parenthetically at the end of the citation:

33. Mark A. Hlatky et al., "Quality-of-Life and Depressive Symptoms in Postmenopausal Women after Receiving Hormone Therapy: Results from the Heart and Estrogen/Progestin Replacement Study (HERS) Trial," *Journal of the American*

Medical Association 287, no. 5 (2002), http://jama.ama-assn.org/issues/v287n5/rfull/joc10108.html#aainfo (accessed January 7, 2002).

B: Hlatky, Mark A., Derek Boothroyd, Eric Vittinghoff, Penny Sharp, and Mary A. Whooley. "Quality-of-Life and Depressive Symptoms in Postmenopausal Women after Receiving Hormone Therapy: Results from the Heart and Estrogen/Progestin Replacement Study (HERS) Trial." *Journal of the American Medical Association* 287, no. 5 (February 6, 2002). http://jama.ama-assn.org/issues/v287n5/rfull/joc10108.html#aainfo (accessed January 7, 2002).

Testa, Bernard, and Lamont B. Kier. "Emergence and Dissolvence in the Self-Organisation of Complex Systems." *Entropy* 2, no. 1 (March 2000): 1–25. http://www.mdpi.org/entropy/papers/e2010001.pdf.

Tornikoski, M., I. Jussila, P. Johansson, M. Lainela, and E. Valtaoja. "Radio Spectra and Variability of Gigahertz-Peaked Spectrum Radio Sources and Candidates." *Astronomical Journal* 121, no. 3 (March 2001): 1306–18. http://www.journals.uchicago.edu/AJ/journal/issues/v121n3/200486/200486.html.

Warr, Mark, and Christopher G. Ellison. "Rethinking Social Reactions to Crime: Personal and Altruistic Fear in Family Households." *American Journal of Sociology* 106, no. 3 (November 2000): 551–78. http://www.journals.uchicago.edu/AJS/journal/issues/v106n3/050125/050125.html.

T: (Hlatky et al. 2002)

(Testa and Lamont 2000, 17)

(Tornikoski et al. 2001)

(Warr and Ellison 2000, under "The Consequences of Fear")

R: Hlatky, M. A., D. Boothroyd, E. Vittinghoff, P. Sharp, and M. A. Whooley. 2002. Quality-of-life and depressive symptoms in postmenopausal women after receiving hormone therapy: Results from the Heart and Estrogen/Progestin Replacement Study (HERS) trial. *Journal of the American Medical Association* 287, no. 5 (February 6). http://jama.ama-assn.org/issues/v287n5/rfull/joc10108.html#aainfo (accessed January 7, 2002).

Testa, B., and L. B. Kier. 2000. Emergence and dissolvence in the self-organisation of complex systems. *Entropy* 2, no. 1 (March): 1–25. http://www.mdpi.org/entropy/papers/e2010001.pdf.

Tornikoski, M., I. Jussila, P. Johansson, M. Lainela, and E. Valtaoja. 2001. Radio spectra and variability of gigahertz-peaked spectrum radio sources and candidates. *Astronomical Journal* 121, no. 3 (March): 1306–18. http://www.journals.uchicago.edu/AJ/journal/issues/v121n3/200486/200486.html.

Warr, M., and C. G. Ellison. 2000. Rethinking social reactions to crime: Personal and altruistic fear in family households. *American Journal of Sociology* 106, no. 3 (November): 551–78. http://www.journals.uchicago.edu/AJS/journal/issues/v106n3/050125/050125.html.

If there is a digital object identifier (DOI) for the source (see 17.14), include it in place of page numbers or other locators:

N: 2. James W. Friedman and Claudio Mezzetti, "Learning in Games by Random Sampling," *Journal of Economic Theory* 98, no. 1 (May 2001), doi:10.1006/jeth.2000.2694, http://www.idealibrary.com/links/doi/10.1006/jeth.2000.2694.

MAGAZINES

17.182   *Definition.* For the use of *magazine* as against *journal,* see 17.150. Many of the guidelines for citing journals apply to magazines also. See also the guidelines for newspapers (17.188–98).

17.183   *Citing by date.* Weekly or monthly magazines, even if numbered by volume and issue, are usually cited by date only. The date, being an essential element in the citation, is not enclosed in parentheses (see 17.166). While a specific page number may be cited in a note, the inclusive page numbers of an article may be omitted, since they are often widely separated by extraneous material. When page numbers are included, a comma rather than a colon separates them from the date of issue.

N: 1. Stephen Lacey, "The New German Style," *Horticulture*, March 2000, 44.

17.184   *Headlines.* A headline or summary, rather than a formal article title, may be capitalized sentence style (see 8.166). See also 17.189.

N: 1. Tracy Metz, "Behnisch, Behnisch & Partner let the environmentalists at the IBN-DLO institute in Holland practice what they preach," *Architectural Record*, January 2000.

R: Ezzell, Carol. 2000. Care for a dying continent. *Scientific American*, May.

17.185   *Departments.* Titles of regular departments in a magazine are capitalized headline style but not put in quotation marks.

N: 2. The Talk of the Town, *New Yorker*, April 10, 2000, 31.
    3. Debra Klein, Focus on Travel, *Newsweek*, April 17, 2000.

B: Wallraff, Barbara. Word Court. *Atlantic Monthly*, April 2000.

A department without a named author is best cited by the name of the magazine.

B: *Gourmet.* Kitchen Notebook. May 2000.

T: (*Gourmet* 2000)

R: *Gourmet.* 2000. Kitchen Notebook. May.

17.186 *Form of date.* If a set of notes contains numerous references requiring specific dates, the day-month-year style, formerly recommended by this manual (see 6.46), will eliminate clutter.

N: 4. Molly O'Neill, Food, *New York Times Magazine*, 18 October 1998, 22 November 1998, 10 January 1999, 9 May 1999, 2 April 2000.

ONLINE MAGAZINES

17.187 *Information to include.* To cite online magazines, follow the relevant examples above. In addition, add a URL and, if the publisher or discipline requires it, or for especially time-sensitive data, the date the material was last accessed (see 17.12).

N: 1. Jessica Reaves, "A Weighty Issue: Ever-Fatter Kids," interview with James Rosen, *Time*, March 14, 2001, http://www.time.com/time/nation/article/0,8599,102443,00.html.

If an access date is required, include it parenthetically, at the end of the citation:

N: 7. Lawrence Osborne, "Poison Pen," review of *The Collaborator: The Trial and Execution of Robert Brasillach*, by Alice Kaplan, *Salon*, March 29, 2000, http://www.salon.com/books/it/2000/03/29/kaplan/index.html (accessed July 10, 2001).

B: Reaves, Jessica. "A Weighty Issue: Ever-Fatter Kids." Interview with James Rosen. *Time*, March 14, 2001. http://www.time.com/time/nation/article/0,8599,102443,00.html.
        Osborne, Lawrence. "Poison Pen." Review of *The Collaborator: The Trial and Execution of Robert Brasillach*, by Alice Kaplan. *Salon*, March 29, 2000. http://www.salon.com/books/it/2000/03/29/kaplan/index.html (accessed July 10, 2001).

T: (Reaves 2001)
        (Osborne 2000)

R: Reaves, Jessica. 2001. A weighty issue: Ever-fatter kids. Interview with James Rosen. *Time*, March 14. http://www.time.com/time/nation/article/0,8599,102443,00.html.

Osborne, Lawrence. 2000. Poison pen. Review of *The collaborator: The trial and execution of Robert Brasillach*, by Alice Kaplan. *Salon*, March 29, http://www.salon.com/books/it/2000/03/29/kaplan/index.html (accessed July 10, 2001).

Note that online articles will generally not carry page numbers; for article-length material, however, descriptive "locators" (see 16.14, 17.181) will rarely be necessary.

NEWSPAPERS

17.188 *Elements of the citation.* The name of the author (if known) and the headline or column heading in a daily newspaper are cited much like the corresponding elements in magazines (see 17.183–86). The month (often abbreviated), day, and year are the indispensable elements. Because a newspaper's *issue* of any given day may include several *editions*, and items may be moved or eliminated in various editions, page numbers are best omitted. In a note or bibliographical entry it may be useful to add "final edition," "Midwest edition," or some such identifier. If the paper is published in several sections, the section number or name may be given (see examples in 17.191). For papers published on the Internet, adding a URL will show that an online edition was consulted (see 17.198). For more on headlines, see 17.189.

N: 1. Editorial, *Philadelphia Inquirer*, July 30, 1990.

2. Mike Royko, "Next Time, Dan, Take Aim at Arnold," *Chicago Tribune*, September 23, 1992.

3. Obituary of Claire Trevor, *New York Times*, April 10, 2000, national edition.

4. "Pushcarts Evolve to Trendy Kiosks," *Lake Forester* (Lake Forest, IL), March 23, 2000.

17.189 *Headlines.* Whether to capitalize headlines "headline style" (see 8.167) or sentence style (8.166) depends not on the original headline cited but on the bibliographic style of the work in which the citation appears. Chicago has traditionally used headline style for citing headlines in notes and bibliographies. Since headlines are often grammatical sentences, however, sentence style works well for them—and is, indeed, used in the headlines of many major newspapers. In documentation, either style is acceptable if used consistently.

"Justices Limit Visiting Rights of Grandparents in Divided Case"

or

"Justices limit visiting rights of grandparents in divided case"

Full capitals in the original are always converted to upper- and lowercase in documentation. For quoting headlines in text rather than in documentation, see 7.50.

17.190 *Regular columns.* Many regular columns carry headlines as well as column titles. When such columns are cited, both may be used or, to save space, the column title alone.

N: 5. Gretchen Morgenson, "Applying a Discount to Good Earnings News," Market Watch, *New York Times*, sec. 3, April 23, 2000.

or

5. Gretchen Morgenson, Market Watch, *New York Times*, sec. 3, April 23, 2000.

17.191 *Citing in text.* Newspapers are more commonly cited in notes or parenthetical references than in bibliographies. A list of works cited need not list newspaper items if these have been documented in the text. No corresponding entry in a bibliography or reference list would be needed for the following citation:

In an article on rampage killers (*New York Times*, April 10, 2000), Laurie Goodstein and William Glaberson describe the warning signs either missed or unreported by colleagues, friends, teachers, family members, and others.

If, for some reason, a bibliographic entry were included, it would appear as follows:

B: Goodstein, Laurie, and William Glaberson. "The Well-Marked Roads to Homicidal Rage." *New York Times*, April 10, 2000, national edition, sec. 1.

17.192 *Unsigned articles.* Unsigned newspaper articles or features are best dealt with in text or notes. But if a bibliographic or reference-list entry should be needed, the name of the newspaper stands in place of the author.

B: *New York Times*, "In Texas, Ad Heats Up Race for Governor," July 30, 2002.

T: (*New York Times* 2002)

R: *New York Times*. 2002. In Texas, ad heats up race for governor. July 30.

17.193 *Letters to the editor.* Published letters to the editor are treated generically, without headlines.

N: 6. David Clemens, letter to the editor, *Wall Street Journal*, April 21, 2000.

17.194 *Weekend supplements, magazines, and the like.* Articles from Sunday supplements or other special sections are treated in the same way as material from magazines (see 17.183–86). They are usually dealt with in notes or parenthetical references rather than in bibliographies.

> N: 45. Bruce Barcott, review of *The Last Marlin: The Story of a Family at Sea*, by Fred Waitzkin, *New York Times Book Review*, April 16, 2000, 7.

17.195 *Names of newspapers.* An initial *The* is omitted (see 8.180). A city name, even if not part of the name of an American newspaper, should be added, italicized along with the official title. The name (usually abbreviated) of the state or, in the case of Canada, province may be added in parentheses if needed.

> *Chicago Tribune*   *Ottawa (IL) Daily Times*
> *Hackensack (NJ) Record*   *Saint Paul (Alberta or AB) Journal*

For such well-known national papers as the *Wall Street Journal* or the *Christian Science Monitor*, no city name is added.

17.196 *Names of foreign newspapers.* Names of cities not part of the titles of foreign newspapers may be added in parentheses after the title, not italicized. An initial *The* is omitted in English-language papers, but in foreign-language papers the article is retained if part of the name.

> *Frankfurter Zeitung*   *Guardian* (Manchester)
> *Times* (London)   *Le Monde*

17.197 *News services.* Names of news services, as opposed to newspapers, are capitalized but not italicized.

> the Associated Press (AP)   United Press International (UPI)

> N: 1. Associated Press, "Westchester Approves Measure on Gun Safety," *New York Times*, June 12, 2000.

17.198 *Online newspapers, news services, and other news sites.* Citations to online newspapers or news articles posted by news services are identical to their print counterparts, with the addition of a URL. If the publisher or discipline requires it, or for especially time-sensitive data (see 17.12), also add the date the material was last accessed, as shown in the first example.

N: 1. Alison Mitchell and Frank Bruni, "Scars Still Raw, Bush Clashes with Mc-
Cain," *New York Times*, March 25, 2001, http://www.nytimes.com/2001/03/25/
politics/25MCCA.html (accessed January 2, 2002).
        13. Richard Stenger, "Tiny Human-Borne Monitoring Device Sparks Privacy
Fears," *CNN.com*, December 20, 1999, http://www.cnn.com/1999/TECH/ptech/
12/20/implant.device/.

If a URL becomes invalid before publication of the work in which it is
cited, or if the article was obtained from an online archive for a fee, include
only the main entrance of the newspaper or news service (e.g., http://
www.nytimes.com/). Note that main entrance ("home page") and other
directory-level URLs end with a slash.

N: 33. Reuters, "Russian Blasts Kill 21, Injure More Than 140," *Yahoo! News*, March
24, 2001, http://dailynews.yahoo.com/.

B: Mitchell, Alison, and Frank Bruni. "Scars Still Raw, Bush Clashes with McCain."
        New York Times, March 25, 2001. http://www.nytimes.com/2001/03/25/
        politics/25MCCA.html (accessed January 2, 2002).
        Reuters. "Russian Blasts Kill 21, Injure More Than 140." *Yahoo! News*, March 24,
        2001. http://dailynews.yahoo.com/.
        Stenger, Richard. "Tiny Human-Borne Monitoring Device Sparks Privacy Fears."
        CNN.com, December 20, 1999. http://www.cnn.com/1999/TECH/ptech/12/
        20/implant.device/.

T: (Mitchell and Bruni 2001)
        (Reuters 2001)
        (Stenger 1999)

R: Mitchell, Alison, and Frank Bruni. 2001. Scars still raw, Bush clashes with McCain.
        New York Times, March 25. http://www.nytimes.com/2001/03/25/politics/
        25MCCA.html (accessed January 2, 2002).
        Reuters. 2001. Russian blasts kill 21, injure more than 140. *Yahoo! News*, March
        24. http://dailynews.yahoo.com/.
        Stenger, Richard. 1999. Tiny human-borne monitoring device sparks privacy fears.
        CNN.com, December 20. http://www.cnn.com/1999/TECH/ptech/12/20/
        implant.device/.

Online news articles generally will not carry page numbers; they are usually short, however, so descriptive "locators" (see 16.14, 17.181) will rarely
be necessary.

CITING REVIEWS

17.199   *Overview.* The following paragraphs are concerned only with *citing* reviews. For listing a title in the heading to a review, see 1.156.

17.200   *Elements of the citation.* In citations to reviews, the elements are given in the following order: name of reviewer if the review is signed; title of the review if any (a headline should be included only if needed for location); the words *review of,* followed by the name of the work reviewed and its author (or composer, or director, or whomever); location and date (in the case of a performance); and finally the listing of the periodical in which the review appeared. If a review is included in a bibliography or reference list, it is alphabetized by the name of the reviewer or, if unattributed, by *Review of.*

17.201   *Book reviews*

N: 1. Ben Ratliff, review of *The Mystery of Samba: Popular Music and National Identity in Brazil,* by Hermano Vianna, ed. and trans. John Charles Chasteen, *Lingua Franca* 9 (April 1999): B13–B14.

2. Thomas Fischer, review of *Color Encyclopedia of Ornamental Grasses,* by Rick Darke, *Horticulture,* May 2000.

B: Gibbard, Allan. "Morality in Living: Korsgaard's Kantian Lectures." Review of *The Sources of Normativity,* by Christine M. Korsgaard. *Ethics* 110, no. 1 (1999): 140–64.

T: (Boehnke 2000)

R: Boehnke, Michael. 2000. Review of *Analysis of human genetic linkage,* 3rd ed., by Jurg Ott. *Am J Hum Genet* 66:1725. http://www.journals.uchicago.edu/AJHG/journal/issues/v66n5/001700/001700.html.

17.202   *Reviews of plays, movies, television programs, concerts, and the like*

N: 3. Ben Brantley, review of *Our Lady of Sligo,* by Sebastian Barry, directed by Max Stafford-Clark, Irish Repertory Theater, New York, *New York Times,* April 21, 2000, Weekend section.

4. Jon Pareles, review of *Men Strike Back* (VH1 television), *New York Times,* April 18, 2000, Living Arts section.

5. Joe Morgenstern, review of *U-571,* directed by Jonathan Mostow, *Wall Street Journal,* April 21, 2000, Weekend Journal section.

B: Kozinn, Allan. Review of concert performance by Timothy Fain (violin) and Steven Beck (piano), 92nd Street Y, New York. *New York Times*, April 21, 2000, Weekend section.

R: Kauffman, Stanley. 1989. Review of *A dry white season* (MGM movie). *New Republic*, Oct. 9, 24–25.

17.203 *Unsigned reviews.* Unsigned reviews are treated similarly to unsigned articles (see 17.192).

N: 34. Unsigned review of *Geschichten der romanischen und germanischen Völker*, by Leopold von Ranke, *Ergänzungsblätter zur Allgemeinen Literatur-Zeitung*, February 1828, nos. 23–24.

Interviews and Personal Communications

17.204 *First element of citation.* In whatever form interviews or personal communications exist—published, broadcast, preserved in audiovisual form, available online—the citation normally begins with the name of the person interviewed or the person from whom the communication was received. The interviewer or recipient, if mentioned, comes second.

FORMAL INTERVIEWS

17.205 *Unpublished interviews.* Unpublished interviews are best cited in text or in notes, though they occasionally appear in bibliographies or reference lists. Citations should include the names of both the person interviewed and the interviewer; brief identifying information, if appropriate; the place or date of the interview (or both, if known); and, if a transcript or tape is available, where it may be found. Permission to quote may be needed; see chapter 4.

N: 7. Andrew Macmillan (principal adviser, Investment Center Division, FAO), in discussion with the author, September 1998.
      8. Benjamin Spock, interview by Milton J. E. Senn, November 20, 1974, interview 67A, transcript, Senn Oral History Collection, National Library of Medicine, Bethesda, MD.
      9. Macmillan, discussion; Spock, interview.

R: Hunt, Horace [pseud.]. 1976. Interview by Ronald Schatz. Tape recording. May 16.
       Pennsylvania Historical and Museum Commission, Harrisburg.

17.206 *Unattributed interviews.* An interview with a person who prefers to remain anonymous or whose name the author does not wish to reveal may be cited in whatever form is appropriate in context. The absence of a name should be explained (e.g., "All interviews were conducted in confidentiality, and the names of interviewees are withheld by mutual agreement").

N: 10. Interview with health care worker, August 10, 1999.

17.207 *Published or broadcast interviews.* An interview that has already been published or broadcast is treated like an article in a periodical or a chapter in a book.

N: 10. McGeorge Bundy, interview by Robert MacNeil, *MacNeil/Lehrer NewsHour*,
       PBS, February 7, 1990.

B: Bellour, Raymond. "Alternation, Segmentation, Hypnosis: Interview with Ray-
       mond Bellour." By Janet Bergstrom. *Camera Obscura*, nos. 3–4 (Summer 1979):
       89–94.

If an interview is included or excerpted in the form of a direct quotation within an article or chapter by the interviewer, the interviewer's name may come first.

N: 11. Michael Fortun and Kim Fortun, "Making Space, Speaking Truth: The Insti-
       tute for Policy Studies, 1963–1995" (includes an interview with Marcus Raskin
       and Richard Barnet), in *Corporate Futures*, ed. George E. Marcus, Late Editions 5
       (Chicago: University of Chicago Press, 1998), 257.

PERSONAL COMMUNICATIONS

17.208 *Citing in text or in a note.* References to conversations (whether face-to-face or by telephone) or to letters, e-mail messages, and the like received by the author are usually run into the text or given in a note. They are rarely listed in a bibliography or reference list. For references to electronic lists, see 17.236. See also 11.3.

In a telephone conversation with the author on October 12, 1999, Colonel William Rich
revealed that . . .

N: 2. Constance Conlon, e-mail message to author, April 17, 2000.

An e-mail address belonging to an individual should be omitted. Should it be needed in a specific context, it must be cited only with the permission of its owner. (Note also that e-mail addresses change frequently.) For breaking an e-mail address at the end of a line, see 7.44.

17.209 *Personal communications, unpublished data, and such.* In a parenthetical citation, the terms *personal communication* (or *pers. comm.*), *unpublished data*, and the like are used after the name(s) of the person(s) concerned, following a comma. Reference-list entries are unneeded. The abbreviation *et al.* should be avoided in such citations.

> T: (H. J. Brody, pers. comm.)
>
> (E. Simpkins, S. Warren, M. Turck, and S. Gorbach, unpublished data)

Unpublished and Informally Published Material

17.210 *Use of parentheses in notes.* In note citations to *published* material, parentheses are generally used to enclose information that is useful but not essential to tracking down a source. The publication details of a book, for example, are not needed for finding the work in a library catalog or other listing by author and title. For the *unpublished* material discussed in the following paragraphs, however, the material in parentheses is essential.

17.211 *"Unpublished" material online.* More and more material that once would have gone unpublished is apt to be "posted" on the Internet, and such material is then technically considered published. Many of the recommendations for citing "unpublished material" will apply to such "informally published" material, but see 17.234–37 for special considerations and additional categories.

17.212 *Other material.* For letters, memoranda, and the like, see 17.208–9. For archived collections of letters and other manuscript material, see 17.222–33.

17.213 *Title.* The title of an unpublished work—whether book, thesis, speech, essay, or whatever—is not italicized. In notes and bibliographies it is capitalized headline style and put in quotation marks; in reference lists it is capitalized sentence style, with no quotation marks.

> N: 23. David Hanson, "The Provenance of the Ruskin-Allen Letters" (computer printout, Department of English, Southeastern University, 2001), 16.

17.214 *Theses and dissertations.* The kind of thesis, the academic institution, and the date follow the title. Like the publication data of a book, these are enclosed in parentheses in a note but not in a bibliography or reference list. The word *unpublished* is unnecessary. For dissertations issued on microfilm, see 17.242. For published abstracts of dissertations, see 17.245.

N: 1. Dorothy Ross, "The Irish-Catholic Immigrant, 1880–1900: A Study in Social Mobility" (master's thesis, Columbia University, n.d.), 142–55.

B: Murphy, Priscilla Coit. "What a Book Can Do: *Silent Spring* and Media-Borne Public Debate." PhD diss., University of North Carolina, 2000.

R: Schwarz, G. J. 2000. Multiwavelength analyses of classical carbon-oxygen novae (outbursts, binary stars). PhD diss., Arizona State Univ.

17.215 *Lectures, papers presented at meetings, and the like.* The sponsorship, location, and date of the meeting at which a speech was given or a paper presented follow the title. This information, like that following a thesis title, is put in parentheses in a note but not in a bibliography or reference list.

N: 2. Stacy D'Erasmo, "The Craft and Career of Writing" (lecture, Northwestern University, Evanston, IL, April 26, 2000).

B: Nass, Clifford. "Why Researchers Treat On-Line Journals Like Real People." Keynote address, annual meeting of the Council of Science Editors, San Antonio, TX, May 6–9, 2000.

R: O'Guinn, T. C. 1987. Touching greatness: Some aspects of star worship in contemporary consumption. Paper presented at the annual meeting of the American Psychological Association, New York.

A paper included in the published proceedings of a meeting may be treated like a chapter in a book (see 17.68–71). If published in a journal, it is treated as an article (see 17.154–81).

17.216 *Poster papers.* Papers presented at poster sessions are treated like other unpublished papers.

R: Ferguson, Carolyn J., and Barbara A. Schaal. 1999. Phylogeography of *Phlox pilosa* subsp. *ozarkana*. Poster presented at the 16th International Botanical Congress, St. Louis.

17.217 *Working papers and other unpublished works.* Most unpublished papers can be treated in much the same way as the material presented in 17.214–15.

> N: 3. Deborah D. Lucki and Richard W. Pollay, "Content Analyses of Advertising: A Review of the Literature" (working paper, History of Advertising Archives, Faculty of Commerce, University of British Columbia, Vancouver, 1980).

> R: Ferber, R. 1971. Family decision-making and economic behavior. Faculty Working Paper 35, College of Commerce and Business Administration, Univ. of Illinois at Urbana-Champaign.

In the second example above the term *working paper* is part of a formal series title, therefore capitalized (see 17.90–95). It is sometimes useful to add *photocopy* or some other term to indicate the form in which an unpublished document exists.

> B: Alarcón, Salvador Florencio de. "Compendio de las noticias correspondientes a el real y minas San Francisco de Aziz de Río Chico . . . de 20 de octubre [1771]." Photocopy, Department of Geography, University of California, Berkeley.

17.218 *Preprints.* Not being subject to peer review, preprints are treated as unpublished material.

> R: Lockwood, G. W., and B. A. Skiff. 1988. Air Force Geophys. Lab., preprint (AFGL-TR-88-0221).

17.219 *Patents.* Patents are cited under the names of the creators and dated by the year of filing.

> R: Petroff, M. D., and M. G. Stapelbroek. 1980. Blocked impurity band detectors. US Patent 4,586,960, filed Oct. 23, 1980, and issued Feb. 4, 1986.

17.220 *Private contracts, wills, and such.* Private documents are occasionally cited in notes but rarely in bibliographies. More appropriately they are referred to in text (e.g., "George J. Wilson, in his will dated January 20, 1976, directed . . .") or in notes. Capitalization is usually a matter of editorial discretion.

> N: 4. Samuel Henshaw, will dated June 5, 1806, proved July 5, 1809, no. 46, box 70, Hampshire County Registry of Probate, Northampton, MA.
>
>   5. Agreement to teach in the Publishing Program of the Graham School, University of Chicago, signed by Jane Doe, May 29, 2004.

17.221 *Other materials.* For letters, memoranda, and the like, see 17.208–9. For archived collections of letters and other manuscript material, see 17.222–33.

MANUSCRIPT COLLECTIONS

17.222 *General.* The *Guide to the National Archives of the United States* (bibliog. 4.5) offers the following excellent advice: "The most convenient citation for archives is one similar to that used for personal papers and other historical manuscripts. Full identification of most unpublished material usually requires giving the title and date of the item, series title (if applicable), name of the collection, and name of the depository. Except for placing the cited item first [in a note], there is no general agreement on the sequence of the remaining elements in the citation. . . . Whatever sequence is adopted, however, should be used consistently throughout the same work" (761).

17.223 *Note forms versus bibliographic entries.* In a note, the main element of a manuscript citation is usually a specific item (a letter, a memorandum, or whatever) and is thus cited first. In a bibliography, the main element is usually the collection in which the specific item may be found, the author(s) of the items in the collection, or the depository for the collection. Collections, authors, and depositories are therefore entered in alphabetical order. Specific items are not included in a bibliography unless only one item from a collection is cited.

> N: 38. James Oglethorpe to the Trustees, 13 January 1733, Phillipps Collection of Egmont Manuscripts, 14200:13, University of Georgia Library.
>
> 39. Alvin Johnson, memorandum, 1937, file 36, Horace Kallen Papers, YIVO Institute, New York.
>
> 40. Revere's Waste and Memoranda Book (vol. 1, 1761–83; vol. 2, 1783–97), Revere Family Papers, Massachusetts Historical Society, Boston.

> B: Egmont Manuscripts. Phillipps Collection. University of Georgia Library.
>
> Kallen, Horace. Papers. YIVO Institute, New York.
>
> Revere Family Papers, Massachusetts Historical Society, Boston.

For more examples, see 17.230–31. For citing manuscript collections in author-date style, see 17.233.

17.224 *Specific versus generic titles.* In notes and bibliographies, quotation marks are used only for specific titles (e.g., "Canoeing through Northern Minnesota"), but not for generic names such as *report* or *minutes*. Generic names of this kind are capitalized if part of a formal heading actually appearing on the manuscript, lowercased if merely descriptive. Compare 17.230, note examples 46–49.

17.225 *Dates.* Names of months may be spelled out or abbreviated, as long as done consistently. If there are many references to specific dates, as in a collection of letters or diaries, the day-month-year form (8 May 1945), used in some of the examples below, will reduce clutter. See also 6.46.

17.226 *Folios, page numbers, and such.* Older manuscripts are usually numbered by signatures only or by folios (*fol., fols.*) rather than by page (see 17.135–37). More recent ones usually carry page numbers; if needed, the abbreviations *p.* and *pp.* should be used to avoid ambiguity. Some manuscript collections have identifying series or file numbers, which may be included in a citation.

17.227 *Papers and manuscripts.* In titles of manuscript collections the terms *papers* and *manuscripts* are synonymous. Both are acceptable, as are the abbreviations *MS* and (pl.) *MSS.* If it is necessary to distinguish a typescript or computer printout from a handwritten document, the abbreviation *TS* may be used.

17.228 *Depositories.* The location (city and state) of such well-known depositories as major university libraries is rarely necessary (see examples in 17.230).

University of Chicago Library   Oberlin College Library

17.229 *Letters and the like.* A note citation to a letter starts with the name of the letter writer, followed by *to*, followed by the name of the recipient. Given names may be omitted if the identities of sender and recipient are clear from the text. (Identifying material may be added if appropriate; see 17.205.) The word *letter* is usually omitted—that is, understood—but other forms of communication (telegram, memorandum) are specified. If such other forms occur frequently in the same collection, it may be helpful to specify letters also. For capitalization and the use of quotation marks, see 17.224. For letters and the like not in formal collections, see 17.208–9, 17.232. For date form, see 6.46, 9.35.

17.230 *Examples of note forms*

40. George Creel to Colonel House, 25 September 1918. Edward M. House Papers, Yale University Library.

41. James Oglethorpe to the Trustees, 13 January 1733, Phillipps Collection of Egmont Manuscripts, 14200:13, University of Georgia Library (hereafter cited as Egmont MSS).

42. Burton to Merriam, telegram, 26 January 1923, Charles E. Merriam Papers, University of Chicago Library.

43. Minutes of the Committee for Improving the Condition of Free Blacks, Pennsylvania Abolition Society, 1790–1803, Papers of the Pennsylvania Society for the Abolition of Slavery, Historical Society of Pennsylvania, Philadelphia (hereafter cited as Minutes, Pennsylvania Society).

44. Hiram Johnson to John Callan O'Laughlin, 13 and 16 July 1916, 28 November 1916, O'Laughlin Papers, Roosevelt Memorial Collection, Harvard College Library.

45. Memorandum by Alvin Johnson, 1937, file 36, Horace Kallen Papers, YIVO Institute, New York.

46. Undated correspondence between French Strother and Edward Lowry, container 1-G/961 600, Herbert Hoover Presidential Library, West Branch, Iowa.

47. Memorandum, "Concerning a Court of Arbitration," n.d., Philander C. Knox Papers, Manuscripts Division, Library of Congress.

48. Joseph Purcell, "A Map of the Southern Indian District of North America" [ca. 1772], MS 228, Ayer Collection, Newberry Library, Chicago.

49. Louis Agassiz, Report to the Committee of Overseers . . . [28 December 1859], Overseers Reports, Professional Series, vol. 2, Harvard University Archives, Cambridge, MA.

50. Gilbert McMicken to Alexander Morris, 29 November 1881, Glasgow (Scotland), Document 1359, fol. 1r, Alexander Morris Papers, MG-12-84, Provincial Archives of Manitoba, Winnipeg.

The content of subsequent citations (*short forms*) will vary according to the proximity of the earlier notes, the use of abbreviations, and other factors. Absolute consistency may occasionally be sacrificed to readers' convenience.

51. R. S. Baker to House, 1 November 1919, House Papers.

52. Thomas Causton to his wife, 12 March 1733, Egmont MSS, 14200:53.

53. Minutes, 15 April 1795, Pennsylvania Society.

17.231 *Examples of bibliographic entries.* The style of the first six examples below is appropriate if more than one item from a collection is cited in the text or notes. In the second and third examples, commas are added after the initials to avoid misreading. See also 17.223.

Egmont Manuscripts. Phillipps Collection. University of Georgia Library.

House, Edward M., Papers. Yale University Library.

Merriam, Charles E., Papers. University of Chicago Library.

Pennsylvania Society for the Abolition of Slavery. Papers. Historical Society of Pennsylvania, Philadelphia.

Strother, French, and Edward Lowry. Undated correspondence. Herbert Hoover Presidential Library, West Branch, Iowa.

Women's Organization for National Prohibition Reform Papers. Alice Belin du Pont files, Pierre S. du Pont Papers. Eleutherian Mills Historical Library, Wilmington, DE.

If only one item from a collection has been mentioned in text or in a note and is considered important enough to include in a bibliography, the entry will begin with the item.

Dinkel, Joseph. Description of Louis Agassiz written at the request of Elizabeth Cary Agassiz. Agassiz Papers. Houghton Library, Harvard University.

17.232 *Letters and the like in private collections.* Letters, memoranda, and such that have not been archived may be cited like other unpublished material. Information on the depository is replaced by such wording as "in the author's possession" or "private collection," and the location is not mentioned.

17.233 *Author-date style.* Manuscript collections are rarely cited in author-date style. When they are, however, the date is usually mentioned in text, outside the parentheses, since most collections contain items from various dates.

Oglethorpe wrote to the trustees on January 13, 1733 (Egmont Manuscripts), to say . . .

Alvin Johnson, in a memorandum prepared sometime in 1937 (Kallen Papers, file 36), observed that . . .

R: Egmont Manuscripts. Phillipps Collection. University of Georgia Library.
Kallen, Horace. Papers. YIVO Institute, New York.

If only one item from a collection has been mentioned in text, the entry may begin with the writer's name (if known).

T: (Dinkel n.d.)

R: Dinkel, Joseph. n.d. Description of Louis Agassiz written at the request of Elizabeth Cary Agassiz. Agassiz Papers. Houghton Library, Harvard University.

INFORMALLY PUBLISHED
ELECTRONIC MATERIAL

17.234 *Lack of standard publishing information.* One of the most valuable roles the Internet plays is in the rapid sharing of information. This information is often posted without clear indication of authorship, title, publisher, or date—that is, without standard facts of publication.

17.235 *URL plus descriptive phrase.* If no facts of publication, or very few, can be determined, it is still necessary to include information beyond the URL. If only a URL is cited and that URL changes or becomes obsolete, the citation will have become just a more or less unintelligible string of characters. The URL tells *where* a source is or at least was located; a complete citation must also indicate *what* a source is.

17.236 *Electronic mailing lists.* To cite material from an electronic mailing list that has been archived online, include the name of the list, the date of the individual posting, and the URL. Also record an access date, if the publisher or discipline requires it. Citations to such material should generally be limited to text and notes.

Charges of a Microsoft monopoly don't change the fact that software is still highly specialized, even theirs. Microsoft Word wouldn't win any awards for its drawing tools, but its editing tools are formidable. According to John Powell, one might choose Word just for its pattern-matching capabilities.[17] But would anyone choose Word to *produce* their publication?

N: 17. John Powell, e-mail to Grapevine mailing list, April 23, 1998, http://www .electriceditors.net/grapevine/issues/83.txt.

Material that has not been archived will not have an associated URL:

N: 17. John Powell, e-mail to Grapevine mailing list, April 23, 1998.

17.237 *Site content.* For original content from online sources other than periodicals, include as much of the following as can be determined: author of the content, title of the page, title or owner of the site, URL. Citations of site content are best relegated to notes; in works with no notes, they may be included in the reference list or bibliography. For the addition of access dates, see 17.12, 17.187.

N: 14. Evanston Public Library Board of Trustees, "Evanston Public Library Strategic Plan, 2000–2010: A Decade of Outreach," Evanston Public Library, http:// www.epl.org/library/strategic-plan-00.html (accessed July 18, 2002).

B: Evanston Public Library Board of Trustees. "Evanston Public Library Strategic Plan, 2000–2010: A Decade of Outreach." Evanston Public Library. http://www .epl.org/library/strategic-plan-00.html.

If there is no author per se, the owner of the site may stand in for the author.

N: 19. The Bahá'ís of the United States, "History," *The Bahá'í Faith*, http://www .us.bahai.org/history/index.html.
25. Federation of American Scientists, "Resolution Comparison: Reading License Plates and Headlines," http://www.fas.org/irp/imint/resolve5.htm.

B: The Bahá'ís of the United States. "History." *The Bahá'í Faith*. http://www.us.bahai .org/history/index.html.

T: (Federation of American Scientists)

R: Federation of American Scientists. Resolution comparison: Reading license plates and headlines. http://www.fas.org/irp/imint/resolve5.htm.

For content from very informal sites, such as personal home pages and fan sites, where titles may be lacking, descriptive phrases may be used.

N: 1. Camp Taconic Alumni, 1955 photo gallery, http://www.taconicalumni.org/ 1955.html.
4. Pete Townshend's official Web site, "Biography," http://www.petetownshend .co.uk/petet_bio.html.

If a site ceases to exist before publication, as did the site in note 4 above, include such information parenthetically at the end of the citation, separated from the access date, if any, by a semicolon.

N: 4. Pete Townshend's official Web site, "Biography," http://www.petetownshend .co.uk/petet_bio.html (accessed December 15, 2001; site now discontinued).

Special Types of References

17.238 *Reference works.* Well-known reference books, such as major dictionaries and encyclopedias, are normally cited in notes rather than in bibliographies. The facts of publication are often omitted, but the edition (if not the first) must be specified. References to an alphabetically arranged work cite the item (not the volume or page number) preceded by *s.v.* (*sub verbo*, "under the word"; pl. *s.vv.*)

N: 1. *Encyclopaedia Britannica*, 15th ed., s.v. "Salvation."
      2. *Dictionary of American Biography*, s.v. "Wadsworth, Jeremiah."

Certain reference works, however, may appropriately be listed with their publication details.

N: 3. *The Times Guide to English Style and Usage*, rev. ed., comp. Tim Austin (London: Times Books, 1999), s.vv. "police ranks," "postal addresses."
      4. *MLA Style Manual and Guide to Scholarly Publishing*, 2nd ed., ed. Joseph Gibaldi (New York: Modern Language Association of America, 1998), 6.9.4.

B: *Diccionario de historia de Venezuela*. 3 vols. Caracas: Fundación Polar, 1988.

R: Filippelli, R. L., ed. 1990. *Labor conflict in the United States: An encyclopedia*. Garland Reference Library of Social Science 697. New York: Garland.
      Garner, Bryan A. 2003. *Garner's modern American usage*. New York: Oxford University Press.

17.239 *Reference works online.* Online versions of encyclopedias are subject to continuous updates and should therefore be considered databases rather than standard reference works with standard edition numbers. For this reason, Chicago recommends always including an access date in addition to the URL. Though the version of the article accessed on a given date may not be the one available to a reader at a later date, an access date will at least indicate the timeliness of the source citation. Well-known online reference works, such as major dictionaries and encyclopedias, are normally cited, like their printed counterparts, in notes rather than in bibliographies. The facts of publication are often omitted. Note that some reference works will indicate the appropriate URL to cite for a specific entry; use this rather than the less stable URL generated by search engines.

N: 1. *Encyclopaedia Britannica Online*, s.v. "Sibelius, Jean," http://search.eb.com/bol/topic?eu=69347&sctn=1 (accessed January 3, 2002).

Sometimes it may be appropriate to include the author of an entry.

      2. *The New Grove Dictionary of Music and Musicians*, s.v. "Sibelius, Jean" (by James Hepokoski), http://www.grovemusic.com/ (accessed January 3, 2002).

17.240 *Exhibition catalogs.* An exhibition catalog is often published as a book and is treated as such.

B: *Mary Cassatt: Modern Woman.* Edited by Judith A. Barter. Chicago: Art Institute of Chicago, in association with Harry N. Abrams, 1998. Published in conjunction with the exhibition "Mary Cassatt: Modern Woman" shown at the Boston Museum of Fine Arts, the National Gallery in Washington, DC, and the Art Institute of Chicago.

       or, if space is tight,

       . . . with Harry N. Abrams, 1998. An exhibition catalog.

A brochure—the kind often handed to visitors to an exhibition—may be treated similarly.

17.241   *Pamphlets, reports, and the like.* Pamphlets, corporate reports, brochures, and other freestanding publications are treated essentially as books. Data on author and publisher may not fit the normal pattern, but sufficient information should be given to identify the document. For special issues of journals, see 17.170.

N: 34. Hazel V. Clark, *Mesopotamia: Between Two Rivers* (Mesopotamia, OH: End of the Commons General Store, [1957?]).

       35. *Lifestyles in Retirement*, Library Series (New York: TIAA-CREF, 1996).

       36. Merrill Lynch Advisory Services Group, *Merrill Lynch Consults Service*, Disclosure Statement, April 2000.

17.242   *Microform editions.* Works issued commercially in microform editions, including dissertations, are treated much like books. The form of publication, where needed, is given after the facts of publication. (In the first example below, the page number is to the printed text; the other numbers indicate the fiche and frame, and the letter indicates the row.)

N: 5. Beatrice Farwell, *French Popular Lithographic Imagery*, vol. 12, *Lithography in Art and Commerce* (Chicago: University of Chicago Press, 1995), text-fiche, p. 67, 3C12.

B: Tauber, Abraham. *Spelling Reform in the United States.* Ann Arbor, MI: University Microfilms, 1958.

Microform or other photographic processes used only to preserve printed material need not be mentioned in a citation. The source is treated as it would be in its published version.

17.243   *Loose-leaf services.* Documentation of material obtained through loose-leaf services is handled like that of books.

N: 13. Commerce Clearing House, *1990 Standard Federal Tax Reports* (Chicago: Commerce Clearing House, 1990), ¶20,050.15.

17.244 *News release.* A news release, though published in a sense, is treated like an unpublished document. For sentence-style versus headline-style capitalization, see 17.189.

N: 6. National Transportation Safety Board, "Airline fatalities for 1994 climbed to five-year high," news release, January 19, 1995.

17.245 *Abstract.* An abstract is treated like a journal article, but the word *abstract* must be added.

R: Lovejoy, C. O. 1979. A reconstruction of the pelvis of A1-288 (Hadar Formation, Ethiopia). Abstract. *Am J Phys Anthropol* 40:460.

In citing a published abstract of an unpublished dissertation, give details of the original as well as of the abstract.

R: Schwarz, G. J. 2000. Multiwavelength analyses of classical carbon-oxygen novae (outbursts, binary stars). PhD diss., Arizona State Univ., 1999. Abstract in *Dissertation Abstracts International*, publ. nr. AAT9937424, DAI-B 60/07 (Jan. 2000): 3327.

SCRIPTURAL REFERENCES

17.246 *Stylebook.* Any scholarly writer or editor working extensively with biblical material should consult *The SBL Handbook of Style* (bibliog. 1.1), which offers excellent advice and numerous abbreviations.

17.247 *Chapter and verse.* References to the Jewish or Christian scriptures usually appear in text citations or notes rather than in bibliographies. Parenthetical or note references to the Bible should include book (in roman and usually abbreviated), chapter, and verse—never a page number. A colon is used between chapter and verse. Note that the traditional abbreviations use periods but the shorter forms do not. For guidance on when to abbreviate and when not to, see 15.48–49. For full forms and abbreviations, see 15.50–53.

Traditional abbreviations:

N: 4. 1 Thess. 4:11, 5:2–5, 5:14.

T: (Heb. 13:8, 13:12)
        (Gen. 25:19–36:43)

Shorter abbreviations:

N: 5. 2 Sm 11:1–17, 11:26–27; 1 Chr 10:13–14.

T: (Jo 5:9–12)
        (Mt 26:2–5)

17.248 *Versions of the Bible.* Since books and numbering are not identical in different versions, it is essential to identify which version is being cited. For a work intended for general readers, the version should be spelled out, at least on first occurrence. For specialists, abbreviations may be used throughout. For abbreviations of versions, see 15.54.

N: 6. 2 Kings 11:8 (New Revised Standard Version).
        7. 1 Cor. 6:1–10 (NRSV).

17.249 *Other sacred works.* References to the sacred and revered works of other religious traditions may, according to context, be treated in a similar manner to biblical or classical references. The Qur'an is set in roman, and citations to its sections use arabic numerals and colons (e.g., Qur'an 19:17–21). Such collective terms as the Vedas or the Upanishads are normally capitalized and set in roman, but particular parts are italicized (e.g., the *Rig-Veda* or the *Brihad-Aranyaka Upanishad*). For authoritative usage, consult *History of Religions,* an international journal for comparative historical studies (bibliog. 5).

CLASSICAL GREEK AND LATIN REFERENCES

17.250 *Where to cite.* Classical primary source references are ordinarily given in text or notes. They are included in a bibliography only when the reference is to information or annotation supplied by a modern author (see 17.254, 17.259).

The eighty days of inactivity reported by Thucydides (8.44.4) for the Peloponnesian fleet at Rhodes, terminating before the end of Thucydides' winter (8.60.2–3), suggests . . .

17.251 *Identifying numbers.* The numbers identifying the various parts of classical works—books, sections, lines, and so on—remain the same in all editions, whether in the original language or in translation. (In poetry, line content may vary slightly from the original in some translations.) Arabic numerals are used. Where letters also are used, they are usually lower-cased but may be capitalized if the source being cited uses capitals. Page numbers are omitted except in references to introductions, notes, and the like supplied by a modern editor or to specific translations. See also 17.253, 17.258.

> 3. Ovid *Amores* 1.7.27.
> 4. Aristotle *Metaphysics* 3.2.996b5–8; Plato *Republic* 360e–361b.

17.252 *Abbreviations.* Abbreviations of authors' names as well as of works, collections, and so forth are used extensively in classical references. The most widely accepted standard for abbreviations is the list included in the *Oxford Classical Dictionary* (bibliog. 5). When abbreviations are used, these rather than *ibid.* should be used in succeeding references to the same work. (Abbreviations are best avoided when only two letters are omitted, and they must not be used when more than one writer could be meant—Hipponax or Hipparchus, Aristotle or Aristophanes.)

> 1. Thuc. 2.40.2–3.
> 2. Pindar *Isthm.* 7.43–45.

17.253 *Punctuation.* No punctuation intervenes between classical author and title of work, or between title and number, but a comma follows the author in references to specific editions (see 17.254, 17.259). Numerical divisions are separated by periods with no space following each period. Commas are used between two or more references to the same source, semicolons between references to different sources, and en dashes between continuing numbers. If such abbreviations as *bk.* or *sec.* are needed for clarity, commas separate the different elements.

> 5. Aristophanes *Frogs* 1019–30.
> 6. Cic. *Verr.* 1.3.21, 2.3.120; Caes. *B Gall.* 6.19; Tac. *Germ.* 10.2–3.
> 7. Sappho *Invocation to Aphrodite*, st. 1, lines 1–6.

17.254 *Editions.* Details of the edition used, along with translator (if any) and the facts of publication, should be specified the first time a classical work is cited or given elsewhere in the scholarly apparatus. If several editions are used, the edition (or an abbreviation) should accompany each citation. Although many classicists will recognize a well-known edition merely from the last name of the editor or translator, a full citation, at least in the bibliography, should be furnished as a courtesy.

8. Epictetus, *Dissertationes*, ed. Heinrich Schenkl (Stuttgart: Teubner, 1916).
9. Herodotus, *The History*, trans. David Grene (Chicago: University of Chicago Press, 1987).
10. Solon (Edmonds's numbering) 36.20–27.

17.255 *Titles.* Titles of works and published collections are italicized whether given in full or abbreviated (see 17.252). Latin and transliterated Greek titles are capitalized sentence style (see 8.166, 10.2, 10.60).

11. Cato's uses of *pater familias* in *Agr.* (2.1, 2.7, 3.1, 3.2) are exclusively in reference to estate management. For the *diligens pater familias* in Columella, see *Rust.* 1.1.3, 1.2.1, 5.6.37, 9.1.6, 12.21.6.
12. *Scholia graeca in Homeri Odysseam*, ed. Wilhelm Dindorf (Oxford, 1855; repr. 1962).
13. *Patrologiae cursus completus, series graeca* (Paris: Migne, 1857–66).

17.256 *Superscripts.* In classical references, a superior figure is sometimes used immediately after the title of a work (or its abbreviation), and preceding any other punctuation, to indicate the number of the edition.

14. Stolz-Schmalz *Lat. Gram.*[5] (rev. Leumann-Hoffmann; Munich, 1928), 390–91.
15. *Ausgewählte Komödien des T. M. Plautus*[2], vol. 2 (1883).

In former practice, the letters accompanying numerals in citations to classical works (see 17.251) sometimes appeared as superscripts (e.g., 3.2.996[b]5–8).

17.257 *Collections of inscriptions.* Arabic numerals are now used in references to volumes in collections of inscriptions. Periods follow the volume and inscription numbers, and further subdivisions are treated as in other classical references.

16. *IG* 2[2].3274. [= *Inscriptiones graecae*, vol. 2, 2nd ed., inscription no. 3274]
17. *IG Rom.* 3.739.9.10. [*IG Rom.* = *Inscriptiones graecae ad res romanas pertinentes*]
18. *POxy.* 1485. [= *Oxyrhynchus papyri*, document no. 1485]

Some collections are cited only by the name of the editor. Since the editor's name here stands in place of a title, no comma is needed.

19. Dessau 6964.23–29. [= H. Dessau, ed., *Inscriptiones latinae selectae*]

17.258 *Fragments.* Fragments of classical texts (some only recently discovered) are not uniformly numbered. They are published in collections, and the numbering is usually unique to a particular edition. Two numbers separated by a period usually indicate fragment and line. The editor's name, often abbreviated in subsequent references, must therefore follow the number.

> 20. Empedocles frag. 115 Diels-Kranz.
> 21. Anacreon frag. 2.10 Diehl.
> 22. Hesiod frag. 239.1 Merkelbach and West.
> 23. Anacreon frag. 5.2 D.
> 24. Hesiod frag. 220 M.-W.

In citations to two or more editions of the same set of fragments, either parentheses or an equals sign may be used.

> 25. Pindar frag. 133 Bergk (frag. 127 Bowra).
>
> *or*
>
> 26. Pindar frag. 133 Bergk = 127 Bowra.

17.259 *Modern editions of the classics.* When Greek, Latin, or medieval classics are cited by page number, the edition must be specified, and the normal rules for citing books are followed. See also 17.254.

> N: 35. Propertius, *Elegies*, ed. and trans. G. P. Goold, Loeb Classical Library 18 (Cambridge, MA: Harvard University Press, 1990), 45.
>
> B: Aristotle. *Complete Works of Aristotle: The Revised Oxford Translation.* Edited by J. Barnes. 2 vols. Bollingen Series. Princeton, NJ: Princeton University Press, 1983.
>
> T: (Maimonides 1965, 74)
>
> R: Maimonides. 1965. *The code of Maimonides, book 5: The book of holiness.* Trans. and ed. L. I. Rabinowitz and P. Grossman. New Haven, CT: Yale Univ. Press.

17.260 *Medieval references.* The form for classical references may equally well be applied to medieval works.

> N: 27. Augustine *De civitate Dei* 20.2.
> 28. Augustine, *The City of God*, trans. John Healey (New York: Dutton, 1931), 20.2.
> 29. *Beowulf*, lines 2401–7.
> 30. Abelard *Epistle 17 to Heloïse* (Migne *PL* 180.375c–378a).
> 31. *Sir Gawain and the Green Knight*, trans. Theodore Silverstein (Chicago: University of Chicago Press, 1974), pt. 3, p. 57.

CLASSIC ENGLISH POEMS AND PLAYS

17.261 *When to cite edition.* Classic English poems and plays can often be cited by book, canto, and stanza; stanza and line; act, scene, and line; or similar divisions. Publication facts can then be omitted. For frequently cited works—especially those of Shakespeare, where variations can occur in wording, line numbering, and even scene division—the edition is normally specified in the first note reference or in the bibliography. The edition must be mentioned if page numbers are cited (see 17.259).

N: 1. Chaucer, "Wife of Bath's Prologue," *Canterbury Tales*, fragment 3, lines 105–14.

2. Spenser, *The Faerie Queene*, bk. 2, canto 8, st. 14.

3. Milton, *Paradise Lost*, bk. 1, lines 83–86.

4. *King Lear*, ed. David Bevington et al. (New York: Bantam Books, 1988), 3.2.49–60. References are to act, scene, and line.

B: Shakespeare, William. *Hamlet*. Arden edition. Edited by Harold Jenkins. London: Methuen, 1982.

T: (Dryden 1912)

R: Dryden, John. 1912. *Dramatic essays*. Everyman's Library. New York: Dutton.

17.262 *Short forms.* A citation may be shortened by omitting *act, line*, and the like, as long as the system used has been explained. Arabic numerals are used, separated by periods. In immediately succeeding references, it is usually safer to repeat all the numbers. The author's name may be omitted if clear from the text. For citing sources in text, see 11.75–76, 16.39–40.

N: 5. Pope, *Rape of the Lock*, 3.28–29.

6. *Lear* (Bevington), 4.1.1–9, 4.1.18–24. (*or, if space is tight*, 4.1.1–9, 18–24)

7. "Wife of Bath's Prologue," 115–16.

Musical Scores

17.263 *Published scores.* Published musical scores are treated in much the same way as books.

N: 1. Giuseppe Verdi, *Il corsaro* (*melodramma tragico* in three acts), libretto by Francesco Maria Piave, ed. Elizabeth Hudson, 2 vols., The Works of Giuseppe

Verdi, ser. 1, Operas (Chicago: University of Chicago Press; Milan: G. Ricordi, 1998).

B: Mozart, Wolfgang Amadeus. *Sonatas and Fantasies for the Piano.* Prepared from the autographs and earliest printed sources by Nathan Broder. Rev. ed. Bryn Mawr, PA: Theodore Presser, 1960.

Schubert, Franz. "Das Wandern (Wandering)," *Die schöne Müllerin (The Maid of the Mill).* In *First Vocal Album* (for high voice). New York: G. Schirmer, 1895.

In the last example above, the words and titles are given in both German and English in the score itself. See also 17.65.

17.264   *Unpublished scores.* Unpublished scores are treated in the same way as other unpublished material in manuscript collections (see 17.222–33).

N: 2. Ralph Shapey, "Partita for Violin and Thirteen Players," score, 1966, Special Collections, Joseph Regenstein Library, University of Chicago.

Audiovisual Materials

17.265   *Form of citation.* Only note and bibliography (or discography) forms are illustrated in the following paragraphs, since the author-date system is inappropriate for most audiovisual materials. In a work using the author-date system, such materials are best mentioned in running text and grouped in the reference list under a subhead such as "Sound Recordings."

17.266   *Elements to include.* Documentation of a recording usually includes some or all of the following pieces of information: the name of the composer, writer, performer, or other person primarily responsible for the content; the title, in italics; the name of the recording company or publisher; the identifying number of the recording; and the medium (compact disc, audiocassette, audiovisual file, etc.). The copyright date or date of production (or both), the number of discs in an album, the URL and size of an audiovisual file, and other information may also be given.

17.267   *Discographies.* Discographies are lists of audiovisual materials such as audio recordings, video recordings, and multimedia packages. For advice on discographies, see Suzanne E. Thorin and Carole Franklin Vidall, *The Acquisition and Cataloging of Music and Sound Recordings* (bibliog. 5). For an example, see figure 16.16.

SOUND RECORDINGS

17.268 *Music.* For the typographic treatment of musical compositions in running text, see 8.201–5. Those guidelines, however, do not necessarily apply to recordings when listed in a discography (see fig. 16.16), bibliography, or note. *Symphony* or *sonata,* for example, is capitalized when part of the title of a recording. Note too that the name of the conductor or performer, if the focus of the recording or more relevant to the discussion than that of the composer, may be listed first. The symbol ℗ means published.

N: 1. *The Fireside Treasury of Folk Songs,* vol. 1, orchestra and chorus dir. Mitch Miller, Golden Record A198:17A–B, 33 rpm.

2. The New York Trumpet Ensemble, with Edward Carroll (trumpet) and Edward Brewer (organ), *Art of the Trumpet,* compact disc, Vox/Turnabout, PVT 7183, ℗ and © 1982 The Moss Music Group.

3. Beethoven, *Piano Sonata no. 29 "Hammerklavier,"* Peter Serkin, Proarte Digital CDD 270.

4. Janet Baker, *Schubert Songs,* EMI CDC 7 47861 2.

B: Anderson, Doug. *Frostwork.* OAR 1001, Dolby HX PRO. Audiocassette.

Weingartner, Felix von. *150 Jahre Wiener Philharmoniker.* Preiser Records, PR90113. ℗ 1992 by Preiser Records. (Includes Beethoven symphonies nos. 3 and 8.)

Mozart, Wolfgang Amadeus. *Le nozze di Figaro.* Vienna Philharmonic. Riccardo Muti. With Thomas Allen, Margaret Price, Jorma Hynninen, Ann Murray, Kurt Rydl, and the Konzertvereinigung Wiener Staatsopernchor. ℗ 1987. Original sound recording made by EMI Records Ltd. CDS 7 47978 8 (3 compact discs).

Bernstein, Leonard, dir. *Symphony no. 5,* by Dmitri Shostakovich. New York Philharmonic. CBS IM 35854.

Recordings are usually listed in a separate discography (see fig. 16.16) rather than in a bibliography. If included in a bibliography, they are best grouped under an appropriate subhead (see 16.80).

17.269 *Literature, lectures, and such.* Recordings of drama, prose or poetry readings, lectures, and the like are treated much the same as musical recordings. Facts of publication, where needed, follow the style for print media.

N: 5. Dylan Thomas, *Under Milk Wood,* performed by Dylan Thomas and others, Caedmon TC-2005 (audiocassette), CDLS-2005 (compact disc).

6. M. J. E. Senn, *Masters and Pupils,* audiotapes of lectures by Lawrence S. Kubie, Jane Loevinger, and M. J. E. Senn presented at meetings of the Society for Research in Child Development, Philadelphia, March 1973 (Chicago: University of Chicago Press, 1974).

B: Auden, W. H. *Poems*. Read by the author. Spoken Arts 7137. Compact disc.
       Twain, Mark. *The Humor of Mark Twain*. Commuters' Library. Arlington, TX: En-
       tertainment Software. 6 cassettes.

ONLINE MULTIMEDIA

17.270   *General principles.* To cite online multimedia, follow the principles and relevant examples presented above. In addition, include a URL and, if the
publisher or discipline requires it, or for especially time-sensitive material, an access date (see 17.12). Finally, include the type of medium. Not
only is such information more relevant by definition when it is a question
of "multi*media*," but, given the wide variety of medium types, such information will give some indication of what software or hardware may be
needed to gain access to the source.

N: 1. A. E. Weed. *At the Foot of the Flatiron* (American Mutoscope and Biograph
       Co., 1903), 2 min., 19 sec.; 35 mm; from Library of Congress, *The Life of a City:
       Early Films of New York, 1898–1906*, MPEG http://lcweb2.loc.gov/ammem/papr/
       nychome.html (accessed August 14, 2001).

B: Weed, A. E. *At the Foot of the Flatiron*. American Mutoscope and Biograph Co.,
       1903; 2 min., 19 sec.; 35 mm. From Library of Congress, *The Life of a City: Early
       Films of New York, 1898–1906*. MPEG, http://lcweb2.loc.gov/ammem/papr/
       nychome.html (accessed August 14, 2001).

In the following example, the audiovisual material is associated with a
specific article in an electronic journal. For citing electronic journals, see
17.180–81.

3. *Naraya* no. 2, "Ghost Dancing Music" (MP3 audio file), Richard W. Stoffle,
Lawrence Loendorf, Diane E. Austin, David B. Halmo, and Angelita Bulletts,
"Ghost Dancing the Grand Canyon," *Current Anthropology* 41, no. 1 (2000), http://
www.journals.uchicago.edu/CA/journal/issues/v41n1/001001/001001.html.

CD-ROMS OR DVD-ROMS

17.271   *Similarity to printed works.* Works issued on CD-ROM are treated similarly
to printed works. Place of publication and date may be omitted unless
relevant.

B: *Complete National Geographic: 110 Years of National Geographic Magazine*. CD-
       ROM. Mindscape, 2000.
       Oxford English Dictionary. 2nd ed. CD-ROM, version 2.0. Oxford University Press.

SLIDES, FILMSTRIPS, AND VIDEOS

17.272   *Slides and filmstrips.* Slides and filmstrips may be treated much like sound recordings (see 17.268–69).

> N: 1. Louis J. Mihalyi, *Landscapes of Zambia, Central Africa* (Santa Barbara, CA: Visual Education, 1975), slides.

> B: *The Greek and Roman World.* Chicago: Society for Visual Education, 1977. Filmstrip.

17.273   *DVDs and videocassettes.* Facts of publication for video recordings generally follow that of books, with the addition of the type of medium. Scenes (individually accessible in DVDs) are treated as chapters and cited by title or by number. Ancillary material, such as critical commentary, is cited by author and title. Note that in the second example, the citation is to material original to the 2001 edition, so the original release date of the film is omitted.

> N: 7. "Crop Duster Attack," *North by Northwest*, DVD, directed by Alfred Hitchcock (1959; Burbank, CA: Warner Home Video, 2000).

> B: Cleese, John, Terry Gilliam, Eric Idle, Terry Jones, and Michael Palin. "Commentaries." Disc 2. *Monty Python and the Holy Grail*, special ed. DVD. Directed by Terry Gilliam and Terry Jones. Culver City, CA: Columbia Tristar Home Entertainment, 2001.

> B: Handel, George Frederic. *Messiah*, selections. VHS. Atlanta Symphony Orchestra and Chamber Chorus, Robert Shaw. Batavia, OH: Video Treasures, 1988.

Citations Taken from Secondary Sources

17.274   *"Quoted in."* To cite a source from a secondary source ("quoted in . . .") is generally to be discouraged, since authors are expected to have examined the works they cite. If an original source is unavailable, however, both the original and the secondary source must be listed.

> N: 1. Louis Zukofsky, "Sincerity and Objectification," *Poetry* 37 (February 1931): 269, quoted in Bonnie Costello, *Marianne Moore: Imaginary Possessions* (Cambridge, MA: Harvard University Press, 1981), 78.

In author-date style, the original author and date would be used in the text citation and would appear first in the reference-list entry. The "quoted in" data would be given either as an annotation to the entry or in a separate entry with a cross-reference. In a humanities bibliography, the same device could be used, with appropriate adjustments (authors' full names, etc.).

T: (Zukofsky 1931)

R: Zukofsky, L. 1931. Sincerity and objectification. *Poetry* 37 (February 1931): 269.
       Quoted in B. Costello, *Marianne Moore: Imaginary possessions* (Cambridge, MA:
       Harvard Univ. Press, 1981), 78.

       or

       Costello, B. 1981. *Marianne Moore: Imaginary possessions*. Cambridge, MA: Har-
       vard Univ. Press.
       Zukofsky, L. 1931. Sincerity and objectification. *Poetry* 37 (Feb.): 269. Quoted in
       Costello 1981, 78.

Legal Citations

17.275   *Stylebooks.* Citations in predominantly legal works may follow one of three guides: (1) *The Bluebook: A Uniform System of Citation,* 17th edition, published by the Harvard Law Review Association in 2000; (2) the newest style guide, the *ALWD Citation Manual: A Professional System of Citation,* prepared and published by the Association of Legal Writing Directors and Darby Dickerson in 2000; or (3) *The University of Chicago Manual of Legal Citation,* 2d edition (2000), edited by the staff of the *University of Chicago Law Review* (see bibliog. 1.1 for all these sources). For Canada, see 17.325. Whichever system you choose, follow it consistently throughout a work. Any editor working extensively with legal materials should have one or all of these manuals on hand. *The Bluebook* is the most widely used citation guide; its conventions predominate in law reviews. The *ALWD Citation Manual* differs in some elements but is much simpler; it has been widely adopted by law-school writing courses. The rules below are based on both the *Bluebook* and *ALWD* systems (including, for example, the use of *2d* and *3d* rather than *2nd* and *3rd* and other minor deviations from the style set forth in earlier sections of this manual). Examples of each style are presented here. In nonlegal works, the rules may be adjusted to the style of the surrounding documentation; providing adequate information to help readers find a source is more important than slavishly following prescribed forms of abbreviation and the like.

17.276 *Note form.* Since almost all legal works use notes for documentation and few use bibliographies, the examples in this section are given in note form only. For conversion to humanities style (notes and bibliographies) or author-date style (parenthetical citations and reference lists), see chapter 16.

17.277 *Typefaces.* In both *Bluebook* and *ALWD* style, italic is used for case names, titles of articles and chapters (a major difference from nonlegal usage), uncommon words or phrases in languages other than English (but not such well-known terms as "de facto" or "ex parte"), and emphasis. All other material is presented in roman except that in *Bluebook* style caps and small caps are used for the titles of books and their authors and for the names of periodicals and newspapers.

17.278 *Abbreviations.* Periods are omitted from acronyms and abbreviations that are explained or are easily recognized. For example, most people understand that IRS stands for Internal Revenue Service. Symbol abbreviations used without periods include § (section) and ¶ (paragraph). But periods are not omitted from most other abbreviations, including those for versus, *v.* (in italic); chapter, "ch." (in roman); or note, "n." (in roman). Legal style uses *id.* rather than *ibid.* (both in italic).

> 1. *NLRB v. Somerville Constr. Co.*, 206 F.3d 752 n. 1 (7th Cir. 2000).

17.279 *Full citations.* As in nonlegal works, sources, including authors' names, are given in full at first citation. When a work has three or more authors or editors, usually only the first is listed, followed by "et al." (in roman, with a period). For examples, see 17.280.

17.280 *Books and treatises.* Long titles may be shortened. For abbreviations of elements, see 17.278. Notable differences from nonlegal style are the placement of elements, the omission of certain commas and periods, and the omission of the place of publication (and often the publisher). In *Bluebook* style, both titles and authors' names are in caps and small caps. An ampersand is used between two authors' names or between the second and third of three names (see also 17.279). The citation format for a particular book depends on various factors. Usually all publication information except the edition and date is omitted. But the citation for a book that has been reprinted or issued in a new edition by a different publisher requires two parentheticals. The first identifies the publisher and date of the edition cited. The second gives the original edition's publication date.

> 2. CLARENCE DARROW, VERDICTS OUT OF COURT 273 (Arthur Weinberg & Lila Weinberg eds., Ivan R. Dee 1989) (1963).

If the original publisher issues multiple editions, give only the edition and year of publication.

> 3. GEORGE CAMERON COGGINS ET AL., FEDERAL PUBLIC LAND AND RESOURCES LAW ch. 9 (3d ed. 1993).
> 4. STEPHEN G. BREYER & RICHARD B. STEWART, ADMINISTRATIVE LAW AND REGULA-TORY POLICY 719 (2d ed. 1985).

If a work is published in multiple volumes, the volume number is placed before the authors' names.

> 5. 2 PATRICIA LOVE & TIMOTHY P. NAMSSORG, LITIGATION IN UNFRIENDLY BUYOUTS § 18.2, at 20 (1991).

In *ALWD* style, titles are italicized and capitalized in headline style (see 8.167). All citation information follows the title except for the edition number, which precedes the publisher's name.

> 6. Clarence Darrow, *Verdicts Out of Court* 273 (Ivan R. Dee 1989).
> 7. George Cameron Coggins, Charles F. Wilkerson, & John D. Leshy, *Federal Public Land and Resources Law* ch. 9 (3d ed., Found. Press 1993).
> 8. Stephen G. Breyer & Richard B. Stewart, *Administrative Law and Regulatory Policy* 719 (2d ed., Little, Brown 1985).
> 9. Patricia Love & Timothy P. Namssorg, *Litigation in Unfriendly Buyouts* vol. 2, § 18.2, at 20 (Castleworth 1991).

17.281 *Chapters in edited books.* When reference is made to a chapter in a multi-author work (sometimes called a contributed work), both the first page of the chapter and, where appropriate, the page specifically cited are given. In *Bluebook* style, the chapter title is italicized, and the book title is in caps and small caps.

> 10. Mark Tushnet, *Corporations and Free Speech*, in THE POLITICS OF LAW 253, 256 (David Kairys ed., 1982).

In *ALWD* style, the chapter title and the book title are both italicized.

> 11. Mark Tushnet, *Corporations and Free Speech*, in *The Politics of Law* 253, 256 (David Kairys ed., Pantheon 1982).

17.282   *Articles in periodicals.* Titles of articles are italicized and in headline style. Well-known journal names are usually abbreviated. Volume numbers are in arabic and appear *before* the journal name; page numbers—first the opening page of the article and then the specific page cited—follow the journal name; the date, in parentheses, is the final element. *Bluebook* style uses caps and small caps for the journal name.

> 12. Michael Stokes Paulsen, *Abrogating Stare Decisis by Statute: May Congress Remove the Precedential Effect of Roe and Casey?* 109 YALE L.J. 1535, 1546–47 (2000).
>
> 13. Chris Heck, Comment, *Conflict and Aggression: Appointing Institutional Investors as Sole Lead Plaintiffs Under the PSLRA,* 66 U. CHI. L. REV. 1199, 1203 (1999).

In *ALWD* style, the journal name is set in roman. If the author is a student (i.e., if the author is identified as a JD candidate), or if the article is designated as a note, comment, case comment, or recent development, then "Student Author" is added, set off by commas, immediately after the author's name.

> 14. Michael Stokes Paulsen, *Abrogating Stare Decisis by Statute: May Congress Remove the Precedential Effect of Roe and Casey?* 109 Yale L.J. 1535, 1546–47 (2000).
>
> 15. Chris Heck, Student Author, *Conflict and Aggression: Appointing Institutional Investors as Sole Lead Plaintiffs under the PSLRA,* 66 U. Chi. L. Rev. 1199, 1203 (1999).

If a volume number is omitted—in a citation to a magazine, for example—the full date of the issue is given. In *Bluebook* style, the page numbers cited follow the date.

> 16. Albert Gore Jr., *Stability for Two,* NEW REPUBLIC, Nov. 17, 1986, at 19, 21.

In *ALWD* style, the page numbers precede the date, which is in parentheses.

> 17. Albert Gore Jr., *Stability for Two,* New Republic 19, 21 (Nov. 17, 1986).

17.283   *Cases or court decisions: basic elements.* Case names, including the abbreviation *v.*, are italicized. Full citations include volume number (arabic), name of the reporter series (abbreviated), the ordinal series number (if applicable), the abbreviated name of the court and the date (together in parentheses), and other relevant information (see 17.286). A single page number designates the opening page of a decision; an additional number designates an actual page cited. The *Bluebook* and *ALWD* styles are identical.

18. *U.S. v. Christmas*, 222 F.3d 141, 145 (4th Cir. 2000).

19. *Profit Sharing Plan v. Mbank Dallas, N.A.*, 683 F. Supp. 592 (N.D. Tex. 1988).

When a loose-leaf service or similar source is cited, the publisher is indicated parenthetically.

20. *In re Saberman*, 3 Bankr. L. Rep. (CCH) ¶67,416 (Bankr. N.D. Ill. 1980).

17.284 *U.S. Supreme Court decisions.* All Supreme Court decisions are published in the *United States Supreme Court Reports* (abbreviated U.S.) and are preferably cited to that reporter. Cases not yet published there may be cited to the *Supreme Court Reporter* (abbreviated S. Ct. or, sometimes, Sup. Ct.), which publishes decisions more quickly. Because the court's name is identified by the reporter, it is not repeated before the date.

21. *AT&T Corp. v. Iowa Utils. Bd.*, 525 U.S. 366 (1999).

22. *Old Chief v. U.S.*, 117 S. Ct. 644 (1997).

17.285 *Lower federal courts.* Lower federal-court decisions are usually cited to the *Federal Reporter* (F.) or to the *Federal Supplement* (F. Supp.). If relevant, the Supreme Court's grant or denial of certiorari may be indicated.

23. *United States v. Dennis*, 183 F. 201 (2d Cir. 1950).

24. *Am. Trucking, Inc. v. EPA*, 175 F.3d 1027 (D.C. Cir. 1999), *cert. granted*, 120 S. Ct. 2003 (2000).

25. *Eaton v. IBM Corp.*, 925 F. Supp. 487 (S.D. Tex. 1996).

17.286 *State- and local-court decisions.* Decisions of state and local courts are cited much like federal-court decisions. Citation to official state reporters is preferred. If both the official and the commercial reporters are cited, they are separated by a comma. If the court's name is identified by the reporter, it is not repeated before the date. If a case was decided in a lower court, the abbreviated court name appears before the date.

26. *Williams v. Davis*, 27 Cal. 2d 746 (1946).

27. *Henningsen v. Bloomfield Motors, Inc.*, 32 N.J. 358, 161 A.2d 69 (1960).

28. *Bivens v. Mobley*, 724 So. 2d 458, 465 (Miss. Ct. App. 1998).

17.287 *Subsequent citations.* Subsequent citations are shortened to the first nongovernmental party's name, reporter volume, reporter series, and "at" (in roman) preceding the particular page being cited. Absence of "at" implies reference to the decision as a whole. The year is omitted. The following examples are based on those in the preceding paragraphs.

29. *AT&T*, 525 U.S. at 370.

30. *AT&T*, 525 U.S. 366.

31. *Old Chief*, 117 S. Ct. at 645.

32. *Id.* at 646.

33. *Am. Trucking*, 175 F.3d at 1033.

34. *Williams*, 27 Cal. 2d 746.

In nonlegal works, a subsequent citation may consist of the case name and, if needed, a page number.

35. *United States v. Christmas*, 146.

36. *Georgia v. Brailsford*, 2.

17.288 *Constitutions.* In citations to constitutions, the article and amendment numbers appear in roman numerals; other subdivision numbers in arabic. (For nonlegal style see 9.32, 17.289.) In *Bluebook* style the name of the constitution is given in caps and small caps; other abbreviations are lowercased. *ALWD* does not use caps and small caps but capitalizes some abbreviations.

Bluebook: 37. U.S. CONST. art. I, § 4, cl. 2.

38. U.S. CONST. amend. XIV, § 2.

39. ARIZ. CONST. art. VII, § 5.

40. ARK. CONST. of 1868, art. III, § 2 (superseded 1874).

ALWD: 41. U.S. Const. art. I, § 4, cl. 2.

42. U.S. Const. amend. XIV, § 2.

43. Ariz. Const. art. VII, § 5.

44. Ark. Const. of 1868 art. III, § 2 (superseded 1874).

17.289 *Legal citations in nonlegal works.* The styles outlined above may be modified in general works—for example, *par.* or *sec.* may be used rather than ¶ or §; and *Fourteenth Amendment* may be more appropriate than *amend. XIV* or *Amend. XIV*.

Public Documents

17.290 *Stylebooks.* The number and variety of government publications preclude comprehensive treatment in this manual. For documents that do not fit the patterns outlined below, and for lists of abbreviations, consult *The Bluebook: A Uniform System of Citation*, the *ALWD Citation Manual: A Pro-*

fessional System of Citation, or *The University of Chicago Manual of Legal Citation* (see 17.275). See bibliog. 1.1 for all these sources. For Canada, see 17.325; for the United Kingdom, see 17.336.

17.291 *Form of documentation.* Since the author-date style is generally inappropriate for citing public documents, examples in this section (except for 17.293) are given in note or bibliographic form only. Should conversion to author-date style be necessary, refer to the principles outlined in chapter 16 or the examples in 17.293.

17.292 *Abbreviation style.* In a legal work following one of the styles mentioned in 17.275, abbreviations prescribed there should be used. This section is addressed primarily to nonlegal writers and editors, so the examples follow Chicago's traditional style. Note that although *2d* is used for consistency throughout the section on public documents, *2nd* could be substituted in other contexts for internal consistency (see 9.8, 17.300). On *U.S.* versus *US,* see 15.5.

17.293 *Elements required.* References to printed public documents should include the elements needed to find the work in a library catalog, including some or all of the following:

- Country, state, city, county, or other government division issuing the document
- Legislative body, executive department, court bureau, board, commission, or committee
- Subsidiary divisions, regional offices, and so forth
- Title, if any, of the document or collection
- Individual author, editor, or compiler, if given
- Report number or other identifying information
- Publisher, if different from the issuing body
- Date
- Page, if relevant

N: 1. Senate Committee on Foreign Relations, *The Mutual Security Act of 1956,* 84th Cong., 2d sess., 1956, S. Rep. 2273, 9–10.

B: U.S. Congress. Senate. Committee on Foreign Relations. *The Mutual Security Act of 1956.* 84th Cong., 2d sess., 1956. S. Rep. 2273.

T: (U.S. Senate Committee 1956, 9–10)

R: U.S. Congress. Senate. Committee on Foreign Relations. 1956. *The Mutual Security Act of 1956.* 84th Cong., 2d sess. S. Rep. 2273.

17.294   *Discretion.* The order in which elements listed in 17.293 appear may differ from work to work, according to the subject matter. Discretion and common sense should dictate how much information is necessary for a reader to locate the material and, if both notes and a bibliography are used, which elements may be omitted from the notes (see, e.g., 17.287).

UNITED STATES

17.295   *Government Printing Office.* Publications are issued by both houses of Congress (Senate and House of Representatives), by the executive departments (State, Justice, Labor, etc.), and by government agencies (Federal Trade Commission, General Services Administration, etc.). Most such publications are printed and distributed by the Government Printing Office (GPO) in Washington, DC. Notes and bibliographies may use, consistently, any of the following forms, with relevant date. See also 17.292.

Washington, DC: U.S. Government Printing Office, 2000
Washington, DC: Government Printing Office, 2000
Washington, DC: GPO, 2000
Washington, DC, 2000

These facts of publication are often omitted when other identifying data are given, such as the data for congressional documents.

17.296   *Catalog.* The *Monthly Catalog of United States Government Publications* (see bibliog. 4.5) lists a large array of technical literature, including government-sponsored research, development, and engineering reports; foreign technical reports; and other analyses prepared by national or local government agencies and their contractors. Many of these materials are available through such information services as the National Technical Information Service (NTIS) and the Educational Resources Information Center (ERIC). Citations to these sources should include as much identifying information as possible.

17.297   *Congressional publications.* Congressional publications include the journals of both the House of Representatives and the Senate; the *Congressional Record*; bills and statutes; and committee reports, hearings, and other documents.

17.298   *Inclusion of "U.S. Congress" and such.* Bibliographical listings of congressional debates, hearings, and the like usually begin with "U.S. Congress," followed by "Senate" or "House"; committee and subcommittee, if any;

title of document; number of the Congress and session; date of publication (which may be omitted when the session is identified); and the number and description of the document (e.g., H. Doc. 487) if available. Since "Congress" is usually understood, a listing may simply begin "U.S. Senate" or "U.S. House," but for consistency's sake in this section, the full forms are given in examples. In notes, where alphabetical order does not apply, "U.S." is usually omitted (see examples in 17.293). See also 17.292.

17.299 *The 3-em dash.* Only where no ambiguity could occur should the 3-em dash be used in a bibliography for repeated references to the same congressional source. See also 16.84, 16.103.

B: U.S. Congress. House. Committee on Foreign Affairs. *Background Material* . . .

————. Committee on Interior and Insular Affairs. *International Proliferation* . . .

————. Committee on Interior and Insular Affairs. *Dangers of* . . .

U.S. Congress. Senate. Committee on Foreign Relations. *The Mutual* . . .

17.300 *Congress and sessions.* Both Congress number and session number must be identified. (The form *2nd* may be preferred if used elsewhere in the work; see 9.8.)

97th Cong., 2d sess.

17.301 *Congressional journals.* The Senate and House journals (as distinct from the *Congressional Record*; see 17.302) contain motions, actions taken, and roll-call votes and are published at the end of each session.

N: 2. *Senate Journal*, 16th Cong., 1st sess., December 7, 1819, 9–19.

B: U.S. Congress. *Senate Journal*. 16th Cong., 1st sess., December 7, 1819.

17.302 *Congressional Record.* Since 1873, congressional debates have been published by the government in the *Congressional Record* (in notes often abbreviated as *Cong. Rec.*). Daily issues are bound in paper biweekly and in permanent volumes (divided into parts) yearly. Since material may be added, deleted, or modified when the final volumes are prepared, pagination will vary between the different editions. Whenever possible, citation should be made to the permanent volumes, with the relevant year or, if a precise reference is not needed, a run of years.

N: 16. *Food Security Act of 1985*, HR 2100, 99th Cong., 1st sess., *Congressional Record* 131 (October 8, 1985): H 8461.

B: U.S. Congress. *Congressional Record.* 71st Cong., 2d sess., 1930. Vol. 72, pt. 10.

———. *Congressional Record.* 1940–45. Washington, DC.

Unless required in order to keep all such references in the same neigh-borhood in a bibliography, "U.S. Congress" may be omitted.

17.303   *Identity of a speaker.* Occasionally it may be necessary to identify a speaker, the subject, and a date in a note.

N: 4. Senator Kennedy of Massachusetts, speaking for the Joint Resolution on Nu-clear Weapons Freeze and Reductions, on March 10, 1982, to the Committee on Foreign Relations, S.J. Res. 163, 97th Cong., 1st sess., *Congressional Record* 128, pt. 3:3832–34.

17.304   *Debates.* Until 1873, congressional debates were privately printed in *Annals of the Congress of the United States* (also known by other names and cov-ering the years 1789–1824), *Congressional Debates* (1824–37), and *Congressional Globe* (1833–73). Note that the publication dates differ from the years covered.

N: 5. *Congressional Globe,* 39th Cong., 2d sess., 1867, 39, pt. 9:9505.
       6. *Annals of Congress,* 18th Cong., 1st sess., 358, 361.

B: U.S. Congress. *Annals of the Congress of the United States, 1789–1824.* 42 vols. Washington, DC, 1834–56.
       U.S. Congress. *Congressional Globe.* 46 vols. Washington, DC, 1834–73.

As with the *Congressional Record,* "U.S. Congress" may be omitted.

17.305   *Journals of the Continental Congress.* The complete thirty-four-volume edi-tion of the *Journals of the Continental Congress,* published by the Library of Congress, is cited the same way as any other multivolume work (see 17.85). After the first citation, the abbreviation *JCC* may be used in notes.

N: 7. *Journals of the Continental Congress, 1774–1789,* ed. Worthington C. Ford et al. (Washington, DC, 1904–37): 15:1341.
       8. *JCC* 25:863.

B: Continental Congress. *Journals of the Continental Congress, 1774–1789.* Edited by Worthington C. Ford et al. 34 vols. Washington, DC, 1904–37.

17.306   *Reports and documents.* References to reports and documents of the Sen-ate (S.) and the House (H.) should include both Congress and session numbers and, if possible, the series number.

N: 9. Senate Committee on Foreign Relations, *The Mutual Security Act of 1956,* 84th Cong., 2d sess., 1956, S. Rep. 2273, 9–10.

10. *Declarations of a State of War with Japan, Germany, and Italy,* 77th Cong., 1st sess., 1941, S. Doc. 148, serial 10575, 2–5.

11. Senate Committee, *Mutual Security Act,* 9.

12. *Reorganization of the Federal Judiciary,* 75th Cong., 1st sess., 1937, S. Rep. 711.

B: U.S. Congress. House. *Report of Activities of the National Advisory Council on International Monetary and Financial Problems to March 31, 1947.* 80th Cong., 1st sess., 1947. H. Doc. 365.

17.307   *Hearings.* Records of testimony given before congressional committees are usually published with titles, which should be cited. The relevant committee, even if not classified as author in the published hearing, should be so listed in a note reference or a bibliographic entry.

N: 13. House Committee on Banking and Currency, *Bretton Woods Agreements Act: Hearings on H.R. 3314,* 79th Cong., 1st sess., 1945, 12–14.

14. House Committee, *Bretton Woods,* 13.

B: U.S. Congress. Senate. Committee on Foreign Relations. *Famine in Africa: Hearing before the Committee on Foreign Relations.* 99th Cong., 1st sess., January 17, 1985.

17.308   *Committee Prints.* Committee Prints (most often congressional research reports) are usually numbered. If so, the number follows the words *Committee Prints* with no intervening punctuation; page numbers, if given, follow a comma. The relevant committee is usually listed as author, but the person(s) who prepared the document, if more relevant to the discussion, may appear as primary author.

N: 15. House Committee on Interior and Insular Affairs, Subcommittee on Energy and the Environment, *International Proliferation of Nuclear Technology,* report prepared by Warren H. Donnelly and Barbara Rather, 94th Cong., 2d sess., 1976, Committee Print 15, 5–6. (*or, if no print number were listed,* . . . Committee Print, 5–6.)

or

15. Warren H. Donnelly and Barbara Rather, *International Proliferation of Nuclear Technology,* report prepared for the Subcommittee on Energy and the Environment of the House Committee on Interior and Insular Affairs, 94th Cong., 2d sess., 1976, Committee Print 15, 5–6.

B: U.S. Congress. House. Committee on Foreign Affairs. *Background Material on Mutual Defense and Development Programs: Fiscal Year 1965.* 88th Cong., 2d sess., 1964. Committee Print.

17.309   *Bills and resolutions.* Congressional bills (proposed laws) and resolutions are published in pamphlet form (slip bills). In citations, bills or resolutions originating in the House of Representatives are abbreviated *HR* or *HR Res.,* and those originating in the Senate, *S* or *S Res.* (all in roman). The title of the bill is italicized; it is followed by the bill number, the congressional session, and (if available) publication details in the *Congressional Record.*

N: 16. *Food Security Act of 1985,* HR 2100, 99th Cong., 1st sess., *Congressional Record* 131, no. 132, daily ed. (October 8, 1985): H 8461.

B: U.S. Congress. House. *Food Security Act of 1985.* HR 2100. 99th Cong., 1st sess. *Congressional Record* 131, no. 132, daily ed. (October 8, 1985): H 8353–8486.

If the title of a bill has been mentioned in text, it may be omitted from the note. The date a bill was introduced, as distinct from the date published in the *Congressional Record,* may be added in parentheses after the congressional session.

N: 17. S 2404, 97th Cong., 2d sess. (April 13, 1982), *Cong. Rec.* 128 (April 20, 1982): S 7091.

17.310   *Laws and statutes.* Bills or resolutions that have been passed into law— "public laws," or statutes—are first published separately, as slip laws, and then collected in the annual bound volumes of the *United States Statutes at Large* (abbreviated in legal style as *Stat.*). Later they are incorporated into the *United States Code.* Laws may be cited to *Statutes,* the *U.S. Code,* or both.

N: 18. *Atomic Energy Act of 1947,* Public Law 585, 79th Cong., 2d sess. (August 1, 1946), 12, 19.
      19. *Telecommunications Act of 1996,* Public Law 104-104, *U.S. Statutes at Large* 110 (1996): 56.
      20. *National Environmental Policy Act,* Public Law 91-190, *U.S. Statutes at Large* 83 (1970): 853, codified at *U.S. Code* 42 (1982), § 4332.
      21. *National Environmental Policy Act,* § 4333.
      22. *Declaratory Judgment Act, U.S. Code* 28 (1952), §§ 2201 et seq.

17.311   *Earlier statutes.* The *United States Statutes at Large* (abbreviated as *Stat.*) began publication in 1874. Before that, laws were published in the seventeen-volume *Statutes at Large of the United States of America, 1789–1873* (abbreviated as *Stats at Large of USA*). Citations to this collection include the volume number and the publication date of that volume.

17.312 *State laws and municipal ordinances.* State laws and municipal ordinances are set in roman; codes (compilations) are italicized. A name is included in parentheses where necessary to indicate the version of a code cited. The date a specific law was passed may be included in parentheses. The date following a code indicates the year the volume was updated or supplemented to include the law being cited.

In legal style:

N: 41. *Ohio Rev. Code Ann.* § 3566 (West 2000).

       42. *Ky. Rev. Stat. Ann.* § 520.020 (Banks-Baldwin 1985).

In nonlegal style:

N: 43. *Baldwin's Ohio Revised Code Annotated.*

       44. *Ohio Revised Code Annotated*, sec. 3566 (West 2000).

       45. An Act Guaranteeing Governmental Independence (January 3, 1974), *Kentucky Revised Statutes Annotated*, sec. 520.020 (Banks-Baldwin 1985).

17.313 *American State Papers.* Documents printed privately for the early Congresses are collected in the thirty-eight-volume *American State Papers* (1789–1838; sometimes abbreviated as *Am. St. P.*). The papers are organized into ten classes (e.g., 1. *Foreign Relations*; 3. *Finance*), each class having several volumes. Both class and volume numbers are usually cited, as in the first example. When the former is omitted, as in the second example, a colon appears between collection title and class title. One or the other of the two forms illustrated should be used consistently in a work.

N: 23. *American State Papers*, 5, *Military Affairs* 2:558.

       24. Mifflin to Washington, July 18, 1791, *Am. St. P.: Misc.* 1:39.

17.314 *Other collections.* An excellent source covering legislative documents and collections is Laurence F. Schmeckebier and Roy B. Eastin's *Government Publications and Their Use* (bibliog. 4.5).

17.315 *Presidential documents.* Presidential proclamations, executive orders, vetoes, addresses, and the like are published in the *Weekly Compilation of Presidential Documents* and in *Public Papers of the Presidents of the United States*. Proclamations and executive orders are also carried in the daily

Federal Register and then published in title 3 of the *Code of Federal Regulations*; if already published in the *Code*, they are best so cited.

N: 25. President, Proclamation, "Caribbean Basin Economic Recovery Act, Proclamation 5142, Amending Proclamation 5133," *Federal Register* 49, no. 2 (January 1984): 341.
       26. Executive Order no. 11,609, *Code of Federal Regulations*, title 3, sec. 586 (1971–75).

17.316 *Compilations of presidential papers.* The public papers of U.S. presidents are collected in two multivolume works: *Compilation of the Messages and Papers of the Presidents, 1789–1897*, and for subsequent administrations, *Public Papers of the Presidents of the United States*.

N: 27. *House Miscellaneous Document no. 210*, 53d Cong., 2d sess., in *Compilation of the Messages and Papers of the Presidents, 1789–1897*, ed. J. D. Richardson (Washington, DC: GPO, 1907), 4:16.
       28. *House Misc. Doc. no. 210*, 17.

B: Hoover, Herbert. *Public Papers of the Presidents of the United States: Herbert Hoover, 1929–33.* 4 vols. Washington, DC: Government Printing Office, 1974–77.

17.317 *Executive department documents.* Reports, bulletins, circulars, and miscellaneous materials are issued by executive departments, bureaus, and agencies. When authors are identified, their names should be cited; for different locations, see examples below. In a bibliography, cross-reference between author and department may be appropriate.

N: 30. U.S. Department of the Treasury, *Report of the Secretary of the Treasury Transmitting a Report from the Register of the Treasury of the Commerce and Navigation of the United States for the Year Ending the 30th of June, 1850*, 31st Cong., 2d sess., House Executive Document 8 (Washington, DC, 1850–51).
       31. Ralph I. Straus, *Expanding Private Investment for Free World Economic Growth*, special report prepared at the request of the Department of State, April 1959, 12.

B: LaBelle, Robert P. *See* U.S. Department of the Interior.
       U.S. Census Office. *Agriculture of the United States in 1860: Compiled from the Original Returns of the Eighth Census.* Washington, DC: Government Printing Office, 1864.
       U.S. Department of the Interior. Minerals Management Service. *An Oilspill Risk Analysis for the Central Gulf (April 1984) and Western Gulf of Mexico (July 1984)*, by Robert P. LaBelle. Open-file report, U.S. Geological Survey. Denver, 1984.

U.S. Department of Labor. Employment Standards Administration. *Resource Book: Training for Federal Employee Compensation Specialists.* Washington, DC, 1984.

T: (EPA 1999)

R: U.S. Environmental Protection Agency. Office of Air Quality Planning and Standards. 1999. *Haze: How air pollution affects the view.* http://www.epa.gov/ttn/oarpg/t1/fr_notices/haze.pdf.

17.318 *Series numbers.* When the series number for departmental publication is given, publication facts may be omitted.

B: U.S. Department of State. *Postwar Policy Preparation, 1939–1945.* General Policy Series, no. 15.

17.319 *Census Bureau.* Publications of the Census Bureau may be listed under "U.S. Department of Commerce, Bureau of the Census" or simply under "U.S. Bureau of the Census."

B: U.S. Bureau of the Census. *Median Gross Rent by Counties of the United States, 1970.* Prepared by the Geography Division in cooperation with the Housing Division, Bureau of the Census. Washington, DC, 1975.

17.320 *Government commission publications.* Bulletins, circulars, reports, and study papers issued by such government commissions as the Federal Communications Commission or the Securities and Exchange Commission are cited much like legislative reports. They are often classified as House (H) or Senate (S) documents; for more examples, see 17.307.

N: 32. Senate, *Report of the Federal Trade Commission on Utility Corporations,* 70th Cong., 1st sess., 1935, S. Doc. 91, pt. 71A.

B: U.S. Securities and Exchange Commission. *Annual Report of the Securities and Exchange Commission for the Fiscal Year.* Washington, DC: GPO, 1983.

17.321 *Constitutions.* The U.S. Constitution and state constitutions are cited by article or amendment, section, and, if relevant, clause. For legal style see 17.288.

N: 32. U.S. Constitution, art. 2, sec. 1, cl. 3.
33. U.S. Constitution, amend. 14, sec. 2.
34. New Mexico Constitution, art. 4, sec. 7.

17.322 *Treaties.* The texts of treaties signed before 1949 are published in *United States Statutes at Large (Stat.;* see 17.311); the unofficial citation is to the *Treaty Series* or the *Executive Agreement Series,* each of which assigns a number to a treaty covered. Those signed in 1949 and later appear in *United States Treaties and Other International Agreements (UST,* 1950–), or *Treaties and Other International Acts Series (TIAS,* 1946–), which also assigns a number. Treaties involving more than two nations may be found in the United Nations *Treaty Series: Treaties and International Agreements Registered or Filed or Recorded with the Secretariat of the United Nations* or, from 1920 to 1946, in the League of Nations *Treaty Series.* Titles of treaties are set in roman and put in quotation marks. The publications, whether technically multivolume works or series, are italicized. An exact date indicates the date of signing and is therefore preferable to a year alone, which may differ from the year the treaty was published in one of the works above. Page numbers are given where relevant.

N: 34. "Nuclear Weapons Test Ban," August 5, 1963, *United States Treaties and Other International Agreements* 14, pt. 2.

35. "Denmark and Italy: Convention concerning Military Service," July 15, 1954, *Treaties and Other International Acts Series* 250, no. 3516 (1956): 45.

36. "Treaty with Iraq on Commerce and Navigation, 1939," *United States Statutes at Large* 53:1790, *Treaty Ser.* no. 960.

37. "Nuclear Weapons Test Ban."

38. "Denmark and Italy," 43.

B: United States. "Naval Armament Limitation Treaty." February 26, 1922. *United States Statutes at Large* 43, pt. 2.

Legal style omits quotation marks and makes other minor adjustments; see the manuals mentioned in 17.275.

17.323 *State and local governments.* Citations to state and local government documents follow a form similar to that used for federal documents.

N: 39. Illinois General Assembly, Law Revision Commission, *Report to the 80th General Assembly of the State of Illinois* (Chicago, 1977), 14–18.

B: Illinois Institute for Environmental Quality (IIEQ). *Review and Synopsis of Public Participation regarding Sulfur Dioxide and Particulate Emissions.* By Sidney M. Marder. IIEQ Document no. 77/21. Chicago, 1977.

For state laws and municipal ordinances, see 17.312.

17.324 *Unpublished government documents.* For general guidelines and many examples, which can be adapted to government documents, see 17.222–31. Most unpublished documents of the United States government are housed in the National Archives (NA) in Washington, DC, or in one of its branches. All, including films, photographs, and sound recordings as well as written materials, are cited by record group (RG) number. A list of the record groups and their numbers is given in the *Guide to the National Archives of the United States* (see bibliog. 4.5). Names of specific documents are given in quotation marks.

N: 40. Senate Committee on the Judiciary, "Lobbying," file 71A–F15, RG 46, National Archives.

B: National Archives Branch Depository, Suitland, MD. Records of the National Commission on Law Observance and Enforcement. RG 10.

CANADA

17.325 *Reference works.* The major reference work for citing Canadian public documents and legal cases is *Canadian Guide to Uniform Legal Citation,* edited and published by the Carswell/McGill Law Journal (see bibliog. 1.1). Also valuable are Douglass T. MacEllven, Michael J. McGuire, and Denis LeMay, *Legal Research Handbook* (bibliog. 5); *Canadian Almanac and Directory,* especially section 3, "Government Directory," and section 10, "Legal Directory" (bibliog. 4.4), and Gerald L. Gall, *The Canadian Legal System,* 4th edition (bibliog. 5). All should be referred to by writers or editors of specialized works in Canadian history and law. The following paragraphs are addressed primarily to generalists.

17.326 *Parliament, legislatures, and executive departments.* Government documents are issued by both houses of the federal Parliament (the Senate and the House of Commons), by the provincial and territorial legislatures, and by various executive departments.

17.327 *Date form and abbreviations.* Canadians generally prefer the day-month-year form of dates (2 January 2002), and the examples below reflect that form. *Chapter* and *section* are abbreviated as *c.* and *s.* In a publication containing only occasional references to Canadian documents, date and number forms and abbreviations may be made consistent with the style used elsewhere in the work (*chap.*, *sec.*, *2nd*, etc.).

17.328 *Inclusion of "Canada."* Citations should begin with "Canada" unless it is obvious from the context.

N: 1. "Report of the Royal Commission to Enquire into Railways and Transportation in Canada," *Sessional Papers*, 1917, no. 20g, p. xiii.

B: Canada. Manitoba. Legislative Assembly. *Debates and Proceedings*, 17 August 2000.

17.329   *Debates.* Parliamentary debates are published in separate series, *House of Commons Debates* and *Senate Debates.* Where relevant, the name of the person speaking may be added.

N: 2. Canada, *House of Commons Debates* (3 June 2000), p. 7904 (Mrs. Lalonde, MP).

Provincial and territorial legislatures publish their own debates.

N: 3. Manitoba, Legislative Assembly, *Debates and Proceedings* (17 August 2000), p. 5326 (Joy Smith, MLA).

17.330   *Bills.* Parliamentary bills are cited by bill number, title, session number, Parliament number, year, and any relevant additional information.

N: 3. Bill C-40, *Extradition Act*, 2d sess., 36th Parliament, 1998, cl. 1 (assented to 17 June 1999), *Statutes of Canada* [or *SC*] 1999, c. 18.

17.331   *Statutes.* Canadian statutes are first published in the annual *Statutes of Canada* (*SC*) and were most recently consolidated in 1985 in the *Revised Statutes of Canada* (*RSC*). They should be cited, wherever possible, to the latter and identified by chapter, section, and year.

N: 4. *Canada Wildlife Act*, *RSC* 1985, c. W-9, s. 1.
        5. *Extradition Act*, *Statutes of Canada* [or *SC*] 1999, c. 18, s. 1.

17.332   *Regulations.* Regulations are created by Canadian executive ministries pursuant to enabling legislation. They are published first as *Statutory Orders and Regulations* (*SOR*) in the *Canada Gazette*, Part II, and are now available on the Web site of *Consolidated Regulations of Canada* (*CRC*). They are identified by calendar year, chapter (c.), and section (s.).

N: 6. *Cost of Borrowing (Banks) Regulations*, *SOR*/92-320, s. 1.
        7. *Collision Regulations*, *Consolidated Regulations of Canada* [or *CRC*], c. 1416, s. 4 (1978).

17.333   *Gazettes.* The federal government and the provincial and territorial governments each issue a *Gazette*. The *Gazettes* contain public notices, registration of corporate names, subordinate legislation, and other materials, which are published as Part I of a *Gazette*. Ministerial regulations are in Part II of a *Gazette*. The most recent acts of Parliament appear in Part III of the federal *Canada Gazette* (*C. Gaz.*). Roman numerals are used to denote parts.

N: 8. *An Act to Amend the Municipal Governments Act, Canada Gazette* [or *C. Gaz.*] 2000, III.

         9. *Notice of Amalgamation, Manitoba Gazette* [or *M. Gaz.*] 1999, I, 905 (Corporations Act).

17.334   *Citing legal cases*. The following examples illustrate the style recommended by the *Canadian Guide to Uniform Legal Citation* (see 17.325). In a work following the style of *The Bluebook*, the *ALWD Citation Manual*, or *The University of Chicago Manual of Legal Citation* (see bibliog. 1.1), minor adjustments may be made for consistency. The basic elements are similar to those used in U.S. law citations; the volume number precedes the reporter, which is abbreviated, and the page number follows.

N: 10. *Manitoba Attorney General v. Lindsay* [2000] 5 W.W.R. 30 (2000), 145 Man. R. (2d) 187 (C.A.).

         11. *Arsenault-Cameron v. Prince Edward Island* [2000] 1 S.C.R. 3 at para. 26, 2000 SCC 1.

         12. *Manitoba v. Health Sciences Centre* 141 Man. R. (2d) 161, 2000 MQB 6.

Two reporters may be cited, as in the first example above (W.W.R. = Western Weekly Reports; Man. R. = Manitoba Reports). In the second and third examples, SCC stands for Supreme Court of Canada and MQB for Manitoba Queen's Bench.

17.335   *Unpublished Canadian government documents*. The National Archives of Canada (NAC) houses the unpublished records of the federal government, both individually written and institutional. In the absence of a printed guide to the entire NAC collections, consult the official NAC Web site. Each province and territory has its own archives; these too may be accessed on the Internet, though certain printed guides are available. For citing unpublished material, see the guidelines and examples in 17.222–31.

UNITED KINGDOM

17.336   *Reference works*. Among numerous guides to British records are *Guide to the Contents of the Public Record Office*; Frank Rodgers, *A Guide to British*

Government Publications; and John E. Pemberton, ed., *The Bibliographic Control of Official Publications* (all in bibliog. 4.5).

17.337 *First element in citations.* Citations to British government documents, as to U.S. documents, should begin with the name of the authorizing body—whether Parliament, Public Record Office, Foreign Office, or whatever, preceded (unless obvious from the context) by "United Kingdom." ("UK" is best used adjectivally, as in 17.338.)

17.338 *Government publisher.* The publisher of most UK government material is Her (His) Majesty's Stationery Office (HMSO) in London.

17.339 *Date and number form.* The British generally prefer the day-month-year form of dates (2 January 2002), and the examples below reflect that form. In an American work, however, dates pertaining to British documents should be given in a form consistent with the usage elsewhere in the work. Dates that are part of a quoted title must remain unchanged. Similarly, *2d* and *3d* may be changed, as appropriate, to *2nd* and *3rd*.

17.340 *Parliamentary publications.* Parliamentary publications include all materials issued by both houses of Parliament, the House of Commons (HC) and the House of Lords (HL): journals of both houses (sometimes abbreviated *CJ* and *LJ*); votes and proceedings; debates; bills, reports, and papers; and statutes.

17.341 *Publication of parliamentary debates.* Before 1909, debates from both houses were published together; since then they have been published in separate series.

Hansard Parliamentary Debates, 1st series (1803–20)
Hansard Parliamentary Debates, 2d series (1820–30)
Hansard Parliamentary Debates, 3d series (1830–91)
Parliamentary Debates, 4th series (1892–1908)
Parliamentary Debates, Commons, 5th series (1909–80)
Parliamentary Debates, Commons, 6th series (1980/81–)
Parliamentary Debates, Lords, 5th series (1909–)

17.342 *Citing debates.* Citations include series, volume number, and dates; specific references include column (or occasionally page).

N: 1. *Hansard Parliamentary Debates*, 3d ser., vol. 249 (1879), cols. 611–27.
       2. *Parliamentary Debates*, 4th ser., vol. 13 (1893), col. 1273.
       3. *Hansard*, 3d ser., vol. 249, col. 628.
       4. *Parl. Deb.*, 4th ser., vol. 13, col. 1270.

5. Churchill, Speech to the House of Commons, 18 January 1945, *Parliamentary Debates*, Commons, 5th ser., vol. 407 (1944–45), cols. 425–46.

B: Churchill, Winston. Speech to the House of Commons, 18 January 1945. *Parliamentary Debates*, Commons, 5th ser., vol. 407 (1944–45), cols. 425–46.

United Kingdom. *Hansard Parliamentary Debates*, 3d ser., vol. 249 (1879).

———. *Parliamentary Debates*. Commons, 5th ser., vol. 26 (1911).

Although no longer the official name, *Hansard* (less often, *Hansard's*) is still sometimes used in citations to all series of parliamentary debates. Such usage is best avoided, however.

17.343 *Citing debates, British style.* The following British style may be used if consistent with other citations within a work—for example, in a work using formal legal citation style.

N: 6. 188 *Parl. Deb.* 4s., cols. 1356–1406.

7. 393 *HC Deb.* 5s., col. 403.

17.344 *Parliamentary bills, reports, and papers.* The bills, reports, and papers issued separately by Parliament are published together at the end of each session in volumes referred to as *Sessional Papers*. Each volume includes a divisional title (*Prison Education* in the example below).

N: 8. House of Commons, "Present and Future Role of the Assistant Chief Education Officer," *Sessional Papers, 1982–83, Prison Education*, 25 April 1983, vol. 2, par. 9.14, p. 102.

17.345 *Command papers.* Command papers are so called because they originate outside Parliament and are ostensibly presented to Parliament "by command of Her [His] Majesty." The different abbreviations for "command" indicate the series and must not be altered. No *s* is added to the plural (Cmnd. 3834, 3835).

No. 1 to No. 4222 (1833–69)	Cmd. 1 to Cmd. 9889 (1919–56)
C. 1 to C. 9550 (1870–99)	Cmnd. 1–9927 (1956–86)
Cd. 1 to Cd. 9239 (1900–1918)	Cm. 1– (1986–)

Command papers may consist of a pamphlet or several volumes. Dates may include a month or just a year.

N: 9. *The Basle Facility and the Sterling Area*, Cmnd. 3787 (October 1968), 15–16.

10. *First Interim Report of the Committee on Currency and Foreign Exchanges after the War*, Cd. 9182 (1918).

11. Committee on the Working of the Monetary System [Radcliffe Committee], *Principal Memoranda of Evidence*, vol. 1 (London, 1960).

12. *Review Boards on Doctors' and Dentists' Remuneration, Thirteenth Report*, Cmnd. 8878 (1983).

13. *Basle Facility*, 16.

B: United Kingdom. Parliament. *Report of the Royal Commission on Indian Currency and Finance*. Vol. 2, Appendices. Cmd. 2687. 1926.

17.346   *Statutes.* More often cited in notes than in bibliographies, the Acts of Parliament are identified by title (in roman), date (regnal year through 1962, calendar year after 1962), and chapter number (c. or cap. for chapter; arabic numeral for national number, lowercase roman for local). Monarchs' names in regnal year citations are abbreviated: Car. (Charles), Edw., Eliz., Geo., Hen., Jac. (James), Phil. & M., Rich., Vict., Will., W. & M. The year precedes the name; the monarch's ordinal, if any, follows it (15 Geo. 6), both in arabic numerals. An ampersand may be used between regnal years and between names of dual monarchs (1 & 2 W. & M.).

Act of Settlement, 12 & 13 Will. 3, c. 2.
Consolidated Fund Act, 1963, c. 1.
Manchester Corporation Act, 1967, c. xl.

17.347   *Compilations of statutes.* The three chief compilations of statutory material for the United Kingdom are the following:

· *Statutes of the Realm.* Statutes from 1235 through 1948, with the exception of the years 1642–60.
· *Acts and Ordinances of the Interregnum*, ed. C. H. Firth and R. S. Rait, 3 vols. (London, 1911). Statutes for the years 1642–60.
· *Public General Acts and Measures*, published annually since 1831 by HMSO (see 17.338).

Statutes of the Realm (sometimes abbreviated as *Statutes*) is the most commonly cited. The calendar date may be given as well as the regnal year.

N: 14. King's General Pardon, 1540, *Statutes of the Realm*, 32 Hen. 8, c. 49.

         15. *Statutes of the Realm*, 31 Vict., c. xiv, 2 April 1868.

In citing more recent statutes, the regnal year is usually omitted, and the statute may be given in short form.

16. *Crown Proceedings Act* (1947).

17.348 *Foreign and state papers.* Citations to the publication *British Foreign and State Papers* include the name of the originating agency, the title of the paper (in quotation marks), the years covered (in roman), and, where relevant, the volume and page reference.

> N: 17. Foreign Office, "Austria: Proclamation of the Emperor Annulling the Constitution of 4th March 1849," *British Foreign and State Papers*, 1952–53, 41: 1289–99.

A bibliographic entry would begin like this: United Kingdom. Foreign Office.

17.349 *Reports in pamphlet form.* Reports issued in pamphlet form by ministries, committees, and the like are cited as follows:

> B: United Kingdom. Office of the Minister of Science. Committee on Management and Control of Research. *Report*, 1961.

17.350 *Other published records.* There are many compilations of British historical records, some of them transcriptions of the documents preserved in the Public Record Office.

> B: United Kingdom. *Acts of the Privy Council of England*. Edited by J. R. Dasent. 32 vols. London, 1890–1907.
> ———. *Rotuli parliamentorum* . . . (1278–1504). 6 vols. N.p., n.d.
> ———. *Statutes of the Realm*. Edited by A. Luders and others. 11 vols. London, 1810–28.

In notes, abbreviations may be used.

> N: 19. *Rot. parl.*, vol. 2 (1341) (n.p., n.d.).

17.351 *Calendars.* Early records preserved in the Public Record Office and available in printed form, called *Calendars*, are arranged more or less chronologically. It is essential to give the date of the item cited.

> B: United Kingdom. Public Record Office. "Queen Mother to Queen," 18 February 1581. *Calendar of State Papers, Foreign Series, of the Reign of Elizabeth [I]* (January 1581–April 1582). London, 1907.

A note could omit "United Kingdom" (if clear from the context) and end with the item number and page reference.

> . . . (London, 1907), no. 85, p. 63.

17.352 *Unpublished UK government documents.* For general guidelines and many examples, which can be adapted to government documents, see 17.222–31. The main depositories for unpublished government documents in the United Kingdom are the Public Record Office (PRO) and the British Library (BL), both in London. (The British Library is a division of the British Museum; before it was called the British Library, citations to documents housed there used the abbreviation BM.) References usually include such classifications as Admiralty (Adm.), Chancery (C), Colonial Office (CO), Exchequer (E), Foreign Office (FO), or State Papers (SP) as well as the collection and volume numbers and, where relevant, the folio or page number(s).

17.353 *Frequently cited collections.* Among important collections in the British Library are the Cotton Manuscripts, with subdivisions named after Roman emperors (e.g., Cotton MSS, Caligula [Calig.] D.VII), the Harleian Manuscripts, the Sloane Manuscripts, and the Additional Manuscripts (Add. or Addit.).

17.354 *Examples*

N: 19. Patent Rolls, 3 Rich. 2, pt. 1, m. 12d (Calendar of Patent Rolls, 1377–81, 470).

20. Hodgson to Halifax, 22 Feb. 1752, PRO, CO 137:48.

21. Clarendon to Lumley, 16 Jan. 1869, PRO, FO Belgium/133, no. 6.

22. [Henry Elsynge], "The moderne forme of the Parliaments of England," BL, Add. MSS 26645.

23. Minutes of the General Court, 17 Apr. 1733, 3:21, BL, Add. MSS 25545.

24. Letter of a Bristol Man, BL, Add. MSS 33029:152–55.

B: United Kingdom. Public Record Office. Patent Rolls, Philip and Mary. C66/870. London.

———. Public Record Office. Lisle Papers. SP3. 18 vols.

INTERNATIONAL BODIES

17.355 *Elements to include.* Citations to documents of international bodies such as the United Nations should identify the authorizing body (and the author or editor where appropriate), the topic or title of the paper, and the date. Series and publication numbers, place of publication, and a page reference may be included. Abbreviations may be used in notes and, to avoid duplication, in bibliographies (UN = United Nations, LoNP = League of Nation Papers, WTO = World Trade Organization, and so forth).

N: 1. League of Nations, *Position of Women of Russian Origin in the Far East*, ser. LoNP, 1935, IV.3.

2. League of Nations, *International Currency Experience: Lessons of the Inter-war Period* (Geneva, 1944), II.A.4.

3. UN General Assembly, Ninth Session, Official Records, Supplement 19, *Special United Nations Fund for Economic Development: Final Report*, prepared by Raymond Scheyven in pursuance of UN General Assembly Resolution 724B (VIII), A/2728, 1954.

4. I. Clark, "Should the IMF Become More Adaptive?" Working Paper WP/96/11 (Washington, DC: International Monetary Fund, 1996).

5. P. Low, "Trade Measures and Environmental Quality: The Implications for Mexico's Exports," in *International Trade and the Environment*, ed. P. Low, chap. 7, Discussion Paper 159 (Washington DC: World Bank, 1992).

B: General Agreement on Tariffs and Trade. *The Results of the Uruguay Round of Multilateral Trade Negotiations: The Legal Texts*. Geneva: GATT Secretariat, 1994.

Organization for Economic Cooperation and Development. *Liberalization of Capital Movements and Financial Services in the OECD Area*. Paris: OECD, 1990.

United Nations Conference on Trade and Development. *Controlling Carbon Dioxide Emissions: The Tradeable Permit System*. Geneva: UNCTAD, 1995.

World Trade Organization. *International Trade: Trends and Statistics*. Geneva: WTO, 1995.

PUBLIC DOCUMENTS ONLINE

17.356   *General.* To cite online public documents, follow the relevant examples presented above. In addition to the complete standard citation, include a URL and, if the publisher or discipline requires it, or for especially time-sensitive data, an access date (see 17.12).

N: 1. Illinois Constitution, art. 2, sec. 2, http://www.legis.state.il.us/commission/lrb/conmain.htm.

39. U.S. Census Bureau, "Health Insurance Coverage Status and Type of Coverage by Sex, Race, and Hispanic Origin, 1987 to 1999," Health Insurance Historical Table 1, 2000, http://www.census.gov/hhes/hlthins/historic/hihistt1.html.

107. L. A. Adamic and B. A. Huberman. "The Nature of Markets in the World Wide Web," working paper (Xerox Palo Alto Research Center, 1999), http://www.parc.xerox.com/istl/groups/iea/www/webmarkets.html (accessed March 1, 2001).

B: Adamic, L. A., and B. A. Huberman. "The Nature of Markets in the World Wide Web." Working paper, Xerox Palo Alto Research Center, 1999. http://www

.parc.xerox.com/istl/groups/iea/www/webmarkets.html (accessed March 1, 2001).

Illinois Constitution, art. 2, sec. 2. http://www.legis.state.il.us/commission/lrb/ conmain.htm.

U.S. Census Bureau. "Health Insurance Coverage Status and Type of Coverage by Sex, Race, and Hispanic Origin, 1987 to 1999." Health Insurance Historical Table 1, 2000. http://www.census.gov/hhes/hlthins/historic/hihisttl.html.

T: (Illinois Constitution)
      (U.S. Census Bureau 2000)
      (Adamic and Huberman 1999)

R: Adamic, L. A., and B. A. Huberman. 1999. The nature of markets in the World Wide Web. Working paper, Xerox Palo Alto Research Center. http://www .parc.xerox.com/istl/groups/iea/www/webmarkets.html (accessed March 12, 2001).

Illinois Constitution, art. 2, sec. 2. http://www.legis.state.il.us/commission/lrb/ conmain.htm.

U.S. Census Bureau. 2000. Health insurance coverage status and type of coverage by sex, race, and Hispanic origin, 1987 to 1999. Health Insurance Historical Table 1. http://www.census.gov/hhes/hlthins/historic/hihisttl.html.

Databases

17.357   *General.* Though all information stored electronically may be said to constitute a database, for this discussion on documentation a database is a collection of electronic information or records organized, stored, and updated for the sole purpose of providing information. In this sense the computerized record of the human genome has become a database, and any online encyclopedia or dictionary is considered a database. (For citing online reference works, see 17.239.)

17.358   *Scientific databases.* In the sciences especially, it has become customary to cite databases as follows: list, at a minimum, in this order, the name of the database, the URL, a descriptive phrase or record locator (such as a data marker or accession number) indicating the part of the database being cited or explaining the nature of the reference, and finally an access date. In bibliographies or reference lists, list under the name of the database.

N: 1. NASA/IPAC Extragalactic Database, http://nedwww.ipac.caltech.edu/ (object name IRAS F00400+4059; accessed August 1, 2001).

5. GenBank, http://www.ncbi.nlm.nih.gov/Genbank/ (for RP11-322N14 BAC [accession number AC017046]; accessed August 6, 2001).

7. Unified Database (Bioinformatics Unit and Genome Center, Weizmann Institute of Science), http://bioinformatics.weizmann.ac.il/udb/ (for mapping data on candidate genes; accessed July 29, 2001).

B/R: NASA/IPAC Extragalactic Database. http://nedwww.ipac.caltech.edu/ (object name IRAS F00400+4059; accessed August 1, 2001).

GenBank. http://www.ncbi.nlm.nih.gov/Genbank/ (for RP11-322N14 BAC [accession number AC017046]; accessed August 6, 2001).

Unified Database. Bioinformatics Unit and Genome Center, Weizmann Institute of Science. http://bioinformatics.weizmann.ac.il/udb/ (for mapping data on candidate genes; accessed July 29, 2001).

T: (NASA/IPAC Extragalactic Database [object name IRAS F00400+4059])

(Unified Database)

(Genbank [accession number AC017046])

17.359 *News and journal databases.* For citations to news or journal articles obtained by searching a third-party Internet database that archives and offers such material whether by subscription or otherwise, follow the recommendations in the sections on journals and other periodicals in this chapter. In addition, include the URL of the main entrance of the service, as in the first and third examples (note that main entrance and other directory-level URLs end with a slash). Some services will provide stable URLs to articles in their databases, as in the second example, but usually the main entrance is easier to reproduce, especially in printed material. If the publisher or discipline requires it, or for especially time-sensitive data, also record in parentheses the date the material was last accessed (see 17.12).

N: 2. Beth Daley, "A Tale of a Whale: Scientists, Museum Are Eager to Study, Display Rare Creature," *Boston Globe*, June 11, 2002, third edition, http://www.lexis -nexis.com/.

B: Thomas, Trevor M. "Wales: Land of Mines and Quarries." *Geographical Review* 46, no. 1 (1956): 59–81. http://links.jstor.org/sici?sici=0016-7428%28195601 %2946%3A1%3C59%3AWLOMAQ%3E2.0.CO%3B2-O.

or

Thomas, Trevor M. "Wales: Land of Mines and Quarries." *Geographical Review* 46, no. 1 (1956): 59–81. http://www.jstor.org/.

18

Indexes

Introduction

18.1   *Scope.* This chapter offers basic guidelines for preparing and editing an index. It covers both general principles of indexing and specifics of Chicago's preferred style in matters of typography, alphabetizing, and the like. Many of the guidelines apply equally to electronic works, which often require indexes (see 1.186).

18.2   *Who should index a work?* The ideal indexer sees the work as a whole, understands the emphasis of the various parts and their relation to the whole, and knows—or guesses—what readers of the particular work are likely to look for and what headings they will think of. The indexer should be widely read, scrupulous in handling of detail, analytically minded, well acquainted with publishing practices, and capable of meeting almost impossible deadlines. Although authors know better than anyone else their subject matter and the audience to whom the work is addressed, not all can look at their work through the eyes of a potential reader. Nor do many authors have the technical skills, let alone the time, necessary to prepare a good index that meets the publisher's deadline. Some authors produce excellent indexes. Others would do better to enlist the aid of a professional indexer.

18.3   *The indexer and deadlines.* Most book indexes have to be made between the time page proof is issued and the time it is returned to the typesetter—usually about four weeks. (For an illustration of how indexing fits into the overall publishing process for books, see appendix B.) An author preparing his or her own index will have to proofread as well as index the work in that short time span. Good indexing requires reflection; the indexer needs to stop frequently and decide whether the right choices have been made. A professional indexer, familiar with the publisher's requirements, may be better equipped for such reflection. For journals that publish a volume index, the indexer may have several months to prepare a preliminary index, adding entries as new issues of the journal arrive. The final issue in the volume is typically indexed from page proofs, however, and the indexer may have as little as a week to work on the last issue and prepare the final draft of the index.

18.4   *Computer software.* Computers and special indexing software can streamline the indexing process and substantially reduce the time required. No computer can produce a good index on its own, however; human intervention is always required. A computer can search, record, and alphabetize terms and can arrange numbers far more efficiently than a person. But it cannot distinguish between a term and a concept or between a relevant and an irrelevant statement. At best it can generate a concordance—a simple list of major words that appear in a document. Without human intervention, a computer cannot create appropriate subentries or cross-references.

18.5   *Resources.* For greatly expanded coverage of the present guidelines, along with alternative usages, consult Nancy Mulvany's *Indexing Books* (bibliog. 2.5). Anyone likely to prepare a number of indexes should acquire that work. For further reference, see Hans H. Wellisch, *Indexing from A to Z*, and Linda K. Fetters, *Handbook of Indexing Techniques* (bibliog. 2.5).

Kinds of Indexes and Components of an Index

18.6   *Single versus multiple indexes.* A single index, including subjects and names of persons, is usually the easiest to use. It is frustrating to hunt for a name or term only to find you are in the wrong index. Further, cross-referencing between subjects and persons is much simpler in a single index. Certain publications, however, such as journals and lengthy scientific works that cite numerous authors of other studies, may include an index of names (or author index; see 18.115–16) in addition to a subject index. An anthology may include an author-and-title index, and a collection of poetry or hymns may have an index of first lines as well as an index of titles. If two or more indexes must appear in one work, they should be visually distinct so that users know immediately where they are. In a biological work, for example, the headings in the index of names will all be in roman type and will begin with capital letters, and there will be no subentries, whereas most of the headings in the general subject index will begin lowercase and many subentries will appear; and if there is a taxonomic index many entries will be in italic. The running heads should carry the titles of each index.

MAIN HEADINGS, SUBENTRIES, AND LOCATORS

18.7 *The entries.* An entry consists of a heading (or main heading), locators (see 18.12), and subentries and cross-references as needed.

18.8 *Main headings.* The main heading of an index entry is normally a noun or noun phrase—the name of a person, a place, an object, or an abstraction. An adjective alone should never constitute a heading; it should always be paired with a noun to form a noun phrase. A noun phrase is sometimes inverted to allow the keyword—the word a reader is most likely to look under—to appear first. For capitalization, see 18.10.

agricultural collectivization, 143–46, 198	Communist Party (American), 425
Aron, Raymond, 312–14	Communist Party (British), 268
Bloomsbury group, 269	war communism, 90, 95, 125
Brest-Litovsk, Treaty of, 61, 76, 85	World War I, 34–61
capitalism, American commitment to, 383	Yalta conference, 348, 398
cold war, 396–437	

18.9 *Subentries.* An entry that requires more than five or six locators (page or paragraph numbers) is usually broken up into subentries to spare readers unnecessary excursions. A subentry, like an entry, consists of a heading (usually referred to as a subheading), page references, and, rarely, cross-references. Subheadings often form a grammatical relationship with the main heading, whereby heading and subheading combine into a single phrase, as in the first example below. Other subheadings form divisions or units within the larger category of the heading, as in the second example. Both kinds can be used within one index. See also 18.129. For sub-subentries, see 18.26–28.

capitalism: and American pro-Sovietism, 273, 274; bourgeoisie as symbol of, 4, 13; as creation of society, 7; Khrushchev on burying, 480; student protests against, 491, 493	Native American peoples: Ahualucos, 140–41; Chichimecs, 67–68; Huastecs, 154; Toltecs, 128–36; Zapotecs, 168–72

18.10   *Initial lowercase letters in main headings.* The first word of a main heading is normally capitalized only if capitalized in text—a proper noun (as in the second example in the previous paragraph), a genus name, the title of a work, and so on. Indexes in the sciences often avoid initial capitals because the distinction between capitalized and lowercased terms in the text may be crucial. Traditionally, all main headings in an index were capitalized; Chicago recommends the practice only where the subentries are so numerous that capitalized main headings make for easier navigation.

18.11   *Capitalization of subentries.* Subentries are always lowercased unless, as in the second example in 18.9, the keyword is capitalized in text (a proper noun, a genus name, the title of a work, etc.).

18.12   *Locators.* In a printed work, locators are usually page numbers, though they can also be paragraph numbers (as in this manual), section numbers, or the like. When discussion of a subject continues for more than a page, paragraph, or section, the first and last numbers (inclusive numbers) are given: 34–36 (if pages), 10.36–41 (if paragraphs), and so on (see 18.13). The abbreviations *ff.* or *et seq.* should never be used in an index. Scattered references to a subject over several pages or sections are usually indicated by separate locators (34, 35, 36; 8.18, 8.20, 8.21). The term *passim* may be used to indicate scattered references over a number of not necessarily sequential pages or sections (e.g., 78–88 passim). Trivial mentions are best either ignored or, if needed for some reason, gathered at the end of the entry under a subentry "mentioned." For use of the en dash, see 6.83; for inclusive numbers, see 9.64, 18.13.

18.13   *Inclusive numbers.* Publishers vary in their preferences for the form of inclusive numbers (also known as continuing numbers). Although the simplest and most foolproof system is to give the full form of numbers everywhere (e.g., 234–235), Chicago prefers its traditional system (presented below), which more or less corresponds to the way numbers would be read aloud. The system is followed in all examples in this chapter. Whichever form is used in the text should be used in the index as well.

FIRST NUMBER	SECOND NUMBER	EXAMPLES
1–99	Use all digits	3–10, 71–72, 96–117
100 or multiples of 100	Use all digits	100–104, 1100–1113
101 through 109, 201 through 209, etc.	Use changed part only	101–8, 1103–4

110 through 199, 210 through 299, etc.	Use two or more digits as needed	321–28, 498–532, 1087–89, 11564–615, 12991–13001
	But if three digits change in a four-digit number, use all four	1496–1504, 2787–2816

Roman numerals are always given in full, for example, xxv–xxviii, cvi–cix. For use of the en dash between numerals, see 6.83, 9.62–63.

CROSS-REFERENCES

18.14 *General principles.* Cross-references should be used with discretion; an overabundance can be irritating. They are of two main kinds—*see* references and *see also* references. Both are treated differently according to whether they refer to a main heading or to a subheading. *See* and *see also* are set in italics (but see 18.21).

18.15 *"See" references.* See references direct a reader from, for example, an informal term to a technical one, a pseudonym to a real name, an inverted term to a noninverted one, or vice versa. They are also used for variant spellings, synonyms, aliases, abbreviations, and so on. The choice of the term under which the full entry appears depends largely on where readers are most likely to look. *See* references should therefore be given only where the indexer believes many readers might otherwise miss the full entry. If the entry to which the *see* reference refers is about the same length as the *see* reference itself, it is often more useful to omit the *see* reference and simply give the page numbers under both headings. Such duplication will save readers a trip. Further, the indexer and anyone editing an index must make certain that no *see* entry merely leads to another *see* entry (a "blind cross-reference"). See also 18.46.

Federal Bureau of Investigation, 145–48
FBI (Federal Bureau of Investigation),
    145–48

18.16 *"See" references following a main entry.* When a *see* reference follows a main entry, as it usually does, it is preceded by a period and *See* is capitalized. If two or more *see* references are needed, they are arranged in alphabetical order and separated by semicolons. They reflect the capitalization of the main entry.

adolescence. *See* teenagers; youth

American Communist Party. *See* Communist Party (American)

baking soda. *See* sodium bicarbonate

Clemens, Samuel. *See* Twain, Mark

de Kooning, Willem. *See* Kooning, Willem de

Den Haag ('s Gravenhage). *See* Hague, The

Lunt, Mrs. Alfred. *See* Fontanne, Lynn

Mormons. *See* Latter-day Saints, Church of Jesus Christ of

Roman Catholic Church. *See* Catholicism

The Hague. *See* Hague, The

Turwyn. *See* Terouenne

universities. *See* Harvard University; Princeton University; University of Chicago

van Gogh, Vincent. *See* Gogh, Vincent van

Virgin Queen. *See* Elizabeth I

18.17 *"See" references following a subentry.* When a *see* reference follows a subentry, it is put in parentheses and *see* is lowercased.

statistical material, 16, 17, 89; coding of, for typesetter (*see* typesetting); proofreading, 183

18.18 *"See" references to a subheading.* Most *see* references are to a main entry, as in the examples in 18.16. When a cross-reference directs readers to a subentry under another main heading, *see under* may be used.

lace making. *See under* Bruges

Pride and Prejudice. See under Austen, Jane

An alternative, to be used when a *see under* reference might fail to direct readers to the right spot, is to drop the word *under* and add the wording of the subentry, following a colon. (Although a comma is sometimes used, a colon is preferred.) The wording of the cross-reference must correspond to that of the relevant subentry so that readers can find it quickly.

lace making. *See* Bruges: lace making

Pride and Prejudice. See Austen, Jane: *Pride and Prejudice*

18.19 *"See also" references. See also* references are placed at the end of an entry when *additional* information can be found in another entry. They follow a period. *See* is capitalized, and both words are in italics. If the cross-reference is to a subentry under another main heading, the words *see also under* may be used. If two or more *see also* references are needed, they are arranged in alphabetical order and separated by semicolons. As with *see* references, *see also* references must never lead to a *see* entry.

copyright, 95–100. *See also* permission to
 reprint; source notes
Maya: art of, 236–43; cities of, 178; present
 day, 267. *See also under* Yucatán

If *see also under* does not work in a particular context—for example, when one of the *see also* references is to a main entry and another to a subentry—the word *under* should be dropped and the wording of the subentry added after a colon.

Maya: art of, 236–43; cities of, 178. *See also*
 Mexican art; Yucatán: Maya

When a *see also* reference comes at the end of a subentry—a rare occurrence, and somewhat distracting—it is put in parentheses and *see* is lowercased.

equality: as bourgeois ideal, 5–6, 7; contractual quality, 13; in democracy's
 definition, 24 (*see also* democracy);
 League of the Rights of Man debate on,
 234–35

18.20 *Accuracy.* In all cross-references, headings (and subheadings, if used) should generally be cited in full, with capitalization, inversion, and punctuation exactly as in the entry referred to. But a long heading may occasionally be shortened if no confusion results. For example, in an index with frequent references to Beethoven, "*See also* Beethoven, Ludwig van" could be shortened to "*See also* Beethoven" if done consistently.

18.21 *Italics.* The words *see, see under,* and *see also* are normally italicized. But if what follows (e.g., a book title or a foreign word) is in italics, the words are preferably set in roman to distinguish them from the rest of the cross-reference. This is not necessary when they follow italics.

Austen, Jane. See *Pride and Prejudice*
but
Pride and Prejudice. See Jane Austen

18.22   *Generic cross-references.* Both *see* and *see also* references may include generic references; that is, they may refer to a type of heading rather than to several specific headings. The entire cross-reference is then set in italics.

> public buildings. *See names of individual*
>   *buildings*
> sacred writings, 345–46, 390–401, 455–65.
>   *See also specific titles*

When generic cross-references accompany specific cross-references, the former are placed last, even if out of alphabetic order.

> dogs, 35–42. *See also* American Kennel
>   Club; shelters; *and individual breed names*

RUN-IN VERSUS INDENTED INDEXES

18.23   *Flush-and-hang style.* In printed works, all indexes are set in flush-and-hang (or hanging-indention) style. The first line of each entry, the main heading, is set flush left, and any following lines are indented. When there are subentries, a choice must be made between run-in and indented styles.

18.24   *Run-in style.* In run-in style, the subentries follow one another without each one's starting a new line. They are separated by semicolons. If the main heading is immediately followed by subentries, it is separated from them by a colon (see first example below). If it is immediately followed by locators, these are preceded by a comma and followed by a semicolon (see second example below). Further examples of run-in entries may be seen in 18.9, 18.19, 18.145.

> coordinate systems: Cartesian, 14; distance within, 154–55; time dilation and, 108–14. *See also* inertial systems; moving systems

> Sabba da Castiglione, Monsignor, 209, 337; against cosmetics, 190; on whether to marry, 210–11; on wives' proper behavior, 230–40, 350

Chicago and many other scholarly publishers generally prefer run-in style because it requires less space. It works best, however, when there is only one level of subhead (but see 18.27). For the examples above in indented style, see 18.25.

18.25   *Indented style.* In indented style (also known as stacked style), each subentry begins a new line and is indented (usually one em). No colon appears before the first subentry, and subentries are not separated by semicolons. Runover lines must therefore be further indented (usually two ems) to distinguish them clearly from subentries; whether runover lines belong to the main heading or to subentries, their indention should be the same. (Indention is always measured from the left margin, not from the first word in the line above.) Cross-references appear at the end of the list of subentries. A period is used only before *See,* which immediately follows the main entry, not before *See also. See* and *see under* references are treated in the same way as in run-in indexes (see 18.24).

coordinate systems
  Cartesian, 14
  distance within, 154–55
  time dilation and, 108–14
  See also inertial systems; moving systems

Sabba da Castiglione, Monsignor, 209, 337
  against cosmetics, 190
  on whether to marry, 210–11
  on wives' proper behavior, 230–40, 350

Indented style is usually preferred in scientific works and reference works (such as this manual). It is particularly useful where sub-subentries are required (see 18.28).

18.26   *Sub-subentries.* If an index requires a second level of subentries (sub-subentries), a mixture of run-in and indented styles can be used (see 18.27–28, 18.146).

18.27   *Sub-subentries in run-in indexes.* If more than a handful of sub-subentries are needed in an index, the indented format rather than the run-in type should be chosen (see 18.26). A very few, however, can be accommodated in a run-in index or, better, avoided by repeating a keyword (see example A). If repetition will not work, subentries requiring sub-subentries can be indented, each starting a new line but preceded by an em dash flush with the margin; the sub-subentries are then run in (see example B). Em dashes are *not* used where only one level of subentry is needed.

Example A (run-in index: sub-subentries avoided)

Inuits: language, 18; pottery, 432–37;
  tradition of, in Alaska, 123; tradition of,
  in California, 127

Example B (run-in index: subentries requiring sub-subentries indented with em dash, sub-subentries run in)

Argos: cremation at, 302; and Danaos of Egypt, 108; Middle Helladic, 77; shaft graves at, 84
  Arkadia, 4; Early Helladic, 26, 40; Mycenaean, 269, 306

Armor and weapons 152, 244, 258, 260, 311; greaves, 135,
—attack weapons (general): Early Hel- 179, 260; helmets, 101, 135, 147, 221,
ladic and Cycladic, 33; Mycenaean, 225, 243, 258
255, 258–60; from shaft graves, 89, —bow and arrow, 14, 99, 101, 166, 276
98–100; from tholos tombs, 128, 131, Asine: Early Helladic, 29, 36; Middle Hel-
133 ladic, 74; Mycenaean town and trade,
—body armor: cuirass, 135–36, 147, 233, 258, 263; tombs at, 300

18.28 *Sub-subentries in indented indexes.* In an indented index, sub-subentries are best run in (see example A below). If, in a particular index, running them in makes the index hard to use, they have to be indented more deeply than the subentries (example B). When the first method is used, runover lines need not be indented more than the standard two ems, already a fairly deep indention. When the second is used, runover lines have to be indented three ems, and some very short lines appear. See also 18.146–47.

Example A (indented index: run-in sub-subentries)

nutritional analysis of bamboo, 72–81 organic constituents, 73–79, 269, 270;
  digestible energy, 94–96, 213–14, 222   amino acids, 75–76, 86, 89; amino
  inorganic constituents: minerals, 81,   acids compared with other foods,
    83–85, 89; silica (*see* silica levels in   77; cellulose, 73, 78, 269, 270; crude
    bamboo); total ash, 73, 79, 80, 91   protein, 73–75, 80, 89–91, 213, 269,
    269, 270   270; standard proximate analysis of,
  methods used, 72–73   78–80; vitamin C, 78, 79

Example B (indented index: sub-subentries indented)

nutritional analysis of bamboo, 72–81   cellulose, 73, 78, 269, 270
  digestible energy, 94–96, 213–14, 222   crude protein, 73–75, 80, 89–91, 213,
  inorganic constituents: 269, 270
    minerals, 81, 83–85, 89   standard proximate analysis of,
    silica (*see* silica levels in bamboo)   78–80
    total ash, 73, 79, 80, 91, 269, 270   vitamin C, 78, 79
  methods used, 72–73
  organic constituents, 73–79, 269, 270
    amino acids, 75–76, 86, 89
    amino acids compared with other
      foods, 77

If sub-sub-subentries are required (which heaven forbid!), style B must be used, and they must be run in.

General Principles of Indexing

18.29   *Style and usage.* An index is a tool for one particular work. By the time the index is prepared, the style used in the work has long been determined, and the index must reflect that style. If British spelling has been used throughout the text, it must be used in the index. Shakspere in the text calls for Shakspere in the index. Hernando Cortez should not be indexed as Cortés. Older geographical terms should not be altered to their present form (Constantinople, Istanbul; Siam, Thailand; etc.), though a cross-reference may be appropriate. The use of accents and other diacritical marks must be observed exactly as in the text (Schönberg, *not* Schoenberg). Only in the rare instance in which readers might not find information sought should a cross-reference be given. Any terms italicized or enclosed in quotation marks in the text should be treated similarly in the index. If inclusive numbers are given in full in the text (see 18.13), that style should be used in the index.

18.30   *Choosing terms.* The wording for all entries should be concise and logical. As far as possible, terms should be chosen according to the author's usage. If, for example, the author of a philosophical work uses *essence* to mean *being*, the main entry should be under *essence*, possibly with a cross-reference from *being*. If the terms are used interchangeably, the indexer must choose one; in this case a cross-reference is imperative. An indexer relatively unfamiliar with the subject matter may find it useful to ask the author for a brief list of terms that must appear in the index, though such terms will usually suggest themselves as the indexer proceeds through the proofs. Common sense is the best guide. For journals, terms may have been established in advance, either by a predetermined list of keywords within the discipline or by previous journal indexes. See also 18.20.

18.31   *Terms that should not be indexed.* Although proper names are an important element in most indexes, there are times when they should be ignored. In a work on the history of the automobile in the United States, for example, an author might write, "After World War II small sports cars like the British MG, often owned by returning veterans, began to make their appearance in college towns like Northampton, Massachusetts, and Ann Arbor, Michigan." An indexer should resist the temptation to index these place-names; the two towns mentioned have nothing to do with the theme of the work. The MG sports car, on the other hand, should be indexed, given the subject of the work. Similarly, names or terms that occur in passing references and scene-setting elements that are not essential to the theme of a work need not be indexed. (An exception might be made if many readers of a publication would be likely to look for their own names in the index. Occasional vanity entries are not forbidden.)

Proper Names and Variants

18.32   *Choosing between variants.* When names appear in the text in more than one form, or in an incomplete form, the indexer must decide which form to use for the main entry and which for the cross-reference (if any) and occasionally must furnish information not given in the text. Few indexes need to provide the kind of detail found in biographical or geographical dictionaries, though reference works of that kind will help in decision making.

18.33   *Familiar forms of personal names.* Personal names should be indexed as they have become widely known. Note that brackets are used in the following examples to distinguish Chicago's editorial glosses from parenthetical tags, such as those in some of the examples in 18.34–38, which would actually appear in a published index.

> Cervantes, Miguel de [*not* Cervantes Saavedra, Miguel de]
> Fisher, M. F. K. [*not* Fisher, Mary Frances Kennedy]
>
> London, Jack [*not* London, John Griffith]
> Poe, Edgar Allan [*not* Poe, E. A., *or* Poe, Edgar A.]

But in a work devoted to, say, M. F. K. Fisher or Cervantes, the full form of the name should appear in the index.

18.34   *Pseudonyms.* Persons who have used pseudonyms or other professional names are usually listed under their real names. If the pseudonym has become a household word, however, it should be used as the main entry, often with the real name in parentheses; a cross-reference is seldom necessary.

> Ouida. *See* Ramée, Marie Louise de la
> Ramée, Marie Louise de la (pseud. Ouida)
> Æ. *See* Russell, George William
> Russell, George William (pseud. Æ)
> *but*
> Voltaire (François-Marie Arouet)
> Molière (Jean-Baptiste Poquelin)

Twain, Mark (Samuel Langhorne Clemens)
Monroe, Marilyn (Norma Jean Baker)

The real name should be included only where it is relevant to the work.

18.35 *Persons with the same name.* Persons with the same name should be distinguished by a middle initial (if either has one) or by a parenthetical tag.

Campbell, James
Campbell, James B.
Field, David Dudley (clergyman)

Field, David Dudley (lawyer)
Pitt, William (the elder)
Pitt, William (the younger)

In works that include many persons with the same last name (often a family name), parenthetical identifications are useful. For example, in *Two Lucky People,* by Milton Friedman and Rose D. Friedman (University of Chicago Press, 1998), the following identifications appear.

Friedman, David (son of MF and RDF)
Friedman, Helen (sister of MF)
Friedman, Janet (daughter of MF and RDF)

Friedman, Milton (MF)
Friedman, Rose Director (RDF)
Friedman, Sarah Ethel Landau (mother of MF)

18.36 *Married women's names.* Married women who are known both by their birth names and by their married names should be indexed by their birth names unless the married name is the more familiar. Parenthetical clarifications or cross-references may be supplied as necessary.

Sutherland, Joan (Mrs. Richard Bonynge)
Marinoff, Fania (Mrs. Carl Van Vechten)
Van Vechten, Mrs. Carl. *See* Marinoff, Fania
but
Browning, Elizabeth Barrett
Besant, Annie (née Wood)
Dole, Elizabeth

18.37 *Monarchs, popes, and the like.* Monarchs, popes, and others who are known by their official names, often including a roman numeral, should be indexed under the official name. Identifying tags may be omitted or expanded as appropriate in a particular work.

Anne, Queen
Elizabeth II (queen)
John Paul II (pope)

18.38   *Princes, dukes, and other titled persons.* Princes and princesses are usually indexed under their given names. Dukes, earls, and the like are indexed under the title. A cross-reference may be needed where a title differs from a family name.

Charles, Prince of Wales	Cooper, Anthony Ashley. *See* Shaftesbury,
William, Prince	7th Earl of
Shaftesbury, 7th Earl of (Anthony Ashley Cooper)	

Unless necessary for identification, the titles *Lord* and *Lady* are best omitted from an index, since their use with given names is far from simple. *Sir* and *Dame*, while easier to cope with, are also unnecessary in most indexes. If used, they are ignored in alphabetizing. Brackets are used here to denote Chicago's editorial glosses (see 18.33).

Churchill, Winston [*or* Churchill, Sir Winston]
Hess, Myra [*or* Hess, Dame Myra]
Thatcher, Margaret [even if referred to as Lady Thatcher in text]

But in a work dealing with the nobility, or a historical work such as *The Lisle Letters* (University of Chicago Press, 1981), from which the following examples are taken, titles may be an appropriate or needed element in index entries. The last two examples illustrate distinctions for which expert advice may be needed.

Arundell, Sir John	Grenville, Sir Roger
Audley, Thomas Lord	Grey, Lady Jane ["Lady Jane Grey" in text]
Courtenay, Gertrude, Marchioness of	Whethill, Elizabeth (Muston), Lady
Exeter	["Lady Whethill" in text]
Grenville, Sir Richard	

18.39   *Clerical titles.* Like titles of nobility, such abbreviations as *Rev.* or *Msgr.* should be used only when necessary for identification (see 18.38). They are ignored in alphabetizing.

Jaki, Rev. Stanley S.
Manniere, Msgr. Charles L.
George E. Councell (rector of the Church of the Holy Spirit)
Cranmer, Thomas (archbishop of Canterbury)

18.40   *Academic titles and degrees.* Academic titles such as *Professor* and *Doctor*, used before a name, are not retained in indexing, nor are abbreviations of degrees such as *PhD* or *MD*.

18.41 *"Jr.," "Sr.," "III," and the like.* Suffixes such as *Jr.* are retained in indexing but are placed after the given name and preceded by a comma.

King, Martin Luther, Jr.
Stevenson, Adlai E., III

18.42 *Saints.* Saints are indexed under their given names unless another name is equally well or better known. Parenthetical identifications or cross-references (as well as discretion) may be needed. See also 18.73.

Catherine of Siena, Saint
Thomas, Saint (the apostle)
Thomas Aquinas, Saint

Aquinas. *See* Thomas Aquinas, Saint
Borromeo, Saint Charles
Chrysostom, Saint John

18.43 *Persons whose full names are unknown.* Persons referred to in the work by first or last names only should be parenthetically identified if the full name is unavailable.

John (Smith's shipmate on *Stella*)
Thaxter (family physician)

18.44 *Names incomplete or alluded to in text.* Even if only a shortened form of a name or an epithet is used in the text, the index should give the full form.

TEXT	INDEX
the lake	Michigan, Lake
the bay	San Francisco Bay
the Village	Greenwich Village
the Great Emancipator	Lincoln, Abraham

18.45 *Confusing names.* When the same name is used of more than one entity, identifying tags should be provided.

New York (city)   *or*   New York City
New York (state)   *or*   New York State

18.46 *Abbreviations and acronyms.* Organizations that are widely known under their abbreviations should be indexed and alphabetized according to the abbreviations. Parenthetical glosses, cross-references, or both should be added if the abbreviations, however familiar to the indexer, may not be known to all readers of the particular work. Lesser-known organizations are better indexed under the full name, with a cross-reference from the abbreviation if it is used frequently in the work. See also 18.15.

EEC (European Economic Community)
MLA. *See* Modern Language Association
NATO

Titles of Publications and Other Works

18.47   *Typographic treatment.* Titles of newspapers, books, journals, stories, poems, artwork, musical compositions, and such should be treated typographically as they appear in text—whether italicized, set in roman and enclosed in quotation marks, or simply capitalized (see 8.164–210).

18.48   *Newspapers.* English-language newspapers should be indexed as they are generally known, whether or not the city of publication appears on the masthead. The name is italicized, as in text, and *The* is omitted.

Chicago Sun-Times	*Wall Street Journal*
Cleveland Plain Dealer	*New York Times*
Christian Science Monitor	*Times* (London)

For foreign-language newspapers, the place of publication may be included in parentheses, not italicized. Any article (*Le, Die*, etc.) follows the name, separated by a comma. See also 18.52.

Monde, Le (Paris)
Prensa, La (Buenos Aires)
Süddeutsche Zeitung, Die

18.49   *Periodicals.* Magazines and journals are indexed in the same way as newspapers. *The* is omitted in English-language publications, but the article is included, following the name, in foreign ones.

JAMA (*Journal of the American Medical Association*)
New England Journal of Medicine
Spiegel, Der
Time

18.50   *Titles of works.* A published work, a musical composition, or a piece of art is usually indexed both as a main entry and as a subentry under its creator. The main entry is followed by the creator's name in parentheses (except in an index in which all titles cited have the same creator).

Look Homeward, Angel (Wolfe), 34–37
Wolfe, Thomas: childhood, 6–8; early
    literary influences on, 7–10; *Look*
    Homeward, Angel, 34–37; and Maxwell
    Perkins, 30–41

Several works by a single creator are sometimes treated as subentries under a new main heading, following a main entry on the creator. This device is best employed when many works as well as many topics are listed. Separate main entries may also be included for the works.

Mozart, Wolfgang Amadeus, 49–51, 55–56;   Mozart, Wolfgang Amadeus, works of:
    early musical compositions of, 67–72,   *La clemenza di Tito*, 114; *Don Giovanni*,
    74–80; to Italy with father, 85–92; Salz-   115; *Idomeneo*, 105–6; *Jupiter* Sym-
    burg appointment, 93–95; in Vienna,   phony, 107; *The Magic Flute*, 111–13;
    98–105   *The Marriage of Figaro*, 109–12

18.51   *English-language titles beginning with an article.* In titles beginning with *The, A,* or *An,* the article is traditionally placed at the end of the title, following a comma, when the title forms a main heading. When such a title occurs as a subheading, it appears in its normal position in a run-in index, where inversion would be clumsy and unnecessary, but is inverted in an indented index for easier alphabetic scanning.

Professor and the Madman, The   Winchester, Simon
    (Winchester), 209–11   *Pacific Rising*, 190–95
Winchester, Simon, *Pacific Rising*, 190–95;   *Professor and the Madman, The*, 209–11
    The Professor and the Madman, 209–11;   *River at the Center of the World, The*,
    The River at the Center of the World,   211–15
    211–15

If numerous titles with initial articles appear in one index, clutter may be eliminated by simply omitting the articles. An article should be omitted, however, only if the full title appears elsewhere in the work (whether in text, notes, or bibliography). See also 18.55.

Dickens, Charles, 38–46; *Old Curiosity*
    Shop, 45; *Tale of Two Cities*, 39
Old Curiosity Shop (Dickens), 45

18.52   *Foreign-language titles beginning with an article.* Since initial articles in foreign titles sometimes modify the following word, they are usually retained in an index. They follow the rest of the title in main headings but remain, as in English titles, in their normal position in run-in subentries (see 18.51). Articles are ignored in alphabetizing.

Bohème, La (Puccini)
clemenza de Tito, La (Mozart), 22
kleine Nachtmusik, Eine (Mozart), 223
Mozart, Wolfgang Amadeus: *La clemenza*
   de Tito, 22; *Eine kleine Nachtmusik*, 23
trovatore, Il (Verdi), 323
but
"Un deux trois" (Luboff) [alphabetize under *U*]

An indexer unfamiliar with the language of a title should make sure that the article is indeed an article and not a number (see last example above). French *un* and *une,* for example, and German *ein* and *eine* can mean *one* as well as *a*. In the absence of verification, the indexer will do better to alphabetize all foreign titles just as they appear in text, without inversion. Inversion is customary but not mandatory, whereas faulty inversion will confuse or irritate the user and embarrass the publisher.

18.53   *Titles beginning with a preposition.* Prepositions beginning a title always remain in their original position and are never dropped, whether in English or foreign titles.

Auf meines Kindes Tod
Of Mice and Men

18.54   *Subtitles.* Subtitles of books or articles are omitted both in main headings and in subentries unless essential for identification.

Alphabetizing

18.55   *Main headings: the basic rule.* To exploit the virtues of alphabetizing and thus ease the way for readers, the first word in a main heading should always determine the location of the entry. Thus *A Tale of Two Cities* is inverted as *Tale of Two Cities, A,* and alphabetized under *T,* where readers would naturally look first. Or the article may simply be omitted. See also 18.49, 18.51–52.

LETTER BY LETTER OR WORD BY WORD?

18.56 *Two systems.* The two principal modes of alphabetizing—or sorting—indexes are the *letter-by-letter* and the *word-by-word* systems. A choice between the two should be made before indexing begins, though occasionally an indexer will find, as indexing progresses, that a change from one to the other is appropriate. Dictionaries are arranged letter by letter, library catalogs word by word. Chicago, most university presses, and many other publishers have traditionally preferred the letter-by-letter system but will normally not impose it on a well-prepared index that has been arranged word by word. In an index including many open compounds starting with the same word, the word-by-word system may be easier for users. Both systems have their advantages and disadvantages, and few users are confused by either. Most people simply scan an alphabetic block of an index until they find what they are looking for. The indexer must understand both systems, however, and the following paragraphs offer guidelines for each. For a fuller discussion, consult Nancy Mulvany, *Indexing Books* (bibliog. 2.5).

18.57 *The letter-by-letter system.* In the letter-by-letter system, alphabetizing continues up to the first parenthesis or comma; it then starts again after the punctuation point. Word spaces and all other punctuation marks are ignored. Both open and hyphenated compounds such as *New York* or *self-pity* are treated as single words. The order of precedence is one word, word followed by a parenthesis, and word followed by a comma, number, or letters. The index to this manual, in accordance with Chicago's traditional preference, is arranged letter by letter.

18.58 *The word-by-word system.* In the word-by-word system, alphabetizing continues only up to the end of the first word (counting hyphenated compounds as one word), using subsequent words only when additional headings begin with the same word. As in the letter-by-letter system, alphabetizing continues up to the first parenthesis or comma; it then starts again after the punctuation point. The order of precedence is one word, word followed by a parenthesis, word followed by a comma, word followed by a space, and word followed by a comma, number, or letters.

18.59 *The two systems compared.* In both systems a parenthesis or comma interrupts the alphabetizing, and other punctuation marks (hyphens, slashes, quotation marks, periods, etc.) are ignored. The columns below illustrate the similarities and differences between the systems.

LETTER BY LETTER	WORD BY WORD
NEW (Neighbors Ever Watchful)	NEW (Neighbors Ever Watchful)
NEW (Now End War)	NEW (Now End War)
New, Arthur	New, Arthur
New, Zoe	New, Zoe
new-12 compound	New Deal
newborn	new economics
newcomer	New England
New Deal	new math
new economics	New Thorndale
newel	new town
New England	New Year's Day
"new-fangled notions"	new-12 compound
Newfoundland	newborn
newlyweds	newcomer
new math	newel
new/old continuum	"new-fangled notions"
news, lamentable	Newfoundland
News, Networks, and the Arts	newlyweds
newsboy	new/old continuum
news conference	news, lamentable
newsletter	*News, Networks, and the Arts*
news release	news conference
newt	news release
NEWT (Northern Estuary Wind Tunnel)	newsboy
New Thorndale	newsletter
new town	newt
New Year's Day	NEWT (Northern Estuary Wind Tunnel)

GENERAL RULES OF ALPHABETIZING

18.60 *Same name.* When a person, a place, and a thing have the same name, they are arranged in normal alphabetical order.

hoe, garden	London, England
Hoe, Robert	London, Jack

Common sense must be exercised. If Amy London and Carolyn Hoe were to appear in the same index as illustrated above, adjustments in the other entries would be needed.

garden hoe	London (England)
hoe. *See* garden hoe	London, Amy
Hoe, Carolyn	London, Jack
Hoe, Robert	

18.61 *Initials versus spelled-out names.* Initials used in place of a given name come before any spelled-out name beginning with the same letter.

Oppenheimer, J. Robert	Oppenheimer, K. T.
Oppenheimer, James N.	Oppenheimer, Keven S.

18.62 *Abbreviations.* Acronyms, initialisms, and most abbreviations are alphabetized as they appear, not according to their spelled-out versions, and are interspersed alphabetically among entries. See also 18.46, 18.73.

faculty clubs	NATO
FBI	North Pole
Feely, John	NOW (National Organization for Women)
LBJ. *See* Johnson, Lyndon B.	

18.63 *Numerals.* Numerals, when isolated entries, are alphabetized as though spelled out.

1984 (Orwell) [*alphabetized as* nineteen eighty-four]	10 Downing Street [*alphabetized as* ten downing street]
125th Street [*alphabetized as* one hundred twenty-fifth street]	

If many numerals occur in an index, they may be listed together in numerical order at the beginning of the index, before the *A*s.

18.64 *Headings with numerals.* When two or more similar headings with numerals occur together, they are ordered numerically, regardless of how they would be spelled out.

Henry III	L7	section 9
Henry IV	L44	section 44
Henry V	L50	section 77

The *L* entries above would be placed at the beginning of the *L* section.

18.65 *Accented letters.* Words beginning with or including accented letters are alphabetized as though they were unaccented. (Note that this rule is intended for English-language indexes that include some foreign words. The alphabetizing practices of other languages are not relevant in such instances.)

Ubeda	Schoenberg
Über den Gipfel	Schomberg
Ubina	Schönborn

SUBENTRIES

18.66 *Alphabetical order.* Introductory articles, prepositions, and conjunctions are disregarded in alphabetizing subentries, whether the subentries are run in or indented.

> Churchill, Winston: as anti-Fascist, 369;
>   on Curzon line, 348, 379; and de Gaulle,
>   544n4

Especially in indented style, where alphabetizing functions more visually, such introductory words should be used only where needed for clarity. The subheadings could be edited as follows.

> Churchill, Winston
>   anti-Fascism of, 369
>   Curzon line, views on, 348, 379
>   de Gaulle, relations with, 544n4

18.67 *Numerical order.* Occasional subentries demand numerical order even if others in the same index (but not the same entry) are alphabetized.

> Daley, Richard (mayor): third term, 205;
>   fourth term, 206–7
> flora, alpine: at 1,000-meter level, 46,
>   130–35; at 1,500-meter level, 146–54;
>   at 2,000-meter level, 49, 164–74

18.68 *Chronological order.* In a run-in index, an entry for the subject of a biography may be arranged chronologically rather than alphabetically so as to provide a quick summary of the subject's career and to avoid, for example, a subheading "death of" near the beginning of the entry.

PERSONAL NAMES

18.69   *Names with particles.* In alphabetizing family names containing particles, the indexer must consider the individual's personal preference (if known) as well as traditional and national usages. *Merriam-Webster's Biographical Dictionary* (bibliog. 4.1) provides a safe guide; library catalogs are another useful source. Cross-references are often advisable (see 18.16). Note the wide variations in the following list of actual names arranged alphabetically as they might appear in an index. See also 8.7, 8.11–13.

Beauvoir, Simone de	Keere, Pieter van den
Ben-Gurion, David	Kooning, Willem de
Costa, Uriel da	La Fontaine, Jean de
da Cunha, Euclides	Leonardo da Vinci
D'Amato, Alfonse	Medici, Lorenzo de'
de Gaulle, Charles	Van Rensselaer, Stephen
di Leonardo, Micaela	

Chicago occasionally deviates from Webster when a name is invariably accompanied by a particle and thus likely to be sought by most readers under the particle—de Gaulle, for example.

18.70   *Compound names.* Compound family names, with or without hyphens, are usually alphabetized according to the first element. See also 8.8, 8.14.

Lloyd George, David	Sackville-West, Victoria
Mies van der Rohe, Ludwig	Teilhard de Chardin, Pierre

18.71   *Names with "Mac" or "Mc."* Names beginning with *Mac* or *Mc* are alphabetized letter by letter, as they appear. (Here Chicago parts company with *Merriam-Webster's Biographical Dictionary.*)

Macalister, Donald	Madison, James
MacAlister, Paul	McAllister, Ward
Macauley, Catharine	McAuley, Catherine
Macmillan, Harold	McMillan, Edwin M.

18.72   *Names with "O'."* Names beginning with *O'* are alphabetized as if the apostrophe were missing.

Onassis, Aristotle
O'Neill, Eugene
Ongaro, Francesco dall'

18.73 *Names with "Saint."* A family name in the form of a saint's name is alphabetized letter by letter as the name is spelled, whether *Saint, San, St.,* or however. (Here too Chicago differs from Webster.) A cross-reference may be useful if *Saint* and *St.* are far apart in an index. See also 18.42, 18.91.

Sainte-Beuve, Charles-Augustin	San Martin, José de
Saint-Gaudens, Augustus	St. Denis, Ruth
Saint-Saëns, Camille	St. Laurent, Louis Stephen

FOREIGN PERSONAL NAMES

18.74 *Arabic names.* Modern Arabic names consisting of one or more given names followed by a surname present no problem.

Himsi, Ahmad Hamid
Sadat, Anwar

Arabic surnames prefixed by *al-* or *el-* (the) are alphabetized under the element following the particle; the article is treated like *de* in French names.

Hakim, Tawfiq al-
Jamal, Muhammad Hamid al-

Names beginning with *Abu, Abd,* and *ibn,* elements as integral to the names as *Mc* or *Fitz,* are alphabetized under those elements.

Abu Zafar Nadvi, Syed
Ibn Saud, Aziz

Context and readership may suggest cross-references. For example, in an index to a work likely to have readers unfamiliar with Arabic names, a cross-reference "al-Farabi. *See* Farabi, al-" may be useful.

18.75 *Burmese names.* Burmese persons are usually known by a given name of one or more elements and should be indexed under the first element. If the name is preceded in text by a term of respect (*U, Daw,* etc.), that term either is omitted or follows in the index.

Aung San Suu Kyi [alphabetize under *A*]
Thant, U [alphabetize under *T*]

18.76 *Chinese names.* Chinese names should be indexed as spelled in the work, whether in the pinyin or the Wade-Giles system. Cross-references are needed only if alternative forms are used in the text. Since the family name precedes the given name in Chinese usage, names are not inverted in the index, and no comma is used.

Li Bo [pinyin; alphabetize under *L*]
Mao Tse-tung [Wade-Giles; alphabetize under *M*]

Persons of Chinese ancestry or origin who have adopted the Western practice of giving the family name last are indexed with inversion and a comma.

Kung, H. H.
Tsou, Tang

18.77 *Hungarian names.* In Hungarian practice the family name precedes the given name—for example, Bartók Béla, Molnár Ferenc. In English contexts, however, such names are usually inverted; in an index they are therefore reinverted, with a comma added.

Bartók, Béla
Molnár, Ferenc

18.78 *Indian names.* Modern Indian names generally appear with the family name last and are indexed accordingly. As with all names, the personal preference of the individual as well as usage should be observed.

Gandhi, Mohandas Karamchand
Krishna Menon, V. K.
Narayan, R. K.

18.79 *Indonesian names.* Usage varies. Some Indonesians (especially Javanese) use only a single, given name. Others use more than one name; since the family name comes first, these are indexed like Chinese names, with no inversion or punctuation (see third and fourth examples). Indonesians with Muslim names and certain others whose names may include a title or an honorific are indexed by the final element, with inversion. The indexer must therefore ascertain how a person's full name is referred to in text and which part of the name is used for a short reference.

Suharto   Hatta, Mohammed
Sukarno   Suryojusumo, Wiyono
Pramoedya Ananta Toer   Habibi, B. J.
Marzuki Darusman

18.80 *Japanese names.* In Japanese usage the family name precedes the given name; names are therefore not inverted in the index, and no comma is used. If the name is westernized, as it often is by authors writing in English, the family name comes last. The indexer must therefore make certain which practice is followed in the text so that the family name always appears first in the index.

Tajima Yumiko [alphabetize under *T*]
Yoshida Shigeru [alphabetize under *Y*]
but
Kurosawa, Noriaki [referred to in text as Noriaki Kurosawa]

18.81 *Portuguese names.* The Portuguese, unlike the Spanish (see below), index surnames by the last element. (Where both Portuguese and Spanish names appear in the same context, cross-references may be necessary.)

Vasconcellos, J. Leite de
Martins, Luciana de Lima

18.82 *Spanish names.* In Spain and in some Latin American countries a double family name is often used, of which the first element is the father's family name and the second the mother's birth name (*her* father's family name). The two names are sometimes joined by *y* (and). Such compound names are alphabetized under the first element. Cross-references will often be needed, especially if the person is generally known under the second element or if the indexer is uncertain where to place the main entry. Webster is a good guide for persons listed there. Where many Spanish names appear, an indexer not conversant with Spanish or Latin American culture should seek help.

Ortega y Gasset, José
Sánchez Mendoza, Juana
García Lorca, Federico
Lorca, Federico García. *See* García Lorca, Federico

When the particle *de* appears in a Spanish name, the family name, under which the person is indexed, may be either the preceding or the following name (depending in part on how a person is known). If it is not clear from the text and the name is not in Webster, a cross-reference will be needed.

Esquivel de Sánchez, María
Fernández de Oviedo, Gonzalo
Navarrete, Juan Fernández de

Traditionally, a married woman replaced her mother's family name with her husband's (first) family name, sometimes preceded by *de*. Her name should be alphabetized, however, by the first family name (her father's).

Mendoza Salinas, María Carmen [woman's name before marriage]
Peña Montalvo, Juan Alberto [husband's name]
Mendoza de Peña, María Carmen [woman's name after marriage]

In telephone directories and elsewhere, some women appear under the husband's family name, but this is not a recommended bibliographic or indexing practice. Many modern women in Spanish-speaking countries no longer take the husband's family name. See also 8.14.

18.83 *Thai names.* Although family names are used in Thailand, Thais are normally known by their given names, which come first, as in English names. The name is often alphabetized under the first name, but practice varies. Seek expert help.

Supachai Panitchpakdi
Sarit Thanarat [*or* Thanarat, Sarit]
Sivaraksa, Sulak [*or* Sulak Sivaraksa]

18.84 *Vietnamese names.* Vietnamese names consist of three elements, the family name being the first. Since Vietnamese persons are usually referred to by the last part of their given names (Premier Diem, General Giap), they are best indexed under that form.

Diem, Ngo Dinh [*cross-reference under* Ngo Dinh Diem]
Giap, Vo Nguyen [*cross-reference under* Vo Nguyen Giap]

18.85 *Other Asian names.* Throughout Asia, many names derive from Arabic, Chinese, the European languages, and other languages, regardless of where the bearers of the names were born. In the Philippines, for example, names follow a Western order, giving precedence to the family name, though the names themselves may be derived from local languages. In some parts of Asia, titles denoting status form part of a name as it appears in written work and must be dealt with appropriately. When the standard reference works do not supply an answer, query the author.

NAMES OF ORGANIZATIONS AND BUSINESSES

18.86 *Omission of article.* In indexing organizations whose names begin with *the* (which would be lowercase in running text), the article is omitted.

University of Chicago
Sutherland Group

18.87 *Personal names as corporate names.* When used as names of businesses or other organizations, full personal names are not inverted, and the corporate name is alphabetized under the first name or initials. An organization widely known by the family name, however, should be indexed under that name. In both instances, cross-references may be appropriate.

A. G. Edwards & Sons, Inc. [alphabetize under *A*]
Penney, J. C. *See* J. C. Penney Company, Inc.
Saphir, Kurt. *See* Kurt Saphir Pianos, Inc.
but
John G. Shedd Aquarium. *See* Shedd Aquarium

A personal name and the name of that person's company should be indexed separately.

J. S. Morgan & Company, 45–48. *See also*
  Morgan, Junius S.
Morgan, Junius S., 39, 42–44; J. S.
  Morgan & Company, 45–48

NAMES OF PLACES

18.88 *Names beginning with "Mount," "Lake," and such.* Proper names of mountains, lakes, and so forth that begin with a generic name are usually inverted and alphabetized under the nongeneric name.

Geneva, Lake
Japan, Sea of
McKinley, Mount

Names of cities or towns beginning with topographic elements, as well as islands known as "Isle of . . . ," are alphabetized under the first element.

Isle of Pines   Isle of Wight

Lake Geneva, WI   Valley Forge
Mount Vernon, NY

18.89 *Names beginning with the definite article.* Aside from such cities as The Hague (unless the Dutch form *Den Haag* is used; see 18.90) or The Dalles, where *The* is part of the formal name and thus capitalized, an initial *the* used informally with place-names is omitted in indexing.

Bronx   Netherlands
Hague, The   Ozarks
Loop (Chicago's downtown)   Philippines

18.90 *Names beginning with foreign definite articles.* Names of places beginning with *El, Le, La,* and such, whether in English- or non-English-speaking countries, are alphabetized according to the article.

Den Haag   La Mancha
El Dorado   Le Havre
El Paso   Les Baux-de-Provence
La Crosse   Los Alamos

18.91 *Names with "Saint."* Names of places beginning with *Saint, Sainte, St.,* or *Ste.* should be indexed as they appear in the text, that is, abbreviated only if abbreviated in text. Like personal names, they are alphabetized as they appear. Note that French hyphenates place-names with *Saint.*

Saint-Cloud (in France)   Ste. Anne de Beaupré
Sainte-Foy   St. Louis
Saint-Luc   St. Vincent Island
St. Cloud (in Florida)

Merriam-Webster's Geographical Dictionary (bibliog. 4.2) spells out English-language place-names beginning with *Saint.* Because *St.* is widely used in references to St. Paul, St. Petersburg, St. Louis, and the like, Chicago no longer insists on spelling it out in such place-names. Cross-references may be appropriate (e.g., "Saint. *See* St.," or vice versa).

Punctuation: A Summary

18.92 *Overview.* The following paragraphs merely summarize conventions of punctuation in an index. See further examples throughout this chapter.

18.93 *Comma.* In both run-in and indented indexes, when a main heading is followed immediately by locators (usually page or paragraph numbers; see 18.12), a comma appears before the first locator. Commas appear between locators. Commas are also used when a heading is an inversion or when a main entry is qualified, without subentries. The first example illustrates three uses of the comma.

Sabba da Castiglione, Monsignor, 209,
   337; against cosmetics, 190, 195, 198
lighthouses, early history of, 40-42

18.94 *Colon.* In a run-in index, when a main heading is followed immediately by subentries, a colon appears before the first subentry. In an indented index, no punctuation is used after the main entry. A colon is also used in a cross-reference to a subentry. See also 18.19.

Maya: art of, 236–43; cities of, 178. *See*   Maya
   also Yucatán: Maya   art of, 236–43
                                                                      cities of, 178
                                                                      See also Yucatán: Maya

18.95 *Semicolon.* When subentries or sub-subentries are run in, they are separated by semicolons. Cross-references, if more than one, are also separated by semicolons.

astronomy: Galileo's works on, 20–21,
   22–23, 24; skills needed in, 548–49.
   See also Brahe, Tycho; comets;
   Flamsteed, John

18.96 *Period.* In a run-in index a period is used only before *See, See also,* or *See under.* In an indented index a period is used only before *See.* When a *see* reference in parentheses follows a subentry in either a run-in or an indented index, no period is used. No period follows the final word of any entry.

18.97 *Parentheses.* Parentheses enclose identification or supplementary information.

Charles I (king of England)
Charles I (king of Portugal)
Of Human Bondage (Maugham)

18.98   *Em dash.* For use of the em dash in run-in indexes that require occasional sub-subentries, see example B in 18.27.

18.99   *En dash.* The en dash is used for page ranges and all other inclusive locators (e.g., "dogs, 135–42"). See 6.83, the index to this manual, and examples throughout this chapter.

The Mechanics of Indexing

BEFORE INDEXING BEGINS: TOOLS AND DECISIONS

18.100   *Schedule.* Anyone making an index for the first time should know that the task is intensive and time consuming. An index for a three-hundred-page book could take as much as three weeks' work. See also 18.3.

18.101   *Proofs.* The indexer must have in hand a clean and complete set of proofs before beginning to index. For a printed work, page proofs are required; for an electronic work, the indexer typically requires a printout showing both content and locators. For a journal volume, the work may begin when the first issue to be indexed has been paginated, and it may continue for several months, until page proofs for the final issue in the volume have been generated. For a nonprint work, the final version must be available. See also 18.107–8, 18.118–27.

18.102   *Publisher's preferences.* Before beginning work, the indexer should know the publisher's preferences in such matters as alphabetizing, run-in or indented style, inclusive numbers, handling of numeric entries, and the like (all matters dealt with in earlier sections of this chapter). For a journal volume index, the style is likely to be well established, and the indexer must follow that style. If the publisher requests an index of a particular length, the indexer should allow more than the normal time for editing (see 18.133). See also 18.134.

18.103   *Software.* Software programs commonly used by professional indexers require more learning time than most authors can afford. Less complicated ones are becoming available (check with your publisher or the American Society of Indexers). But an index can be prepared with patience and an ordinary word processor.

18.104   *Using the text files.* Authors often request a copy of the final electronic files that correspond exactly to the page proofs and thus include page numbers or other locators. Unfortunately, those files are heavily formatted for type-setting and perhaps other uses; to convert them for use by the indexer is therefore extremely expensive. A copy of the publisher's edited files could be used for searches and other tasks, but it may not include locators.

18.105 *Typing and format.* Before beginning to type—*typing* is used here to mean keyboarding on a computer as well as on a typewriter (see 18.106)—consult the publisher about the format in which the index is to be submitted (see 18.134). Although the index will eventually appear in flush-and-hang style, you may find it easier to type it in the form of simple paragraphs, flush left, with a hard return at the end of each entry. In indented style, use the hanging-indent feature after the main entry and all but the final subentries; use a hard return only at the end of the entire entry. Avoid the tab; just let the runover lines wrap normally. Use your regular software to create italics and boldface, if needed.

18.106 *The old-fashioned way.* Indexers used to handwrite or type preliminary entries and subentries on 3 × 5-inch index cards, then alphabetize and edit the cards, and finally type the index, while further refining it, on 8¹/₂ × 11-inch sheets. For details, consult Nancy Mulvany, *Indexing Books* (bibliog. 2.5), or the thirteenth or fourteenth edition of this manual (no longer in print but available in large libraries). The procedures described in the following sections can be adapted to the index-card method.

WHEN TO BEGIN

18.107 *Preliminary work.* Although some planning can be done at the manuscript stage, most indexes are prepared as soon as a work is in page proof or, if electronic, in its final form. For indexes in which the locators are paragraph or section numbers rather than page numbers, galley proof or, for an electronic work, a nonfinal printout can be used. Authors who are not preparing their own indexes may compile a list of important terms for the indexer, but doing much more is likely to cause duplication or backtracking.

18.108 *Pagination of printed works.* Once an indexer has started work on an index that uses page numbers, adding or moving an illustration or more than two or three words of text will affect pagination. No index using page numbers should be begun, let alone completed, until page numbering is final.

WHAT PARTS OF THE WORK TO INDEX

18.109 *Text, front matter, and back matter.* The entire text of a book or journal article, including most notes (see next paragraph), should be indexed. Much of the front matter, however, is not indexable—title page, dedication, epigraphs, lists of illustrations and tables, and acknowledgments. A preface, or a foreword by someone other than the author of the work, may be indexed if it concerns the subject of the work and not simply how the work came to be written. A true introduction, whether in the front matter or, more commonly, in the body of the work, is always indexed (for introduction versus preface, see 1.53). Book appendixes should be indexed if they contain information that supplements the text, but not if they merely reproduce documents that are discussed in the text (the full text of a treaty, for example, or a questionnaire). Appendixes to journal articles are indexed as part of the articles. Glossaries, bibliographies, and other such lists are not indexed.

18.110 *Notes.* Notes, whether footnotes or endnotes, should be indexed if they continue or amplify discussion in the text (substantive notes). Notes that merely document statements in the text (reference notes) need not be indexed if the source is clearly implied in the text itself. But if a note documents an otherwise unattributed statement or idea discussed in the text, the author of that statement or idea should indeed be indexed. And in works that contain no bibliography, reference notes—at least those giving full details—should be carefully indexed.

18.111 *Endnote locators.* Endnotes in printed works are referred to by page, the letter *n* (for *note*), and—extremely important—the note number, with no internal space (334n14). If two or more consecutive notes are referred to, two *n*'s and an en dash are used (e.g., 334nn14–16). Nonconsecutive notes on the same page are treated separately (334n14, 334n16, 334n19). Occasionally, when reference to a late note in one chapter of a book is followed by reference to an early note in the next, nonchronological order will result (334n19, 334n2). To avoid the appearance of error, the chapter number may be added in parentheses after the lower note number.

dogs, 334n19, 334n2 (chap. 9), 335n5

18.112 *Footnote locators.* Footnotes in a printed work are generally referred to in the same way as endnotes. When a footnote is the only one on the page, however, the note number (or symbol, if numbers are not used) may be omitted (156n). Note numbers should never be omitted when several notes appear on the same page. If there is indexable material in a text passage and in a related footnote, only the page number need be given. But if the text and the footnote materials are unrelated, both text and note should be cited (156, 156n, 278, 278n30).

18.113   *Notes spanning more than one printed page.* For endnotes or footnotes that continue onto another page, normally only the first page number is given. But if the reference is specifically to a part of a note that appears on the second page, the second page number should be used. Referring to a succession of notes, however, may require inclusive page numbers, e.g., 234–35nn19–23.

18.114   *Parenthetical text citations.* Documentation given as parenthetical author-date citations in text is not normally indexed unless the citation documents an otherwise unattributed statement in the text (see 18.110). Any author discussed in text should be indexed. In some fields it is customary to index every author named in the text; check with the publisher on the degree of inclusiveness required. See also 18.115–16.

18.115   *Author indexes: time involved.* Preparing an author index, though somewhat mechanical, takes more time than often supposed. Since most authors are cited in text by last name and date only, full names must be sought in the reference list. Occasional discrepancies between text and reference list, not caught in editing, have to be sorted out or queried. Is L. W. Dinero, cited on page 345, the same person as Lauren Dinero, discussed on page 456? If so, should she be indexed as Dinero, Lauren W.? (Answer: only if all or most authors are indexed with full first names.)

18.116   *Author indexes: multiple authors.* Where a work by two or more authors is cited in text, the indexer must determine whether each author named requires a separate entry. Should Jones, Smith, and Black 1999 share one index entry, or should three entries appear? And what about Jones et al.? Chicago recommends the following procedure: Make separate entries for each author whose name appears in text. Do not index those unfortunates whose names are concealed under *et al.* in text.

TEXT CITATION	INDEX ENTRIES
(Jones, Smith, and Black 1999)	Black, M. X., 366
	Jones, E. J., 366
	Smith, R. A., 366
(Sánchez et al. 2001)	Sánchez, J. G., 657
(Sánchez, Cruz, et al. 2002)	Cruz, M. M., 435
	Sánchez, J. G., 435

18.117   *Illustrations, tables, charts, and such.* Illustrative matter may be indexed if it is of particular importance to the discussion, especially when such items are not listed in or after the table of contents. References to illustrations may be set in italics (or boldface, if preferred); a headnote should then be inserted at the beginning of the index (see 18.145 for an example).

reptilian brain, 199, 201–3, *202*

Alternatively, references to tables may be denoted by *t*, to figures by *f*, plates by *pl*, or whatever works (all set in roman, with no space following the page number). Add an appropriate headnote (e.g., "The letter *t* following a page number denotes a table"). If the number of an illustration is essential, it is safer to use *table, fig.*, and so on, with no comma following the page number.

titi monkeys, 69, 208t, 209t, 210f
authors and printers, 88 table 5, 89–90,
    123–25, 122 fig. 7

MARKING PROOFS AND PREPARING ENTRIES

18.118   *The initial review.* Experienced indexers usually begin by perusing the table of contents and scanning the rest of the proofs to establish what is in the work and where.

18.119   *Highlighting terms and beginning to type.* Highlighting terms to be used as main headings or subentries is the first essential step in preparing an index. It is normally done by hand-marking a set of proofs. Inexperienced indexers are advised to mark the proofs—at least in the early stages—with the same kind of detail as is illustrated in figure 18.1. Most indexers prefer to mark one section (or chapter or journal issue) at a time and to type and alphabetize the marked terms in that section before going on to the next section. The notes belonging to the section, even if endnotes, should be checked and, if necessary, indexed at the same time (see 18.110–13). As the indexer becomes more skilled in marking the proofs, less underlining and fewer marginal notes may suffice.

18.120   *How many terms to mark.* The number of terms to mark on any one printed page obviously depends on the kind of work being indexed. As a very rough guide, an average of five references per text page in a book will yield a modest index (one-fiftieth the length of the text), whereas fifteen or more will yield a fairly long index (one-twentieth the length of the text). If the publisher has budgeted for a strictly limited number of pages, the indexer should work accordingly. Remember that it is always easier to drop entries than to add them; err on the side of inclusiveness. See also 18.30–31, 18.102, 18.114–17, 18.133.

18.121 *Marking entries.* To visualize the method advocated here, suppose you are indexing a chapter from Wayne Booth's *For the Love of It* (University of Chicago Press, 1999), a discussion of work and play and work as play (see fig. 18.1). You have read through the chapter once and now have to go back and select headings and subheadings for indexing this particular section (of which only the first paragraphs are shown here). You decide that the whole section (pp. 54–56) will have to be indexed under both *work* and *play*, so you mark the section head as shown. (On the marked proofs, a colon separates a proposed principal heading from a proposed subheading.) Going down the page, you underline *Bliss Perry* (noting that it is to be inverted—Perry, Bliss—as a heading; similarly for the other personal names). You also underline *amateur* and *professional* (modifying them to the plural). In the second paragraph, you underline *work* and *love*, with proposed subheads, and Churchill (if you have to look up the first name, note it in the margin). You pass by *Chicago Symphony Orchestra* as tangential, but politicians may be considered as a heading.

18.122 *Planning subentries.* For each term marked, you should write in a modification—a word or phrase that narrows the application of the heading, hence a potential subentry. Although some such modifications may eventually be dropped, they should be kept on hand in case they are needed. Otherwise you may end up with some headings that are followed by nothing but a long string of numbers, which makes for an all but useless index entry. The modifications can be altered and added to as the indexing proceeds.

18.123 *Inclusive numbers.* If a text discussion extends over more than one page, section, or paragraph, both beginning and ending numbers—which will depend on what locator system is being used (see 18.12)—must be written in.

18.124 *Typing and modifying entries.* Each entry at this stage should include three elements: a heading, a modification (or provisional subentry), and a locator (page or paragraph number). While typing, you will probably modify some of the headings and add, delete, or alter subentries and locators. After typing each entry, read it carefully against the page proof. You are unlikely to have time to read the final printout against the marked-up proofs,

54 ❧ CHAPTER THREE

those who find the hurting of others fun, no arguments against it can fully succeed, and the history of efforts to explain why "human nature" includes such impulses and what we might do to combat them could fill a library: books on the history of Satan and the Fall, on the cosmogonies of other cultures, on our genetic inheritance, including recently the structure of our brains, on sadism and why it is terrible or defensible. And so on. I'll just hope that here we can all agree that to hurt or harm for the fun of it is self-evidently not a loving choice.[1]

One embarrassing qualification: we amateurish amateurs do often inflict pain on others. We just don't do it on purpose.

Work and Play, Work as Play: *as play −56*   *work as −56*

To celebrate playing for the love of it risks downgrading the work we do that we love. In fact we amateurs are often tempted to talk snobbishly about those who cannot claim that what they do they do for the love of it. As Bliss Perry put the danger: "[T]he prejudice which the amateur feels toward the professional, the more or less veiled hostility between the man who does something for love which another man does for money, is one of those instinctive reactions—like the vague alarm of some wild creature in the woods—which give a hint of danger."   *∫ : loving one's*

The words "professional" and "work" are almost as ambiguous as the word "love." Some work is fun, some gruesome. Churchill loved his work—but needed to escape it regularly. I hated most of the farm work I did as an adolescent, and escaped it as soon as possible. I hated having to dig ditches eight hours a day for twenty-five cents an hour. Yet working as teacher and a scholar, I have loved most of my duties—even the drudgery parts. A member of the Chicago Symphony Orchestra told me that he hates his work—his playing—and is eager for retirement. Politicians celebrate work as what will save welfare recipients from degradation; for them, to require people to work, even if they're underpaid and even if the job is awful, is a virtuous act.   *: of one's work*   *: work celebrated by*

Such a mishmash of implied definitions makes it impossible to place work in any simple opposition to play or pleasure. In *Homo Ludens* Huizinga occasionally writes as if the whole point of life were to have fun by *escaping*

Winston
Johan
Walter

1. A fine discussion of the dangers threatened by "doing things for the love of the doing" is given by Roger Shattuck in *Forbidden Knowledge*. Shattuck argues that the art-for-art's-sake movement, with its many echoes of Pater's celebration of "burning" with a "hard, gemlike flame" and living for the "highest quality" of a given moment, risks moving us toward "worship of pure experience without restraint of any kind." The temptations of sadistic ecstasies lurk in the wings. As I shall insist again and again, to make sense out of a title like *For the Love of It* requires careful distinction among diverse "loves," many of them potentially harmful.

Fig. 18.1. Sample page of proof from Wayne Booth's *For the Love of It*, marked up for indexing.

though you should certainly retain the proofs for reference until the work has been printed. See also 18.105.

18.125 *Alphabetizing.* Many indexers alphabetize as they type; others let their software do it, intervening as necessary. By this time the indexer should have decided whether to use the letter-by-letter or the word-by-word system (see

18.57–59). If the system chosen proves unsatisfactory for the particular work as the index proceeds, a switch can be made if the publisher agrees.

18.126 *Final check of proofs.* After typing all the entries, read quickly through the marked-up proofs once again to see whether anything indexable has been omitted. You may find some unmarked items that seemed peripheral at the time but now, in the light of themes developed in later chapters, declare themselves significant. Or you may have missed major items. Now is the time to remedy all omissions.

18.127 *Noting errors.* Although not engaged to proofread, the indexer has to read carefully and usually finds a number of typographical errors and minor inconsistencies. If indexing a book (rather than a journal volume, most of which will already have been published), keep track of all such errors and send a list to the publisher (who will be very grateful) when, or before, submitting the index.

EDITING AND REFINING THE ENTRIES

18.128 *Deciding on terms for main headings.* The assembled entries must now be edited to a coherent whole. You have to make a final choice among synonymous or closely related terms—*agriculture, farming,* or *crop raising; clothing, costume,* or *dress; life, existence,* or *being*—and, if you think necessary, prepare suitable cross-references to reflect those choices. For journals, the terms may have been established in the indexes for previous volumes and should be retained.

18.129 *Main headings versus subentries.* You also have to decide whether certain items are best treated as main headings or as subentries under another heading. Where will readers look first? In a work dealing with schools of various kinds, such terms as *kindergarten, elementary school, middle school,* and *public school* should constitute separate entries; in a work in which those terms appear but are not the primary subject matter, they may better be treated as subentries under *school.* An index with relatively few main entries but masses of subentries is unhelpful as a search tool. Furthermore, in an indented index an excessively long string of subentries may begin to look like a set of main entries, so that users lose their way alphabetically. Promote subentries to main entries and use the alphabet to its best advantage.

18.130 *When to furnish subentries.* Main entries unmodified by subentries should not be followed by more than five or six locators. If, for example, the draft index of a work on health care includes an entry like the first example below, it should be broken up into a number of subentries, such as those in the second example, to lead users quickly to the information sought. The extra space needed is a small price to pay for their convenience.

hospitals, 17, 22, 23, 24, 25, 28, 29–31, 33, 35, 36, 38, 42, 91–92, 94, 95, 96, 98, 101, 111–14, 197
hospitals: administration of, 22, 96; and demand for patient services, 23, 91–92;

efficiency of, 17, 29–31, 33, 111–14; finances of, 28, 33, 36, 38, 42, 95, 112; and length of patient stay, 35, 94, 98, 101, 197; quality control in, 22–25, 31

18.131 *How to phrase subentries.* Subentries should be as concise and informative as possible and begin with a keyword likely to be sought. The, a, and an are omitted whenever possible. Example A below, *not* to be emulated, shows poorly worded and rambling subentries. Example B shows greatly improved subentries that conserve space. Example C adds sub-subentries, making for quicker reference but requiring more space (see 18.26–28). For arrangement of subentries, see 18.66–68.

Example A (*not* to be emulated)

house renovation
  balancing heating system, 65
  building permit required, 7
  called "rehabbing," 8
  correcting overloaded electrical circuits, 136
  how wallboard is finished, 140–44
  installing ready-made fireplace, 191–205
  painting outside of house adds value, 11
  plumbing permit required, 7
  removing paint from doors and woodwork, 156–58

repairing dripping faucets, 99–100
replacing clogged water pipes, 125–28
replacing old wiring, 129–34
separate chimney required for fireplace, 192
straightening sagging joists, 40–42
termite damage to sills a problem, 25
three ways to deal with broken plaster, 160–62
violations of electrical code corrected, 135
what is involved in, 5

Example B (improvement with fairly inclusive subentries)

house renovation, 5, 8
  electrical repairs, 129–34, 135, 136
  fireplace, installing, 191–205
  heating system, balancing, 65
  legal requirements, 7, 135, 192

painting and decorating, 11, 156–58
plaster repair, 160–62
plumbing repairs, 99–100, 125–28
structural problems, 25, 40–42
wallboard, finishing, 140–44

Example C (improvement with sub-subentries)

house renovation, 5, 8
  electrical repairs: circuit overload, 136;
    code violations, 135; old wiring,
    129–34
  heating system: balancing, 65;
    fireplace installation, 191–205
  legal requirements: electrical code, 135;
    permits, 7; separate chimney for
    fireplace, 192
  painting and decorating: painting
    exterior, 11; stripping woodwork,
    156–58
  plumbing repairs: clogged water pipes,
    125–28; dripping faucets, 99–100
  structural problems: sagging joists,
    40–42; termite damage, 25
  wall and ceiling repairs: broken plaster,
    160–62; wallboard, finishing, 140–44

If it looks as though an index is going to require a great many sub-subentries, the indexer should check with the publisher before proceeding.

18.132 *Cross-referencing.* Make sure that all cross-references match the edited headings (see 18.15–22).

SUBMITTING THE INDEX

18.133 *Gauging length.* If the publisher has specified a maximum number of pages for a printed index, you can gauge whether you are within the limit by temporarily formatting your index to a narrow line width (but see next paragraph). The publisher can tell you (or has already told you) whether the printed index is to appear in two or three columns, how wide each column is to be, and how many lines are to appear on each page. If necessary, you then may do further editing and cutting. See also 18.120.

18.134 *Submission format.* Having carefully proofread the draft and checked all cross-references, punctuation, and capitalization to ensure consistency, you will now send the final draft in electronic and printout form to the publisher. Allow margins of at least one inch both left and right, and leave the right margin unjustified. Do not waste paper by using a very narrow line length; the index will probably be edited online in any case. (Do not attempt to print double columns.) Avoid hyphenation except for hard hyphens (see 2.15). Leave an extra line space between alphabetical sections. Unless otherwise instructed, double-space the entire printout (though the electronic file can remain single spaced). Ask the publisher whether hanging indention is required (see 2.14, 18.105). If there is more than one index, give each an appropriate title (Author Index, Subject Index, etc.); each index should be in a separate file, and pages should be numbered. To avert disaster, keep a copy of the final draft that you send to the publisher, as well as your set of marked-up proofs, until the work has been published. For a book, send the publisher a list of any errors you have found (see 18.127).

Editing an Index Compiled by Someone Else

18.135   *Quality of the index.* Editing a well-prepared index can be a pleasure. Little work should be needed. A poorly prepared one, however, presents serious problems. As an editor, you cannot remake a really bad index. If an index cannot be repaired, you have two choices: omit it or have a new one made by a professional indexer—thereby delaying publication.

18.136   *Editing an index.* Copyediting an index requires some or all of the following steps, not necessarily in the order given here. *Checking* does not mean referring to the page proof for every entry—which would take forever— but merely reading carefully and referring to the page proof as necessary.

1. Check headings for alphabetical order.
2. Check the spelling, capitalization, and font of each heading, consulting the page proofs if in doubt.
3. Check punctuation—commas, colons, semicolons, en dashes, etc.— for proper style.
4. Check cross-references to make sure they go somewhere and that headings match. Make sure they are needed; if only a few locators are involved, substitute these for the *see* reference (see 18.15–18). Ensure that the placement of all cross-references within entries is consistent.
5. Add cross-references you believe are necessary.
6. Check to make sure there are no false locators such as "193–93" or "12102," and make sure the locators are in ascending order.
7. Check subentries for consistency of order, whether alphabetical or chronological.
8. If some entries seem overanalyzed (many subentries with only one locator or, worse, with the same locator), try to combine some of them if it can be done without sacrificing their usefulness. If subentries are more elaborate than necessary, try to simplify them.
9. If awkward or unnecessary sub-subentries appear, correct them by adding appropriate repeated subentries or by adjusting punctuation (see 18.26–28).
10. Look for long strings of unanalyzed locators and break them up, if possible, with subentries (see 18.9, 18.131).

11. Evaluate the accuracy of locators by a random check of five to ten entries. If more than one error shows up, consult the author or the publisher; every locator may have to be rechecked.
12. If the index needs trimming, delete any entries that you know from your work on the book are trivial, such as references to persons or places used only as examples of something. But be careful. You may offend someone or let yourself in for a lot of work. A handful of unnecessary entries, if they are very short, does not mar an otherwise good index.

18.137 *Instructions for typesetting.* At this stage the typesetter should have the specifications in hand, and few instructions are needed. To avoid problems, a brief note such as the following (for an indented index) may be attached to the index manuscript (usually consisting of an electronic file and a printout).

Set two columns, flush and hang, ragged right; indent subentries one em; indent runovers two ems; set en dashes between all continuing numbers; leave one line space between alphabetical chunks. Set headnote across both columns. See specs for size and measure.

Typographical Considerations

18.138 *Type size and column width.* In print works, indexes are usually set in smaller type than the body of the work, often two sizes smaller. That is, if the body copy is set in ten-on-twelve-point type, and the extracts, bibliography, and appendixes in nine-on-eleven, the index will probably be set in eight-on-ten. Indexes are usually set in two columns; with a type page twenty-seven picas wide, the index columns will each be thirteen picas, with a one-pica space between them. In large-format print works, however, the index may be set in three or even four columns.

18.139 *Unjustified right-hand margin.* For very short lines, such as those in an index, justifying the right-hand margin usually results in either gaping word spaces or excessive hyphenation, making for difficult reading. Chicago therefore sets all indexes with unjustified right-hand margins ("ragged right").

18.140 *Indention.* All runover lines are indented, whether the subentries are run in or indented. In indexes with indented subentries (see 18.25), runover lines have to be indented more deeply than the subentries; all runovers, whether from a main heading or a subentry (or even a sub-subentry, should these too be indented), should be indented equally from the left margin. Thus, in an indented index the subentries may be indented one em, the sub-subentries two ems, and the runovers three ems. For avoiding sub-subentries, see 18.27–28. These matters must be determined before type is set.

18.141   *Bad breaks.* What cannot be solved before type is set are problems connected with page and column breaks. A line consisting of only one or two page numbers should not be left at the top of a column, for example. A single line at the end of an alphabetic section (followed by a blank line) should not head a column, nor should a single line at the beginning of an alphabetic section remain at the foot of a column. Blemishes like these (called bad breaks) are eliminated by transposing lines from one column to another, by adding to the white space between alphabetic sections, and sometimes by lengthening or shortening all columns on facing pages by one line.

18.142   *"Continued" lines.* If an entry breaks at the foot of the last column on a right-hand page (a recto) and resumes at the top of the following left-hand page (a verso), the main heading is repeated, followed by the word *continued* in parentheses, above the carried-over part of the index.

> ingestive behavior *(continued)*
> > network of causes underlying, 68;
> > physiology of, 69–70, 86–87; in rat,
> > 100; in starfish, 45, 52–62

In an indented index with indented sub-subentries it may be necessary to repeat a subentry if the subentry has been broken.

> house renovation *(continued)*
> > structural problems *(continued)*
> > > termite damage, 25–27
> > > warped overhangs, 46–49

18.143   *Special typography.* A complicated index can sometimes be made easier to read by using different type styles or fonts. If, for example, names of writers need to be distinguished from names of literary characters, one or the other might be set in caps and small caps. Page references to illustrations might be in italic type (see 18.117) and references to the principal treatment of a subject in boldface. If devices of this kind are used, a headnote to the index must furnish a key (see 18.145, 18.147).

Examples

18.144   *Five formats.* The following examples, some of which illustrate styles described earlier in this chapter, are presented here for overview and comparison. For discussion, see the paragraphs referred to.

18.145   *A run-in index.* See 18.23–24, 18.26–27, 18.93–97.

Page numbers in italics refer to figures and tables.

Abbot, George, 241–42
ABC, printing of, 164
Abridgement (Croke), *302–3*
Abridgment (Rolle), *316*, 316–17
abridgment: cases of, 246n161; as offense, 455–56, 607; of *Philosophical Transactions*, 579n83; restrictions on, 226, 227; works as, *302–3, 316*, 316–17

absolutism: absence of in England, 48; arbitrary government and, 251–52, 252n182; Cromwell and, 273–74; Hobbes and, 308; patronage and, 24; property and, 253, 255; royal authorship of laws and, 312, 317, 336n29; royal prerogative and, 251, 253–54
Académie Royale des Sciences (France), 436, 491n91, 510, 554

If occasional sub-subentries are required in a run-in index, you may resort to the style illustrated in 18.27, example B, using an em dash.

18.146   *An indented index with run-in sub-subentries.* See 18.26, 18.28, 18.66.

American black bear
  compared with giant panda: activity, 216–17; habitat, 211–12; home range, 219; litter size, 221; movement patterns of males, 124–26, 219
  delayed implantation in, 191
  reproductive flexibility of, 221
  see also bears

amino acid content of bamboo, 75–76, 86, 89; compared with other foods, 77
artificial insemination, 179
Ascaris schroederi, 162
Asiatic black bear
  constructing sleeping nests, 140
  giant panda serologically close to, 228
  see also bears

18.147   *An indented index with indented sub-subentries and highlighted definitions.* Note the deep indention for runover lines. A boldface page number indicates that the term is defined on that page. Italics could also be used for that purpose. Similarly, either boldface or italics can be used to indicate illustrations. If any of these devices is used, an explanatory headnote should appear at the beginning of the index. See 18.28, example B, 18.66, 18.117.

Page numbers for definitions are in boldface.

brightness temperatures, 388, 582, 589, 602

bright rims, **7**, 16, 27–28 (*see also* nebular forms)

B stars, **3**, 7, 26–27, 647

bulbs (in nebulae). *See* nebular forms

cameras, electronic, 492, 499

carbon flash, 559

Cassiopeia A (3C461). *See* radio sources; supernovae

catalogs
  of bright nebulae, 74
  of dark nebulae, 74, 120
    Lundmark, 121

Lynds, 123
Schoenberg, 123
Herschel's (of nebulae), 119
of planetary nebulae, 484–85, 563
  Perek-Kohoutek, 484, 563
  Vorontsov-Velyaminov, 484
of reflection nebulae, 74

3C catalog of radio sources, revised, 630

central stars. *See* planetary nebulae

Cerenkov radiation, **668**, 709

chemical composition, 71. *See also* abundances; *and names of individual elements*

If occasional sub-sub-subentries are essential (they should be avoided if at all possible), they must be run in to the sub-subentries in the same way as sub-subentries are run in at 18.28, example B.

18.148 *An index of first lines.* Unless all the poems, hymns, or songs indexed have very short lines, indexes of this kind are often set full measure for easier reading. Letter-by-letter alphabetizing is normally used. Note that lines beginning with *A, An, or The* are alphabetized under *A* or *T*.

After so long an absence, 295
A handful of red sand, from the hot clime, 108
An old man in at a lodge within a park, 315
Beautiful valley! through whose verdant meads, 325
From this high portal, from where upsprings, 630
O'er all the hill-tops, 617
Of Prometheus, how undaunted, 185
O hemlock tree! O hemlock tree! how faithful are thy branches, 614
There is no flock, however watched and tended, 107
The young Endymion sleeps Endymion's sleep, 316

18.149 *Authors, titles, and first lines combined.* To distinguish the elements, authors' names may be set in caps and small caps, titles of poems in italics, and first lines in roman type, sentence style, without quotation marks. If needed, a headnote to this effect could be furnished. Letter-by-letter alphabetizing should be used.

Cermak, it was, who entertained so great astonishment, 819	*Coming Homeward Out of Spain,* 73
Certain she was that tigers fathered him, 724	Commemorate me before you leave me, Charlotte, 292
CHESTERVILLE, NORA M., 212	*Complaint of a Lover Rebuked,* 29
Come, you whose loves are dead, 394	COMPTON, WILBER C., 96
	Confound you, Marilyn, confound you, 459

In a general index, poem titles would be set in roman and enclosed in quotation marks, as in text or notes (see 8.191–92).

Appendix A: Design and Production— Basic Procedures and Key Terms

~~~~~~

Introduction

This appendix provides writers and editors with an overview of how publications are designed and produced. It is not necessary to understand the design and production processes in all their detail—indeed, technology advances so rapidly that any full discussion would soon become obsolete. But it is essential for everyone who works with designers and production personnel to have some knowledge of what happens between the submission of an edited manuscript and the delivery of a finished work. (For more detailed coverage of these processes, consult the sources listed in the bibliography, section 2.6. For definitions of specialized terms, including many not mentioned here, see the list of key terms at the end of this appendix [pp. 823–40]. For an illustration of how the stages described fit into the overall publishing sequence for books and journals, see appendix B.)

New technology has changed the way authors, editors, and production personnel work together. The use of word-processing and page-layout programs to prepare, edit, and design manuscripts for publication is now common. Authors are almost always required to submit their work in electronic format, eliminating the need for rekeying. At the same time, typesetting and printing stages are being streamlined through the use of digital technology. In such a climate, a successful publishing program must continually adapt its production methods.

Despite these advances, the fundamentals of designing and producing a publication remain remarkably constant. Authors are asked to follow specific guidelines when preparing manuscripts for publication (see chapter 2). Designers create a visual format for a work that complements—even enhances—the content of that work. And production controllers coordinate the efforts of in-house staff and vendors to ensure timely publication and adherence to acceptable manufacturing and electronic publication standards.

A general note on production schedules: since even a short delay at any point in the sequence described below can jeopardize a publication date, everyone involved with a project should be aware of the key deadlines, which are often summarized in a production schedule. The details of the schedule vary by publisher and type of publication and depend on such factors as the length and complexity of the text; the number of authors or editors who will review proof; and, for a printed work, the decision whether to print it domestically or overseas. A typical timetable for a book printed domestically (see fig. A.1) would allow six to nine months from the submission of the edited manuscript to the delivery of bound copies. The timetable for a journal ranges from a few days (for an article published individually on the World Wide Web) to three or four months (for a printed journal issue). Figure A.2 represents a typical publication schedule for a quarterly journal published in both print and electronic forms.

Design

CHARACTERISTICS OF THE WORK

At the initial stage of planning a design, the designer needs information about the nature of the project and the audience for whom it is intended. Although the same basic concerns underlie the design of both books and journals, a journal usually maintains the same typographical specifications (or "specs") for years and as such is designed to accommodate general categories rather than specific pieces of text (see 1.162–64). Books are usually designed individually, although those in a particular series may follow a single set of specifications. (Electronic forms of both journals and books present additional issues for a designer that are not covered here.

	CALENDAR DAYS	DATES	
Transmittal	n/a	06/25/04	
Contract OK	n/a	06/25/04	
Begin MS edit	7	07/02/04	
MS to author	63	09/03/04	*In editing*
MS design in	21	09/24/04	*three months*
MS from author	7	10/01/04	
MS design OK	7	10/08/04	
Final MS to production	7	10/15/04	
Sample pages in	14	10/29/04	
Sample pages OK	3	11/01/04	*In production*
Pages in/to author	11	11/12/04	*six months*
Pages from author	28	12/10/04	
Pages to design	4	12/14/04	
Pages to production	4	12/18/04	
Pages to typesetter	1	12/19/04	
Index MS to typesetter		12/19/04	
Revised pages in	19	01/07/05	
Index pages in		01/07/05	
Mfg quotes requested		01/07/05	
Mfg quotes received	7	01/14/05	
Revised pages to typesetter		01/14/05	
Index pages to typesetter		01/14/05	
Estimate and release routing	2	01/16/05	
Page revisions completed	12	01/28/05	
Final lasers requested	7	02/04/05	
Final lasers in	7	02/11/05	
Final lasers OK	14	02/25/05	
Estimate and release approved		01/30/05	
Cover/dust jacket copy in/OK		12/18/04	
Cover/dust jacket design in		01/14/05	
Cover/dust jacket design OK		01/21/05	
Keyline in		02/11/05	
Keyline OK		02/25/05	
Order date text/cover/dust jacket		02/25/05	
Blues in	21	03/18/05	
Blues OK	1	03/19/05	
F&Gs in	10	04/05/05	
F&Gs OK		04/03/05	
Advances in	7	04/09/05	
Books in warehouse		04/09/05	

Fig. A.1. Sample design and production schedule for a book printed domestically.

	DAYS	JAN ISSUE	APR ISSUE	JUL ISSUE	OCT ISSUE
MSS at Press		08/02	11/01	01/31	05/02
MS files converted / to Press editorial	7	08/13	11/12	02/11	05/13
MSS edited / typeset / proofed	21	09/11	12/11	03/12	06/11
Proofs to authors	1	09/12	12/12	03/13	06/12
Proofs from authors to journal office / journal office check / back to Press editorial	21	10/11	01/10	04/11	07/11
Revised proofs generated / checked	10	10/25	01/24	04/25	07/25
Revised proofs to journal office	1	10/26	01/25	04/26	07/26
Revised proofs back from journal office to Press editorial	10	11/09	02/08	05/10	08/09
Final proofs (generated by Press editorial) to production	3	11/14	02/13	05/15	08/14
Production paginates issue	5	11/21	02/20	05/22	08/21
Final check (1 day Press editorial, 1 day journal office)	2	11/23	02/22	05/24	08/23
PostScript file to printer	3	11/28	02/27	05/29	08/28
Post electronic issue	3	12/03	03/04	06/03	09/02
Mail print edition	15	12/19	03/20	06/19	09/18

Fig. A.2. Sample production schedule for a quarterly journal published in both print and electronic forms.

The design of dust jackets, paperback covers, and packaging for electronic storage media also involves technical and marketing considerations beyond the scope of this appendix. For works covering these topics, see section 2.6 of the bibliography.)

To develop specifications for a publication, the designer must know about such elements as the categories of text that appear in the manuscript; the placement of notes (footnotes or endnotes?); the kind and number of illustrations, including tables, graphs, or charts; and the material to be included in the preliminary pages and the back matter. Many book publishers, including Chicago, communicate such information internally through an editorial transmittal sheet that accompanies the manuscript to the design and production department (see fig. A.3). Such fact sheets are often not enough; subsequent conferences between editor and designer may be necessary to clarify any unusual features of a project.

The length of the original manuscript and the desired length of the published work are crucial pieces of information for the designer. Because the overall cost of services and materials used in the production and manufacture of a printed work depends on its length, a publisher will often specify a target page count for the publication, taking into account the length of the manuscript. From this starting point, the designer can calculate the number of words or characters that must fit onto a page. (Works published electronically are not necessarily subject to the same length restrictions as their print counterparts; see 1.130 and 1.189–90.)

The character count of a book manuscript can be determined through a castoff, which is performed on a version of the manuscript that is final (at least in terms of the number, nature, and length of its parts) and complete in all essentials. Ideally, a castoff involves counting each character—that is, every letter, mark of punctuation, and space between words—in the text. With heavily edited material, this would be the only way to ascertain a manuscript's true length. A more common and less time-consuming method is to count both the number of characters in an average line and the number of lines in the entire manuscript and then multiply these numbers to get a total character count. The "character count" function in many word-processing programs will also provide a quick record of a document's length, but this function does not necessarily tell the designer everything essential about the nature of the characters being counted.

Since each category of text will likely be given its own set of type characteristics, the designer needs not just a total character count for the work but a count broken down by type of material. For front matter, manuscript closely mirrors typeset pages, so character counts are not as useful. Similarly, for material in which certain line breaks must be observed—poetry, notes, bibliographies, and glossaries—calculating the number of lines is often more helpful than performing a character count. With these two exceptions in mind, a typical character count might read as follows:

	CHARACTERS	LINES
Text	700,000	. . .
Extracts	50,000	. . .
Appendix	85,000	. . .
Notes	. . .	360
Bibliography	. . .	240

The number of illustrations and tables and any peculiarities of size and formatting should be noted along with the text character count; characters in tables and legends need not be counted. Dividing the numbers in the castoff by the target number of characters per printed page—taking into account illustrations and other nontext materials—will give a fair estimate of the length of the finished publication (see figs. A.4–6).

BOOK TRANSMITTAL   Date: 5/26/00

Acquisitions editor: **   Season: S01   Proposed delivery date: 5/01

Author: Laura Hostetler

Full title: *Qing Colonial Enterprise: Ethnography and Cartography in Early Modern China*

Description: Laura Hostetler studies the process of empire building in China during the early modern period (1500–1800) and explores the uses that the Qing state made of cartographic and ethnographic representation. Technologies of representation usually thought to have originated in Europe were widely used in the Qing period. In mapping the contours of an expanding empire, the Qing court chose to use the same idiom or map language in which its competitors functioned—a style of cartography characterized by accurate, to-scale representations. The Kangxi emperor (r. 1662–1722) commissioned a team of European Jesuit missionaries to survey and map the growing empire in much the same manner as Peter the Great commissioned maps of Russia, and the French and Spanish courts commissioned maps of their own countries and their colonies in the New World. In addition to examining the Qing maps, Hostetler examines other forms of representation of the newly acquired territories, focusing particularly on the Miao Albums of Guizhou Province. These are colorful illustrated manuscripts showing depictions of the native peoples. Twenty of these captivating watercolors will be reproduced in color in the book. Hostetler's book will be of interest to historians of cartography, ethnographers, and historians of China's early modern period.

Contract, Rights, Permissions
Contract no: **   Series contract no: N/A   Any contractual pieces missing? ■No □Yes; see contract summary

■Book represents all new work by one or more authors under contract to us.
□Translation (*Note to manuscript editing: AAs must be kept to a minimum; charge index to translation account.*)
          Original publisher: Year of original publication:
□Other; specify:

Paperback or other nonstandard clauses: None

Copyright: ■University of Chicago   □Other; specify:
Rights: ■We have world rights, all languages, all editions.   □Other; specify:
Permissions: □None needed   □All in/free to Press   ■See permissions summary

Unusual permissions problems: None

Manuscript Editing
Type of manuscript: ■Electronic   □Conventional   Mark each item as here (X), N/A (—), or to come (date required):
Type and version of software: Text is in WordPerfect 9.0;
  appendix and glossary are in MS Word (incl. Chinese characters)
Manuscript and proof to be handled by: Author
Preferred address: **

Half title	X
Series title	—
Title page	X
Copyright page	X
Dedication	X

Phone number: **
Fax number: **
E-mail address: **

Epigraph	—
Contents	X
List of illus.	X (three separate ones)
List of tables	X
Foreword	—

Will contact person be away/unavailable during the next year?
Please provide dates, details. No

Preface	X
Acknowledgments	X
Introduction	X
Complete text	X
Notes	X

Does author have any special requests regarding type/level of editing? Please specify. No, but we should remove the subheads from the table of contents and the credit lines from the various lists of illustrations.
Index to be prepared by: Author

Appendix(es)	X
Glossary	X
Bibliography	X
Index	to come
Captions	X
Disks	X

Manuscript editor assigned:

**Some personal or proprietary information omitted.

Fig. A.3. Sample editorial transmittal sheet for a book manuscript, including information for the design and production department.

<u>Design and Production</u>
Typesetting: ■Electronic □Conventional   Notes: ■Footnotes □Endnotes □Other; specify:
No. words: Text: Notes/biblio: Total: 88,400
Est. no. pages: 240   Proposed trim: 6 x 9

Artwork:	No. here	No. to come (w/dates)	Total
Color plates	20*	0	20
B/w halftones	12	1 (by 7/1)	13
Maps	6*	0	6
Line drawings	3	1	4
Musical ex's	0	0	0
Tables	4	0	4

Notes on missing art: Glossies here but better slides to follow for plates 7–10, 12b, 13b, and 15b. Note that components labeled (a) for image and (b) for accompanying Chinese text in plates 7–10, 12b, and 15b are to be set side-by-side with labels dropped so images and text represent a single illustration. Author is having map 2 reshot.

Art to run: □In text   □As gallery   ■Combination; specify: color plates in 16-page gallery; rest interspersed

Interior design suggestions: Note that Chinese characters appear in appendix and glossary but not in text (transliterated). All four tables are unusually long (several pages).
Jacket/cover design suggestions: 4-color; use one of the color plates

Design manager's comments: *Wpp:*

                                                       Quark?:

Proposed to-production date:

Proposed delivery date: 5/01   *Advance jacket/cover needed? Date?*

Designer assigned: *Production controller assigned:*

<u>Marketing</u>
Proposed publication plan: **Cloth**   **Paper**
  Print run   **
  Price/discount $35.00/sp

Subjects:
  Bookstore: Asian History
  Complete catalog: Asian Studies—East Asia; History—Asian History; Geography—Cartography; Anthropology

Suggestions for/comments on seasonal catalog treatment: 1/2 page

Meetings and dates for which advances are needed: Asian Studies; proofs OK.

Is the book designed for use as a text? Please specify course area(s). No

Other notes on marketing: None

Promotions manager assigned:

**Some personal or proprietary information omitted.

Necessary calculation to determine the final, typeset length of a printed book. The estimator begins with the raw manuscript and calculates how many printed pages the manuscript copy will run based on the following:

(1) Type size: Size of letters, measured in points
(2) Typeface: Style of type (e.g., Stempel Garamond, Adobe Caslon, etc.). Also now referred to as "font" in desktop publishing industry
(3) Line measure: Length of typeset line, measured in picas
(4) Page fill: Number of lines per page

(These four items are derived from the book design.)

Original manuscript

Number of characters per line __62__ × Number of lines per page __27__ × Number of

manuscript pages __400__ = __669,600__ [TOTAL NUMBER OF CHARACTERS IN MANUSCRIPT]

Typeset page

Number of characters per pica __2.8__ × Number of picas per line __26__ × Number of lines

per page __40__ = __2912__ [TOTAL NUMBER OF CHARACTERS PER TYPESET PAGE]

Approximate number of typeset pages*

Number of characters in original manuscript ÷ number of characters per typeset page

= __256__

*add extra amount—about 5–10%—for slippage

Fig. A.4. Formula for estimating the length of a book manuscript based on a castoff. The numbers in this example come from the manuscript excerpted in figure A.5 and are reflected in the typeset page in figure A.6.

TEXT DESIGN

With the manuscript and the information from the castoff in hand, and knowing the desired length of the publication, the designer can make some key decisions about the design of the text. Which typefaces and sizes of type to use for running text, notes, and other parts of the document is perhaps the most important. A number of considerations affect this decision: Is the text peppered with foreign words requiring a variety of diacritical marks available only in certain typefaces? Is the text highly technical, contain-

Take as an example the finale of Haydn's Opus 64, No. 5, D
Major. The violin plays, according to my quick, indeed impatient
count, 857 notes, most of them sixteenths, most of them entailing a change not just of bowing but of fingering from the preceding note. The viola plays 368 notes, many of them sixteenths, and most requiring finger changes. Meanwhile the cello
is asked to play only 122 notes, with only 72 rapid sixteenths,
and with 32 of those sixteenths resting comfortably either on

Approximate number of characters per line, including word spaces: 62

Fig. A.5. Sample text from a book manuscript used to determine the total number of characters in the manuscript. See figure A.4 for the formula used to calculate this information.

ing mathematics or other material requiring special symbols that are likewise available in a limited number of typefaces? Are there several levels of
subheadings that might call for a second, complementary typeface to help
readers navigate the text? What kind of display type is appropriate to the
subject matter? Experienced designers know how to evaluate the typographical requirements of a particular project and to make choices that will
transform the manuscript into a visually appealing publication.

Other key decisions for the designer concern the dimensions of the
printed publication. One such dimension is the size of the type page,
which is the area occupied by the running head, the text proper (the text
page or text area), the footnotes (if any), and the page number (or folio).
The dimensions of the type page are measured in picas, with one pica
equaling approximately one-sixth of an inch. In addition to the width and
length of the type page, the designer typically specifies the number of text
lines on a full text page and on any special types of pages, such as a chapter opening. A final variable is the publication's trim size, which is measured in inches (stated as width by depth; for example, 6″ × 9″) and refers
to the size of the whole page on which type and illustrations are printed
(see fig. A.7). A large trim size may allow more characters to be fitted on a
page or may be appropriate to a work containing many illustrations. In
general, however, the choice of a trim size is usually made before a project
reaches the designer and is based on the expectations of the marketplace
as well as the relative cost of producing the publication in various trim
sizes.

A complete design should include full type specifications and representative layouts for all the various categories of text in the publication.

sic. I knew that the piano was out, because on it I could never come close to the skill needed for even the simplest chamber music parts, providing real musical pleasure to others. On the other hand, if I took up a string instrument, it seemed obvious that I could soon be doing a not-bad job of playing some of the easier chamber music, depending on Phyllis and other better players to do the harder stuff on the other parts.

But which string instrument? I here offer as evidence for the rightness of my choice a meticulous, unprecedented calculation of the Ratio of the Disparity of Instrumental Difficulties, or RDID. Take as an example the finale of Haydn's Opus 64, No. 5, D Major. The violin plays, according to my quick, indeed impatient count, 857 notes, most of them sixteenths, most of them entailing a change not just of bowing but of fingering from the preceding note. The viola plays 368 notes, many of them sixteenths, and most of them requiring finger changes. Meanwhile the cello is asked to play only 122 notes, with only 72 rapid sixteenths, and with 32 of those sixteenths resting comfortably either on the tonic or dominant. Many of them are followed by a lovely rest period providing time to seek out the next note. Now there we have a clear measure of why it was wiser for me to take up the cello than the violin or even the viola: an RDID of viola to cello of precisely 3 to 1 and of violin to cello of about 7 to 1.

The fact is that there are many wonderful moments with RDIDs even better than that, when the only challenge to the cellist is to produce a single tolerable note sustained for measure after measure. At one point in the Haydn I am offered a comfortable low A while the first violin plays 63 notes! Timeless moments like that rightly tempted me—the chance to dwell lovingly on a single note while feeling as if I were playing all the parts.

Of course I am not saying that anything even remotely like that RDID holds for all chamber music. I'm glad it doesn't. But if I were to count piano and cello notes for an early piano trio by Beethoven, say, the RDID would be even more striking. In more modern works a greater democratic balance is sought and sometimes achieved, but the cello still has far more occasions to rest easy while one or more of the others capers.

Even without counting the RDID I already had a strong enough hunch to guide my choice. Though I loved listening to some of the "display" cello concertos that at many points actually reverse the RDID fraction, I fortunately knew that a lot of chamber literature issued me a simple invitation: not "come and play me, as a star, as a leader" but "come and play me as a deeply feeling accompanist for the stars."

I hope it's clear that I'm not mocking the choice of other string instruments; if you're already good at one of them, get better. Both my playing

Fig. A.6. Typeset page, based on the type specifications indicated at right and generated from the book manuscript shown in figure A.5. The designer used the numbers from the castoff (see fig. A.4) along with information about the desired length of the book to determine how best to fit the type on the page.

sic. I knew that the piano was out, because on it I could never come close to the skill needed for even the simplest chamber music parts, providing real musical pleasure to others. On the other hand, if I took up a string instrument, it seemed obvious that I could soon be doing a not-bad job of playing some of the easier chamber music, depending on Phyllis and other better players to do the harder stuff on the other parts.

But which string instrument? I here offer as evidence for the rightness of my choice a meticulous, unprecedented calculation of the Ratio of the Disparity of Instrumental Difficulties, or RDID. Take as an example the finale of Haydn's Opus 64, No. 5, D Major. The violin plays, according to my quick, indeed impatient count, 857 notes, most of them sixteenths, most of them entailing a change not just of bowing but of fingering from the preceding note. The viola plays 368 notes, many of them sixteenths, and most of them requiring finger changes. Meanwhile the cello is asked to play only 122 notes, with only 72 rapid sixteenths, and with 32 of those sixteenths resting comfortably either on the tonic or dominant. Many of them are followed by a lovely rest period providing time to seek out the next note. Now there we have a clear measure of why it was wiser for me to take up the cello than the violin or even the viola: an RDID of viola to cello of precisely 3 to 1 and of violin to cello of about 7 to 1.

The fact is that there are many wonderful moments with RDIDs even better than that, when the only challenge to the cellist is to produce a single tolerable note sustained for measure after measure. At one point in the Haydn I am offered a comfortable low A while the first violin plays 63 notes! Timeless moments like that rightly tempted me—the chance to dwell lovingly on a single note while feeling as if I were playing all the parts.

Of course I am not saying that anything even remotely like that RDID holds for all chamber music. I'm glad it doesn't. But if I were to count piano and cello notes for an early piano trio by Beethoven, say, the RDID would be even more striking. In more modern works a greater democratic balance is sought and sometimes achieved, but the cello still has far more occasions to rest easy while one or more of the others capers.

Even without counting the RDID I already had a strong enough hunch to guide my choice. Though I loved listening to some of the "display" cello concertos that at many points actually reverse the RDID fraction, I fortunately knew that a lot of chamber literature issued me a simple invitation: not "come and play me, as a star, as a leader" but "come and play me as a deeply feeling accompanist for the stars."

I hope it's clear that I'm not mocking the choice of other string instruments; if you're already good at one of them, get better. Both my playing and my listening depends on them. But I can't resist a warning to lovers of

A.7. The type page is the part of the page occupied by the text, the running head, and the folio; the size is the entire area of the page.

Common elements include the front (or preliminary) matter; a chapter opening page; two facing pages showing text, extracts, subheads, footnotes, illustrations, running heads, and folios; and the back (or end) matter (including, as relevant, the appendix, endnotes, glossary, bibliography, and index). A sample text design with complete type specifications appears at the end of this appendix (fig. A.14, pp. 841–56).

Before the project is submitted for typesetting, the designer's layouts are checked to be sure each of the text elements has been assigned a typographical specification. The final edited manuscript (in paper or electronic form) is reviewed to ensure that it has been properly coded (see 2.87–91).

Production

TYPESETTING

In the past, typesetting involved keyboarding text from hard copy prepared by authors and marked up by editors. Today the electronic files originated by authors are often used in both editing and typesetting, although they may require substantial manipulation. The way a manuscript is prepared for typesetting depends on two main factors: the equipment and software that will be used to perform the typesetting and the format in which the work will ultimately be disseminated (print, electronic, or both). Many typesetting programs require the removal or modification of formatting codes used in word-processing programs. Often publications that will be distributed electronically (either solely or in conjunction with a print counterpart) are also tagged in a formal markup language such as SGML or XML (see 2.91); tagging produces an archival file that can be used to create future print or electronic editions. The timing of and responsibility for these tasks vary.

Traditionally, publishers have relied on the services of professional typesetters, or compositors, to produce their publications. Technological advances in areas such as desktop page-layout and illustration programs, however, have given them the option of typesetting manuscripts in-house, commonly using design and production staff. While this option may eliminate outside typesetting fees, it still costs staff time. In addition, desktop programs remain less sophisticated and versatile than professional typesetting systems; they can be prohibitively expensive, and they require substantial expertise. Regardless of which method is used, it is the typesetter's responsibility to be sure the electronic files meet the needs of the printer, who is almost always an outside supplier.

Before typesetting (or composition) begins in earnest, a publisher will often ask the typesetter for sample pages, which are prepared in accordance with the designer's specifications and layouts to show how various typographical elements will look in page form. The publisher either approves the sample pages or sends them back to the typesetter with a request for changes. Once the sample pages have been approved, composition proceeds.

The first full set of proofs supplied by a typesetter is usually in the form of either galley proofs or page proofs. Galley proofs show all of the text set in type but do not reflect how the text and illustrations will fit on individual pages. Improvements in page-layout programs have eliminated the need for galleys in all but the most complicated projects. Page proofs, in contrast, show the text, the illustrations, and all other elements of the design in paginated form. After the proofreading stage (see chapter 3), the typesetter will make any requested corrections and provide revised proofs if necessary.

The final output from the typesetter—usually in the form of laser proofs—reflects the electronic files exactly and should represent the work as the publisher wishes it to appear in print. (Instead of laser proofs, some typesetters may still provide a more traditional photographic output called repro, or reproduction copy.) The typesetter prepares desktop page layout files or, increasingly, PostScript (PS) or Portable Document Format (PDF) files as well as associated graphics and fonts. These files are checked for accuracy and completeness before they are sent to the printer for reproduction (see fig. A.8 for a checklist).

PREPRESS

The prepress phase includes all the steps that occur between the time the printer receives the typesetter's files (and any other materials, such as artwork, needed for printing) and the time the publication is put on press, or printed.

Among the first stages of prepress is the creation of blueline proofs, or bluelines, which are photographic prints prepared from film negatives. Through disk-to-film technology, these negatives can now be generated directly from the typesetter's files. Bluelines are used to examine the layout and position of all elements, including page sequence, before plates are made and the work is printed; they do not, however, represent the quality of the final printing. For works in which the reproduction quality of the illustrations is critical, a publisher may require that the printer supply contact proofs, which can be checked for contrast and quality by the designer and production staff before printing.

Typical Digital Problems:
- ❑ Missing screen and printer fonts, incorrect resolution, and insufficient resolution for high-quality printing in supplied high-resolution files.
- ❑ Inadequate bleed allowance (we need at least 1/8 inch or 3 mm).
- ❑ Digital files that do not match the supplied laser prints.
- ❑ Mixing of outdated versions of the files together with new one on your supplied disk(s).
- ❑ Incorrect file names and missing information about blank pages.
- ❑ Inconsistency in the margins, folios, and styles from page to page and file to file.
- ❑ Customized fonts, not properly referenced or supplied with your files.
- ❑ Disk errors or incompatible drivers on the storage medium.
- ❑ Scanned images with substantial reduction/enlargement in later stage affecting final printing quality.

We Need from You:
- ❑ Complete specifications for your title, such as book title, text stock, trim size, number of supplied images, line screen requirements, proof requirements, quantities, and any special requirements.
- ❑ Originals/photos/slides, all files on disk, laser output at 100% size and with trim marks.
- ❑ Accurate and clear file directories.
- ❑ All corrections, or replacement images, on a new disk together with all artwork and needed screen and printer fonts, along with updated laser proofs.

Useful Tips:
- ❑ Send all the files, fonts, graphics, laser proofs, and full specifications at one time.
- ❑ Make sure all files are well organized on the disk(s). It is better to include all graphic files for text and application files in one folder, and the text fonts in a separate folder.
- ❑ Do not put multiple jobs on a single disk.
- ❑ Label all supplied disks with job name. Number each disk (1 of 3, 2 of 3, 3 of 3, etc.).
- ❑ Do not leave outdated versions of the files on the disks.
- ❑ Provide all screen and printer fonts.
- ❑ Do not use TrueType or non-PostScript fonts.
- ❑ Be sure to set the trim size in the digital files to match the trim size of the final book block.
- ❑ Provide complete cropping information for your images to achieve a better quality in scanning.

Fig. A.8. Sample list of items to be checked before sending the typesetter's files to the printer. Each printer has its own checklist.

Increasingly, printers have eliminated the need for traditional blue-lines by using computer-to-plate (CTP) technology. By converting the typesetter's files to PostScript or PDF, this technology bypasses the photographic phase and allows the pages to be imposed directly onto offset printing plates. Files for works that contain art must have high-resolution scans of the art embedded in them before this conversion takes place. Instead of bluelines, the publisher receives digital proofs, which are generated from the typesetter's files and checked for completeness and layout but not for reproduction quality.

Another stage of prepress may involve scanning original artwork to produce images for incorporation into the typesetter's files. With the increasing availability of high-quality scanners and color-calibrated computer monitors, such scanning can theoretically be done at an earlier stage of production by the publisher or even by the author, provided the pub-

Submitting Scans

BLACK AND WHITE SCANS

Glossy photographs are superior to author-generated scans as a starting point for image reproduction. The original photograph or drawing gives designers and printers the most options for determining how best to reproduce the original. Modern print shops have systems that are calibrated from the scanning stage all the way through to the printing press, and taking advantage of this work flow ensures the best possible reproduction.

Unfortunately, the widespread availability of inexpensive desktop scanners encourages the illusion that submitting images in the form of scans is a cost-saving convenience. Scanning introduces a plethora of quality and technical issues that are all too often unseen by the novice. These issues can entail unnecessary delays and costs.

If submitting original art is not possible, then it is best to use an established graphic arts service or library service for scanning.

SUBMISSION REQUIREMENTS FOR BLACK-AND-WHITE SCANS

Form. Black-and-white continuous-tone scans should be provided in the grayscale mode.
Format. Scans should be saved in the TIFF or EPS format
Quality. Scans should be made from sharp, clear originals by a graphic arts service, a professional photo lab, or a library service.
Size. 5 × 7 inches or 8 × 10 inches
Resolution. 300 pixels per inch.
Documentation. Each scan must be accompanied by a laser print representing the scan at actual size.

TO BE AVOIDED

If you must submit scans with the following features, please consult your publishing team before doing so.
Form. Scans submitted in the RGB and CMYK modes that are intended for black-and-white reproduction. Converting these scans often yields unexpected and disappointing results.
Quality. Scans made from muddy, blurry, or damaged originals. Scans made from previously printed material such as books and magazines. Scans made from slides. Scans meant for use on the World Wide Web.
Size. Scans smaller than 5 × 7 inches and larger than 8 × 10 inches
Resolution. Resolution less than 300 pixels per inch.

INCORPORATING TEXT AND GRAPHICS

If you wish to incorporate graphic identifiers (such as a numbering scheme or arrow indicators) with a continuous-tone black-and-white image, import the scan into a drawing program such as Adobe Illustrator or Macromedia Freehand and incorporate the elements there.

COLOR SCANS

Submitting color scans is discouraged even more than submitting black-and-white scans. Four-color printing requires more planning between designer and print shop than black-and-white printing does.

If you have no alternative and must submit color scans, you should also provide a flat art facsimile of the scan that accurately portrays the color makeup of the image. Our printers will need this when they convert the scan from RGB to CMYK format. Submit color scans in RGB mode in the TIFF or EPS format. Do not submit scans in the CMYK mode. *Please consult your book team before submitting color scans.*

Fig. A.9. Sample guidelines for the submission of scanned artwork to a publisher.

lisher's guidelines are followed (see fig. A.9 for an example of such guidelines and chapter 12 for more detailed discussion of illustration preparation). But printers are typically the best prepared to do this kind of work since they have both highly trained personnel and sophisticated scanning devices. These devices outperform most publishers' desktop scanners, and they can be calibrated to work directly with the printing press and with the type of paper to be used. In-house scanners should, however, be adequate for works to be published electronically, since such publications have different requirements from those of their printed counterparts for image resolution, color, and so forth.

PAPER

One of the most important responsibilities of design and production personnel working on print publications is selecting paper. Paper comes in varying weights, sizes, shades, coatings, and degrees of opacity and smoothness, and each of these variables affects the overall appearance of a printed work. In consultation with the printer or a paper merchant, the publisher must determine which type of paper best suits a particular publication and which will print on and run through a given printing press most efficiently. Other considerations for the publisher are the cost and availability of the paper.

The choice of a trim size is heavily influenced by the fact that paper is manufactured to standard roll and sheet sizes. Because printing presses and bindery equipment are set up to accommodate these roll and sheet sizes with minimal waste of paper, publishers usually find it most economical to choose one of a handful of corresponding trim sizes for their books and journals—in the United States, these are $5^1/_2 \times 8^1/_2$ inches, 6×9 inches, 7×10 inches, and $8^1/_2 \times 11$ inches. When the special needs of a publication dictate a nonstandard trim size, the costs of both the printer's labor and the paper are likely to rise.

Growing concerns about the durability of printed publications and about environmental contamination related to the paper industry also enter into the choice of paper. Publications that are printed on acid-free paper have a longer life expectancy than those that are not, and they usually carry a notice on the copyright page indicating their compliance with the durability standards of the American National Standards Institute (see 1.35). Certain types of works may be printed on recycled paper, a combination of virgin fiber and pre- and postconsumer wastepaper. The proportion of each kind of fiber required to legitimate the label *recycled*, however, is subject to some debate. A related issue is that the bleaching

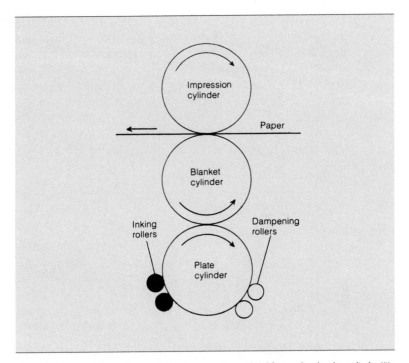

Fig. A.10. Principle of offset printing. A plate is wrapped around and fastened to the plate cylinder. Water applied by the dampening rollers adheres only to the background area of the plate; ink applied by the inking rollers adheres only to the dry image of the type on the plate. As the plate cylinder revolves, it transfers the ink to the rubber blanket of the blanket cylinder, which in turn transfers (or offsets) it onto the paper, which is held in place by the impression cylinder.

methods used to make recycled papers employ varying amounts of chlorine. An elemental chlorine-free (ECF) paper is made with a chlorine derivative that contains hazardous substances, including dioxin; a totally chlorine-free (TCF) paper is not. Publishers seeking to minimize the environmental impact of printing should keep these issues in mind when selecting paper.

PRINTING

The most common type of printing used to produce books and journals is offset printing, or offset lithography. This process involves the transfer of images (text, illustrations, and any other marks that will be distinct from the background color of the page) from the printer's plates to the paper

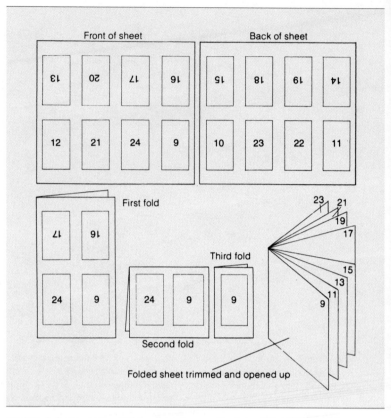

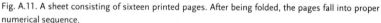

Fig. A.11. A sheet consisting of sixteen printed pages. After being folded, the pages fall into proper numerical sequence.

through an intermediate cylinder. The printer applies ink to each plate, and the inked images are offset onto the paper through the rubber-blanketed intermediate cylinder (see fig. A.10). The printing press itself may be either sheet-fed, using sheets of paper that have been precut, or web-fed, using rolls of paper that will be folded and trimmed at the end of the printing stage.

A newer method, digital printing, uses technology similar to that of the traditional photocopier, in which images are printed directly onto paper through ink jets or thermal transfer. The quality of the reproduction is generally not as high as that achieved through the offset process. But digital printing makes it economically viable to print small quantities of a publication (three hundred copies or fewer) on demand, preferably from archived electronic files, and can assist publishers with inventory management.

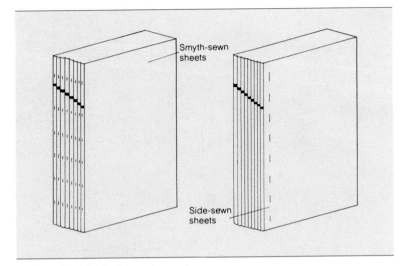

Fig. A.12. Two methods of sewing used in binding. In Smyth sewing the sheets are stitched individually through the fold; in side sewing they are stitched from the side, close to the spine. The black rectangles printed on the folds in both methods help the binder recognize whether a signature is missing, duplicated, out of order, or upside down.

BINDING

The final element in the production of a print publication is binding, which begins with the folding and trimming of the press sheets, or printed sheets, that emerge from the printing press. A press sheet bears printed pages on both sides, each side created from a single plate, and when it is folded in half, and then in half again—continuing until only one page is showing—all the pages fall into proper sequence (see fig. A.11). The folded sheet, called a signature, usually consists of thirty-two pages, but this number may vary depending on the bulk and flexibility of the paper and the size of the offset printing press. When all the signatures have been gathered in the proper order, they are referred to as folded and gathered sheets, or F&Gs. The F&Gs can then be bound in either hardcover or paperback format.

Hardcover Binding

Binding hardcover books typically requires sewing the signatures together, usually by either Smyth sewing or side sewing (see fig. A.12). An alternative method, adhesive binding, involves notching or fraying the

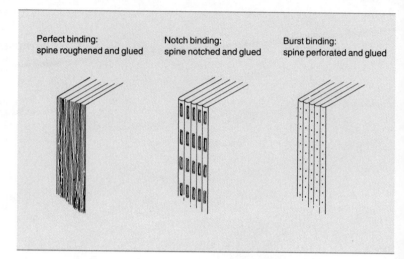

Perfect binding:
spine roughened and glued

Notch binding:
spine notched and glued

Burst binding:
spine perforated and glued

Fig. A.13. Three methods of adhesive binding: perfect, notch, and burst binding.

folded edges and then applying adhesive to the signatures to hold them together. Smyth- or side-sewn books have a sturdier binding and hold up better over time, but adhesive binding is faster and less costly. In any of these methods, the hardcover case is fashioned by the application of cover material (such as cloth, synthetic fabric, leather, or paper) to boards. The case is then affixed to the body of the book, and a dust jacket may be wrapped around the case.

Paperback Binding

Journals and paperback books are almost always adhesive-bound through one of three methods: perfect, notch, or burst binding (see fig. A.13). In the perfect-binding method, about an eighth of an inch is mechanically roughened off the spine of the tightly gathered F&Gs, reducing them to a series of separate pages. The roughened spine is then coated with a flexible glue, and a paper cover is wrapped around the pages. In the other two methods, the spine is either scored by a series of notches (notch binding) or perforated (burst binding) and then force-fed with glue. Unlike perfect binding, these methods prevent the loss of part of the back margin and ensure that signatures remain intact, reducing the risk of pages coming loose. For paperbound books of higher quality, the signatures can be sewn and the covers (sometimes with flaps) then affixed, as with adhesive-bound books; this style of binding is known as flexibinding or limpbinding.

ELECTRONIC VERSIONS

An electronic version of a publication may be produced in conjunction with, or even instead of, a print version (see chapter 1). Many of the basic production stages for an electronic publication are the same as those for a print publication.

One procedure that can enhance the usefulness of a file intended for publication in an electronic format is to add formal markup in SGML or XML (see 2.91). The point at which markup is added varies widely from one publisher to another. Chicago, for example, adds markup to its journal articles before editing begins; it is present throughout editing and production. For Web presentation, the final edited files are converted to HTML; elements that cannot be rendered reliably in HTML—such as figures and images of complex math—are specially generated for Web presentation. The presence and functioning of all elements, including hypertext links and any other electronic-only features, must be confirmed before publication (see 3.42–43).

Publication in an electronic storage medium, such as a CD-ROM or a DVD, involves specific technical production tasks beyond markup that are suitable to the medium and that are not detailed here.

Key Terms

AA. An abbreviation for *author's alteration*. See also **alteration**.

acid-free paper. Paper having a pH of 7, or close to 7. Acid-free paper deteriorates at a much slower rate than paper with a lower pH, giving publications printed on it a longer life expectancy. See also **pH**.

adhesive binding. A method of binding that employs glue instead of stitching to hold the pages or signatures together and is widely used for journals and paperback books. Three types of adhesive binding are currently used: perfect binding, notch binding, and burst binding. Contrast **case binding; flexibinding.**

alteration. A change from the manuscript copy introduced in proof, as distinguished from a *correction* made to eliminate a printer's error. See also **AA; DA; EA.**

arabic numerals. The familiar digits used in arithmetical computation. In many type fonts they are available in two forms: *lining*, or *aligning* (1 2 3 4 5 6 7 8 9 0), and *old style* (1 2 3 4 5 6 7 8 9 0), abbreviated *OS* and characterized by ascenders and descenders. Contrast **roman numerals.**

artwork. Illustrative material (photographs, drawings, maps, and so forth) intended for reproduction.

ascender. The portion of a lowercase letter that extends above the x-height, as in *b* and *d*. Contrast **descender.**

ASCII file. See **text file.**

back margin. The inner margin of a page; that is, the margin along the binding side of the page. See also **gutter.**

baseline. In type, an imaginary common line that all capital letters, x-heights, arabic numerals, and ascenders rest on. See also **x-height.**

basis weight. The weight in pounds of a ream (five hundred sheets) of paper cut to a standard size (25 × 38 inches for book papers). Book papers generally range from forty to eighty pounds. See also **grammage.**

beta testing. The final checking of a computer application (such as a Web site) before it is released. Such testing is ideally carried out under normal operating conditions by users who are not directly involved in developing the application.

binding. (1) A covering for the pages of a publication, using such materials as leather, cloth, and paper. (2) The process by which such a covering is attached. See also **adhesive binding; case binding.**

binding cloth. Cloth (usually cotton or rayon) for use in book covers that has been sized, glazed, or impregnated with synthetic resins and is available in a large variety of weights, finishes, colors, and patterns.

bitmap. A digital representation of an image consisting of an array of pixels, in rows and columns, that can be saved to a file. Each pixel in the grid of the bitmap contains information about the color value of its position, which is used, for example, to display an image on a monitor or print it to a page.

blanket. In offset printing, the resilient rubber covering of the blanket cylinder, which receives the ink impression from the plate cylinder and offsets it onto the paper.

bleed. To run an illustration or ink coverage beyond the edge of the paper (or "off the page").

blind embossing. See **embossing.**

blind folio. See **folio.**

blind stamping. See **stamping.**

block quotation. Quoted material set off typographically from the text (see 11.11). Also called *extract*. Contrast **run in.**

bluelines. An abbreviation for *blueline proof;* also called *blues* or (in Europe and Asia) *ozalids*. A type of photographic proof generated by a printing firm either from repro or from the typesetter's electronic files. Bluelines should reflect all the changes made in the galley and page proof stages and should be checked for completeness and placement of material but not for color or quality of type. See also **digital proof.**

boards. Stiffening material used in binding to form the foundation of the cover; formerly wood, now generally a paper product such as binder's board (the finest quality), pasted board (often used in case binding), or chipboard (low quality). Redboard is used for flexible bindings. The bare board is sheathed in one of a variety of cover materials.

body type. Type used for the running text of a work, as distinguished from the display type used for chapter openings, subheads, and so forth.

boldface. Type that has a darker and heavier appearance than standard type (as in the entries in this list of key terms).

book paper. Paper made principally for the manufacture of books, journals, and magazines, as distinguished from newsprint and from writing and cover stock. Book paper is usually wood-free.

broadside. Designed to be read or viewed normally when the publication is turned ninety degrees. In University of Chicago Press practice, the *left* side of a broadside table or illustration is at the *bottom* of the page. Because most publications are longer than they are wide, broadside images are usually landscape, but not all landscape images are broadside. See also **landscape.**

bulk. The thickness of paper measured in number of pages per inch; also used loosely to indicate the thickness of a publication, excluding the cover.

burst binding. A type of adhesive binding in which the untrimmed spine is perforated and force-fed with glue.

camera-ready copy (CRC). Artwork and text that are ready to be photographed for reproduction without further alteration.

caps. An abbreviation for *capital letters.* See also **small caps.**

case. A hard cover or binding made by a casemaking machine or by hand and usually printed, stamped, or labeled before being glued to the gathered signatures. A case that is covered entirely by one type of material is a one-piece case; a case in which the spine is covered by one type of material and the front and back cover boards by another (often in a different color) is a three-piece case.

case binding. A method of encasing a book in a rigid cover, or *case.* The gathered signatures can be Smyth sewn or side sewn together or adhesive bound; endpapers are glued to the first and last signatures; a hinge of heavy gauze (the *super*) is glued to the spine of the sewn signatures; and the case is secured to the book by being glued to the flaps of the super and to both endpapers. Contrast **adhesive binding; flexibinding.**

castoff. An estimate of the space, or number of printed pages, that a manuscript will occupy when typeset.

CD-ROM. An abbreviation for *compact disc read-only memory.* A type of compact disc used for storing digital data that can be read optically and processed by a computer. The storage capacity of CD-ROMs is about 700 megabytes. See also **DVD.**

character. A letter, numeral, symbol, or mark of punctuation.

character count. An approximate measure of the length of a manuscript made by multiplying the number of characters and spaces in an average line by the number of lines in the manuscript. The "character count" feature of many word-processing programs can also provide such a total. See also **copyfitting.**

clothbound. Bound with a rigid cover, usually cloth wrapped around boards. Contrast **paperback.**

CMYK. An abbreviation for the basic colors used in process color printing—cyan (C), magenta (M), and yellow (Y), plus black (K)—to approximate all the colors in the spectrum.

code. A generic marker that identifies a particular type of text throughout a manuscript. A code is usually associated with a set of formatting instructions specified by the designer and followed by the typesetter. See also **tag.**

colophon. A statement, usually at the back of a publication (as in this manual), about the materials, processes, and individuals or companies involved in its preparation, production, and manufacturing.

color printing. See **process color printing; spot color printing.**

color separation. (1) The analysis of color copy for reproduction in terms of the three process colors (plus black) to be used in printing; separation is achieved by shooting through filters or by electronic scanning. (2) A film negative or positive, or a digital file, so produced for preparation of the printing plate. See also **process color printing.**

comp. An abbreviation for *comprehensive layout*, as for a dust jacket, and also for *composition* or *compositor*.

composition. Typesetting.

computer-to-plate (CTP) technology. A process in which a typesetter's electronic files are imposed directly onto offset printing plates, thus eliminating the need for an intermediate stage involving film. See also **digital proof.**

contact proof. A photographic proof used to show the reproduction quality of an image. Also called *velox*.

continuous tone. An image, such as a photograph, with gradations of tone from dark to light, in contrast to an image formed of pure blacks and whites, such as a pen-and-ink drawing. See also **halftone.**

copyfitting. Estimating the space required to print a given quantity of copy in a desired type size or the quantity of manuscript that, when printed, will fill a given space. The former is also called *casting off* copy. See also **character count.**

cover. The two hinged parts of a binding, front and back, and the center panel, or *spine*, that joins them; also the four surfaces making up the covers in this sense, when used to carry printed matter. See also **dust jacket.**

crop. To cut down an illustration, such as a photograph, to improve the appearance of the image by removing extraneous areas.

cyan. A greenish blue, one of the three colors (plus black) used in process color printing.

DA. An abbreviation for *designer's alteration*. See also **alteration.**

descender. The portion of a lowercase letter that extends below the x-height, as in *g* and *p*. Contrast **ascender.**

descreen. To remove evidence of the original halftone screen pattern in a previously printed image using software or mechanical filters. If such an image is not descreened before a new halftone screen is added, the printed version may include visually disruptive patterns called *moirés.*

die. See **stamping.**

digital. Transmitted or stored in an electronic format consisting of a sequence of discrete bits (0s and 1s), as with data such as text and images.

digital printing. A type of printing in which the transfer of electronic images to paper is accomplished with ink-jet or laser printers. Contrast **offset printing.**

digital proof. (1) In general, a type of proof generated directly from electronic files and output on a laser printer or other device. (2) A subset of the type above that takes the place of traditional bluelines and should reflect all the changes made in the galley and page proof stages; it should be checked for completeness and placement of material but not for color or quality of type. See also **bluelines.**

disk-to-film (DTF) technology. A process in which film negatives or positives are imposed from a typesetter's electronic files, eliminating the need for repro and the manual assembly of negatives from single pages of film.

display type. Type that is larger than or otherwise distinguished from body type and is used for title pages, chapter openings, subheads, and so on.

dpi. An abbreviation for *dots per inch*. A measurement of the resolution of a printed image. The term is also used to describe the maximum resolution of an output device (as in a 1,200-dpi printer).

drop cap. An uppercase character set in a type size larger than the text and "dropped," or nested, into lines of text, usually as the first character in the opening paragraph of a chapter or other section of text.

drop folio. See **folio.**

dropout halftone. A halftone in which the highlights have been whitened by removing all dots. Also called *highlight halftone.*

DTD. An abbreviation for *document type definition*. In SGML or XML, a set of rules about the structure of a document that dictate the relationship among different tags and allowable text or elements within specified tags. See also **tag.**

dummy. A mock-up of a publication (or part of a publication) intended to suggest the appearance and size of the completed work. Individuals involved in various phases of production may make different kinds of dummies to serve their purposes. (1) A designer's dummy usually consists of galley proofs and FPOs cut and pasted to show the relation between text and illustrations. (2) A printer's dummy consists of the specified paper and binding materials assembled to show the exact bulk and spine width of the publication.

dummy folio. See **folio.**

duotone. A halftone reproduction consisting of two tones, whether (1) two intensities of the same color, (2) black and a color, (3) black and gray, or (4) two colors other than black.

dust jacket. Also called *jacket.* A protective wrapping, usually made of paper, for a clothbound book; its *flaps,* which fold around the front and back covers, usually carry promotional copy. See also **cover.**

DVD. An abbreviation for *digital versatile* (or *video*) *disc.* A type of compact disc that can store up to seventeen gigabytes of digital video, audio, or computer data. See also **CD-ROM.**

EA. An abbreviation for *editor's alteration.* See also **alteration.**

ECF paper. An abbreviation for *elemental chlorine-free.* Paper bleached with a chlorine derivative that releases hazardous substances, including dioxin, into the environment. Contrast **TCF paper.**

edition. (1) A publication in its original form, and each subsequent reissue of the publication in which its content is significantly revised. (2) More informally, a term used to refer to each format in which a publication appears (for example, a book published in both cloth and paperback bindings, or a journal published in both electronic and print forms). However, the designation *second edition* would not be applied to the secondary format, or to a second or subsequent *impression* of the publication, in the absence of significant content changes. See also 1.22; **impression; reprint.**

em. A unit of type measurement equal to the point size of the type in question; for example, a six-point em is six points wide. See also **point.**

embossing. Forming an image in relief (that is, a raised image) on a surface such as a case or a paper cover or dust jacket. If the process does not involve metallic leaf or ink, it is called *blind embossing.* See also **stamping.**

em dash. A short typographical rule measuring the width of an em. See also 6.87–94.

en. A unit of type measurement half the size of an em.

en dash. A short typographical rule measuring the width of an en. See also 6.83–86.

endpapers. Folded sheets pasted or, rarely, sewn to the first and last signatures of a book; the free leaves are then pasted to the inside of the front and back covers to secure the book within the covers. Sometimes endpapers feature printed text or illustrations. Also called *endsheets.*

entity reference. A series of characters representing a single character, usually a letter with a diacritical mark (such as é for é) or a symbol (such as £ for £).

EPS file. An abbreviation for *Encapsulated PostScript* file. A type of file used to encode graphics so they can be embedded in a larger PostScript file.

extract. See **block quotation.**

F&Gs. See **folded and gathered sheets.**

figure. An illustration printed with the text (hence also called a *text figure*), as distinguished from a plate, which is printed separately.

file. A block of digital information with a unique name and location in a computer system or external storage medium (such as a disk) that can be accessed and manipulated by users of the system or by the system itself. Programs, documents, and images are all examples of data stored in files.

film laminate. A plastic film bonded to a dust jacket or a paperback cover to protect the surface.

finish. The character of the surface of paper, usually described in terms of smoothness and opacity.

flaps. See **dust jacket.**

flexibinding. Also called *limpbinding*. A method of binding in which the pages or signatures are sewn together and the cover (sometimes with flaps) is then affixed, as in adhesive binding. The result is a publication that is lighter and less bulky than a casebound book but sturdier and more flexible than an adhesive-bound paperback. Contrast **adhesive binding; case binding.**

flopped. Erroneously inverted, as with a photograph, so that a mirror image of the original is produced.

flush. Even, as with typeset margins. Lines that are set *flush left* are aligned vertically along the left-hand margin; lines set *flush right* are aligned along the right-hand margin. Contrast **ragged right.**

flush-and-hang style. A copy-setting style in which the first line begins flush left and subsequent, or runover, lines are indented (as in this list of key terms). Also referred to as *hanging indention* or *hanging indent*.

folded and gathered sheets. Also called *F&Gs* or *sheets*. The collection of all printed signatures in a publication, folded into proper page sequence and gathered for binding. See also **imposition; signature.**

folio. A page number, often placed at the outside of the running head at the top of the page. If it is placed consistently at the bottom of the page, the number is a *foot folio*; if it is placed at the bottom of the page on display pages only, it is a *drop folio*. A folio counted in numbering pages but not printed (as on the title page) is a *blind folio* or *dummy folio*; any folio printed is an *expressed folio*.

font. A complete assortment of a given size and style of type, usually including capitals, small capitals, and lowercase together with numerals, punctuation marks, ligatures, and the commonly used symbols and accents. The italic of a typeface is considered a part of the equipment of a font of type but is often spoken of as a separate font. See also **typeface.**

foot folio. See **folio.**

fore edge. The trimmed outer edge of the leaves of a publication. The outer margin of a page is called the *fore-edge margin.*

form. In offset printing, all the pages that print together on one side of a sheet.

format. The shape, size, style, and general appearance of a publication as determined by type, margins, and so forth.

four-color process. See **process color printing.**

FPO. An abbreviation for *for placement only.* A copy of a graphic element used as a placeholder in proof.

FTP. An abbreviation for *file transfer protocol.* The protocol, or set of instructions and syntax, for moving files between computers on the Internet.

gallery. A section of illustrations grouped on consecutive pages rather than scattered throughout the text.

galley proof. Proof showing typeset material that has not yet been paginated, with text usually set in continuous columns. See also **page proof.**

grammage. In the metric system for specifying the basis weight of paper, the weight in grams of one square meter of paper (that is, grams per square meter, or gsm). See also **basis weight.**

gutter. The two inner margins (back margins) of facing pages of a book or journal.

hair space. A very small space—variously defined as one-quarter point, one-half point, or one-fifth of an em—added between characters. See also **thin space.**

halftone. An image formed by breaking up a continuous-tone image, such as a photograph, into a pattern of dots of varying sizes. When printed, the dots, though clearly visible through a magnifying glass, merge to give an illusion of continuous tone to the naked eye. See also **dropout halftone; duotone.**

halftone screen. A grid used in the halftone process to break an image up into dots. The fineness of the screen is denoted in terms of lines per inch, as in *a 133-line screen.*

H&J. An abbreviation for *hyphenation and justification,* a stage in typesetting. See also **justified.**

hanging indention. See **flush-and-hang style.**

hard copy. A paper copy of text, artwork, or other material, as opposed to a copy that has been stored in digital form.

headband. A decorative band at the top (and usually also the bottom) of the spine of a clothbound book, originally intended to take the strain of a person's finger pulling a book from a shelf.

head margin. The top margin of a page.

HTML. An abbreviation for *HyperText Markup Language*. A specific set of tags used to describe the structure of hypertext documents that make up most Web pages. Web browsers interpret these tags to display the text and graphics on a Web page. HTML is an application of SGML.

hypertext. The organization of digital information into associations connected by links. In a hypertext environment, objects such as text and images can contain links to other objects in the same file or in external files, which users can choose to follow. See also **HTML**.

imposition. Arranging pages before printing so that, when the resulting press sheets are printed and folded, the pages will be in the proper order. See also **press sheet; signature.**

impression. (1) The inked image on the paper created during a single cycle of a press; the speed of a sheet-fed printing press is given in terms of impressions per hour. (2) A single printing of a publication; that is, all the copies printed at a given time. See also 1.22; **edition; reprint.**

indent. To set a line of type so that it begins or ends inside the normal margin. In *paragraph* indention the first line is indented from the left margin and the following lines are set full measure. In *hanging* indention (also referred to as *flush and hang*) the first line is set full measure and the following lines are indented.

Internet. A global, public network of computers and computer networks that communicate using TCP/IP (Transmission Control Protocol/Internet Protocol). The Internet is used for such applications as electronic mail and the World Wide Web.

italic. Slanted type suggestive of cursive writing (*like this*). Contrast **roman.**

jacket. See **dust jacket.**

justified. Spaced out to a specified measure, as with printed lines, so that both margins are aligned. Contrast **ragged right.**

kern. The part of a letter that extends beyond the edge of the type body and overlaps the adjacent character, as the *j* in *adjacent* or the *T* in *To.*

kerning. The selective adjustment of space between particular characters to improve appearance or ease of reading. See also **letterspacing.**

keyline. Copy for offset reproduction showing the placement of artwork and type as well as instructions regarding color. Also called a *mechanical.*

landscape. Having a greater dimension in width than in length, as with an image or a publication. Contrast **portrait;** see also **broadside.**

layout. A designer's plan of how the published material, including illustrative content, should appear.

leading. Also called *line spacing.* The visual space between lines of type, usually measured in points from baseline to baseline. This word, derived from the element *lead*, rhymes with "heading."

letterspacing. The consistent adjustment of space between letters in a block of copy to improve appearance or ease of reading, as in display lines. See also **kerning.**

ligature. A single character formed by joining two characters, such as *æ, fi, ff*, and so forth. Older, more decorative forms (such as *ct*) are known as *quaint characters.*

line art. Copy for reproduction that contains only solid blacks and whites, such as a pen-and-ink drawing. Contrast **continuous tone.**

line spacing. See **leading.**

lining figures. See under **arabic numerals.**

lowercase. The uncapitalized letters of a font. Contrast **uppercase.**

macro. A sequence of operations that is saved for reuse in a software application. For example, a macro can be used to perform the steps to clean up a manuscript file in a word-processing application.

magenta. A bluish red, one of the three colors (plus black) used in process color printing.

makeready. A series of operations performed by the printing firm to ensure that all parts of a form print evenly and that binding operations are done correctly, with folds straight and signatures in proper order.

makeup. Arranging of type lines and illustrations into page form.

margin. The white space surrounding the printed area of a page, including the back, or gutter, margin; the head, or top, margin; the fore-edge, or outside, margin; and the tail, foot, or bottom margin. Contrast **type page.**

markup. (1) A sequence of characters, often called *tags* or *codes*, that indicate the logical structure of a manuscript or provide instructions for formatting it. (2) The insertion of such tags in an electronic manuscript; also, traditionally, editing and coding a paper manuscript.

measure. The length of the line (usually in picas) in which type is set. *Full measure* refers to copy set the full width of the type page. *Narrow measure* refers to a block of copy (such as a long quotation) indented from one or both margins to distinguish it from surrounding full-measure copy, or to copy set in short lines for multicolumn makeup.

mechanical. See **keyline.**

metadata. Data about data. The metadata for a given publication may include, among other things, copyright information, an ISBN or ISSN, and a volume or issue number.

moiré. In printing, an undesirable wavy pattern caused by poor screen angles in an image that has not been properly descreened. See also **descreen; halftone screen.**

negative. (1) A photographic image in which light values are reversed (that is, black appears as white). (2) Film used in offset printing.

notch binding. A type of adhesive binding in which the untrimmed spine is notched and force-fed with glue.

numerals. See **arabic numerals; roman numerals.**

OCR. An abbreviation for *optical character recognition.* A technology that converts images of text into character data that can be manipulated like any other digital text.

offprint. An article, chapter, or other excerpt from a larger work printed from the original plates and issued as a separate unit.

offset printing. Also called *offset lithography.* The most common type of printing used for books and journals. The pages to be printed are transferred either photographically or through computer-to-plate technology to a thin, flexible metal plate, curved to fit one of the revolving cylinders of the printing press. The image on this plate is then transferred to, or *offset* onto, the paper by means of a rubber blanket on another cylinder. Contrast **digital printing.**

old style figures. See under **arabic numerals.**

opacity. The measurement of transparency of paper. The higher a paper's opacity, the less tendency there is for text and images printed on one side of a sheet to show through to the other side.

orphan. A short line appearing at the bottom of a page, or a word or part of a word appearing on a line by itself at the end of a paragraph. Orphans can be avoided by changes in wording or spacing that either remove the line or lengthen it. Contrast **widow.**

out of register. See **register.**

overlay. A hinged flap of paper or transparent plastic covering a piece of artwork. It may be there merely to protect the work, or it may bear type or other artwork intended for reproduction along with what lies underneath.

overrun. A quantity of printed material beyond what was ordered.

page. One side of a leaf, or sheet, of paper. See also **type page.**

page proof. Proof showing typeset material that has been paginated to reflect the placement of text, illustrations, and other design elements. Some publications may require one or more stages of *revised page proof* for checking corrections.

paperback. Bound with a cover stock rather than a cloth-and-board cover. Also called *paperbound.* Contrast **clothbound.**

PDF. An abbreviation for *Portable Document Format.* An Adobe file format to which a PostScript file can be converted without loss of fonts, formatting, or graphics. This format is preferable to PostScript in certain situations because it allows some editing, compresses the amount of memory needed for the graphics, and is more uniform, causing fewer problems at the printer. See also **PostScript (PS).**

PE. An abbreviation for *printer's error.* See also **printer's error.**

penalty copy. Copy difficult to compose (heavily corrected, faint, in a foreign language, and so forth) for which the typesetter charges more than the regular rate.

perfect binding. A type of adhesive binding that involves mechanically roughening off about an eighth of an inch from the spine of the folded and gathered sheets. This treatment produces a surface of intermingled fibers to which an adhesive is applied, and a cover (usually paper) is wrapped around the pages.

perfector press. A press designed to print both sides of the paper in one pass. Also called *perfecting press.*

pH. A designation, on a scale of 0 to 14, of the acidity or alkalinity of a substance: pH 7 is neutral; lower numbers are progressively acidic, and higher numbers progressively alkaline. Paper with a pH value of 7 is desirable for any artwork or printed matter intended to have a long life.

pica. A unit of type measurement equal to twelve points (approximately one-sixth of an inch).

pica em. A twelve-point em.

pixel. The basic unit that constitutes a digital image. Each pixel contains black and white, grayscale, or color information about the square it represents. See also **resolution.**

plate. (1) An image-bearing surface that, when inked, will produce one whole page or several pages of printed matter at a time. (2) A printed illustration, usually of high quality and produced on special paper, tipped or bound into a publication; when so printed, plates are numbered separately from other illustrations.

point. (1) The basic unit of type measurement—0.0138 inch (approximately one seventy-second of an inch). (2) A unit used in measuring paper products employed in printing and binding—0.001 inch.

Portable Document Format. See **PDF.**

portrait. Having a greater dimension in length than in width, as with an image or a publication. Contrast **landscape.**

positive. A photographic image on paper or film that corresponds to the original subject in values of light and shade.

PostScript (PS). An Adobe programming language used to describe pages (in terms of trim size, font, placement of graphics, and so forth) and to tell output devices how to render the data.

ppi. (1) An abbreviation for *pages per inch.* A measurement of the bulk of a specific weight of paper. (2) An abbreviation for *pixels per inch.* A measurement of the resolution of a digital image.

prepress. The processes undertaken by a printing firm between the receipt of the electronic files and other materials from the typesetter and the printing of the publication. These processes include platemaking and makeready.

preprint. Part of a book or journal printed and distributed before publication for promotional purposes. See also **offprint.**

press run. See **print run.**

press sheet. Also called *printed sheet.* In offset printing, a large sheet of paper that emerges from the press with pages printed on both sides, each side printed from a single plate. The sheet must then be folded so that the pages fall into proper sequence. See also **imposition; signature.**

presswork. The actual printing of a publication, as distinguished from composition, which precedes it, and binding, which follows.

printer's error (PE). An error made by the compositor, as distinguished from an *alteration* made in proof by the author or editor.

print run. The number of copies printed. Also called **press run.**

process color printing. The halftone reproduction of full-color artwork or photographs using several plates (usually four), each printing a different color. Each plate is made with a halftone screen. *Process colors* are cyan, magenta, and yellow, plus black (CMYK). See also **halftone screen;** contrast **spot color printing.**

proof. The printed copy made from electronic files, plates, negatives, or positives and used to examine and correct a work's text, illustrations, and design elements before final printing. A publication may involve several stages of proof; see **bluelines; contact proof; digital proof; galley proof; page proof; repro.**

PS. See **PostScript (PS).**

ragged right. Set with an uneven right-hand margin, as with printed lines. Contrast **justified.**

recto. The front side of a leaf; in a book or journal, a right-hand page. To *start recto* is to begin on a recto page, as a preface or an index normally does. Contrast **verso.**

recycled paper. Paper made from a combination of virgin fiber and pre- and postconsumer wastepaper. The proportion of each kind of fiber required to legitimate the label *recycled* is subject to debate.

register. To print an impression on a sheet in correct relation to other impressions already printed on the same sheet; for example, to superimpose exactly the various color impressions in process color printing. When such impressions are not exactly aligned, they are said to be *out of register.*

reprint. A publication in its second or subsequent printing, or *impression.* A reprint may include corrections or new material or both and may be published in a format different from the original printing (for example, as a paperback rather than a clothbound book). The extent of the changes usually determines whether the reprint is considered a new *edition* of the publication. See also **edition.**

repro. An abbreviation for *reproduction copy.* A type of photographic proof generated by the typesetter that reflects the changes made in galley and page proof stages. Many typesetters now provide final laser proof, generated from the electronic files, instead of repro.

resolution. (1) The number of pixels per unit of measure used to form an image. In the United States, image resolution is calculated per inch; the more pixels per inch, the higher the quality of the image. (2) The number of actual dots per unit of measure at which an image or page is output, usually by a printer or an image-setting device. In the United States, output resolution is usually expressed per inch; the more dots per inch, the higher the quality of the output.

reverse out. To manipulate an image of type or of a drawing so that it appears in white surrounded by a solid block of color or black. This technique makes it possible to use the white paper as a "color."

right-reading. Having a right-to-left orientation in a photographic image that appears as in the original subject. *Wrong-reading* is the opposite— that is, a mirror image, in which case the photograph is said to be *flopped.* The terms are not to be confused with positive and negative, which refer to light values.

river. An undesirable streak of white space running more or less vertically through several lines of type, often the result of excessive spacing between words.

roman. The primary type style (like this), as distinguished from italic.

roman numerals. Numerals formed from traditional combinations of roman letters, either capitals (I, II, III, IV, etc.) or lowercase (i, ii, iii, iv, etc.). Contrast **arabic numerals.**

rounding. Imparting a convex curve to the spine of a bound publication.

run. (1) A print run. (2) A quantity of material produced in one continuous operation by a paper or cloth mill or printer.

run in. (1) To merge a paragraph or line with the preceding one. (2) To set quoted matter continuously with text rather than setting it off as a block quotation.

running heads. Copy set at the top of printed pages, usually containing the title of the publication or chapter, page number, or other information. Such copy is sometimes placed at the bottom of the pages, in which case it is referred to as *running feet.*

runover. (1) The continuation of a heading, figure legend, or similar copy onto an additional line. (2) In flush-and-hang material, all lines after the first line of a particular item. (3) Text that is longer than intended, running onto another page, or reset material that is longer than the material it was meant to replace.

saddle stitching. Also called *saddle wiring.* A method of binding that involves inserting thread or staples through the folds of gathered sheets, as in pamphlets and magazines.

sans serif. A typeface with no serifs (like this). See also **serif.**

scale. To calculate (after cropping) the proportions and finish size of an illustration and the amount of reduction or enlargement needed to achieve this size.

scan. To produce a digital bitmap of an image (text or graphics) using a device that senses alternating patterns of light and dark and of color. The resolution and scaling percentage of the desired output should be considered before the image is scanned.

screen. A halftone screen; also the dot pattern in the printed image produced by such a screen. See also **descreen.**

script. (1) Type that imitates handwriting. (2) An abbreviation for *manuscript* or *typescript*. (3) A computer program written in an interpreted or scripting language to perform a sequence of tasks.

serif. A short, light line projecting from the top or bottom of a main stroke of a letter; originally, in handwritten letters, a beginning or finishing stroke of the pen. Sans serif typefaces lack serifs.

set. The horizontal dimension of type. The set width of a given character in one typeface may vary from the set width of that character in another typeface.

sewing. Stitching signatures together as part of binding. See also **side sewing; Smyth sewing.**

SGML. An abbreviation for *Standard Generalized Markup Language,* an international standard for constructing sets of tags. SGML is not a specific set of tags but a system for defining *vocabularies of tags* (the names of the tags and what they mean) and using them to encode documents. See also **tag.**

sheet. A piece of paper (or other material) cut to a specific size, as distinguished from a roll. See also **folded and gathered sheets; press sheet; web.**

sheet-fed press. A printing press using paper in sheet form. Contrast **web-fed press.**

side heads. Subheads that (1) are aligned with, or lie partly outside, the margin of the text and are set on a line of their own; (2) lie wholly outside the text margin; or (3) begin a paragraph and are continuous with the text. Subheads of the third sort are sometimes called *run-in side heads.*

side sewing. In binding, a method of sewing that involves stitching the signatures from the side, close to the spine, before attaching the case. Libraries typically rebind books in this manner. A side-sewn book is more durable than a Smyth-sewn book but will not open flat. See also **Smyth sewing.**

signature. A press sheet as folded, ready for binding. A signature is usually thirty-two pages but may be only sixteen, eight, or even four pages if the paper stock is very heavy, or sixty-four pages if the paper is thin enough to permit additional folding. The size of the press also affects the size of the signature. See also **folded and gathered sheets; press sheet.**

slipcase. A protective box in which a book or set of books fits with the spine (or spines) visible.

small caps. An abbreviation for *small capitals*. Capital letters set at the x-height of a font (LIKE THIS), usually for display.

Smyth sewing. A method of sewing that involves stitching the signatures individually through the fold before binding them. A Smyth-sewn book has the advantage of lying flat when open, unlike a side-sewn or perfect-bound book. See also **perfect binding; side sewing.**

spec. An abbreviation for *specification* (plural, *spex* or *specs*).

spine. The "back" of a bound publication; that is, the center panel of the binding, hinged on each side to the two covers, front and back, and visible when the book or journal is shelved. Typically the title of the publication is printed on the spine. Also called the *backbone*.

spot color printing. The reproduction of isolated graphic elements or display type in a single ink of an exact color. Contrast **process color printing.**

spread. Two facing pages, a verso and a recto.

stamping. Imprinting the spine of a case and sometimes the front cover with hard metal dies. Stamping may involve ink, foil, or other coloring material; if it does not, it is called *blind stamping*. See also **embossing.**

subheads. Headings, or titles, for sections within a chapter or an article. Subheads are usually set in type differing in some way from that of the text; for example, in boldface, all capitals, caps and small caps, or upper- and lowercase italic. See also **side heads.**

subscript. A small numeral, letter, fraction, or symbol that prints partly below the baseline, usually in mathematical material or chemical formulas.

superscript. A small numeral, letter, fraction, or symbol that prints partly above the x-height, often in mathematical or tabular material.

tag. (1) In SGML, a generic marker used to specify and (when paired) delimit an element in the structure of a document. Adding tags to a manuscript is known as *tagging* or *markup*. (2) More informally, a synonym for *code*. See also **code; markup; SGML.**

TCF paper. An abbreviation for *totally chlorine-free* paper. Paper bleached using nonhazardous elements. Contrast **ECF paper.**

text file. An informal term for a file that contains data encoded using ASCII (American Standard Code for Information Interchange) codes and that includes only letters, numerals, punctuation marks, spaces, returns, line feeds, and tabs with no additional formatting. Text files are often referred to as *ASCII files*, although other kinds of data (such as SGML and PostScript) can also be stored as ASCII files.

text page. Also called *text area*. The area of a typeset page occupied by the main text block, excluding folios, running heads, and marginalia.

text type. See **body type.**

thick space. A small space, defined as one-third of an em, added between characters.

thin space. A very small space, defined as one-fifth of an em, added between characters. See also **hair space.**

thumbnail. A miniature rendition of a page or an image. In electronic publications, a thumbnail is often used to indicate a link to a larger electronic object.

TIFF. An acronym for *Tagged Image File Format*. A file format developed by Aldus and Microsoft and used to store bitmapped graphics, including scanned line art and color images.

tip-in. A separately printed leaf tipped (pasted) into a book or journal.

trim marks. Marks used to indicate the edges of illustrations or pages in proof.

trim size. The dimensions, in inches, of a full page in a publication, including the margins.

two-up. Having the printing image on the plate duplicated so that two copies of the piece are printed at the same time. The terms *three-up, four-up*, and so forth are analogous.

typeface. A collection of fonts with common design or style characteristics. A typeface may include roman, italic, boldface, condensed, and other fonts. The various typefaces are designated by name: Baskerville, Caslon, and Times Roman, for example. See also **font.**

type page. The area of a typeset page occupied by the type image, from the running head to the last line of type on the page or the folio, whichever is lower, and from the inside margin to the outside margin, including any area occupied by side heads.

typesetter. A person, firm, facility, or machine that sets type. Also called *compositor.*

type styles. See **boldface; italic; roman.**

unjustified. See **ragged right.**

uppercase. The capital letters of a font. Contrast **lowercase.**

verso. The back side of a leaf; in a book or journal, a left-hand page. Contrast **recto.**

web. A roll of paper (or other material), as distinguished from a sheet.

web-fed press. A printing press using paper in roll form. Contrast **sheet-fed press.**

Web page. A virtual document delivered via the World Wide Web and viewed in a Web browser.

widow. A short, paragraph-ending line appearing at the top of a page. Widows should be avoided when possible by changes in wording or spacing that either remove the line or lengthen it. Contrast **orphan.**

World Wide Web. Also called *the Web*. The Internet's most widely used information-retrieval service. The World Wide Web uses Hypertext Transfer Protocol (HTTP) to allow users to request and retrieve documents ("Web pages" and multimedia objects) from other computers anywhere on the Internet.

wrong font (WF). A designation for type that has been set in the wrong typeface, style, or size.

wrong-reading. See **right-reading.**

WYSIWYG. An acronym for *what you see is what you get.* Pronounced "wizzy-wig." Text and graphics shown formatted on a computer screen as they will appear when printed.

x-height. In type, a vertical dimension equal to the height of the lowercase letters (such as *x*) without ascenders or descenders.

XML. An abbreviation for *Extensible Markup Language.* A subset of the SGML standard, used for structuring documents and data on the Internet. See also **SGML.**

Composition and Page Makeup Specifications
The University of Chicago Press • 1427 E. 60th Street • Chicago, IL 60637

Date: 14 August 1998	Designer:	Phone:
Author: **Wayne C. Booth**	Controller:	Phone:
Title: **For the Love of It**	MS Editor:	Phone:
Series:		

FORMAT
Trimmed size: **6" x 9"**   inches

MARGINS
Head: **9/16"**   inches, trim to base of running head
Back: **3/4"**   inches

COMPOSITION
Text typeface: **Janson**
Display typeface: **Shelley Allegro**
Other: **Poetica Supplemental Ornaments**
Measure: **26p**
Lines per page: **41**
(excluding running heads and folios)
Words per page: (approx.) **497**
Based on: **2.87**   characters per pica
    41   lines per page
    6   characters per word
Ligatures: (see no. 7 on "House Style" page)

PAGINATION
Roman numerals for front matter
Arabic page numbers begin with
❑ Second half title
◙ First part title
❑ Introduction, opening page
❑ First chapter opening page

TYPE SIZES (point size/leading/line length)
1. Main text: **10/13 Janson x 26p**
Paragraph indent: **1p** pts.
  ❑ Modern numbers   ◙ Old Style numbers
  Letterfit: ❑ Track 1   ❑ Track 2 ❑ Track 3
2. Running heads/feet
    Verso: **8.5pt Janson small caps w/ Poetica orn**
    Recto: **8.5pt Janson small caps w/ Poetica orn**
3. Folios: **8.5pt Janson oldstyle figures**
4. Extracts: **Many Styles: SEE LAYOUTS**
5. Epigraphs: **Many Styles: SEE LAYOUTS**
6. Poetry: **10/13 Janson, indent 1p, line-for-line**
7. Lists: **SEE LAYOUT**
8. Table heading: **n/a**
    Table rule: **n/a**
    Table body: **n/a**
9. Equations: **n/a**
10. Footnotes: **7/10 Janson x 26p justified**
    Endnotes: **n/a**
    End of chapter notes: **n/a**
11. Figure captions **n/a**
12. Appendixes: **Glossary: SEE LAYOUT**
13. Bibliography: **10/13 Janson x 26p. 1p hanging indent**
14. Index: **8/11 Janson , 2-cols**

See layouts for detailed Specifications

	# b/b above	# b/b below
15. Subheads		
A. **12/15 Janson Text Italic**	**32.5pts**	**19.5pts**
B. **10pt Janson all small caps, l-spaced**	**26 pts**	**(run-in)**
C.		
D.		
E.		

16. Display
PART TITLE: 14/26 Janson all small caps
PART SUBTITLE: 12/21 Janson italic
CHAP NUMBER: 10pt Janson italic
CHAPT TITLE: 16/19.5 Janson c/lc

17. Illustrations
  ❑ Gallery
  ◙ Text
18. ❑ Dummy, provide blue keyline boards
19. Other (specify):

More extensive specifications and instructions follow. The categories correspond by number to the list above. (See also University of Chicago Press Composition and Page Makeup style sheets.)

Fig. A.14. Sample text design with complete composition and page layout specifications.

1. MAIN TEXT
- ☑ Text spreads may be 1 line short.
- ☐ Text spreads may be 1 line long.
- ☐ Drop initial:
    Spec:
- ☐ Aligning initial:
    Spec:

2. RUNNING HEADS/FEET
- ☑ Running heads (Designate below what is to appear verso
- ☐ Running feet   and recto: i.e., part title, chapter title,etc.)
    Verso: **Part title**
    Recto: **Chapter title**
    Space between heading and text, b/b: **21pts**
- ☑ Running heads and folios will be left off any page that
    contains a full-page upright table or illustration.
- ☐ Running heads and folios will be left off all broadside
    figures or tables
- ☐ Include ☐ running head, ☐ folio on pages containing a full-
    page upright table or figure.

3. FOLIOS
- ☑ In running heads
- ☐ at foot
- ☐ drop folios for chapter openings
- ☐ centered
- ☐ indented:
- ☑ aligns with outside margin
- ☐ left
- ☐ right
- ☐ modern
- ☑ oldstyle
- ☐ Space between text and drop folio: pts. b/b
- ☐ Space between text and running foot: pts. b/b
- ☐ Folios or running feet at the bottom of the page will maintain
    the same position throughout the book
    (i.e., they will not bounce).

4. EXTRACTS
- ☐ Full measure: **VARIES: SEE** picas
- ☐ Indent left: **LAYOUTS** picas
- ☐ Indent right: picas
- ☐ Justified:
- ☐ Ragged right:
    Space above: pts. b/b
    Space below: pts. b/b

5. EPIGRAPHS
In text:
- ☐ Type specs: **VARIES: SEE LAYOUTS**
- ☐ Justified:
- ☐ Ragged right:
- ☐ Source specification:
    Space above: pts. b/b
    Space below: pts. b/b
As part of chapter opener:
- ☐ Type specs:
- ☐ Source specification:
    Space above: pts. b/b
    Space below: pts. b/b

6. POETRY/VERSE
- ☐ Center on longest line
    All poems that fall on the same page of text will hold the same
    left alignment; poetry that continues to a new page will be cen-
    tered on the longest line appearing on that page.
- ☐ Fixed indention:
- ☑ Indent left: **1p**   pts.
- ☐ Indent right: pts.
- ☐ Source specification:
- ☐ Flush right
- ☐ Run in
- ☐ Indent from right: pts.
- ☐ Indent runovers: pts.
- ☐ Space between stanzas: pts.

7. LISTS
- ☐ Outline style. Indent each new level: pts.
- ☐ Numbered: **SEE**
- ☐ Paragraph style **LAYOUT**
- ☐ Flush and hang: pts.

8. TABLES
- ☐ **Upright tables** should not exceed type page width
- ☐ **Upright tables** may extend up to   picas into the right and
    left margins.
- ☐ **Large upright tables** may run across facing pages with no less
    than 4 picas (total) between the two halves.
- ☐ Center column heads
- ☐ Set column heads flush left
- ☐ Minimum space between columns: pts.
- ☐ Show table number, the word "*continued*", and column heads
    when table continues on a new page
- ☐ Spacing above: pts. b/b
- ☐ Spacing below: pts. b/b
- ☐ Space between table and text can vary
    from   pts. to   pts.
- ☐ **Broadside tables**
- ☐ **Run-on broadside tables** (two or more pages) begin on verso,
    repeat column heads on verso only.

9. EQUATIONS
- ☐ Centered on type page width
- ☐ Fixed indention: pts.

Equation numbers:
- ☐ Flush left with text margin
- ☐ Flush right with text margin
- ☐ Bold face
- ☐ In parentheses
    Space above: pts. b/b
    Space below: pts. b/b

10. NOTES/ENDNOTES/FOOTNOTES
- ☑ Aligning figures
- ☐ Superior figures
- ☑ Paragraph indention: 12   pts
- ☐ Flush and hang
- ☐ Ragged right

Space between last line of text and first footnote:
Minimum   pts. b/b.
Maximum   pts. b/b.
Number consecutively through ☐ page, ☐ section,
   ☐ chapter, ☐ book
- ☑ Footnotes that appear on the last, short page of a chapter will follow the text (they will not drop to the bottom of the page).
Space above note: pts. b/b.

11. LEGENDS/CAPTIONS
(Legends fall below a figure, Captions are above)
- ☐ Legends
- ☐ Captions
- ☐ Ragged right
- ☐ Ragged left
- ☐ Hyphenation
- ☐ No hyphenation
- ☐ Measure varies. Set as specified
- ☐ Space between bottom of figure, or table and base of first line of *legend*:   pts.

Space between base of last line of *caption* and top of figure: pts.

12. APPENDIXES
Begin first appendix ☐ recto, ☐ verso, ☐ run on:
- ☐ Subsequent appendixes recto or verso
Space between text and first line of appendix: pts. b/b

13. BIBLIOGRAPHY
- ☐ Flush and hang **SEE LAYOUT**
- ☐ Other style:

14. INDEX
- ☑ Column width   12p6 picas.
- ☑ No. of columns: 2
- ☑ Alley: 12   pts.
- ☑ Flush and hang: 6   pts
- ☐ Ragged right
- ☐ Subentries indent: pts
- ☑ Run-in subentries indent: 6   pts
- ☑ Space between alphabet breaks 22   pts.
- ☐ Use display initials for alphabet breaks.
Specification:

- ☐ Space may not vary between alphabet breaks when necessary reset for even columns.
- ☐ Continued lines will be used for index entries that break from a recto to a verso page.
- ☐ Name index precedes subject index.

15. SUBHEADS
- ☑ Subheads at the top of a page are to sink the minimum amount so that the first line following the subhead aligns with a text line on a normal page grid, or as follows:

- ☐ **Spacing variables:** Space may be varied above subheads, and equally above and below extracts, equations, poetry, lists, etc., if necessary to make facing pages align or to avoid bad page breaks.
Minimum: pts.
Maximum: pts.

16. DISPLAY
Parts:
- ☑ New recto
- ☐ Two page spread
- ☐ Separate half titles

Chapters:
- ☐ New pages
- ☐ Two page spread
- ☑ Chapter opening following part title starts recto
- ☐ All chapters start recto
- ☑ Recto or verso
- ☐ Run on   pts. b/b between chapters

17. ILLUSTRATIONS
Line figures:
Number:
- ☑ Originals herewith
- ☐ Camera-ready art provided actual size, ready for page makeup
- ☐ Reduce or enlarge as specified. Provide camera-ready stats and put in position with text repro.
- ☐ Figures not herewith. Allow space. List of sizes included.

Halftones:
Number:
- ☐ Compositor to provide halftone film
- ☐ Actual size position copies provided. Crop as indicated and use as position proofs. Position accurately with legends and text on repro pages.
- ☐ Originals not included. Provide 1/2 pt. ruled keyline boxes in position. List of sizes included.
- ☐ Halftone screen: ☐ 133, ☐ 150, ☐ Other:

18. DUMMY
- ☐ Set of galleys needed for dummy
- ☐ Complete dummy will be provided to compositor
- ☐ Combination dummy and marked galleys will be provided to compositor.
- ☐ Compositor to provide printed dummy sheets with non-repro blue ink (reflecting grid supplied to compositor by designer).
- ☐ If galleys are requested, all figure, table, etc., must be indicated by their number in the margin. **Galleys will not be accepted without.**

19. SPECIMEN PAGES

Please show trim corner marks on all pages and base-of-running-head corner marks on all sink pages.

Provide specimen pages:

☑ Contents Page
☑ Chapter Opening
☑ Part Title
☐ Text spread showing:
   ☑ folios and running heads
   ☑ extract
   ☑ all levels of subheads
   ☐ table
   ☑ footnote
   ☑ poetry
   ☑ list
   ☐ figure captions
   ☐ other:

20. U. OF C. PRESS GRID SPECIFICATIONS

Back and head margins are specified in inches. The top of the type page is measured from the trim to the base of the running head. All display drops and other drops within the type page area are measured in picas (base to base) from the running head base line. Compositor should show trim corner marks on all page proofs and base-of-running-head corner marks on all sink pages only.

BACK AND HEAD MARGINS MEASURED IN INCHES

TRIM

BASE OF RUNNING HEAD

BACK MARGIN

ALL DROPS FROM RUNNING HEAD ARE MEASURED BASE TO BASE IN PICAS

ADDITIONAL INSTRUCTIONS, COMMENTS: (list by category number)

IN ADDITION: PLEASE PROVIDE LAYOUTS TITLE PAGE, OF ALL EXTRACT STYLES, AND SPACE BREAKS

SET PARAMETERS SO THAT WORDSPACING AND GENERAL TEXT LETTERSPACING IS FAIRLY TIGHT, AS IN LAYOUTS.

House Style for Composition and Page Makeup
The University of Chicago Press • 1427 E. 60th Street • Chicago, IL 60637
(Unless otherwise specified, these standing specifications apply.)

TYPOGRAPHY

1. Vertical spacing is specified as baseline to baseline.

2. Letter spacing: Text and smaller type is to be set at the standard character fit designed for the typeface unless specified otherwise.

3. Word spacing: Tight horizontal word space is the preference with no extra space after punctuation. Wordspace should average the width of a lowercase n, and be no tighter than the width of a lowercase i.

4. Line Breaks and Hyphenation:
- Standards call for a minimum of two characters at the end of the line, with a minimum of three carried down.
- No more than three consecutive end of line hyphens or punctuation (or a combination of hyphens and punctuation)are allowed.
- Up to 8 hyphens are allowed per 35-40 line page.
- Hyphenated compound words should be broken only at the hyphen.
- The final word of a paragraph is allowed to hyphenate except that a minimum of four characters (not counting periods, commas, and quotation marks) is required on the final line.
- It is best not to have a hyphenated word as the last word on a page. However, it is allowable if the syllable or syllables leave little doubt as to the identity of the full word.
- It is preferable not to break proper names but allowable when difficult to avoid. Line breaks are allowed after a first name or middle initial; names using two initials will not break between the initials.
- More guidelines on word division are found in the CHICAGO MANUAL OF STYLE. Follow it for more detailed guidance.

5. "Carding": Adding extra space between lines or paragraphs to make facing pages align is not allowed.

6. Density: Type density must be consistent from page to page throughout the book, and patches and reruns must match the original type. Repros will be returned if there are variations in density.

7. Ligatures: Use for lower case Roman and italic letter combinations such as ti ff fl ffi and ffl, and other combinations (except ae, oe) when available in the font.

PAGE MAKEUP

1. Type page depth: The depth of the type page is measured from the base of the running head to the base of the last line of the standard text page. If there is no running head, the depth is measured from the base of the first line of text to the base of the running foot, or of the last line of the text if there is no running foot.

2. Corner marks: The compositor is to include corner marks left and right at the base of the running head position on all sink pages (i.e, front matter, part title, chapter openings, end matter).

3. Chapter opening text: The number of lines on chapter opening pages may by up to two short lines if necessary to avoid a bad page break. Keep chapter drop position.

4. Subheads:
- The text page may be up to 4 lines short if there is no room for a subhead at the bottom of a page. The subhead begins at the top of the next page.
- The minimum number of lines of text below a subhead at the bottom of a page is 2.
- If a subhead falls near the top of a page, minimum number of lines of text above is 2.

5. Line minimums for breaking elements:
- A minimum of 2 text lines must appear above or below a separate text element such as an extract, poem, list, etc.
- A minimum of 2 lines of a separate text element may fall at the top or bottom of a page.
- The minimum number of lines of text that may appear on a page with an illustration or table is 5.
- The minimum number of lines on the last page of a chapter is 5.
- If a designated spacebreak in text falls between pages, the extra space will be left at the foot of the preceding page.

6. Page length: Facing text pages should be of equal depth and must align.

7. Orphans and widows: The first line of a paragraph (orphan) may fall at the foot of a page. The last line of a paragraph (widow) may not fall at the top of a page unless it is full measure.

8. Variable vertical space: The space above a subhead should not vary unless specified otherwise. The space above and below a separate text element may be adjusted if necessary to avoid a widow or to make a text spread align. Space must be adjusted equally; 4 pts. maximum to be added above and 4 pts. below, or 2 pts. maximum to be subtracted above and 2 pts. below.

9. Back matter: In bibliographies and end notes, facing pages may differ by one line if necessary to avoid a widow. Index columns on the same page or across a spread may differ in length by one line if necessary. There should be a minimum of 5 lines in each column on the last page of the index. Columns on the last page of an index may vary in length by one line or more if necessary, with the left column being longer. Widows are permitted at the top of columns in back matter and index provided the line is at least three-fourths full.

10. Illustrations and tables: Figures and tables are to be positioned as close to their text citation as possible, preferably after the citation but before the next major subhead; at the top of the type page if possible, or at the foot if necessary. When figures/tables of different depths occur on facing pages, place one at the **top** and the other at the bottom of their respective pages. Full page broadside figures/tables should fit within the text measure and align with the top of the first line of text. No running head or folio should appear on broadside pages unless otherwise specified. Where more than one table/figure appears on a page with text, table-table-text or text-table-table is preferable to table-text-table.

11. Footnotes/endnotes: Long footnotes may be broken from one page to the next. Ideally, at least two lines of the footnote should appear on each page and the note should be broken in mid-sentence. A 5-pica 1/4 pt. rule will be inserted above the continued portion of the footnote, with no extra space below.

- Short footnotes/endnotes (those running at most to 1 pica short of a half-line measure) may be double-columned when there are three or more in a row on one page. Doubling should be vertical:

1	3		1	2
2	4	not	3	4

- When three or more very short notes (e.g., " ibids") occur in succession on one page, tripling is permissible.

12. Corrections:
- Please mark type sections that have been rerun since the last stage of page proof. We assume that there have been no changes in type or line breaks within type blocks not so marked.

- All queries should be marked on proofs (not on manuscript) and, if possible, keyed to manuscript pages.

Half title

16pt Janson c/lc,
centered on 13th text
line

For the Love of It

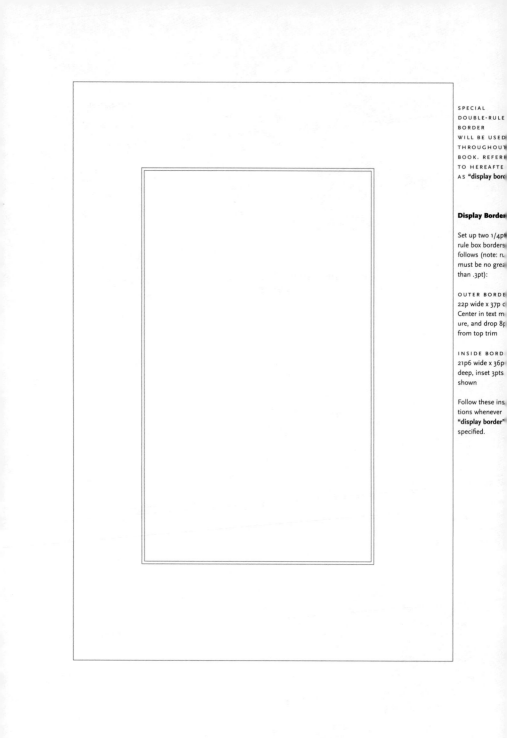

SPECIAL
DOUBLE-RULE
BORDER
WILL BE USED
THROUGHOUT
BOOK. REFER
TO HEREAFTE
AS **"display bord**

Display Border

Set up two 1/4pt
rule box borders
follows (note: ru
must be no grea
than .3pt):

OUTER BORDE
22p wide x 37p d
Center in text m
ure, and drop 8p
from top trim

INSIDE BORD
21p6 wide x 36p
deep, inset 3pts
shown

Follow these ins
tions whenever
"display border"
specified.

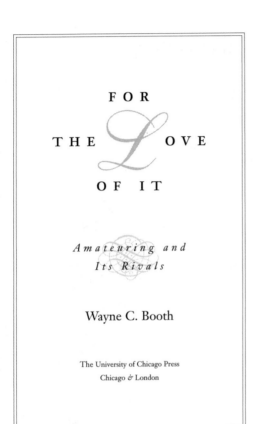

F O R

T H E 〜 O V E

O F I T

A m a t e u r i n g a n d
I t s R i v a l s

Wayne C. Booth

The University of Chicago Press
Chicago & London

Title Page

Sets within "display
border."

Title
22/50 Janson all
small caps, letter-
spaced as shown,
with 92pt Shelley
Allegro initial "L";
unit centers on text
measure. Shelley
Allegro initial prints
10% black and
sinks 27pts from
baseline. Break title
as shown, and
observe spacing.
Set unit so that
baseline of second
line sets on 13th
text line of text grid.

Subtitle:
12/21 Janson italic,
centered on text
measure. Set on
22nd text line.

GRAPHIC
FURNISHED ON
DISK:
filename = "title
page ornament."
Place behind subtitle
as shown. Prints
10% black, centers
on text measure,
and sets 12pts b/b
below second line
of half title.

Author:
14pt Janson, c/lc,
centered 28th text
line

Publisher
8.5/15 Janson, c/lc,
begin 32nd text line,
and center on text
measure. NOTE:
use Janson italic
ampersand.

Contents

Contents

Head
16pt Janson c/lc
center on 5th te
line.

Body
Begin 9th text li
center on text p

PRELIMS + B
MATTER
Same as chapte
titles

PART PAGE
NUMBERS
9.5/16 Janson o
style figures
PART TITLES
9.5/16 Janson al
small caps, lette
space as shown
PART SUBTITE
9.5/16 Janson c
PART ORNAM
8pt Poetica
Ornament (key-
stroke "N"). 18
b/b above and a
follows:
—when followe
a part page num
40pts b/b below
—when followe
a chapter title 1
b/b below.

CHAPTER NO
9.5pt Janson old
figures. Colon s
rates chapter n
from titles (one
space before an
after).
CHAPTER TIT
9.5/16 Janson it
CHAPTER PAC
NOS.
9.5pt Janson ita
old-style figures
en space to pag
nos.

Hank, whose hearing has just plain gone too far, or Louise, who has begun to lose control. Sooner or later Hank or Louise will be seeking some way to cut back on time spent with Wayne Booth, whose intonation will be even worse than it used to be.

❀

The good side is that I find many rather surprising benefits from aging— at least so far. Being older, I can experience the wonders of music in ways quite different from how those young twerps, with all their muscular flexibility and mental "openness"—not to say flabbiness and sheer ignorance— can manage. Those proud half-blind oblivious show-offs probably don't even have the word "twerp" in their impoverished vocabularies . . .

No, no, drop that attempt at ironic self-display. There's no point in playfully insulting the young, even though you do envy them. Of course you'd like to have their skin tone, their unfilled molars, their quick, comfortable thirty-second notes, their seductive vibratos . . . But let's just think a bit about what they *don't* have.

Their most obvious deprivation is of the "petite madeleine" effect. *Remembrance of Things Past*—or if you prefer the new translation, *In Search of Things Past*, or if you prefer the original, *A la recherche du temps perdu*— Proust's fabulous book, is on my mind partly because Phyllis and I read a lot of it aloud together not long ago, in French: at least one-fortieth of the more than 2,000 pages. That's not what you could call full amateuring.

As you no doubt know, Marcel, the narrator, consuming a cup of tea and a small cake called a petite madeleine, finds himself overwhelmed with the memory of the taste of another madeleine when he was very young. The joining of the two sensations sends him on a prolonged trip through the past, encountering many such overlappings of sensation and memory. The trip ends as the aging Marcel pursues the meaning of such layering of the moments, identical but not identical. To experience any sensation a second time, years later, turns both sensations into an entirely new experience, one that escapes the time-bound world in which the particular sensations occur.

Resisting the temptation to quote him here, I must dwell for a moment on that bland phrase, "identical but not identical." When I experience the "Grosse Fuge" today, more than a half century after almost memorizing it, I juxtapose, as a gift of my aging, at least three, or really five, six, or seven works, "identical but not identical": the Busch Chamber Orchestra recording I heard at Ft. Meade, anticipating my doom; the much more heavily

---

Main Text

Book Trim
6" x 9"

Margins
TOP: 5/8" top
trim to base of
running head
INSIDE: 3/4"

Main text
10/13 Janson x 26p
justified. 40 lines
per standard text
page. OK one line
short ONLY for good
page makeup, if
necessary. Old-style
figures throughout;
1p paragraph indent.

Running Heads

VERSO + RECTO:

Folios
8.5pt Janson old-style
figures, flush outside.

Text
8.5pt Janson all
small caps, letter-
spaced as shown.
Separate from folio
with 8.5pt Poetica
Supplemental
Ornament (key-
stroke: "N") Allow
one em space before
and after
ornament, as
shown.

Set 5/8" from top
trim to base of
running head. Main
text begins 21pts b/b
below running head.

laden version I heard in my head on that cattle car during the thirty-two hours that we wandered through France toward Belgium; the far more joyful one I heard played by the string quartet back in Paris a few months later; and on to my first struggles to play it with various friends decades later. (It is usually hard these days to talk any group, even the semipros, into attempting it, it is so aggressively resistant.)

All of these versions are with me—not greatly different in musical detail but with differing depths and qualities of emotional association. I'm not claiming that my older responses are more intense or more valuable than my first one; no mechanical register could ever compare the intensity of my emotions now with those in 1944, and no argument could prove the superiority of either one over the other. But I need no computerized text to tell me that what I lacked then and have now is a *bridging* of the intensities, a broad encounter of a third kind.

Even if that claim seems doubtful, what is certain is that I am having a new . . . but in seeking the right noun for what I'm having I meet again my old problem of the "ineffability of musical experience." Should I call what happens to the old man, as he plays the fugue with his companions, a "new experience"? That's not exactly a falsehood, but it's flat. Should I talk of "a new thrill"? Not false, but too Hollywood. "New transport"? Not false, but pretentious. "New memory"? Both flat and misleading: the experience is not just memory. "Fresh spiritual engagement"? "A love bout of the aging kind"?

Something new happens, some happening worth happening happens that could not have happened when I was young.

Often I can't even distinguish the apparent losses of aging from the apparent gains. So I must leave it to you to pursue the invitations of the following three sections. I'll be surprised if you inform me that none of them prove pertinent to the hours and years you spend as an amateur.

Why Waste Time on Jeremiads?

Since my father's death when I was six, I have never been unaware of the fragility of this fallen world. Some people say they didn't even discover their own mortality until, in their thirties or fifties, a loved one died or a near-fatal accident occurred. I remember concluding that I myself must surely die before surpassing my father's age at death: thirty five. That sense of my life's fragility was underlined by the death of my favorite grandmother when I was seven and then of my closest friend when I was fourteen. The lesson

A Head
12/15 Janson ita
c/lc, FL, RR. Allc
32.5pts b/b abo
and 19.5pts b/b
below.

In t e r l u d e

The Amateur Writer Quarrels
with the Amateur Player

I SUPPOSE THAT most of you, if you saw my list of published books and articles and my annual royalty checks, however modest, would deny me the title of amateur writer. "You may not be a highly successful pro, but you're still a pro. You've not only written and published for most of your life, but you've actually had the chutzpah to write about *how* to write. If that isn't aspiring to the title 'professional,' what would be? Where's the love?"

Obviously I can't claim that all of my writing has been done for the love of doing it. Some bits have been produced with absolute passion, my "self" forgotten for hours or days on end. Others—this chapter would make a good example—have almost torn me apart as I've torn *them* apart and tried and tried again. My journals reveal about most projects a thick goulash of wholehearted inquiry, egotistical ambition, greed, and diverse levels of professed do-goodism.

Once the choice was made to do this book a new anxiety tore in:

NOTEBOOK, 1994 [UNDATED]—As I work on *Amateur*, feel more and more amateur*ish* as a writer. "Whatever claims to 'pro' you could make as a writer apply to territory entirely different from the land you're raiding now." Celebrating *homo ludens*, the *player plays* at the role of amateur writer, dealing with a playful cost-benefit analysis of becoming an amateur *player*, in order to *play up* the blessing of the gift he's been *playing with*.

How does my writing-playing relate to the playing? Doesn't it actually harm it? Last night in the middle of practicing I was thinking, "How

Chapter Opener

Chapter Number
10pt Janson italic
c/lc, letterspaced as
shown and centered
on 10th text line
GRAPHIC
FURNISHED ON
DISK: filename =
"chapter number
ornament." Place
behind chapter
number. Prints 10%
black, centers on
text measure, and
sinks 11pts b/b
below chapter
number.

Chapter title
16/19.5 Janson c/lc,
centered on 13th text
line

Opening text
Begin 17th text line.
First few words set
all small caps, letter-
spaced as shown.

Journal/Diary Entry
TEXT: 10/13 x 26p,
justified. Set on 1p
hanging indent, as
shown 1p paragraph
indent.
DATE: set 10pt
Janson all small
caps, letterspaced as
shown. Sets FL, and
runs in with Journal
text. Use one em
dash to separate
date from text.

Allow 26pts b/b
above and below.

Glossary

9/13 Janson x
FL, RR, set or
hanging inde
TERMS set 9
Janson italic.

humoring: Adjusting pitch; has nothing to do with humor

la: Pronounced "law," by most Americans; second note of a minor third

lusinghiero: Seductive, flattering, coaxing: proper instructions for chapter 2

major mode: The scale you rely on when you sing something like the opening of "The Star-Spangled Banner"

mi: Pronounced "mee"; sing "can" in "Oh-oh, say can you see, by the dawn's early light . . ."

minor mode: Sing to yourself almost any sad song you know.

minor second: Half step; sing "Oh, dear!" sadly, with the second word lower but as close to the first as feels comfortable

minor third: Half-step above a major second; three half-steps above "do"; imagine yourself singing an insult to an enemy: "Nyah, nyah"

morendo: Dying, with a dying fall: rival title for chapter 6

opera: Plural of opus. How it ever came to mean "opera" I'll never know.

opus: Opus

religioso: "You figure it out"; rival title for chapter 11

ritardando: Just drop the last four letters and slow down; proper instructions for reading the whole book

scherzando: Jesting, playful, watch out for ironies

sixteenth: The torture chamber for amateur cellists; in England known as semi-quaver: a note one-fourth as long as an ordinary beat, or one-sixteenth as long as a full measure of four beats. If the tempo is allegro, the quarter notes are going at about 150 per minute, which means that if you're thrown a passage with sixteenths, you have to play 600 notes per minute or 10 notes per second. You'll hear famous pros achieving them clearly. You'll never hear me.

sol: Pronounced "so"; the fifth tone of a diatonic scale. The "dominant"

strings: Both the strings on the instruments and the players in any string section

subito pianissimo: Suddenly, startlingly, extremely quiet

thirty-second: See *sixteenth* and multiply by two

timbre: The quality of sound produced

tonic: See *do* and *fundamental*

tremolo: With shaky trepidation, anxiety, real or faked; rival title for whole book

turn: Sort of a quick trill, without enough time to get it right.

Well-tempered clavier: The untempered keyboard, used until the eighteenth century, would play in tune only on a small number of scales. By tempering—adjusting so that the intervals between all twelve notes in an octave are equal—organists and pianists were enabled to play roughly in tune in any key. Sold on tempering, Bach did forty-eight fabulous preludes and fugues to illustrate the new freedom of scale-choice that the "tempered" scale had produced. But the

10/13 Janson x 26p
FL, RR, set on 1p
hanging indent

Amateur Chamber Music Players Newsletter (1123 Broadway, Room 304, New York, N.Y. 10010. The November 1986 issue has a good bibliography, "Books about Chamber Music.")

"The Amateur Scientist." *Scientific American.* (415 Madison Ave., New York, N.Y. 10017. Regular monthly column, currently edited by Shawn Carlson. The column "Mathematical Recreations" also often engages with amateuring.)

Anderson, Nels. *Man's Work and Leisure.* Leiden: E. J. Brill, 1974.

Angier, Natalie. "An Amateur of Biology Returns to His Easel." *New York Times,* April 28, 1998, B11–12. (About Gary Larson, the cartoonist/biologist/novelist.)

Aristotle. *Ethics.* Esp. book 7.11 and book 8 (friendship).

———. *Metaphysics.* (Everything under *eudaimonia*—happiness—relates to themes addressed here.)

———. *Politics.* Most of book 8.

Atlas, James. "The Art of Failing." *New Yorker,* May 25, 1998, 67–73. (Pursues the problem of how to escape the culture of "making it.")

———. "The Whistle of Money: Watching the Era of Success Pass You By." *New Yorker,* Feb. 2, 1998, 34–37. (Without mentioning Podhoretz, portrays the harm that the ideal of "making it" does to our culture.)

Aulich, Bruno, and Ernst Heimeran. *The Well-tempered String Quartet: A Book of Counsel and Entertainment for All Lovers of Music in the Home.* Trans. D. Millar Craig. Sevenoaks, England: Novello, 1951. (Orig. *Das stillvergnügte Streichquartett,* Munich, 1936.)

Barenboim, Daniel. *A Life in Music.* New York: Charles Scribner's Sons, 1992.

Barrett, Cyril. "Leisure in Western Painting." In Winnifrith and Barrett, 69–80.

Barzun, Jacques. *Pleasures of Music: An Anthology of Writing about Music and Musicians from Cellini to Bernard Shaw.* Chicago: University of Chicago Press, 1951. (Fascinating quotations, some of which I've used in epigraphs.)

Benjamin, Walter. "The Work of Art in the Age of Mechanical Reproduction." *Illuminations.* New York: Schocken Books, 1969. (Orig. 1936.)

Berlin, Isaiah. *The Sense of Reality: Studies in Ideas and Their History.* Ed. Henry Hardy. New York: Farrar, Straus and Giroux, 1997. (One of many philosophers wrestling with the "incommensurability" of values that I refer to often and rely on always.)

Bernstein, Leonard. *The Joy of Music.* New York: Simon and Schuster, 1959.

Index

8/11 Janson c/
two columns c
each, FL, RR, s
6pt hanging in

1-pica gutter

Alphabet brea
22pts b/b

Appendix B: The Publishing Process for Books and Journals

The following diagrams represent the basic stages involved in the editorial and production processes described throughout this manual. The first shows a sequence of stages commonly followed for books; the second shows a sequence followed for journals. Keep in mind that the exact order of the stages may vary from one publisher to the next and may include steps not illustrated here.

Both diagrams incorporate stages relevant to the production of electronic publications in specific formats (CD-ROMs and online editions for books; online editions only for journals). Because these processes are still evolving throughout the publishing industry, they are presented in somewhat simplified form here.

For more information about the stages represented in the diagrams, consult the relevant chapters of this manual, which are indicated by the bars at the top and bottom of each diagram.

Abbreviations used:
au = author
cx = corrections
jnl = journal
MS = manuscript

Books

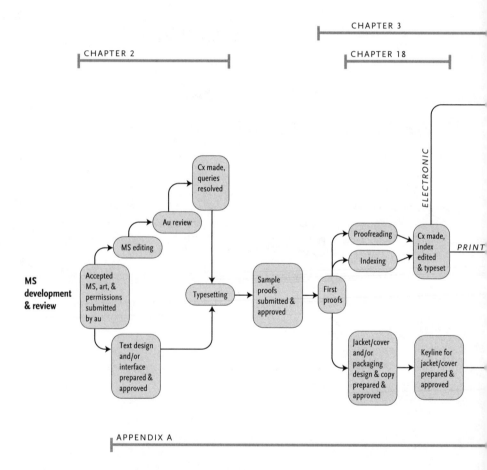

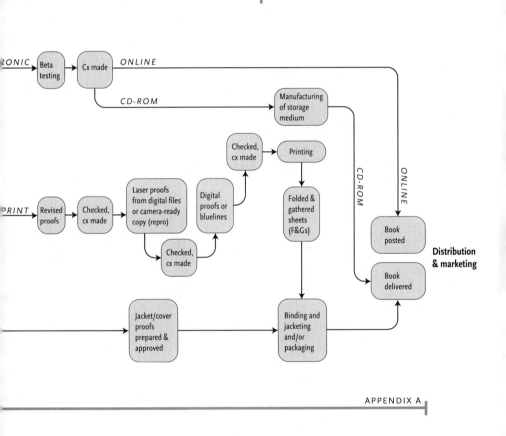

Beta testing

Cx made

ONLINE

CD-ROM

Manufacturing of storage medium

Checked, cx made

Printing

Laser proofs from digital files or camera-ready copy (repro)

Digital proofs or bluelines

CD-ROM

ONLINE

PRINT

Revised proofs

Checked, cx made

Checked, cx made

Folded & gathered sheets (F&Gs)

Book posted

Distribution & marketing

Book delivered

Jacket/cover proofs prepared & approved

Binding and jacketing and/or packaging

Journals

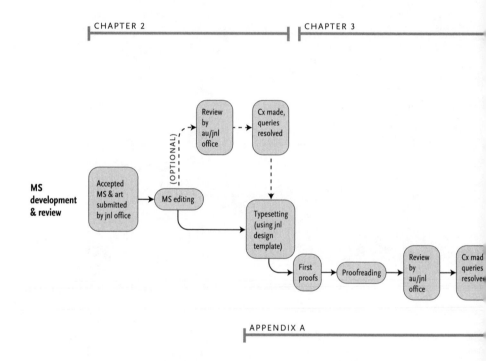

CHAPTER 2

MS development & review

860

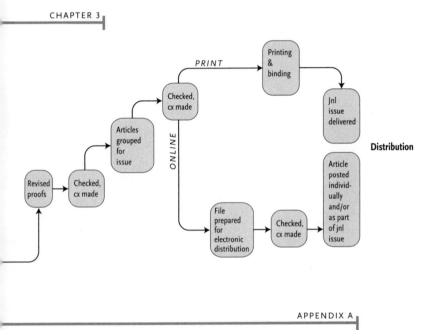

PRINT

ONLINE

Distribution

Bibliography

~~~~~~

The works listed here are a starting point for writers, editors, and others involved in publishing who would like more information about topics covered in this manual. The list includes all the works cited in the text as further resources along with other useful references. Although some make recommendations that diverge from those of this manual, they reflect the specific demands of different disciplines and traditions of writing, editing, and publishing.

1   Works on Writing and Editing

1.1 STYLE

ACS Style Guide: A Manual for Authors and Editors. 2nd ed. Edited by Janet S. Dodd. Washington, DC: American Chemical Society, 1997.

AIP Style Manual. 4th ed. New York, NY: American Institute of Physics, 1990. Also available online at http://www.aip.org/pubservs/style/4thed/toc.html.

ALWD Citation Manual: A Professional System of Citation. Edited by the Association of Legal Writing Directors and Darby Dickerson. Gaithersburg, MD: Aspen Law and Business, 2000.

American Medical Association Manual of Style. 9th ed. Edited by Cheryl Iverson. Baltimore: Williams and Wilkins, 1998.

ASM Style Manual for Journals and Books. Washington, DC: American Society for Microbiology, 1991.

The Associated Press Stylebook and Briefing on Media Law. Rev. ed. Edited by Norm Goldstein. Reading, MA: Perseus Books, 2000.

The Bluebook: A Uniform System of Citation. 17th ed. Cambridge, MA: Harvard Law Review Association, 2000.

Canadian Guide to Uniform Legal Citation. 4th ed. Scarborough, ON: Carswell/ McGill Law Journal, 1998.

Catholic News Service. *Stylebook on Religion 2000: A Reference Guide and Usage Manual.* Washington, DC: Catholic News Service, 2000.

CBE Manual. See *Scientific Style and Format*

The Complete Guide to Citing Government Information Resources: A Manual for Writ-

ers and Librarians. Rev. ed. Edited by Diane L. Garner and Diane H. Smith. Bethesda, MD: Congressional Information Service for the Government Documents Round Table, American Library Association, 1993.

Garner, Bryan A. *The Elements of Legal Style.* 2nd ed. New York: Oxford University Press, 2002.

Harnack, Andrew, and Eugene Kleppinger. *Online! A Reference Guide to Using Internet Sources.* Boston: Bedford/St. Martin's, 2001.

Holoman, D. Kern. *Writing about Music: A Style Sheet from the Editors of "19th-Century Music."* Berkeley and Los Angeles: University of California Press, 1988.

ISO (International Organization for Standardization). *Information and Documentation—Bibliographic References, Part 2, Electronic Documents or Parts Thereof.* ISO 690-2. New York: American National Standards Institute, 1997.

Li, Xia, and Nancy B. Crane. *Electronic Styles: A Handbook for Citing Electronic Information.* 2nd ed. Medford, NJ: Information Today, 1996.

MLA Style Manual and Guide to Scholarly Publishing. 2nd ed. Edited by Joseph Gibaldi. New York: Modern Language Association of America, 1998.

The New York Public Library Writer's Guide to Style and Usage. New York: HarperCollins, 1994.

The New York Times Manual of Style and Usage. Rev. ed. Edited by Allan M. Siegal and William G. Connolly. New York: Times Books, 1999.

The Oxford Guide to Style. Edited by Robert Ritter. New York: Oxford University Press, 2002. Successor to *Hart's Rules for Compositors and Readers at the University Press, Oxford.*

Publication Manual of the American Psychological Association. 5th ed. Washington, DC: American Psychological Association, 2001.

The SBL Handbook of Style: For Ancient Near Eastern, Biblical, and Early Christian Studies. Edited by Patrick H. Alexander et al. Peabody, MA: Hendrickson, 1999.

Scientific Style and Format: The CBE Manual for Authors, Editors, and Publishers. 6th ed. Compiled by the Style Manual Committee of the Council of Biology Editors. Cambridge: Cambridge University Press, 1994.

Strunk, William, Jr., and E. B. White. *The Elements of Style.* 4th ed. Boston: Allyn and Bacon, 2000.

Style Manual for Political Science. Rev. ed. Washington, DC: American Political Science Association Committee on Publications, 2002.

The Times Guide to English Style and Usage. Rev. ed. Compiled by Tim Austin. London: Times Books, 1999.

Turabian, Kate L. *A Manual for Writers of Term Papers, Theses, and Dissertations.* 6th ed. Revised by John Grossman and Alice Bennett. Chicago: University of Chicago Press, 1996.

United States Government Printing Office Style Manual 2000. Washington, DC: Government Printing Office, 2000. Also available online at http://www .access.gpo.gov/styleman/2000/Style001.html.

U.S. Geological Survey. *Suggestions to Authors of the Reports of the United States Geological Survey.* 7th ed. Washington, DC: Government Printing Office, 1991.

The University of Chicago Manual of Legal Citation. 2nd ed. Edited by the *University of Chicago Law Review.* 2000. http://lawreview.uchicago.edu/.

Walker, Janice R., and Todd Taylor. *The Columbia Guide to Online Style.* New York: Columbia University Press, 1998.

The Wall Street Journal Guide to Business Style and Usage. Edited by Paul R. Martin. London: Free Press, 2002.

Words into Type. 3rd ed. Based on studies by Marjorie E. Skillin, Robert M. Gay, and other authorities. Englewood Cliffs, NJ: Prentice Hall, 1974.

1.2 GRAMMAR AND USAGE

Aitchison, James. *Cassell Dictionary of English Grammar.* London: Cassell, 1996.

Baron, Dennis. *Grammar and Gender.* New Haven: Yale University Press, 1986.

Bernstein, Theodore M. *The Careful Writer: A Modern Guide to English Usage.* New York: Atheneum, 1965.

———. *Miss Thistlebottom's Hobgoblins: The Careful Writer's Guide to the Taboos, Bugbears, and Outmoded Rules of English Usage.* New York: Noonday Press, 1971.

Burchfield, Robert W. *Unlocking the English Language.* New York: Hill and Wang, 1991.

Chalker, Sylvia, and Edmund S. C. Weiner. *The Oxford Dictionary of English Grammar.* New York: Oxford University Press, 1998.

Copperud, Roy H. *American Usage and Style: The Consensus.* New York: Van Nostrand Reinhold, 1980.

Ebbitt, Wilma R., and David R. Ebbitt. *Index to English.* 8th ed. New York: Oxford University Press, 1990.

E-What? A Guide to the Quirks of New Media Style and Usage. Alexandria, VA: EEI Press, 2000.

Follett, Wilson. *Modern American Usage: A Guide.* 1st rev. ed. Revised by Erik Wensberg. New York: Hill and Wang, 1998.

Fowler, H. W. *A Dictionary of Modern English Usage.* 2nd ed. Revised and edited by Sir Ernest Gowers. Oxford: Oxford University Press, 1965. (See also *The New Fowler's Modern English Usage.*)

Garner, Bryan A. *Garner's Modern American Usage.* New York: Oxford University Press, 2003.

Gordon, Karen Elizabeth. *The Deluxe Transitive Vampire: The Ultimate Handbook of Grammar for the Innocent, the Eager, and the Doomed.* New York: Pantheon, 1993.

———. *The New Well-Tempered Sentence: A Punctuation Handbook for the Innocent, the Eager, and the Doomed.* New York: Ticknor and Fields, 1993.

Gowers, Ernest. *The Complete Plain Words*. Edited by Sidney Greenbaum and Janet Whitcut. Boston: D. R. Godine, 1988.

Greenbaum, Sydney. *Oxford English Grammar*. New York: Oxford University Press, 1996.

Hale, Constance. *Sin and Syntax: How to Craft Wickedly Effective Prose*. New York: Broadway Books, 1999.

Hale, Constance, and Jessie Scanlon, eds. *Wired Style: Principles of English Usage in the Digital Age*. Rev. ed. New York: Broadway Books, 1999.

Johnson, Edward D. *The Handbook of Good English*. New York: Pocket Books, 1991.

Maggio, Rosalie. *Talking about People: A Guide to Fair and Accurate Language*. Phoenix: Oryx Press, 1997.

The New Fowler's Modern English Usage. Revised 3rd ed. Edited by R. W. Burchfield. New York: Oxford University Press, 2000.

O'Conner, Patricia T. *Woe Is I: The Grammarphobe's Guide to Better English in Plain English*. New York: Putnam, 1996.

Palmer, Frank. *Grammar*. 2nd ed. New York: Penguin, 1984.

Schwartz, Marilyn. *Guidelines for Bias-Free Writing*. Bloomington: Indiana University Press, 1995.

Trask, R. L. *Language: The Basics*. 2nd ed. New York: Routledge, 1999.

Trimble, John R. *Writing with Style: Conversations on the Art of Writing*. 2nd ed. Upper Saddle River, NJ: Prentice Hall, 2002.

Wallraff, Barbara. *Word Court: Wherein Verbal Virtue Is Rewarded, Crimes against the Language Are Punished, and Poetic Justice Is Done*. New York: Harcourt, 2000.

Walsh, Bill. *Lapsing into a Comma: A Curmudgeon's Guide to the Many Things That Can Go Wrong in Print—and How to Avoid Them*. Chicago: Contemporary Books, 2000.

Webster's Dictionary of English Usage. Springfield, MA: Merriam-Webster, 1989.

Williams, Joseph M. *Style: Toward Clarity and Grace*. With two chapters coauthored by Gregory G. Colomb. Chicago: University of Chicago Press, 1990.

Zinsser, William. *On Writing Well: An Informal Guide to Writing Nonfiction*. 5th ed. New York: HarperPerennial, 1995.

1.3 RESEARCH AND WRITING

Barzun, Jacques, and Henry F. Graff. *The Modern Researcher*. 5th ed. Boston: Houghton Mifflin, 1992.

Becker, Howard S. *Writing for Social Scientists: How to Start and Finish Your Thesis, Book, or Article*. Chicago: University of Chicago Press, 1986.

Booth, Wayne C., Gregory G. Colomb, and Joseph M. Williams. *The Craft of Research*. 2nd ed. Chicago: University of Chicago Press, 2003.

Cook, Claire Kehrwald. *Line by Line: How to Improve Your Own Writing*. Boston: Houghton Mifflin, 1985.

Day, Robert A. *How to Write and Publish a Scientific Paper.* 5th ed. Phoenix: Oryx Press, 1998.

Lanham, Richard A. *Revising Prose.* 4th ed. Boston: Allyn and Bacon, 2000.

Lerner, Betsy. *The Forest for the Trees: An Editor's Advice to Writers.* New York: Riverhead Books, 2000.

McMillan, Vicky. *Writing Papers in the Biological Sciences.* 3rd ed. Boston: Bedford/St. Martin's, 2001.

2 Works on Publishing

2.1 MANUSCRIPT EDITING AND PROOFREADING

Butcher, Judith. *Copy-editing: The Cambridge Handbook for Editors, Authors, and Publishers.* 3rd ed. New York: Cambridge University Press, 1992.

Copy Editor: Language News for the Publishing Professional. Bimonthly newsletter published by McMurry Newsletters. Also available online at http://www.copyeditor.com.

The Editorial Eye. Monthly newsletter published by EEI Communications. Also available online at http://www.eeicommunications.com/eye/.

Einsohn, Amy. *The Copyeditor's Handbook: A Guide for Book Publishing and Corporate Communications.* Berkeley and Los Angeles: University of California Press, 2000.

Judd, Karen. *Copyediting: A Practical Guide.* Revised ed. London: Hale, 1995.

Smith, Peggy. *Mark My Words: Instruction and Practice in Proofreading.* 3rd ed. Alexandria, VA: EEI Press, 1997.

Stainton, Elsie Myers. *The Fine Art of Copyediting.* 2nd ed. New York: Columbia University Press, 2002.

Stoughton, Mary. *Substance and Style: Instruction and Practice in Copyediting.* 2nd ed. Alexandria, VA: EEI Press, 1996.

2.2 RIGHTS AND PERMISSIONS

Fischer, Mark A., E. Gabriel Perle, and John Taylor Williams. *Perle and Williams on Publishing Law.* 3rd ed. Gaithersburg, MD: Aspen Law and Business, 1999.

Goldstein, Paul. *Copyright.* 2nd ed. New York: Aspen Law and Business, 1996.

Kirsch, Jonathan. *Kirsch's Handbook of Publishing Law.* Los Angeles: Acrobat Books, 1996.

Nimmer, Melville. *Cases and Materials on Copyright and Other Aspects of Entertain-*

ment Litigation, Including Unfair Competition, Defamation, Privacy. 6th ed. New York: Matthew Bender, 2000.

——. *Nimmer on Copyright*. Rev. ed. 10 vols. New York: Matthew Bender, 1978–. Looseleaf updates.

Nimmer, Melville, and Paul Edward Gellner, eds. *International Copyright Law and Practice*. New York: Matthew Bender, 1988–. Looseleaf updates.

Patry, William F. *Copyright Law and Practice*. Washington, DC: Bureau of National Affairs, 1994. Annual supplements.

——. *The Fair Use Privilege in Copyright Law*. 2nd ed. Washington, DC: Bureau of National Affairs, 1995.

Strong, William S. *The Copyright Book: A Practical Guide*. 5th ed. Cambridge: MIT Press, 1999.

2.3 ILLUSTRATIONS

Briscoe, Mary Helen. *Preparing Scientific Illustrations: A Guide to Better Posters, Presentations, and Publications*. 2nd ed. New York: Springer-Verlag, 1996.

CBE Scientific Illustration Committee. *Illustrating Science: Standards for Publication*. Bethesda, MD: Council of Biology Editors, 1988.

Monmonier, Mark. *Mapping It Out: Expository Cartography for the Humanities and Social Sciences*. Chicago: University of Chicago Press, 1993.

Ross, Ted. *The Art of Music Engraving and Processing: A Complete Manual, Reference, and Text Book on Preparing Music for Reproduction and Print*. Miami: Hansen Books, 1970.

Tufte, Edward R. *Envisioning Information*. Cheshire, CT: Graphics Press, 1990.

——. *The Visual Display of Quantitative Information*. 2nd ed. Cheshire, CT: Graphics Press, 2001.

——. *Visual Explanations: Images and Quantities, Evidence and Narrative*. Cheshire, CT: Graphics Press, 1997.

Zweifel, Frances W. *A Handbook of Biological Illustration*. 2nd ed. Chicago: University of Chicago Press, 1988.

2.4 MATHEMATICS

Clapham, Christopher. *Concise Dictionary of Mathematics*. 2nd ed. New York: Oxford University Press, 1996.

Higham, Nicholas J. *Handbook of Writing for the Mathematical Sciences*. 2nd ed. Philadelphia: Society for Industrial and Applied Mathematics, 1998.

The International System of Units (SI). Edited by David T. Goldman and R. J. Bell. NBS Special Publication 330, U.S. Department of Commerce, National Bureau of Standards, 1986. Washington, DC: Government Printing Office, 1986.

Knuth, Donald E. *The TeXbook*. Boston: Addison-Wesley, 2000.

Lamport, Leslie. *LaTeX: A Document Preparation System. User's Guide and Reference Manual*. 2nd ed. Reading, MA: Addison-Wesley, 1999.

A Manual for Authors of Mathematical Papers. 8th ed. Providence, RI: American Mathematical Society, 1990.

Spivak, Michael. *The Joy of TeX: A Gourmet Guide to Typesetting with the AMS-TeXMacro Package*. 2nd ed. Providence, RI: American Mathematical Society, 1990.

Steenrod, Norman E., et al. *How to Write Mathematics*. Providence, RI: American Mathematical Society, 1981.

Swanson, Ellen. *Mathematics into Type*. Updated edition by Arlene O'Sean and Antoinette Schleyer. Providence, RI: American Mathematical Society, 1999.

Taylor, B. N. *Guide for the Use of the International System of Units (SI)*. Washington, DC: U.S. Department of Commerce, Technology Administration, National Institute of Standards and Technology, 1995. Also available online at http://www.physics.nist.gov/Pubs/SP811/sp811.html.

2.5 INDEXING

Ament, Kurt. *Indexing: A Nuts-and-Bolts Guide for Technical Writers*. Norwich, NY: William Andrew, 2001.

Booth, Pat F. *Indexing: The Manual of Good Practice*. Munich: K. G. Saur, 2001.

Fetters, Linda K. *Handbook of Indexing Techniques: A Guide for Beginning Indexers*. 2nd ed. Corpus Christi, TX: FimCo Books, 1999.

Mulvany, Nancy. *Indexing Books*. Chicago: University of Chicago Press, 1994.

Wellisch, Hans H. *Indexing from A to Z*. 2nd ed. New York: H. W. Wilson, 1995.

2.6 DESIGN AND PRODUCTION

Beach, Mark, and Eric Kenly. *Getting It Printed*. 3rd ed. Cincinnati: North Light Books, 1999.

Bookman's Glossary. 6th ed. Edited by Jean Peters. New York: R. R. Bowker, 1983.

Bringhurst, Robert. *The Elements of Typographic Style*. 2nd ed. Point Roberts, WA: Hartley and Marks, 2001.

Burdett, Eric. *The Craft of Bookbinding*. Newton Abbot, UK: David and Charles, 1978.

Chappell, Warren, and Robert Bringhurst. *A Short History of the Printed Word*. 2nd ed. Point Roberts, WA: Hartley and Marks, 1999.

Dowding, Geoffrey. *Finer Points in the Spacing and Arrangement of Type*. Point Roberts, WA: Hartley and Marks, 1995.

Dreyfus, John. *Into Print: Selected Writings on Printing History, Typography, and Book Production*. Boston: D. R. Godine, 1995.

Eckersley, Richard, Richard Angstadt, Charles M. Ellertson, Richard Hendel, Naomi B. Pascal, and Anita Walker Scott. *Glossary of Typesetting Terms.* Chicago: University of Chicago Press, 1994.

Gill, Eric. *An Essay on Typography.* Boston: David R. Godine, 1988.

Glaister, Geoffrey Ashall. *Encyclopedia of the Book.* 2nd ed. New Castle, DE: Oak Knoll Press, 2001.

Hackos, JoAnn, and Dawn Stevens. *Standards for Online Communication.* New York: John Wiley, 1997.

Hendel, Richard. *On Book Design.* New Haven: Yale University Press, 1998.

Hochuli, Jost, and Robin Kinross. *Designing Books: Practice and Theory.* New York: Princeton Architectural Press, 1996.

Johnston, Edward. *Writing and Illuminating and Lettering.* Mineola, NY: Dover, 1995.

Kinross, Robin, Jaap van Triest, and Karel Martens, eds. *Karel Martens: Printed Matter.* New York: Princeton Architectural Press, 1997.

Lee, Marshall. *Bookmaking: The Illustrated Guide to Editing/Design/Production.* 3rd ed. New York: W. W. Norton, 1997.

Lynch, Patrick J., and Sarah Horton. *Web Style Guide: Basic Design Principles for Creating Web Sites.* 2nd ed. New Haven: Yale University Press, 2001.

McLean, Ruari. *The Thames and Hudson Manual of Typography.* New York: Thames and Hudson, 1992.

Pocket Pal. 18th ed. Memphis: International Paper Company, 2000.

Rogondino, Michael, and Pat Rogondino. *Process Color Manual: 24,000 CMYK Combinations for Design, Prepress, and Printing.* San Francisco: Chronicle Books, 2000.

Romano, Frank J. *Pocket Guide to Digital Prepress.* Albany: Delmar Thomson Learning, 1995.

Stein, Lincoln D. *How to Set Up and Maintain a Web Site.* 2nd ed. Boston: Addison-Wesley Longman, 1996.

Tschichold, Jan. *The Form of the Book: Essays on the Morality of Good Design.* Point Roberts, WA: Hartley and Marks, 1995.

———. *The New Typography: A Handbook for Modern Designers.* Berkeley and Los Angeles: University of California Press, 1998.

Williamson, Hugh. *Methods of Book Design.* 3rd ed. New Haven: Yale University Press, 1983.

2.7 THE PUBLISHING INDUSTRY

Derricourt, Robin. *An Author's Guide to Scholarly Publishing.* Princeton: Princeton University Press, 1996.

Germano, William. *Getting It Published: A Guide for Scholars and Anyone Else Serious about Serious Books.* Chicago: University of Chicago Press, 2001.

Greco, Albert N. *The Book Publishing Industry.* Boston: Allyn and Bacon, 1997.

Harman, Eleanor, and Ian Montagnes, eds. *The Thesis and the Book.* Toronto: University of Toronto Press, 1976.

ILMP (International Literary Market Place). New York: R. R. Bowker. Published annually. Also available online at http://www.literarymarketplace.com/lmp/us/index_us.asp.

Journal of Electronic Publishing. Published quarterly by the University of Michigan Press. http://www.press.umich.edu/jep/.

Journal of Scholarly Publishing. Published quarterly by the University of Toronto Press.

LMP (Literary Market Place). New York: R. R. Bowker. Published annually. Also available online at http://www.literarymarketplace.com/lmp/us/index_us.asp.

Luey, Beth. *Handbook for Academic Authors.* 4th ed. New York: Cambridge University Press, 2002.

Rabiner, Susan, and Alfred Fortunato. *Thinking Like Your Editor: How to Write Great Serious Nonfiction—and Get It Published.* New York: W. W. Norton & Company, 2002.

Smith, Datus C., Jr. *A Guide to Book Publishing.* Rev. ed. Seattle: University of Washington Press, 1989.

Suzanne, Claudia. *This Business of Books: A Complete Overview of the Industry from Concept through Sales.* 3rd ed. Edited by Carol J. Amato and Thelma Sansoucie. Tustin, CA: Wambtac, 1996.

3   Dictionaries

3.1 ENGLISH DICTIONARIES

American Heritage Dictionary of the English Language. 4th ed. Boston: Houghton Mifflin, 2000.

Merriam-Webster's Collegiate Dictionary. 11th ed. Springfield, MA: Merriam-Webster, 2003. Also available online at http://www.Merriam-WebsterCollegiate.com and as a CD-ROM.

New Oxford American Dictionary. Edited by Elizabeth J. Jewell and Frank Abate. New York: Oxford University Press, 2001.

New Shorter Oxford English Dictionary. 2 vols. Oxford: Clarendon Press, 1993.

Oxford English Dictionary. 2nd ed. 20 vols. Oxford: Oxford University Press, 1989. Also available as a CD-ROM.

Random House Dictionary of the English Language. 2nd ed. New York: Random House, 1987.

Roget's 21st Century Thesaurus. Nashville: Thomas Nelson, 1992.

Roget's 21st Century Thesaurus in Dictionary Form. 2nd ed. Edited by Barbara Ann Kipfer. New York: Dell, 1999.

Webster's New World College Dictionary. 4th ed. Cleveland: Webster's New World, 2001.

Webster's Third New International Dictionary of the English Language, Unabridged. Springfield, MA: Merriam-Webster, 1993.

3.2 FOREIGN-LANGUAGE DICTIONARIES

ABC Chinese-English Dictionary. Edited by John DeFrancis. Honolulu: University of Hawaii Press, 1996.

Cassell's Italian Dictionary. Edited by Piero Rebora et al. New York: John Wiley, 1994.

Gale, James S. *Han-Yong Chajon: A Korean-English Dictionary*. Soul-si: Kukhak Charyowon, 1996.

Grand dictionnaire Larousse-Chambers, anglais-français/français-anglais. Edited by Ralf Brockmeier. New York: Larousse, 1999.

Kenkyūsha's New English-Japanese Dictionary. 5th ed. Tokyo: Kenkyusha, 1980.

Oxford-Duden German Dictionary. 2nd ed. Edited by Werner Scholze-Stubenrecht et al. Oxford: Oxford University Press, 1999.

Oxford English-Arabic Dictionary of Current Usage. Edited by N. S. Doniach. Oxford: Clarendon Press, 1972.

Oxford-Hachette French Dictionary. Edited by Marie-Hélène Corréard et al. Oxford: Oxford University Press, 2001.

Oxford Latin Dictionary. Combined ed. Edited by P. G. W. Glare. New York: Oxford University Press, 1982.

Oxford-Paravia Italian Dictionary. Edited by Cristina Bareggi. Oxford: Oxford University Press, 2001.

Oxford Russian Dictionary. 3rd ed. Edited by Marcus Wheeler et al. Oxford: Oxford University Press, 2000.

Oxford Spanish Dictionary. 2nd ed. Edited by Beatriz Galimberti Jarman and Roy Russell. Oxford: Oxford University Press, 2001.

The University of Chicago Spanish Dictionary. 5th ed. Edited by David Pharies. Chicago: University of Chicago Press, 2002.

4 General Reference Works

4.1 BIOGRAPHY

American Men and Women of Science. 20th ed. 8 vols. New York: R. R. Bowker, 1998.

American National Biography. 24 vols. New York: Oxford University Press, 1999. Supplements. Also available online at http://www.anb.org.

Burke's Genealogical and Heraldic History of the Peerage, Baronetage, and Knightage. Multiple vols. London: Burke's Peerage, 1826–.

Canadian Who's Who. Toronto: University of Toronto Press. Published annually, with semiannual supplements.

Concise Dictionary of National Biography. 3 vols. New York: Oxford University Press, 1992.

Dictionary of American Biography. 11 vols. New York: Scribner's, 1995. Supplements.

Dictionary of Canadian Biography. 14 vols. Toronto: University of Toronto Press, 1966–. Supplements.

Dictionary of National Biography. Multiple vols. Prepared under various editors. New York: Oxford University Press, 1885–1990.

Directory of American Scholars. 10th ed. 6 vols. Detroit: Gale Group, 2002.

International Who's Who. London: Europa. Published annually.

Merriam-Webster's Biographical Dictionary. Springfield, MA: Merriam-Webster, 1995.

Who's Who: An Annual Biographical Dictionary. New York: St. Martin's Press. Published annually.

Who's Who in America. Chicago: A. N. Marquis. Published biennially.

4.2 GEOGRAPHY

Cambridge World Gazetteer: A Geographical Dictionary. Edited by David Munro. New York: Cambridge University Press, 1990.

Columbia Gazetteer of North America. Edited by Saul B. Cohen. New York: Columbia University Press, 2000. Also available online at http://www.bartleby.com/69/.

Merriam-Webster's Geographical Dictionary. 3rd ed. Springfield, MA: Merriam-Webster, 1997.

Omni Gazetteer of the United States of America. Edited by Frank R. Abate. Detroit: Omnigraphics, 1991.

Oxford Atlas of the World. 8th ed. New York: Oxford University Press, 2000.

Road Atlas and Trip Planner: United States, Canada, and Mexico. Skokie, IL: Rand McNally, 2001.

The Times Atlas of the World. 10th ed. New York: Times Books, 1999.

4.3 ENCYCLOPEDIAS

Britannica Concise Encyclopaedia. London: Encyclopaedia Britannica, 2000.

Canadian Encyclopedia. 2000 ed. Toronto: McClelland and Stewart, 1999.

Columbia Encyclopedia. 6th ed. New York: Columbia University Press, 2000.

Encyclopedia Americana. 30 vols. Danbury, CT: Grolier, 2002.

Encyclopaedia Britannica, 2002 edition. 32 vols. Chicago: Encyclopaedia Britannica, 2001. Also available online at http://www.britannica.com and as a CD-ROM.

4.4 ALMANACS AND YEARBOOKS

Canadian Almanac and Directory. Toronto: Copp-Clark. Published annually.
Europa World Yearbook. London: Europa. Published annually.
New York Times Almanac. New York: Penguin Group. Published annually.
Statesman's Year-Book. New York: St. Martin's Press. Published annually.
Time Almanac: With Information Please. Boston: Information Please. Published annually.
Whitaker's Almanack. London: Stationery Office. Published annually.
World Almanac and Book of Facts. New York: St. Martin's Griffin. Published annually.
World of Learning. London: Allen and Unwin. Published annually.

4.5 GUIDES TO BOOKS, PERIODICALS, AND OTHER SOURCES

ABI/Inform. Ann Arbor, MI: University Microfilms International. http://tls.il .proquest.com/cgi-bin/TitleForm?cfg=LibTitles.cf (updated weekly) and on CD-ROM.
Anglo-American Cataloguing Rules. 2nd ed. Prepared by the American Library Association, the British Library, the Canadian Committee on Cataloguing, the Library Association, and the Library of Congress. Edited by Michael Gorman and Paul W. Winkler. Chicago: American Library Association; Ottawa: Canadian Library Association, 1998.
Ashley, Lowell E. *Cataloging Musical Moving Image Material: A Guide to the Bibliographical Control of Videorecordings and Films of Musical Performances and Other Music-Related Moving Image Material.* Canton, MA: Music Library Association, 1996.
Australian Books in Print. Melbourne: D. W. Thorpe. Published annually.
The Bibliographic Index. New York: H. W. Wilson, 1938–.
Book Review Digest. New York: H. W. Wilson. Published monthly, except for February and July, with annual cumulations. Also available online at http://www .hwwilson.com (updated twice weekly).
Book Review Index. Detroit: Gale Research Company. Published monthly, with quarterly and annual cumulation.
Books in Print. New York: R. R. Bowker. Published annually. Also available online at http://www.booksinprint.com.

Butcher, David. *Official Publications in Britain*. 2nd ed. London: Library Association, 1991.

Canadian Books in Print. Toronto: University of Toronto Press. Published annually.

Dissertation Abstracts International. Ann Arbor, MI: University Microfilms International. Published monthly with annual cumulation.

Guide to Reference Books. 11th ed. Compiled by Robert Balay. Chicago: American Library Association, 1996.

Guide to the Contents of the Public Record Office. 3 vols. London: Her Majesty's Stationery Office, 1963–68.

Guide to the National Archives of the United States. Washington, DC: Archives, 1987.

Guide to U.S. Government Publications. Edited by Donna Batten. Formerly known as *Andriot*. Detroit: Gale Research Company. Updated annually.

Humanities Index. New York: H. W. Wilson. Published quarterly with annual cumulation. Also available online at http://www.hwwilson.com (updated twice weekly).

Index Islamicus. London: Mansell. Published quarterly with quinquenniel cumulation.

Index Medicus. Washington, DC: U.S. Department of Health and Human Services/ National Library of Medicine. Published annually. Also available online at http://www.ncbi.nlm.nih.gov/entrez/query.fcgi.

Library of Congress Subject Headings. Washington, DC: Library of Congress Cataloging Distribution Service. Published annually.

List of Journals Indexed in Index Medicus. Bethesda, MD: National Library of Medicine. Published annually.

Livres disponibles. [French Books in Print]. Paris: Electre. Published annually.

Monthly Catalog of United States Government Publications. Washington, DC: Government Printing Office.

New York Times Index. New York: New York Times Company. Annual cumulations.

PAIS International in Print. New York: Public Affairs Information Service. Published monthly, with every fourth issue being cumulative.

Pemberton, John E., ed. *The Bibliographic Control of Official Publications*. New York: Pergamon, 1982.

Periodical Title Abbreviations. Vol. 1, By Abbreviation. Vol. 2, By Title. 13th ed. Detroit: Gale Research, 2001.

Reader's Guide to Periodical Literature. New York: H. W. Wilson. Published annually. Also available online at http://www.hwwilson.com (updated twice weekly).

Rodgers, Frank. *A Guide to British Government Publications*. New York: H. W. Wilson, 1980.

Schmeckebier, Laurence F., and Roy B. Eastin. *Government Publications and Their Use*. 2nd ed. Washington, DC: Brookings Institution, 1969.

Science Citation Index. Philadelphia: Institute for Scientific Information. Published bimonthly with annual cumulations.

Social Science Index. New York: H. W. Wilson. Published quarterly with annual cumulation. Also available online at http://www.hwwilson.com (updated twice weekly).

Ulrich's International Periodicals Directory. New York: R. R. Bowker. Published annually. Supplemented quarterly by Ulrich's Update. Also available online at http://www.ulrichsweb.com.

Verzeichnis Lieferbarer Bucher. [German Books in Print]. Frankfurt am Main: Verlag der Buchhändler-Vereinigung. Published annually.

Walford's Guide to Reference Material. 8th ed. London: Library Association, 1999–2000.

Whitaker's Books in Print: The Reference Catalogue of Current Literature. London: J. Whitaker. Published annually. Before 1988 titled *British Books in Print.*

4.6 QUOTATIONS

Bartlett, John. *Bartlett's Familiar Quotations: A Collection of Passages, Phrases, and Proverbs Traced to Their Sources in Ancient and Modern Literature.* 17th ed. Edited by Justin Kaplan. Boston: Little, Brown, 2002.

Crystal, David, and Hilary Crystal. *Words on Words: Quotations about Language and Languages.* Chicago: University of Chicago Press, 2000.

The Oxford Dictionary of Quotations. 5th ed. Edited by Elizabeth Knowles. Oxford: Oxford University Press, 1999.

4.7 ABBREVIATIONS

Acronyms, Initialisms, and Abbreviations Dictionary: A Guide to Acronyms, Abbreviations, Contractions, Alphabetic Symbols, and Similar Condensed Appellations. 27th ed. 3 vols. Edited by Mary Rose Bonk. Detroit: Gale Research, 2000.

Davis, Neil M. *Medical Abbreviations: 15,000 Conveniences at the Expense of Communications and Safety.* 10th ed. Huntington Valley, PA: Neil M. Davis Associates, 2001.

Jablonski, Stanley. *Dictionary of Medical Acronyms and Abbreviations.* 4th ed. Philadelphia: Hanley and Belfus, 2001.

Polmar, Norman, Bruce Warren, and Eric Wertheim. *Dictionary of Military Abbreviations.* Annapolis, MD: Naval Institute Press, 1994.

Stahl, Dean, and Karen Kerchelich. *Abbreviations Dictionary.* 10th ed. Originated by Ralph De Sola. Boca Raton, FL: CRC Press, 2001.

Webster's Guide to Abbreviations. Springfield, MA: Merriam-Webster, 1985.

5 Miscellaneous Works Cited in Text

ALA-LC Romanization Tables: Transliteration Schemes for Non-Roman Scripts. Compiled and edited by Randall K. Barry. Washington, DC: Library of Congress, 1991.

American Naturalist. Journal published monthly by the University of Chicago Press for the American Society of Naturalists. Also available online at http://www.journals.uchicago.edu/AN/home.html.

Astronomical Journal. Journal published monthly by the University of Chicago Press for the American Astronomical Society. Also available online at http://www.journals.uchicago.edu/AJ/home.html.

Astrophysical Journal. Journal published three times a month by the University of Chicago Press for the American Astronomical Society. Also available online at http://www.journals.uchicago.edu/ApJ/front.html.

Baker, A. D., III. *The Naval Institute Guide to Combat Fleets of the World, 2002–2003: Their Ships, Aircraft, and Systems.* Annapolis, MD: Naval Institute Press, 2002.

Beuschel-Menze, Hertha, and Frohmut Menze. *Die neue Rechtschreibung: Wörter und Regeln leicht gelernt.* Reinbek: Rowohlt, 1996.

BIOSIS Serial Sources. Philadelphia: BIOSIS. Published annually. Also available online at http://www.biosis.org and as a CD-ROM.

Daniels, Peter T., and William Bright, eds. *The World's Writing Systems.* New York: Oxford University Press, 1996.

Duden Rechtschreibung der deutschen Sprache. 21st ed. Vol. 1. Mannheim: Dudenverlag, 1996.

French Review. Journal published bimonthly by the American Association of Teachers of French.

Gall, Gerald L. *The Canadian Legal System.* 4th ed. Scarborough, ON: Carswell, 1995.

Grevisse, Maurice. *Le bon usage: Grammaire française.* 12th ed. Edited by André Goosse. Paris-Gembloux: Éditions Duculot, 1986.

History of Religions. Journal published quarterly by the University of Chicago Press.

Horticulture. Magazine published ten times a year. Also available online at http://www.hortmag.com.

Human Gene Nomenclature Committee Database. http://www.gene.ucl.ac.uk/nomenclature/.

International Code of Botanical Nomenclature (St. Louis Code). Prepared and edited by W. Greuter et al. Königstein: Koeltz Scientific Books, 2000.

International Code of Zoological Nomenclature. 4th ed. London: International Trust for Zoological Nomenclature, 1999.

International Journal of Middle East Studies. Journal published quarterly by Cambridge University Press for the Middle East Studies Association of North America. Also available online at http://www.jstor.org/journals/00207438.html.

MacEllven, Douglass T., Michael J. McGuire, and Denis LeMay. *Legal Research Handbook*. 4th ed. Toronto: Butterworths, 1998.

Mouse Genome Database. Mouse Genome Informatics. http://www.informatics .jax.org/.

Noel, John V., Jr., and Edward L. Beach. *Naval Terms Dictionary*. 5th ed. Annapolis, MD: Naval Institute Press, 1988.

Oxford Classical Dictionary. 3rd ed. Edited by Simon Hornblower and Anthony Spawforth. Oxford and New York: Oxford University Press, 1996. Also available as a CD-ROM.

Physical Review Letters. Published semimonthly by the American Physical Society. Also available online at http://prl.aps.org/.

PMLA. Journal published bimonthly by the Modern Language Association of America.

Pullum, Geoffrey K., and William A. Ladusaw. *Phonetic Symbol Guide*. 2nd ed. Chicago: University of Chicago Press, 1996.

Raymond, Eric S. *The New Hacker's Dictionary*. 3rd ed. Cambridge, MA: MIT Press, 1996.

Real Academia Española. *Ortografía de la lengua española*. Madrid: Espasa, 1999.

Romanic Review. Journal published quarterly by the Columbia University Department of Romance Languages.

Thorin, Suzanne E., and Carole Franklin Vidall. *The Acquisition and Cataloging of Music and Sound Recordings: A Glossary*. Canton, MA: Music Library Association, 1984.

USP Dictionary of USAN and International Drug Names. Rockville, MD: U.S. Pharmacopeial Convention. Revised annually.

Valli, Clayton, and Ceil Lucas. *The Linguistics of American Sign Language: An Introduction*. 3rd ed. Washington, DC: Gallaudet University Press, 2001.

Zurick, Timothy. *Army Dictionary and Desk Reference*. 2nd ed. Harrisburg, PA: Stackpole Books, 1999.

Index

compounds (*continued*)
hyphens in, 2.15, 5.92–93, 6.81, 6.85,
7.85, 7.88–89
as modifiers before or after noun, 7.86
of nouns, new, 5.33
of nouns, proper, 5.6
omission of second part of, 7.89
phrasal adjectives and, 5.92–93, 5.102
plurals of, 5.6, 5.19, 7.8–9
possessives of, 7.25
prepositions as, 5.163
of pronouns, 5.53, 5.63
readability of, 7.85
resources on, 7.1–2
types of, 7.83, 7.90
See also prefixes; suffixes; word division
computer software
character-count function of, pp. 807, 826
for editing manuscripts, 2.83–85
"hairline rules" in, 12.28
for indexing, 18.4, 18.103
for keyboarding manuscript, 2.11
for mathematical copy, 14.1, 14.60
months abbreviated in, 15.42
for notes, 16.20
slash in directory paths of, 6.119
special characters in, 10.14
spelling and capitalization of, 7.81
style tags in, 2.90 (*see also* codes and
coding)
terminology of, 7.81
for typesetting, pp. 814–15
computer terms
brackets in, 6.109
capitalization in, 7.77, 7.81
font in, 7.79–80
plus sign in, 7.78
resources on, 6.8, 7.81
typographic variations in, 7.76
words to be typed in, 7.80
computer-to-plate (CTP) technology,
pp. 816, 826
concepts
personified, 8.40
religious, 8.116–17
transcendent, 8.101
concerts, reviews of, 17.202
conclusions, format of, 1.80
concordance, definition of, 18.4
conferences, 8.76, 17.215. *See also* proceedings of conferences and symposia

Congress, congressman, 8.25, 8.67. *See also*
United States Congress
Congressional Debates, 17.304
Congressional Globe, 17.304
Congressional Record, 17.302–3, 17.309
conjunctions
ampersand vs. *and,* 8.174, 16.117, 17.27,
17.52, 17.106
beginning sentence with, 5.191
for coordinate adjectives, 5.91
definition of, 5.180
dependent clauses with, 6.37
independent clauses with, 6.32–34, 6.36
in index subentries, 18.66
interrogative verbs as, 5.189
participial prepositions as, 5.164
as prepositions, 5.172
relative pronouns as, 5.189
semicolon preceding, 6.59
in series of items or clauses, 6.19–20,
6.33
slash as, 6.113
types of: adversative (contrasting), 5.184;
coordinate, 5.181; copulative (additive), 5.183; correlative, 5.182; disjunctive (separative), 5.185; final
(illative), 5.186; subordinate, 5.187–
88, 5.189
with used as, 5.190
Consolidated Regulations of Canada (CRC),
17.332
constitutions
documentation of, 17.288–89, 17.321,
17.356
numbers vs. words for divisions in, 9.32
contact proofs, pp. 815, 826
continents, names of, 8.47, 8.50
continued lines, 13.61, 18.142
contractions, 5.104, 7.31, 15.3, 15.5
contracts, 4.53–57, 17.220. *See also* publication agreement
contributors
information for, 1.145
list of, 1.67, 1.89–90, 1.159, 2.39,
fig. 1.11
publication agreement for, 4.53–57
responsibilities of, 2.39
submission information for, 1.141–42,
1.145, 1.175
See also author's name; manuscripts, author's responsibilities

illustrations
  alterations to (e.g., cropping), 12.18,
    12.21
  appearance of, 12.29
  author's own material as, 12.40, 12.44
  author's responsibilities for, 2.30, 2.33–
    35, 2.44, 12.1, 12.17, 12.19
  callouts for, 2.22, 2.30, 2.33, 12.10
  captions (*see* captions)
  credits (*see* credits and credit lines)
  definition of, 12.3
  documentation of, 17.141
  editing and preparation of, 2.66
  editorial changes to, 12.23
  electronic files of, 2.19, 2.22, 2.34,
    12.25–27
  in electronic publications, 1.127, 1.185
  fair use of, 4.81
  frontispiece, 1.8, 1.45
  galleries: definition of, 12.7, p. 830;
    noted in front matter, 1.43, 1.45,
    12.54, figs. 1.7, 1.9; numbering of,
    2.35, 12.16; pagination and, 1.100,
    12.7; plates in, 12.6
  halftones, 12.4, 12.7, fig. 12.1; vs. contin-
    uous tone, 12.4; definition of, p. 830;
    dropout, p. 827; duotone, p. 828; ex-
    ample of, fig. 12.1; galleries com-
    posed of, 12.7
  identification of, 2.35, 12.17, 12.25
  indexing of, 18.117, 18.143
  inventory of, 12.19–20, 12.26
  in journals, 1.140, 1.154
  labels within, 12.9, 12.23, 12.60–61, figs.
    12.2–3
  lists of, 1.44, 12.52, figs. 1.7–9; editing
    of, 12.55; in electronic works, 1.127,
    1.185, 12.53; format of, 1.45; gal-
    leries and, 12.54; location and form
    of, 12.53; titles in, 1.46
  musical examples as, 12.62–63, fig. 12.7
  numbering of: 2.33–34, 12.11, 12.34;
    continuous vs. separate, 12.12;
    double or multiple system, 1.76,
    12.13; numbers and letters for,
    12.14, figs. 12.4, 12.6
  pagination and, 1.104
  permission to use, 4.91–94, 12.41
  placement of, 12.10
  preceding text, 1.59

illustrations (*continued*)
  proofreading of, 3.10, 3.40–41
  running heads and, 1.99
  scale changes to, 12.22
  shading in, 12.30
  in text and gallery both, 12.16
  text references to, 2.33, 9.30, 12.10–11
  unnecessary, 12.15
  unnumbered, 12.15, fig. 12.2
  as works made for hire, 4.67, 12.45
  See also captions; illustration reproduc-
    tion
image agencies, 4.92–94, 12.50
impressions
  copyright dates of, 1.20–22, 1.24, 1.26
  definition of, p. 831
  edition compared with, 1.19, 1.22
  electronic books and, 1.123
  impression numbers, 1.26, 1.123
  publication date of, 17.116
  See also reprints
imprint, definition of, 1.13, 17.111–12. *See
  also* publisher's name
Inc., 6.50, 15.24, 17.104, 17.108
inclusive (continuing) numbers, 9.64, 18.13
  abbreviations and symbols with, 9.18
  alternative systems of, 9.65
  appropriate use of, 18.12, 18.123
  in citations, 17.130, 17.152, 18.113
  with commas, 9.66
  consistency in, 18.29
  en dashes between, 6.83, 9.62, 18.99
  for specific chapters, 17.68–69
  spelled out, 9.50–54, 9.63
  in titles, 9.68
  words between, 9.63
  for years, 9.67–68
  See also numbers
indented style
  continued lines in, 18.142
  description of, 18.23, 18.25–26
  examples of, 18.146–47
  indention guidelines in, 18.140
  runover lines in, 18.140
  sub-subentries in, 18.26, 18.28,
    18.146–47
  See also flush-and-hang style
indention
  with block quotations, 2.25–26, 11.11,
    11.24–25, 11.27

United States Congress
   acts of, 8.86–87, 17.302, 17.306,
      17.309–10
   capitalization of, 8.67
   committees of, 17.306–8
   documents of: *American State Papers,*
      17.313; bills and resolutions, 17.309;
      commission publications, 17.320;
      Committee Prints, 17.308; congres-
      sional journals, 17.301; *Congressional
      Record,* 17.302–3, 17.309; debates,
      17.302–4; hearings, 17.307; *Journals
      of the Continental Congress (JCC),*
      17.305; laws and statutes, 9.32,
      17.310–11; reports and documents,
      17.306, 17.308; speaker identified,
      17.303; 3-em dash for repeated
      sources, 17.299; treaties, 17.322;
      types of, 17.297; unpublished,
      17.324; "U.S. Congress" with, 17.298
   members of, 8.25
   numbers of Congresses and sessions,
      17.300
United States Constitution
   documentation of, 17.288–89, 17.321,
      17.356
   numbers vs. words for divisions in, 9.32
United States Supreme Court, 4.55, 17.284
United States Statutes at Large, 17.310,
   17.322
*United States Treaties and Other International
   Agreements,* 17.322
Universal Copyright Convention, 4.40
Universal Product Code, 1.114
university, 6.86, 8.73–74, 16.100, 17.104. *See
   also* academic concerns
*University of Chicago Manual of Legal Cita-
   tion,* 17.275. *See also* legal cases; legal
   style
unpublished and informally published
   works
   books not under contract as, 17.121–22
   copyright duration for, 4.25
   documentation of, 17.210–21; Canadian,
      17.335; contracts, 17.220; electronic,
      17.234–37; government, 17.324; mu-
      sical scores, 17.264; news release,
      17.244; online, 17.211, 17.356;
      papers presented at meetings,
      17.215; patents, 17.219; poster

unpublished and informally published
   works (*continued*)
      papers, 17.216; preprints, 17.218;
      theses and dissertations, 8.195,
      17.214; titles, 17.212; UK, 17.352–
      54; use of parentheses in notes,
      17.210; wills, 17.220; working
      papers, 17.217
   fair use of, 4.79
   permission to use, 4.72, 11.3
   resources on, 17.324
   titles of, 8.195, 17.212
   See also interviews; letters (correspon-
      dence); manuscript collections; per-
      sonal communications
uppercase. *See* capitalization; capitals
URLs (uniform resource locators)
   access dates for: citation with (example),
      17.181; online books, 17.143; online
      periodicals, 17.148, 17.198; prefer-
      ences on, 17.12, 17.187; reference
      works, 17.239; scientific, 17.358
   colons in, 6.63
   for databases, 17.358
   description of, 17.9
   descriptive phrase added to, 17.235,
      17.237
   documentation of, 17.15, 17.142–43,
      17.148–49
   hyphens in, 6.82
   line breaks and, 6.17, 7.44, 17.11
   for main entrance ("home page") only,
      17.198
   for multimedia, 17.270
   period (dot) in, 6.17
   punctuation of, 17.9–10
   revision dates for, 17.13
   slash in, 6.119, 17.198
U.S., use of, 15.5, 15.34. *See also* United
   States
Utopia, 8.54

verbs
   as adjectives/adjectives as, 5.95–96
   auxiliary (modal or helping), 5.132–40;
      can and *could,* 5.133; definition of,
      5.132; *do, does, did,* and *done,* 5.134;
      have, has, and *had,* 5.135; *may* and
      might, 5.136; *must,* 5.137; *ought,*
      5.138; principal verb compared with,

Weekly Compilation of Presidential Docu-
ments, 17.315
well, 5.93, 5.192, 6.29
West, western, and such, 8.48–50
what, 5.56–58, 5.60–61, 5.63
whether, 6.53
which
appropriate use of, 5.56–63, 5.202
comma with, 6.38
preposition with, 5.162
vs. *that,* 5.202
who, whom, whose, 5.56–58, 5.60–63, 5.162
why, 5.192
widows (lines), 3.11–12, p. 839. *See also* orphans (lines)
will and *would,* 5.118, 5.121, 5.140
wills, documentation of, 17.220
with, 5.190
word division
of abbreviations, 7.42
of compounds, 7.37
in foreign languages, 10.13; Arabic,
10.99; classical Greek, 10.139–42;
French, 10.37–40; German, 10.46–48;
Hebrew, 10.113; Italian, 10.56–58;
Latin, 10.61–64; Polish, 10.69; Russian, 10.123–28; Spanish, 10.80–82
of gerunds, 7.38
hyphens in, 5.92–93, 6.81
of numbers, 7.41
pronunciation as basis for, 7.35
proofreading for correct, 3.7
of proper nouns, 7.40
resources on, 7.33
in run-in lists, 7.43
of two-letter word endings, 7.39
typographic considerations in, 7.45
of URLs and e-mail addresses, 6.17,
7.44, 17.11
after vowel, 7.36
words not appropriate for, 7.34
words
coinages, 5.33, 7.14, 8.64
derived from names, 5.67, 8.2, 8.64–65,
8.97, 10.29
emphasizing particular, 7.49–50, 7.57–
59, 11.70, 16.52
hyphens in spelled-out, 6.82
introductory, punctuation of, 6.25,
6.27–29

words (*continued*)
italicized on first use, 7.55, 7.57
marking spacing changes between,
3.25–26
missing or illegible, 11.66–67
missing or omitted, 6.95
"scare quotes" for, 7.58, 10.53
scholarly, 7.55, 15.45–46
table alignment and, 13.38, tables 13.10,
13.11
used as words (e.g., the term *zero*),
7.62
See also foreign words; historical and
cultural terms; *and specific areas (e.g.,
chemical terminology)*
word usage
bias-free, 5.43, 5.51, 5.203–6
dialect and, 5.31, 5.200
grammar vs., 5.198
prepositions, list of, 5.209
in Standard Written English, 5.199,
5.201
troublesome words, list of, 5.202
working papers, academic, 17.217
works, titles of. *See* titles of works
works cited, 16.75, fig. 16.15. *See also* bibliographies; reference lists
works made for hire
authorship of, 4.9–12, 4.23
categories of, 4.10
contributors' chapters as, 4.52
copyright and, 4.9–12, 4.23
employer as author of, 4.9
illustrations as, 4.67, 12.45
works ineligible as, 4.11
works on demand, 4.60
world, parts of, 8.47–54. *See also* place-
names
World Bank, 17.355
World Trade Organization, 17.355
World Wide Web, pp. 839–40
WYSIWYG, p. 840

XML, 2.91, pp. 814, 823, 840
x-rays, 8.160

years
arabic numbers for, 9.33–34, 9.59
in astrophysical contexts, 9.12
at beginning of sentence, 9.5

THE CHICAGO MANUAL OF STYLE

Designed by Jill Shimabukuro
Typeset by Graphic Composition, Inc., Athens, Georgia
Printed and bound by Quebecor World, Kingsport, Tennessee
Dust jacket printed by Phoenix Color Corp., Hagerstown, Maryland

Composed in Scala and Scala Sans, typefaces designed by Martin Majoor in 1994
Printed on 50# Glatfelter Offset
Bound in Arrestox Linen

DISTRIBUTED BY THE CHICAGO DISTRIBUTION CENTER